100 OF THE GREATEST SCULPTURES IN

THE

WESTERN WORLD

Learn the story behind the art....

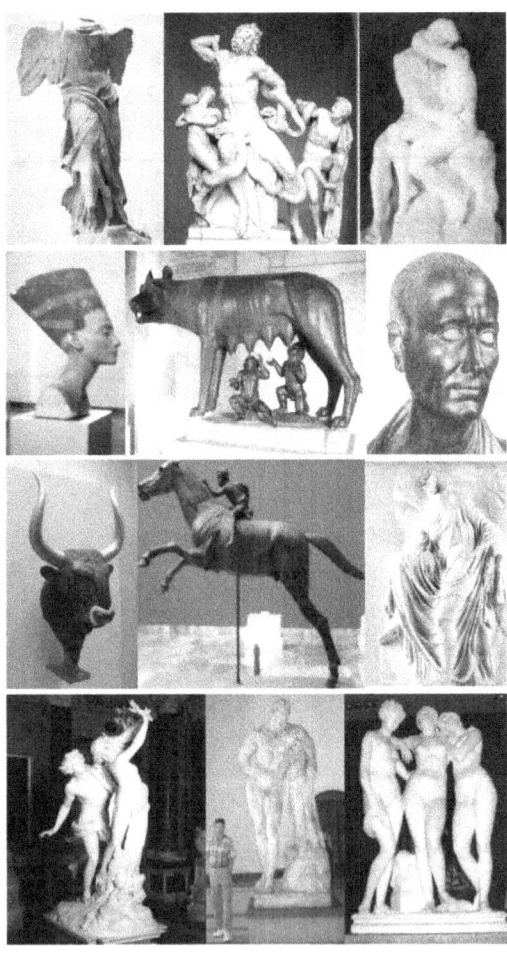

100 OF THE GREATEST SCULPTURES IN

THE

WESTERN WORLD

A *Compendium* of 153 Art References

ROBERT LAWRENCE HOLT

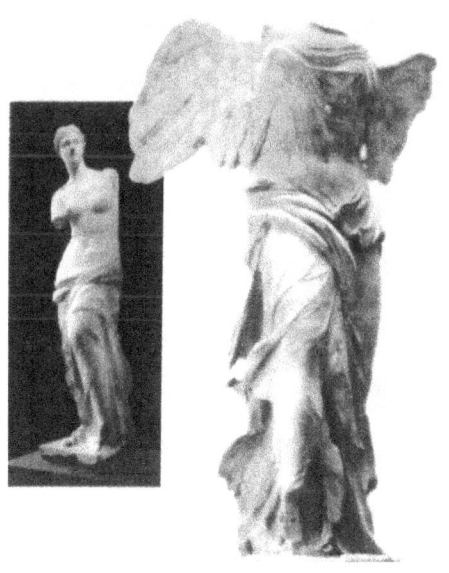

Dedicated to the 'pursuit of happiness'
of all grandchildren

In 2009, an Associated Press-Stanford University poll reported: "Three of every 4 Americans view Climate-Change as a <u>serious</u> problem that will harm <u>future generations</u> if not addressed." [*San Diego Union*, 12-20-09]

In 2017, it appears our future grandchildren will be in <u>harm's way</u>... due to a coalition of corporate CEOs and politicians who control Congress by majorities in each house.

They persist in denying Climate-Change is <u>serious</u>.

Nine 'exemplars' of leadership essential in 21st Century:

Moses... #68

L. Junius Brutus... #33

Alexander the Great... #28 & #45

Julius Caesar... #54

Augustus... #57

Marcus Aurelius... #60 & #61

Constantine the Great... #62

Washington... #83

Lincoln... #93

ROBERT LAWRENCE HOLT

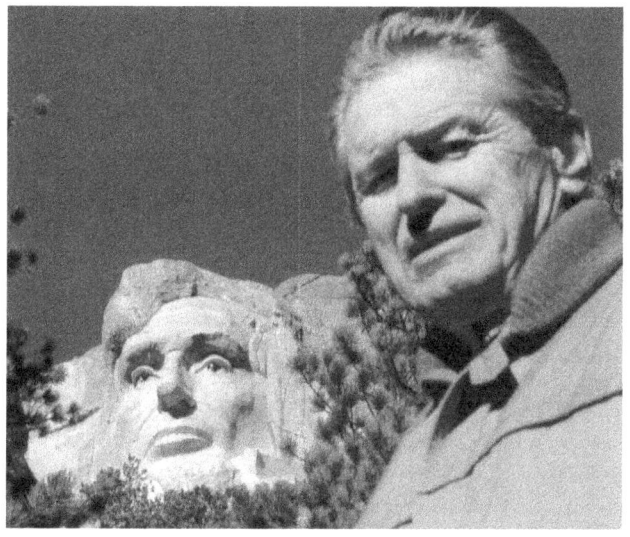

New York Times Bestselling Author, *Good Friday** – 1988
*foretold 1990-1991 Persian Gulf War by 24 months

The *Author* has visited each of the 100 sculptures. His qualifications include sufficient recall to coalesce data from 153 references. A "New York Times" best-seller – *Good Friday* – suggests aptitude for research and some writing skill...as do several other fiction and non-fiction titles. From the age of 8, museums and sculpture parks became and remain among his favorite habitats. He resided primarily in Europe from 7 to 17...and often returns. His BA was taken at St. Univ. of Iowa. He is a former U. S. Marine Corps officer. Following his service, he worked as an investment counselor for 12 years in Los Angeles...and became an author.

Photo Credits: Jane Barry, Martha Hertelendy,
Russel Keen, and John M. Holt II

Cover Design: Ken Fraser, GRAFXedge@gmail.com

SCULPTURE-CHAPTERS

27 Ares, with Eros	335 BC	Lysippos/Scop	Rome,Altemps
28 Alexander Herm	330 BC	Lysippos	Louvre
29 4 Horses – San Marco	330 BC	Lysippos	Venice
30 Crowned Athlete	320 BC	Lysippos	Getty, LA
31 Hercules–Farnese	320 BC	Lysippos	Naples Mus
32 Demosthenes	280 BC	Polyeuktos	Vatican
33 L. Junius Brutus	250 BC	Greco-Roman	Rome (Capt)
34 Jockey of Artemsion	240 BC	Greek	Athens Mus
35 Crouching Aphrodite	240 BC	Diodalus	Rome (Terme)
36 Gaul Chieftain	230 BC	Epigonos	Rome.Altemps
37 Dying Gaul	225 BC	Epigonos	Rome (Capt))
38 Winged Victory of Samothrace	200 BC	Pythokritos	Louvre
39 Old Market Woman	200 BC	Greco-Roman	New York Met
40 Drunken Old Woman	200 BC	Myron of Smyrna	Rome (Capt)
41 Pseudo-Seneca	200 BC	Greco-Roman	Naples Mus
42 Hellenistic Ruler	180 BC	Greco-Roman	Rome.Massimo
43 Great Altar of Zeus	166-156	Menekrates	Berlin
44 Farnese Bull	150 BC	Apoll. & Taur.	Naples Mus
45 Alexander Mosaic	120 BC	Greco-Roman	Naples Mus
46 Man of Delos	100 BC	Agasius	Athens Mus
47 Borghese Warrior	90 BC	Agasius	Louvre
48 Venus de Milo	80 BC	Alexandros	Louvre
49 Belvedere Torso	60 BC	Apollonius	Vatican
50 Seated Boxer	50 BC	Apollonius	Rome (Terme)
51 Venus Genetrix	46 BC	Arcelaus/Call.	Getty, Palantine
52 Laocoon	30 BC	Aga/Polyd/Ath	Vatican
53 Spinario	25 BC	Greco-Roman	Rome (Capt)
54 Black Caesar	45 BC	Greco-Roman	Berlin
55 Ara Pacis	9 BC	Roman	Rome -Tiber
56 Portland Vase	10 AD	Dioscurides	Brit Mus
57 Augustus Primaporta	15 AD	Roman	Vatican

89 End of the Trail	1894	Fraser	Okla. City
90 Bronco Buster	1895	Remington	White House, etc
91 Coming Thru the Rye	1902	Remington	Okla,/Met/ White House
92 Little Mermaid	1913	Erikson	Copenhagen
93 Lincoln Memorial	1922	Wm Fr. Smith	Washington
94 Christ the Redeemer	1926	Landowski	Rio de Janeiro
95 Recumbent Figure	1938	Moore	London, Tate
96 Mt. Rushmore	1941	Borglum	Rapid City, SD
97 Vigeland Park	1947	Vigeland	Oslo
98 Marine Memorial	1954	Rosent/Weldon	Washington
99 Einstein	1979	Berks	Washington
100 the Wall (Vietnam Memorial)	1982	Lin	Washington

ACKNOWLEDGMENTS

Among the 153 art references, 10 are highly recommended as the most thorough and reliable.

Arts of the Ancient Greeks ... Richard Brilliant
Gardner's Art Through the Ages ... a host of contributors
The Story of Art ... Sir E. H. Gombrich
Greatest Works of Art of West. Civilization ... T. Hoving
A Basic History of Western Art ... Janson & Janson
Encyclopedia of Sculpture [3 vol.] ... a host of contributors
Our Oriental Heritage, Life of Greece, Caesar & Christ, and
      Age of Napoleon ... Will & Ariel Durant

PREFACE

This compendium – 16 years in preparation – presents 100 of the 'greatest sculptures' in the Western world. The 100 sculpture-chapters reflect the scholarship of more than 153 prominent educators, historians, and museum curators.

[42 more sculptures – also significant – are listed at *Preface* end]

Primary criteria for selection as one of the '100 sculptures' is frequency of favorable review in the 153 references.

Second criteria: sculptures are readily accessible [excepting 6]. Ninety-four [94] are located in or near 15 major cities of the Western World: Washington ... New York ... Los Angeles ... London ... Paris [+Ve rsailles] ... Berlin ... Copenhagen ... Oslo ... Venice ... Florence ... Rome ... Naples ... Athens [+ Delphi & Mycenae] ... Cairo ... and Rio de Janeiro.

Six exceptions are: Knossos, Crete [2] ... Oklahoma City [2] ... Mt Rushmore, So. Dakota ... and Hearst Castle, California.

Third criteria: response of the viewing public. Thomas Hoving* describes 'response' as: "The 'blink test,' or your 100th-of-a-second initial impression ... If a work of art is any good, it will talk to you. Art will talk quicker if you happen to be able to recognize all sorts of [background] influences – but essentially a great work will reach your own heart and do it on its own." [*LA Times*, 6-13-2005]

*former director, New York Met. Museum of Art

Sculptures appear in chronological order ... according to the date of the original sculptor ... not a copyist. Before 1261 AD, most dates are approximate.

Each sculpture-chapter includes quotes from art scholars and historians. Where they do not agree, divergent opinions are included. Occasionally, the *Author* expresses views that disagree with a scholar or historian ... but no more than they disagree among each other.

The 100 sculptures are listed by era: Ancient Egypt & High Minoan ... Assyrian Empire & Etruscan ... Greek Classic & Hellenistic ... Roman Republic & Empire ... Mannerism & Baroque ... French Rococo & High Baroque ... Neo-Classic & Romantic ... Impressionism & Art Deco ... Realistic & Modern.

For the Convenience of Travelers:

14 sculptures are in the United States
10 in London
16 in Paris
34 in Rome
6 in Naples
4 in Florence
5 in Athens (+2 Delphi & 1 Mycenae)
2 in Knossos, Crete
    *a majority of statues have multiple locations *[google]*

[it is possible to visit 82 sculptures in London, Paris, Berlin, Florence, Rome, and Naples in 2 to 3 weeks ... via the Chunnel train and overnight-sleeper trains ... booking rooms near city centers]

Within this Compendium, 7 Themes
Appear [with overlapping]

Artistic	30 .... ancient 17, recent 13 [*after 1581*]
Deities	29 .... ancient 23, recent 6
Rulers	22 .... ancient 19, recent 3
Love	17 .... ancient 10, recent 7
Democracy	15 .... ancient 6, recent 9
Athletes	10 .... ancient
Climate	2 ... *Vigeland Park* #97, *Einstein* #99

26 Sculptures represent Historic Persons

Nefertiti #4 – queen of ancient Egypt

King Tut #5 – boy-king of ancient Egypt

Tyrannicides #9 – actions led Athens to first democracy

Pericles #18 – strong leader of early Greek democracy

Agias the Athlete #26 – undefeated in Ancient Olympics

Alexander #28 & #45 – spread Hellenic culture outside Greece

Demosthenes #32 –finest Greek orator, defender of democracy

L Junius Brutus #33 – began Roman Republic [of 503 years]

Caesar #54 – introduced Roman concept of *strong central leader*

Augustus #57 – 1st emperor of *Imperial* Rome

Titus #58 – Roman emperor, originally atop Arch

Trajan #59 – Roman emperor, originally atop Column

M. Aurelius #60 & #61 – Roman emperor & philosopher

Constantine the Great #62 – shifted center of Roman Empire

Mary Magdalena #65 – follower of Jesus Christ

David #67 & #70 – defeated Goliath, later King of Israelites

Moses #68 – led Israelites out of Egypt, 10 Commandments

Milo of Croton #75 – undefeated in Ancient Olympics

Pauline Bonaparte #80 – Napoleon's sister, a striking beauty

Washington #83 – president of first modern democracy

Lincoln #94 – ended slavery, preserved American union

Einstein #99 – discovered photo-electric effect (solar power)

Sculptures displaying 'Supreme Unrestrained Spirit'

250 BC	Jockey of Artemsion #34
220 BC	Winged Victory of Samothrace #38
120 BC	Alexander Mosaic #45
1775	Nymph & Satyr #77
1836	Departure of Volunteers #82
1865	Le Dance! #84
1902	Coming Through the Rye #91
1954	Marine Corps War Memorial #98

Statues Often Mis-Identified by References:

#9 Tyrannicides .... they did not kill the Tyrant

#23 Mausolus .... identity as Mausolus is unlikely

#33 L Junius Brutus .... identity by 'custom'

#39 Old Market Woman .... she is not going to 'market'

#40 Old Drunken Woman .... she is not necessarily an 'alcoholic'

#41 Pseudo Seneca .... unlikely to be Seneca

This edition is prepared primarily for an American audience. Foreign editions will involve minor changes in sculpture selection. The *Author* condenses words, #s, dates, and oft-repeated titles.

the 42 Additional Significant Sculptures:

Aenaes, Anchises, & Ascanius	1619	Bernini	Rome
Alexander Sarcophagus	240 BC	unknown	Istanbul
Aphrodite Kneeling at Bath	100 BC	unknown	Rhodes
Aphrodite of Satala [head]	100 BC	unknown	Brit. Museum
Apollo & Nymphs of Thetis	1675	Girardon	Versailles
Augustus Cameo	100 AD	unknown	Vienna
Baker Dancer	200 BC	unknown	NY Met
Balzac	1897	Rodin	Rodin Mus.
Chios, Maid of [head]	320 BC	unknown	Boston
Churchill [*the British Bull*]	1973	Roberts-Jones	Parliament Sq.
Clytie [or Antonia]	50 AD	unknown	Brit. Museum
Continuity in Space	1913	Boccioni	NY Mod. Art
Crazy Horse	1998	Ziolkowski	Black Hills, SD
Diogenes & Alexander	1689	Puget	Louvre
Eiffel Tower	1889	Eiffel	Paris
Franklin D. Roosevelt Memorial	1997	Estern	Washington

Gates of Hell	1890	Rodin	Mus. Orsay
Grant Memorial	1922	Shrady	Washington
Hand of God	1898	Rodin	Paris
Hermes & Dionysus	340 BC	Praxiteles	Olympia, Gr.
Hygieia [head]	350 BC	Scopus	Athens
Julius Caesar [standing]	1696	Coustou	Mus. Orsay
Kennedy [JFK]	1980	Berks	Washington
Lions of Trafalgar	1867	Landseer	London
Madame du Barry	1773	Pajou	Louvre
Mercury	1580	Giambologna	Washington
Odysseus/Ulysses [head]	125 BC	Ages/Plyd	Sperlonga Mus.
Old Fisherman	200 AD	unknown	Louvre
Philosopher of Antikythera	240 BC	unknown	Athens
Queen of the Night	1800 BC	unknown	Brit Mus.
Riace Bronzes	450 BC	unknown	Calabria, Italy
Spiral Jetty	1970	Smithson	Grt. Salt Lake
Satyros the Pugilist	330 BC	Silanian	Athens
Salt Cellar	1543	Cellini	Vienna
the Sphinx	2500 BC	unknown	Cairo
Standing Woman, Elev.	1927	Lachaise	NY Met Mus.
St. George	1415-6	Donatello	Florence
UNESCO Reclining Figure	1956-8	Moore	Paris
Venus of Willendorf	25,000 BC	unknown	Vienna
Venus Baigneuse	1757	Falconet	Louvre
Voltaire [bust]	1781	Houdon	Victoria-Albert

1

THE SCRIBE

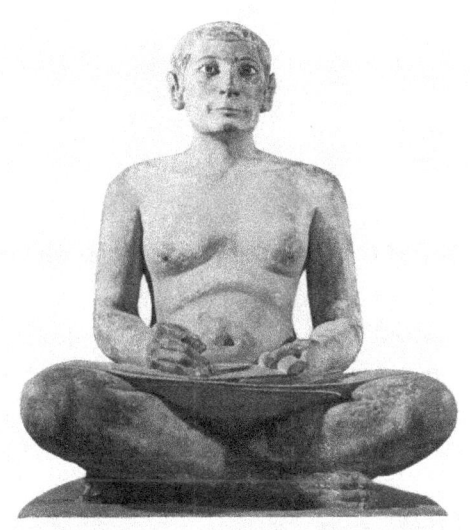

"with such treasures as the Louvre's fabled *Seated Scribe*...
Memphis stood as capital from the 3rd to 11th dynasty...
the golden age of Egyptian sculpture..."
...*Sculpture: Origins to Today*, Janneau & Hoog, p 41

Found in tomb of Kai, Saqqara [near Cairo] – now, Louvre
Egyptian sculpture – approx. 2450 BC – naturalistic
Ht. 21 in. [54 cm] – painted limestone
Sculptor: unknown Egyptian

V isitors in the Louvre catch the eye of *the Scribe* and pause.
Gardner's *Art Through the Ages* observes: "The personality, that of a sharply intelligent and alert individual, is read by the sculptor with a penetration and sympathy seldom achieved at such an early date. Despite the stiff upright posture...its color lends a life-like quality to the statue...<u>The head displays an extraordinary sensitivity.</u>" [p 77]

Durant's *Our Oriental Heritage* adds: "The scribe has come down to us in many forms...the most illustrious is the squatting *Scribe of the Louvre*...on the very verge of writing." [p 186-7]

Sculpture, Origins to Today explains: "the modeling magnetically draws the viewer's eye to the face and torso. Here is remarkable individuality of features and a sincerely fresh approach untainted by any formalism." [p 41]

[*formalism* refers to cold idealism in ancient Egyptian statuary]

Bachechi's *The Louvre* notes the: "extraordinary expression, despite the passage of the millennia, still gives the person represented a natural look...and keen gaze." The gaze is accomplished by its components – each pupil is carved from ebony...the iris is rock crystal...the cornea is white quartz. [p 34-5]

A mirror-like device – "a little strip of silver set behind the iris reflects light..." – gives both depth and authenticity to the eyes. [*History of World Sculpture*, Bazin, p 110]

Subject:

The earliest human statues of Egypt are either standing or seated in a chair [or throne]. In about 2450 BC, a third pose was added – that of a scribe cross-legged in a squatting position.

Janson's *History of Art* reveals: "the finest of these scribes dates from the beginning of the 5th Dynasty...we must not think of him as a lowly secretary waiting to take dictation...rather, the figure represents a high court official, a 'master of sacred-and secret-letters'. Our example stands out not only for the vividly alert expression of the face, <u>but also for the individual handling of the torso, which records the somewhat flabby body of a man past middle age</u>." [p 59-60]

Realism is rarely seen again until the reign of the revolutionary Pharaoh Ikhenaton/Akhenaton and his wife Nefertiti...some 1,100 years later. [see *Nefertiti* #4]

The *Scribe* was discovered in the tomb of an individual named Kai, at a settlement called Saqqara [near present-day Cairo]. Saqqara is the location of the famed Step Pyramid...known as the oldest stone monument and the first built to house the body of a Pharaoh. It was completed in about 2,700 BC, a few 100 years before *the Scribe* was created. [Perring, p 10]

30,000 Years of Art states: "Although the figure bears no inscriptions, we can be fairly certain that it represents the tomb owner himself." Kai is "apparently holding a reed pen [now lost] ... his left hand grasps a papyrus roll – on which he is writing – spread on his firmly stretched kilt. The face of the man conveys concentration, suggests intelligence, and gives the impression of individuality... the quality of this piece is such that we must assume that it was made in one of the workshops that normally specialized in the production of royal sculptures." [p 69]

The above lends credence to the likelihood the *Scribe* in the Louvre was born of royal blood...possibly, even the son of a pharaoh. The pharaohs [kings] of Egypt were known for having many wives and many more children. Janson affirms this possibility: "the solid, incisive treatment of form bespeaks the dignity of his station [which, in the beginning, seems to have been restricted to sons of Pharaohs]." [p 60]

In any case, *the Scribe* was an important person and elevated in society; otherwise, his image would not have been sculpted in limestone.

Bachechi emphasizes: "The office of the scribe was one of the most distinguished in the Egyptian administration, and the numerous artistic statues of these functionaries bear witness to the importance attached to the art of writing... the ability to write was an essential condition for admission to the highest posts... it was not only necessary to the performance of administrative and financial functions but also played a fundamental part in religious life and acts of worship." [p 34]

Durant is specific: "He keeps a record of work done and goods paid, of prices and costs, of profits and loss; he counts the cattle as they move to the slaughter, or corn as it is measured out in sale; he draws up contracts and wills...He is sedulously attentive and mechanically industrious; he has just enough intelligence not to be dangerous. His life is monotonous, but he consoles himself by writing essays on the hardships of the manual worker's existence, and the princely dignity of those whose food is paper and whose blood is ink." [p 161]

Hayes' *Everyday Life in Ancient Times* suggests: "A young man fortunate enough to have passed through the great school of scribes at Memphis, or later Thebes, was expected not only to be able to read, write, and draw with a skill approaching perfection but also to have a thorough knowledge of the language, literature, and history of his country. Furthermore he must be well versed in mathematics, bookkeeping, law, general administrative procedure, and even such subjects as mechanics, surveying, and architectural design...a scribe automatically became a member of the educated official class.... and he could rise through a series of recognized stages to the very highest office in the land." [p 102]

Early Writing:

The ancient scribe of Egypt wrote from right to left. His slender brush had "a carefully frayed and trimmed tip. His excellent paper is made of narrow strips of the pith of the papyrus reed, crossed in two directions, pressed together, and subsequently burnished. His writing pigments – black and red – are contained in two bowls of an alabaster palette, or ink-stand..." [Hayes, p 102]

Individual trade-marks or numbers were likely the first writings by man. Numbers were parallel lines [indicating fingers]...leading to Roman numerals. The word *five* goes back to a root meaning hand. "V represented an expanded hand, and X was merely 2

V's connected at their points." [Durant, p 76] Among the earliest surviving inscriptions on stone which record complex thought are those of the ancient Sumerians in about 3,600 BC. [p 131]

Sculptor:

The sculptor of this statue is unknown. He likely was among the most highly-skilled in his time. Other fine examples of Egyptian scribes are found in the Cairo Museum and the State Museum in Berlin.

Major References:

Art Through the Ages, Gardner, 1996, p 77-8

Sculpture: From its Origins to Today, 1970, Janneau & Hoog, p 41

History of Art, 1977, Janson, p 59-60

The Louvre, 2007, Bachechi, p 34-5

30,000 Years of Art, 2006, editors of Phaidon Press, p 69

Our Oriental Heritage, 1935, Durant, p 76, 130-31, 161, 186, Fig 13

Everyday Life-Ancient Times 1951, Nat. Geog. Soc., Hayes, p 102-03

History of World Sculpture, 1968, Bazin, p 110

Art: A History of Painting, Sculpture..., 1989, Hartt, p 83

Then & Now: Wonders of the Ancient World, 1991, Perring, p 10

2

BULL'S HEAD RHYTON

OF KNOSSOS

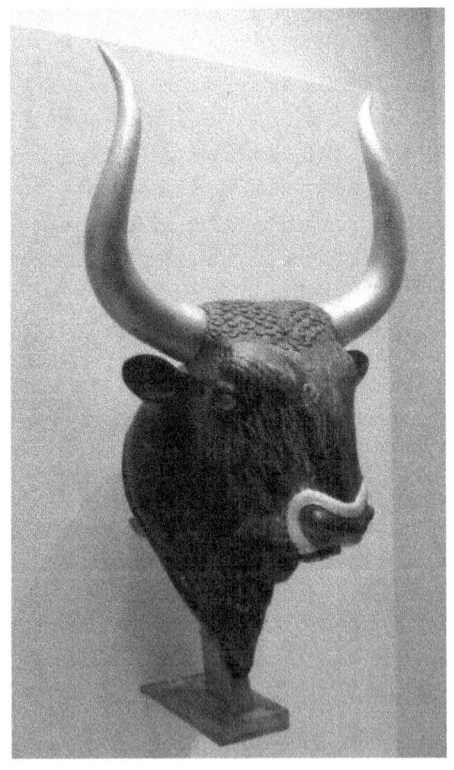

"...a masterpiece of Cretan sculpture..." designed
"to hold liquid in a sacred libation – perhaps bull's blood."
... *Ancient Greece*, Durando, 1997, p 23

Found, 1903, Knossos palace – now, Iraklion Mus., Crete *
Minoan [Crete] sculpture – approx. 1550 BC – naturalistic
Ht. 14 in. [35.6 cm] – black steatite stone & gilded wood horns
Sculptor: unknown Minoan artisan
   *a similar *Bull's Head* is in Athens Arch. Museum

At first sight of this sacrificial vessel, we are struck by its majesty and realism. It was created some 3,500 years ago.

Durant's *Life of Greece* observes: "...in this startling relic <u>the fixed wild eyes, the snorting nostrils, the gasping mouth, and the trembling tongue achieve a power that Greece itself will never surpass.</u>" [p 17]

Matz concurs: "With this rhyton, Minoan 'naturalism' reached its apogee." [*Art of Crete & Greece*, p 124]

30,000 Years adds: "of the stone vessels...produced and used on Crete during the Bronze Age [3300-1500 BC]...it is one of the most elaborate and technically accomplished." [p 104]

After discovery in a chamber of the Little Palace of Knossos, its original form – from a block of black steatite – required restoration on the left side. [steatite is also known as soapstone] The horns, originally gilded, are restorations.

Higgins' *Minoan and Mycenaean Art* states: The right eye has "a lens of rock-crystal, painted on the underside with red for the pupil, black for the iris, and white for the rest of the eye. The crystal is set in a surround of red stone to give a frighteningly blood-shot effect. Around the nostril is an inlaid bank of white shell. Such a natural and sympathetic study of an animal was not seen again in Greek lands until the 5th century BC." [p 162]

Matz says: "...in Minoan pictorial representation, the bull symbolizes a sacrificial animal." [p 125] By the bloody eyes of a 'bull in sacrifice', the sculptor may have meant to indicate its suffering and fate.

After ritual use, Minoan priests – or priestesses, such as the *Snake Goddess* #3 – stored the rhyton in a secret stone repository under a floor in the Little Palace of Knossos. This explains why it [and other fine artifacts] survived more than 3,000 years of earthquakes, fires, and invasions.

The ancient island of Crete, in the eastern Mediterranean Sea, accumulated the wealth to build its great palaces by being "... strategically placed, for trade or war, midway between Phoenicia and Italy, and between Egypt and Greece." Wise leaders "held sway with a powerful fleet over most of the Aegean Sea and part of mainland Greece...and developed...one of the most artistic civilizations in history." [Durant, p 5]

Though the island was far smaller than Greece, the sea-faring people of Crete some 4,000 years ago possessed sufficient sea-faring and the military ability to demand rich tribute from the ancient ports of Greece. This tribute included Grecian youths to engage in dangerous Cretan bull-jumping games/ceremonies...to which the *Bull's Head Rhyton* may be related.

Subject:

Rhytons [ritual stone vessels] were fashioned in various shapes – including vase, goblet, or cup – for the pouring of 'liquid libation' during a sacred rite...usually in honor of a deity. The rarest were modeled with the heads of deer, lions, horses, bulls, or hybrids. "In Crete the vessels were usually decorated with scenes in low relief. From flakes of gold leaf found adhering to some of these rhytons, it would appear they were originally gilt..." [Higgins, p 153]

In ancient accounts, Homer mentions the practice of gilding the horns of bulls before sacrifice. Higgins adds: "Long shaggy hairs are engraved on the animal's forehead, brows, and cheeks...and other engraved lines indicate dappling." [p 162-4]

The *Bull's Head* was filled through a hole in its neck. During the rite of pouring a fluid, it emptied through a hole within the nostrils. [p 162-4] It may have been wine, oil, or the blood of a bull as suggested by Durando. It is possible the people of Crete drank from ritual rhytons...or, that the fluid was spilled over their bodies, a practice of later Romans. [p 23]

Durant adds the citizenry of Crete: "...have apparently no temple, but raise altars in the palace court, in sacred groves or grottos, and on mountaintops. They adorn these sanctuaries with tables of libation and sacrifice, a medley of idols, and 'horns of consecration' [statuary] ... perhaps, representative of the sacred bull." [p 14]

On the island of Crete, the bull also was a central figure in Minoan myths and sports. One has Zeus disguising himself as a bull to abduct Europa. Another legend describes the man-eating Minotaur in the labyrinth under the Knossos Palace.

In this relatively well-preserved ancient palace [partially rebuilt by Dr. Arthur Evans], a famed fresco – known as the *Bull-Game** – displays youths engaging in the dangerous sport of bull-leaping. *now in Herakleion Museum

Durant says: "... the Cretan's greatest thrill comes when he wins his way into the crowd that fills the amphitheater on a holiday to see men and women face death against huge charging bulls. Time and again, he views this lusty sport... the skilled performer, slim and agile, meeting the bull in the arena, grasping its horns, leaping into the air, somersaulting over its back, and landing feet first on the ground...." [p 12-3]

Mary Renault – recognized for historically-accurate fiction – provides an account of Cretan bull-leaping in *The King Must Die*: "A trumpet sounded. In the wall, the great bull-gate opened, and out came the bull. He was a kingly beast, white spatch-cocked with brown; thick-barreled, short-legged, wide-browed, and very long-horned. The horns curved upward and forward, then dipped and rose again at the tips. They were painted lengthwise with stripes of red and gold. [p 207] He [Theseus] ran smoothly up to the sullen bull. He grasped the horns, and swung up between them, going with [the head toss of] the bull... then he soared free. He turned in the air, a curve as lovely as a bent bow's, and on the broad back his slim feet touched down together... then they sprang up again. He seemed not to leap, but to hang above the bull, like a dragonfly over the reeds... then he came down to earth, feet still together, and lightly touched the catcher's hands with his, like a civility... he had no need of steadying. Then he danced away." [p 208]

Sculptor:

The artisan who carved and created this ritual vessel is unknown. It is generally accepted he was from the island of Crete. He may have been influenced by artists of Egypt to the south...and, to a lesser degree, by artists of Syria and Mesopotamia to the east.

The *Bull's Head Rhyton* was discovered at Knossos during excavations begun by the British archeologist Dr. Arthur Evans in 1900. The work of Evans continued until 1936, when he published his 4-volume report, *The Palace of Minos*.

The Athens Archeological Museum displays a somewhat similar *Bull's Head Rhyton*...discovered at the citadel of Mycenae.

Major References:

Herakleion Museum, 2005, Prof. J.A. Sakellarakis, 34-5

Palace of Knossos, 2005, Anna Michailidou, p 113-14

Life of Greece, 1939, Durant, p 13, 14, 17, 20

30,000 Years of Art, 2007, editors, Phaidon Press, p 104

Ancient Greece, Dawn of the Western World, 1997, Durando, p.23

National Arch Museum, Athens, 1980, Newsweek Publ., p.29-3

Art of Crete, Mycenae, and Greece, 1968, German Hafner, p 41

The King Must Die, 1958, Mary Renault, p 207-08

Art: A History of Painting, Sculpture..., 1989, Hartt, p 128-29

Minoan and Mycenaean Art, 1989, Higgins, p 153-64

Art of Crete and Early Greece, 1962, Matz, p 124-25, 130

3

THE SNAKE GODDESS

OR PRIESTESS

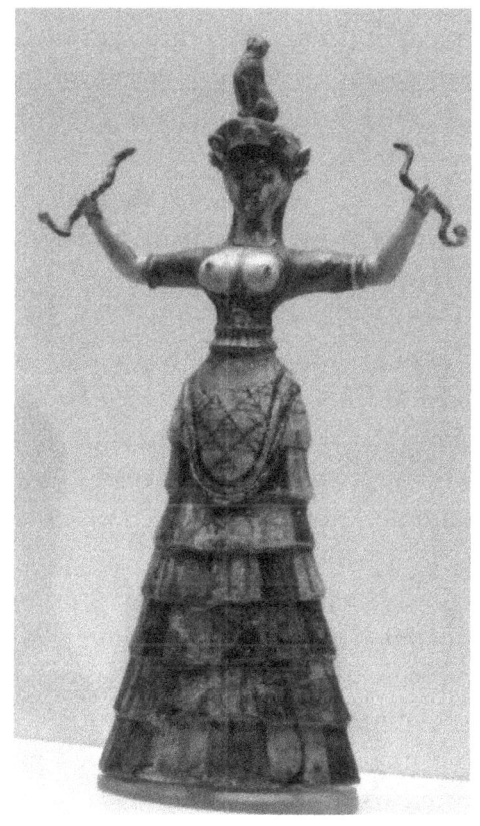

"... an exemplar of Cretan art,
combining ... grace and naturalism."
... Higgins, *Minoan & Mycenaean Art*, p 17

Found 1903, Knossos Palace – now, Iraklion Mus., Crete*
Minoan sculpture – approx. 1500 BC – naturalistic
Ht. 11.5 in. [295 cm] – faience [colored glazed earthenware]
Sculptor: unknown Minoan artisan
    *also, see *Snake Priestess/Goddess* in Boston Museum

At 11.5 inches in height, this statuette of a Minoan goddess [or priestess] is among the smallest major sculptures in the Western world…yet, its beauty and intricate charm continue to draw and captivate the largest crowds at the world-class Iraklion [Herakleion] Museum on the island of Crete.

As a masterpiece of Cretan sculpture… *the Snake Goddess* also is a <u>universal icon representing the spiritual and/or fertility powers of women</u>. Prior to 1,000 BC, most statuary of the female form attests to one or another of these attributes.

Gardner concurs: "… these faience figurines stand in a long line of prehistoric <u>fertility images</u> that are usually considered to be <u>divinities</u>." [*Art Through the Ages,* p 110]

This statuette was discovered in 1903 by Sir Arthur Evans, who devoted most of his adult life to the excavation and preservation of the Palace of Knossos. The *Goddess* had been hidden in a temple repository – a rectangular chamber sunk in the stone floor near the Throne Room of the Palace of Knossos. [with other precious items and works of art associated with the sacred rites of the Minoans].

Several references suggest it represents a priestess more than a goddess. [Michailidou, p 70, 74-5] [Hafner, p 21] [Matz, p 125] Whatever the Minoans of 1500 BC intended, <u>this statuette is as mesmerizing now as it must have been 3,500 years ago</u>.

The head is a modern restoration. Though her beret [round headdress] and its leopard-like feline figure were found in the same deposit with the statuette, it is uncertain whether they belong together." [Janson & Janson, p 63]

The art of ancient Crete was far more expressive and vigorous than the art of neighboring Greece or Egypt.

Burdick, in *Encyclopedia of Sculpture,* offers an explanation. "From approximately 3,000 to 1450 BC, the Minoans led a seemingly ideal lifestyle with few enemies, enjoyable weather, and a bountiful sea. The sculpture of Minoan Crete reflects this carefree lifestyle in its organic form and frivolous subject matter." [p 387]

The design of the *Snake Goddess* bears remarkable resemblance to the *Queen of the Night* – a terracotta relief [height 49.5 cm] depicting a Babylonian goddess dating to about 1775 BC – now, in the British Museum. Both display upright stances, narrow waists, prominent bosoms, raised arms, and hand-held objects which may refer "to the cult of the snake as a deity of the earth." [Robb & Garr., p 403]

Quite likely, the image of the *Snake Goddess* is descended from *Ishtar* – the goddess of love and war, venerated by both the Babylonians and Assyrians. The Phoenicians worshiped her as *Astarte*... the Semites called her *Ashtoreth*... and the Sumerians idolized her as *Inanna*. More recently, the Greeks named her *Aphrodite* and the Romans called her *Venus*.

Subject:

Durant describes the 'worship' of the ancient people of Crete: "Since his death rate is high, he pays devout homage to fertility... and when he rises to the notion of a human divinity, he pictures a mother goddess with generous mannae [nourishment] and sublime flanks... with reptiles creeping up around her arms and breasts, coiled in her hair, or rearing themselves proudly from her head. He sees in her the basic fact of nature – that man's greatest enemy, death, is overcome by woman's mysterious power, reproduction... and he identifies this power with deity." [*Life of Greece*, p 13]

Frescoes found on the walls of the Palace of Knossos indicate that open blouses and long, richly-adorned, flounced skirts were normal court attire of Minoan noble women in the warm climate of Crete. [*Encyclo Sculpt.*, p 388]

Jansons' *Basic History of Western Art* suggests this statuette was associated with a votary... a priestess or one who takes religious vows to a god or goddess. "Snakes are associated with earth deities and male fertility in many ancient religions, just as the startlingly bared breasts of this statuette radiate fecunity [reproduction]." [p 64] Snakes, by periodic skin-shedding, signify renewal of life and fertility.

In both ancient and modern societies, snakes also were accepted as 'guardians of the granary' and 'protectors of the kitchen' for their ability to control common pests...which contributes to their veneration. Branigan & Vickers in *Hellas* describe this statuary as "protectress of the household." [p 44]

Matz maintains: "...the term *Snake Goddess* is not really appropriate. This is a votive [to express devotion]...and probably represents a priestess...The concentration of power expressed in the laced waist may be regarded as typically Minoan..." [*Art of Crete and Early Greece*, p 125]

R. Brilliant, in *Arts of the Ancient Greeks*, says: "Certainly one of the most typical, even emblematic Minoan images, occurs in the well-known faience statuette of an earth goddess...Lithe and slim with fashionable wasp waist, flounced skirt...her form grows organically in swelling and contracting curves with little attention to anatomical accuracy, yet is physically vital." [p 3]

The headdress of the goddess/priestess includes a divine attribute of the lion/leopard. Some references suggest the priestesses of Knossos were dominant in religious matters, accounting for the presence of a 'lion'.

Renault's *The King Must Die* provides this description of the Minoan priestess: "Horns blew. A door opened behind the shrine. There she stood...like a field lily...upright and small...round breasts and thighs...a waist to snap in your fingers. But now she was stiff with gold; you could only see the red of her dress when the flounces stirred. Her foot-high diadem was crested with a golden leopard. If she had not moved, I should have taken her for jeweler's work." [p 206]

Durant explains life in the Palace: "The halls of the king are noisy with scribes taking inventories of goods distributed or received, with artists making statuary, paintings...while wasp-waisted princes and jeweled duchesses, alluringly *decollete*, crowd to a royal feast served on tables shining with bronze and gold. Their clothing is tightly-laced about the middle, for men as well as women ... To rival the men ... the women of the later periods resort to stiff corsets, which gather their skirts snugly around their hips ... the bodice is laced below the bust, opens in a careless circle, and then, in a gesture of charming reserve, may close in a Medici collar at the neck." [p 8-9]

Sculptor:

The artisans who created these faience figures may have been either Cretan or Egyptian. Faience is the term applied to earthenware which has been glazed ... similar to the creative process for porcelain.

Two additional goddess/priestess figures were found at Knossos ... one is exhibited at the Iraklion Museum. It is slightly larger, but less intricate and dramatic, often referred to as the 'mother'. The other figure, now in the Boston Museum, is smaller and carved in ivory with 2 gold snakes coiled about its outstretched arms. [*30,000 Years*, p 107].

Major References:

Minoan and Mycenaean Art, 1989, Higgins, p 16-7, 32-3
Basic History of Western Art, 2006, Janson & Janson, p 63-4
Palace of Knossos, 2005, Prof. Anna Michailidou, p 70, 74-5
Herakleion Museum, 2005, Prof. J.A. Sakellarakis, p 36-7, 39
30,000 Years of Art, 2007, editors of Phaidon Press, p 107
Arts of the Ancient Greeks, 1972, Richard Brilliant, 1972, p 3
Art through the Ages, 1996, Gardner, p 110
Life of Greece, 1939, Durant, p 8, 9, 13, Fig 3
Encyclopedia of Sculpture, 2004, Bostrom, p 17, 387-8
Art in the Western World, 1953, Robb and Garrison, p 402-03, 587
The King Must Die, 1958, Mary Renault, p 206
Ancient Greece, 1997, Durando, p 23
Art of Crete, Mycenae, and Greece, 1968, Hafner, p 21
Art of Crete and Early Greece, 1962, Matz, p 109, 125

4
THE NEFERTITI

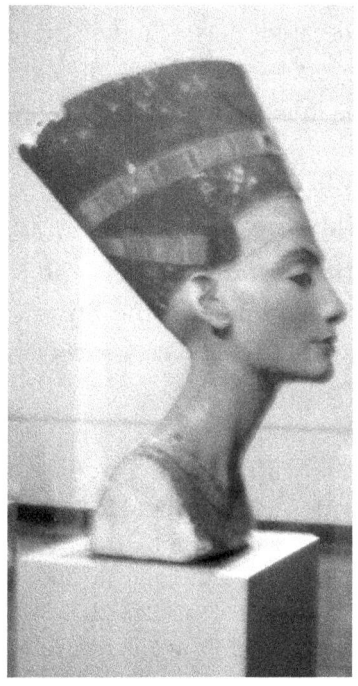

"... timeless beauty of *Nefertiti* has made this sculpture
one of the most famous works of art in the world."
... Berlin Neues Mus., 2007

Found 1912, Tell-el-Amarna – now, Neues Mus., Berlin*
Egyptian – approx. 1365 BC – naturalistic and stylized
Height: 20 in. [50.8 cm] – life-size – painted limestone
Sculptor: Thutmosis, owner of artist's studio in Amarna
    *also copy in NY Met. Mus. of Art

A fter *the Nefertiti* was discovered in 1912, its beauty created her fame.

Gardner describes this sculpture of the Egyptian queen as "...a supremely elegant bust...a masterpiece of cosmetic art." [*Art Through the Ages*, p 91-2]

Gatlein adds: "While enchanted by *Nefertiti's* beauty, the modern viewer is perhaps even more taken by how contemporary she seems, how she appears to bridge the gap of more than 3,000 years to our own world." [*Living with Art*, p 343]

"Her name means 'the beautiful one has arrived'," reveals Janson. "Its perfection comes from a command of geometry that is at once precise – the face is completely symmetrical – and wonderfully subtle." However, the artist did alter her skull and neck to resemble the 'royal' misshapen skull and elongated neck' of her husband, Pharaoh Akhenaten. [*History of Western Art*, p 43-4]

Hoving declares: "Nothing quite equals her shell-like ears, nose and lips of inexpressible elegance, and impossibly thin, long neck...we know that Akhenaten demanded total realism in his artists, even when they portrayed him in an unflattering manner. Whoever he was, he married the most beautiful woman of all time." [*Greatest Works of Art*, p 165]

Gardner adds: "In a daring mixture of naturalism and stylization...the famous painted limestone *Nefertiti* bust exhibits an expression of entranced musing..." [p 91-2]

In April 2009, the medical journal *Radiology* reported researchers in Berlin [after performing a CT scan of the bust] discovered: "a detailed stone carving that differs from the external stucco face...that the stone core of the statue is a highly detailed sculpture of the queen." However, Dr. Huppertz, who led the research team, identified the differences between the 2 faces as slight...the original stone core was distinguished by a bump on her nose, plus creases at the corners of her mouth. [*LA Times*, p D3]

Vanity may have played a role in the omission of the original 'creases'. Perhaps, the earlier stone version adhered to the order of the king ... while the added stucco version followed the pleas of his vain queen.

Another mystery is why this masterpiece was discovered in the studio of an artist – Thutmos, the chief court sculptor to Pharaoh Akhenaten – and not, as one might expect, in a royal tomb or in the ruins of an ancient temple.

Some references suggest the *Nefertiti Bust* was in the artist's studio to serve as a model for other court sculptors and artists. This would explain why the left eye socket is finished but has no inlay, "for this showed the [next] sculptor exactly how to make the hollow in which the eyeball would finally be set in carved stone." [Wildung, p 73, 75]

Bostrom in *Encyclopedia of Sculpture* in 2004 differs: "Termed a model from which apprentice sculptors might learn, the bust appears too accomplished for that purpose. Its design is unlike anything else from Ancient Egypt. Viewed from profile, the face lunges forward, like a streamlined wedge, but it retains its equilibrium ..." [p 494-95]

The *Nefertiti Bust* was found near Tel el-Amarna, the site of the main palace erected by the Pharaoh Akhenaten, who died at the age of 30. Janson says: "It was abandoned with a nearly identical head in the workshop of the royal sculptor Thutmos ... when he moved back from Amarna to Memphis after Akhenaten's death." [p 44]

After his death, Akhenaten's palace at Amarna was abandoned, and Amarna ceased to be the capital of Egypt. The corrupt, multi-god, temple priesthood swiftly regained the dominance they had lost during Akhenaten's reign – when he had introduced the one god, Aton. [Durant, p 210-11]

Perhaps, the *Nefertiti Bust* was 'abandoned' for safekeeping ... to hide it from vandalism or the destruction that leveled most of the monuments created during the reign of her husband, Akhenaten.

Hoving explains how this treasure reached Berlin in 1912: "*Nefertiti* was discovered by a teenage worker in an archeological crew of German excavators ... He gave it to the foreman Mohammed who handed it over to archaeologist Ludwig Borchardt who was struck dumb by its beauty. Borchardt promptly had it smuggled out of Egypt, in violation of his contract with the Egyptian government requiring him to show them everything found on the dig and make 'appropriate' partage [division]. The Egyptians have complained bitterly ever since..." [p 165]

Subject:

Nefertiti was the chief wife of Pharaoh Akhenaten from about 1353 to 1337 BC, during the 18th Dynasty. They "had 7 daughters, but no son; and though by law he might have sought an heir by his secondary wives, he would not, but preferred to remain 'faithful' to Nefertiti." [Durant, p 211]

Durant also reveals Akhenaten "allowed artists to depict him riding in a chariot through the streets, engaged in pleasantries with his wife and children... on ceremonial occasions the Queen sat beside him and held his hand, while their daughters frolicked at the foot of the throne. He spoke of his wife as 'Mistress of his Happiness... at whose voice the King rejoices'... and for an oath he used the phrase, 'As my heart is happy in the Queen and her children'." [p 212]

From depictions of Akhenaten and his wife Nefertiti on surviving reliefs, some sources suggest Akhenaten may have shared his power with his wife... even making her a partner in introducing his new state religion. [*30,000 Years*, p 118-19]

There is uncertainty concerning the parentage of a succeeding pharaoh, Tutankhamun, famed for the riches of his tomb. [see next sculpture] Some suggest Akhenaten was his uncle [Janson, p 44]... or half-brother [Hartt, p 97] Other references suggest Nefertiti was the mother-in-law of Tut.

Sculptor:

The *Nefertiti Bust* is attributed to Thutmos – the chief court sculptor to Pharaoh Akhenaten – in whose studio it was found.

Gardner offers a possible explanation why this bust appears so refreshingly realistic. "We know that Egypt had commercial relations with Crete... and the livelier, less convention-bound art of the Minoans could have proved suggestive and stimulating to the Amarna artists. It may be that some Cretan artists, finding refuge in Egypt and a sympathetic artist climate under Akhenaten's rule, fertilized the Amarna style." [p 86-7]

Prior to the 2009 discovery of the bust's original stone core [under current layers of stucco], the Egyptian Museum of Berlin in 2006 said: "In reality, the bust depicts a mature woman on whose features life has begun to leave its mark. The [faint] lines under the eyes, the slightly sunken cheeks, the creases and pockmarks around the nose and mouth give the face austere appeal of a poignant humanity. The subject of this portrait is not eternal youth, but mortality, as formulated in Akhenaten's own theology. Life is understood to find its fulfillment in the here and now, in the short space of time between birth and death." [Egypt. Mus.-Berlin, p 75]

Nefertiti would not have been the first queen to order a 'face-lift' of her official image.

Or...after the death of her husband Akhenaten, more conservative elements of Egyptian society may have demanded a more perfect image of Nefertiti. It is possible she ruled Egypt a few years after the death of her husband.

A copy of the *Nefertiti Bust* appears in the NY Metropolitan Museum of Art.

Major References:

Basic History of Western Art, 2006, Janson & Janson, p 43-44

Egyptian Mus. & Papyrus Collection-Berlin, 2006, Wildung, p 73, 75

Greatest Works of Art, 1997, Hoving, p 164-65

Los Angeles Times, April 1, 2009, 'Nefertiti Is Really Two-Faced', p D3

Associated Press, May 2010

Encyclopedia of Sculpture, 2004, Bostrom, p 494-95

30,000 Years of Art, 2007, editors-Phaidon Press, p 119

Our Oriental Heritage, 1935, Durant, p 188, 206-12

Art through the Ages, Vol I, 1980, Gardner, p 86-7, 91-2

Living with Art. 2002, Gatlein, p 343

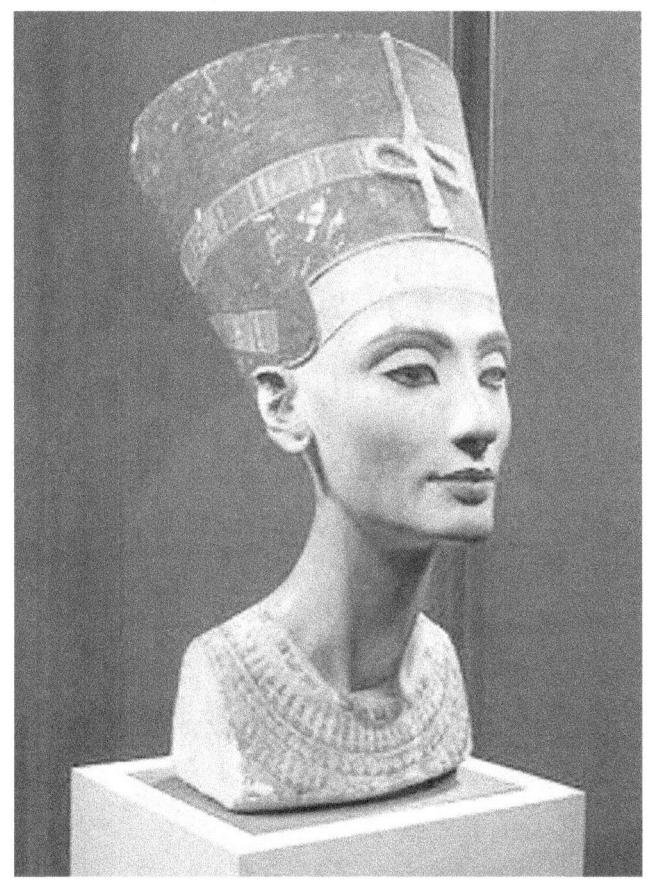

5

GOLD MASK OF
TUTANKHAMUN
OR KING TUT

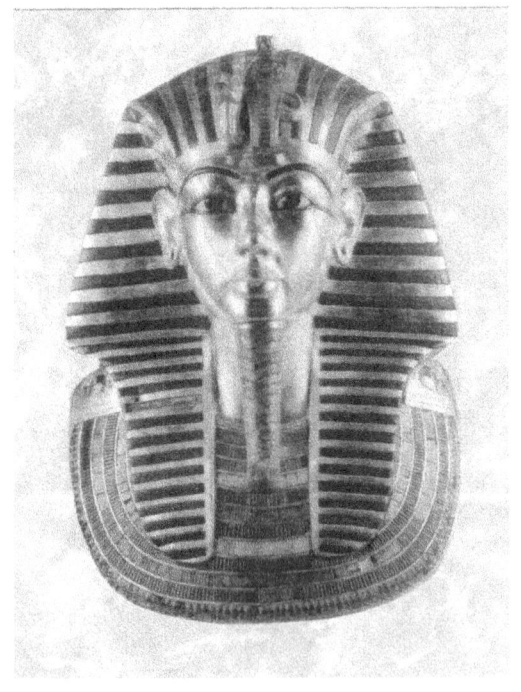

"... one of most beautiful and evocative works of art to have
survived antiquity... among the top portraits ever achieved."
... Hoving, *Greatest Works of Art in Western Civilization*, p 186-7

Found 1922, Valley of Kings – now, Egyptian Museum, Cairo
Egyptian funeral mask – approx. 1323 BC – naturalistic
Ht. 21 inches [54.5 cm], Wt. 24.5 lb – solid gold, w/inlays
Sculptor: unknown Egyptian artisan

The Boy-King Tutankhamun [also known as King Tut] lived from about 1344 to 1323 BC.

"The discovery of his tomb in Egypt's romantic Valley of the Kings in the late evening of November 26, 1922 – and the removal from it [over 10 years] of nearly 5,000 dazzling works of art – caused a sensation throughout the world. It was, and remains, the richest discovery in the history of archaeology." [*Greatest Works of Art*, Hoving, p 186]

In the late 1970s, when Egypt sent the *Gold Mask* and related treasures on a world museum tour, it was "estimated the collection attracted the greatest number of visitors recorded for any single tour of works of art." [Gardner, p 93]

Millions marveled at the mask's "solid beaten gold … eyes of quartz and obsidian … eyelids and eyebrows of lapis lazuli … on the chest a broad collar encrusted with lapis lazuli, quartz and green feldspar … the falcon's head of gold … and also the cobra, whose head was covered with dark blue faience, the hood inlaid with lapis lazuli …" [MacQuitty, 26]

> [when the *Gold Mask* was created … other precious
> jewels such as diamonds, rubies, sapphires, and
> pearls were unknown to the artisans of Egypt]

Tut's tomb had been discovered by British archaeologist Howard Carter after a search of 15 years. He and his sponsor Lord Carnarvon were inspired by discoveries of earlier archaeologists [from 1900 to 1910] in the Valley of Kings. These finds included an elegant blue cup with the name 'Tutankhamun' inscribed upon it … and, later, a grave and tomb yielding more inscriptions with Tut's name. [Nardo, p 16, 18]

The *Atlas of Legendary Places* reveals: "After several seasons of largely fruitless digging, Carnarvon almost decided to close down the operation. But Carter, who knew that nearly all of the tombs of the pharaohs of the 18th Dynasty [c.1570-1320 BC] had been found in the Valley, was convinced Tut's tomb lay waiting to be unearthed. He persuaded Carnarvon to let him dig for one more season ..." [p 93]

Carter had a hunch the entrance of Tut's tomb was obscured by mounds of dirt and rubble left by ancient grave-robbers looting a subsequent tomb [of Ramses VI]. Workers who constructed this tomb – 200 years after the reign of Tut – "built their week-days huts above the spot where Tut was buried. No one [not even thieves] thought to look under the workers' huts for a tomb. This saved King Tut from robbers [including pharaohs who plundered their predecessor's tombs to decorate their own] for more than 3,000 years ... until Carter came along." [Hawass, p 14]

On Nov. 26, 1922, a porter of water-jars – scooping out a hole to prop a jar – uncovered the top of a step carved into rock. He rushed to Carter's tent, anxious to be the first to tell him ... and get a reward. Carter soon brushed away more sand and exclaimed, "This is the tomb!" [p 18]

Carter ordered the descending staircase cleared of debris to bedrock. After uncovering 16 steps, a solid mud-brick door [finished with plaster] appeared ... showing signs of having been broken, repaired, and re-plastered. This dismayed Carter, as it indicated grave-robbers had preceded him. Removal of more debris revealed: "The [original] seal on the door had been broken ... a tell-tale sign that thieves had entered." [p 22]

Then, Carter was greatly relieved to find that a new seal had been placed over the re-plaster in ancient times ... suggesting the tomb had not been disturbed for some 3 millennia.

Halting work, Carter sent an urgent telegram to Lord Carnarvon in London to come quickly. He arrived 18 days later ... and the doorway was completely cleared: "They soon found the name of Tutankhamun, stamped in the plaster." [p 19] They broke through the door and cleared a 25-foot, rubble-filled passageway leading to a second 'repaired' door. Carter cut a small hole … to insert a candle to test the air. He then enlarged the hole and peered into the first of 4 chambers. '… as my eyes grew accustomed to the light, details of the room within emerged slowly from the mist – strange animals, statues, and gold – everywhere the glint of gold … I was struck dumb with amazement'." [MacQuitty, p 9] "… and Lord Carnarvon, unable to stand the suspense any longer, inquired anxiously, 'Can you see anything?' It was all I could do to get out the words, 'Yes, wonderful things'." [p 4]

"Scattered and overturned funeral objects" indicated intruders had searched in haste and most likely taken easily-carried gold objects which could be quickly melted down. [MacQuitty, p 12]

In 1926, after almost 4 years of methodically cleaning and documenting an amazing array of artifacts in the 4 chambers of the tomb, the archeologists opened and dismantled the huge gold-gilded, wooden shrine that filled the 'burial chamber' room. Within the first shrine, they found 3 successively-smaller decorated shrines before reaching a yellow quartz sarcophagus. After its granite cover [weighing a ton] was removed, they saw a golden effigy of the boy-king on the lid of the first of 3 human-shaped coffins. The eyes of Tutankhamun "stared up at them" in "a lifelike portrait." [Harpur, p 96, & MacQuitty, p 19]

The first and second coffins were both wood covered in sheet gold. On the second coffin, "The face wears a look of suffering – the sadness of death in youth." [MacQuitty. p 19] A third and last coffin was "wrapped in a red linen shroud." To the astonishment of Howard Carter and the world, the third coffin "was found to be solid 22-carat gold, weighing an incredible 243 pounds … The face was calm and reposed. The eyes had lost their look of anguish, and the expression was tranquil and profoundly moving." [p 24]

An even greater surprise came as they raised the lid of the final inner coffin and saw the *Gold Mask of King Tut* – "the <u>finest funerary</u>

mask ever discovered and the most important object in the magnificent treasure of the tomb." [MacQuitty, 26]

"The stylized portrait mask [over the face of the mummy] shows the features relaxed in a kind of musing serenity that betokens his confidence in eternal life. ... the general effect is one of grandeur and richness... expressive of Egyptian power, pride, and affluence at the time of the onset of the empire." [Gardner, p 94]

Tut's mummy remains in its original tomb in the Valley of Kings. His invaluable 22-carat, gold coffin and the *Gold Mask* were transferred to the Egyptian Museum in Cairo.

Subject:

Durant states: "...the world would hardly have heard of Tut had not unprecedented treasures been found in his grave." [p 213]

Much of what is known concerning the life of Tutenkhamun is speculative...including that his parents may have been the Pharoah Akhenatan and a secondary wife named Kiya.

Born about 1342 BC, Tut was crowned at the age of 8 and reigned as Pharoah for 9 years. It is unlikely the Boy-King had more than a ceremonial role in the affairs of state.

"The leading royal advisor, Ay, and a powerful general, Horemheb, took the young Tut to Memphis where he was crowned king. Under their influence, the new pharaoh restored the old gods...After the boy-king died [under mysterious circumstances] ... Ay saw to it that he was embalmed and placed in a [temporary?] tomb. But the ceremony was rushed and done in secret.... Ay now took the throne...4 years later, Ay himself was dead, and Horemheb was the new pharaoh. Horemheb ordered the names of Akhenatan, Nefertiti, Smenkhare, Tutankhamun, and Ay chiseled off all monuments. He even forbade people from speaking their names. The strange circumstances surrounding Tut and those he knew were eventually forgotten, just as his tomb was...buried by drifting sands." [Nardo, p 6, 10-14]

Nardo's research may explain the smallness of Tut's burial chambers, but not the mystery of the magnificence of his solid gold coffin weighing 243 pounds, plus the exquisite *Golden Mask*. In addition, 4 shrines and 4 coffins [all gilded and/or decorated] had enclosed and protected the *Golden Mask*.

This repeated grand artistry suggests a lengthy time period was required for the multiple creations. This raises the possibility that Tut's 'permanent' tomb and his *Golden Mask* were not completed until many years after his death.

If, as some suspect, Tut was a son of Pharoah Akhenatan, then followers of Akhenatan's one-god religion [though banned] might have secretly created Tut's hidden tomb. Their *religious fervor* might also explain why the tomb – though limited in size – was gloriously furnished.

Tombs of better-known pharaohs were far larger... and we can only imagine how richly they were adorned. The tomb treasures of Ramses II the Great – who built half of the surviving temples and other ancient edifices of Egypt during his 67-year reign – undoubtedly dwarfed those of Tut.

Sculptor:

The artisan(s) who created Tut's funeral mask remain unknown. Ancient Egypt, like ancient Rome, rarely gave artists recognition for their works. Instead, 'recognition' normally went to those who commissioned the works.

Gold for the coffin and mask came from gold-bearing regions of Nubia to the south, near the source of the Nile. These gold mines were developed in about 1500 BC and had made Egypt a wealthy nation by the time Tutankhamum became a pharoah.

Major References:

Art Through the Ages, Gardner, 1996, p 93-4

Tutankhamun, the Last Journey, William MacQuitty, 1978, p 9, 12, 19, 24-6

Tutankhamun: Mystery of Boy King, 2005, Hawass, p 14, 18, 19, 22

Atlas of Legendary Places, 1997, Harpur/Westwood, p 93, 96-7

History of Art, 1977, Janson, p 65

Our Oriental Heritage, 1935, Will Durant, p 213

Treasures of Tutankhamun, 1978, LA Museum of Art

Greatest Works of Art of Western Civilization, 1997, Hoving, p 186-87

30,000 Years of Art, 2007, editors Phaidon Press, p 121

King Tut, 2005 June, National Geographic, Williams, p 2-21

King Tut's Tomb, 2005, Nardo, p 4-12

6

THE LION GATE

OF MYCENAE

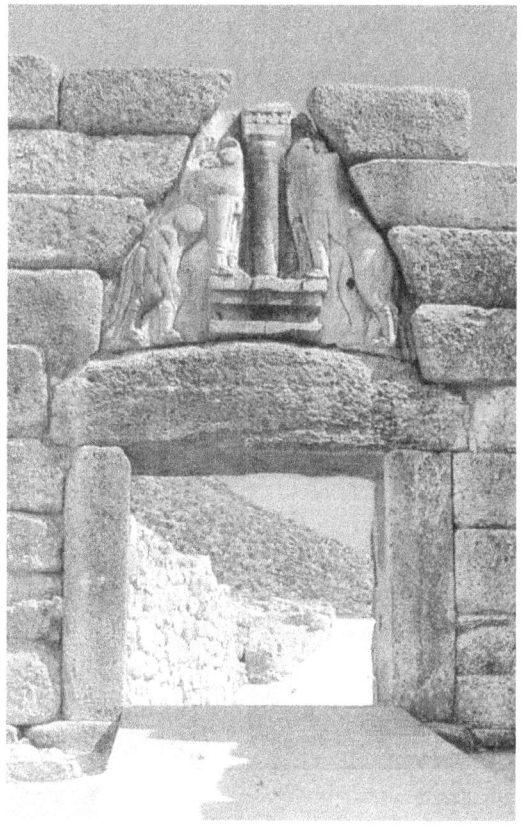

"The lions are carved with breadth and vigor…harmonizing
in dignity, strength, and scale with the massive stones that form
the walls and gate."…Gardner, *Art Through Ages*, p 112

Sculpted approx. 1250 BC – at Citadel of Mycenae, Greece
Mycenaean reliefs – naturalistic [w/Hittite & Minoan styling]
Ht. of relief: 9 ft. 10 in. [300 cm] – dark limestone
Sculptor: unknown ... Hittite, Minoan, or Egyptian

This ancient, majestic portal is <u>an astonishing masterpiece of symmetry.</u>

The "royal beasts standing guard" atop the *Lion Gate* comprise <u>the oldest monumental relief sculpture in all of Europe</u>. [Durant, p 28, Hafner, p 37-8] Their heads would have become 'prizes' in antiquity.

The Mycenaean Age – 1950 BC to 1100 BC – takes its name from the Citadel of Mycenae, the strongest palace-fortress of pre-historic Greece. It is located 12 miles from the Aegean Sea ... a distance that lessened the element of surprise by raiding pirates. The fortress commanded land trading routes in the region.

Today, it can be a humbling experience to enter *the Lion Gate*. We follow in the footsteps of King Agamemnon – who ruled Mycenae [and led the Greeks in the Trojan War]. His brother Menelaus [king of neighboring Sparta] passed through the massive stone entrance with his wife Helen [renowned for her beauty]. Another visitor was Paris of Troy. Since then – more than 3,000 years ago – many hundreds of other kings and queens would have passed under the long-standing *Lion Gate*.

Durant describes ancient Mycenae as "a forbidding cita-del ... housing a busy population of peasants, merchants, artisans, and slaves ..." Homer called this fortress: "a well-built city, broad-avenued and abounding in gold." [p 28]

Three millennia ago ... at the zenith of Mycenae, the lion heads are said to have been gold [or gilded] ... to impressively greet all who entered.

The *Author*, approaching *the Gate* near noon, squinted into the bright sunlight. Had the heads been present and in gold, the lions could not have been more spell-binding.

The missing heads – which might have confirmed their gen-der – were sculpted as separate pieces. The *Encyclopedia of Sculpture* says: "The heads faced out toward those entering the gate and were probably of a more distinctive stone, although gold or bronze has also been suggested." [p 17]

Ancient kings normally preferred the male lion to signify power and majesty; however, the sleekness of these lions suggests they might have been female. If not...the male heads are carved inordinately slim.

Higgins states: "This famous relief was never lost to sight. Athenian audiences of the play 'Agamemnon of Aeschylus' [in the 5th century BC] could have visualized King Agamemnon passing through this very gate to his death on his return from Troy." [*Minoan and Mycenaean Art,* p 93] Pausanias [Greek traveler/author] also saw it in the 2nd century AD.

From 3,200 years ago...Homer describes the forbidding Citadel of Mycenae ruled by Agamemnon. The ancient story-teller invites us to believe the lovely Helen fell in love with the Trojan prince Paris during his royal visit to Sparta...and later, from Mycenae, they secretly fled to Troy. If so, they may have escaped in the night through the less-adorned, still-standing North Gate of the Citadel.

As Homer relates, the Trojan War soon followed.

Subject:

The upright stance of the lions is unique in art...and may represent the coat of arms of one of Europe's oldest royal families...the line of Atreus, father of Agamemnon and Menelaus. R. Brilliant's *Arts of the Ancient Greeks* concurs the lions are: "... the emblem of Mycenae and its ruling house." [p 16]

30,000 Years of Art states: "Lions are common symbols of royalty in the ancient Mediterranean...and the [Mycenae] arrangement with an altar has recently been linked to divinely-sanctioned order and prosperity. The clean lines and powerful musculature of these felines would have made them an impressive sight as one approached the gate, particularly since monumental sculpture was virtually unknown in the Bronze Age Aegean." [p 124]

The *Lion Gate* not only guarded the Citadel, it protected 'Grave Circle A' just inside the gate. Here, in December 1876, Heinrich

Schliemann discovered 5 royal graves, containing 15 skeletons. He wrote: "The bodies were literally covered with gold and jewelry." [Ceram, p 48] Later research determined "they were not the graves of Agamemnon and his followers, but of people who most likely had lived some 400 years earlier." [p 49]

"The golden relics found by Schliemann were of enormous value ... and not exceeded in opulence until the finds of Carnarvon and Carter [King Tut #5] in Egypt." [Ceran, p 50] Durant adds: "Here were male skulls with crowns of gold and golden masks on the bones of the faces ... ladies with golden diadems." [p 19]

Visitors to Mycenae are advised to bring a powerful flashlight ... to enter the [unlighted] "90-foot underground passageway from the Citadel down to its secret water supply [cistern] ... fed by the spring called *Persea* outside the walls of the fortress. [Miller, p 226]

Sculptor:

The architect and sculptor of the *Lion Gate* are unknown. The Mycenaens may have imported artists from Anatolia [Turkey], Mesopotamia, or Egypt.

The Jansons say the Mycenaen hilltop palaces were: "... surrounded by defensive walls of huge, irregular shaped stone blocks. This type of construction, unknown in Crete, was similar to fortifications of contemporary Hittite centers in Asia Minor [modern Turkey] ... The two lions have a grim, heraldic majesty. Their function as guardians of the gate ... and symmetrical design again suggest contact with the Hittites ... who often employed such 'beasts' to protect their citadels and palaces." [p 65]

Treasury of Atreus:

Most tours to Mycenae include the remarkable, 'misnamed' *Treasury of Atreus* – a well-preserved and intact beehive [tholos] tomb on the slope of the same hill. Its interior vault, without supports, remained the largest unified space in the known world for 1500 years ... until the Romans built the Pantheon.

Major References:

Minoan and Mycenaean Art, 1989, Higgins, p 93

Arts of Ancient Greeks, 1972, Brilliant, p 12, 15-6

Mycenae, 2001, Spathari, p 18, 20, 26

Gods, Graves, and Scholars, 1954, Ceram, p 44-50

Life of Greece, 1939, Durant, p 28-32

Encyclopedia of Sculpture, 2004, Bostrom, p 17

Art Through the Ages, Vol I, 10th edition, 1996, Gardner, p 112-13

Greek Art, 1973, Boardman, p 19-21

History of Art, 2006, Janson, p 65-7

Mycenae-Epidaurus-Tiryns-Nauplion, 1978, Papahatzis, p 74

30,000 Years of Art, 2007, editors Phaidon Press, p 124

Art of Crete, Mycenae, and Greece, 1968, Hafner, p 37-8

Greece Through the Ages, 1972, Miller, p. 226-28

Greek Art, 1973, Boardman, p 20

Art in the Western World, 1953, Robb & Garrison, p 403

7
WINGED BULL
OF KHORSABAD

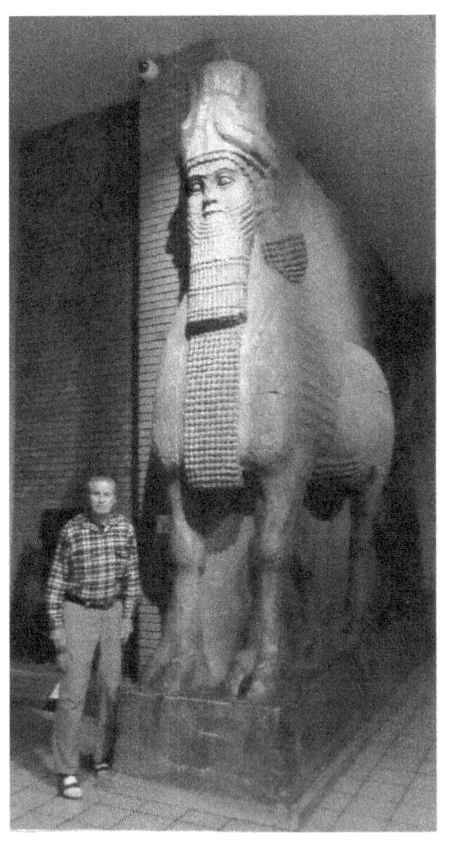

"The gigantic size, the bold vigorous carving, and
fine sweep of wings...produce a splendor and a
stupendous strength that are awesome even today."
...Gardner, *Art Through the Ages*, I, 1954, p 52

Excavated 1824, Khorsabad, Iraq – now, British Museum*
Assyrian – approx. 720 BC – naturalistic and stylized
Ht. 16.5 ft. [tallest; Wt. 40 tons [largest] – limestone
Sculptor: Egyptian, possibly Babylonian, or even Assyrian
*and Louvre, NY Met. Mus. & Chicago Oriental Art Inst.

[*Autho*r, beside *Man-Bull*, can attest few domesticated animals strike fear into the heart of man as much as an angered
bull]

T he primary purpose of the *Winged Bulls* – created by the ancient
Assyrians – was to serve as symbolic warnings to their enemies.
Janson tells us: "<u>Awesome in size and appearance, they were
meant to impress the visitor with the power [potential terror] and
majesty of the king</u>." [*History of Art*, p 74]

Immense wealth was necessary to carve the colossal *Bulls*… and
to build the Assyrian palaces "of unprecedented size and magnificence." The accumulated riches of the 300-year Assyrian Empire
were the result of superior military technology. "The Assyrians
were the first to equip armies with weapons of iron. They also
exploited a new military arm, horse cavalry." [*Ancient Engineers,*
De Camp, p 63, 65]

Their empire stretched from the Sinai peninsula of Egypt to
Armenia in the north… subjecting the ancient Syrians, Phoenicians,
Babylonians, Sumerians, Armenians, Palestinians, Cypriots, and
Egyptians.

De Camp reports that in the land of ancient Babylon: "resounded
the tramp of the dreaded soldiery of Assyria – burly, bearded, hook-
nosed men in heavy boots and crested bronze helmets. For 300
years, one of the most ferociously militaristic governments known
to history held 'the Land Between the Rivers' [Mesopotamia] in its
merciless grip." [p 62]

Gardner says: "Centuries of unremitting warfare against their
neighbors and often rebellious subjects hardened the Assyrians
into a cruel and merciless people whose atrocities in warfare were

bitterly decried throughout the ancient world." [*Art Through the Ages*, p 50]

Subject:

Due to the great size of the *Winged Bulls* – as tall as 16.5 feet and weighing as much as 40 tons – they survived the eventual devastation of the grand Assyrian palaces during the rapid fall of their empire.

In ancient times, the massive man-beasts – carved from single blocks of limestone – were positioned at principal gateways to palaces and at ceremonial entrances to throne rooms.

Gardner states: "They wear the horned crowns of the god-kings of Akkad and the large-eyed, bearded masks familiar ever since Sumer...Dazzling brilliance seems also to have been part of the Assyrian plan to overwhelm the visitor. The bull and lion bodies of the gate figures and their eagles' wings suggest the superhuman strength and fierceness of the king and his swiftness to bring justice or vengeance." [p 52-3]

Bazin adds: "These terrifying beasts – man, eagle, and bull all at once – were powerfully defined under the sheathing of minutely-detailed surfaces. The artist has sought to express not life, but rather a kind of pitiless machine capable of crushing any hostile visitor." [*History of World Sculpture*, p 121]

In 1824, the French archeologist, Paul Emil Botta, discovered two 'bulls' in the ruins of King Sargon II's summer palace [under village of modern Khorsabad near Mosul in northern Iraq]. This massive palace was built into the perimeter of a citadel some 500 feet square." [Hartt, p 112] The Louvre swiftly acquired the two bulls.

As the palace was further excavated, additional colossal *Bulls* appeared. In 1849, British archeologists cut their 2 *Bulls* into sections light enough to be transported to London. [this pair of *Bulls* are said to have been left behind by the French because they were too heavy]

Similar bulls have been excavated in other Assyrian palaces at Nineveh. Due to the addition of a 5th leg – immediately behind the front pair of legs – a person viewing the bull from the side gains a sense of movement.

The Oriental Institute of Chicago has the largest *Bull* at 16' 4" and weighing 40 tons... excavated in 1929 just outside the entrance to the king's throne room. The smallest *Bull* – from another palace in Nimrud – is now in the Metropolitan Museum of New York.

Sculptors:

The sculptors of the *Winged Bulls* are unknown. From earlier massive stone monuments in Egypt, it is likely Egyptian artisans played a role in designing and carving them. It is also possible the Assyrians developed the expertise to carve these stone monuments themselves, as they had been importing sculptors from other lands for some 200 years.

Since the Assyrians borrowed much of their culture from nearby Babylonia – 300 miles to the south – artisans from Babylon also may have contributed.

Major References:

History of World Sculpture, 1968, Bazin, p 121
The Ancient Engineers, 1960, De Camp, p 62-70
Art Through the Ages, Vol I, 1980, Gardner, p 52-3
History of Art, 1977, Janson, p 73-5
Art: History of Painting, Sculpture..., 1989, Hartt, p 112
Our Oriental Heritage, 1935, Durant, p. 266, 272, 278-81
30,000 Years of Art, 2007, Phaidon Press, p 172
www.thebritishmuseum.ac.uk
www.oi.uchicago.edu/research/projects/kho

8

THE DYING LIONESS

OF THE ROYAL HUNT

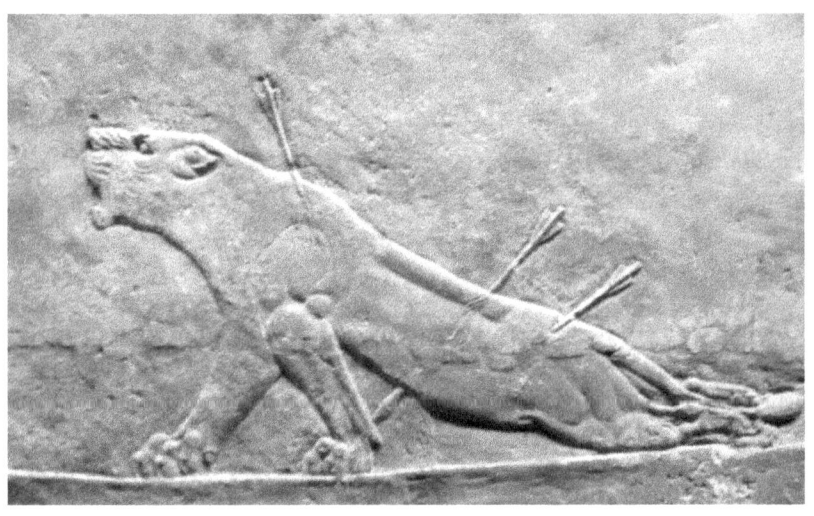

"...one of most beautifully carved pieces on earth...intricate
anatomical details rendered to perfection...gripping drama."
....Hoving, *Greatest Works of Art of Western Civilization*, p 40

Found 1854 in ruins of Nineveh palace* – now, Brit. Museum
Assyrian relief – approx. 645 to 635 BC – naturalistic
Ht. lion: 23 in., relief panel: 66 in. – alabaster stone
Sculptor: unknown Egyptian, Assyrian, or Babylonian
 Nineveh, near Mosul in Iraq

The plight of the courageous lioness draws both admiration and sympathy. This scene is one of a series of Assyrian reliefs – known as the *Royal Hunt of Ashurbanipal II* – recognized as among of the earliest and finest narrative reliefs to appear in sculptural art.

The reliefs portray the ancient sport of lion-hunting ... but, from the point of view of *the hunted*.

Durant enthusiastically declares: "In the heyday of the [Assyrian] kings Sargon II and Ashurbanipal – and presumably through their lavish patronage – the art of bas-relief created new masterpieces ... never before or since have pictured animals been carved so successfully." [*Our Oriental Heritage, p 278*]

Janson adds: "Images such as the 'dying lioness' have an unforgettable tragic grandeur." [*History of Art, p 75*]

On the *Royal Hunt* reliefs in the British Museum, 27 grievously-wounded or dying lions are depicted ... several of whom boldly persevere in attacking the chariot of the Assyrian King Ashurbanipal II [668-627 BC].

In particular, the drama of one mortally-wounded lioness draws our attention. Three arrows from the bow of the King have penetrated her back and crippled her hind-legs. Still, the defiant animal fights on, snarling with flattened ears and supporting herself by forelegs only ... "maintaining surpassing dignity in her final agony." [Hoving, p 41]

Gardner adds: "The artist gives a ruthless reading of straining muscles, the swelling veins, the corrugations of the muzzle ..." [*Art Thru Ages, p 55*]

The sculptor, by depicting the defeated lions as brave and bold-spirited opponents, enhances the glory of the victorious king. In ancient times, the giving of 'artistic dignity through courage' to a fallen opponent was relatively rare.

[some 400 years later, 'artistic dignity' appears in statuary of ancient Pergamon ... see *Gaul Chieftain & Wife* and *Dying Gaul*. #36 & 37]

In 1845, Austen Henry Layard, an amateur antiquarian discovered the foundations of Nineveh's palaces and other great buildings... along the Tigris River near modern Mosul in Iraq. King Ashurbanipal II had built his royal palace in Nineveh – a major city of 300,000... named for the goddess, Nina [the Ishtar of Assyria].

During excavations, Layard also found giant winged lions and bulls, alabaster friezes, and countless other artifacts. This included a vast collection of 'books' in the form of cuneiform tablets... now referred to as the 'Library of Ashurbanipal II'. The king had commissioned scribes to make copies of all the classics of Sumerian and Babylonian literature... found intact after the passage of 2,500 years.

Hoving concludes: "The array of Assurbanipal's Nineveh's stones, in their own way, rivals the sculptures of the Parthenon." Both 'collections' are displayed near each other in the British Museum.

Subject:

The ancient Assyrians – like many other archaic civilizations – viewed the lion as 'the king of the beasts', a noble creature, and therefore an animal worthy of being hunted by a king. To display their prowess in killing lions, the uncommonly cruel kings of Assyria decorated their palaces with relief panels of lion hunts... as Ashurbanipal II did for his throne room [about 640 BC].

At the British Museum, 'display cards' offer another explanation why these kings hunted lions. After many years of heavy rainfall in mid-7th century Assyria, lions had become overly plentiful. An ancient document relates:

"The hills resounded with their roaring, the wild animals tremble.

They pull down the cattle, spill human blood as well."

Therefore, it became the king's duty to thin the lions threatening his people. [see the lion-hybrid *Chimaera of Arezzo* #21, whose Near East origin appears similar]

Hartt reveals the fate of the captured beasts: "Lions were released from their cages, after having been goaded into fury, so that the king could display his strength and courage by shooting down the maddened beasts from his chariot.... these heroic reliefs unleash an astonishing explosion of forces...the swift flight of the horses, the resolute power of the monarch, the rage of the tormented beasts." [*Art: History of Painting, Sculpture,* p 115]

Fourteen years after Ashurbanipal II died in 626 BC, armies from Babylon and Susa plus Scythians from the Caucasus banded together to defeat the new Assyrian king. Durant writes: "Nineveh was laid waste as ruthlessly and completely as her kings had once ravaged Susa and Babylon...the city was put to the torch...the population was slaughtered or enslaved...and the palace so recently built by Ashurbanipal was sacked and destroyed. At one blow, Assyria disappeared from history." [p 283]

Sculptor:

The sculptors of the *Dying Lioness* and related reliefs are unknown. They may have been Assyrian, Egyptian, or from Babylonia [300 miles to the south]. The alabaster stone they carved is translucent gypsum, often used for statues and vases by the ancient Assyrians. Their relief panels "were originally painted, apparently in quite bold colors, traces of paint still survive on some." [*30,000 Years,* p 180]

Note: Visitors to the British Museum often head directly for the famed *Parthenon Marbles*...unknowingly passing narrow Hall 10A [on their left] devoted to the *Royal Hunt of Assurbanipal*. Display cards for each relief panel offer ample descriptions of the scenes on the panels.

Major References:

History of Art, 1977, Janson, p 74-5

Display references in British Museum

Greatest Works of Art of Western Civilization, 1997, Thomas Hoving, p 40-1

British Museum Book of Greek & Roman Art, 1991, Lucilla Burn

Art Through the Ages, Vol I, 1980, Gardner, p 54-5

Our Oriental Heritage, 1935, Durant, p. Fig 31, 279, 266-283

Saudi Aramco World, 1962, February, p. 18-20

Art: A History of Painting, Sculpture..., 1989, Hartt, p 114-15

Gods, Graves, and Scholars, 1954, Ceram, p 265

9

'THE TYRANNICIDES'

ARISTOGEITON & HARMODIUS

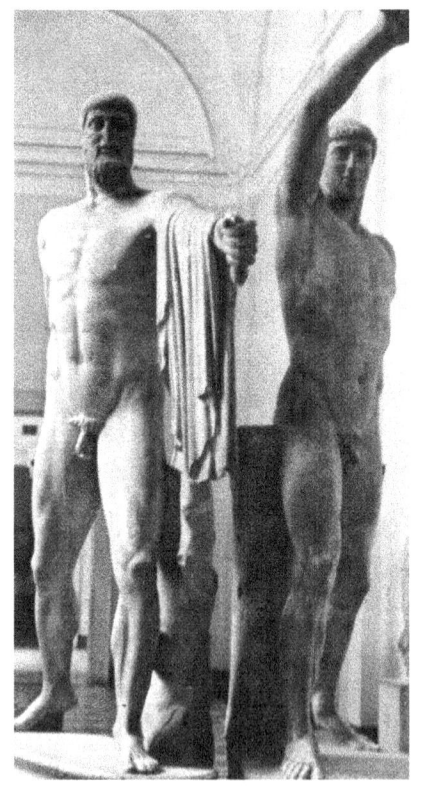

"...most famous group of Athenian statuary"
in the Early Greek Classical era
...Durant, *Life of Greece*, p 221

[see their backs at chapter end]
Found 1770, Hadrian's Villa – now, Naples Arch. Museum
Roman copy – approx. 130 AD – Early Greek Classical style
From: lost Original Greek bronze – [approx. 505 BC]
Ht: 6 ft. 7 in. – marble – originally painted
Sculptors: Antenor [1st bronze], Kritios & Nesiotes [2nd bronze]

T his violent, convoluted event – an attempted assassination gone awry – occurred in Athens in 514 BC. Though the 2 figures are identified as *Tyrannicides*... neither killed a tyrant. [instead... they were 'instrumental' in causing a tyrant to abdicate and leave Athens]

Durant accurately reveals in 514 BC, two Athenian conspirators, *Aristogeiton* and *Harmodius,* lost their lives... in a courageous act that eventually enabled Athens to form the world's first democracy in 507 BC. [*Life of Greece*, p 123-4]

Therefore, Durant identifies the conspirators as "the martyrs of liberty." [p 124]

Lawrence agrees. For the ancient Greeks, the [mis-named] *Tyrannicides* – mature *Aristogeiton* and his young protege *Harmodius* – personified the birth of 'self-government'. [*Greek & Roman Sculpture,* p 114]

'Entangled' Sequence of the Failed Act of Tyrannicide:

Tyrant Hippias... rules prosperous Athens, his reign is quiet
Hipparchos... Tyrant's foolish brother, who *pursues* Harmodius
Harmodius. ... protege and lover to the older Aristogeiton
Aristogeiton ... decides to kill both Hipparchos and Tyrant
Aristogeiton & Harmodius only succeed in killing Hipparchos
Tyrant Hippias, surviving, kills both Aristogeiton & Harmodius

[4 years later , in 510 BC, Hippias abdicates & leaves Athens]
Cleisthenes... seizes power in Athens, assumes a dictatorship...
507 BC, he establishes first democracy

Today…in the Naples Arch. Museum, *Harmodius* raises his sword high…as the bearded, older *Aristogeiton* holds a drapery to shield the coming blow from their victim Hipparchos [unseen].

In the next instant, the sword will strike Hipparchos.

Barr says: "…the two *Tyrannicides* who assassinated [the infatuated] 'Hipparchos'… had planned to assassinate [Tyrant] Hippias, too…" [*The Will of Zeus*, p 123]

Meletzis adds: "The long years of Peisistratid Clan rule were…"so hateful to the Athenians that they felt *the Tyrannicides* should receive due honor for their deed. After all, [indirectly] they owed them their liberty! Therefore, the sculptor Antenor was commissioned to create *the Tyrannicides*…." [*Acropolis*, p 12]

The original bronze stood in the ancient agora [marketplace] of Athens beginning about 505 BC…where Durant states it became "the most famous group in Athenian statuary…" [p 221]

Its renown spread throughout the Mediterranean world.

It gained additional fame 25 years later [480 BC], when the Persian king Xerxes captured Athens and seized *the Tyrannicides*. At the ensuing Battle of Salamis, Xerxes lost to the Greeks…however, he still carried his 'bronze prize' back to Persia. The Athenians quickly commissioned a replacement, sculpted by Critius and Nesiotes.

Further fame [149 years later] for the original bronze group resulted when Alexander the Great conquered Persia…recaptured the original *Tyrannicides*…and had it returned to Athens.

The current Roman marble version in Naples was carved about 130 AD. It was found at Hadrian's Villa outside Rome. Emperor Hadrian [117-138 AD] likely commissioned this marble copy from one of the original bronzes in Athens. He had spent several winters [125 and 128 AD] in Athens…where he began a building program more extensive than his public works in Rome…and "left Athens…a more beautiful city than ever before in its history." [*Caesar & Christ*, p 418]

Eventually…both bronze versions disappeared.

The surviving marble copy may have been displayed in Hadrian's gardens…"so crowded with famous works of art that every major museum in Europe has enriched itself from the ruins." [p 421]

The original Greek bronze *Tyrannicides* was unique among the Early Greek Classical works in that it represented 'mortal men in action'. Prior to this era, the Greeks generally sculpted male and female figures in rigid, frontal standing positions...essentially lifeless.

Encyclo Sculpt. states: "The new Early Classical style completely changed the concept of the human figure, being chiefly preoccupied with mobility and action and its expression of the body." [p 711]

R. Brilliant adds: "...the dignified, mature image of *Aristogeiton* may be compared in every aspect of physique and countenance with the great bronze statue of *Zeus of Artemision* #12. The calm nobility of the face, so grandly conceived, is contained within the type of mature, bearded god that is used as well for Poseidon...the type of *Harmodius* also served the sculptor Myron in his *Discus Thrower* #14 of 460 BC." [*Arts of Ancient Greeks*, p 145]

Subject:

Branigan & Vickers describe the 'heroic' *Aristogeiton & Harmodius.* "They were popularly revered as the liberators of Athens from the Peisistratid tyranny...the truth, according to Thucydides, was neither so simple, nor so heroic." [*Hellas*, p 112]

Durant's 'uncensored' account in *Life of Greece* explains how this failed tyrannicide occurred in 514 BC.

Thirteen years earlier, Hippias had become the Tyrant of Athens, following the death of his father Peisistratus.

"Hippias had continued the policies of his father. The younger brother Hipparchos [to Hippias] was devoted to love and poetry...Athens was prosperous, and the quiet reign of Hippias might have gone on to a peaceful close had it not been for the unsmooth course of Greek love." [p 123]

"*Aristogeiton*, a man of middle age [married, with children] had won the love of the young *Harmodius* 'in the flower of youthful beauty'... [young *Harmodius* also had a mistress, Leaena] ...but Hipparchos [equally careless of gender] solicited the lad's love."

"When *Aristogeiton* heard of this, he resolved to kill Hipparchos...and simultaneously [his brother, the tyrant] Hippias...then describe both killings as necessary to overthrow the tyranny of Hippias. *Harmodius* [and others] joined *Aristogeiton* in this 514 BC conspiracy. They murdered Hipparchos...but the tyrant Hippias eluded the conspirators and had them slain." [Durant, 123]

Hippias, frightened by this revolt, "replaced his hitherto mild rule with a regime of suppression, espionage, and terror...as the dictatorship grew harsher, the cry for freedom grew louder...and *Harmodius* and *Aristogeiton* – who had conspired for love and passion rather than for democracy – were transformed by popular imagination into the martyrs of liberty." [Durant, p 124]

In the ensuing rebellion, Cleisthenes – leader of the Alcmaeonid Clan – marched on Athens to overthrow Hippias...but without immediate success.

Later, in 510 BC, Hippias "consented to abdication and exile" in order to ransom his family who had been captured during another Greek uprising.

Cleisthenes again marched on Athens and, after much political and military maneuvering, set up a popular dictatorship...this eventually led Cleisthenes in 507 BC to establish the first democracy in Athens. [Durant, p 124]

With the new Athenian democracy, Barr adds: "...free men, rich and poor alike...had a master, the Law...equality before the law. And they demanded equality of discussion in the Agora before a rule was voted into law. In short, they governed themselves, and that was a new and exhilarating thing to do. They were determined to achieve, not only freedom, but law and justice." [p 123-24]

Hafner reveals: "The first [Greek] victory over the Persians at Marathon [490 BC] proved the superiority of the new political structure. Despite the later destruction of Athens by the Persians [480 BC], this mighty foe was soon defeated both at sea [later in 480] and on land [479], and driven from Greek soil. This victory proved the validity of the new ideas...and forms the background for the magnificent flowering of Greek genius in all fields during the 5th Century BC." [p 127]

Another appropriate title for *the Tyrannicides* is the *Spark of Democracy*.

Did Greek Events Inspire Romans to Overthrow Tarquins?

Many historians 'ignore' that news of the Athenian success in deposing their Tyrant Hippius in 510 BC would have spread swiftly throughout the numerous Greek trading colonies in southern Italy and Sicily. [*C & C*, Durant, p 15-7] [*Will of Zeus*, Barr, p. 79, 123]

Durant mentions "the defeat of the Etruscans [Tarquins] by Greek colonists at Cumae [near Naples] in 524 BC." This triumph [16 years prior to *the Tyrannicides*] also would have been well-known in Rome ... [only 120 miles north of Cumae].

These events of 524 BC and 510 BC by Greek colonists and natives may have inspired the Romans to overthrow their own tyranny [Etruscan] in 509-8 BC ... and then establish the 'Roman Republic' which would provide its citizens a 'varying' yet moderate liberty for the following 500 years. [see *L. Junius Brutus*, #33]

That "self-rule" should blossom in both Athens and Rome within the same two decades may be more than coincidental.

Sculptor:

Ancient Greek coins and other artworks reproduce recognizable images from the original bronze *Tyrannicides*.

For sculptors, an increasing use of bronze eliminated many problems concerning equilibrium and permitted more projections ... such as extended arms [and weapons] to display greater physical action.

When the Roman marble copy of the elder *Aristogeiton* was found in Hadrian's Villa, it was minus its head [now believed to be wrongly mounted on a *Pherecydes* bust in Madrid]. The right arm of *Aristogeiton* is also restored. The Roman copy of *Harmonius* required restoration of the arms, the right leg, and lower left leg.

Sculptors in ancient times normally colored their limestone and marble statues to match natural skin, clothes, or armor. In the final finish or polishing of a marble statue, Boorstin reveals: "...tinted wax was worked into the pores of the marble to give the desired color to sculptured parts like hair, eyes, lips, and costumes..." [*The Creators,* p 99]

Gurewitsch suggests if Phidias – designer and head sculptor of the Parthenon and its sculptures – could view his statues today without their added color: "the bare stone would look ravaged to him, even cadaverous." [*Smithsonian,* p 68]

For the next 3 centuries, Grecian artists would predominate in the Western world.

Durant states: "The Greco-Persian War [480-479 BC] was the most momentous conflict in European history...for it made Europe possible. It won for Western civilization the opportunity to develop its own economic life...and its own political institutions...it stimulated the pride and lifted up the spirit of the Greek people...out of gratitude they felt called upon to do unprecedented things...<u>Greece entered upon its Golden Age, 480 to 399 BC</u>." [p 242]

He also explains how the equally self-liberated Romans – borrowing significantly from the Greeks – "<u>achieved a democracy of freemen</u> [even with the corrupt Senate]...and molded a government of separated legislative and executive powers whose checks and balances inspired the makers of constitutions as late as revolutionary America and France." [C&C, 1944, Durant, p 670]

Sculptures in this book voicing man's quest for freedom include *the Tyrannicides...Pericles...Lucius Brutus...She-Wolf...Winged Victory of Samothrace...Demosthenes...Moses...La Marseillaise...Washington...Statue of Liberty...End of the Trail...Lincoln Memorial...Mount Rushmore...and the Vietnam Veteran's Memorial.*

Some would add the two *Alexander* works [#28 & #45]...as his military victories led to the establishment of Alexandria and introduced Greek ideals throughout the lands he conquered.

Major References:

Hellas, 1980, Branigan & Vickers, p 112

The Life of Greece, 1937, Durant, p 123-6, 221, 242

The Will of Zeus, 1961, Stringfellow Barr, p 79, 99, 123-24

Acropolis, 1979, Meletzis and Papadakis, p 10-12

Arts of the Ancient Greeks, 1972, Brilliant, p 144-46, 158, 303

Greek and Roman Sculpture, 1972, Lawrence, p 86, 114-6, 21b

Art of Crete, Mycenae, and Greece, 1968, Hafner, p 126-27

Encyclopedia of Sculpture, 2004, Bostrom, p 711, 1367

Smithsonian Magazine, July 2008, Gurewitsch, p 66-72

The Creators, 1992, Boorstin, p 99

The Rise of the Greeks, 1987, Grant, p 62

Caesar & Christ, Durant, 1944, p 15-7, 418, 421

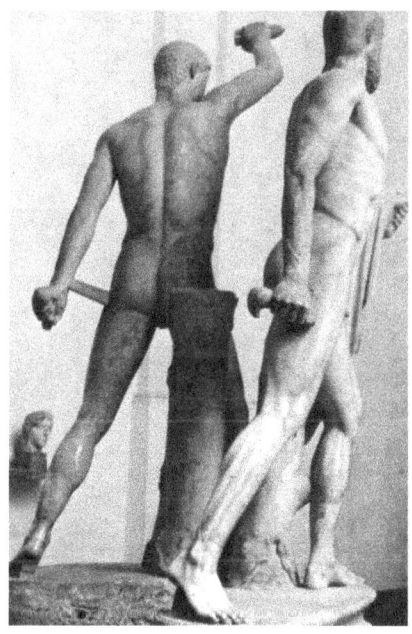

10

SHE-WOLF

OR CAPITOLINE WOLF

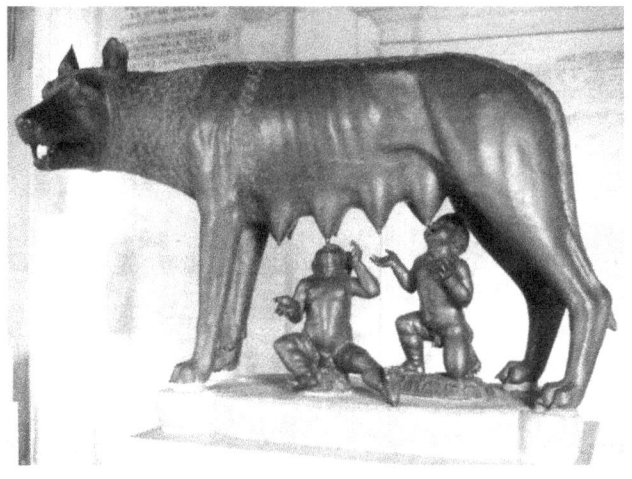

"...one of the most memorable portrayals of
an animal in the history of world art."
...Gardner, *Art Through the Ages*, p 193

Since 296 BC, in Roman Forum – now, Capitoline Mus., Rome*
Etruscan/ Roman/ Greco-Roman – 490 BC – natural & stylized
Height: 33.5 inches [85 cm] – bronze
Sculptor: unknown Etruscan, Roman, or Greco-Roman
    *copies Nat. Gallery, Washington & NY Met Mus. Art

With bared fangs, the savage-eyed beast issues stern warning of imminent violence: *Offend me – or Rome – at your risk!*

The *She-Wolf* is among the most ancient masterpieces of Etruscan, Early Roman, or Greco-Roman sculpture...a sacred image of Rome's legendary beginning.

Durant describes the figure as: "alive in every muscle and nerve...a masterpiece of the highest order." [*Caesar & Christ*, p 82]

Art historians estimate her creation between 500 BC to 480 BC...within a few decades following that of *the Tyrannicides* #9 in Athens. The inception of both sculptures within a narrow time-frame suggests the first may have inspired the other.

Gardner says: "The *She-Wolf* seems to have been made for the new Roman Republic after the expulsion of Tarquinius [508 BC monarchy]...It became the totem of the new state...the appropriately defiant image has remained the emblem of the city of Rome to this day." [*Art Through the Ages*, p 193]

Thomas states: "The cult of Romulus and Remus was as old as the 4th century BC...we know that a statue of a _she-wolf_ was dedicated on the Capitoline Hill in Rome in 296 BC [from an inscription]...and placed in the Forum under a sacred *Ruminal* fig tree. [by legend, Romulus and Remus were found on the Tiber River under a fig tree]. The fullness of her teats suggests she was nursing. The two human babies are later additions...attributed to the 15th century Florentine artist Pollaiuolo.. We do not know whether the present *She-Wolf* is the original. Its dating has been hotly debated...but its Etruscan-origin is now widely accepted." [*Encyclo. Sculpt.*, p 190, 254-55]

Roman coins of the Republican era often display a *She-Wolf* suckling two boys.

Gardner adds the statue is: "...one of the most memorable portrayals of an animal in the history of world art...vitality is concentrated in the tense, watchful body...with her spare flanks, gaunt ribs, and taut, powerful legs. The lowering of the neck and head, alert ears, glaring eyes, and ferocious muzzle capture the psychic intensity of the fierce and protective beast as danger approaches.

Not even the great animal reliefs [#8] of Assyria can match, much less surpass, this profound rendering of animal temper." [p 193-94]

Hoving says the *She-Wolf* is: "the most enthralling work of art to have survived from Etruscan times... the artist has imbued the creature with a fearsome urgency – a killing feeling – combined with a memorable tenderness. It is the combination of exceptionally well-crafted detail with a timeless overall form that makes this beautiful work of art so stunning." [*Greatest Works of Art,* p 254]

The image of the *She-Wolf* may appear bizarre... until we learn its legend and ponder the possible truths within the legend.

Subject:

According to historian Will Durant, the story/legend of Rome's origin begins with the Trojan prince Aeneas [son of Aphrodite] fleeing the burning city of Troy after defeat by the Greeks. Aeneas, carrying his father, wanders westward with his young son [Ascanius] in tow.*

Note: the Villa Borghese in Rome displays Bernini's statue of *Aeneas Fleeing Troy* "who carries on his shoulders his aged father, paralyzed by Jupiter in revenge for his affair with Venus. Behind them stumbles the young Ascanias, carrying a torch not only to illuminate his father's path but also to ensure the continuity of the spirit of Troy." [Croft, p 12]

They arrive in Italy... where Aeneas marries Lavinia [daughter of the king of Latium, 20 miles south of current Rome]. Eight generations later, their descendent Numitor is king.

A usurper [younger brother] Amulius expels Numitor, kills the sons of Numitor, and forces his only daughter Rhea to become a virgin priestess of Vesta.

"But Rhea lies down by the banks of a stream and 'opened her bosom to catch the breeze'... and falls asleep. Mars [the god], overcome by her beauty, 'left her rich with twins'. King Amulius orders them to be drowned. [Durant, p 12]

"They are placed on a raft, which kind waves carried to land... they were suckled by a she-wolf or – said a skeptical variant – by a shepherd's wife nicknamed Lupa because, like a wolf, her love-making knew no law. When Romulus and Remus grew up, they killed King Amulius, restored Numitor, and went resolutely forth to build a kingdom for themselves on the hills of Rome." [p 12]

Over some 2,500 years, variations of this legend arose. One has Lupa as the original mother…who claims the god Mars to be the father. In ancient times, such claims were not uncommon…intended to screen the identity of the true father…and ease the jealousy of a husband.

[theme is similar to that of the *Farnese Bull* #44…wronged mother of twin sons, who both right the wrong, one son becomes king]

In 2007, Italian archaeologist Andrea Carandini announced discovery of a long-lost cave under the Palatine Hill [adjacent to Capitoline Hill]…said to be a cave which ancient Romans held sacred as the location where Romulus and Remus were nursed by the *She-Wolf.* Carandini's support of this legend "has earned him the admiration of the Roman public but the disapproval of his colleagues." [*Archaeology Magazine,* July 2007]

According to Cicero, the *She-Wolf* was hit by lightning in 65 BC. It is said to have been struck again in 44 BC, on the day Julius Caesar* was assassinated. Marks of possible lightning strikes appear on the left hind leg.

*Caesar claimed descent from Ascanius, son of Aenaes. [Durant, p 167]

After the fall of the Roman Empire, the *She-Wolf* was displayed at the Pope's Lateran Palace. In the 10th century, near the Lateran, trials and executions were held "at the Wolf" down to 1450. In the late 12th or early 13th century, the *She-Wolf* 'stalked' a bronze ram in the portico of the Lateran Palace. [*Encyclo.Sculpt.* p 254]

Later, holes were drilled into the teats from which water spouted for citizens to wash their hands. In 1471, Pope Sixtus IV gave the *She-Wolf* to conservators of Rome. By 1509, the fore-mentioned twin baby brothers were cast and added to the mother wolf. About

1536, the group was placed above the entrance to the Palazzo dei Conservatori on the Capitoline Hill. By 1544, it was transferred inside the Conservatori. [p 255]

Sculptor:

The sculptor is unknown. During the Archaic period, it was not unusual for patrons of ancient Rome to commission works from either Etruscan artisans or Greek craftsmen. The *Encyclo Sculpt* proposes the Roman School of Vulca. [p 254]. The same source adds: "the mane-like fur...suggests the mixed appearance of lion and wolf. Perhaps, the animal's leonine aspect was meant to render her more ferocious..." Except for its restored tail and damaged hind legs, *the She-Wolf* is exceptionally well-preserved for her age.

Hoving states: "Many art historians believe the Etruscan artists, especially of the early 7th century BC, had the Greeks beat hands down. In many of the bronzes...there's a taut and earnest directness, combined with a pleasing lack of idealism."

Strangely...the city-fathers of modern Rome have yet to select a suitable site for their distinguished icon. Currently, *the She-Wolf* is off to the side in a large gallery that showcases the notable equestrian statue of Emperor Marcus Aurelius [#60].

Copies of the *She-Wolf* are displayed at the National Gallery in Washington and at the New York Met. Museum of Art.

Major References:

History of Western Art, 1994, Turner, p 181

Basic History of Western Art, 2006, Janson & Janson, p 108-10

Art Through the Ages, 1996, Gardner, p 193

Roman Mythology, 1974, Peter Croft, p 11-23

The Eternal City of Rome, Vol. II, Clement, p. 356, 715-6, 721-2

Encyclopedia of Sculpture, 2004, Thomas, p. 43, 190, 254-5

Ancient Rome, Liberati, p. 20-1

Caesar and Christ, Durant, p. 11-33, 82

Archaeology Magazine, July 2007

Greatest Works of Art, 1997, Hoving, p 254-55

Archaeology Magazine, July 2007, Carandini

Art: History of Paintings, Sculptures..., 1989, Hartt, p 213-14

11

THE CHARIOTEER

OF DELPHI

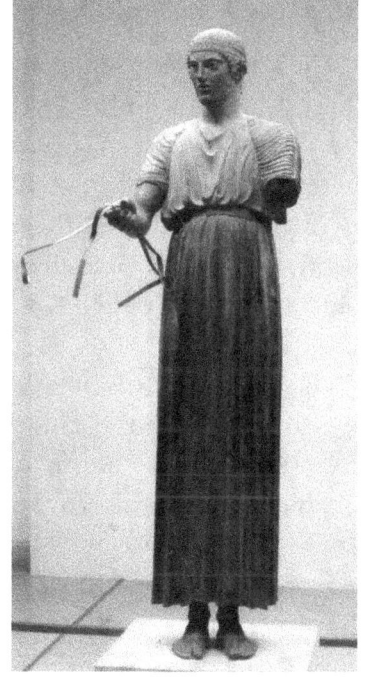

"masterpiece in bronze" ... Durant, *Life of Greece*, p 143

Found 1896, Delphi [100 mi. NW of Athens] – now, Delphi Mus.
Orig. Greek Bronze – 478 or 474 BC – Early Classic [Severe]
Ht. 5 feet 11 in. – bronze – life-size
Sculptor: Pythagorus the Rhegion, or Kalamis of Athens
　　　[see 'face photo' at chapter end]

The watchful *Charioteer of Delphi* – surprisingly, almost intact – is one of few bronzes to survive from the Early Classic era. Found at Delphi in 3 pieces, its good fortune was to be preserved within a landslide, due to an earthquake. Minor fragments from his chariot and 4 horses are also displayed in the Delphi Museum.

In 1896, excavations by the French School of Athens uncovered *the Charioteer* between remains of the Temple of Apollo [now only its terrace & 6 columns] and the well-preserved amphitheater of Delphi. Lawrence reveals it was "at a spot where a wall was built in the 4th century BC to prevent rocks and earth of the mountain slope from tumbling onto the temple terrace." [*Greek & Roman Sculpture,* p 117]

Durando states: "The famous bronze *Charioteer of Delphi* – a masterpiece of Severe [Early Classic] sculpture – was among the votive offerings to the tyrant Polyzalus of Gela." [*Ancient Greece,* p 132]

Polyzalus governed Gela [in Sicily] from about 478 to 466 BC. Since his name is inscribed on the base of the statue, he is believed to be the owner of the winning chariot driven by *the Charioteer*... during the Pythian Games at Delphi in either 478 or 474 BC.

Subject:

It is doubtful Polyzalus drove his winning chariot. Racing a chariot was a hazardous profession... owners normally hired professional drivers. Talented servants or slaves also drove chariots. [*Olympic Games,* Finley & Pleket, p 30-1]

The chariot race – opening event of the Games – was the most spectacular and costly contest. Two-wheeled chariots lined up at one end of the hippodrome. A single post near the far end indicated the turning point. Incredibly... the charioteers could approach the post from either side.

"For 12 laps – more than 9 kilometers – the flying horses pulled the light carts in short bursts of speed punctuated by 180-degree turns at the posts. Although the rules forbade swerving in front of a competitor... bumps, crashes and head-on collisions were the rule rather than the exception...." [p. 29]

"...the largest number [of chariot entries at Pythian Games] on record was 41 in 462 BC when the race was won by Arcesilas, king of Cyrene...whose chariot was the only one to complete the course. His victory as the lone finisher was not normal, but it is not very surprising." [p 28]

Note: see movie Ben Hur for example of chariot racing.

Owners of racing chariots were members of leading families and the wealthy. An inscription on the stone base of *the Charioteer* states: "Polyzalus set me up...prosper him glory, Apollo." Since victorious owners were looked upon as blessed by the gods, they often commissioned statues "to perpetuate these signs of divine grace." [*Encyclo*, p 289] It is possible Polyzalus [or his family] ordered the sculptor to portray his face on the bronze *Charioteer*.

With *the Charioteer*, Polyzalus [or family] may have intended to make 'a display of wealth' at Delphi...as the Sanctuary of Apollo enjoyed a constant stream of travelers from throughout the Mediterranean world. They arrived to consult the famed oracle and/or to enjoy its festivals, games, monuments...plus, a spectacular setting alongside a steep mountain.

According to the Delphi Museum, the chariot driver displays – "an immortal Olympian calm..." [*Delphi, p 118*] Janson adds: "The face has a pensive, somewhat faraway look. The bearing of the entire figure conveys the solemnity of the event...for chariot races and similar contests at that time were competitions for divine favor, not sporting events in the modern sense." [*History of Art*, p 128]

His 'immortal Olympian calm' is one of the earliest examples of facial expression by a Greek sculptor. This 'modest decorum' by a victor' coincides with the precepts of Apollo and Delphi.

Agard explains Apollo: "is a more intellectual type, an incarnation of the moral precepts *'Know Thyself'* and *'Nothing in Excess'* [moderation is preferred] ..." [*Classical Myth in Sculpture*, p 14]

These precepts "were carved in stone above the entrance to Apollo's temple at Delphi." [*Art & Physics*, Shlain, p 412] [*Hellas*, Branigan & Vickers, p 214]

The charioteer's face exhibits a subtle expression and movement... as it *turns slightly right* and *gazes* in that direction... possibly, in reaction to roaring approval from the stadium crowd... particularly those who wagered on his chariot.

Janson says: "The garment is severely simple, yet compared with Archaic drapery the folds seem softer and more pliable; we feel – probably for the first time in the history of sculpture – that they reflect the behavior of real cloth. ... the slightly parted lips [as if stunned] give the face a more animated expression." [p 128]

Gombrich describes how ancient Greek sculptors 'borrowed' skills from the Egyptians two millennia earlier [see *Scribe* #1]. "The eyes – which often look so blank and expressionless in [Greek] marble statues or are empty in bronze heads – are marked in colored stones... The hair, eyes and lips were slightly gilt, which gave an effect of richness and warmth to the whole face... a convincing image of a human being, of wonderful simplicity and beauty." [*Story of Art*, p 89-90]

Lawrence adds: "The lips are parted, to show a line of teeth rendered in silver... The eyes are straight set, with a filling of white enamel and onyx; eyelashes of inserted bronze spikes also remain." [p 118]

Oracle of Delphi:

Delphi is 100 miles northwest of Athens... and, after the Acropolis, one of the most visited sites in Greece. In the Mycenaean period [1950 BC to 1100 BC], Greeks and others began to consult the Oracle of Delphi whose priestess sat on a tripod over a rock fissure.

A Homeric hymn has Apollo– the Greek god of Light/ Sun – proclaiming:

"Here I intend building a temple which shall serve as an Oracle for all mankind, where people from all over – from fertile Peloponnesus, from Europe, and from the isles among the waves – will bring me perfect hecatombs [sacrifices], and will ask for counseling, and I shall give them my infallible advice."

The Greek city-states – at the start of the 6th century BC – formed a political league [the Amphictyony] with common aims. It met at Delphi and Thermopylae in spring and autumn, respectively. The league agreed not to attack each other ... never to alter the water supply of a member ... to protect the treasury of Apollo ... and to attack anyone who violated these pledges. During the next 200 years, the fame of the Oracle of Delphi spread far beyond the Greek city-states. Worshippers – including kings – from throughout the ancient world sought the advice of the oracle. [Durant, p 198]

In modern times, archeologists John Hale and Jelle de Boer searched the Delphi ruins and: "discovered two intersecting fault lines ... the base of the ancient Apollo Temple stood squarely at their intersection. De Boer posited that limestone deposits buried deep beneath the ground might have released hydrocarbon gases – specifically, methane, ethane, and ethylene – into the air. Ethylene is what gives fruits their sweet smell, which seems to match the note that Plutarch had made of the odor. The Greek historian spoke of a spring that emitted 'fragrance and breeze' into the Oracle's temple. In low doses, ethylene can induce a trance." [*U.S. News*, p 46]

Sculptor:

Lawrence suggests: "A contemporary of Critius and Nesiotes – sculptors of *the Tyrannicides* #9 – must be responsible for the life-size bronze *Charioteer of Delphi*." [p 117]

Opper agrees: "... the facial structure and general composition can be linked to other early Classical sculptures such as the *Harmodius* from *the Tyrannicides* #9 group ..." [*Encyclo Sculpt*, p 289]

Opper adds: "A re-examination of *the Charioteer* base has reportedly uncovered traces of a previously overlooked signature by Pythagoras of Rhegion, a renowned artist from southern Italy. According to the Roman writer Pliny the Elder in *Natural History* [1st C. BC], this Pythagoras had been 'the first sculptor to show the sinews and veins and to represent the hair more carefully,' and indeed *the Charioteer's* feet have always been noted for the strong naturalistic detail that contrasts with other parts of the statue." [p 289]

A 'companion' to *the Charioteer* is the equally rare equestrian sculpture known as *the Jockey of Artesium* #34 exhibited at the Nat. Arch. Museum of Athens.

Note: most guided bus-tours to <u>Delphi fail</u> to include its world-famed *Athena Tholos*. Though mostly in ruins, enough survives to confirm it was one of the loveliest of ancient circular temples. Visitors, when selecting bus-tours, should <u>demand</u> 'written evidence' their itinerary includes a guided-visit to the *Athena Tholos*. Otherwise, visitors must jog a half-mile from the Apollo Temple [as did the *Author*] ... then rush back for what may be a too-brief visit at the Delphi Museum.

Major References:

The Olympic Games, 1976, Finley & Pleket, p 27-31, plate II

The Life of Greece, 1939, Durant, p 197-98, 242

Encyclopedia of Sculpture, 2004, Bostrom, p 288-9

U.S. News & World Report, Dec. 3, 2007, Hale and de Boer, p 46

History of Art, 1977, Janson, p 127-28

Delphi, Monuments & Museum, 2004, Tsaroucha, p 115-18

30,000 Years of Art, 2007, Phaidon Press, p 217

The Story of Art, 1995, Gombrich, p 88-9

Greek & Roman Sculpture, 1972, Lawrence, p 117-121

Delphi, 1978, Yalouris, p 17-20

Greek Sculpture, 1960, Carpenter, p 85, 127, plate X

Classical Myths in Sculpture, 1951, Agard, p 14

Art & Physics, 1991, Shlain, p 412

Hellas, 1980, Branigan & Vickers, p 214

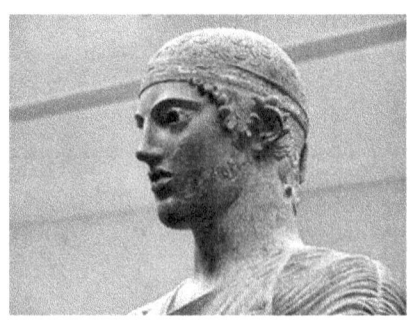

12

Zeus

of Artemision

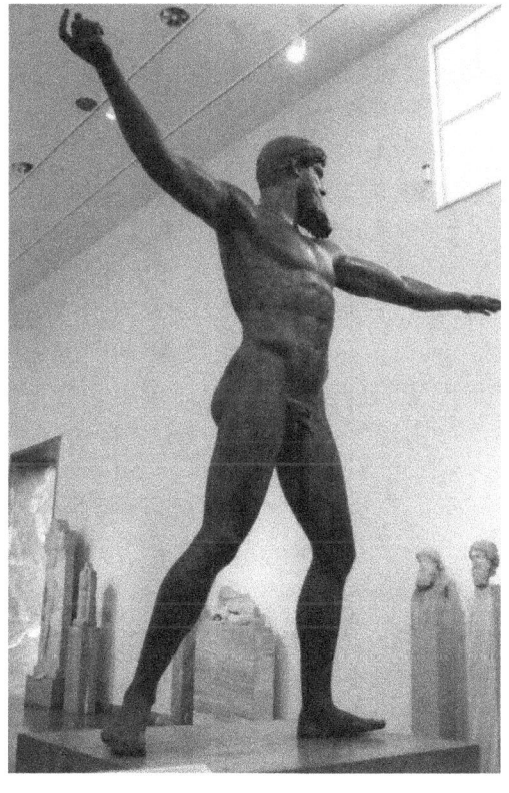

"Scholars ascribed the Artemision bronze, considered
a masterpiece of the Early Classical period,
to the leading sculptors of that time..." ...
Opper, *Encyclo. of Sculpture*, 2004, p 95

Found 1926, Cape Artemision, Gr. – now, Nat Mus. Athens & NYC
Orig. Greek sculpture – approx. 460 BC – Early Classic style
Ht. 6'10" [2.09 m] – slightly over life-size – bronze
Sculptor: Kalamis of Athens ... or Myron, Onatas, Hageladas
    [see face of *Zeus* at chapter end]

The extraordinary power and grandeur of *Zeus of Artemision* compares with the *Winged Victory of Samothrace* #38. Both are near-colossal Greek masterpieces and outstanding examples of dynamic action.

Hoving states: "It is the sublime depiction of courage, indomitability, and sheer beauty of mankind ... this brave and all-powerful god in the fullness of his immortal prime of life is, I believe, the most perfect image of classical humanity that has survived. No other example of Greek art of the 5th century BC has the same delicate combination of idealism and practicality, the muscular and intellectual. This god is ... the quintessential creator and avenger of almost every religion – and what mankind would like to be in its wildest dreams." [*Greatest Works of Art*, p 12]

In 1926 and 1928, pieces of this bronze were found underwater near Cape Artemision in an ancient shipwreck. [off the north coast of Euboea – the 100-mile-long island bordering the eastern coast of central Greece] The statue appeared to have been deliberately divided into pieces ... to be more readily transported and/or smuggled out of Greece.

The mixed cargo of the ancient ship yielding this statue indicates the vessel "carried spoils of war rather than works produced for the art market." Pottery aboard was dated approximately 100 BC and may have been made in Pergamon, suggesting the ship's port. "Analysis of the clay core seems to point to an Attic [near Athens] provenance, which would indicate the statue was made there." [*Encyclo Sculpt*, p 94]

The doomed vessel may have been en route to either Constantinople [now Istanbul], Pergamon, or Rome ... before sinking off the Cape of Artemision in a stormy sea.

The same shipwreck carried the famed *Jockey of Artemision* #34.

Subject:

The Jansons identify this statue as: "a magnificent nude bronze Zeus, almost 7 feet tall, hurling his thunderbolt [missing] at some unseen enemy. The pose is that of an athlete, yet it is not so much the arrested movement in a continuous motion as the awe-inspiring gesture that reveals the god's cosmic power. Hurling a weapon becomes a divine attribute rather than an act aimed at a specific foe in the heat of battle." [*Basic History of Western Art,* p 92-3]

Bazin agrees: "The god, no doubt, brandished his thunderbolts in his right hand, his glance bent on the adversary to whom he points with his outstretched left arm. His weight rests mostly on his left leg, and the right is slightly flexed, ready for the recoil. Dominating the athletic vigor of the body is a proud head that radiates intelligence. The figure's hard-drawn outline is softened by the supple curls of the beard and hair." [*History of World Sculpture,* p 135]

Though middle-aged, the body is finely-muscled like that of an athlete in his prime. Most references believe the bronze represents Zeus...the Greek god of both the earth and sky...supreme among the deities of Mt. Olympus.

Opper declares: "The statue's size, larger than life [6' 10"], and the lack of any other specific attribute leaves no doubt that the imposing figure with its highly realistic anatomy represents a god, not an athlete...The heavily muscled body, long hair, and beard are characteristic of Zeus, the senior Olympian, and his brother Poseidon..." [*Encyclo Sculpt.,* p 94]

Poseidon was god of the seas...during the Trojan War, he angrily sent two serpents to crush a Trojan priest* for warning his people, in vain, to beware of gifts from the Greeks. [*see *Laocoon* #52]

Lawrence offers a third identity: "The same pose occurs on coins which represent Zeus throwing a thunderbolt, but in this instance the position of the fingers suggest they were holding a thong from which to project a javelin or spear. If so, the subject is not Zeus, nor probably would Poseidon cast his trident in that manner ... though a heroized mortal might do so." [*Greek & Roman Sculpture,* p 129]

The choice of Meletzis & Papdakis is also a javelin-thrower: "The left arm is outstretched to direct the throw and balance the body, the head is turned left toward a target, feet are apart hardly touching the ground – the characteristic position of a javelin thrower. The coiffure is arranged according to the Archaic style of this period. Two pigtails crossed at the back, are disposed around the head, over a fringe of waved hair adorning the forehead. The entire statue radiates a divine majesty and vigor." [*1988 Museum Athens,* p 56]

The reach of his outstretched arms is 210 cm, essentially the same as his 209 cm height. Originally, the lips and brows were inlaid with silver or copper foil, and the eyes were inlaid with colored materials. The mouth and nipples were cast separately with a copper alloy, creating a lifelike reddish tone. [*Encyclo,* p 94]

Ragghianti suggests the sculptor's inspiration: "The figure was unquestionably derived – as far as the general distributive system of its triangular components is concerned – from the initial figures of *the Tyrannicides* of Kritos #9 ...." [*1980 Museum Athens,* p 110, 114]

R. Brilliant agrees: "the dignified mature image of *Aristogeiton* #9 may be compared in every aspect of physique and countenance with the great bronze statue of *Poseidon* from Cape Artemision." [p 145]

Sculptor:

Several references link this statue to Kalamis of Athens, the master Athenian sculptor. Other possibilities include Onatas, Myron, and Hageladas. Whoever he is, the sculptor was supremely talented and renowned in his time. His skill suggests he may have worked on or with the Athenians who created the Parthenon. [*Encyclo,* p 95]

The same pose – Zeus about to throw a thunderbolt – is seen in high relief on the *Great Altar of Zeus* #43 in Berlin. The Berlin State Museum has "a small early Classical bronze figure in virtually the same attitude as the Artemsion bronze ..." [*Encyclo.,* p 95]

This statue also appears in the Metropolitan Museum of Art in New York City.

Major References:

Greek and Roman Sculpture, 1972, Lawrence, p 129

Greatest Works of Art, 1997, Hoving, p 12

Art of Crete, Mycenae, and Greece, 1968, Hafner, p 142-3

Basic History of Western Art, 7th Ed, 2006, Jansons, p 92-3

Arts of the Ancient Greeks, 1972, Brilliant, p 145-6, 158, 169, 351

Ancient Greece: Dawn of the Western World, 1997, Durando, p. 132-39

Encyclopedia of Sculpture, 2004, Opper, p 94-5

Greek Art, 1964, Boardman, p. 113-4

Nat. Arch Museum of Athens, Ragghianti, 1980, p 110-14

Nat. Arch Museum of Athens, Meletzis & Papadakis, 1988, p 56, 60-1

Nat. Arch Museum of Athens, 1979, Voutsas, p 18, 53-4

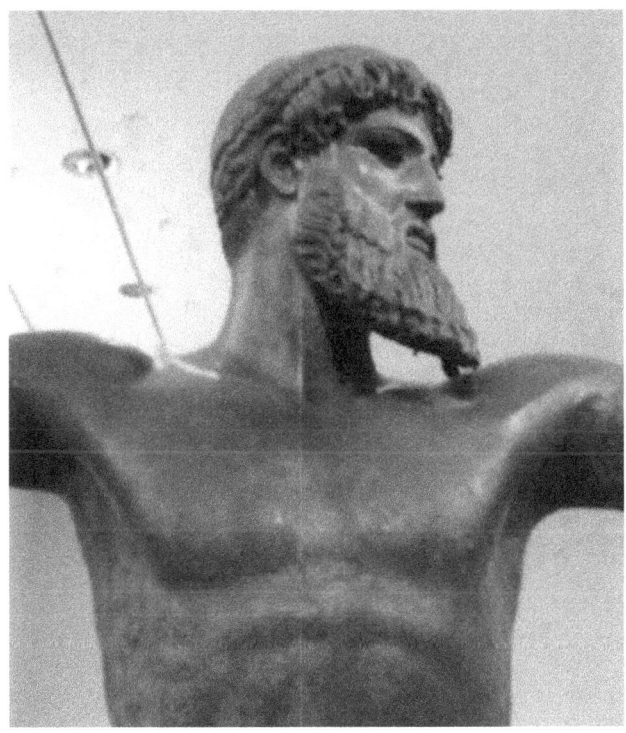

13
ALTAR OF APHRODITE
[AKA BIRTH OF APHRODITE OR LUDOVISI THRONE]

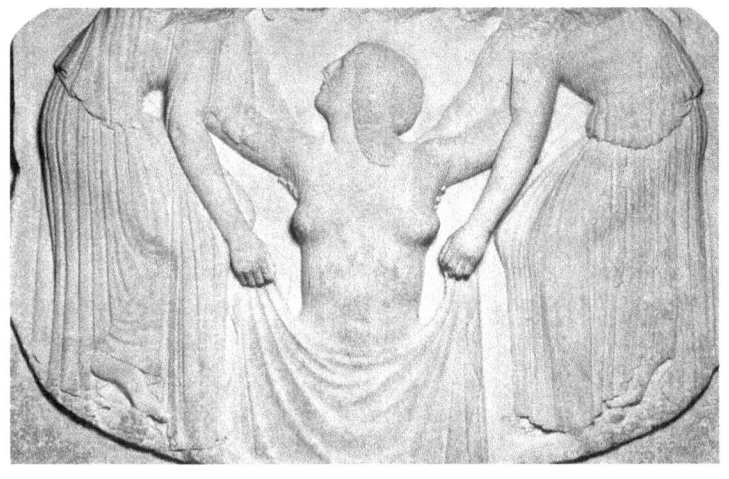

"a masterpiece of Early Classic Greek sculpture"
... Opper, *Encyclo Sculpture*, p 982

Found 1877, Ludovisi Villa, Rome – now, Palazzo Altemps, Rome
Orig. Greek reliefs – approx. 460 BC – Early Classical style
Ht. 1.04 m., Width 1.44 m. – dolomitic marble [Thasos]
Sculptor: unknown ... likely Ionian Greek
    [see both side-reliefs at chapter end]

The graceful symmetry of *the Aphrodite Altar* is immensely pleasing. According to the 6th Homeric Hymn, the youthful *Aphrodite* emerges from the foamy waves and seed of Croton along the seashore of Cyprus. [*Encyclo.* Opper, p 981]

Durant says: "Two goddesses are raising *Aphrodite* from the sea ... her thin wet garment clings to her form and reveals it in all the splendor of maturity ... the head is semi-Asiatic, but the drapery of the attendant deities, and the soft grace of their pose, bear the stamp of the sensitive Greek eye and hand." [*Life of Greece,* p 319]

The handmaiden-goddesses assisting *Aphrodite* hold a cloth to veil her lower half. Other maidens appear on side-reliefs ... one plays a double-flute, the other holds a box of incense. Some references describe this sculpture as a 'throne'... it is more likely an altar.

Among surviving relief-statuary of the ancient Greeks, this *Altar* includes the first life-size, female nude [the flute-playing girl on side-relief] ... and the first Greek female displaying the 'wet-look' [*Aphrodite*'s semi-transparent gown]. Prior to this time, conservative elements in Greek society discouraged images of the unclothed female ... though male nudes were acceptable.

As sculptors progressed to thinner garments and the clinging or wet-look, this modicum of restraint gradually gained favor ... and satisfied the desire of sculptors to create with greater sensuality. [Lawrence, p 123] [Electa, p 138]

Within a few decades, *the Three Goddesses* #17 on the east pediment of the Parthenon would appear in wet-drapery ... and, later, this style appeared with the famed *Victory Loosening Sandal* #19 on the parapet of the Temple of Athena Nike ... on the Acropolis. [original #19 now in Acropolis Museum]

Brilliant states the *Aphrodite Altar* is "the lovely invocation of femininity ... in the flowing movement of her rise, the water has caused her thin garment to cling to her luscious body ... the sense of the moment is very strong ... and so too is the underlying dependence on triangular patterns of composition ..." [*Art of the Ancient Greeks,* p 146-48]

Bazin adds: her handmaidens "modestly hold before her a cloth whose beautiful dipping horizontal folds complement and flow into the vertical pleats of their own clothing." [*History of World Sculpture*, p 136]

Subject:

Most references agree the central figure of the altar is *Aphrodite* emerging from the sea at 'birth'... though it is remotely possible the central figure is rising from a ritual bath. [*30,000...*, p 216]

The 3 reliefs – found in 1887 buried upright in ruins of the Villa Ludovisi [named for papal family] in Rome – originally are believed to have been part of an altar within the *Temple of Aphrodite* in Locri Epizefiri ... a Greek colony in southern Italy.

In this temple, the 3 pieces stood facing outwards, forming a screen around a sacred, rectangular space [pit]. The sacred pit received precious vessels and other votive offerings. The bases of the 3 reliefs fit perfectly into blocks of this pit. Terracotta plaques from the site are also similar in style. [*Encyclo*, p 982] [Lawrence, p 122]

The life-sized, female figures on the 2 side-reliefs illustrate different aspects of the goddess *Aphrodite*. The young flute-playing nude sits cross-legged on a cushion with her hair gathered in a *sakkos*... indicating she may be "a highly-cultivated courtesan". [*Encyclo*, p 981]

Bazin suggests "She may represent 'profane love', of which *Aphrodite* is the patroness. The flute-player's attitude is awkward, but her dimpled body is full of charm, with its curves and its soft modeling echoed in the folded cushion." [p 135]

The clothed female appears to hold an incense box from which she places grains into an incense brazier ... suggesting she may be "a priestess or ... more likely a bride giving an offering." [*Encyclo*, p 981] Bazin adds: "she is of sacred love" the other aspect of *Aphrodite*. [p 135] Durant offers a different perspective: "a veiled woman prepares her lamp for the evening; perhaps the face and garments here are even nearer to perfection than on the central piece." [p 319]

The history of this statuary is described as 'speculative' by the *Encyclo Sculpt*: "When the Ludovisi Throne [*Aphrodite Altar*] was dug up, it was found upright with no fragments or built structures around it, strongly indicating it had been moved there from its previous position. A few 100 meters to the east... archeologists discovered traces of a round building possibly identified as the *Temple of Venus Erucina*... founded in 181 BC... some have speculated the *Ludovisi Throne* was brought to Rome to decorate it... either from Sicily... or Locri Epizefiri [described above]" [p 982]

In Antiquity, the Roman *Temple of Venus Erucina* was on property – the Gardens of Sallust – owned by Roman emperors with huge parklands... upon which Caesar's Villa was built, and later the Villa Ludovisi... from which the statuary took its initial name when unearthed in 1887. [Lawrence, p 123]

Since there is no record of eyewitnesses to the 1887 'discovery' of the 3 relief panels, it is possible the reliefs were secretly brought to Rome from southern Italy... following the 1748-49 re-discovery of Pompeii... which generated growing demand for ancient artworks by wealthy collectors throughout Europe.

Sculptor:

The creator of the *Aphrodite Altar* is unknown. Brilliant says it was "carved by a western Greek artist in southern Italy or Sicily." [p 146] An Ionian Greek or a Greek-trained Roman is suggested by other references.

The Museum of Fine Arts in Boston has a similar three-sided altar with reliefs... of the same marble and age... said to have been found within a few hundred yards of the *Aphrodite Altar.*

In June of 2000, a stunning and similarly-draped ancient female figure was found in the sea near Alexandria, Egypt. It was "a life-size, headless, black-granite statue of the [Egyptian] goddess Isis, sculpted as if wearing a diaphanous cloth held together by knots at her breast." It was exhibited at a news conference after being raised from its underwater location of 2,500 years. [*SD Union-Tribune*, 6/4/2000, AP]

When visiting the Hearst Castle in San Simeon, note the stunning *Birth of Venus* by Charles Cassou [1930]. It is the centerpiece of the Neptune Pool ... 2 mermen hold Venus aloft, standing upon a seashell with 3 cherubs and Eros.

Major References:

Arts of the Ancient Greeks, 1972, Brilliant, p 146-49

The Esthetic Basis of Greek Art, 1959, Carpenter, p 52

Encyclopedia of Sculpture, 2004, Opper, p 981-1

History of World Sculpture, 1968, Bazin, p 135

Museo Nazionale Romano, 2005, Mondadori Electa, p 135-39

Life of Greece, 1939, Durant, p. 319

Greek and Roman Sculpture, 1972, Lawrence, p 122-23

History of World Sculpture, 1968, Bazin, p 135

30,000 Years of Art, 2007, Phaidon, p 219

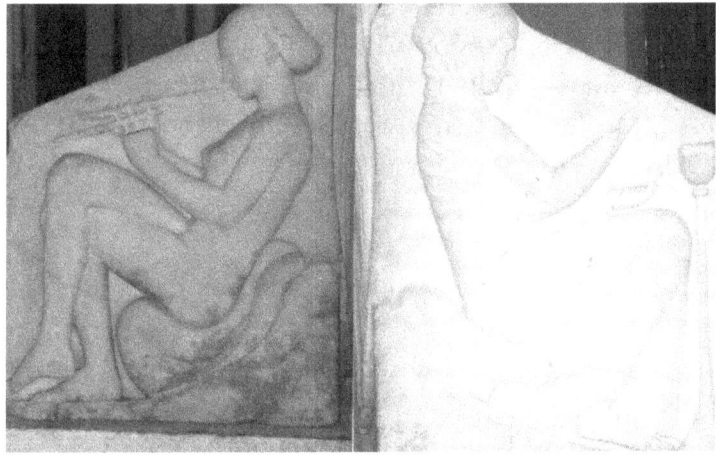

14
DISCOBOLOS – DISCUS
THROWER

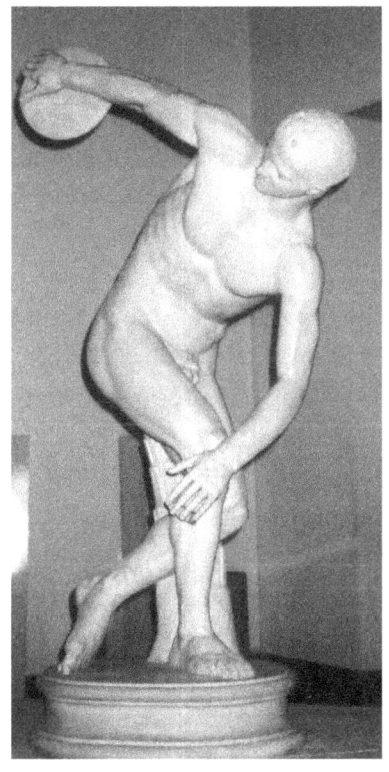

"one of the most famous statues of antiquity."
... Thliveri, *Encyclo..of Sculpture*, p 1135

Found 1781, Hadrian's Villa – now, Terme Mus., Rome*
Roman marble copy – 140 AD – Early Classical style
From: lost Orig. Greek bronze – 470 to 450 BC
Ht: 5 ft. 1 in [155 cm] – marble
Sculptor: orig. bronze by Myron, Roman copy: unknown
    *also Brit.Mus., Munich, NY Met.Art, Naples, etc.

Olympic Games: every 4 summers, from 776 BC to 261 AD, peoples from the lands of the Mediterranean gathered at Olympia in southern Greece for *the Games*. Travel to Olympia was also a pilgrimage to the sacred precinct of Zeus. After a grand parade of athletes and dignitaries, 100 oxen were sacrificed to Zeus, and the sports festival began!
... *The Olympic Games*, Finley & Pleket, 1976

F inley & Pleket state: "This is probably the most famous, most admired, and most frequently copied athletic statue ever made...it is thought that the discus was thrown [in ancient Greek] in much the same way as today...though not with the circling movement within the marked ring." [*Olympic Games,* p 33]

In 708 BC, discus-throwing became a competitive sport when it was introduced as part of the Greek pentathlon – a contest involving 5 events: the discus, the standing long jump, the javelin, a 200-meter sprint, and wrestling. The winning contestant gained the highest total of wins among the 5 events. If a competitor won 3 events before the 4th or 5th event, the contest ended. [p 32]

Ancient historian Pliny the Elder wrote: "Myron is the first sculptor who appears to have enlarged the scope of realism, having more rhythms in his art than Polycleitus and being more careful of his proportions." [Brilliant, p 170] Modern historian E.H. Gombrich observes: "Myron conquered movement just as the painters of his time conquered space. [*Story of Art,* p 90]

Durant adds: "Myron saw the athlete, not like Polycleitus before or after the contest, but in it...and realized his vision so well in bronze that no other sculptor in history has rivaled him in portraying the male body in motion. The wonder of the male frame is here complete … the body carefully studied in all those movements of muscle, tendon, and bone that are involved in the action … the legs and arms and trunk bent to give fullest force to the throw … the face not distended with effort, but calm in the confidence of ability … the head not heavy or brutal, but that of a man of blood and refinement…" [*Life of Greece*, p 323]

Hafner states: "Here is one of the finest examples of an artist's choice of the 'pregnant moment.' It is this brief pause – at the highest point of the upswing of the arm, just before the downward swing which will hurl the discus into the distance – that Myron recognized as the most characteristic instant in the complicated process of discus throwing." [*Art of Crete, Mycenae, & Greece*, p 146]

Authors of *30,000 Years of Art* say: "the sculpture is a masterful study of torsion and movement … his body twisted and arm raised, every muscle straining and the veins in his arms swelling with physical effort." [p 221]

Janson adds: "The conquest of movement in the free-standing statue now exerted a liberating influence on pedimental sculpture as well … endowing it with a new spaciousness, fluidity, and balance." [*History of Art*, p 130]

On the grounds of ancient Olympia in Greece, many pedestals inscribed to triumphant athletes have been found … however, their statues have long since disappeared. "That Pausanias [about 170 AD] reports the names of other victorious athletes portrayed by Myron and seen in Olympia … but not *the Discobolos*, suggests that the statue may have been moved to Rome earlier, possibly plundered by Nero during his trip to Greece in 66-67 AD." [*Encyclo*, 1136]

If Nero seized the statue and took it to Italy, the bronze *Discobolos* likely passed into a private collection eventually … where it disappeared. The statue now exists in numerous marble copies carved by the ancient Romans … the finest of which are said to be in Rome and London.

Gardner reveals the fate of many ancient masterpieces, even their copies: "In war, statues made of precious metals were often pillaged and bronze statues melted to make weapons or utensils…During the barbarian invasions in the time of the fall of the Roman Empire, marble statues were used to make lime for mortar." [p 138]

Subject:

In his bent position, the *Discus Thrower* briefly pauses at the highest point of his initial movement – the rearward uptrust of his throwing arm. His other arm poises freely, and his legs are gracefully crossed. In the next moment, his body will execute a three-quarter turn as his right arm explodes forward, hurling the spinning discus high and long across the field of play.

Carpenter's *Greek Sculpture* says: "Like a pendulum…the *Discobolus* has drawn himself back for the forward throw. No one can view a figure so engaged without anticipating the movement which must follow… So precise is Myron's formulation that 'Myronic moment' has become a textbook phrase for motion presented through its dynamic suggestion." [p 84]

In ancient Greek athletic contests, the discus was normally bronze and shaped like the modern discus, but slightly heavier. Each contestant made 5 throws, the best one being marked with a peg.

The Discus-Thrower is unclothed because that is how he would have competed. Every 4 years at ancient Olympia in Greece during the Games, the athletes "entered the stadium through a ground-level tunnel nude. They ran or jumped unencumbered by robes, cloaks, or shorts. The women of those early times could not attend these events… though there were a few specific horseraces in which they could attend and compete.

Historians at the Univ. of Athens have determined that two groups of people were barred from playing or watching games – women and undesirables [slaves and convicts]." [Oates, D11]

A recent reference – *A Visitor's Guide to the Ancient Olympics* by Faulkner – states: "The only woman allowed into the stadium to watch the contests was, in fact, the high priestess of Demeter of the Earth-Bed…a 'relic' of an age when the goddesses dominated Olympia." [*Wall Street Journal*, 5/19/2012]

Of course, a highly-determined and clever woman might watch the games surreptitiously.

"In 404 BC, a widow, who came from a great sporting family of wealthy Rhodian exiles, wished to watch her son box in the boys' event at the Olympic Games. She went disguised as a trainer...but, in her excitement when the boy won, she leaped over the barrier behind which the trainers were stationed and exposed herself. The judges let her off without penalty 'out of respect for her father and her brothers and her son...all of whom were Olympic winners'... but a rule was immediately introduced requiring trainers henceforth to attend the contests as naked as the participants." [Finley & Pleket, p 45-6]

Just before the Christian era, short races for girls were introduced...including a sprint of about 160 meters.

The strong emphasis on sports by the ancient Greeks is affirmed by Prof. Papaspyropoulos, a Director of Ancient Studies at the Univ. of Athens: "The ancient Greeks believed human beings are 3 things in one – mind, body, and spirit – and all 3 should be developed equally.... in school, they spent as much time on music as math, and they boxed and wrestled as often as they competed in debating. Their ideal was the man of well-balance – the sound mind in the sound body. They played hard, but they also studied hard. Many of their best poets, musicians, and writers of plays were also great soldiers and great athletes." [Oates, p D11]

Sculptor:

Myron, an Athenian citizen, was one of the earliest and most important Greeks to sculpt 'moving' figures. His working life spanned the period from 475 to 440 BC. He is recorded as the sculptor of 3 other statues of victorious athletes...in 456. 448, and 444 BC. [Lawrence, p 130] Other notable sculptures include his *Running Ladas*, and his *Marsyas*.

Carpenter states: "According to established Greek judgement and the opinion of Roman collectors...sculpture of real worth was not produced until the lifetime of Myron..." [p 57]

Brilliant reveals: "As an athlete, the type of *Harmodius* [from the *Tyrannicides* #9] served the Early Classical sculptor Myron in his *Discobolos* of 460 BC." [p 145] Myron is also one of the several sculptors suspected of having the necessary skill to create the *Zeus of Artemisium* #12.

Major References:

Ancient Greece, 1997, Durando, p 140-41

Los Angeles Times, May 31, 2004, Bob Oates, p D11

The Story of Art, 1995, Gombrich, p 90-1

The Olympic Games, 1976, Finley and Pleket, p 32-3

Encyclopedia of Sculpture, 2004, Thliveri, p 1135-37

Life of Greece, 1939, Durant, p 323

Art Through the Ages, I, 1980, Gardner, p 127-8, 137-8

Art of Crete, Mycenae, and Greece, 1968, Hafner, p 146 (+photo)

Greek and Roman Sculpture, 1972, Lawrence, p 130-33

Arts of the Ancient Greeks, 1972, Brilliant, p 146-7, 170-1

Greek Sculpture, 1960, Carpenter, p 57, 84

30,000 Years of Art, 2007, Phaidon, p 221

History of Art, 1977, Janson, p 130

A Visitor's Guide to the Ancient Olympics, 2012, Faulkner

15

SPEAR BEARER

OR DORYPHOROS

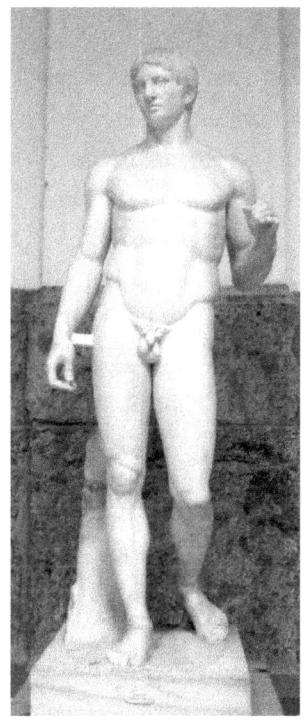

"This studied poise ... and harmonious proportions made *the Doryphorus* renowned as the Classical ideal of human beauty."
...Jansons, *Basic History of Western Art*, p 94

Excavated in Pompeii – now, in Naples Nat. Mus.*
Roman marble copy – approx. 25 BC to 25 AD – Classic style
From: lost Original Greek bronze, approx. 440 BC
Ht. 6 ft-6 in. [193 cm] – marble
Sculptor: Orig. by Polycleitus [480 to 400 BC]
    *also in Vatican, the Uffizi, and Minneapolis Art Inst.

B ol in *Encyclopedia of Sculpture* states: "No other Classical master-piece has had an impact on succeeding generations compara-ble to that of *the Doryphoros*. During the period of late Hellenism, the reception of *the Doryphoros* continued to gain strength, and in Roman art there is scarcely a revered pictorial statue that does not allude to it, either in the design of the posture or in the formation of the details..." [p 1328]

Four centuries after Polycleitus created this masterpiece, the first Roman emperor Augustus selected its Classic pose as the model for his famed *Augustus Prima-Porta* #57. Only the raised right arm of *Augustus* differs from *the Doryphoros*.

R. Brilliant explains why *the Doryphoros* became the model for virtually all Classical sculptors: "this statue offers some-thing totally new... harmony. Balanced between grace and solid-ity... about to walk but still at rest... relaxed yet alert... the statue exists as a totally realized human object – as a being." [*Arts of Ancient Greeks,* p 170-1]

Gardner concurs, it is "... one of the most frequently copied Greek statues... a work that epitomizes the intellectual rigor of Classical statuary design." One of the two finest surviving copies – now in the Naples National Museum – originally "stood in a pal-estra at Pompeii, where it served as a model for Roman athletes exercising..." [*Art Thru the Ages,* 1996, p 145]

Delivorrias says: "Its bronze original is generally believed to have portrayed Achilles [Greek hero of Troy] and to have stood in Argos [ancient city of southeast Greece], where its nearly contemporary reflec-tion on a relief has been found. It was in this creation that Polycleitus applied his theoretical notions about the relationship of the parts to the whole... that is, the proportions of the standards of harmony that compose the beauty of the human body." [*Encyclo.*,p 1325]

Polycleitos' polished-bronze *Doryphoros* provided a 'cleaner' appearance than later Roman marble copies. Jansons' *Basic History of Western Art* observes marble copies of the bronze "convey little of the beauty and power of the original..."

Consequently, a German sculptor, Georg Roemer, made a modern reconstruction in bronze... from a composite of several Roman marble copies. However, it was destroyed in 1944 during World War II. [its photo can be viewed online or in Jansons' *Basic History Western Art*, 2006 edition, p 94]

The sculptor of the marble statue in the Naples Museum found it necessary to add a 'tree stump' support behind the right leg... to strengthen the marble. "Without it, the legs of the brittle stone would have broken under the weight of the body. This same consideration led to insertion of the bar between the right arm and the hip." [Robb, p 422] Similar supports had been necessary to strengthen the marble copy of the *Tyrannicides* #9.

Branigan & Vickers declare the *Spear-Bearer*... the *Scraper* #25... and *Agias* #26 "depict Classical Greek art in its full flowering. The last of them [*Agias*] dates to 336 BC... close to the death of Alexander the Great, the generally-accepted terminal date for classical Hellenic civilization." [*Hellas*, p 9]

Subject:

Delivorrias identifies the *Spear-Bearer* as: "a successful warrior... a victorious strategist... a victory statue of an athlete [from its swollen ear]... or the *Canon* of Polycleitus. 'Canon' is the title of a tract by Polycleitus on the laws of sculpture." [*Encyclo Sculpt*, p 1326]

Gardner suggests the aim of Polycleitus was: "to impose order upon human movement, to make it 'beautiful,' to perfect it. He achieved this through a system of chiastic, or cross-balance. What appears at first to be a casually natural pose is, in fact, the result of extremely complex and subtle organization of various parts of the figure. [p 146-47]

To this day, some 2,500 years later, the subtle lessons of Polyclietus continue to inspire artists. His "laws of *chiasmus* – the response to every action or form with its opposite – determine the stance and construction of the figure." [*Encyclo*, Bol, p 1327]

A study of *the Spear-Bearer* reveals opposing relationships ... every action/position harmonizes with an opposite action/position:

1. arms and legs oppose each other diagonally
2. flexed and forward left arm, brandishing spear ... *versus* the right arm down, in a relaxed position,
3. engaged right leg strides forward [to rest bearing weight of body] ... *versus* left leg bent back [momentarily still], preparing to lift off,
4. shoulders, due to the weight-bearing right leg, slant forward ... the right shoulder is lowered ... *versus* left shoulder slightly-raised,
5. even curls of hair over mid-forehead achieve a rhythm of opposites.
   [Robb & Garrison, p 421] [Brilliant, p 170-71] [Bol, p 1327]

Sculptor:

Polycleitus was born in the city-state of Argos on the Peloponnesus peninsula of Greece. Most of his statues were erected in temples and shrines in this region. In addition to bronze, he also worked with great skill in marble, gold, and ivory.

In a competition between Polycleitus and Pheidias [famed sculptor of Parthenon, 448-432 BC] for commissions to produce bronze versions of Amazons, the ancient writer Pliny identifies Polycleitos as winning the prize over Pheidias. [*Encyclo*, p 1324]

Polycleitus is also renowned for creating "the bronze *Aphrodite of Amyklai* recently identified by copies of the famous *Hera Borghese* [in Carlsberg Glyptothek, Copenhagen]." [p 1325]

On occasion, the new style of Polycleitus was criticized as being too squarish ... since it presented only four basic and distinct views of the human figure – front, rear, right, and left. This 'squarishness' may have been due to his preference of muscular, wide-shouldered athletes and warriors as models.

It was not until about 360 BC – some 80 years after *the Spear-Bearer* – that the Greek sculptor Praxiteles introduced a new style of grace and elegance with taller and slimmer figures – a competing 'canon' that continued into the statuary of Christian Europe.

Slightly later, in about 335 BC, Lysippus and his followers further refined the art of sculpting the human figure by presenting expressive contours from all viewpoints.

Major References:

Hellas, 1980, Branigan & Vickers, p 9
Encyclopedia of Sculpture, 2004, Peter Bol, p 1326-28
Encyclopedia of Sculpture, 2004, Delivorrias, p 1324-5
Art Through the Ages, 10th Ed., 1996, Gardner, p 145-47
The Life of Greece, 1939, Durant, p 322-23
Arts of the Ancient Greeks, 1972, Brilliant, p. 170-73
Basic History of Western Art, 2006, Jansons, p 93-4
Art in the Western World, 1953, Robb and Garrison, p 420-22
Ancient Greece, 1997, Durando, p 140-41
History of World Sculpture, 1968, Bazin, p 136-37

16
WOUNDED NIOBID
[CHILD OF NIOBE]

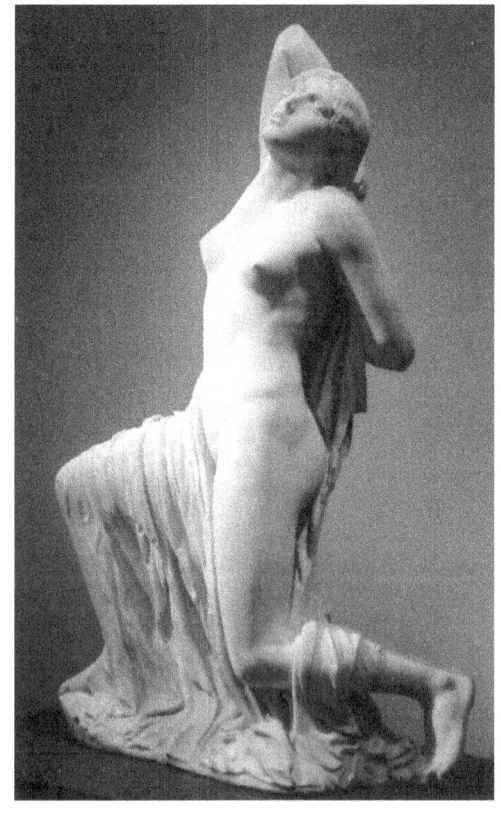

"This statue is to many the most pleasing of its age ..."
... Lawrence, Greek & Roman Sculpture, p. 156

Found 1906 Gardens of Sallust, Rome – now Terme Mus. Rome*
Original Greek marble – approx. 440 BC – Classic style
Or, possibly: Roman marble copy [about 100 BC to 100 AD]
Height: 4 ft. 11 in. – Parian marble
Sculptor: possibly Agorakritos
    *other Niobid youths are in Copenhagen & Florence [Ufizzi].

L awrence states: "This statue is to many the most pleasing of its
    age ... because of its mingling of naturalism, idealism, and for-
malism, its singularly fine proportions, and firm modeling." [*Greek
& Roman Sculpture,* p 156]

As pleasing as this statue appears, it is also disconcerting. The
young woman is mortally wounded ... and struggles to pull an arrow
from her back. She has done nothing to deserve this fate.

The consummate skill of the sculptor draws us nearer.

Bazin describes this distressed yet "radiantly beautiful" daughter of Queen Niobe: "The strong, naked body is represented real-
istically ... The young *Niobid* is arrested in her flight by the celestial
arrow that has struck her back ... she is falling, her left knee nearly
touching the ground ... her torso stiffening with pain ... her mouth
open in a cry which is interrupted by death. With her right hand
she tries to pull out the arrow, while her left hand holds up her
peplos." [*History of World Sculpture,* p 138]

The Jansons explain: "What separates the *Niobid* from the
world of Archaic art is summed up in the Greek word *pathos. Pathos*
means suffering, but particularly suffering conveyed with nobility
and restraint ... so that it touches us rather than horrifies us." [*Basic
History of Western Art,* p 96]

The delicately-carved figure is renowned for being the "earliest known large female nude in Greek art." It is also the first
to be carved in-the-round. After the *Niobid* is "shot in the back
while running ... the violent movement of her arms has made
her garment slip off. Her nudity is thus a dramatic device,
emphasizing her helplessness in the face of divine wrath ..."
[Jansons, p 96]

Carpenter explains: the theme of *the Niobid* involved "a mortal arrow"... therefore, semi-nudity could be justified. [*Greek Sculpture,* p 216-17]

In 1906, *the Niobid* was discovered in Rome within the Gardens of Sallust... where the *Aphrodite Altar* #13 had been found in 1887.

Subject:

Niobe, in Greek mythology, is identified as the first 'mortal' with whom the god Zeus mated... she would give birth to 7 sons and 7 daughters. Eventually, she became the queen of ancient Thebes, a Greek city-state north of Athens.

Bullfinch's Mythology reveals Queen Niobe's fatal error was on the: "occasion of the annual celebration in honor of the goddess Latona* [immortal wife of Zeus] and her offspring... the gods Apollo and Diana. The people were assembled... and paying their vows.

"Queen Niobe appeared and surveyed the people with haughty looks before shouting: 'What folly is this! – to prefer beings you never saw to those who stand before your eyes? Why should Latona be honored with worship, and none paid to me? Is my form and presence unworthy of a goddess? Let me add, I have 7 sons and 7 daughters... have I not cause for pride? Will you prefer me to this Latona, the Titan's daughter, with her 2 children? I have 7 times as many! Were I to lose some of my children, I should hardly be left as poor as Latona with her 2 only. Away with you from these solemnities! – put off the laurel from your brows – have done with this worship!

"The people of Thebes obeyed their queen... and left the sacred services uncompleted. [p 115-16]

"When the goddess Latona learned she had been 'deprived of my worship' from the people of Thebes, she informed her own children of Niobe's tirade. Apollo and Diana swiftly flew to the towers of Thebes from where they loosed arrows that dispatched the children of Niobe. Each child turned to stone... and, at the end, Niobe too changed to stone... borne on a whirlwind to her native mountain, she still remains, a mass of rock, from which a trickling stream flows, the tribute to her never-ending grief." [p 117-18]

[see the *Gardens of Versailles* #74 for the 'Fountain of Latona' which appears first... nearest the Palace]

When Queen Niobe boasted she possessed 7 daughters and 7 sons, she violated a morality message from the Greek gods to all mortal beings: avoid *hubris* – the display of arrogance through excessive pride.

To the Greeks in the 5th century BC, the *Niobid* statue illustrated the penalty for ignoring this important lesson. [*Bullfinch*, p 115-16]

[*hubris* appears again with *Milo of Croton* #75 by Puget]

Originally... the 'slaughter of Niobe's children' is believed to have been displayed on a Greek or Roman temple – possibly the Temple of Apollo Sosianus in Rome. [*Hellenistic Sculpture,* p 108]

Lawrence suggests: "They are likely to have occupied a pediment, because they range from the tall *Niobe* to quite low figures and all were carefully designed to extend sideways rather from front to back. The attitude and faces express despair, terror, or defiance... while drapery worn by the youngest daughter is meant to be damp with sweat of fear." [*Greek & Roman Sculpture,* p 227]

Sculptor:

A statue of the mother Niobe – attempting to shield an adolescent daughter – is in the Uffizi Museum in Florence. Two other Niobids – a son and daughter – are in Copenhagen.

Smith says: "The Niobids [in Florence] formed an open group of probably 16 figures... Pliny adds that no one knew if the group was by Praxiteles or Skopas..." [*Hellenistic Sculpture,* p 107-08]

It has been suggested these works "were copied from a group of *Wounded Niobids* made by an artist of the Parian school working in Athens after 440 BC, perhaps Agorakritos." [Bazin, p 138]

If, instead, they are Roman copies, a highly-skilled Roman created them.

Lawrence and the Jansons identify the *Niobid* as an original Greek marble. Brilliant says it is either an original Greek marble or a Roman replica.

Boardman adds: "Many Greek sanctuaries and towns were plundered for works of art to adorn villas or temples in Italy. The group of the *Niobids* was no doubt loot of this sort..." [p 226]

Major References:

Hellenistic Sculpture, 1991, Smith, p 107-08

Arts of the Ancient Greeks, 1972, Brilliant, p 232-3

Greek Mythology, 1973, Pinsent, p 87-8

Bullfinch's Mythology, 1968, Doubleday, p 115-9

Greek and Roman Sculpture, 1972, Lawrence, p 155-6, 227, 37b, 66b

Basic History of Western Art, 2006, Janson & Janson, p 96

Classical Myths in Sculpture, 1951, Agard, p 192

The Life of Greece, 1939, Durant, p 182

Greek Sculpture, 1960, Carpenter, p 216-17

History of World Sculpture, 1968, Bazin, p 138

17

THE THREE GODDESSES

OF THE PARTHENON

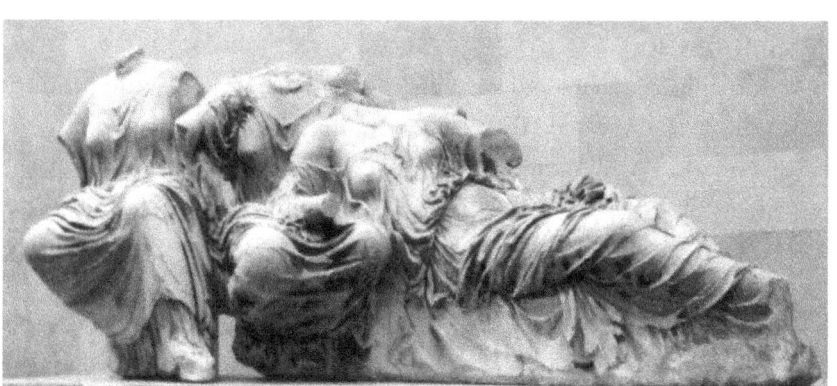

"As works of sculpture, they are matchless. Not only are
they carved with a perfection that has never been equaled,
they possess an astonishing sense of life..."
...Hoving, *Greatest Works of Art...*, 1997

Seized by Elgin from Parthenon, 1801 – now in Brit. Mus.
Original Greek statuary – 439-432 BC – Classic style, wet
Ht. 3 to 4 feet – over life-size – Pentelic marble
Sculptor: Pheidias, with Alcamenes and Agoracritus
  visit early or late in day... to avoid crowds & tour groups

W*hat a grand setting!*
    In the British Museum, we enter the spacious Duveen Gallery and to our right find a pair of marble dais [raised platforms] displaying over-sized Greek figures...the surviving statuary from the east pediment of the Parthenon.

The nearest dais displays the *Three Goddesses*...among the finest of surviving Classic Greek statuary.

Grecian gods and goddesses of Mt. Olympus were surprisingly capricious and wanton...unpredictable and impulsive...quick to anger and quick to love...always entertaining. The Greeks revered their gods...yet, also relished poking fun at them.

The *Three Goddesses* are lightly attired for a warm summer day...and pretentious enough to boldly make a display of their bountiful beauty.

R. Brilliant states: "The curving masses of their mature femininity push through the varied drapery – equally expressive in concealment and revelation of the anatomical forms beneath; they are monumentally disposed...as if the surface of the marble were a rich landscape that delights the eye, but quietly." [*Arts of the Ancient Greeks*, p 202]

Robb & Harrison add: "The whole group is a masterpiece of effective detail...the forms themselves are never obscured by the drapery but rather made more clear through them." [*Art in the Western World*, p 426]

The *Brit. Mus. Book of Greek & Roman Art* says: "Particularly fine are 3 seated female figures... *Aphrodite* reclining in the lap of *Dione*, her mother...and perhaps *Hestia*, goddess of the hearth [seated]. Treatment of the drapery is astonishing...the smooth polished flesh of the goddess' necks and arms...plus, the sensuously clinging, pleated *chitons* that mold the forms of their breasts and stomachs..." [p 65-6]

Lapatin describes Pheidias as "the most renowned artist of Antiquity." After an illustrious career sculpting major commissions throughout Greece, he was selected by Pericles to design and supervise the creation of each statue on the Parthenon. Pheidias may have sculpted several himself..." [*Encyclo Sculpt.*, p 1269-70]

The *Three Goddesses* are symbolic of the Parthenon...of Athens...and of Greece.... icons that remind us this is the birthplace of the cultural and democratic models from which Western Civilization derives.

Subject:

The *Three Goddesses* enjoy revealing their perverse nature as Greek deities. *Aphrodite* and her mother *Dione* dare to face away from the momentous, divine birth of Athena [unseen] a few feet to their right.

Athena...miraculously conceived within the brain of Zeus...bursts forth "from his forehead, fully armed..." [the figures of Athena & Zeus were lost in 450 AD when Christians 'altered' the Parthenon into a church]

The *Goddesses* care little whether mighty Zeus takes offense as they ignore the 'arrival' of Athena. By legend, her 'birth' was the most important event in the rise of Athens...she became patron, protector, and mother goddess of the city-state. [Pinset, 31-2]

As *Aphrodite* lounges against her seated mother *Dione,* they both look in the opposite direction of Athena's birth. They watch the disappearing chariot [unseen] of Selene, the Moon Goddess [unseen]. Both 'Selene' and 'chariot' are represented by the head of a fatigued horse...the *Horse of Selene.* The 'descending head' rests on a cornice of the dais to indicate the end of day.

Due to Ottoman Turks in 1795, the heads of the goddesses are missing. The skill with which Pheidias [or others] sculpted the heads is suggested by the marble *Head of Athena Lemna* now in Bologna – copied from an original bronze which appeared on the Acropolis. [Robb, p 426]

On the other dais [your left] is a group from the other side of the Parthenon's east pediment. The reclining, nude Dionysus also ignores Athena's divine birth. The Greek god of wine and fertility leans back on his elbows...perhaps, exhausted from a night of revelry. Each year, in his name, ancient Greece celebrated 3-day harvest festivals of unrestrained feasting, drinking, and dancing.

Dionysus watches the far end of the dias where "the sun-god Helios [unseen] ascends from the sea in a 4-horse chariot to usher in the new day."

Unlike other figures on the east pediment, Dionysus retains his head … the Turks, possibly favoring him, made an exception.

The Parthenon:

The Temple stands on an outcropping of stone [Acropolis] offering a natural fortress in the middle of Athens. It was built 448 to 438 BC … and dedicated to Athena Parthenos *(maiden/virgin)* … for her assistance in victories over the Persians.

The 'east pediment' of the Parthenon was the triangular section at the top of the east facade. Less than half its original sculptures exist … due to losses in 450 to 500 AD when Christians converted the temple into a church. [*Brit. Mus. Book*, p 62]

After 2,400 years, the Parthenon continues to provide majestic views … from hilltops and roof terraces of Athens in daytime … and especially in evening when flood-lighted.

Lord Elgin:

In 1801, the Earl of Elgin, British ambassador to the Ottoman [Turkish] Empire [which had governed Greece since 1453] obtained a permit from the Sultan to make casts and drawings of antiquities on the Acropolis … to tear down walls to view antiquities … and to take sculptures. From 1801 to 1804, Elgin took – without permission of the Greek people – the cream of available Parthenon sculptures and other works on the Acropolis. They were transported to England and remained in damp storage until sold in 1816 to the British Museum.

A wall plaque in the Duveen Gallery states only 50% of the original sculpture on the Parthenon survives … divided among museums in Athens, London, Paris, the Vatican, Copenhagen, Wurzburg, and Palermo. The plaque also says the British Museum has "much of the sculpture that survives from the *east pediment*, and about half of that which survives from the *west pediment*." Some two-thirds of the original 160-meter frieze survives – of this, about 40% is in Athens and 60% is in the British Museum.

Today, if we compare the 'deteriorated state' of Parthenon statuary Elgin left in Athens to statuary he removed to London – the latter avoiding the acidic smog of Athens – we can be thankful the British Museum became 'caretaker' of so many Parthenon sculptures.

[the future 'home' of these works remains a point of contention between the two nations]

The new Acropolis Museum [at base of Acropolis] provides a safe haven for many surviving sculptures of the Acropolis.

The Classic perfection of the Parthenon is seen <u>intact</u> in the Lincoln Memorial, the La Madeleine Church of Paris, and in a full-scale replica in Nashville, Tennessee. Most major cities in the Western world have borrowed the Parthenon style for civic buildings... particularly Washington, DC.

The *Three Goddesses* are a powerful reminder of the crowning achievements of the ancient Greeks in the 100 years between 510 and 410 BC... as summarized in *Life of Greece* by historian Will Durant:

"Greek civilization is alive; it moves in every breath of mind that we breathe... We know its defects... its insane and pitiless wars... its corrupt individualism... But those who cherish <u>freedom, reason, and beauty</u> will not linger over these blemishes. They will hear... the voices of Solon and Socrates, of Plato and Euripides, of Pheidias and Praxiteles... they will be grateful for the existence of such men, and will seek their company across alien centuries. They will think of Greece as <u>the bright morning</u> of that Western civilization which, with all its kindred faults, is our nourishment and our life." [p 670-71]

Sculptor:

As Pheidias designed the Parthenon statuary, Alcamenes and Agoracristus were among his most able assistant sculptors. Durant says: "No one expected him [Pheidias] to carve with his own hands the hundreds of figures that filled the metopes, frieze, and pediments of the Parthenon ... he left it to his pupils ... and, above all, to Alcamenes to execute his plans." [p 324]

Pheidias also is recognized as the master sculptor/creator of the colossal gold and ivory statue of *Athena* which stood in the cella [inner temple of Parthenon]. The 12-meter-high *Athena* was large enough to hold a life-size golden statue of *Nike* [*Victory*] in her right hand.

Later, at the site of the ancient Olympic Games, Pheidias created another masterpiece, the colossal statue of *Zeus* ... "which came to be ranked among the *Seven Wonders of the Ancient World* ..." [*Encyclo,* p 1270]

Two millenniums later, the American sculptor Horatio Greenough would model his colossal *George Washington* #83 in the "calm grandeur" of the Classic style introduced by Pheidias.

Pericles, Athen's elected leader, initiated and commissioned the Classic Doric-columned Parthenon. He financed its construction largely by unauthorized withdrawals of funds from the treasury of the Delian League ... a political and defensive confederation of mainland Greece and islands in the Aegean Sea. The *Bust of Pericles* follows.

[to view full-scale replica of the original Parthenon, visit Nashville. This temple, built for the Tennessee Centennial Exposition of 1897, includes the *Athena Parthenos* statue]

Major References:

British Museum Book of Greek & Roman Art, 1991, Burn, p. 62, 65-6

Wonders of the World, 2002, Burton & Cavendish, p 14-5

Basic History of Western Art, 2006, Janson and Janson, p 83, 97-8

Art in the Western World, 1953, Robb & Harrison, p 425-8

The Esthetic Basis of Greek Art, 1959, Carpenter, p 65-7

Greek Mythology, 1973, Pinset, p 31-2

Mythology, 1942, Hamilton, 29, 33, 53-76

Arts of the Ancient Greeks, 1972, Brilliant, p 191-203, 232

Encyclopedia of Sculpture, 2004, Lapatin, p 1269-70

The Life of Greece. II, 1966, Durant, p 324-5, 332-36, 670-1

Art of Crete, Mycenae, and Greece, 1968, Hafner, p 148-9

Greek Art, 1964, Boardman, p 118-119

Greek and Roman Sculpture, 1972, Lawrence, p 144-8

Bulfinch's Mythology, 1968, (foreword-Robert Graves), p 6-7

Greatest Works of Art of Western Civilization, 1997, Hoving, p 260-1

Art Through the Ages, Vol I, Gardner, p 132-135

18

PERICLES BUST

OR PERICLES HERM

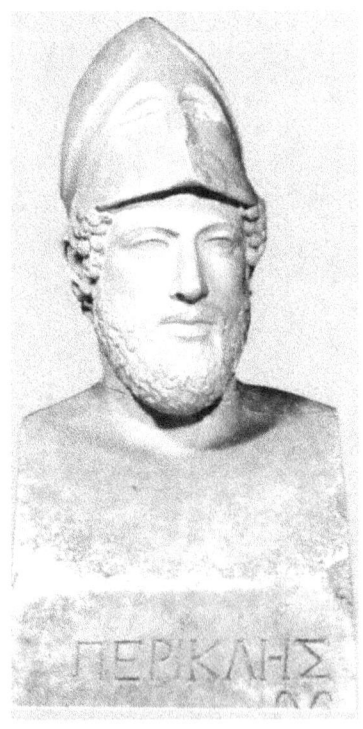

"... commander in chief of all the physical and spiritual
forces of Athens during her greatest age ... the
most complete man that Greece produced."
.... Durant, *Life of Greece*, 1939, p 248

Found, Roman villa, Tivoli – now, Vatican & British Mus.
Roman marble copy – 200 BC & 50 BC – Classic style
From: lost Orig. Greek bronze – 440 to 429 BC
Ht. 19.75 in. [59 cm] – marble – originally painted
Sculptor: Cresilas [orig. Greek bronze]

Universal fame of the *Pericles Bust* derives from its subject. Though Pericles was both a great orator and military leader, he is best remembered as the Athenian responsible for restoring the Acropolis...and, in particular, for building the Parthenon [448 to 432 BC].

The *Golden Age of Pericles* – also described as the *Classical Period* – spanned three decades, from 460 BC to 429 BC. Pericles, born about 495 BC, died in 429 BC. Durant states: "he was, so far as we know, the most complete man that Greece produced." [p 248]

Robb & Garrison declare: "The statue is an ideal embodiment of the powerful personality that made Athens the foremost city in the Greek world...in the fifth century BC." [*Art in the Western World*, p 431]

Hartt states: "The vision and vitality of a single statesman, Pericles, brought Athens to her new political hegemony [dominance]...and it was Pericles who commissioned the monuments for which Athens is eternally renowned...in some 20 dizzying years, Pericles and the great architects and sculptors who worked under his direction created a series of monuments that have been the envy of the civilized world ever since...perhaps because they first proclaimed the new ideal of a transfigured humanity, raised to a plane of superhuman dignity and freedom." [*Art: History of Painting, Sculpture*, p 167]

On the Acropolis, ruins of these works remain impressive. Though their original funding was controversial, "they still stand as visible reminders of the power of the polis...citizens of the original Greek city-states operating independently in a democracy. [Boorstin, p 92]

Gardner asserts: "The Periclean Acropolis saw the concentration of more creative genius than has been seen in any other place or time in the history of the Western World." [*Art Through the Ages*, p 148]

Subject:

Pericles was born about 495 BC. Plutarch [AD 46-120] reveals: "His family was one of the most considerable in Athens, both on his father's and mother's side. His father Xanthippus – who defeated the King of Persia's generals at Mycale [Ionia] – married Agarista, the niece [or grandchild] of Cleisthenes ... who expelled the Peisistratid clan, and abolished their tyranny ..." [*Plutarch's Lives*, 1758, p 5-6] As previously described in *the Tyrannicides* #9, Cleisthenes then introduced democracy to Athens.

The *History of Herodotus* explains the legendary birth of Pericles by his mother, Agarista. "She married Xanthippus; and, when she was with child by him, had a dream, wherein she fancied that she was delivered of a lion; after which, within a few days, she bore Xanthippus a son, to wit, Pericles." [Rawlinson, p 350]

Durant reveals: "In his development, Pericles absorbed the rapidly growing culture of his epoch, and united in his mind and policy all the threads of Athenian civilization – economic, military, literary, artistic, and philosophical." [p 248]

Plutarch explains: "... Pericles acquired not only an elevation of sentiment, and a loftiness and purity of style ... but likewise a gravity of countenance ... a firm and even tone of voice ... and an easy deportment which no vehemence of speaking [hecklers] ever put into disorder. These things, and others of the like nature, excited admiration in all who saw him. [*Plutarch's Lives*, Ellis, p 51]

In 469 BC, at the age of 27, Pericles entered public affairs and quickly became the dominant leader in Athens and therefore in the Greek world. Plutarch adds: "... such was the solitude of Pericles, when he had to speak in public, that he always first addressed a prayer to the gods: *'That not a word might unawares escape him unsuitable to the occasion'.*" [p 52]

Though born an aristocrat, Pericles did not act like one. He advocated liberal reforms, which were strongly opposed by the landed aristocrats.

Durant observes: "History through him illustrated again the principle that liberal reforms are most ably executed and most permanently secured by <u>the cautious and moderate leadership of an aristocrat</u> enjoying popular support." [p 249]

Pericles undoubtedly intended to impress the Mediterranean world with his new Parthenon and other temples on the Acropolis. His extended years of construction on the Acropolis also provided financial rewards to his political supporters – the working trades and professions.

To pay for these new monuments, Pericles proposed the treasury of the Delian Confederacy – funds accumulated for the common defense of Greek city-states – be transferred from Delos to Athens...which many Athenians considered the true capital of the Greek world. When his opponents in the Assembly of Athens opposed this 'confiscation' of funds, Pericles told them, "Very well, let the cost of these buildings go not to your account but to mine; and let the inscription upon them stand in my name." The Assembly quickly acceded to Pericles' plan to seize a portion of the gold in Delos and spend it. [Durant, p 251]

The Jansons add that Pericles "...argued the chief danger [foreign invasion] was no longer real and that Athens – the chief victim and victor of the Persian Wars in 480-479 BC – was justified in using the money to rebuild what the Persians had destroyed. His act...<u>increased the allies' [other Greek city-states] resentment</u> against Athens' growing power...indirectly contributing to <u>the disastrous outcome</u> of the Peloponnesian War." [*Basic History of Western Art*, p 83]

Pericles remained Athen's leader until 430 BC, when he was not re-elected to the 'board of 10 generals'. Due to illness, his life ended in 429 BC.

The long Peloponnesian War [431 – 404 BC] devastated Athens and weakened Sparta. Though the Athenian democracy survived only sporadically...it continued to serve as a model to the rest of the Mediterranean world.

Amazingly...for more than 800 years, the great monuments on the Acropolis built under the leadership of Pericles survived intact.

The new Christians were the first to defile the Parthenon...and were followed by others.

Sculptor:

Cresilas, born in Crete, became a sculptor in Greece between 450 and 428 BC. One of his commissions [from a private-citizen group] was for a bronze statue of Pericles, full-length in heroic nudity – either about 445-40 BC, or soon after Pericles' death in 429 BC. The statue was dedicated on the Acropolis. There are 5 remaining marble copies of the head of this statue. The busts in the British Museum and the Vatican are said to be the finest. By the inscription on the British bust, it is known to be late Hellenistic. [Lawrence, p 151] [Bazin, 144]

Robb & Harrison add: "...certain personal traits are suggested such as the slight tilt of the head and the full sensual lips...the bust is rather an ideal embodiment of the powerful personality...the creases and wrinkles that would normally appear in the face are absent. It is not a portrait of Pericles the man as much as it is the representation of Pericles the statesman." [p 431, 458]

In his era, Greek artistic tradition was to idealize the heads of statesmen...above all, giving them a solemn dignity. On the *Pericles Bust*, his Attic helmet with a movable cheek-guard is a: "symbol of the function of stategos – *that he once commanded an army in the field –* a distinction he held for 15 years in a row. It is believed Pericles preferred this helmet...as it minimized the appearance of his egg-shaped skull.

Cresilas was a contemporary and competitor of the sculptor Pheidias, designer and supervisor of the Parthenon sculptures. When Cresilas participated in a competition at Ephesus [about 440 BC] to produce the finest bronze of a wounded *Amazon*, 5 competing sculptors included Pheidias, Cresilas, Polycleitus, Cydon, and Phradmon. Cresilas took second place to Polycleitus.

A Roman copy of the *Wounded Amazon* by Cresilas can be seen in the Vatican.

Major References:

Plutarch's Lives, MDCCLVIII,(1758), translated Tonson, p 5-6

Plutarch's Lives, Modern Library (publ. by Random House), p 183

Plutarch's Lives, 1917, translated by Ellis, p 50-56

British Museum Book of Greek & Roman Art, 1991, Burn, p 60

History of World Sculpture, 1968, Bazin, p 144

Art: History of Painting, Sculpture..., 1989, Hartt, p 167

History of Herodotus, 1928, translated by Rawlinson, p 350

Lives, Pericles, 100 AD, Plutarch (also known as "Parallel Lives")

Greek and Roman Sculpture, 1972, Lawrence, p 151-2, Plate 35b

Ancient Greece, 1997, Durando, p 48, 145

Life of Greece, 1939, Durant, Fig, 15, p 248-255

The Creators, 1992, Boorstin, p 92, 95-100

Art in the Western World, 1953, Robb & Harrison, p 431, 458

Basic History of Western Art, 2006, Janson & Janson, p 83

Art Through the Ages. Vol. I, 1996, Gardner, p 147-48

Arts of the Ancient Greeks, 1972, Brilliant, p 128

The Will of Zeus, 1961, Barr, p 122-24

Vatican Collections (Met), 1982, O'Neill, p 206

19

NIKE LOOSENING SANDAL

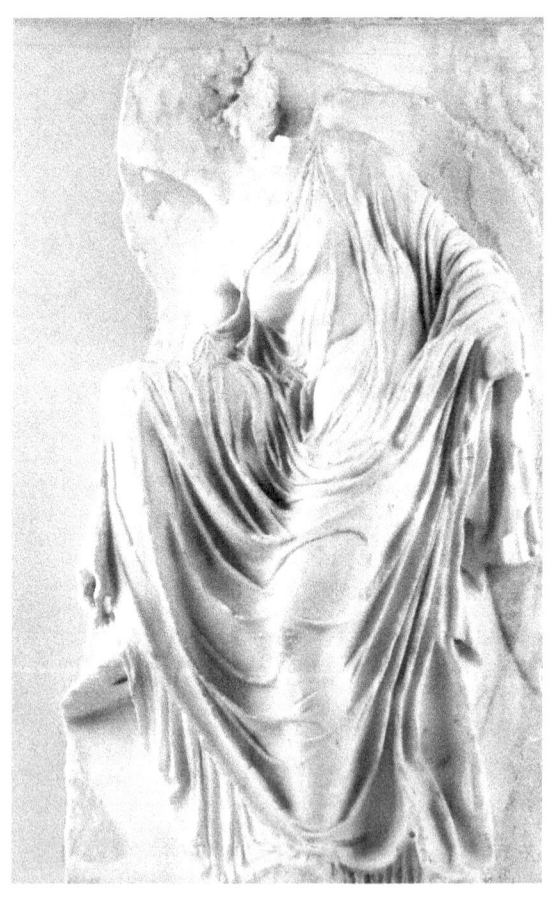

"...one of the triumphs of Greek art."
...Durant, *Life of Greece*, 1939, p 331

Originally on Athena Nike Temple – now, Acropolis Museum
Orig. Greek sculpture – approx. 408 BC – Classic style, wet
Ht. 41.75 inches [106 cm] – Pentelic marble
Sculptor: likely Alcamenes or Agoracritus or Callimachus
   Nike is Greek term for the ancient goddess of victory

For grace and charm, the *Nike Loosening Sandal* has few equals in the Western world.
   As she prepares to enter a sacred temple on the Acropolis, her lithe figure pauses to remove her sandals. She is veiled in a thin, wet chiton … suggesting it is a humid, summer day … and perspiration moistens her skin.
   Burn describes the 'original' Nike figures on the marble parapet of the Athena Nike temple [on Acropolis] as "among the most beautiful figures of Classical art … their clinging, transparent draperies more finely-carved even than that of the Parthenon." [*Brit. Mus. Book of Greek & Roman Art,* p 66]
   When the Temple of Athena Nike was built in about 420 BC, Athens was a decade into the Peloponnesian War with Sparta [431-404 BC]. By dedicating a temple to Athena [their mother goddess], Athenians sought her favor in the long, self-destructive conflict.
   The winged Nike goddesses were added to the temple between 411 and 407 BC. "They were intended to extol the victories of Alcibiades who had raised the Athenian hopes of a successful outcome to the war. But … by 404 BC, the defeat of the Athenians was already sealed." [*Acropolis,* Meletzis/Papadakis, p 21]

Subject:

With the arrival of *Nike Loosening her Sandal* in 408 BC, the 'wet' look became an art form unto itself.
   Janson describes her. "The balustrade around the Temple of Athena Nike shows a festive procession, but the participants are winged Nike goddesses rather than citizens of Athens. The *Nike* is removing her sandals – in conformity with an age-old tradition – indicating she is about to step on holy ground. Her wings – one

open, the other closed – are effectively employed to help keep her balance … so that <u>she performs with consummate elegance of movement</u> what is ordinarily a rather awkward act." [*History of Art,* p 133]

The Nike goddesses bring gifts and sacrifices to the 'mother goddess' Athena* seated at the end of the parapet wall. Two Nike goddesses approach the sacrificial altar with a prize calf … another goddess kneels on a cow's back to kill it with a knife … others construct a trophy by placing a helmet atop a pole. *model for original *Britannia* on English coinage

The real 'subject' in the mind of the sculptor(s) who created these *Nike* goddesses may have had less to do with the "victories of Alcibiades" than it did with the sculptors' desire to fully display their new skills.

Sir Ernst Gombrich's *Story of Art* avows the figures: "… show the change of taste towards delicacy and refinement … one goddess of victory stoops to unfasten a sandal as she walks … with what charm the sudden halt is portrayed, and how softly and richly the thin drapery falls over the beautiful body. We can see in these works … gradually, the approach to art changed … <u>statues earned their reputation more 'by virtue of their beauty' as works of art</u>." [p 99-101]

R. Brilliant observes: "in the lovely figures of the *Nike Balustrade* … we have <u>the introduction of precious grace</u> … of pleasure in a beautiful statement …" [p 214] "The supple, fully-developed figure of *Nike* stands momentarily arrested … The 'wet' clinging drapery – a provocatively diaphanous second skin – draws the eye to the graceful movement of the *Nike* and to the physical beauty of her form." [*Arts of the Ancient Greeks,* p 239]

Robb & Garrison add: "… solid stone is made more ephemeral than the finest silk, completely revealing the charming, gracefully poised figure. No longer does the observer breathe the rarified atmosphere of Mt. Olympus, for here is no goddess but a human being. The *Victory* untying her sandal represents not an ideal of divinity but rather a divinely beautiful mortal." [*Art in the Western World,* p 437]

Gardner suggests the master sculptor had a far different goal: "The artist has carried the style … even further and has given us a figure whose garments cling so tightly to the body that they seem almost transparent… The sculptor is, however, interested in much more than revealing the supple beauty of the young female body. The folds of the draperies form intricate linear patterns that are unrelated to the anatomical structure of the body and have a life of their own as abstract designs. Deep carving produces pockets of shade to contrast with the polished surfaces of the marble and enhances the ornamental beauty of what is admittedly a highly mannered design." [*Art Through the Ages,* p 157]

Bazin also mentions abstract design: "The sculptor's chief concerns seem to have been the virtuoso play [of light] on the figure's nudity under her transparent robe, and the ornamental combinations of drapery folds, which make up a quasi-abstract pattern of light and shade. The firm design and broad curves of the figure give an impression of elegance and weightlessness." [*History of World Sculpture,* p 145]

The *Three Goddesses* #17 on the Parthenon were originally displayed 34 feet above ground level. Initially, the *Nike Goddesses* on the Athena Nike Temple also were displayed far above eye-level… perhaps, to appease conservative elements of society.

Sculptor:

The sculptor of this *Nike* was most likely Alcamenes, based on his comparable *Aphrodite in the Gardens* [after the Athena Nike temple had been completed]. Durant says Alcamenes, "made an *Aphrodite of the Gardens* which Lucian ranked with the highest masterpieces of statuary… a *Draped Venus* in the Louvre may be a copy of this statue." [p 326]

Lawrence adds: "… the *Victory* fastening her sandal… is executed with the same perfection as in the *'Genetrix'…*" [p 166] This refers to the *Venus Genetrix* #51 of which the finest examples are in the Palatine Museum and the Getty Villa.

Major References:

History of Art, 1977, Janson, p 133
Art in the Western World, 1953, Robb & Garrison, p 436-37
Art through the Ages, Vol I, 1996, Gardner, p 157

The Story of Art, 1995, Sir Ernst Gombrich, p 99-101, Pl. 61

Acropolis, 1967, Meletzis and Papadakis, p 7, 21, 30

British Museum Book of Greek & Roman Art, 1991, Burn, p 66

Life of Greece, 1939, Will Durant, p 331, Fig 28

Greek & Roman Sculpture, 1972, Lawrence, p 161-62, 164-66,

Arts of the Ancient Greeks, 1972, Brilliant, p 214, 239

History of World Sculpture, 1968, Bazin, p 145

20

APHRODITE OF CYRENE
ADAPTATION OF LOST APHRODITE
OF CNIDUS

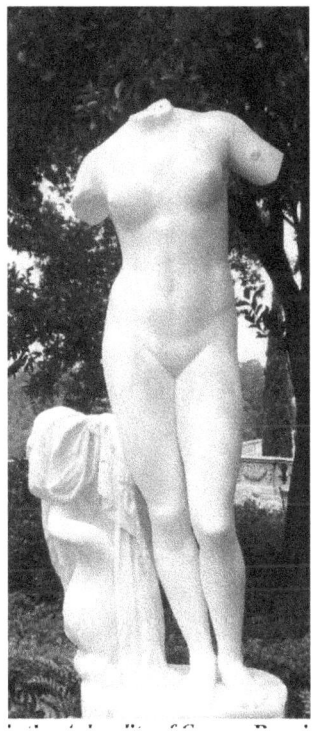

"More original is the *Aphrodite of Cyrene*. Rangier in build than
Praxiteles's *Aphrodite*, the Cyrene figure has, in addition to its
beautiful silhouette, a wealth of subtle modulations...."

... Classical Myths in Sculpture, Agard, p 19, 20

Dis. 1913, Cyrene – now Libya; copies: Rome & Hearst Castle*
Greek marble – approx. 150 BC – Hellenistic style
adapted from: Orig. Greek marble – 350 BC – Praxiteles
Ht. 4 ft. 8.25 inches – Parian marble
Sculptor of *Cyrene* figure: possibly, Euphranor of Corinth
   *above photo is Hearst Castle copy in California

The original *Aphrodite of Cnidus* by Praxiteles in 350 BC – "the first completely nude monumental cult statue of a goddess in Greek art" – drew immediate fame throughout the Mediterranean world. [Jansons, p 100] It became "the most highly praised sculpture of antiquity." [Brilliant, p 368]

At an unknown date, this statue left Cnidus and arrived in Constantinople [capital of the eastern Roman Empire] where it was lost by fire in 476 AD. [Curtiss, p 179]

Throughout the ancient Greek and Roman worlds, wide demand for thousands of reproductions of the *Cnidian Aphrodite* [some 60 versions] resulted in mass production of the figure. Virtually all were by low-skilled copyists... explaining the bland copies in the Louvre, Uffizi, Vatican, and Capitoline museums. Janson describes these copies as "no more than pallid reflections of the original." [*History of Art*, p 137]

However... Gardner states: "*Aphrodite of Cnidus* was widely regarded in antiquity as the most beautiful of statues... its charm can be best understood – not from the inferior Roman copies of it – but from a much later Hellenistic work, *the Aphrodite of Cyrene*, which, at one century remove, conveys a Praxitelean poetry of sensual beauty." [*Art Through the Ages*. p 141]

Aphrodite of Cyrene

The left arm of the above *Aphrodite* is in a raised position, suggesting she dries her hair after bathing in the sea.

Or... following birth at sea "the goddess is represented nude... rising from the waves at the moment of her first appearance to mortals... and all wet and just pressing water from her hair..." [*Art & Archaeology*, Feb, 1921] [*Rome*, 1965, Editrice Parthenon, p 111]

In 1913, this *Aphrodite* was unearthed in Libya by an occupying Italian army and shipped to Rome. [in 2007, Italy repatriated the figure to Libya]

Agard states: "More original is the *Aphrodite of Cyrene*. Rangier in build than Praxiteles's *Aphrodite*, the Cyrene figure has, in addition to its beautiful silhouette, a wealth of subtle modulations in the modeling." [*Classical Myths in Sculpture,* p 19, 20]

[Agard also describes Rodin's reaction to the *Cyrene* figure: "Rodin declared that only by candlelight can all of its subtlety of modeling be appreciated." [p 19] Rodin often sculpted with a candle]

After 1914, two copies of *the Cyrene* figure were created. One is displayed at the Hearst Castle in California. Commissioned by William Randolph Hearst in the mid-1920s, it stands in the garden terrace above the Neptune Pool of the Castle.

The National Museums of Rome display the other copy...irregularly.

[on *Author's* 3 most recent visits to Rome, this copy was not at any location suggested by tourist booths. At Terme Museum, an official 'disclaimed' it. Privileged Romans are known to 'borrow' public art for private use – a la Tiberius & *the Scraper* #25]

The 1913 discovery of the original *Aphrodite of Cyrene* is described by British journalist Barnaby Rogerson: "The temple-encrusted Sanctuary of Apollo [at Cyrene] can be compared only to that at Delphi...the nymph's spring still supplies a trickle of cool water. The miraculous is still tangible here, as was witnessed when a torrential shower washed away the soil to reveal the famous statue of *Aphrodite of Cyrene* to an incredulous Italian army encampment in 1913. It was found in the ruins of the Roman baths in Cyrene." [*Independent of London,* Oct. 14, 2000]

Rhys Carpenter [former director, Amer. School of Classical Studies/Athens] states: "the lovely *Aphrodite of Cyrene*...embodies in the guise of effortless composure a supremely self-conscious artistry of skill...broader hips and higher waist and narrower shoulders are now recorded correctly and sympathetically. All exuberant ostentation...all dramatic diversion...all calculated display of technical capacity have been avoided by an artist who has relied on only the subtlest elements of sculptural appeal...Perhaps, this marks a culmination [peak] in Greek sculptural art..." [*Greek Sculpture,* p 196-97, Pl. 36]

Clark describes the *Cyrene* as a "combination of elegance and naturalism [that] takes our eyes at the first glance...she is more delicately carved than almost any other Aphrodite...and still imparts some thrill of refined sensuality such as was the glory of the *Cnidian.*" [*Nude, Study in Ideal Form,* p 90-1]

R. Brilliant dates the *Cyrene* figure as "late Hellenistic" and says: "...the transient imagery of pretty sexuality may be realized in the sleek elegance of the late Hellenistic *Aphrodite of Cyrene*..." [p 368]

Lucas observed: "She is less glorious than *Venus de Milo*, but far more human than the *Venus of the Capitoline.* Her charm is irresistible...in no other statue has the sculptor come so near the miracle of turning flesh to stone or stone to flesh." [*Wanderer in Rome,* p 193, 214]

History – the lost *Aphrodite of Cnidus* by Praxiteles

Praxiteles, known for both charm and wit, created his *Aphrodite* leaning forward, preparing to step into a bath...her gown partially draped over a water jug...she is surprised by a visitor...her hand moves.

Lucian, a Greek rhetorician [117-180 AD] who observed the original statue in person, wrote: "When we had taken sufficient delight in the garden plants, we passed on into the temple. The goddess is set there in the middle of it – an exceedingly beautiful work of Parian marble – with a look of proud contempt and a slight smile which just reveals her teeth. The full extent of her beauty is unhidden by any clinging raiment, for her nudity is complete except insofar as she holds one hand in front of her to hide her modesty." [Gardner, 1996, p 162]

Lucian also notes the: "dewy quality of *Aphrodite's* eyes." [p 162]

Gardner agrees: "We can get a good idea of the 'look' of the *Aphrodite of Cnidus* from original works by sculptors who emulated the master's manner. One of the finest of these is the head of the *Woman from Chios*... the chisel has been wielded to suggest the softness of the young girl's face and the 'dewy' gaze of the eyes." [p 162]

Lawrence quotes the Roman historian Pliny [AD 23-79]: "the finest statue, not only by Praxiteles but of the whole world, is the *Aphrodite*, for the sight of which many have sailed to Cnidus [Greek settlement on coast of Asia Minor]. Praxiteles had carved two statues; the other, a draped figure, was preferred by the people of Cos, who considered it more dignified and modest. The nude statue Cos refused was bought by the Cnidians, and its reputation grew out of all proportion to the Cos statue. At a later date, King Nicomedes wished to buy it from the Cnidians, offering to redeem the whole debt of the state, but they preferred to put up with anything [declined] ... and not unwisely, because by that statue Praxiteles cast a glory on Cnidus." [p 190]

Durant adds: "Tourists came from every nook of the Mediterranean to see the work... critics pronounced it the finest statue yet made in Greece...." [*Life of Greece*, p 495]

Sculptor – *Aphrodite of Cnidus*

Praxiteles – born about 390 BC – is described by art historian Sir Ernest Gombrich as "the greatest artist of that century." Most active as a sculptor from about 370 to 330 BC, he introduced a new style – taller and slimmer statues distinguished by their grace. [*Story of Art*, p 103]

The 'Cnidian curve of Praxiteles' – the seductively uneven hip position of his female figures – was adopted by all his imitators.

Phyrne, the famed model of Praxiteles, is described by Durant: "The beauty of Phyrne is the talk of 4th century Athens, since she never appears in public except completely veiled... but, at the Eleusinian festival, and again on the feast of the Poseidonia, she disrobes in the sight of all... lets down her hair... and goes to bathe in the sea. For a time she loves and inspires Praxiteles, and poses for his *Aphrodite*." [p 300]

Clark informs us Praxiteles created: "…a nude statue of her in gilt bronze" and it "was erected in the sacred precincts of Delphi by a grateful community." [p 83]

Boorstin confirms the existence of this statue: "In the 2nd Century AD, Pausanias, at Delphi along the Sacred Way…saw relics of a gilded statue of the courtesan *Phyrne* erected by her lover Praxiteles next to two statues of Apollo…" [*The Creators*, p 96]

Major References:

Classical Myths in Sculpture, 1951, Agard, p 18-20

The Nude, a Study in Ideal Form, 1990, Clark, p 83, 90, 91

Greek Sculpture, 1960, Carpenter, p 196-7, 216-8, pl 36

Art and Archaeology, February 1921

A Wanderer in Rome, 1926, Lucas, p 193, 214

Rome, 1965, Editrice Parthenon, p 111

How To Look At Sculpture, 1989, Finn, p 85-6

The Birth of Western Civilization, 1964, Grant, p 156

Disarmed, 2003, Curtiss, p 179

The Independent (of London), 10/14/2000, Rogerson, "Miracle of the Desert"

Arts of the Ancient Greeks, 1972, Brilliant, p 368

Life of Greece, II, 1939, Durant, fig. 51, p 185, 300-01, 494-7, 504

Caesar and Christ, III, 1944, Durant, p 216, 548, 559*

Art Through the Ages, Vol I, 1980, Gardner, p 141

Art Through the Ages, 1996, Gardner, p 162

Hellenistic Science & Culture in Last 3 Centuries BC, George Sarton, p 511

The Story of Art, 1989 edition, Gombrich, p 103-6

30,000 Years of Art, 2007, Phaidon Press, p 248

Greek and Roman Sculpture, 1972, Lawrence, p 189-90

The Creators, 1992, Boorstin, p 92

Amores 13, Lucian, 2nd C. AD, translated by J.J. Pollitt

Art in the Western World, 1953, Robb and Garrison, p 440

History of Art, 1977, Janson, p 137

Art & Arch…Rome, 2005, Hintzen-Bohlen, p 137

21

CHIMAERA

OF AREZZO

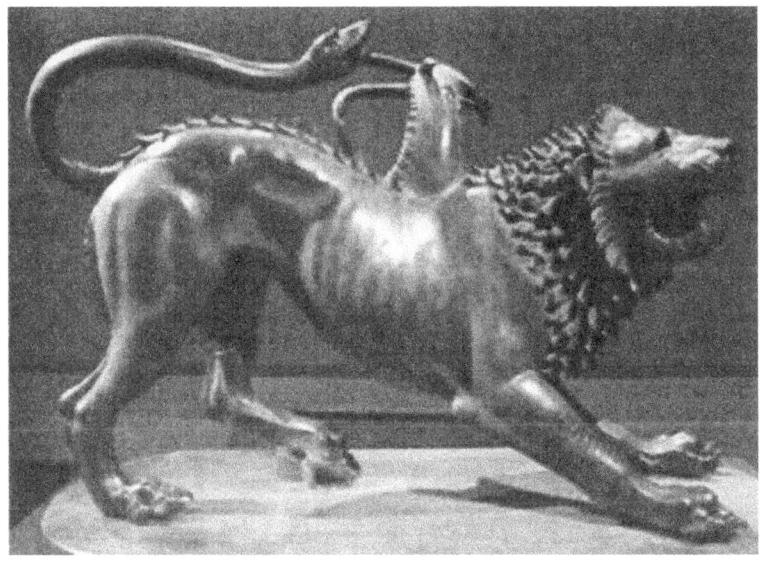

"the magnificent hollow-cast statue shows the 3-headed
mythical monster responding to an attack"
...Checci , *Encyclopedia of Sculpture*, p 295

Found 1553, Arezzo, Tuscany – Nat. Arch. Mus., Florence
Orig. Etruscan bronze – 375-350 BC – Naturalistic Hybrid
Ht. 31 in.[65 cm]; Length: 4.25 feet
Sculptor: unknown Etruscan

T he wounded *Chimaera* has been "famous since its discovery on 15 November 1553...near the Porta [gate] San Lorenzo of the Etruscan city of Arrezo." [*30,000 Years of Art*, p 219]

Durant declares *the Chimaera* "a masterpiece." [*Caesar & Christ*, p. 9]

He adds the Etruscan statue is: "...a disagreeable figure...presumably the monster slain by Bellerophon – head and body of a lion, a serpent for a tail, a goat's head growing out of the back...its power and finish reconcile us to its biological extravagance. No other art [than Etruscan] has produced so many distortions of the human frame, so many hideous masks, uncouth animals, monstrous demons, and terrifying gods." [p. 9-10]

30,000 Years says: "The lean naturalistic forms of the smooth body – with muscular legs, bony paws, and protruding ribs and veins – contrast with the intensely textured, flame-like tongues of the long mane. Such stylization...is found in [other] Archaic Etruscan works, such as the well-known *She-Wolf* #10 of Rome." [p 239]

Knight describes the unknown sculptor as "a supremely gifted artist" and the lion-hybrid as "a surely amazing sculptural grouping...a magnificent bronze...a marvelously animated dynamism...a masterpiece." [*LA Times*, p D5]

Originally, before restoration, the snake-head may have hovered over the back of the lion, prepared to strike in any direction. Horns of the goat offered protection to *the Chimaera's* back, neck and shoulders.

The origins of this Etruscan bronze are believed to be from the exotic East...possibly ancient Lycia in Asia Minor [now southwest coast of Turkey]. Shortly after 900 BC, the ancient Etruscans began to migrate from this coastal region to central Italy. Their motivation may have been over-population, prolonged drought, foreign invasion, or some other catastrophe.

Bulfinch's Mythology states: "*The Chimaera* was a fearful [lion-like] monster, breathing fire...no one could withstand its fiery breath. It made great havoc in Lycia so that the king Iobates sought for some hero to destroy it...there arrived at his court a gallant young warrior, Bellerophon. He brought letters from Proetus [son-in-law of Iobates] recommending Bellerophon in the warmest terms as an unconquerable hero … but added, at the close, a request to his father-in-law to put Bellerophon to death … Proetus was jealous of him, suspecting his wife Antea looked too much in admiration on the young warrior." [p 129-30]

[travelling storytellers – to earn more coin – embellished the exploits of their heroes … and freely assigned special attributes to their foes.]

However … the 'fearful monster' above may not be wholly myth. Lions did roam the ancient lands of Turkey … just as they ranged in nearby Assyria [see *the Dying Lioness* #8] Certain renegade lions may have acquired a reputation for creating 'great havoc' by devouring livestock and even humans. Hunters of these lions could gain fame and reward by killing such beasts.

30,000 Years adds *the Chimaera* "was surely a votive offering in some sanctuary located just outside the walls of the city [Arrezo] … its pose and wounds – bleeding gashes on the goat's neck, just visible below the head and on the lion's [injured] left hind leg – have been taken as evidence that it was part of a group portraying the mythical slaying of the monster by Bellerophon." [p 239]

The hero Bellerophon would have been mounted on Pegasus, a winged horse. Neither a figure of Bellerophon nor Pegasus was found with *the Chimaera*. The larger figures [if they had existed] may have been melted down for bronze by marauders … while the smaller *Chimaera* could have been hidden easily.

Checci says: "Cosimo I [Medici] considered the discovery of the Arezzo *Chimaera* a good omen … the Medici [ruling family in nearby Florence] saw the defeated monster as a symbol of their vanquished enemies. … a beautiful marble statue of Pegasus [by Costoli in 1865] still dominates the Boboli Gardens in Florence …" [*Encyclo Sculpture*, p 296]

Cosimo I "claimed the newly-unearthed bronze *Chimaera* and immediately had it installed in his Florentine palace … now he had a brilliant work of ancient art to rival Rome's *She-Wolf*. History was symbolically asserted to be on Cosimo's side – no small thing in an age that was mad for building on the glory and grandeur of the ancient world." [*LA Times*, Knight, 8-4-2010, p D5]

Durant states: "The bronze casters of Etruria were at the top of their craft... one city alone is reported to have had 2,000 statues in bronze. Among these... two masterpieces stand out: *the Orator*... and *the Chimaera*." [*Caesar & Christ*, p 9-10]

Subject:

Checci observes: "...the magnificent hollow-cast statue shows the '3-headed' mythical monster responding to an attack. The animal seems contracted in a moment of terrible stress... anger and pain mix in a tragic representation. The body rests firmly on the front paws, with the neck twisted to the right and the goat-head turning in dialectic tension to the left. The beast's terrible jaws are wide open... the paws are equipped with powerful claws." [*Encyclo. Sculpt.*, 296-97]

Knight describes the restored snake. "The serpent rises in a long Rococo S-curve straight over the beast's spine, splitting the difference between the other two heads curving left and right. The composition meant that the snake's fangs would clamp down on the goat's right horn. It's a startling vision – a ferocious beast wildly biting itself in the chaotic throes of life-or-death combat." [*LA Times*, 8-4-2010]

Pinsent describes Bellerophon as "remarkable for his beauty... When Bellerophon arrived at the court of King Iobates of Lycia, the rules of hospitality discouraged the king from following the request of his son-in-law Proetus to kill Bellerophon. [*Greek Mythology*, p 70-2]

Bulfinch reveals the king of Lycia decided "to send Bellerophon to do combat with *the Chimaera*. ... the soothsayer Polyidus advised Bellerophon to procure the horse Pegasus for the conflict... and directed him to pass the night in the Temple of Minerva... as he slept, Minerva came to him and gave him a golden bridle. When he awoke, the bridle remained in his hand... Minerva also showed him Pegasus drinking in the well of Pirene, and at the sight of the bridle the winged steed came willingly and suffered himself to be taken. Bellerophon mounted him, rose with him in the air, soon found *the Chimaera*, and gained an easy victory over the monster." [p 130]

Checci explains the victory is made possible since the wings of Pegasus permit it to fly: "...enabling the hero to attack and kill *the Chimaera* from above." [p 296]

Bazin observes: "...the monster is depicted with muscles tensed and back arched in a last desperate effort; but the goat-head on its back is already dying from a wound to the neck...the bronze forms quiver with life and pain." [*History of World Sculpture*, p 168]

Knight advises: "Look closely and you'll spot a couple of stylized floral rosettes on the goat's neck and the lion's hind end – engorged drops of blood, spurting from stabbed flesh." [p D5]

Sculptor:

The Chimaera is believed to have been sculpted by an Etruscan master sculptor.

Upon discovery of the statue, a length of serpent's tail was also excavated. From this, a Renaissance artist restored the tail...also replacing the missing snakehead and attaching it to the goat's horn, probably for stability and strength. [Gardner, p 164]

Cellini is believed to have reconstructed the left rear paw...which is raised as if injured. [Checchi, p 295]

"The slaying of *the Chimaera* was a popular motif in Etruscan art, and like the *She-Wolf,* has inspired artists ever since its discovery. The animal appears in Medieval art as a hybrid monster, with human face and serpent tail...later versions often morph into a sphinx-like creature." [*30,000 Years*, p 239]

Major References:

Bulfinch's Mythology, 1968, Rbt. Graves foreword, p 129-31
Greek Mythology, 1973, Pinsent, p 70-2
Mythology, 1942, Hamilton, p 184-90
Encyclopedia of Sculpture, 2004, Checci, p 295-96
History of World Sculpture, 1968, Bazin, p 168-69
Art Through the Ages, 1980, Gardner's, p 164
Los Angeles, Times, 8-4-10, Knight, p D1, D5
Caesar and Christ, 1944, Durant, p 9-10
30,000 Years of Art, 2007, Phaidon, p 239

22

THE BALL PLAYER

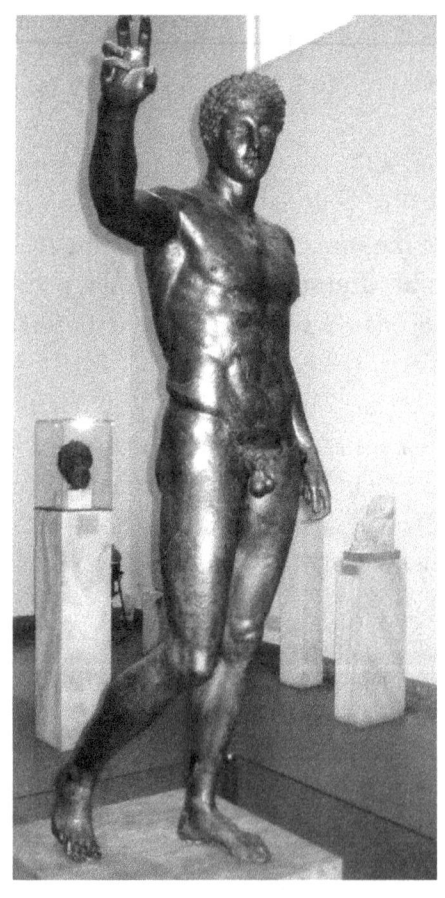

"magnificent statue of a young man"
...Brilliant, *Arts of Ancient Greeks*, p 266

Found 1900, ancient shipwreck – now Athens Arch. Mus.
Orig. Greek bronze – 350 to 340 BC – Late Classic
Ht. 6 ft. 5 in. [194 m.] – over life-sized bronze
Sculptor: unknown master of the Polykleitan school

At the sight of this 2,300-year-old Greek statue, many Americans visiting the Athens Arch. Museum may immediately visualize a baseball player. The stance of the figure and the grip of his raised hand give the impression he is throwing or catching a ball with another person. The forward position of the opposite foot suggests he is throwing.

Notably ... the *Ball Player* is refreshingly dynamic in a museum exhibiting a vast collection of 'static' statuary.

That this statue has survived is extraordinary, as few ancient Greek sculptures – bronzes or marbles – are both intact and masterpieces. The good fortune of the surviving *Ball Player* may be due to a covetous Roman citizen ... and a severe storm at sea.

In 1900 the statue was discovered in fragments at the site of a shipwreck [approx.100 BC] off the small island of Anticythera, south of the Peloponnesian peninsula of Greece.

The doomed ship carrying this Classic bronze was likely headed west and bound for Italy where the prized bronze could be sold to a wealthy Roman citizen. Or ... delivered to the villa of a Roman general who had 'procured' it. Or ... delivered to an imperial residence ... among many possibilities. [Carpenter, p 161]

Subject:

By its 'quality of execution', this bronze likely represented a famed athlete. His eyes are inlaid with semiprecious stones.

The facial expression conveys concern for the [unseen] ball either in hand or in flight from a companion.

Some references suggest it is the golden apple Paris awards to Aphrodite ... but, this is improbable due to the shoulder-high arm plus the vertical hand-grasp.

Another suggestion is Perseus holding the snake-haired head of Medusa ... except the bent-finger position is not that of a hand gripping hair, and the youth wears no sword-belt. [Lawrence, p 200]

Durant's *Life of Greece* describes ball contests in ancient times: "Ball games were as varied then as now, and as popular ... at Sparta the terms *ballplayer* and *youth* were synonyms. Special rooms were built in the palaestra [place of exercise] for games of ball ... these rooms were called *sphairisteria* ... and teachers were *sphairistai*. On a relief we see men bouncing a ball against the floor or the wall, and striking it back with the flat of the hand ... Another game resembled Canadian lacrosse, being a form of hockey played with racquets." [p 212]

Durant offers the observation of the ancient writer Antiphanes: "When he got the ball, he delighted to give it to one player while dodging another; he knocked it away from one and urged another with noisy cries. Outside, a long pass, beyond him ... overhead, a short pass ..." [p 212] This is similar to modern rugby and football.

Galen, a Greek physician/writer of Pergamon in the 2nd century AD, favored: "quiet all-round gymnastics and especially exercise with a small ball ... a man stood between two rows of players and tried to intercept the ball as they passed it; hence a game in which there were no winners, no contests and no spectators other than friends and family." [Finley, p 120]

Carpenter's *Greek Sculpture* comments: "Except for the tilt of the head and the more sharply-raised and out-thrust arm, the pose is the mirror image [reverse] of *the Spear Bearer/Doryphoros* #15. Classic abstract formalism is becoming modified into formalized naturalism. But the past is still strong upon it and within it, to give it stylistic character and structural power." [p 162]

Sculptor:

Though the sculptor cannot be identified, some authorities note an association with the school of Polykleitos due to the statue's athletic structure. Brilliant adds: "This larger than life-size bronze reveals another adaptation of the Polykleitan tradition, in the direction of 3-dimensional movement, reduction of bulk ... and enhanced modeling…as well as the agitated hair, projecting forehead, and shadowy eyes and mouth…" [p 266]

Lawrence states while: "the face reveals the influence of Praxiteles…the heavy build of the trunk follows the Polykleitan tradition." [p 199]

The sculptor of this statue broke tradition by not exaggerating the hip muscles – along the lower torso – as was common among earlier sculptors seeking 'structural eloquence'. Overly-enlarged hip muscles are clearly evident in the previously-discussed *Zeus of Artemision* #12 and the *Doryphoros* #15.

According to Carpenter: "it is the enormous hip muscle which gives most offense to the modern anatomist. It was allowed to survive in the classic canon because it helped to give structural articulation and definition. The bronze *Ballplayer* preserves it intact, but with the divisional boundaries now less sharply-lined, and the transitions from part to part more tempered." [p 43-4]

Major References:

Greek Sculpture, 1960, Carpenter, p 43-5

Greek and Roman Sculpture, Lawrence, 1972, p 199-200, Pl. 51b

Nat. Arch. Mus. Athens, Ragghianti, 1980, p. 136, 138

Nat. Arch. Mus. Athens, Meletzis & Papadakis, 1988, p. 130, 150-1

Art of Crete, Mycenae, and Greece, Hafner, 1968, p.192

Arts of the Ancient Greeks, 1972, Brilliant, p. 266

Ancient Greece, 1997, Durando, p 153

The Life of Greece, 1939, Durant, p 212

The Olympic Games, 1976, Finley and Pleket, p 120

23

'THE MAUSOLUS'

OF HALICARNASSUS

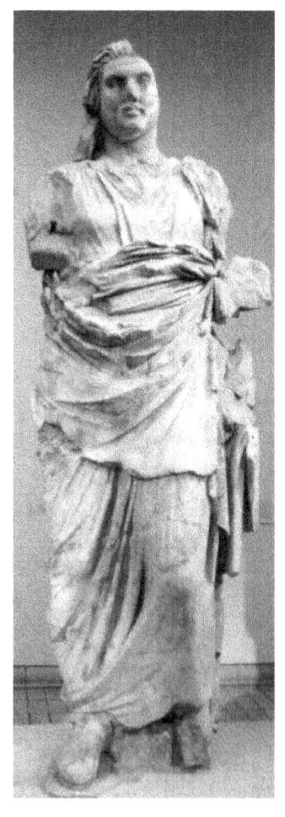

"... a masterpiece of regal portraiture"
...Brilliant, *Arts of the Ancient Greeks*, p 250

Found 1857, ruins Mausoleum of Halicarnassus* – Brit. Mus.
Orig. Greek [Ionian] statue – 340 BC – late Classic style
Height: 9 ft. 8 in. [3 m.] – marble – nearly twice life-size
Sculptor: Greek, likely Bryaxis, Scopas, or Leochares
  *now Bodrum, southwest coast of modern Turkey

Of surviving ancient Greek sculpture, this <u>famed monumental masterpiece is one of the first to display strong facial character</u>... and, therefore, possibly a particular person. However, we are uncertain who.

The figure displays '<u>a regal bearing</u>' and – for lack of a viable alternative – became known as *Mausolus*, a king of Caria. However, there is no inscription or other evidence to confirm this identity.

As the Hellenized king of Caria [in southwest Turkey], Mausolus reigned from 377 to 353 BC. From his huge and magnificent tomb [no longer standing], the word 'mausoleum' derives. It means outsized funerary monument.

The structure rose in 3 stages to a height of some 160 feet and was crowned by a chariot with statues of the deceased. Of its 3 friezes, the 'Greeks fighting Amazons' was considered the finest.

The Jansons describe the Mausoleum of Halicarnassus as "the only project of the 4th century BC that corresponds to the Parthenon in size and ambition." [*Basic History of Western Art,* p 98] It became known as one of the 'Seven Wonders of the Ancient World'.

In 1857, when Englishman Charles Newton discovered the statue near the remains of a chariot in the ruins of the Mausoleum, he assigned it the name *Mausolus.*

Burns says: "...most modern authorities believe the [funerary] building must have been started by King Mausolus in his own lifetime. The most complete and impressive of the surviving, free-standing sculptures are the colossal male and female figures that Newton 'understandably' christened *Mausolos* and *Artemisia.* <u>Particularly fine is the male figure,</u> clearly a portrait of an individual with his shaggy hair, mustache and beard, deep-set eyes and strongly drawn brows..." [*Brit. Mus. Book of Greek & Roman Art,* p 118, 120]

Burns later declares: "It now seems extremely unlikely that Newton's identification is correct; they appear to be two of the large number of figures believed to represent past and present members of the ruling dynasty of Caria... that once stood on the top of the podium..." [p 123]

Bazin adds: "The sculptured decoration of the Mausolus tomb included a number of portrait statues of relatives, ancestors or dignitaries standing round the dead king like a last guard of honor. This figure is robed in heavy theatrical folds of drapery and the head is powerfully individualistic. The fleshy face, oriental in type, has an imperious forehead and nose, a slightly scornful mouth; its short beard and long hair are rendered somewhat summarily, since – owing to the placing of the statue – it would have been seen only from a distance and from below." [*History of World Sculpture*, p 146-47]

Carpenter lends support to Burns: "these statues cannot have been mounted upon the great 4-horse chariot recorded as crowning the pyramidal roof of the tomb... '*Mausolus*' once carried a scepter and sword... neither he nor the woman can be equipped with reins..." [*Greek Sculpture*, p 214]

Caygill agrees: "Because of its scale, it is unlikely that it [the statue] would have fitted into the chariot group [atop the Mausoleum] and it probably represents one of the rulers of Caria whose statues stood between the pillars... below the pyramidal top." [*Treasures of the British Museum*, p 20]

Lawrence – who accepts the identity as *Mausolus* – says: "The head of *Mausolus* was obviously for a portrait, though idealized... his height – 3 meters – is greater than would have been suitable for any other man. The generally excellent preservation of the surface indicates that it originally stood under cover... placed, as a cult-like image, within the cella [enclosed chamber of Classical temples]. In the head, the lines of hair, brows and mustache flare away at exciting angles... likewise emphasized by shadow, in contrast to the wide smooth features that produce an effect of serene majesty." [*Greek & Roman Sculpture*, p 200-01]

Subject:

Hafner fairly states: "This is undoubtedly the statue of a Carian prince ... either a relative of Mausolus or *Mausolus* himself. The corpulence and the long hair give the figure a 'barbaric' appearance. [*Art of Crete, Mycenae, & Greece,* p 199]

[below: Boardman, Durant & Brilliant favor 'Mausolus' identity]

Boardman comments: "The Carian's un-Hellenic features and wild hair are faithfully copied by the Greek sculptor." [*Greek Art,* p 136-37]

Durant describes "a statue of Mausolus" as "calm and strong" and adds: "the 4th century BC tried to realize in stone something of human individuality and feeling. In male statuary, the head and face took on more importance, the body less ... the study of character replaced the idolatry of muscle ... portraits in stone became the fashion for any 'subject' who could pay ... the surface was modeled to let in the living play of light and shade." [*Life of Greece,* p 494-95]

Brilliant says: "The figure of *Mausolus* is ponderously handsome and stands powerfully erect ... heavy folds and masses of drapery rhythmically complement both the stance and the dignity of the subject. The head, <u>a masterpiece of regal portraiture</u>, is broad and round ... The curve of lips, chin, and brows is complemented by full shadows, especially well developed in the deeply-set eye sockets. The weighty presence ... and the dignified bearing modified by feeling are important characteristics of the figure of *Mausolus.*" [*Arts of the Ancient Greeks,* p 250-51]

Mausoleum of Halicarnassus:

The 24-year reign [377-353 BC] of King Mausolus of Caria might have remained a mere footnote in history had it not been for the grandiose plans he and his fond Queen Artemisia developed for their tomb ... of which Durant says: "The sculptural masterpiece of the period [4th century BC] was the great mausoleum dedicated to King Mausolus of Halicarnassus." [p 494]

Halicarnassus [now Bodrum, in Turkey] is only 25 miles north, across a bay, from ancient Cnidus [Knidos] – original home of Praxiteles' famed *Aphrodite* #20 ... and later, the seated *Demeter* #24 now in the British Museum.

Durant describes Mausolus as a petty viceroy under the protection [and service] of the Persian king ... and adds: "Nominally a satrap of Persia, Mausolus had extended his personal sway over Caria and parts of Ionia and Lydia, and had used his rich revenues to build a fleet and beautify his capital. When he died, his devoted wife Artemisia, held a famous oratorical contest in his honor ... and summoned the best artists of Greece to collaborate upon a tomb that should be a fitting memorial to his genius ..." [p 494]

Pliny the Elder [23-79 AD] names the 4 principal sculptors of the Mausoleum – Scopas [east], Bryaxis [north], Timotheos [south], and Leochares [west] – and also states in *Natural History*: "it was through the exertions of these artists ... that this work came to be reckoned one of the 'Seven Wonders of the World' ... before their task was completed, Queen Artemisia died. They did not leave their work, however, until it was finished ... considering that it was at once a memorial of *their own fame* and of the sculptor's art ..." [*Treasures of Brit. Mus.*, Caygill, p 17-8]

Caygill adds: "The building is thought to have been still standing in the 12th century ... after years of neglect and gradual dissolution ... it appears eventually to have been overthrown by an earthquake. Its destruction was completed by the Knights of St. John who began to fortify the town, building the Castle of St. Peter in 1402." [p 18]

Lawrence explains: "The ruins were demolished – partly for building material and partly to be burnt for lime – by the Knights of St. John and by the Turkish inhabitants ... Many of the sculptures were picked out of the 'walls' of the medieval castle and out of the 'walls and chimneys' of private homes by Newton's expedition ... only a few were excavated from the ground upon which they had fallen ..." [p 200]

Sculptor:

Boardman reveals: "The princes of Asia Minor competed with each other in the splendor of their burial places and employed Greek artists for this purpose ... the most famous sculptors of the time executed the rich sculptural decoration." [p 200]

Lawrence identifies Bryaxis and Leochares – of the recorded sculptors who worked on the Mausoleum – as having the most compatible styles to the statuary found on the monument. He says: "Moreover the composition of *the Mausolus* resembles that of *Asclepius*, known from copies, which might be Bryaxis' famous statue of that deity." [p 201]

The *Mausolus* was excavated by Sir Charles Newton along the north side of the great Mausoleum, where Bryaxis is said to have sculpted works. The better known Scopas had a reputation for crafting powerful, stocky heads with intelligent countenances.

*the other *Ancient Wonders of the World* were the Pyramids ... the Colossus of Rhodes ... the Hanging Gardens of Babylon ... the Pharos Lighthouse of Alexandria ... the Temple of Diana at Ephesus, and the Zeus of Olympia.

Major References:

History of Art, 1977, Janson, p 135-37

History of World Sculpture, 1968, Bazin, p 146-47

Treasures of the British Museum, Caygill, p 17-21

British Museum Book of Greek & Roman Art, 1991, Burns, p 123

Arts of the Ancient Greeks, 1972, Brilliant, p 229, 231, 247-51, 254, 257

Greek Sculpture, 1960, Carpenter, p 214-16, 258

Art of Crete, Mycenae, and Greece, 1968, Hafner, p 199-200

The Life of Greece, 1939, Durant, p 134, 494, 497, 618

Greek and Roman Sculpture, 1972, Lawrence, p 200-03, PL 52a, 52b

The Greeks, 1985, Browning, p 147, 171, 191

Greek Art, 1973, Boardman, p 136-37

24
DEMETER

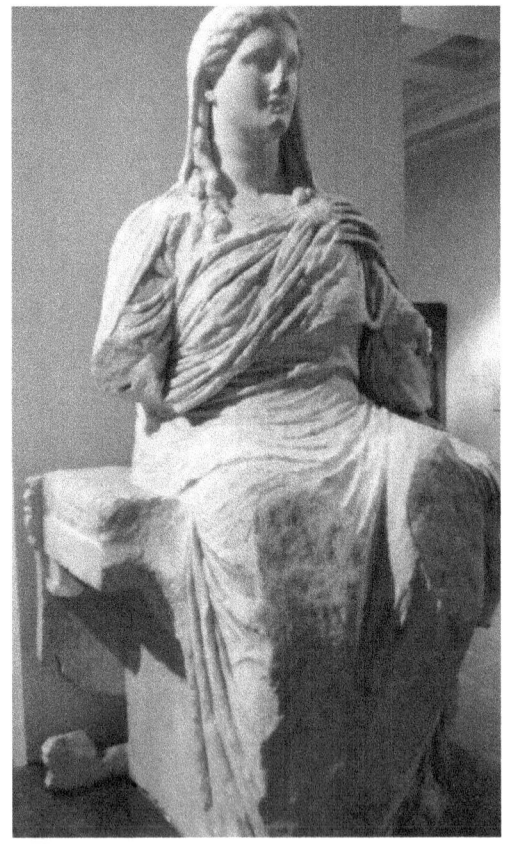

"...in mature beauty and quiet depth of feelings...
among the noblest figures in the British Museum."
...*Life of Greece*, 1939, Durant, p 499

Unearthed in 1857-8, Cnidus [S.W. Turkey] – now, Brit. Museum
Orig. Greek marble – approx. 340 BC – in Classic style
Ht. 6'1" [147 cm] – monumental
Sculptor: perhaps Leochares [370-330 BC]

T he seated *Demeter* was found by Sir Charles Newton in 1857-8 ... among the ruins of ancient temples [to underworld deities] at the Sanctuary of Demeter in Cnidus. In ancient times, Cnidus was an important port of coastal trade ... on a promontory jutting out from what is now the southwest coast of Turkey (north of Rhodes).

[in about 350 BC, Cnidus acquired the *Aphrodite of Cnidus* #20 ... that drew immediate fame in the Mediterranean world]

Demeter, sister of Zeus, is best known as the goddess of motherhood and agricultural fertility. Her name stems from 'da mother' in a pre-Greek language. [Pinsent, 33] On mythic Mt. Olympus, Demeter [*Ceres,* Latin] was one of two deities considered "mankind's best friends ... for their gifts from the earth." The other was Dionysus [*Bacchus,* Latin], god of wine. [Hamilton, p 53]

Burns observes: "Demeter turns her head a little to the left, calm and reposeful in both expression and attitude." [*Brit. Mus. Book Greek & Roman Art,* p 72]

Lawrence describes: "a lingering trace of her normal half-smile of maternal tranquility." [p 203] Hafner adds: "... she is – in contrast to the *Aphrodite* – the epitome of motherliness, that other side of feminine nature." [p 202]

Subject:

Though *Demeter* displays a dignified bearing, her melancholy face silently grieves ... for good reason. Zeus [her brother] secretly gave her daughter Persephone [*Proserpine,* Latin] in marriage to his brutish brother Hades [*Pluto,* Latin] – god of the underworld.

Hades then sought out Persephone gathering flowers and took her forcefully.

Demeter, hearing echoes of her daughter's screams, searches over land and sea, but fails to find Persephone. [see Bernini's *Abduction of Persephone*, Villa Borghese]

"In terrible grief, Demeter withholds her gifts from the Earth, which turned to a frozen desert. The green and flowering land was icebound and lifeless because Persephone had disappeared." [Hamilton, p 57]

That "Earth ... turned to a frozen desert ... icebound" may or may not be myth. It is possible that far-distant ancestors of the ancient Greeks passed down memories of a Glacial Age ... the most recent ended only <u>15,000</u> years ago.

[in 1994, the discovery of Chauvet Cave in southeast France revealed "more than 300 extraordinary paintings and engravings of animals ... radiocarbon tests established them to be over <u>30,000 years old</u> – the oldest known paintings in the world ... they are powerful, sophisticated works of art rather than crude sketches." [*Dawn of Art, Chauvet Cave*, 1996]

If Cro-Magnon artists inside Chauvet Cave were capable of producing such "sophisticated" art, it is not impossible that succeeding generations possessed adequate intelligence to pass down memories of 'a prolonged catastrophe' such as a Glacial Age 15,000 years ago.]

There are different versions how the dilemma of Demeter and Persephone resolves.

One has Demeter – after dwelling on earth in misery – going to Zeus and asking for the return of her daughter. Since Demeter, during the loss of Persephone, has "withheld the kindly fruits of the earth" and "mankind would have perished", Zeus grants her request ... and commands Pluto to return Persephone.

Pluto accedes ... but gives Persephone a pomegranate seed to eat which will force her to stay with him a third of each year ... in the autumn, Persephone descends to Hades and cannot reappear until spring.

A second version – from the *Hymn of Demeter,* attributed to Homer – has Demeter persuading Pluto to let her daughter Persephone live on the earth 9 months of the year – from early spring to late fall – symbolic of rebirth and seasonally dying. [Durant, p 178]

Because the people of Eleusis *(15 miles east of Athens)* comforted Demeter during 'her long year on earth', she taught them and other people of this region 'the secret of agriculture.' Thereafter, in ancient Greece, Eleusis became sacred to Demeter, and the people erected a great temple to her...where 'mysterious rites' were held every 5 years... [Brilliant, p 285]

Cicero, in the century before Christ, wrote: "Nothing is higher than these mysteries. They have sweetened our characters and softened our customs...they have made us pass from the condition of savages to true humanity. They have not only shown us the way to live joyfully, but they have taught us how to die with a better hope." [Hamilton, p 55]

Durant enlightens us: "Essentially, it was the same myth as Isis and Osiris of Egypt, Tammuz and Ishtar in Babylonia, Astarte and Adonis in Syria.... The cult of motherhood survived through classical times to take new life in the worship of Mary the Mother of God." [p 178]

Lucas, in *A Wanderer in London,* describes *Demeter*: "...I know of no Madonna in the painting of any old master more material and serene and wise and holy than this marble goddess...the most beautiful piece of sculpture in the British Museum." [p 225-26]

Sculptor:

The seated *Demeter* provides evidence of influence by Scopas. However, Leochares [370-330 BC] is the more likely sculptor...based on another head Leochares is known to have carved – that of *Alexander the Great* [now, in the Acropolis Museum] which somewhat resembles the head of *Demeter.*

Both have almost identically-shaped mouths [full, parted lips]. Their lips and eyebrows are carved with "precisely the same clean lines". Both have the "hint of smile" and "over-shadowed eye-sockets". This encourages some authorities to accept Leochares as the sculptor of *Demeter*. [Lawrence, p 203 & Burns, p 72]

Many observers of *Demeter* in the British Museum may question why the head of the goddess is so smooth and highly-polished ... compared to the rough drapery of the figure. References point out the head and neck were found buried and separate from the body ... which was more open to the elements and therefore suffered more damage from weathering. Lawrence tells us: "The head and neck were carved out of a single block of marble; the neck is rounded underneath to fit into a hollow concealed by the edge of drapery." [p 203]

The mythical seizing of Demeter's daughter by Hades is somewhat similar to the Spartan marriage. Durant tells us: "Marriages were usually arranged by the parents, without purchase; but after this agreement the bridegroom was expected to carry off the bride by force, and she was expected to resist; the word for marriage was *harpadzein*, to seize." [p 84]

Major References:

Mythology, 1942, Hamilton, p 53-76

Greek Mythology, 1969, Pinsent, p 33-7

Dawn of Art: Chauvet Cave, 1996, Jean Chauvet, dustjacket

Greek and Roman Sculpture, 1972, Lawrence, p 203

British Museum Book of Greek & Roman Art, 1991, Burns, p 110

A Wanderer in London, 1911, E V Lucas, p 225-26

Art of Crete, Mycenae, and Greece, 1968, Hafner, p 202

Arts of the Ancient Greeks, 1972, Brilliant, p. 177, 251, 283

The Life of Greece, 1939, Durant, p 32-3, 68-9, 84, 178, 499

Ancient Greece, 1997, Durando, 42, 80-1

25

THE SCRAPER

OR APOXYOMENOS

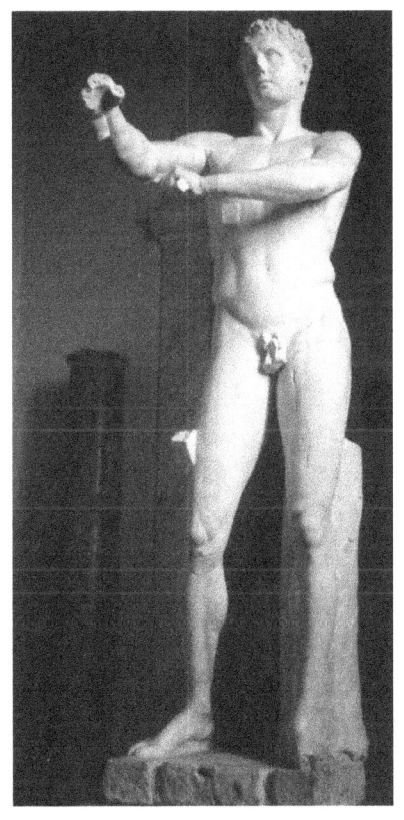

"…most famous work of Lysippos"
…Durando, *Ancient Greece,* p 151

Discovered 1849 in Rome – now, Vatican Museum
Roman marble copy – [30 to 300 AD] – late Classical style
From: lost Orig. Greek bronze [approx. 340 BC]
Ht. 6 ft. 9 in [2.1 m] – marble
Sculptor: Lysippos [370-315 BC]; the copyist unknown

Due the acquisitive eye of Agrippa [admiral/general to Augustus] the original bronze *Scraper* arrived in Rome. [*Encyclo Sculpt,* p 985]

In *Natural History,* Roman historian Pliny the Elder [23-79 AD] reveals Agrippa 'acquired' this bronze in either "Greece, southern Italy, or most likely Asia Minor" sometime shortly after 31 BC. He may have seized the statue upon discovering Alexander's personal sculptor Lysippos created it.

In 19 BC, Agrippa dedicated this 'trophy' in front of the first great public baths of Rome...which he had constructed near the Pantheon [rebuilt by Agrippa]. [p 985-86]

After the next emperor Tiberius came to power in 12 AD, Pliny adds: "Although at the beginning of his reign he kept control of himself, in this case he was unable to resist temptation, and had the [publicly-displayed] bronze statue removed to his bedroom, substituting another in its place. But the Roman people became so obstinately opposed to this that they raised an outcry at the theater, shouting: 'Give us back *the Scraper!*' So although he had fallen quite in love with the statue, the emperor had to restore it." [*Nat. History,* 34.62]

With the bronze *Scraper* returned to its rightful place, it became even more popular...inspiring wealthy art patrons to commission marble copies. Later, in the Great Fire of Rome in 80 AD, the Baths of Agrippa and, presumably the Lysippos bronze, were destroyed. [*Encyclo,* p 986]

In 1849, the Vatican's marble copy was discovered in the Trastevere quarter of Rome...south of the Pantheon and across the Tiber River. At that time, it was restored by Pietro Tenerani, pupil of Antonio Canova [#79, #80, #81]. Its fig leaf is a modern addition. The figure of *the Scraper* swiftly regained its previous fame; and, again, numerous replicas – in marble, plaster and small bronzes – were made for museums and collectors. To support the weight of extended limbs, marble copies required a stump and struts.

Gardner reveals the original sculptor Lysippos: "…was so renowned that he was selected by Alexander the Great to fashion his official portrait.* Lysippos had introduced a new canon of proportions in which the bodies were more slender…where the heads were roughly one-eighth the height of the body rather than one-seventh as in the previous century." [Art Through the Ages, p 165]

*the Alexander Herm #28

Subject:

This young athlete – after applying oil to his skin and exercising – now scrapes off the oil, accumulated sweat, and dirt with a crescent-shaped, bronze strigil. Sometimes, the oil was applied after exercise. His body is more naturally presented than in previous statuary, even his hair is unruly. The muscles are finely-lined and hard, but not emphasized.

The face is barely idealized, if at all. The subtle curve of his brow and eyes suggest "a weariness and a certain melancholy" from his exertions… "but the body is all harmony with the balanced distribution of the weight between the two legs." Soon, he will relax in the baths…and, perhaps, seek a massage. [Bazin, p 150-51]

R. Brilliant explains: "… the right arm of the Scraper is cantilevered directly from the mass of the figure and physically penetrates the spectator's space. In this way the sculptural space of the statue is no longer isolated or self-contained, but relates to the human environment of the spectator…the figure creates the illusion of dynamic elasticity and of movement through space." [Arts of the Ancient Greeks, p 268]

Gardner adds: "A nervous energy runs through the Scraper…the strigil is about to reach the end of the right arm and at any moment it will be switched to the other hand so that the left arm can be scraped…the weight will shift at the same time and the positions of the legs will be reversed. Lysippos encourages the observer to look at his athlete from multiple angles…to comprehend the action, we must move to the side and view the work at a three-quarter angle or in full profile." [p 165]

Robb & Garrison summarize: "By the close of the 4th century BC, man was becoming increasingly aware of his surroundings... the earlier philosophy [based only on consciousness of oneself] was inadequate to interpret experiences..." [p 443-44]

Sculptor:

[also, see his *Agias the Athlete* #26... next]

Brilliant says: "Lysippos, as the greatest sculptor of the 4th century BC, may be compared to Titian or Michelangelo for the length of his creative life... for the continuous quality of his work... for his enjoyment of the greatest fame... and for securing the greatest possible patron – Alexander the Great at the end of his career." [p 266]

The works of Lysippos offered a greater illusion of movement through space than the works of sculptors coming before him. Pliny the Elder adds: "The extreme delicacy of his work, even in the smallest detail, would seem to be its most individual feature." [p 34, 61-65]

Lysippos specialized in heroic athletes and male deities, either as individuals or in groups. He was among the first sculptors to create statues of particular persons with realism. Pliny says that Lysistratus, brother of Lysippos, 'invented' realistic portraits in stone, by first modeling in plaster a living face, pouring wax into the plaster mold, then making final corrections in the wax cast.

Some 2,100 years later, Houdon utilized a similar method in seeking realism. [see *Diana the Huntress* #78]

Agrippa was one of many Roman generals who returned 'spoils of war' to Rome.

Durant describes when the Roman patrician-general Flamininus – upon defeating the Macedonian king Philip V in 197 BC and 'liberating' Greece – seized from "any city that had supported Philip V so much booty" that "in Flamininus' triumph, the spoils of his Grecian campaign passed for 3 days in continuous train before the eye of Rome... on the first day arms, armor, and innumerable marble and bronze statues… on the second day 18,000 pounds of silver, 3,714 pounds of gold, and 100,000 silver coins… and on the third day 114 coronets." [p 664]

Major References:

Art Through the Ages, Vol I, 1996, Gardner, 164-66

History of World Sculpture, 1968, Bazin, p 150-51

Art in the Western World, 3rd Ed., 1953, Robb & Garrison, p 442-44

Natural History, Pliny, 34.61-65 [from Brilliant, 264]

Encyclopedia of Sculpture, 2004, Lapatin, p 982-86

Arts of the Ancient Greeks, 1972, Brilliant, p 268-69

Art of Crete, Mycenae, and Greece, 1968, Hafner, p 10, 216

Art Through the Ages, Vol. I, 1976, Gardner, 142-3

Plutarch's Lives, Vol 4, 1758, J & R Tonson edition, p 227-28

Ancient Greece, 1997, Durando, p 150-1

Classical Myths in Sculpture, 1951, Agard, p 41-4

26
Agias,
The Athlete

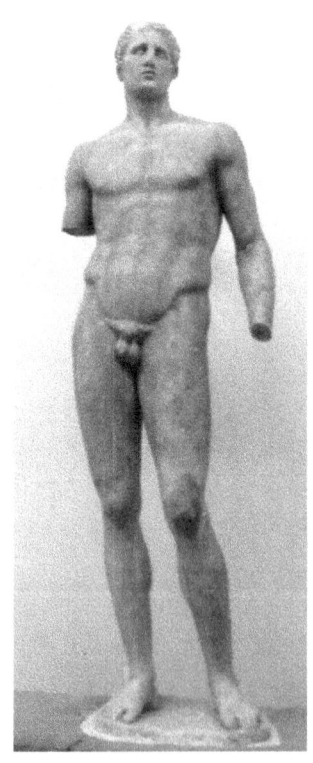

"a masterpiece by Lysippos … his look faraway …
free of stress – like an ancient mythical hero."
… Durando, *Ancient Greece*, p 210

Greek marble, found at Delphi – now, in Delphi Museum
Copy [338-334 BC] – late Classic or early Hellenistic
From: lost Original Greek bronze – 338 BC
Height: 6 ft. 5.5 in.
Sculptor: Lysippos [370-315 BC] or copied by a pupil

The Olympic Games: every 4 summers, from 776 BC to 261 AD, peoples from the lands of the Mediterranean gathered at Olympia in southern Greece for *the Games.* Travel to Olympia was also a pilgrimage to the sacred precinct of Zeus. After a grand parade of athletes and dignitaries, 100 oxen were sacrificed to Zeus, and the sports festival began!
... *The Olympic Games,* Finley & Pleket, 1976

After heated competition, *Agias* stands alone. He gazes overhead and does not hear thunderous acclaim from the great crowd. His expression is sensitive and reserved, that of a man with nothing more to prove.

He has fought here many times ... and can only wonder when and how the streak must end. Though no longer young, he is the victor again. His unmarred face may not be wholly realistic; however, his noble features are said to represent an actual likeness of his face. If so, this is one of the earliest examples of facial realism by the Greeks.

The pride of the aristocrat Agias remains discreet. We recognize the 'immortal Olympian calm' seen previously on the face of the *Charioteer of Delphi* #11.

The excessive pride of the *Crowned/Getty Athlete* #30 is not evident here. Nor is there a bold superiority of pose ... as displayed in the *Hellenistic Ruler* #42, about 150 years later.

This masterpiece in marble [338–334 BC] was created near the conclusion of the Hellenistic era of sculpture ... by or under the close supervision of Lysippos, the finest sculptor during *the Age of Alexander the Great*: [356 to 323 BC].

A few years earlier, he had completed the original bronze *Agias.*

During the lifetime of Lysippos, strong demand for statuary from his workshop – said to have produced some 1,500 bronzes – required the assistance of other artists and studio-pupils. Today, while none of his original works can be positively identified, more than a few clearly suggest his techniques and style.

Lapatin states: "Many of his statues were 'transferred' to Rome [and eventually to Constantinople], where they were favorites of emperors and other elite collectors." [*Encyclo Sculpt,* p 983]

Subject:

Agias was unique among Olympic athletes of any era…in that, he excelled at both boxing and wrestling. Over an unprecedented 30 years, this Greek nobleman repeatedly won the brutal 'pankration' competition – a favorite sport of spectators. It involved a vicious combination of wrestling, judo, and to a lesser degree boxing.

During the early Games, boxing and wrestling had been separate competitions. "In the course of time, as brutality increased, boxing and wrestling were combined into the 'game of all powers' or the pankration. Everything but biting and eye-gouging was permitted, even to a kick in the stomach." [Durant, p 214-5]

There were few rules, no time limits, and no ring boundaries. Competitors wrestled and punched – generally on the ground – until one tapped the back or shoulder of the other in surrender. Serious injury and even death were not unknown. Since major competitions such as the Olympics had no weight-classes, eventually the participants were mostly large men, heavily muscled, and 'rough'. Ancient paintings usually show them with bull necks.

Faulkner says: "most athletes were aristocrats who invested heavily in their training and expected to win big prize money at the hundreds of local athletic festivals around Greece." [*Wall Street Journal,* 5/19/2012]

Seventy years after Agias competed in the Olympics, his great-grandson Daochos commissioned Agias' portrait in bronze for their homeland Pharsalus [city-state in Thessaly, north-central Greece].

Daochos also commissioned a marble copy for Delphi. [Lawrence, p 205] The marble was meant to be a votive offering to Delphi during the period Daochos was a representative from Thessaly [338-334 BC]. In truth, the statue [part of a family group] was likely meant as an 'overt display of prestige' by members of his aristocratic family… to impress the tens of thousands of visitors yearly who arrived at the sacred city of Delphi – a major destination for ancient travelers in the eastern Mediterranean world. [Brilliant, p 266]

Original Sculptor: [see discussion of Lysippos in previous chapter]

Lysippos replaced the stern canon of Polycleitus by introducing less massive figures and greater movement. Legs sculpted by Lysippos were longer, his heads smaller, and often the slender arms and legs were extended to create a more 3-dimensional effect… and thereby more vitality.

The ancient Roman historian, Pliny the Elder [23-79 AD] mentions Lysippos' brother, Lysistratus: "He was the first person who modeled a likeness in plaster of a human being from a living face, and established the method of pouring wax into this plaster mold and then making final corrections in the wax cast…" [Boorstin, p 175]

Brilliant adds: "Something of the character of the original bronze *Agias* may be gathered from a magnificent bronze statue of a young man found in the sea off Antikythera… known as the *Ball Player* #22." [p 266]

In the Louvre, the greatly-weathered but majestic *Alexander-Azara Herm* #28, with Alexander's name inscribed, is most likely a copy of Lysippos' original bronze. The Louvre also has a small bronze replica of the statue *Alexander with a Lance* by Lysippos, which may be related to the 'heroic posture' of *Agias*. An excellent copy of this *Alexander* is also seen in the British Museum. [Brilliant, p 266]

Another marble sculpture believed to be modeled from an original bronze by Lysippos is the *Farnese Hercules* #44 in Naples. For a list of 18 more 'possible' copies from Lysippos' originals, see *Encyclo Sculpture*, p 984.

Major References:

The Creators, 1992, Boorstin, p 174-5

Ancient Greece, 1997, Durando, p 210

The Life of Greece, 1939, Durant, p 214-15, 498

Encyclopedia of Sculpture, 2004, Lapatin, p 982-86

Art of the Ancient Greeks, 1972, Brilliant, p. 265-66. Plate 7-57

The Getty Bronze, 1982, Frel, p 31

Greek and Roman Sculpture, 1972, Lawrence, p 205-6, pl. 57b

Delphi Museum Guide, 2004, Petsas, p 104-5

The Olympic Games, 1976, Finley and Pleket, p 37-44

Natural History, Pliny, 35, 153, 34, 65

Life of Alexander, Plutarch, 2.2

27

ARES W/EROS
OR MARS W/ CUPID

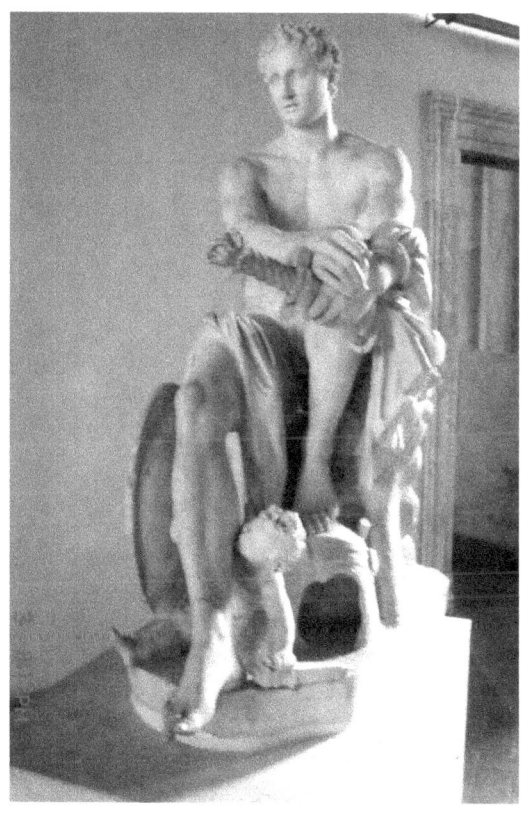

"... a work of considerable quality"
... Bazin, *History World Sculpture*, p 148

Found in Rome, 1621-22 – now Palazzo Altemps Museum, Rome*
Roman marble copy – 140 AD – Hellenistic [323 BC to 31 BC]
From: lost Orig. Greek bronze – 335 BC – Pergamon
Ht. 5 feet – white Pentelic marble
Sculptor: Scopas or Lysippos
   *copy by Marcellini [1929] at Hearst Castle, San Simeon, Calif.

[the Greek _Ares_ _is the_ Roman _Mars..._ as _Eros_ is to _Cupid_]

_A_ _res,_ the Greek god of war – contemplative with a downcast head – day-dreams. The presence of _Eros_ hints of his distraction. Too long at war, _Ares_ sorely misses his paramour _Aphrodite,_ the goddess of love and beauty.

Eros, shown as a young child, was the Greek god of love. In Greek and Roman art, he is normally winged, quite young, and up to mischief. Here...as a 2-year-old cherub, _Eros_ toys with the right leg of _Ares._

The Nat. Mus. of Rome says: "the playful atmosphere suggested by _Eros_...is in keeping with his erotic link with _Aphrodite._" [La Regina, p 132]

The same source describes _Ares_: "...in a position of repose, the left leg lifted languidly and resting on a helmet...sword clasped in hands, crossed on a knee...the face has ideal features and follows the heroic models of the 4th century BC...with a half-open mouth and ruffled hair in the tradition of Scopas and a cranial structure inspired by Lysippos. The point where another statue was attached can be seen on the left shoulder..." likely the hand of _Aphrodite._ [p 132]

This sculpture [aka _Ares Ludovisi_] was found in Rome [1621-22]...some 400 yards east of today's Campo de Fiori [ancient piazza with flowers & produce] directly south of the Pantheon. In ancient times, this was between the Circus Flaminius and the Campus Martius, near the current "remains of a podium of a late-Republican temple to _Mars._ [La Regina, p 132]

Bazin adds: "In a temple dedicated to _Mars_ by L. Junius Brutus #33 [_not the assassin_], near the Circus Flaminius in Rome, there was a colossal seated [bronze] statue of *Ares* by Scopas. The smaller *Ares with Eros*, a work of considerable quality, has sometimes been considered a copy of that original." [*History of World Sculpture*, p 148]

Scopas [or his contemporary Lysippos] is believed to have created the original bronze colossal *Ares* – much admired at Pergamon. If this is accurate, then a Roman general or emperor likely brought the bronze from Pergamon to Rome...where it may have served as the model for the marble Greco-Roman copy currently in the Palazzo Altemps.

This marble statue appears in excellent condition...due to restoration by the young Bernini. In addition to refinishing its surfaces, Bernini added a missing nose, right foot, and sword hilt, plus *Eros'* head and parts of his body. [La Regina, p 132-33]

Shortly after its discovery, the statue became widely-known and was a popular attraction on the 'Grand Tour' of English nobility. The marble *Ares* eventually became part of the Ludovisi collection in Rome...gathered by Cardinal Ludovisi [1595-1632], nephew of a pope.

Subject:

Another well-known statue of *Ares* stands at Hadrian's Villa [outside Rome] – a warrior bearing his shield and wearing the same battle helmet seen on *Pericles* #18. The Greek aspect [indicated by battle helmet] of *Ares* indicates a lust for blood and violence.

The prehistoric Greeks – who established the Mycenaean culture from 1950 BC to 1100 BC – looked upon *Ares* as "the mysterious and divine protector of the warrior spirit" who set an example for the early Greeks to fight well and bravely with a ruthless intelligence. In the insecure society of that time, "the virtues of war outweighed the virtues of peace."

Durant describes the earlier virtues: "The good man is not one that is gentle and forbearing, faithful and sober, industrious and honest...he is simply one who fights bravely and well. A bad man is not one that drinks too much, lies, murders, and betrays; he is one that is cowardly, stupid, and weak." [*Life of Greece*, p 50]

During the next millennium, *Ares* lost favor among the Greeks.

In *Mythology* by Hamilton, he is summed up as "a general pest." Homer in the *Iliad* describes Ares as: "the incarnate curse of mortals."

Ares, typical of many Olympian gods of the Greeks, was ever known for his roguish and mysterious nature. The most outrageous act of *Ares* was to support the enemy in the Trojan War. His lover, *Aphrodite*, also favored Troy.

In *Titans and Olympians*, we are told: "...the [Classic] Greeks felt a certain ambivalence toward *Ares*...they did not relish the idea of war...in disparaging stories, they told: *Ares* was captured by the enemy...he was actually wounded by a mortal...the two untamable horses that pulled his chariot were called Fright and Terror...he was attended by retainers such as Discord, Strife, and Panic...and his altars were kept permanently blood-strewn." *Ares* was considered "chaotic and dangerous." [p 89]

By the Classic Age, the Greeks had learned to practice peaceful colonization in order to expand their trade and wealth. The new political order of the 'city-state' was generally sufficient to preserve security.

Later, the Romans, "whose attitude toward war was more aggressive", adored their war god...who they named '*Mars*' and made the principal patron of Rome. The city "traced its founding [through Aenaes] back to [citizens of] Troy...." [p 89]

Durant writes: "...Rhea [Rhea Silvia, descendant of Aeneas] lay down by the banks of a stream [the Tiber] and 'opened her bosom to catch the breeze.' Too trustful of gods and men, she fell asleep... *Mars*, overcome with her beauty, left her rich with twins." [*Caesar & Christ*, p 12] The twins fathered by Mars were named Romulus and Remus...who became the legendary founders of Rome. [see *She-Wolf*, #10]

For the ancient Romans, *Mars* initially had been a god of tillage [Martius], and they named a month after him. The later Romans of the Republic and the Empire created a more civilized and friendly deity than the Greek version. To the practical-minded Romans, conquest and colonization by war were completely acceptable. [Allan & Maitland, p 89-90]

While the Greeks sculpted relatively few statues of their god of war, the Romans were more enthusiastic. They erected many temples to *Mars* and displayed his statues in "magnificent shining armor, redoubtable and invincible." Three majestic Corinthian columns remain from the Temple of Mars Ultor [Avenger] erected in the Forum of Augustus. The ancient Romans also honored *Mars* with a statue at the staircase of their Senate building...its base survives. [Durant, *C&C*, p 358] [Monumental Rome, p 33]

Originally, the Temple of Mars Ultor had a semi-circular, domed chamber in which the statues of Mars, Venus, and Caesar stood. Venus [*Aphrodite*] was mother to Aeneas, who 'proved' the *divine descent* of the Julian clan – adding 'luster' to both Caesar and his great-nephew Augustus. [*Roman Forum*, Electa]

Augustus built and dedicated this temple to fulfill a vow made before the Battle of Philippi in 42 BC...where he avenged the death of Julius Caesar, his 'adoptive' father. "Before setting out on any expedition, Augustus [as consul, and later emperor] offered prayers at this temple. In solemn ritual, Augustus would shake the spear in the hand of *Mars* and commend the whole city to his protection with the words: 'God of War, watch over the safety of this city'." [Allan & Maitland, p 90]

Sculptor:

References associate the original bronze statue with the work of Scopas or Lysippos. The sculptor of the copy in Rome is unknown. He was likely a Greek hired by a Roman...therefore, the statue can be considered of Greco-Roman origin.

Major References:

Museo Nazionale Romano, 2005, La Regina, p 132-33

History of World Sculpture, 1968, Bazin, p 148

Mythology, 1942, Hamilton p 35-6

Greek & Roman Sculpture, 1972, Lawrence, p 195

Life of Greece, 1939, Durant, p 50, 57-8, 184, 497

Caesar & Christ, 1944, Durant, p 12, 61, 358, 383

Titans & Olympians, 1997, Allan & Maitland, p 89-90

A Wanderer in Rome, 1926, Lucas, p 232-3

Monumental Rome, 2006, Tagliaferri, p 2, 32-3

The Roman Forum, 1998, Electa, insert

Ancient Greece, 1997, Durando, p 81

28

ALEXANDER HERM

OR AZARA HEAD

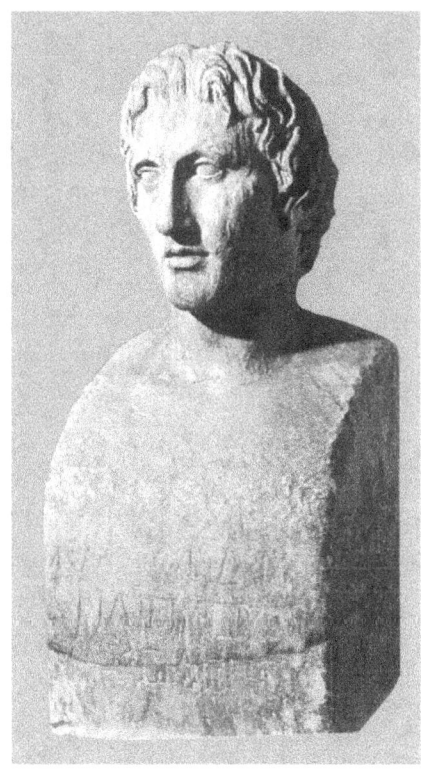

"Lysippos caught the essence of his [Alexander's] nature ...
of which the best is the flame-like portrait bust known as
the Azara Head." ... R. Brilliant, *Arts of Ancient Greeks*, p 273-4

Found 1779, Hadrian's Villa, near Tivoli – now, in Louvre
Imperial Roman copy – approx. 100 AD – early Hellenistic
From: lost Original Greek statue – approx. 330 BC
Ht. 25.6 inches, 68 cm. – Pentelic marble
Orig. Sculptor: Lysippos w/pupil? [370-315 BC]

> "The first quality is courage. Without this, all others
>   are of little value as they can't be used. The 2nd is
>   intelligence,.. which must be strong and
>   fertile in expedients. The 3rd is health."
>   ... *Memoirs: Art of War*, 1744, Marshal Maurice de Saxe

Alexander the Great possessed courage ... intelligence ... and health to an uncommon degree.

Following royal birth and tutoring by Aristotle ... at 18, Alexander "led the Macedonian cavalry with reckless courage, and won the honors of a bitter day"... when the Macedonian army [led by his father, King Philip] defeated the Athenians and their allies at Chaeronea. Two years later, following his father's assassination, Alexander seized the Macedonian throne. [Durant, *Life of Greece*, p 480]

His subsequent military accomplishments – by the age of 33 – have no parallel.

In *Plutarch's Lives*, the Roman historian [46-120 AD] writes: "The statues that most resembled Alexander were those by Lysippos, by whom alone this Prince would suffer his image to be made. The inclination of his head which leaned a little to one side, and the liveliness of his eyes were accurately expressed by the artist. Alexander is said to have been fair, with a mixture of ruddiness [healthy redness] chiefly in his face ..." [*Tonson edition*, 1758, p 227-28]

The *Alexander Herm* [from bronze original by Lysippos] bears the inscription: *Alexander, son of Philip the Macedonian*. While the bust is thought to closely represent Alexander in his full maturity, we also know that Lysippos, to some extent, idealized Alexander ... in accordance with the wishes of his subject.

Bazin states: "In spite of dilapidation and restorations, it seems to be the most authentic Lysippian portrait of *Alexander the Great.* The hair is represented as supple, ruffled locks...the full mouth is slightly open, the chin well marked. His glance is moving because of the melancholy gravity of the eyes, set deep and shadowed by the orbital arch and eyelids. Among the long series of portraits of Alexander, this one is the most convincing in its sincerity." [*History of Western Sculpture,* p 151]

Smith adds: "The inscribed *Alexander Herm*...is an important and impressive image. Alexander has long hair arranged around the head in a 'wreath', brushed up from the forehead in a distinctive, off-center parting, the *anastole* – a personal 'sign' of Alexander seen on all his portraits. The square face combines elements of the real Alexander and a strong ideal structure. He is older, more restrained, more mature than in any other of his portraits – for example, there is no upward turn of the head and neck." [*Hellenistic Sculpture,* p 21, 28]

After *the Herm* was discovered in Hadrian's Villa [outside Rome] in 1779, it came into the hands of Joseph Nicolas Azara – Spanish ambassador to the Vatican. Twenty years later, Azara, then ambassador to France, offered the bust to Napoleon as a 'diplomatic gift'. At that time, it was the 'only known portrait' of *Alexander the Great.*

Napoleon Bonaparte treasured the bust...but, it did not humble the Corsican or encourage him to *'Know Thyself'* [Apollo's counsel at Delphi]. In 1803, Napoleon placed the bust in the Louvre Museum.

When he retreated from Moscow in 1812...and, 3 years later, was defeated at Waterloo, the once brilliant Napoleon became a ruined second to the ancient Macedonian.

The Louvre website states *the Herm* is a copy from a full-size *Alexander* bronze created by Lysippos in about 330 BC. [Louvre, 2009]

Frel summarizes the era when the bust was created: "The art of Lysippos' age portrays much more of the man, not just his appearance but also his psyche, will, and emotions." [*Getty Bronze,* p 36-7]

Subject:

When Alexander [born 356 BC] reached the age of 13, he was educated by Aristotle [selected by his father] for a period of 4 years. Durant tells us: "To some extent, Aristotle made a Hellene out of him... through all his life, Alexander admired Greek literature and envied Greek civilization." [p 525, 536]

Aristotle is said to have counseled the young Alexander: "the only self deserving of self-love is what would now be called the super-ego – the intellectual soul which must be trained to rule, like a king, over all lesser and baser appetites... to spurn the limits of mortality... to covet as riches only honor, nobility, and glory." [*Nature of Alexander*, Renault, p 48]

Alexander is believed to have stated: "I am indebted to my father for living, but to my teacher for living well."

During the 13 years after Alexander became king of the Macedonians and Greeks, he repeatedly led his armies to military victories... twice defeating vastly larger Persian armies. Eventually, his rule extended south into Egypt and east into India... until, finally, his men 'refused' to follow him to China.

Of his courage, Durant says: "When a campaign lagged, he would go hunting and, unaided and on foot, face any animal in combat... once, after an encounter with a lion, he was pleased to hear it said that he had fought as though it had been a duel to decide which of the two would be king." [p 539]

The Louvre reports: "His voice was hard and strong, and there was something fearsome in his attitude. He was brave, tenacious, frugal and generous, but could also be angry and violent." [website, 2009]

Durant adds: "Physically, Alexander was an ideal youth... we know from his contemporaries that he was handsome beyond all precedents for a king. He was good in every sport; a swift runner, a dashing horseman, a brilliant fencer, a practiced bowman, a fearless hunter... on the march his wild energy found vent in alighting from and remounting his chariot at full speed... He helped introduce into

Europe the custom of shaving the beard, on the ground that whiskers offered too ready a handle for an enemy to grasp." [p 538-39]

Finley & Pleket reveal: "...Alexander, though a good runner and splendid horseman, declined to compete in the Olympic Games, saying, 'Only if kings will be my opponents'." His father, Philip II, had scored victories [horse-racing with hired riders] in three successive Olympics..." [*Olympic Games*, p 54]

R. Brilliant aptly summarizes: "Alexander, unbelievably, was the mythic hero living in the midst of normal men. His career gleamed like some incandescent meteor, bright as a star and quickly gone... but unlike the meteor his passage changed everything." [p 273]

The greatest accomplishment of Alexander, according to Durant, was political: "Acting as the agent of 'historical necessity', he put an end to the era of [Greek] city-states, and, by sacrificing a substantial measure of local freedom, created a larger system of stability and order... His conception of government – an absolutism using religion to impose peace upon diverse nations – dominated Europe until the rise of nationalism and democracy in modern times." [p 551]

The 'historical necessity' above was inevitable. In Durant's words: "Greek democracy was corrupt and incompetent... and had to die. But, when it was dead, men realized how beautiful its heyday had been; and all later generations of antiquity looked back to the centuries of Pericles and Plato as the zenith of Greece, and of all history." [p 554]

Alexander ruled for 12 years and 8 months, expiring in 323 BC. Over the succeeding 2,300 years, no mortal man has had more books written about his life and accomplishments. Few men have been commemorated by as many sculptures.

The cause of his death has been in long dispute. In June 1990, research in the *New England Journal of Medicine* reported: "Alexander the Great, long thought to have died from poison or malaria, probably succumbed to typhoid fever. The Macedonian king was drinking heavily in Babylon after a successful campaign when he cried out in pain, saying it felt like he had been hit in the liver by an arrow. He had a raging fever, chills, and sweats before falling into a coma and dying 11 days later on June 10, 323 BC. Signs of decomposition were notably absent several days after his death ... those symptoms fit best with typhoid fever, which is spread by contaminated food or drinking water. The sharp pain suggests that the disease perforated his intestine. Typhoid fever can also cause a paralysis accompanied by very slow breathing, which makes the patient appear dead – this may be why his body did not appear to decompose." [*LA Times*, 6/11/90]

Chapter 31–*Farnese Hercules* briefly describes Alexander's favorite sculpture: *the Herakles Epitrapezios*... also by Lysippos. It was later owned by Hannibal ... then, by the Roman dictator Sulla. Different versions appear in the Naples Arch. Museum.

Sculptor:

R. Brilliant states: "Lysippos, the greatest sculptor of the 4th century BC, may be compared with Titian and Michelangelo for the length of his creative life ... for the continuous quality of his work ... and for the enjoyment of the greatest fame." He also enjoyed: "the pleasure of the greatest possible patron, Alexander the Great, at the end of his career." [p 266]

Alexander, born 14 years after the birth of Lysippos, died 8 years earlier than his sculptor. Alexander's father, King Philip II of Macedonia, had first sat for Lysippos. The sculptor's many portraits of Alexander [even as a boy] "were said to record the development of both a great artist and a great subject." [Boorstin, p 175]

The Greco-Roman sculptor of the *Alexander Herm* may have been one of hundreds of highly-skilled sculptors who made copies of the original by Lysippos. Demand for portrait busts of the most renowned man of his era in the Mediterranean world remained strong for many centuries, extending well into the years of the Roman Republic and Empire.

Note: in the Louvre, the *Alexander Herm* is poorly presented ... his back is to a large, bright window ... consequently, his shadowed face is best viewed by kneeling to his right-front. [unless the Louvre repositions Alexander]

Other Notable Sculptures of Alexander:

Alexander Mosaic [#45] ... in Naples Arch. Museum.
Alexander Sarcophagus – Istanbul
Marble head and statue – Pella, Greece [capital, ancient Macedonia]
Acropolis Head – Acropolis Museum, Athens
Bust (young) – British Museum
Alexander Bust – Geneva

Major References:

Plutarch's Lives, Vol. 4, 1758, Tonson edition, p 227-8
History of World Sculpture, 1968, Bazin, p 151
Hellenistic Sculpture, 1991, Smith, p 19-22, 28
Art History, 2005, 2nd edition, Stokstad
The Getty Bronze, 1982, Frel, p 36-7
Alexander the Great, 1970, Green [Cambridge], p 174-75
Search for Alexander, 1980, Fox, p 98, 99, 163, 173-77, 179
The Nature of Alexander, 1975, Renault, p 48, 66-7, 122, 137
The Life of Greece, 1939, Durant, p 525, 538, 539, 540-54
Alexander Mosaic: Stories of Victory & Defeat, Cohen (new)
World History, Diodorus, 17.34.1-5
Arts of the Ancient Greeks, 1972, Brilliant, p 273, 276
Birth of Western Civilization, 1964, Grant, p 66
Ancient Rome, 1996, Liberati & Bourbon. p 180-1
Alexander the Great, 2004, Cartledge, p 254
The Search for Alexander: Exhibition – 1980-1982, *Hunt Frieze*
The Olympic Games, 1976, Finley and Pleket, Plate VIII.
British Museum Book of Greek & Roman Art, 1991, Burns, p.130

29

FOUR HORSES OF ST. MARK'S

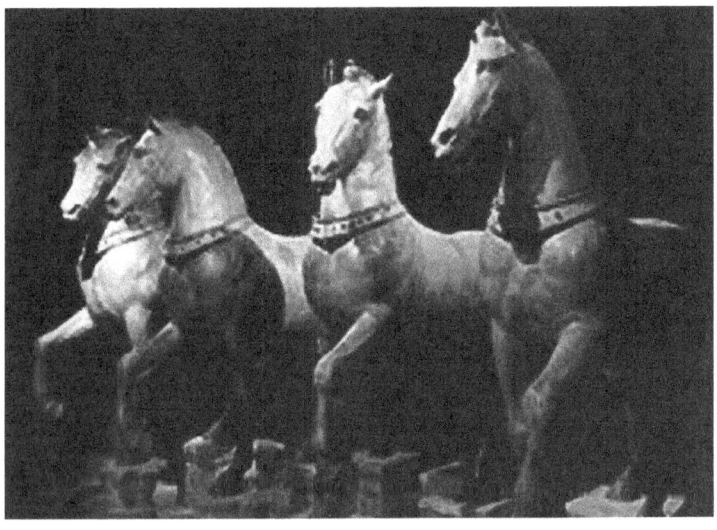

"The fame of Lysippos rests... especially on the 4-horse chariot
... executed for Rhodes." ... Pliny, Nat. History, 34.61-65 [Brilliant, p 264]

Sacked at Constantinople, 1204 AD – now in St. Marks, Venice
Roman orig. [*uncertain*] – 211 AD – late Classic/early Hellenistic
From: lost [*uncertain*] Orig. Greek bronze – approx. 330 BC
Ht. 5'8"; originally gilded with gold [known from traces]
Sculptor: possibly Lysippos , or unknown Greco-Roman

T he *Four Horses* are the only '4-horse team' for a quadriga [char-
iot] to survive from antiquity. Their suggested origin varies
widely. The most likely origins are Rhodian for Delphi...Roman for
Nero...or the island of Chios.

In 1204 AD...Venetians, on their infamous *Fourth Crusade* to
'save' Jerusalem, instead sacked Constantinople [Istanbul]. After
the Venetians pillaged the *Christian* capital of the Byzantine Empire,
they took the *Four Horses* back to Venice.

Carpenter states: "Representations of triumphal arches on coins
and medallions often show them carrying a bronze chariot with 4
horses...The celebrated *Horses of St. Mark's* almost certainly... [stood
upon] such a monument." [*Ancient Rome Brought To Life*, p 308-09]

Prior to 1204, the history of the *Four Horses* is speculative. Pliny
[Roman historian, 23-79 AD] in *Natural History*, recorded: "The
fame of Lysippos rests...especially on his 4-horse chariot, with the
Sun, executed for <u>Rhodes</u>." [Brilliant, p 264] By the breast collars
on the 4 bronze horses, it is assumed they pulled a 4-horse chariot.
[Checci. p 762]

Lawrence says: "Pliny mentions a group of the sun-gods in a
4-horse chariot, made by Lysippos for the Rhodians, and it may have
been the group they dedicated at Delphi...if so, some emperor presumably took it to Constantinople..." [*Greek & Roman Sculpture*, p 205]

Although the *Four Horses* are often said to be Greek originals by
Lysippos in about 330 BC...it is also possible they are Roman copies. <u>A Roman origin</u> – according to the 2004 edition of *Encyclopedia
of Sculpture* – is indicated because "the *Four Horses* are literally blan-
keted with hundreds of irregularly shaped [Roman-style] patches
that the [gold] gilding has concealed for centuries.... the Greeks
are known to have used only square or rectangular patches."
[Checci, p 762]

Two other references say: "these noble steeds were originally
designed and cast for a triumphal arch, to be driven by *Victory*,
in honor of <u>Nero</u>. Filched from Rome by Emperor Constantine,
they were carried to his own city as an ornament to the imperial
Hippodrome." [*Greek Art*, p 10-11] [*Wanderer*, p 21]

Boardman suggests they: "had been taken to the Hippodrome of Constantinople from <u>Chios</u> [island in Aegean] in the 5th C. AD. [p 10-11]

[sketchy sources have Nero plundering the *Horses* from Greece ... or Romans casting them for an arch to be dedicated to Trajan ... or the emperor Septimius Severus ordering a new 4-horse chariot for the Acropolis to replace one he had removed.]

In Constantinople, the *Horses* stood in the ancient Hippodrome, the sporting and social center of the city. Today, a few fragments of the hippodrome remain ... in what is now referred to as 'Horse Square'.

In 1798, Napoleon seized the *Four Horses* from Venice "and took them to Paris where he mounted them on the Arc du Carrousel in the Tuileries. They were not returned until after his fall in 1815 ..." [Boardman, p 10-11]

[after the French made copies of the *Horses*, to which they added a chariot carrying a statue of Peace]

That the *Horses* have survived some 2,000 years may be due to 'the mutual attraction' between humans and horses. Throughout the long history of the *Four Horses* – instead of being melted down for cannons, cups, or coins – they were preserved as a great work of art ... or, simply as 'friends' to man.

In Venice, when citizens spoke of melting down the *Horses*, they were opposed by the poet Petrarch and other citizens who praised the works and claimed they were 'Works of Lysippos himself.' The *Horses* were kept in the Arsenal of Venice some 50 years until an appropriate open terrace had been built over the symbolic triumphal arch on the façade of St. Mark's. [Boardman, p 10-11]

To the Venetians during the Middle Ages, the *Horses* came to symbolize the 4 Evangelists. This Christian symbolism may have aided their survival ... just as it 'aided' the *Marcus Aurelius* equestrian statue #61 in Rome.

Today, viewers standing in St. Mark's Square see bronze replicas of the originals on the terrace above the cathedral's loggia. In the 1960s, due to atmospheric pollution, the originals were moved inside St. Mark's Cathedral.

Subject:

The ancient quadriga normally consisted of 4 horses harnessed abreast and drawing a two-wheeled chariot. In ancient hippodromes, the race of the quadrigas was often the most popular and violent event.

[3 paragraphs below repeat from Chapter 11, the *Charioteer*]

Racing a 4-horse chariot at the Pythian Games of Delphi was a highly hazardous profession. The race was usually the opening athletic event, the most spectacular ... and the most costly. Two-wheeled chariots lined up across the width of one end of the hippodrome. A single post near the far end signified the turning point for all chariots. Drivers could approach this post from either side – which resulted in frequent head-on collisions.

Finley and Pleket reveal: "... the largest number on record [entries in any Greek chariot race] was 41 at the Pythian Games of 462 BC when the race was won by Arcesilas, king of Cyrene ... whose chariot was the only one to complete the course. Arcesilas' victory as the lone finisher was not normal, but it is not very surprising." [p 28]

"For twelve laps [more than 9 kilometers], the flying horses pulled the light carts in short bursts of speed punctuated by 180-degree turns at the posts. Although the rules forbade swerving in front of a competitor, bumps, crashes and head-on collisions were the rule rather than the exception, as chariots raced up and down the narrow un-separated course and made one wide turn after another." [p. 29]

An excellent example of an ancient quadriga competition can be seen in the famed [15-minute] scene in *Ben Hur* where Charlton Heston races his chariot.

Ancient quadriga monuments normally commemorated a great victory or the man who won such a victory. The top the *Mausoleum of Hallicarnassus* [Mausolos #23] displayed a 4-horse chariot...of which the head and chest of one horse are in the British Museum. The famed Berlin quadriga atop the Brandenburg Gate was put in place in 1793.

In Rome, the Monument of Victorio Emanuele II displays 'two' quadrigas on its heights. In London, the Wellington Arch with quadriga was designed in 1912.

Above the entrance to the Minnesota State Capitol in the United States, an impressive gold-leafed quadriga has been displayed since 1906. It was created by Edward Clark Potter and Daniel Chester French. [later, sculptor of *Lincoln* #93]

Sculptor:

According to the Roman historian Pliny, the original sculptor is 'popularly' believed to be either Lysippos or one of his students. Other sources, supporting 'a Roman copy', suggest the copy was made by an unknown Greco-Roman sculptor.

Major References:

Arts of Ancient Greeks, 1972, Brilliant, p 264

Ancient Rome Brought To Life, Carpenter, p 308-09

Greek Art, 1973, Boardman, p 10-11

Encyclopedia of Sculpture, 2004, Checci, p 761-2

A Wanderer in Venice, 1914, E.V. Lucas, p 21

Greek and Roman Sculpture, 1972, Lawrence, p 205

The Olympic Games, 1976, Finley and Pleket, p. 29

All Paris, 1975, Giovanna Magi, p 28

30

THE CROWNED ATHLETE
OR GETTY BRONZE

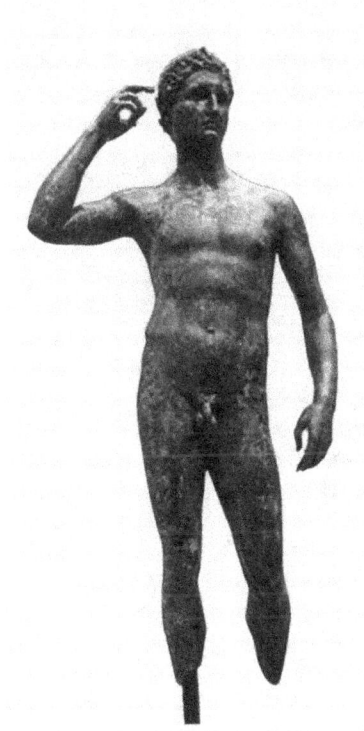

"... so expresses the Lysippic intention to show the human body in natural movement through space ... scholars believe it may be an original from that sculptor's own hands."
... *Encyclopedia of Sculpture*, 2004, p 166

Found 1964, at sea off Fano, Italy – now Getty Museum, LA
Orig. Greek Bronze – 320 BC – late Classic / early Hellenistic
Ht. 5' 7" [170 cm] with feet – bronze
Sculptor: likely Lysippos [390-320 BC] or his studio

"Fano, Italy – On a summer day in 1964, the trawler pushed off from this port before dawn. It motored...through the Adriatic Sea toward a submerged outcropping where fish gathered, 32 nautical miles out. By dusk...the 7-man crew cast their nets and fished all night...Early the next morning, the nets caught on a snag. The boat's engine whined. With a jolt, the nets came free. Crewmen watched as a barnacle-encrusted figure emerged from the sea. *'C'e un morto!'* [There's a dead man!] cried one of the fisherman." [*LA Times*, 5/11/2006]

With the barnacles removed from the life-sized bronze, it revealed a victorious athlete...who would gain the 'plausible' reputation of being <u>the only surviving original statue of 1,500 created by Lysippos</u> [w/assistants & pupils] – the finest sculptor of his era [second half of 4th C. BC] and personal sculptor to Alexander the Great.

This young man is believed to represent an athlete who competed in the Ancient Games at Olympia. In 200 AD, the ancient traveler Pausanias tells of seeing nearly 200 large statues of victorious athletes lining the pathways of Olympia. In the core of the statue, bits of flax were found, a grain that "grew abundantly" in this Greek city. [*LA Times*, Felch, 2006]

The *Encyclo Sculpt.* states the *Crowned Athlete*: "... so expresses the Lysippic intention to show the human body in natural movement through space, that, given its recognizably Lysippic traits, some scholars believe it may be an original from that sculptor's own hands."

Subject:

"The tall, slender, elegant young man ... appears to be gliding past the observer. His gesture, it has been suggested, is that of an athlete at the games, <u>placing on his head the wreath of victory</u>. The facial features are like those we find in the Roman copies of the statues of Lysippos that record his style ..." [p 166]

> [the wreaths were made with leaves of a sacred olive tree located behind the principal shrine in Olympia – the Temple of Zeus. For mythical origin of laurel wreaths, see *Apollo & Daphne* #71]

If he is a runner – suggested by his physique – his victory may have been in "the *stade* or short foot-race, a sprint of just under 200 meters ... always the most important contest ... each particular Olympiad being named after the winner." [*Ancient Olympic Games*, p 234]

In the tradition of Lysippos, the face exhibits a 'spark of life'.

However, this 'spirit' is far from the humble expression expected of an Olympic winner. Frei, in *Getty Bronze*, explains: "To describe athletic victors, the classical Greeks used the word *aidos*, meaning modesty but implying much more. The head was traditionally bowed down, confirming the humility of the winner. Honor was received this way ... <u>while avoiding any suspicion of hubris</u>, not acceptable to the gods and offensive to fellow citizens." [p 15, 20]

Here, instead ... the raised face is <u>haughty, even arrogant</u>.

Durant describes how ancient Olympic athletes were normally crowned by the judges. "When the toils of 5 days were over, the victors received their rewards. Each bound a woolen fillet about his head, and upon this the judges placed a crown of wild olives, while a herald announced the name and city of the winner. An olive wreath was the only prize at the Olympic Games, yet it was the most eagerly contested distinction in Greece. Many cities voted substantial sums to the victors on their return ... some cities made them generals [or, in war, permitted them to fight alongside the commander] ... and the crowd idolized them so openly that jealous philosophers complained. Poets were engaged by the victor or his patrons to write odes in his honor ... which were sung by choruses of boys [in the procession that welcomed him home] ... sculptors were paid to perpetuate him in bronze and stone; and sometimes he was given free sustenance in the city hall." [p 215-16]

Today, we can only speculate why Lysippos chose to sculpt an Olympic winner in the act of' self-crowning'... who also displays a demeanor of contempt.

Perhaps ... Lysippos recorded in bronze an 'historical event' – though now forgotten – which occurred during a highly-competitive race.

The *Crowned Athlete* may have been a novice, unusually young, hardly expected to win against experienced competitors ... but, he runs well ... too well. A mean-spirited competitor – midway in the race – jostles him and forces a stumble. The novice recovers though ... and wins <u>in spite of the skullduggery</u>. Now, his sneer is directed at the other sprinter.

Or ... our novice athlete does not win the race after the stumble ... however, the judges disqualify the sprinter who won by cheating. They declare the novice the 'official' winner, who now holds the wreath firmly to his brow.

Or ... the victor displays contempt to a jeering crowd ... who disparage him because he is Spartan – during a period when Sparta was at war with other Greek city-states.

Or ... the judges, after extended discussion over a 'technicality,' cannot decide whether to 'officially' crown the athlete ... therefore, they simply hand the wreath to him, and he self-crowns himself.

Faulkner's 2012 *Guide to the Ancient Olympics* reveals: "As for politics, the Olympics was nothing if not a pageant of parochial hatreds and city-state rivalries, often laced with class antagonism, where oligarchic states like Sparta clashed on the running track with democracies like Athens." [*Wall Street Journal*, 5/19/2012]

Disputed Ownership:

In 1964...the fishermen from the Italian trawler – who snagged the 280-pound statue – secretly sold it for $5,600 to traffickers in antiquities...who smuggled it out of Italy. Two years later, the smugglers were convicted of trafficking in stolen goods...however, after another 5 years, "the convictions were overturned on the grounds that a discovery in international waters could not be considered stolen property." Though the traffickers violated Italian law restricting the export of such a statue, they were never charged...as they would not reveal to whom they sold it. [*LA Times*, Felch, 5/11/2006]

In 1974... "[billionaire oilman J. Paul] Getty joined forces with the NY Met. Museum of Art to bid on the bronze. Thomas Hoving, the Met's director at the time...urged Getty to jump at the opportunity, comparing the piece's artistic value to that of the *Mona Lisa* if all of Leonardo da Vinci's other works had been destroyed." [Felch, p 25]

In 1976...J. Paul Getty died before the acquisition was concluded.

In 1977... "The trustees of the [Getty] museum bought it from a German dealer for $3.95 million and put it on display the next year." [*LA Times*, 6/3/14]

In 2010... "an Italian judge ordered the seizure of the Getty's iconic bronze statue...citing 'grave negligence' in the museum's acquisition of the ancient statue in 1977...documents show the Getty Museum bought the statue despite legal concerns of the museum's founder [J. Paul Getty] who insisted its purchase be cleared with Italian authorities before he died in 1976." [*LA Times*, Felch, 2-12-10]

In 2017...the controversial *Crowned Athlete* remains at the Getty Villa.

Sculptor:

See '*Sculptor*' sections of earlier 'Lysippos' chapters: *the Scraper* #25...*Agias* #26...and *Alexander Herm* #28.

Major References:

Encyclopedia of Sculpture, 2004, p 166

The Ancient Olympic Games, 1999, Swaddling, p 234-5

The Olympic Games, 1976, Finley and Pleket, p 14-25, 47-58

The Life of Greece, 1939, Durant, p 88, 213-16, 666

Amazing Catch...5/11/2006, "LA Times", Felch, p 1, 24-5

Twist in Getty's Italian Saga, 1/14/2010, "LA Times", Felch, p A9

Judge Orders Statue Seized, 2/12/2010, "LA Times", Felch, p 1, F14

The Getty Bronze, 1982, Frei, p 1-5, 15, 18-20

31

HERCULES,

THE FARNESE

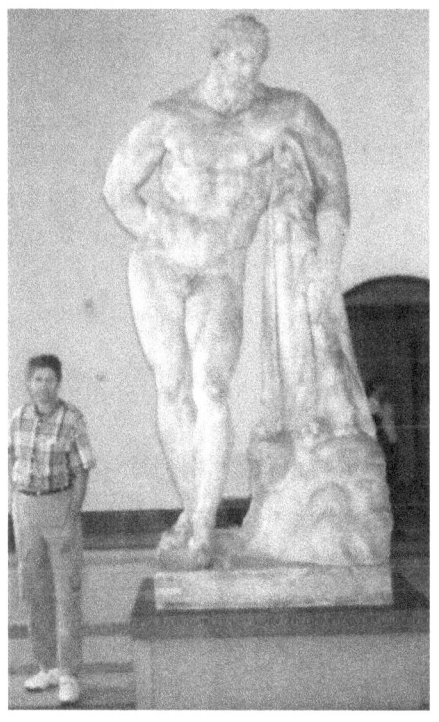

"Leaning on his club, the hero appears astonishingly massive ...
Lysippos also wanted to depict his humanity ... from the sad,
downcast glance and the lax athletic body ... in a moment
of weariness." ... Bazin, *History of World Sculpture*, p 151

Unearthed, Rome, 1540 & 1546 – now, Naples Arch. Museum
Greco-Roman copy – 216 AD – Hellenistic
From: lost Original Greek bronze – 320 BC
Ht. 10 feet, 4 in. – marble
Sculptor: orig. bronze: Lysippos – copy: Glycon of Athens

The ancient Greeks believed Hercules to be the son of Zeus…and the strongest man on Earth. In Naples, when we stand beside *Hercules,* it can be a humbling experience. Our eyes are level with his kneecaps. He is more than 10 feet tall, mounted on a 3.5 foot pedestal.

Brilliant describes the *Farnese Hercules* as "wearily and even sadly leaning on his club after the exhausting efforts of his labors…his powerful body drained of its energy…his spirit vulnerable and depressed…battered by his experiences…and whether joyous or suffering…knows and feels his fate …he will try again." [*Arts of the Ancient Greeks,* p 270-1]

'Farnese' refers to the prominent papal family – including states-men, military leaders, and Pope Paul III – who patronized the arts between the years 1545 and 1731.

30,000 Years of Art adds: "*Hercules* rests on his club, which ordinarily signifies power but here serves as a crutch. This pose gives the figure a sense of vitality and impending motion…" [p 349] Lawrence describes the figure as having a "wide chest, broad shoulders, thick hair, fat buttocks, and powerful arms." [p 208]

Durant observes: "A world away from the academically cold and lifeless Apollo Belvedere…is the Farnese Hercules, copied by Glycon from an original attributed to Lysippos – all muscle in the overdone body…kindliness and wonder in the face." [*Life of Greece,* p 624]

In 1540, the head of *Hercules* was found in a well in Trastevere [across Tiber from Colosseum]. Six years later, his torso was discovered in the Baths of Caracalla [south of Colosseum] completed in 216 AD. We may speculate the head was hidden in the well to prevent its seizure or destruction by an invading army…or early Christians dropped it in the well.

This *Hercules* – and the equally immense *Farnese Bull* #44 – were commissioned by the Emperor Caracalla to adorn his great Baths... among the largest and best preserved of all the baths built by the Romans... remaining in working condition until 537 AD [invading Goths cut off water supply]. An earthquake in 847 AD: "brought down some parts of the building. But the Baths suffered their worst damage through the pontificate [1534-1549] of Pope Paul III, who 'released' them as a 'quarry' for the rebuilding of St. Peter's. It was in this way that many of the sculptures came into the possession of the papal family." [Hintzen-Bohlen, p 389]

The first written record of this *Hercules* has it in the courtyard of the Palazzo Farnese [now French Embassy] in 1556. New legs had been added by Italian architect/sculptor Guglielmo della Porta. More than 200 years later, in 1787, the original legs were restored to the *Farnese Hercules*. "After the death of the last Farnese of the Neapolitan line of the Bourbons [1787], the library and archeological collection [of their Palazzo] were taken to Naples..." [*Palazzi & Villas of Rome*, p 88]

Subject:

Ancient Greeks, according to Hamilton's *Mythology*, considered Hercules to be "the greatest hero of Greece..." Though a god of little intellect and also willful, Hercules "showed greatness of soul" by his "willingness to do anything to" correct a wrongful act... of which he committed many. [p 224-27]

From the three apples *Hercules* grasps in his right hand [behind his back], we can surmise he has returned from the 11th of his "Twelve Labors" – the recovery of the *Golden Apples of Hesperides* – originally wedding gifts to the goddess Hera, who had placed them under the guard of the Hesperides nymphs. [*30,000 Years*, p 349]

Hera, the jealous and vengeful wife of Zeus, made the life of Hercules miserable... with reason. Zeus had fathered Hercules during a 'visit' with a mortal woman, Alcema [wife of Theban general Amphitryon]. The indiscreet dalliance by Zeus infuriated Hera.

When Hercules was a year old, Hera sent two deadly snakes to destroy the child in his cradle. His mother Alcema rushed in and found Hercules tightly gripping the weaving heads of the snakes by their necks as they coiled around his body. Alcema called out to her husband, Amphitryon. When he arrived, the laughing Hercules held up the limp bodies of the now dead snakes and gave them to Amphitryon.

[in Capitoline Mus…see the *Child Hercules* gripping the snakes]

Years later, Hera "sent a madness" upon Hercules which caused him to unknowingly kill those most dear to him – his own wife and children. Seeking purification for this horrid deed, Hercules traveled to Delphi and consulted the oracle, who advised him to seek out his cousin, King Eurystheus of Mycenae. Eurystheus ordered the 'Twelve Labors of Hercules' as "penances to purge Hercules and make him clean again."

To find the fore-mentioned *Golden Apples*, Hercules searched for Atlas – father of the Hesperides nymphs – and found him in the mountains of northwest Africa holding up the sky.

Hercules offered to support the sky if Atlas would obtain the *Golden Apples* from his daughters. Atlas agreed…however, upon returning with the *Apples*, Atlas told Hercules he no longer wished to hold up the sky and said he himself would take the *Apples* to King Eurystheus. Hercules consented, but requested Atlas support the sky for a moment while he placed a pad on his shoulder to soften the burden. When Atlas set down the *Apples* and did as requested, Hercules picked up the *Apples* and left.

In the Naples Museum, we see an exhausted Hercules before his return to Mycenae. Since he holds the *Golden Apples* in his hand, they may be the subject of his thoughts. Hercules was known to have a good soul…he may be regretting his trickery with Atlas. Or…the *Golden Apples* could be a painful reminder of the misery which the goddess Hera continues to cause him. Or…it could be that Hercules knows, upon returning to Mycenae, King Eurystheus will assign him another difficult and dangerous Labor...though it will be the last. [Hamilton, p 224-43]

Sculptor:

The marble *Hercules* is signed by Glycon of Athens, recognized as a fine Greek copyist. Little else is known of him. Due to the great size of the *Hercules*, its head, arms, and legs were carved from separate blocks.

The original bronze *Hercules* – one of many statues believed to have been sculpted by Lysippos – is said to have "stood in the marketplace of Sicyon", the hometown of Lysippos. [Lawrence, p 207]

After the marble *Farnese Hercules* was 'discovered' in the 1540s, many reproductions were made in the following 17th and 18th centuries. In Wilhelmscohe Park near Cassel in Germany, an exceptionally large 9.3 meter, copper version was created and erected in 1717...on a pyramid-shaped pavilion 63 meters high.

See *the Hellenistic Ruler* #42 for the 'Herculean-style'... often adopted in the following century by Roman generals to glorify and commemorate their victorious campaigns.

The *Hercules Epitrapezios*

Some 2,400 years ago, a famed silver statuette by Lysippos – the *Hercules Epitrapezios* [meaning: *at* or *on a table*] – decorated the dining table of Alexander the Great each evening during his long military campaigns. "According to the poets Martial and Statius, this *Hercules* looked up to the stars and invited the guests to the joys of the festive meal." [Hafner, p 215] The 21-inch seated *Hercules* "appears boisterously drunk, but relaxed and full of good feeling..." and holds out a drinking cup, as if offering its contents to guests "as an invitation to conviviality."

Highly-praised in antiquity, the piece passed from Alexander to Hannibal...to the Roman dictator Sulla...and then into the hands of a Roman art collector, Novius Vindex [described by Martial and Statius...] but it has not survived." [Brilliant, p 270]

A fine bronze statuette copy…plus a colossal, Roman marble copy of the *Hercules Epitrapezios* are exhibited in the Naples Arch. Museum. From these and other surviving copies, we know that the muscular physique of its figure is shared by the *Farnese Hercules*…suggesting the same sculptor.

Major References:

History of World Sculpture, 1968, Bazin, p 151
30,000 Years of Art, 2007, Phaidon, p 349
Arts of the Ancient Greeks, 1972, Brilliant, p 270-1
Greek and Roman Sculpture, 1972, Lawrence, p 207-9, 297-8
Art of Crete, Mycenae, and Greece, 1968, Hafner, 214-15
The Life of Greece, 1939, Durant, p 624
Bulfinch's Mythology, 1968, foreword by Graves, p 150-3
Mythology, 1942, Hamilton, p 224-40
Art and Architecture of Rome, 2005, Hintzen-Bohlen, p 159, 388-9
Bulfinch Guide to Art History, 1996, West, p 430

32

DEMOSTHENES

THE GREAT ORATOR

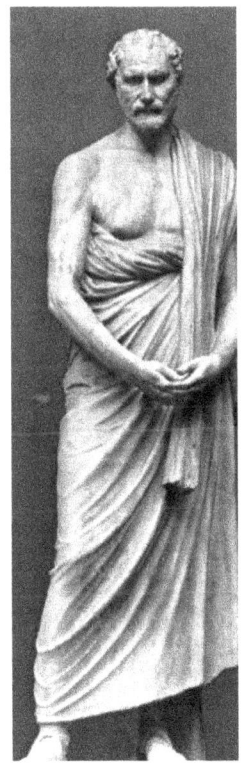

"The Vatican statue of the great orator is one
of the masterpieces of Hellenistic realism."
...Durant, *Life of Greece*, 1939, p 478

Origin unknown – now, in Vatican & Glyptotek of Copenhagen
Greco-Roman copy – approx. 100 BC – Hellenistic
From: lost Original Greek bronze – 280-279 BC
Ht. 2.02 m. – marble
Sculptor: orig. bronze by Polyeuktos

D emosthenes [384-322 BC] is considered the greatest of all
Greek orators...as Cicero is considered among the Romans.
The ancient historian/traveler Plutarch favored Demosthenes over
Cicero. [*Plutarch's Lives*, 1973, p 1070]

On 3 occasions: 338 BC...335 BC...323 BC...the eloquence of
Demosthenes inspired the Greeks to defend their city-states and
democracy against the armies of the Macedonians to the north.
First, against King Phillip II...then Phillip's son Alexander...and,
again, after the death of Alexander. Each time, the Greeks were
overwhelmed and crushed.

R. Brilliant describes *the Demosthenes* as: "a masterpiece of psychological and physical realism...a superbly passionate portrait of
the great orator standing wearily in gloomy seriousness with taut
face and wrinkled brow...head inclined toward his hands, tightly
clasped in tense resolution...Polyeuktos has captured the spirit of
the indomitable, passionate patriot who fought for his country and
lost." [*Art of Ancient Greeks*, p 397]

Smith offers similar praise: "one of the great works of Hellenistic
portraiture...a posthumous monument set up to mark significant
moments in history...erected over 40 years after the orator's death
[323 BC]...to express the apparent vindication in that year of democratic confrontation [280-279 BC] with Macedon. The *Demosthenes*
is pensive, diffident, and has a knitted brow signifying concentration...his appearance is one of troubled introspection." [*Hellenistic
Sculpture*, p 37-8]

When Polyeuktos' original bronze of *Demosthenes* was installed
in the Agora of Athens in 280/279 BC, it was "a nostalgic evocation
of the last great Athenian democrat. The orator's face expresses a
deep inward suffering." [Bazin, p 154]

Durant adds: "The body is thin and wearied; the aspect is that of a man who is about to make a final appeal for a cause that he considers lost... the eyes reveal a restless life, and foresee a bitter death." [p 478]

Though the bronze statue is lost, several excellent Roman marble copies exist, particularly in the Vatican and the Glyptotek of Copenhagen.

Lawrence comments: "The Vatican *Demosthenes* is wrongly restored holding a scroll... for other copies prove that originally the hands were clasped in front of the body. In the pose is revealed the patriot, meditating on the downfall of Athens and his own approaching death at the hands of the Macedonians..." [*Greek & Roman Sculpture*, p 218]

Subject:

From *Plutarch's Lives* [Ellis, 1917] we learn: "At first, Demosthenes was laughed at and interrupted... for his violence of manner and his stammering made it difficult to understand him. He overcame these difficulties by retiring to the country, where he practiced and studied every day, both action and speech. The hesitation and stammering of his tongue he corrected by practicing to speak with pebbles in his mouth... and strengthened his voice by running or walking up hill, and pronouncing some passage in an oration or a poem during the difficulty in breathing. He had, moreover, a looking-glass [mirror] in his house, before which he used to declaim, and adjust all his motions. [p 197]

When Demosthenes no longer stammered, he began as a hired orator... often receiving fees for "preparing pleas for both the opposed parties to a dispute." Eventually, he enriched himself as a professional lawyer and entered politics to excel on a par with Pericles who had led Athens during its Classic Age 100 years earlier. [Durant, p 478]

Durant describes his oratorical style: "On the rostrum he contorted his figure, whirled round and round, laid his hand upon his forehead as in reflection, and often raised his voice to a scream, telling the Athenians they were degenerate slackers who had lost the military virtues of their progenitors. There is little wit in him, little philosophy. Only his patriotism redeems him, and the apparent sincerity of his despairing cry for freedom." [p 483-84]

Demosthenes' Wars with the Macedonians:

In 338 BC, he persuaded the Greeks to oppose the invading army of Philip II [father of Alexander]. Phillip forced the Greek army to flee the field of battle, then generously released Athenian prisoners and forgave Demosthenes. The Athenians were allowed to "retain a large measure of their freedom." [Durant, p 479-80]

In 336 BC, when news of the assassination of Philip reached Athens, Demosthenes "donned festal garb, placed a garland of flowers upon his head, and moved in the Assembly that a crown of honor should be voted to the assassin Pausanias." However, when the son Alexander marched south to Thebes, the Greeks were quick "to renew their allegiance." Alexander "declared all dictatorships abolished in Greece, and decreed that each city should live in freedom according to its own laws." [p 542]

In 335 BC, while Alexander marched north to suppress rebelling barbarians, a rumor arose in Athens that Alexander had been killed. Demosthenes again "called for a war of independence, instigated Thebes into revolting, and Athens sent help to Thebes. Alexander, furious over what seemed to him not a passion for freedom but the crudist ingratitude and treachery, marched his weary troops down again into Greece." [p 542-43]

Alexander soundly defeated the Greeks and burned Thebes, selling its inhabitants [excepting those who could prove they had opposed the revolt] into slavery. Once more, Alexander was lenient with Athens, overlooking the violation of its pledges a year before…and he "did not press his demand for the surrender of Demosthenes and other anti-Macedonian leaders." [p 543] Demosthenes was exiled.

In 323, at the death of Alexander, Demosthenes was recalled to Athens from exile. His voice again helped raise an army to seek freedom from the Macedonians. Antipater, one of Alexander's best generals, destroyed the Greeks and forced Athens "to abandon its democratic constitution and courts." [p 552]

When the surrender of Demosthenes was also demanded, Plutarch tells us: "Demosthenes and his party hastened to escape … as they fled different ways, Antipater sent a company of soldiers, under Archias, the exile hunter, to pursue and capture them. Archias, being informed that Demosthenes had taken 'sanctuary' [protection] in the [island] temple of Poseidon at Calauria, he and his Thracians passed over into it in rowboats. As soon as he landed, he went to the orator and endeavored to persuade him to quit the temple and go with him to Antipater … assuring him that he had no hard measure to expect. On hearing which, Demosthenes retired into the inner part of the temple; and taking some paper as if he meant to write, he put the pen in his mouth, and bit it a considerable time, as he used to do when thoughtful about his composition. He sucked the poison from his pen, after which, he covered his head, fell by the altar, and expired. He died on the 16th of October, BC 322, aged 61, having left behind him a great body of orations." [p 201]

The <u>concept of democracy, nevertheless, survived intact</u> … and thereby, Demosthenes gained immortality for far more than becoming the finest orator of the ancient world.

In an ironic twist, by 323 BC, Alexander the Great carried the torch of 'democracy' into every country he conquered east of Greece, introducing it even at local levels.

Durant instructively adds: "The death of Greek democracy was both a violent and a natural death, in which the fatal agents were the organic disorders of the system; the sword of Macedon merely added the final blow. The weakness and smallness of the city-states of Greece had been a boon to the individual, if not in body, certainly in soul … that freedom, costly though it was, had generated the achievements of the Greek mind. *Individualism in the end destroys the group,* but in the interim it stimulates personality, mental exploration, and artistic creation. Greek democracy was *corrupt and incompetent, and had to die.* But, when it was dead, men realized how beautiful its heyday had been; and all later generations of antiquity looked back to the centuries of Pericles and Plato as the zenith of Greece, and of all history." [p 554]

Historians have long debated whether Demosthenes or Cicero was the better orator. In *Plutarch's Lives* [translated by Dryden], the historian/traveler compares the two: "Demosthenes far surpassed in force and strength of eloquence all his contemporaries in political and judicial speaking, in grandeur and majesty... and in accuracy and science all the logicians and rhetoricians of his day. For Demosthenes' oratory was without embellishment and jesting, wholly composed for real effect and seriousness... whereas Cicero's love of mockery often ran him into scurrility; and in his love of laughing away serious arguments in judicial cases by jests and facetious remarks, with a view to the advantage of his clients, he paid too little regard to what was decent..." [p 1070]

Sculptor:

Polyeuktos was a master sculptor on Attica, the southern peninsula of Greece that includes Athens. Since Polyeuktos created this statue some 40 years after the death of Demosthenes, his portrait is believed to be somewhat idealized.

Smith tells us: "the statue of *Demosthenes* in the Agora endured as a political and cultural landmark. It is 'preserved' in over 50 Roman marble copies." [*Hellenistic Sculpture,* p 38]

Major References:

History of World Sculpture, 1968, Bazin, p 154
Life of Greece, 1939, Durant, p 468-9, 478-80, 483-5, 542, 553-4
Plutarch's Lives, 1917, Ellis, p 197
Plutarch's Live, 1973, Random House (translated by Dryden), p 1070
Greek and Roman Sculpture, 1972, Lawrence, p 218, plates 60d, 61a
Hellenistic Sculpture, 1991, Smith, p 37-8, fig 39
Arts of the Ancient Greeks, 1972, Brilliant, p 219, 396-7

33

'L. Junius Brutus'
[not the assassin brutus]

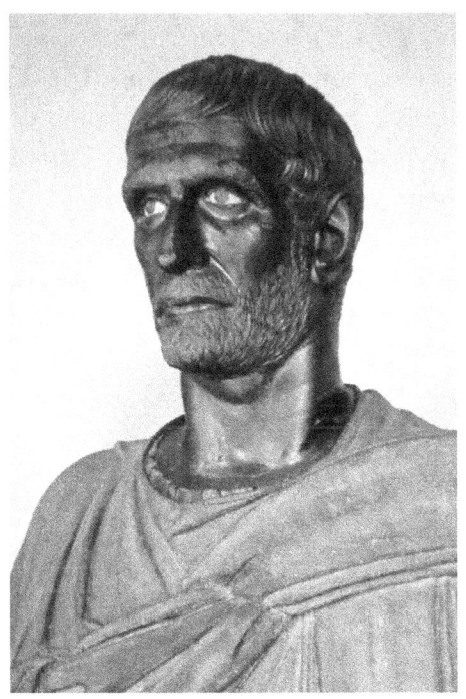

"Some very great 3rd C. BC artist – heir to both the
Etruscan and Italic traditions and knowledgeable about
Greek portraiture – created this bronze masterpiece..."
...Brilliant, *Roman Art*, p 231

Orig. Etruscan/Roman bronze – now Capitoline Mus., Rome
Ht. [head] 1'1", 32 cm; bust: 69 cm – 250 BC – Hellenistic
Eyes: ivory and glass paste – torso added later
Sculptor: unknown Etruscan or Greco-Roman
    *also known as the *Capitoline Brutus* [due to current location]

The eyes on this dark bronze are said to be the most riveting in Rome. The entire face is immensely dignified.

Brilliant observes: "the powerful face is stripped of all super-fluous flesh...the bony skull covered with a dynamic, restless sur-face...the sculptor has thrust an image of intense force into the consciousness of the beholder...who is thus compelled to recognize its power and authority." [*Roman Art*, p 232]

30,000 Years of Art suggests: "The Etruscans were expert bronze-casters...and both the sitter and the artist may have been Etruscans." [p 264]

If the sculptor is Etruscan, it would be ironic...as many Romans accept this bust as representing the Roman patriot L. Junius Brutus who led the overthrow of the Etruscan tyranny in 509-508 BC. He then established the Roman Republic...providing a moderate liberty to Romans. He is often described as the '*Deliverer of Democracy to Rome.*'

Bazin says: "Since the Renaissance, many have believed that this magnificent bust represents *L. Junius Brutus* [Brutus the Elder] who in 509 BC, according to tradition, liberated Rome from the Etruscan yoke and became a first co-consul of the Republic." [*History of World Sculpture*, p 171]

However, Brilliant specifies: "There is no evidence that this is *the* Brutus, patriot and puritan in the formative years of the Roman Republic at the end of the 6th C BC...nor that the head is a portrait of any Roman at all. And yet this shaggy, grim-visaged, tight-lipped, sharp-featured, austere man – intuitively felt as a very redoubtable individual – has come to represent, even typify, the high moral 'Old Roman' of the great days of the Republic." [p 231-32]

The bronze head is believed to have been sculpted some 250 years after the life of *L. Junius Brutus*. Beyond doubt, the unknown Etruscan or Roman who commissioned it was a patrician or wealthy merchant, who could afford the services of the finest sculptors in his time.

30,000 Years adds: "This majestic face seems appropriate for *L. Junius Brutus,* the patrician leader who freed Rome from the Etruscan Tarquin kings...but the name is merely a tradition...we do not know who the sitter was. Aristocratic Roman families originally kept death masks of their venerable forbears for display in the public reception rooms of their houses. This grand gentleman and his family would have been proud of his hard-won position in Roman society...The torso is a later addition, as early Roman portraits comprised just the head." [p 264]

Bazin describes how this 'Roman portrait' differs from older Greek portraits. "The Greek portrait is a character study, but the Roman portrait is a life-like reproduction of the sitter's every feature, so faithful that it allows the spectator to speculate for himself on the person's character...the beautiful bronze *Capitoline Brutus* reflects the Hellenistic manner, although the physiognomies are typically Roman." [p 34]

Though we cannot assume this bronze is *L. Junius Brutus,* we can accept this exceptionally-fine sculpture as symbolic of what the Western World derived from Ancient Rome.

Durant reminds us Rome: "achieved a democracy of freemen...it formed a majestic system of law [initially, borrowing from Greeks] which through nearly all Europe gave security to life and property, incentive and continuity to industry...It molded a government of separated legislative and executive powers whose checks and balances inspired the makers of constitutions as late as revolutionary America and France." [C&C, p 670]

Subject:

[speculating the bust is L.Junius Brutus...and knowing the sources of Roman historian Livy, 59 BC-17 AD, may be mostly legend]

In 509 BC, L. Junius Brutus was a close friend of Collatinus, a relative of Sextus Tarquin – son of the Etruscan King Tarquin.

Durant [from *Livy*] informs us: "Sextus...was debating with Collatinus the comparative virtue of their wives. Collatinus proposed they should take horse to Rome and surprise their ladies in the late hours of the night...They found the wife of Sextus feasting with intimates, but Lucretia [wife of Collatinus] was spinning wool for her husband's clothing...Sextus was inflamed with desire to try Lucretia's fidelity and enjoy her love. A few days later, he secretly returned to the home of Lucretia and overcame her by wile and force...Lucretia sent for her father and her husband Collatinus, told them what had happened, and then stabbed herself to death." [p 16, 56-7]

"Thereupon, L. Junius Brutus called upon all good men to drive the Tarquins from Rome. [Brutus was a nephew to King Tarquin...much earlier, his father and his brother had been put to death by the king] Brutus rode with Collatinus to the capital, told Lucretia's story to the Senate, and persuaded it to banish all the royal family...The King had meanwhile left his army and hurried to Rome. Brutus – apprised of this – rode out to the army, told Lucretia's story again, and won the citizen-soldier's support. Tarquin fled north alone..." [p 16]

[Durant qualifies Livy: "Most students...consign Lucretia to legend and Shakespeare. We do not know where history retires and poetry enters. Some have thought even Junius Brutus to be legend, but here again, skepticism has probably gone too far." p 16]

L. Junius Brutus and Collatinus, after convening an assembly of the citizen-soldiers, were "elected as co-consuls, with equal and rival powers to rule for a year." They are recognized as the first co-consuls of the Roman Republic. [16-7]

Over time, the Senate introduced restrictive requirements for membership, favoring wealthy aristocrats. They also passed laws allowing only the Senate to select candidates for the positions of co-consul – again favoring aristocracy.

For the next 450 years, 2 consuls shared leadership of Rome with the Senate.

Durant concludes: "The revolution [in 509 BC] had two main results: it freed Rome from Etruscan ascendancy and replaced the monarchy with an aristocracy that ruled Rome until Caesar. The victors called the revolution a triumph of liberty; but now and then liberty – in the slogans of the strong – means freedom from restraint in the exploitation of the weak. The political position of the poorer citizens was not improved…they lost the modest measure of protection with which the monarchy had shielded them from aristocratic domination." [p 17, 670]

If the troubled face of this *Brutus* appears grim, it may mirror the personal ill-fortune of the historical man. After the overthrow of the Etruscan king, 2 disloyal sons of Brutus conspired in a plot to restore Tarquin as king.

Durant, in *Caesar and Christ*, says: "The two sons of Junius Brutus were among the arrested conspirators, and the fiery first consul provided an exemplar – *perhaps a myth* – for all later Romans when he witnessed in stoic silence the flogging and [death] of his children." [p 17]

Livy writes: "The youths, all of distinction, stood tied to stakes, but the sons of the consul entirely engaged the eyes of the spectators…The consuls mounted their throne, and the lictors were sent to inflict the punishment: after stripping the criminals…they beat them with rods, and [killed] them; whilst, through the whole process of the affair, the looks and countenance of Brutus afforded an extraordinary spectacle…the feelings of the father often struggling with the character of the magistrate [judge] enforcing the execution of the laws." [*History of Rome, Vol I*, 1833, p 101]

Did Athen's *Tyrannicides* Inspire the 509 BC Roman Revolt?

In 514 BC, the *Tyrannicides* #9 'initiated' a rebellion in Athens against the Tyrant Hippias…in 510 BC, he abdicated…by 507 BC, the Athenians enjoyed democracy. [*The Will of Zeus*, 1961, Barr, p 79, 123]

Even earlier, in 524 BC, a Greek colony – the port of Cumae near Naples [founded 750 BC] – defeated and threw off their Etruscan rulers. At that time, numerous Greek colonies existed in Italy and Sicily, trading with the Romans.

When the Romans learned of the [510 BC] Athenian 'revolt' against their tyrant, it is possible Athen's success encouraged the Romans in [509 BC] to seek their own freedom. [*C & C*, Durant, 1944, p 1-18] [Bazin, p 171]

Sculptor:

The unknown artist who created this bronze bust was highly-skilled...whether Etruscan or Roman. Initially, only the head was cast in bronze...as, in public processions, the head alone would have been easier to carry by members of the family wishing to demonstrate their prestige.

The museum exhibiting *L Junius Brutus* is on the historic Capitoline Hill. In antiquity, day-long triumphs – parades awarded for great victories by Roman generals and emperors – wound through the Forum on the Sacred Way...and culminated at the top of the Hill. [originally crowned by the giant Temple of Jupiter].

Modern visitors to the Capitoline Hill often take the easier western approach – up the wide, gradual marble staircase [designed by Michelangelo] to the Piazza del Campidoglio.

Major References:

History of Rome [Vol. I], 1833, Livy, p 100-01
Roman Art, 1974, Brilliant, p 231-32
Caesar and Christ, 1944, Durant, p 1-18, 670
History of World Sculpture, 1968, Bazin, p 34-5, 171
30,000 Years of Art, 2007, Phaidon, p 264
Ancient Rome, 1996, Liberati and Bourbon, p 36-7
The Eternal City – Rome, 1896, Clara Clement, p 536
Art & Architecture, Rome & Vatican, 2001, Hintzen-Bohlen, p 70
The Will of Zeus, 1961, Stringfellow Barr, p 79, 123

34

JOCKEY OF ARTEMISION

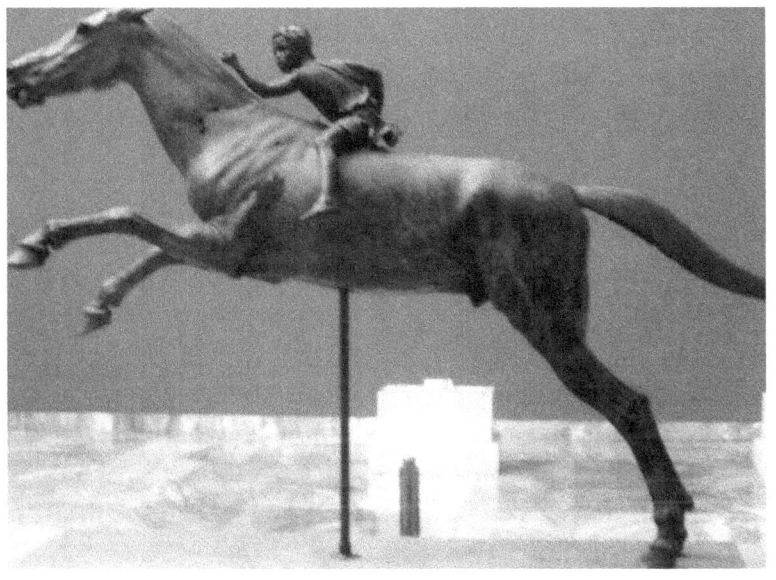

"one of most impressive masterpieces of Hellenistic sculpture."
...Ragghiani, Nat. Museum of Athens, p 154
[in museum, ears of horse are 'flat' as seen above]

Found 1926/1937 off Cape Artemision – now Nat.Mus.Athens
Orig. Greek bronze – 240 to 150 BC
Ht. Horse 7.5 ft., Boy 2.7 ft. – Length: 9 ft. 6 in., 290 cm
Sculptor: unknown Greek, possibly from Corinth
[see face of boy at chapter end]

The exuberance of this bronze equestrian group is yet another example that later sculptors have equaled but not exceeded the creative skills of the ancient Greeks.

In the Nat. Museum of Athens, first-time viewers of the *Jockey of Artemision* often are astounded by the 9 ½ foot horse and slight boy jockey flying through space.

30,000 Years of Art declares: "There are no close parallels for the approximately life-size horse in full gallop, carrying a boy jockey who glances back over his shoulder... most other equestrian statues are of the static, cavalry type, seldom capturing as this does the thrill and vitality of a horserace." [p 280]

The visual experience compares to standing at the finish-line of the Kentucky Derby as the winner flashes past. Smith says: "The *Horse* is a beautiful thoroughbred... and the *Jockey* is a boy... portrayed with vivid genre realism..." [*Hellenistic Sculpture*, p 54]

Fright on the boy's face is genuine. His cheeks are creased and brow heavily-furrowed. Fifteen is a fair estimate of his age. In ancient times on a swift-paced steed, only experience and luck enabled a young jockey to avoid serious injury or death.

Ragghianti describes it as "one of the most impressive masterpieces of Hellenistic sculpture. The reckless agility of this youngster who, having jumped on the back of the horse, makes an effort to control the reins while turning his head as if listening to cries of instruction... the arms and legs explode in alternate rhythms... the keen yet guileless face of the boy protrudes from the fragile diminutive body with urgent, burning emotional tension." [*Athens Museum*, 1980, p 153-55]

Meletzi adds: "The young rider looks very small... legs parted and arms in movement, he still holds part of the reins. He wears a short chiton attached to the left shoulder. All the muscles are tensed. The legs are bare, except for spurs attached to the heels with thongs. The horse is balanced on two hind hooves, its front hooves raised in the air, all the muscles of its body straining, the face with flaring nostrils superb in its intensity – everything testifies to exceptional artistic mastery." [*Athens Museum*, 1988, p 57]

This national treasure rose in pieces over a decade from the Aegean Sea…found in the same ancient shipwreck as the fore-mentioned *Zeus* #12. The doomed vessel may have been en route to either Constantinople [now Istanbul], Pergamon, or Rome…before sinking off the Cape of Artemision in a stormy sea.

Ragghianti adds: "The dating is uncertain…between 240 and 150 BC. It is a work which manifests the vast exchanges of diverse artistic languages that were opened to Greek figurative culture – from Syria to the Aegean Islands, from Pergamon to Alexandria – in what is generally called the Hellenistic period, extending from the death of Alexander in 323 BC to the Roman conquest of Egypt in 31 BC. The period was too long and the area too vast to make it possible to fix the moment and place in which an exceptionally gifted artist might have created this masterpiece." [p 155]

Subject:

The dangers threatening this young boy are revealed in *The Olympic Games* by Finley and Pleket: "The Olympic horse race followed in the Hippodrome immediately after the chariot race, on the same course. No wonder gentlemen preferred not to ride themselves…riding an unshod horse bareback and without stirrups [neither horse-shoe nor stirrup was known in antiquity] over a field that had just been churned up by chariot-teams could not have been much fun." [p 51]

Galen, a Greek physician from Pergamon in the late 2nd century AD, wrote: "Horse-back riding is a strenuous sport and has been known to rupture parts of the region of the kidneys, and has often brought injuries to the chest or sometimes to spermatic passages – to say nothing of the missteps of the horses, because of which riders have often been pitched from their seat and instantly killed." [p 31]

"The Olympic horse race required a fanned-out line of horses to head for the far turning-post and then back, apparently for only a single lap, about 800 meters." [p 31]

When museum visitors in Athens stand back to view the full 9.6-foot wide leap of the half-suspended horse, their attention is drawn to the detailed heads. The wildly-panting horse – with mouth agape – strains forward with the forelegs in what may be a final leap to victory.

The head of the Ethiopian boy – his skin originally had a black patina – may have turned to check his competition as he digs in his spurs. [*30,000 Years*, p 280] Urgency and emotional tension concentrate and distort his facial features … as he struggles to balance his body – slightly off-center – to the rhythm of the horse.

His right hand held a whip, his left the reins. His eyes were once inlaid, but their material is now missing. On the horse's right hind thigh, a brand of Nike [Winged Victory] can be discerned. Ancient jockeys were usually paid-servants of the horse's owner, and their lives might be considered as slightly-less expendable than the horse.

Sculptor:

Due the grand scale and quality of this sculpture, it likely was commissioned by royalty or a wealthy aristocrat. The unknown but gifted sculptor of this work originally cast the horse in sections, then welded the pieces together.

This bronze has spent most of its life – some 2,100 of its approximately 2,300 years – underwater in the Aegean Sea. The fragmented and badly-damaged horse required painstaking restoration and reassembly over a period of some 40 years … which explains why many art references fail to give it notice.

30,000 Years conjectures: "the Roman general Mummius plundered the sculpture from Corinth in 145 BC … only to lose it when the ship sank on its way to Pergamon." Another reference suggests the horse and rider were en route to Constantinople … a nearer destination.

Durant describes the Roman appetite. "Fulvius carried off 1,015 statues from Pyrrhus' collection in Ambracia … Aemilius Paulus filled 50 chariots in his triumph with the art treasures he had taken from Greece as partial payment for liberating her … Sulla, Verres, Nero, and other Romans were to do likewise through 200 years. Greece was denuded to clothe the Roman mind." [*Caesar & Christ*, p 93]

Had the sea not sequestered these masterpieces over two millennia, they might have been melted down for their bronze...in either Greece or Rome.

Major References:

Nat. Arch. Museum of Athens, 1980, Ragghianti, p 153-55

Hellenistic Sculpture, 1991, Smith, p 54, 239, ph. 58

Nat. Arch. Museum of Athens, guidebook, 1988, p. 57, 72-3

30,000 Years of Art, 2007, Phaidon, p 280

The Olympic Games, 1976, Finley and Pleket. p 31

Arts of the Ancient Greeks, 1972, Brilliant, p 376, photo 379

Greek and Roman Art, 1972, Lawrence, p 236

Nat. Arch. Museum of Athens, 1988, Meletzis, p 57

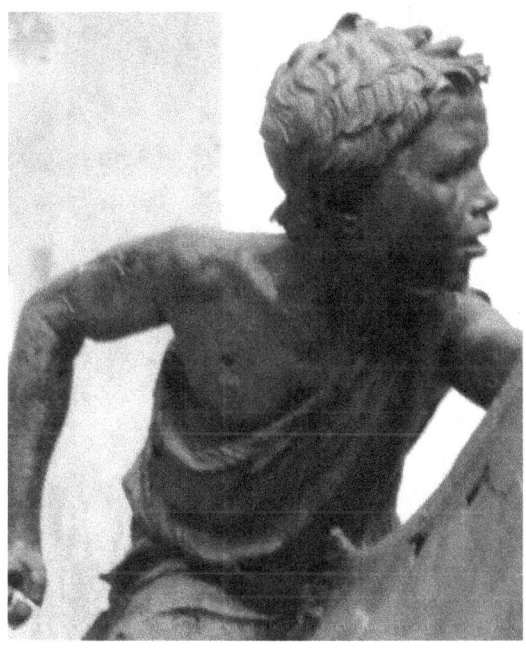

35

CROUCHING APHRODITE

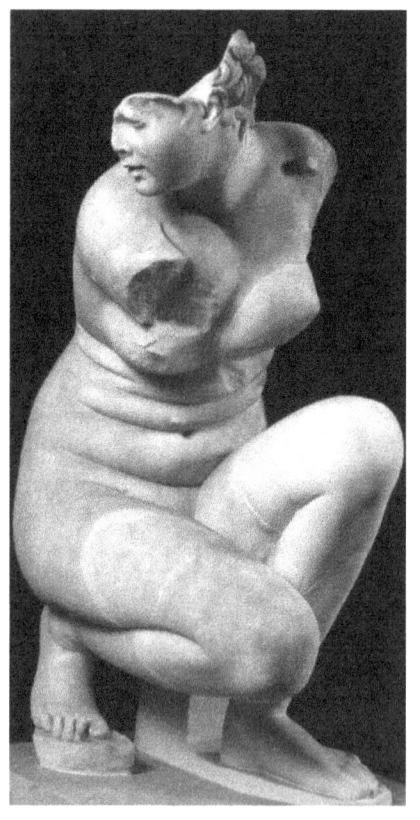

"strongly composed from many points of view...
with harmonious grace...luxuriantly
clad in a rich mantle of soft flesh."
... *Arts of Ancient Greeks*, Brilliant, p 363. 365

Found in baths of Hadrian's Villa – now Terme Mus. Rome*
Greco-Roman Copy: marble – 100 BC – Hellenistic
From: lost bronze Orig. – 240 BC
Ht. 32 in (1.07 m], life-size
Sculptor: Doidalsas [orig.]; marble: unknown sculptor
   *plus, Louvre, Brit. Mus., Vatican, & Hearst Castle

[one century after standing *Aphrodite of Cnidus* #20]

In the middle of the 3rd century BC, the *Crouching Aphrodite* by Doidalsas became one of the most popular statues of the goddess.

Smith says: "The most striking Hellenistic nude Aphrodite is probably the *Crouching Aphrodite*... known in a core of a few but precise copies. The body has a voluptuous sexuality... while the head displays a dynamic turn and unusual strength of expression.

The pose restores the Cnidian's bathing motif... and its 'narrative' crouching posture lessens the direct sexual 'confrontation' posed by the standing Capitoline and Medici figures.

A passage of Pliny mentions – among various Hellenistic statues in the Porticus Octavae at Rome – is a "Venus washing herself." This statue might be the *Crouching Aphrodite* since Pliny seems to contrast it with an Aphrodite standing." [*Hellenistic Sculpture,* p 80-1, fig 102]

R. Brilliant adds: "The bronze original,... took the form of a life-size substantial nude... self-enclosed within its pyramidal shape, yet strongly composed from many points of view... the artist has contained the contrasting movements of limbs and head within a stable but energetic figure realized with harmonious grace as a living female... fully developed and luxuriantly clad in a rich mantle of soft flesh." [*Arts of the Ancient Greeks,* p 363. 365]

The Terme Museum in Rome displays a marble copy of this *Aphrodite*. Over time, it lost both arms and the upper-right quarter of its head. Nevertheless, the balance of the face and the lush figure confirm the fame of the original. The most complete and satisfying view is from the right-side of the kneeling figure, where the left profile of the attractive face is fully available.

Several major Western museums display copies, but none are finely sculpted and also complete. We must view figures from 2 museums – Rome's Terme [above] and the Louvre – to receive a 'combined' view of the goddess.

In the Louvre, their *Crouching Aphrodite* offers the finest torso of any copy. Her shoulders are lovely ... the genuine rolls and curves of the torso tantalize in their realism ... while her skin retains its original smoothness and sheen. Nearby, *Venus de Milo* #48 must 'envy' this final detail.

Though the Vatican copy is complete and reveals the cleverly-placed arms and hands of the original bronze, it is drab compared to the Terme and Louvre figures. Sadly, it also suffers from a gray, severely-mottled surface.

Subject:

Pasquier, in *Louvre: Greek, Etruscan, & Roman Antiquities*, says: "As for the *Crouching Aphrodite*, the theme has never ceased to haunt artist's imaginations ... and reflections of it can be seen in contemporary art. The goddess, at her bath, was accompanied by Eros." [p 47-8]

Hafner states: "Of all Aphrodite statues, this is perhaps the most intimate. The goddess, unaware she is observed, kneels down to her bath with the naturalness of a nymph. She seems to have turned her head in response to a noise which has broken the silence of her solitude." [*Art of Crete, Mycenae, and Greece*, p 247]

In a pretense of shyness, she affects modesty by coyly positioning her limbs. This was an attraction of the earlier *Aphrodite of Cnidus*... yet, here the artist is more subtle.

Hafner explains: "This type of statue became highly popular in the Hellenistic and Roman epochs, because the sculptor makes the goddess use her hands to draw attention to those parts of her body which she affects to hide." [*Art of Crete, Mycenae, and Greece*, p 247]

Regina also describes the Terme figure: "The goddess is portrayed kneeling while she pours water on her back ... she turns to watch it fall, and will rise as soon as she has finished her bath. The unusual position allows the sculptor to depict the full and soft forms of the female body, while creating it within a compact [circular] structure. The 'instability' of the posture … shows the influence of Lysippos, who liked to construct his figures in this way. This type of Aphrodite was a favorite in the decorations of fountains and baths … and, in fact, this statue comes from the Heliocaminus Baths of Hadrian's Villa." [*Museo Nazionale Romano,* p 38]

It is commendable the Roman copyist of the Terme figure – concerned with authenticity – provided the mature woman with an ample abdomen displaying fully <u>realistic wrinkles</u> of a 'crouching' person. [previously noted on *the Seated Scribe* #1]

Sculptor:

Lawrence's *Greek & Roman Sculpture* says: "… the *Aphrodite* crouching in her bath has been ascribed to a Bithynian sculptor, Doidalsas … The series of copies and imitations thus inaugurated grew apace." [p 220, fig 62a]

In 1797, Napoleon took the Vatican copy of the *Crouching Aphrodite* to Paris. It returned in 1815.

The gardens of the Hearst Castle in San Simeon, California display an excellent modern *Crouching Venus* which is complete … sculpted in the Classic style. The artist reversed the positioning of limbs.

Major References:

Louvre: Greek, Etruscan, & Roman Antiquities, 1998, Pasquier, p 46,7

Museo Nazionale Romano, 2005, La Regina, p 38

Greek Art, 1973, Boardman, p. 192, fig 198

Hellenistic Sculpture, 1991, Smith, p 80, (fig. 102)

Arts of the Ancient Greeks, 1972, R. Brilliant, p 363, 365

Greek & Roman Sculpture, 1972, Lawrence, p 220, fig 62a

Art of Crete, Mycenae, and Greece, 1968, Hafner, p 247

Roman Mythology, 1975, Perowne, p 61

36

THE GAUL CHIEFTAIN

OR GAUL KILLING HIMSELF

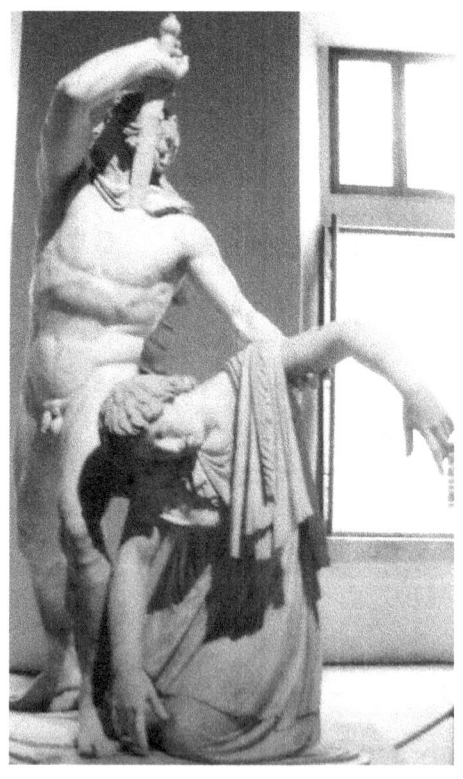

"The circular victory monument" – with the *Gaul Killing
Himself* as its centerpiece – "stands as a masterpiece...
of Hellenistic art." ... Brilliant, *Art of the Ancient Greeks*, p 341

Unearthed, Rome approx. 1623 – now, Palazzo Altemps,* Rome
Greco-Roman copy – 100 to 200 AD – Hellenistic/Baroque style
From: Orig. Greek bronze – 235-230 BC
Ht. 83 in. – marble
Orig. Greek Sculptor: Epigonos
  *museum 1 block north of Piazza Navona

At first sight, this sculpture is shocking and dreadful.
The determined *Gaul Chieftain* – with anguish, yet extreme reason – plunges his sword down through his heart.

Hintzen-Bohlen describes the grievous act. "The prince, striding out powerfully, looks back at his pursuers...as he thrusts his sword into his chest. His left hand holds the arm of his wife, who has already fallen. Details are vividly shown: blood spurts from the Gaul's breast as the point of his sword enters...the mortal wound under his wife's armpit...her closing eyes...her facial expression showing her death agony." [*Art & Architecture*...p 171]

The *Gaul Chieftain* – to save his wife from certain capture, unspeakable abuse, and slavery – has fatally wounded her.

Now, he plunges the sword into his heart to save himself from a similar fate. In the mind of the defeated *Gaul*, the more courageous end is the one now taken.

Carpenter states: "Nowhere else in surviving ancient sculpture – save in *the Laocoon* #51 – has sensationalism been attuned to such a pitch of emotional tension as in the group of the *Gaul Chieftain*." [*Greek Sculpture*, p 222-23]

Gardner advises: "In the best Lysippan tradition, the statuary group can be fully appreciated only by walking around it. From one side, we see the intensely expressive face of the *Gaul*...from another, his powerful body...from a third, the limp and almost lifeless body of the woman. The twisting posture of the man...and the emotional intensity of the suicidal act are hallmarks of the Pergamene 'baroque' style and are closely paralleled later in the frieze on the *Altar of Zeus* #43." [*Art Thru the Ages*, p 177]

The original bronze sculpture was the centerpiece of a raised circular monument – *the Attalid Dedications* – on the acropolis of Pergamon... which included *the Dying Gaul* #37. The circular monument was commissioned by King Attalos after his victories over the Gauls... [or possibly, after the final victory of his son, King Eumenes in approx. 230 BC]. Hafner adds: "Fragments of the pedestal were found, as well as the signature of the famous artist Epigonos." [*Art of Crete, Mycenae.& Greece,* p 234]

Durant is reserved. "These figures show a Classic restraint in the expression of emotion... the conquered suffer the extremes of pain and grief, but die without opera... the conquerors have allowed the artists to portray the virtues, as well as the defeat, of their enemies." [*Life of Greece,* p 623]

King Attalos, by giving dignity to the defeated Gauls, enhances his own status as the victor. These monuments soon became famous and were copied both in his time and later. To Athens, Attalos gave smaller than life-size copies... displayed on the south side of the Acropolis.

Hafner says the marble copy of the *Gaul Chieftain* was "made in Asia Minor and originally intended for Rome. In 222 BC in Italy, the Gauls were decisively beaten, after harassing the Romans for over a century. Attalos, an ally of the Romans, may have underscored their mutual interests through such a gift." [p 234]

When this marble copy arrived in Rome, it was likely put on public exhibit.

Some 150 years later, it became a favorite of Julius Caesar, who is said to have become its owner. It is believed to have been excavated sometime before 1623 in gardens which had belonged to Sallust, an ancient Roman historian.

Subject:

That this Gaul was a chieftain or prince is indicated by the royal cloak, his broad proportions, longer hair, and the squarish facial appearance. His fate, if captured alive, could be a torturous death... or being chained as a slave to work in a mine or other hazardous conditions... until overwork, disease, and deprivation ended his misery.

This Gallic chieftain and his wife are shown as having resolutely chosen to end their own lives rather than suffer the harsh indignities of defeat and capture.

It should be noted the same barbarian Gauls were infamous for inflicting atrocities on their defeated enemies.

These Gauls had emigrated from Europe [France, Switzerland, Belgium, and the Netherlands]. Ancient historian Pausanias provides a description of this Gallic tribe when they first invaded Greece in 279 BC. "They butchered all the males and likewise old women, and babes at their mother's breasts; they drank the blood... High-spirited women and maidens in their flower committed suicide... and those that survived were subjected to every kind of outrage... Some of the Greek women rushed upon the swords of the Gauls, and voluntarily courted death ..." [Durant, p 559]

At Delphi, the Gauls finally were repulsed... and they crossed over to Asia Minor where, for a generation, they terrified the native populations and pillaged its rich coastal city-states. [Smith, p 100-02]

The prominence of Pergamon [*Bergama,* modern Turkey] in histories seldom receives the emphasis it deserves.

Initially, it was a small fortified hill-town on the coast of Asia Minor. "In 282 BC, Lysimachus [Macedonian general and among the 'Successors' to *Alexander the Great*] selected Pergamon for his treasury. He then entrusted Philataerus with the fortified hill and care of 9,000 talents. Philataerus appropriated the money and declared his independence." Conveniently, Lysimachus died one year later. [Durant, p 538, 558, 578]

Under successive Hellenistic rulers, Pergamon rapidly grew and soon became the capital of a minor but prosperous city-state, controlled by a half-Greek monarchy.

In repeated battles between 242 BC and 228 BC, the Gauls attacked the city-state of Pergamon... but were defeated by King Attalos [and his son]. The son, King Eumenes, defeated the Gauls in a final battle in 228 BC. [Carpenter, p 222-23]

The surviving Gauls finally settled in lands well to the north, which they called Galatia [now Turkey]. Its major city was Ancyra, which had been the capital of the Hittites more than 1,200 years earlier. [now Ankara, capital of Turkey]

In the south, Pergamon "became the rival of Alexandria as a center of art and learning…famous for the *Altar of Zeus* #43, its luxurious palaces, its library and theater…The library was second only to Alexandria's in the number of its volumes and the repute of its scholars…for half a century, Pergamon was the finest flower of Hellenic civilization…the last king, Attalos II, bequeathed his kingdom to Rome in 139 BC." [p 578-79]

Sculptor:

The platform of *the Attalid Dedications* is signed 'Work of Epigonos'. Pliny the Elder's *Natural History* [77 BC] mentions Epigonos as the sculptor of *the Dying Gaul* #37

Major References:

Gardner's Art Through the Ages, 1996, Gardner, p 177
Arts of the Ancient Greeks, 1972, Brilliant, p 341-3
Greek Sculpture, 1960, Rhys Carpenter, p 222-23
Life of Greece, 1939, Durant, p 559, 578-79, 623
Hellenistic Sculpture, 1991, Smith, p 100-03
Art and Architecture, Rome & Vatican, 2001, Hintzen-Bohlen, p 171
Art of Crete, Mycenae, and Greece, 1968, Hafner, p 234

37

THE DYING GAUL

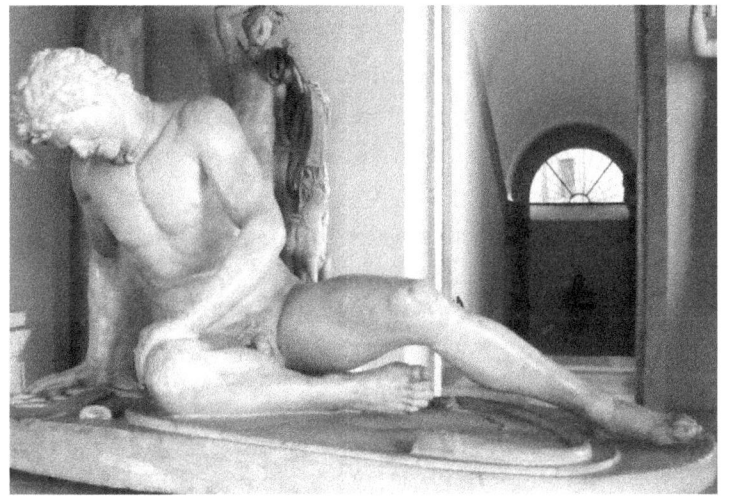

"a magnificent marble statue ... superbly represented"
... *Arts of the Ancient Greeks*, Brilliant, p 341

Unearthed 1623, Rome – now, Capitoline Mus., Rome
Greco-Roman copy – 100 to 200 AD – Hellenistic/Baroque
<u>From:</u> lost Original Greek Ionian bronze – 225 BC
Ht. 28.75 inches, Width. 6 ft. [185 cm] – pale green marble
Orig Greek Sculptor: Epigonos of Pergamon

[see 'face' at chapter end]

W e first notice the uncommon, distinctive, pale-greenish marble. The reclining figure appears to be at rest...supporting
himself by a vertical arm and the left hand on his knee. His face is
contorted. Coming close enough, we notice a stream of blood flowing down his chest.

As life ebbs in his body, the mind of the Gaul warrior strives to
will *death* away. Under his deeply-furrowed brow, his lips part.

The Jansons explain: "Over 6 feet tall, the trumpeter has been
fatally wounded in the chest...as he led his fellow warriors into battle. A
Celtic ethnic is carefully rendered in the leathery body...the distinctive
facial structure...the bristly mustache and shock of hair. The torque
around the neck is specifically Celtic." [*History of Western Art,* p 100]

Robb & Garrison comment: "The use of naturalistic
details...introduced with great restraint...exist not as mere *tours
de force* of technique but to the idea which the figure represents:
<u>the anguish of defeat that kills the spirit</u>...rather than the pain of
physical violence that destroys the flesh." [*Art in the Western World,*
p 448-49]

"Yet...energy diffuses his lithe body in defiance of death...The
supporting right arm generates an opposing force...folds of flesh
at the juncture of pelvis and abdomen emphasize the abdomen's
lateral slide...contending forces are resolved into a state of equilibrium in tension. The warrior is thus <u>suspended in time and space</u>."
[Leigh, *Wall Street Journal:* 1-25-14]

Gardner says: "...the male musculature is rendered in an exaggerated manner – note the tautness of the chest and the bulging
veins of the left leg – implying that the unseen Attalid hero who has
struck down this noble and savage foe must have been an extraordinary man." [*Art Through the Ages,* p 177]

"Clearly, the Gauls were not considered unworthy foes. *'They
knew how to die...barbarians though they were'* is the thought conveyed
by the statue....Death, as we witness it here, is a very concrete physical process..." [Jansons, p 141]

The figure's uniquely green marble, believed from the region
of Pergamon [*Bergama* in modern Turkey] suggests the statue could

have been copied from the original bronze in that ancient city-state. If the sculptor wished to lend an unhealthy pallor to the work, pale green was a good choice.

Monti states when this statuary was unearthed in Rome shortly before 1623: "The finding of the *Dying Gaul* and the *Gaul Chieftain* marked <u>a turning point in the artistic direction of baroque sculpture</u>." [*Capitoline Museums,* p 47, 50]

Within a few years after their discovery, Bernini – famed architect of the new Baroque era – produced his spirited *Apollo & Daphne* #71 ... *David* #70 ... and *Ecstasy of St. Theresa* #72.

Subject:

The *Dying Gaul* appears of high birth by his thick neck band – representing a golden torque – worn by Gauls of wealth and standing. A similar torque is found on statues of Vercingetorix, the great Gallic chieftain who led a revolt against Roman rule until famously conquered by Caesar in 52 BC. Shaven cheeks with a mustache also indicate nobility.

This warrior was a member of Gallic tribes [from northwest Europe] which, in 278-79 BC, invaded Asia Minor and ravaged its population for a generation. [see Chapter #36] Eventually, they were defeated in repeated battles between 241 and 228 BC by King Attalos of Pergamon ... and in a final battle by his son King Eumenes.

Attalos, to celebrate his victories and enhance the fame of Pergamon, commissioned a multi-figured monument [on a raised circular platform] displaying the Gauls as formidable opponents ... giving them noble features and graceful poses. By depicting dignity in the defeated, Attalos intended to elevate his own prestige as the victor.

The bronze group on this circular monument was called the *Attalid Dedications* – "possibly the oldest freestanding sculptural monument for a city square in Western art." [Brilliant, p 341]

[centerpiece of bronze monument was *the Gaul Chieftain* #36]

Attalos, in a generous gesture, gave marble replicas [under-life-size] of his *Attalid* statues to Athens, where they were exhibited on the south side of the Acropolis.

It is possible Attalos commissioned the *Dying Gaul* and gifted it to Rome.

Voorhis says: "The surviving marble version of the statue in the Capitoline Museum was manufactured for display in Rome, where it may have been installed alongside the *Gaul Chieftain* #36." [*Encyclo Sculpt,* p 478]

The *Dying Gaul* was excavated from gardens once belonging to Sallust, an ancient Roman historian. The gardens were in the area of the current Villa Ludovisi, whose inventory recorded the statue in 1623. Other ancient statuary found during these excavations includes the *Aphrodite Altar* #13, the *Ares with Eros* #27, and possibly the *Gaul Chieftain* #36.

[since all 5 sculptures mentioned above were excavated in 'the gardens of Sallust', they may have been deliberately buried to hide them from barbarian invaders]

In 1737, Pope Clement XII purchased the *Dying Gaul.* In 1797, Napoleon took it to Paris…it was returned in 1815.

Sculptor:

A signature on a long platform of the *Attalid Dedications* is signed "Work of Epigonos". Pliny the Elder's *Natural History* [77 BC] mentions Epigonos as the sculptor of a dying trumpeter in bronze. This suggests Epigonos is the original creator of the statue…as, on its shield is a curved trumpet. [*Voorhis*..p 478]

Voorhis adds: "Restorations made to the statue after its discovery include the right arm [in legend attributed to Michelangelo, thus adding to the statue's fame] and large portions of the plinth." [p 477]

Other statues from 'Attalid Dedications' monument:

… *Gaul Chieftain* – in Rome's Museo Nazionale Romano

... *Helmeted Gaul, Wounded* – Naples Nat. Arch. Museum
... *Amazon Warrior* – Naples Nat. Arch. Museum
... *Hooded Persian Head* – Museo Nazionale Romano
... *Head of Bearded Gaul* – Vatican

Major References:

Greek Sculpture, 1960, Rhys Carpenter, p 222-23
Basic History of Western Art, 2006, Janson & Janson, p 100
Wall Street Journal, 1-25-2014, Catesby Leigh, p C13
Arts of the Ancient Greeks, 1972, Brilliant, p 341-2
Encyclopedia of Sculpture, 2006, p. 477-8
30,000 Years of Art, 2007, Phaidon Press, p 268
Hellenistic Sculpture, 1991, Smith, p 100-03
Art Through the Ages, 1996, Vol. I, Gardner, p 177
Life of Greece, 1939, Durant, p 578, 623, 111, p 224
Art of the Western World, 1953, Robb & Garrison, p 448-449
Capitoline Museums, Rome, 1984, Monti, p 47, 50

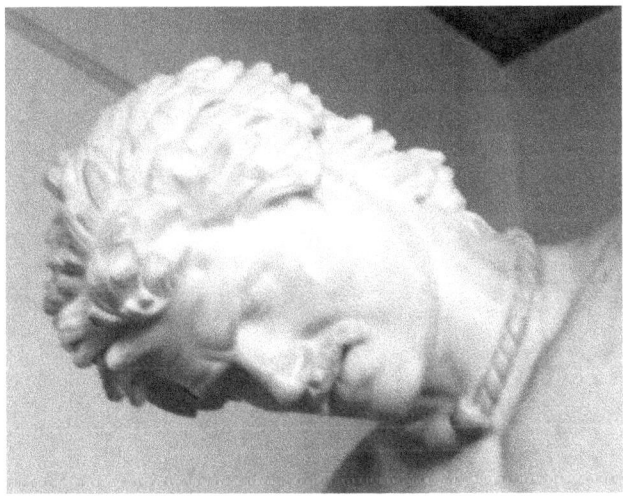

38
WINGED VICTORY
OF SAMOTHRACE

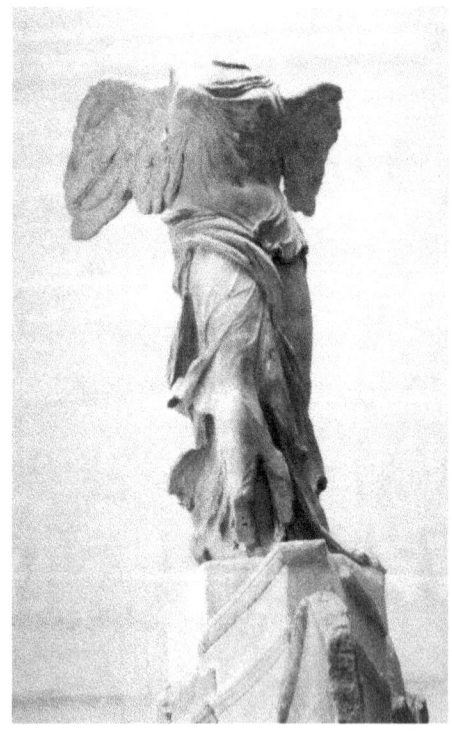

"One of the great masterpieces of the Hellenistic style...
Art and nature are here combined in one of the most
successful works of sculpture ever fashioned."
...Gardner, *Art Through the Ages*, 1996, p 177

Found 1863 on island of Samothrace – now, in Louvre
Orig. Greek – approx. 200 BC – Hellenistic and Baroque
Ht. 9 feet [2.45 m] – white Parian marble [island of Paros]
Sculptor: Pythokritos of Rhodes
  *cleaned 2013- 2014, now close to its original white

R odin declared: "On Sundays – when I go up to the *Samothrace* – I feel an eternal youth…an inspiration of happiness!" [*Rodin*, p 16]

Her elegant figure is 9 feet tall. To the ancient Greeks, she was Nike, their goddess of victory.

Durant considers her: "the sculptural masterpiece of the Louvre." [*Life of Greece*, p 624]

The Jansons state: "The *Nike of Samothrace* deserves her fame as the greatest surviving masterpiece of Hellenistic sculpture." [*Basic History Western* Art, p 103]

[a first-time visitor to this statue – displayed atop the famed Daru Escalier, one of the world's most dignified staircases – is advised to make an unhurried approach from the far west end of the great hall of 'Large Format French Paintings'… on the first floor of Denon Gallery]

This approach permits the *Winged Victory* to gradually unfold.

R. Brilliant offers high compliment: "spectacular magnificence… the dramatic pose of sudden descent fuses in a masterful conception of victory at sea." [*Arts… Greeks*, p 355]

We see *the Winged Victory* as she – having descended from Mt. Olympus – now alights on the prow of a fast-moving Greek trireme [warship] to "crown its commander and crew… following their victory" against a Syrian fleet. [*Encyclo Sculpt*, Dillon, p 1199]

The Jansons add: "A powerful head-wind beats at her body and outspread wings. The invisible onrushing air… not only balances the forward movement of the figure but also shapes every fold of the wonderfully animated drapery. As a result, there is an active relationship between the statue and the space around it such as we have never seen before." [p 102-03]

Salt spray thrown up by the prow of the trireme has saturated the gauze-like, transparent cloth of her chiton [blouse], and her woolen mantle [cloak]. The wetted garments cling to the thrusting torso of the divine goddess and swirl violently behind her.

Her right thigh pushes profoundly forward ... her right arm [missing] raises high in victory ... lifting the right shoulder and chest in bold presentations. The thin chiton slips off her shoulder.

Dillon adds: "The top edge of the garment clings suggestively to the upper curve of her right breast. The broad wings – stretching up and back to steady the landing – are beautifully and meticulously detailed." [*Encyclo Sculpt*, p 1199]

[the right hand – unearthed in 1950 – is in a glass case to the right of the statue. The position of its thumb and index finger suggest they held a thin victory wreath, as seen on other Victory statues. Her missing left arm may have held a trumpet].

She is best viewed from her left ... at three-quarter view ... from below.

When an over-large crowd gathers around her, climb the nearby stairway overlooking and facing the *Winged Victory*. The unobstructed view is peaceful and gratifying.

[another <u>winged woman</u> – brandishing her sword – leads *the Departure of Volunteers* #82 on the Arch of Triumph in Paris. The French know her as their 'Goddess of Liberty']

Subject:

Nike was esteemed and honored by Greek military commanders, competitive athletes, and grateful citizens. Her best-known sculptures depict her flying or standing.

The specific triumph to which the *Winged Victory of Samothrace* was dedicated is believed by many historians to be the Greek-Rhodian fleet's victory over the Syrian fleet of King Antiochus III in about 191 BC...whose ships had been assembled by Hannibal. [Durant, III p 55 – Brilliant p 355 – Curtis p 74]

Greek-Rhodians were extraordinarily grateful for this victory. Had they lost, the Syrian king might have enslaved them. In the Mediterranean world, Greek slaves were the most prized...for their "superior intelligence, language, and culture." [Carpenter, p 302]

Original Location – Sanctuary of the Great Gods:

In the first half of the 4th century BC, the ancient Greeks and Macedonians built a 'Sanctuary of the Great Gods' on Samothrace – an island in the northern Aegean Sea [25 miles off the coast of Greece]

In antiquity, secret and mysterious rites were conducted on the isolated island.

The hillside Sanctuary was near enough to the island's rocky shoreline that its majestic monuments could be displayed to all who sailed the trade route to the Black Sea. Until modern times, this island remained relatively inaccessible due to its lack of safe landings...which discouraged pirates and other marauders.

Use of the Sanctuary was a prerogative of royal families in the region, particularly from Macedonia. The beautiful Olympias – a princess from Epirus who became the mother of Alexander the Great – is said to have met King Philip II of Macedonia when visiting Samothrace.

Barr's *Will of Zeus* reveals: "Although Philip had made a number of political marriages, he married Olympias for love." [p 393-94] "He had met her...during her initiation into a mystery cult...when she was 20 and he was 27. Tradition reports Olympias – an unusually zealous and inspired Bacchante and worshiper of the wine god Dionysus – would distribute to fellow revelers tame serpents, which coiled about the women's wands as they danced wildly, and this spectacle terrified the men." [p 393-94]

Some 150 years after Alexander's birth, the *Winged Victory* was carved and installed on the island...to commemorate the defeat of a 'dynasty' established by one of Alexander's 'successor' generals.

It is likely earthquakes and landslides damaged the statue, though religious intolerance or barbarian invasions may have added to its fragmented condition and missing elements.

From the heights of the island's Mount Fengari, legend suggests *Poseidon* observed the Trojan War to the east. Some 1,200 years later, from the same mile-high summit, an observer could have seen dust rising from the Battle of Philippi – 75 miles northwest – where Octavian [later Augustus] and Mark Antony defeated Brutus and Cassius [assassins of Caesar].

Eleven years later, Octavian [Augustus] would fight his former friend Mark Antony [and Cleopatra] for dominance at the Battle of Actium. Antony and his lover lost, essentially ending the Roman Republic in 31 BC.

This date also is considered the end of the artistically-creative Hellenistic Age – a period in which sculptures [particularly, the *Winged Victory*] were carved with far more complexity and emotional energy than during the preceding Classical age.

In the words of historian Will Durant: "an age of freedom ended and an age of discipline began."

Discoverer – Charles Champoiseau:

Some 1900 years after the end of the Hellenistic Age, Champoiseau [French diplomat and amateur archeologist] wrote a letter to Napoleon III proposing to enrich the Louvre with Hellenistic art. The letter explained, while it was no longer possible to gather statues on the Greek mainland, such treasures could still be secured on many Aegean islands under the control of the Turks. It urged haste as other European countries were rapidly seizing treasures in the region, and locals were using ancient sculptures for building materials. The Greek-speaking French diplomat asked for 55,000 francs per year for four years. Napoleon III agreed.

In March 1863, Champoiseau found 118 fragments of this statue on a terrace in the Sanctuary of the Great Gods. His account: "While workers started to clear ground close to a covered promenade near a large temple, I paced some 50 meters away...my eyes scanning the uneven ground for fragments. My eyes suddenly stopped on some white marble barely sticking out of the ground. I cleared away dirt myself and quickly discovered it was the breast of a woman and quite admirably done...I called my workers over to dig out the rest of the marble, while I continued to search the ground. After the workers had dug down through two feet of dirt and pebbles, a worker screamed out: 'Monsieur! We have found a woman!' After I inspected the fragmented body, I immediately sent a message to the French Ambassador in Constantinople to send a ship so we could remove the find from the island." [*Victoire de Samothrace*, 2000, Ellenberger]

On May 2, 1863, the l'Ajaccio [ship] arrived...4 days were required to clear a 1,200-meter path down to the shoreline to carry the fragmented statue aboard.

[a dozen irregular blocks of grey Rhodian marble – fragments of a pedestal in the form of a ship's prow, 6.5 feet long – were found. Champoiseau, near the end of his funds, decided to take only the statue and left an official document stating the rights of France over the pedestal]

The l'Ajaccio ship transferred the *Winged Victory* to a faster corvette which spirited it across the Mediterranean to a French port near Toulon...from there the statue continued to Paris. The Louvre required 3 years to assemble the fragments, not including wings. The statue was then exhibited in a minor corner of the Hall of Caryatids, where it remained for 20 years.

In 1879, 16 years after Champoiseau found the *Victory*, he returned to the island of Samothrace to recover the pedestal. Finding and assembling these fragments required 4 more years, and the prow was shipped to Paris.

In 1884, *the Winged Victory of Samothrace* was finally installed.

Sculptor:

Scholars A.W. Lawrence, Richard Brilliant, and John Boardman suggest its highly-skilled sculptor was Pythokrites of Rhodes...due to an inscription 'Rhodhios' seen on the pedestal base. Pottery found during excavation of the excedra [its enclosure] has been dated to around 200 BC; and, stylistically, the statue is said to fit best around 200 BC." [Dillon, p 1199-2000]

The inscription 'Rhodhios' also explains why art historians believe a Hellenistic king from Rhodes commissioned the Nike around 200 BC...to celebrate a victory at sea over the Seleucid forces of Antiochus III.

During the original sculpting of this statue and its base, it is likely more than one sculptor was involved.

Most of the body of *the Winged Victory* – below the bust and to the feet – was carved from one block of marble. Other blocks yielded the bust, head, wings, and portions of the drapery. Since the right wing was never found, a plaster wing was created at the Louvre.

For an idea of how the missing head of the *Samothrace* may have appeared, see the serene, bronze head known as the Aphrodite of Satala in the British Museum...originally from Satala, Armenia.

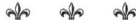

Another Winged Victory...in ruins of ancient Cyrene [Libya]

She stands high on the prow of a 'trireme', with a pair of dolphins below. Her arms and head are missing...plus both wings. This may be a Roman copy. The current status of this sculpture is uncertain...due to instability in the aftermath of Libya's recent revolution.

The image below is on a Libyan postcard, dated Oct 5, 2005.

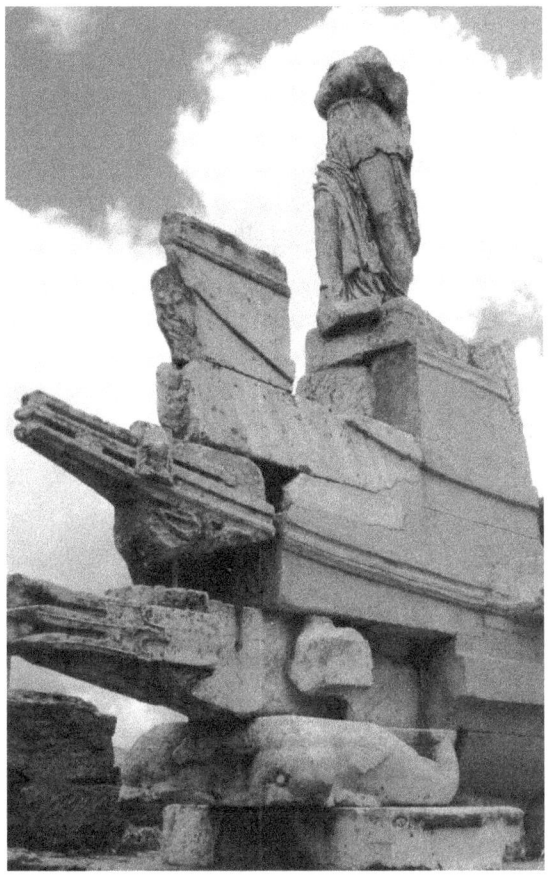

Major References:

Victoire de Samothrace, 2000, Ellenberger, all
Rodin: Sculpture & Drawings, 2001, Nat. Gallery Australia, p 16
Art Through the Ages, 1996, Gardner, p 177
Encyclopedia of Sculpture, 2004, Dillon, p 1199-1200
History of World Sculpture, 1968, Bazin, p 158
30,000 Years of Art, 2007, Phaidon, p 275
Basic History of Western Art, 2006, Janson & Janson, p 102-03
Arts of the Ancient Greeks, 1972, p 355-56
Greek and Roman Sculpture, 1972, Lawrence, p 226
The Will of Zeus, 1961, Barr, p 393-94

Greek Art, 1973, Boardman, p 196

Hellenistic Sculpture, 1991, Smith, p 77-8, fig. 97

The Life of Greece, 1939, Durant, 55, 624

Caesar and Christ, 1944, Durant, p 55, 85-6

The Greek Islands, 1978, Durrell, 1978,

The Louvre, 2007, Francesca Curti, p 74

Everyday Life in Ancient Times, 1958, Carpenter, p 302

39

OLD MARKET WOMAN

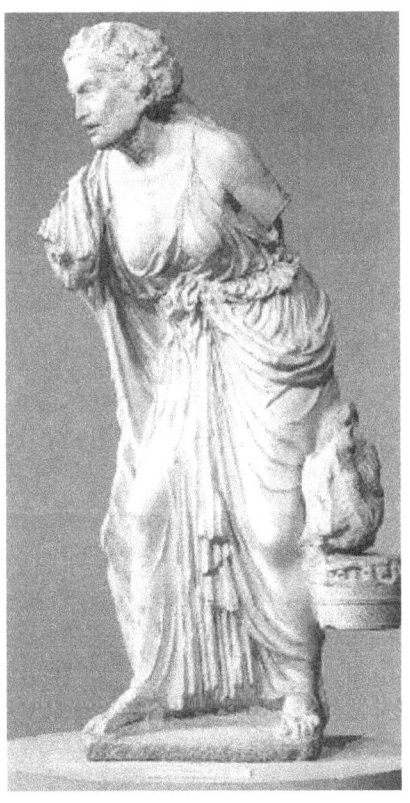

or better, THE OLD FESTIVE WOMAN
"Roman artists developed ideas of their own, notably in studies
of old age... perhaps, the best... is the *Old Market Woman*..."
... *Greek & Roman Sculpture*, Lawrence, p 262-3

Found 1907, in Rome – now, New York Met. Mus. of Art
Greco-Roman copy – approx. AD 14 to 68
From: Orig. Greco-Roman Bronze – 200 BC – late Hellenistic
Ht. 49.6 inches [126 cm] – Pentelic marble
Sculptor: unknown Greek or Roman

In the past, this determined, festive woman has been described as 'a harsh and exaggerated satire of old age'.

The discerning eye perceives far more than 'satire' in this beguiling masterpiece.

Durant cautions: "Youth cannot last forever… nor are its charms supreme… the life of Greece, like every life, had to have a natural subsidence, and accept a ripe old age." [*Life of Greece*, p 625]

[the famed historian overlooks that *ripe old age* may reign *supreme* with the unconditional love between grandparents and grandchildren… plus, the opportunity to pursue whatever makes our hearts sing]

When sculptors in the late Hellenistic era tired of carving gods and 'idealized' generals, politicians, athletes, etc., they turned ever more to stark realism and bizarre subjects in searching for originality. By 200 BC, wealthy art patrons of ancient Rome had begun to commission statuary intended to amuse… shock… and deceive.

Our 'festive' old woman provides all three.

Durant adds: Greek artists of the late Hellenistic age: "took delight in representing… absurdities of human life… they sought unhackneyed subjects in children and peasants… in desolate derelicts like the *Old Market Woman*." [p 624-26]

[the term '*desolate derelicts*' may be undue]

The Roman art patron who commissioned this statue could have displayed it on the manicured grounds of a palatial villa. As he escorted guests about his estate, he might guide them first through his Classic Greek statuary [demonstrating wealth]...then, to his early Hellenistic works [establishing fine taste]...and, finally...he surprises his guests with the *Old Woman*.

After initial aversion, the guests might sense sympathy for the elderly woman carrying her heavy burden.

Gardner's 1980 *Art Through the Ages* harshly declares: "The bent, hobbling creature is offered to the viewer as an object of contempt, pity, or disgust, depending on his temperament." [p 148]

By 1996, Gardner is less harsh, but still short-sighted: "... <u>one of the finest preserved statues of this type</u> depicts a haggard old woman bringing chickens and a basket of fruits and vegetables to sell in the market. Her face is wrinkled, her body bent with age, and her spirit is broken by a lifetime of poverty..." [p 181]

Lawrence's *Greek & Roman Sculpture* opines: "Roman artists developed ideas of their own, notably in their studies of old age. Perhaps, <u>the best of these statues is the *Old Market Woman* at the N.Y. Met Mus of Art</u>. The face – considerably restored, but correctly – is sunken, the neck skinny, and the breasts flabby, while the whole figure is arthritic...only in the legs and feet is there any tempering of the harsh realism. At her left side are some chickens and a basket of fruit, and probably her right arm [missing] held other produce for sale." [p 262-63]

Hafner adds: "The outspoken realism evident in this figure of an old woman is characteristic of this phase of Greek art. The love of detail is in conformity with an attitude of mind that sees the great in the small...." [p 242]

Casual observers – Durant, Gardner, and Lawrence above – miss important aspects of this highly-detailed sculpture.

Subject:

This woman, by her appearance, is certainly old. Yet, we need not pity her.

It's doubtful she is "desolate"... "derelict"... or going to "market."

To Lawrence's credit, he briefly recalls: "The ivy-wreath encircling the handkerchief on the head may point to the celebration of some Bacchic festival." [p 263]

More thorough, Smith in *Hellenistic Sculpture* states the *Old Woman*: "...wears a fine dress and delicate sandals, clearly her best, not for the farmyard. She is walking, on her way to a Dionysus festival...Her basket contains poultry." [p 138, fig 175]

The N.Y. Met Museum of Art fully enlightens: "The woman wears a thin elegant dress, thong sandals, and a crown of Dionysiac ivy leaves. She may be dressed for a festival...and the birds [poultry] and basket of fruit she carries might be offerings [to Dionysus]. Her garment has slipped off her shoulder, a detail often seen in representations of old women...that hints at the liberation of the elderly from restrictions imposed on women of child-bearing years. The piece may be a copy of an older Hellenistic model or a creation of the Roman period in a tradition that was still alive. It seems to have been deliberately damaged, probably in late antiquity, when such a pagan image would have provoked hostility." [website, 2010]

It is comforting to imagine this slow-moving but steadfast woman – at the end of her journey – merrily feasting and celebrating with friends and others. Dionysus is best known as the Greek god of wine...a beverage she can be expected to enjoy in generous measure with many delectable food offerings. Best of all, she and her fellow Dionysians will dance the night away in unrestrained pleasure.

We may envy this elderly festive woman...admire her example...and wish ourselves a similar, joyful destiny.

Brilliant's *Arts of the Ancient Greeks* mentions: "the orgiastic cults of Dionysus and Priapus" in his commentary...and also the *Drunken Old Woman* #40. [p 377, 380]

Note: to view Dionysus, the Greek god of wine & laughter, see *the Dance!* #84

Sculptor:

While the creator of this statue is unknown, his work must have been widely recognized in his time. He was either a Greek working in Sicily or at a settlement in Italy.... or a highly-skilled Roman.

During the great flowering of art accompanying the Hellenistic age, Durant observes: "the spirit of the age was for experiment, individualism, naturalism, and realism, with a strong countercurrent toward imagination, idealism, sentiment, and dramatic effect." [p 625] Greek artists "no longer confined themselves to the perfect and the beautiful ... the impetus of the Greek genius kept Greek art, like Greek science and philosophy, near their zenith to the end. There, Rome would find it, and pass it on." [p 626]

To view other examples of sentimental art during the late Hellenistic period, see the *Old Drunken Woman* #40 ... *the Pseudo-Seneca* #41 ... and *Man of Delos* #46.

Note to Met: your description is refreshingly accurate. Why not correct your title, too?

Major References:

Arts of the Ancient Greeks, 1972, Brilliant, p 377, 380
New York Metropolitan Museum, website, 2010
Hellenistic Sculpture, 1991, Smith, p 138, 153
Art of Crete, Mycenae, and Greece, 1968, Hafner, p 242
Art through the Ages I, 1980, Gardner, p 148
Life of Greece, 1939, Durant, p 626
Greek and Roman Sculpture, 1972, Lawrence, p 262-3, pl. 81a

40
DRUNKEN OLD WOMAN

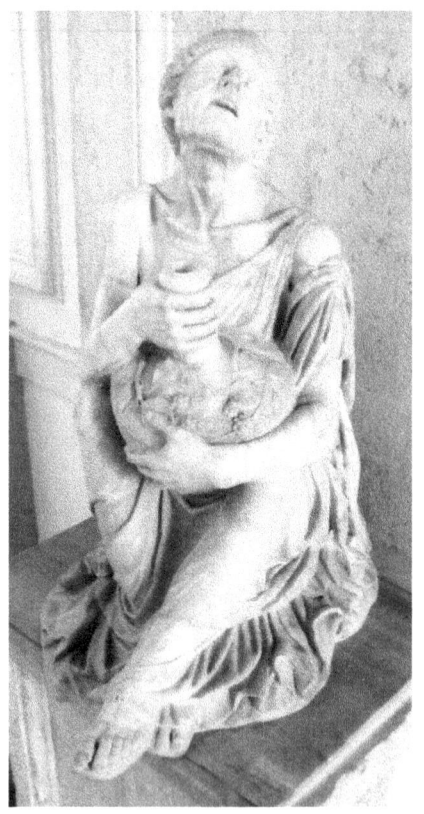

"The expression of rapture on the face of the
Drunken Old Woman... has been wonderfully rendered."
... *Rome: Eternally Beautiful*, Fattorusso, p 266
[see her side-view at chapter end]

Found in Hellenistic villa – now, Capitoline Mus., Rome*
Greco-Roman copy – approx. 50 BC
From: Orig. Greek bronze [lost] – 200 BC – late Hellenistic
Ht. [92 cm] – marble
Orig. Sculptor: Myron of Smyrna [not of *Discus Thrower*]
  * also, Glyptothek Museum, Munich

Here again, as in the *Old Market Woman* #39, the ancient sculptor delights in leading his viewer astray.

In *Rome: Eternally Beautiful*, Fattorusso astutely declares: "The <u>expression of rapture on the face of the *Drunken Old Woman*</u> – who is clasping with arms and legs her friend, a corpulent amphora – <u>has been wonderfully rendered</u>." [p 266]

Lawrence observes: "The drapery may be compared with that on the *Gigantomachy* #43…the Munich [Glyptothek] statue alone preserves the head, with a shrunken wrinkled face and a fatuous gap-toothed smile. The arms hug a wine-jar of the Hellenistic type called a *lagynos*. The subject is not a new one, for drunkenness had long held a place in the repertory of artists…and old age provided the caricaturists of the previous two centuries with abundant material of the same nature. It is a statue intended to exhibit the perfection of the sculptor's technique…artists now rioted in the freedom which their skill had given to them." [*Greek & Roman Sculpture*, p 230]

Carpenter [his word '*Hag*' is inept*] says: "Myron's *Drunken Hag*, famous in antiquity, may be identified in copies familiar to every visitor to the museums in Rome and Munich. The head and neck, and especially the grimacing face of the hag, have presumably been tampered with by the copyist and to a lesser degree by the modern restorer…anxious to emphasize the crass stupor of the figure…." [*Greek Sculpture*, p 134]

*hag defined: *a witch, an ugly often vicious old woman*

Green accurately describes the Munich figure: "The new realism…is hard, tough, direct, brutal…" and he adds: "her dress, the *peronema* [between knee and ankle] indicates respectable social standing." [*Alexander to Actium,* p 576-77]

Smith summarizes: "The jar is a well-known Hellenistic type, and clearly recognizable as a wine container by the Dionysian ivy on its shoulder. The woman is clearly meant to be drunk, but to see her as a genre study of aged alcoholism would reflect a modern perspective. She is, rather, <u>a laughing figure ... in the care of the wine god</u>. She bares her teeth like trouble-free satyrs and maenads ... she is *hilara* – merry or exhilarated. Her body is ruined by age, emphasized by her exposed bony shoulder. Her dress has slipped, in drunkenness perhaps ... but also as an ironical or mock-coquettish reference to her vanished sexual attraction. The figure is both <u>a study of old age and a statement of Dionysus' powers. He can make an old hag laugh at her fate and at the passing viewer.</u>" [*Hellenistic Sculpture,* p 137-38]

Smith reminds us: "Dionysus was a particularly-favored Hellenistic deity. His most popular function ... was as god of wine, laughter, and release." [p 127]

Of the wine jar or *lagynos,* Smith adds: "we know of a particularly drunken Dionysian festival at Alexandria, called the *Lagynophoria* ... established in the later 3rd century BC by Ptolemy IV ... a great devotee of Dionysus and of this festival. The statue might then have been a votive [expressing devotion] connected with such a festival." [p 138]

Note: to view a more recent Dionysus [1869] see *the Dance!* #84

Subject:

This image of old age and inebriation – initially appearing harsh and uncompromising – reveals far more upon close inspection.

Zanker notes "a toothless smile" on the heavily-wrinkled face ... but he also observes "<u>fine earrings and rings, a well-prepared coiffure, and a fancy tunic ... all suggesting this woman was once a prosperous hetaira</u> – a woman in the Greek world who traded her beauty and charm to obtain wealth and social position. Portrayed with strong realism, initially she may appear pathetic ... but her past may have been richly lived and enjoyed. For all her superficial sadness, her memories may be quite fond." It should be noted that the hetaira were often among the best educated Athenian women. [*Modes of Viewing in Hellenistic Poetry and Art,* 2008}

The most famous hetaira of ancient Athens – Phyrne, the lover of sculptor Praxiteles – is said to have posed for the artist when he created his renowned *Aphrodite of Cnidus* #20, the first nude statue of the goddess in Greek art.

Durant describes this distinguished woman: "The beauty of Phyrne is the talk of 4th century Athens, since she never appears in public except completely veiled...but, at the Eleusinian festival, and again on the feast of the Poseidonia, she disrobes in the sight of all, lets down her hair, and goes to bathe in the sea." [*Life of Greece,* Durant, p 300]

It is speculative to assume Myron of Smyrna had in mind the lovely Phyrne [in her later years] when he sculpted the original *Drunken Old Woman.* However, he would have been familiar with Praxiteles' *Aphrodite*...as this statue was created some 170 years earlier...and had become the most famous in the Mediterranean world.

In ancient Greece, it was possible for a hetaera to enjoy a respected position in society...and, of course, she could be 'festive' at any age.

Brilliant provides a summary of both this statue and the *Old Shepheress*: "They are costly, life-size marble replicas of an anonymous reality...Here is sentimentality perfected as a precious attitude, carefully walling off the unpleasantness of life by making amusing images of it...an ideal late Hellenistic remedy for a world in decline. Even if some of these motifs may have had an element of religious significance in connection with the orgiastic cults of Dionysus and Priapus, the mundane exactness of these images is far removed from the idealizations of the Greek classical age." [*Arts of the Ancient Greeks,* p 377, 380]

In the great Roman villas – during the late Hellenistic age – these sentimental masterpieces understandably were more popular and appreciated for their realism than the relatively dull 'idealizations' of the distant past.

Sculptor:

Pliny, in discussing the sculptor of the original Greek version, mentions a Boetian sculptor of the 2nd C BC with the name, Myron of Smyrna. [Smith, p 138] This Myron is not to be confused with the more famed sculptor who created the *Discus Thrower* some 250 years earlier.

Most likely, the *Drunken Old Woman* statues in Rome and Munich are Greco-Roman marble copies, and their sculptors were not 'recognized' at the time they created their works.

Major References:

Ancient Greece, the Dawn of the Western World, 1997, Durando, p 156

Arts of the Ancient Greeks, 1972, Brilliant, p 376-77, 380-81

Modes of Viewing in Hellenistic Poetry and Art, 2008, Graham Zanker

Rome: Eternally Beautiful, 1937, Fattorusso, p 266

Alexander to Actium, 1990, Green, p 576-7

Hellenistic Sculpture, 1991, Smith, p 137-38, pl 174

Greek Sculpture, 1960, Carpenter, p 134-5, pl XX

Greek and Roman Sculpture, 1972, Lawrence, p 229-30

Capitoline Museums, Rome, 1984, Monti, p 16, 1

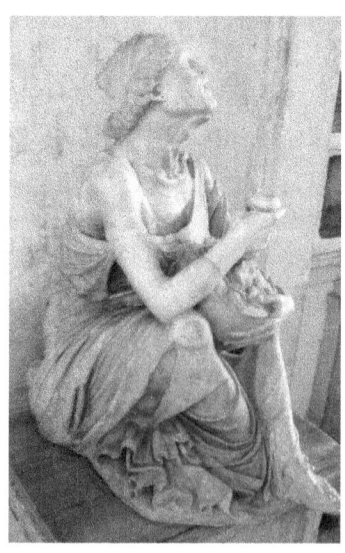

41

PSEUDO-SENECA

OR HESIOD THE POET

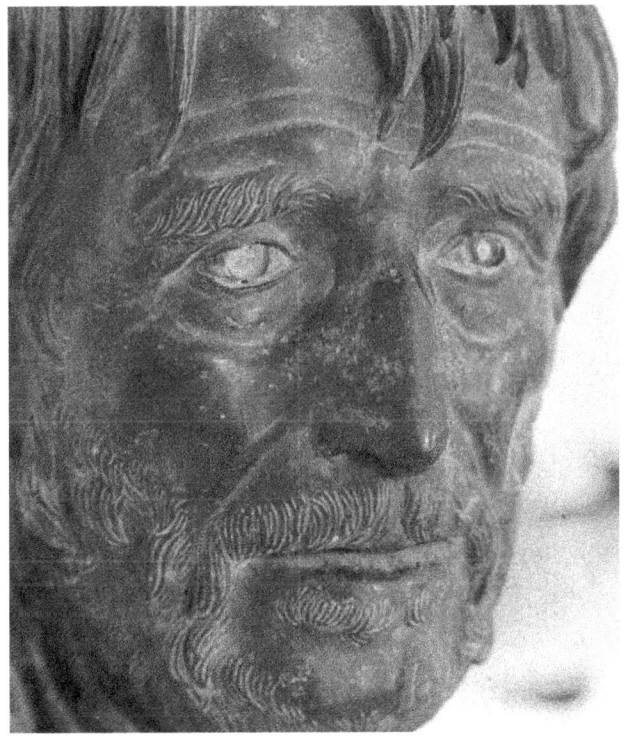

"...apart from *the Cynic*...there is no other even
remotely comparable to this one in its unrestrained
rendering of passion, old age, and dishevelment."
...Zanker, *Mask of Socrates*, 1995, *p 150*

Found 1754, Herculaneum – now, Naples Arch. Mus.
Greco-Roman copy – 22 BC to AD 79 – late Hellenistic
From: Orig. Greek bronze [lost] – 200 BC – late Hellenistic
Ht. 13 in. [33 cm] – bronze
Sculptor: unknown Greco-Roman

The face of this exceptional bronze bust suggests a life spent under the harsh sun ... the survivor of a great calamity ... extreme old age ... or even a tragic actor. His identity remains unknown.

Janneau & Hoog state: "The viewer's eyes are instantly drawn to the strands of hair and beard ... then, one feels and appreciates the structural impact of the head ... and the character of the subject. The portrait's strength stems from the attention to detail ... representing a Roman work." [*Sculpture: Origins to Today,* p 75-6]

Zanker calls this sculpture a "superb copy" and states: "apart from the statue of the Cynic in the Capitoline [Museum], there is no other even remotely comparable to this one in its unrestrained rendering of passion, old age, and dishevelment." [*Mask of Socrates,* p 150]

Smith says: "The formal dissolution and surface plasticity used to represent the bodily shell of 'men of wisdom' is found in extreme form in two major portraits ... the *Hellenistic Blind Homer* and the *Pseudo-Seneca.* The *Pseudo-Seneca* combines exaggerated rhetorical pathos with strong iconographical references to genre works of peasant low life. He is most easily taken as a Hellenistic interpretation of *Hesiod,* the grim poet of agricultural toil." [*Hellenistic Sculpture,* p 36-7]

It also is possible this bronze was created solely for the pleasure of its subject [or the sculptor] ... and, that it does not represent a particular historical figure. The only certain fact of its past is it was excavated in 1754 from the Villa dei Papiri in Herculaneum [near Naples] ... where it had been buried by lava in AD 79 during the historic eruption of Mount Vesuvius.

Subject:

After its discovery, many art authorities were quick to assign the bronze bust to Seneca – the famed Roman philosopher, poet, and statesman who lived from 4 BC to AD 65. Later, other authorities believed the head to be Hesiod, an 8th C. BC poet who lived in poverty... composing verse while herding goats.

Durant suggests it could be a common man from the streets: "When the artist left the palace [where he lived with his patron] and roamed the streets, he could give free play to the Italic imp of humorous truth. Some old man – surely less equipped with wisdom and denarii than the philosopher-premier [Seneca] – posed for the disheveled scarecrow once labeled Seneca." [*Caesar & Christ*, p 351]

Brilliant says the bust is of an "unknown subject... considered by many to be an invented portrait of rough Hesiod or coarse Aristophanes [Greek playwright]. Whoever the *Pseudo-Seneca* represents, his portrait reveals an old man, tough and haggard, but intelligent..." [*Art Through the Ages*, p 397-98]

Lawrence concludes the bronze head originally came from a statue in Pergamon and adds: "None of the many guesses at the subject of this doubtless imaginary portrait has yet carried conviction, though he must have been a very famous personage." [*Greek & Roman Sculpture*, p 251]

Seneca [as choice]:

Since the life of *Seneca* was contemporary to the era in which the Greco-Roman head was cast, it is understandable why the initial identity of *Seneca* was adopted. He died in AD 65... 13 years before Mount Vesuvius erupted in AD 79. If this bust is an original modeled from Seneca in life, it could have been cast sometime between approximately AD 50 and AD 65.

Durant reminds us Seneca wrote: "Abundance of food dulls the wits; excess of food strangles the soul." Durant also reveals Seneca "drank only water and ate so sparingly that when he died his body was emaciated through undernourishment." [*Caesar & Christ*, p 303]

In 1813, the discovery of a double herm – including an inscribed bust of Seneca [now in Berlin] – revealed a thick face with heavy jowls and fleshy shoulders. This is contrary to the 'slim' appearance of the bust found in Herculaneum. Consequently, the bust currently in Naples was re-classified as *Pseudo-Seneca*.

Seneca, born 4 BC into wealth, arrived in Rome from Spain at the age of 5. Well-educated and from an influential aristocratic family, he entered politics and became a member of the Roman Senate ... but he is best remembered as a Stoic philosopher of Rome, whose ideas and writings strongly influenced later thinkers.

During the reign of <u>Caligula</u>, the mad emperor "wished to have him executed for his impertinence, but Seneca's friends saved his life by arguing he would presently die of consumption [progressive wasting away] in any case. Soon afterward, [new emperor] <u>Claudius</u> accused him of improper relations with Julia ... the Senate condemned him to death, but Claudius commuted this to exile in Corsica." [p 301]

Eight years later, Seneca was recalled to Rome when Emperor Claudius' new wife Agrippina wanted him to tutor her 11-year-old son, Nero.

When <u>Nero</u> became emperor, he chose Seneca as one of his two principal administrators [a premier]. After 5 years, Seneca retired to a country estate .... but, 3 years later, he was charged with being a co-conspirator in a death plot against Nero, who ordered Seneca to kill himself ... and he did.

In his lifetime, Seneca was accused of being a hypocrite for his less-than-Stoic lifestyle. While this charge is true, supporters of Seneca suggest he was both a Stoic and realist ... thereby, permitting him to survive and even prosper through the reigns of two of Rome's most notorious emperors.

Durant provides this epitaph: "With all his faults, he was the greatest of Rome's philosophers and, at least in his books, one of the wisest and kindliest of men. Next to Cicero, he was the most lovable hypocrite in history." [p 307]

Hesiod (as choice):

As Smith earlier stated: "He is most easily taken as a Hellenistic interpretation of *Hesiod*, the grim [8th C. BC] poet of agricultural pathos." [p 37]

Zanker is in agreement with Smith that this is a bust of Hesiod. Distinguishing signs which indicate 'peasant low life' include: "the leathery skin dried out by the sun forming ugly furrows on the neck and shoulder...the shriveled body with bones protruding in face and neck...hair falling over the brow in straggly locks...at the nape of the neck, the locks are caked with dirt and sweat...and the crudely trimmed and irregularly growing beard. [*The Mask of Socrates*, p 150]

Zanker adds this bust is in: "no way characterized as sick or dispirited. Instead, he is filled with a passionate energy. The tension in the forehead and eyebrows suggests extreme concentration, as he searches for just the right word...he just has to express himself, as if something is driving him that is stronger than he is. All this seems to point to the peasant-poet Hesiod, who was called to poetry by the Muses while he was tending his goats on Mount Helikon...and, who, in his verses, described a life of inexorable toil, worry, and disappointment." [p 150-51]

Sculptor:

This head might represent an original bronze by an unknown Greek artist who worked at Pergamon in about the year 200 BC. The pathos of the face is similar to faces found on the *Great Altar of Zeus* #43. It is also possible the head was originally created in Rome by an unknown Greek or Roman sculptor.

Zanker compares this bronze head with another impressive head [on a black marble body] of the "pitiful *Old Fisherman*" in the Louvre...a statue "roughly contemporary" with the bronze bust. [p 150]

Lawrence describes the similarity of their realism: "hopelessly brutalized face...a body wrinkled with age and underfeeding...every unpleasant detail is scrupulously carved." [Lawrence, p 283, pl. 90a]

Smith too refers to the notable "*Seneca Fisherman*"in the Louvre. "The exaggerated black marble version...once taken for the Stoic Seneca in his suicide bath...His body is bowed by age, and his head uncompromisingly 'realistic'. The face with short scrappy beard, thick lips, and a high level of pathos has clear connections with the fictional *Pseudo-Seneca* portrait." [p 138]

Major References:

Sculpture: Origins to Today, 1970, Janneau & Hoog, p 75-6

Rome: Art & Architecture, 2001, Hintzen-Bohlen, p 614-15

Arts of the Ancient Greeks, 1972, Brilliant, p 397-8

Art through the Ages, Vol I, Gardner, 1980, p 194

Hellenistic Sculpture, 1991, Smith, p 36-7, 40, 138, fig 36

Greek and Roman Sculpture, 1972, Lawrence, p 251, pl. 76a and pl. 90 (Louvre)

Caesar and Christ, 1944, Durant, p 267, 273-9, 301-7, 351

Nat. Naples Arch. Museum, 1974, Franciscis, p 25

The Mask of Socrates, 1995, Zanker, p 150-1

42

THE HELLENISTIC RULER

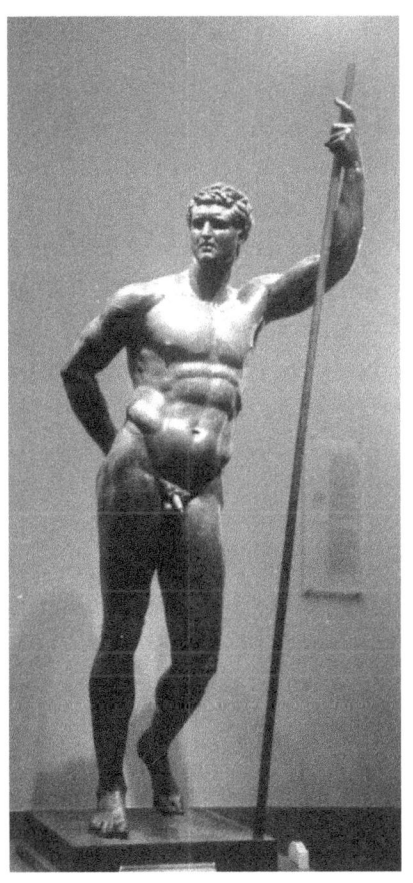

"... finest surviving example of a [Roman] portrait..."
... *Greek Sculpture*, Carpenter, p 245-46

Found 1885, Rome – now Palazzo Massimo alle Terme, Rome
Greco-Roman original [or copy] – 160 BC – Hellenistic
Ht. 7 ft. 4 in – bronze
Sculptor: unknown Greek or Roman … style of Lysippos

This over-sized bronze statue – described as the "finest surviving example of a [Roman] portrait" – spent some 1,300 years underground. [*Greek Sculpture*, Carpenter, p 245-46]

The *Hellenistic Ruler* is believed to have adorned a private estate or the Baths of Constantine, both of which once stood on the Quirinal Hill – east of today's famed Trevi Fountain #76. [Cadario, p 24]

It is possible an imminent barbarian invasion of Rome – either the Visigoths in AD 410, or the Vandals in AD 455 – explains why it was discovered in 1885 deeply buried/hidden under 17 feet of loose dirt and clay … in a vault between the foundation walls of a Roman temple [now in ruins]. If it was 'hidden' from barbarians, the Romans who buried it may have fled the city for their lives and never returned. It was discovered during excavations to build a theater over the site.

Clement's *Rome, the Eternal City, II* describes the discovery: "In the spring of 1885, there were 2 great treasures discovered in Rome … on the western slope of the Quirinal, which had been occupied in ancient times by the Temple of the Sun [built in AD 273 by Aurelian] … the foundation walls crossed each other, and the spaces between … were filled in with clay and loose earth. In one of these spaces, a workman came upon the arm of a bronze statue lying on its back … 17 feet below the level of the platform. The statue was … 7 feet and 4 inches in height and well proportioned. The Baths of Constantine were very near the Temple of the Sun; and it is probable that these two bronzes [the other, *the Boxer* #50] were a portion of their decoration, as they are of such subjects as were much used in Roman baths." [p 736]

Subject:

The scowling brutal face offers a realistic likeness. His narrowing, deep-set eyes [once inlaid with colored enamel] are smaller than the broad nose and the thick-lipped mouth with a cleft chin. An unusually prominent, furrowed brow is firmly set. His short beard and locks of hair are fashionably finished.

The open mouth and beetled brow appear more disbelieving than disdainful. Brilliant, senses "tension ... by abrupt movement of the too small head, turned by the music of some distant drummer and disturbed ..." [p 360]

On the battlefield, this ruler/general may be 'disturbed' by news of a setback that would discourage another man ... but he is confident and knows he will prevail.

E.V. Lucas summarizes the face: "like one who knows his strength, fears none, but has no arrogance." [p 215]

Bazin's *History of World Sculpture* says: "In its heroic character, the proportions and the classicizing rendering of the hair, this powerful figure seems inspired by Lysippos' lost statue of Alexander bearing a lance." [p 158]

It also may have been inspired by the *Farnese Hercules* #31 from the same sculptor. [compare photos of the two figures]

The identity of this statue is unknown. References vary widely, suggesting: a Roman general ... Sulla or Lucullus ... an *Achillean* body ... or a Selucid [Syrian] king.

The Terme museum, in 2005, states: "the light beard ... probably alludes to the condition of a general on military campaign ... The position in repose implies the victorious conclusion of a military campaign, so it is possible to recognize the *Ruler/Prince* as an anonymous victorious general, perhaps Roman, who had attributed his victory in the first half of the 2nd century BC to the protection of Hercules." [Cadario, p 24, 25]

This statue has its head set upon a much larger, heavily-muscled, exaggerated body modeled from heroic images of the mythical warrior *Hercules* "at the end of his labors." To assure viewers of this allusion, the right hand rests upon a buttock in precisely the same manner as the previously-mentioned *Farnese Hercules* #31. [Cadario, p 24]

Carpenter's *Greek Sculpture* paraphrases Pliny and implies the *Hellenistic Ruler* is misnamed and might be better called the *Victorious Roman General*. "Prior to the dictatorship of Julius Caesar, distinguished Romans caused themselves to be represented in the nude and statues of this kind, known as 'Achillean,'... intimating that their physical type was athletic-heroic and classical. Only the head, modeled apart in the 'likeness' of the sitter would be the sculptor's creative and personal contribution. All the rest could be taken bodily from some earlier classic masterpiece – in the case of a work in bronze, by taking molds directly from some prototype. Our finest surviving example of such a portrait pastiche is the so-called *'Hellenistic Ruler'...*" [p 245-46]

Carpenter suspects the life-size head of *the Hellenistic Ruler* was copied from a "mold directly taken from ... a bronze head of a boxer from Olympia ..."

If Carpenter is correct, then the actual face of 'the Roman general' must have been ignored by the sculptor. This was not unusual in Roman times ... as a wealthy family may have preferred to immortalize an ancestor with a more distinguished face than was the case in real life. [p 246]

Bazin says: "it has been suggested – comparing him to Republican [Roman] coins – that he was Sulla or Lucullus ..." Yet, Bazin adds: "... the most convincing hypothesis is that he was the Syrian prince Demetrius I Soter [162-150 BC]." [p 158]

This Demetrius was the last king in a dynasty established by Seleucus [famed general of *Alexander the Grea*]. Demetrius is said to have "fought and died heroically" in 153 BC as he defended his kingdom against the combined forces of Pergamon, Egypt, and Roman mercenaries. [Durant, p 579]

Several references suggest the face resembles those on Syrian coins from the reigns of either Demetrios I Soter or Alexander Bala [150-146 BC]. [Boardman, Brilliant, Lawrence]

Sculptor:

While the Greek and/or Roman sculptors – one for the head, another for the body – remain unknown, their execution is exceptional. The sculptor of the body was certainly influenced by the works of Lysippos ... primarily, *the Farnese Hercules* in Naples.

Major References:

Museo Nazional Rome, 2005, Cadario, p 6, 24, 25
Art of the Ancient Greeks, 1972, Brilliant, p 360-3, fig 9-24
Greek and Roman Sculpture, 1972 A. W. Lawrence, p. 232
Rome, the Eternal City Vol I, 1896, Clement, p 398-9
Rome, the Eternal City Vol II, 1896, Clement, p 735-9
Wanderer in Rome, 1926, Lucas, p 215, fig 208+
Greek Art, 1973, Boardman, p 196-7
Greek Sculpture, 1960, Carpenter, p 245-6, pl. XLVI (a), pl. XLVII (a)
Hellenistic Sculpture, 1991, Smith, p 19-20, fig. 3
History of World Sculpture, 1968, Bazin, p 158

43

GREAT ALTAR OF ZEUS

OR GIGANTOMACHY [BATTLE OF THE GODS & GIANTS]

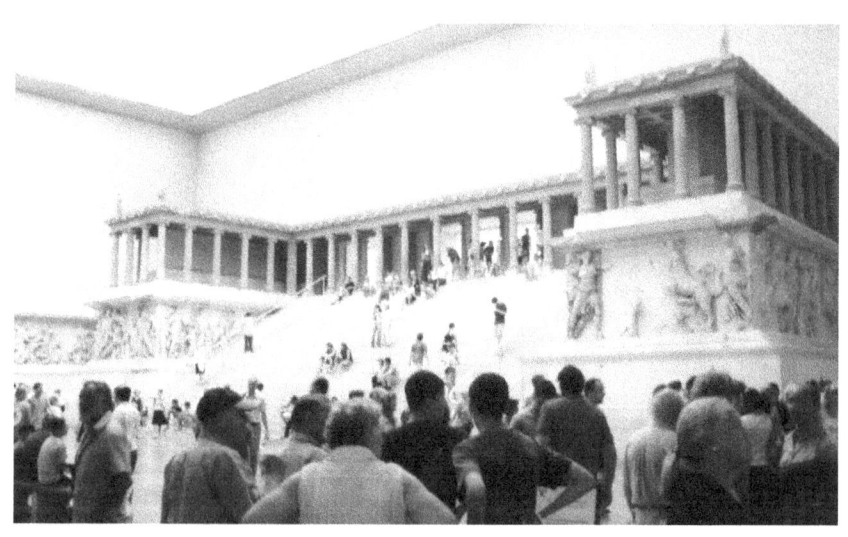

"... the classic statement of Hellenistic art ...
in antiquity, one of the wonders of the world ..."
... *Arts of the Ancient Greeks*, Brilliant, p 347

From Bergama, Turkey, 1871-86 – now, Pergamon Mus, Berlin
Orig. Greek-Ionian temple – 169 BC – Hellenistic Baroque
Temple: Width: 120 ft. [36 m] X 56 ft. [17 m]; Ht. 40 ft. [12 m]

Frieze Ht.: 7.5 feet [2.3 m], Length: 371 feet [113 m] – marble
Master sculptor: Menekrates of Rhodes...with 15 others
   *buy 50-page guidebook to identify & enjoy what is seen

[see *Athena* battling *Alcyoneus* at chapter end]

Today...to experience an ancient Greek temple that is amaz-ingly near-intact, visit the Pergamon Museum in Berlin. We 'step back in time' some 2,200 years.

In 225 AD, Roman author Lucius Ampelius wrote in his *Book of Memorable Facts*: "At Pergamon is a great marble altar, 40 feet high, with remarkable statues, and the entire [platform] is surrounded by the "Battle of the Giants." [Zabern, p 5]

Gardner describes *the Great Altar of Pergamon* as "<u>the most famous of all Hellenistic sculptural ensembles</u>...the most extensive repre-sentation of the *Gigantomachy* ever attempted by Greek artists." [*Art Through the Ages*, p 174-76]

The *Gigantomachy* is the legendary Battle of the Olympian Gods/Goddesses against the Barbarian Giants. These combat-ants – sculpted in high-relief on a 7.5-foot tall frieze – line the 371-foot walls of the *Great Altar*. Most of the figures – considering age and ill-use – are in remarkably good condition.

The western portion of this temple retains 60% of its original statuary. [Zaberrn, p 15]

R. Brilliant says the "titanic battle of the gods and giants" is "a vibrant, palpable display of positive violence expressed in figures of the greatest variety and energy..." [p 350] The temple and its statuary were: "valued in antiquity as <u>one of the wonders of the world</u>..." [p 347]

The *Encyclo Sculpt* adds: "Its marvelously detailed and beauti-fully carved *Gigantomachy* is a spectacular example of the Hellenistic Baroque style." [p 1259]

Museum visitors may sit on *the Altar's* 60-foot-wide, grand staircase.

In 169 BC, this marble staircase was reserved for "the select few [priests, royalty, and foreign emissaries] permitted to mount the great stairway during cult festivals... or to approach the high altar for burnt offerings." [*Guidebook*, p 21]

The wealthy Greek-Ionian kingdom of Pergamon built the *Great Altar* for several reasons: to honor Zeus and Athena... to memorialize victories over the Gauls... and to gain prestige throughout the Mediterranean World for a <u>temple that challenged the Parthenon</u>.

It survived intact nearly 1,000 years... until being dismantled by Byzantine conquerors in the 8th C. AD... for material to build a defensive wall around the hill fortress [acropolis] of Pergamon. Marble slabs of *the Altar* [plus reliefs] were embedded in the fortress wall.

Citizens of Bergama also removed temple marble to construct dwellings.

Consequently – when re-discovered and excavated in 1871 by German engineer Karl Humann and archaeologist Alexander Conze – a majority of the original marble and reliefs had survived with only minor damage. The German government purchased these ruins and statuary for 20,000 marks.

In Berlin, it was reconstructed from 1901 to 1908. The Pergamon Museum of Berlin was specifically built to shelter the temple. [Kunze, p 5, 11-5]

Originally, the *Great Altar* had been erected in Pergamon by the same Attalid kingdom that earlier commissioned the *Gaul Chieftain* #36 and the *Dying Gaul* #37... for display on the acropolis of Pergamon. It is 17 miles from the Mediterranean coast [now, Bergama, Turkey].

Subject:

By Greek myth, the earth mother Gaia and her giant barbarian sons were expected one day to overthrow the divine Olympian gods. An oracle warned the Greeks: unless a mortal man came to the assistance of their gods, they would be unable to oppose the giants. When the Battle between the gods and barbarians began, Hercules arrived to fight by the side of his father Zeus. Hercules was the son of a mortal woman who had been 'visited' by Zeus.

[the ancient Greeks looked upon Hercules as both man and god]

The baroque *Gigantomachy* displays the savagery of this Battle. In violent hand-to-hand combat – with the crucial aid of Hercules – the gods are overpowering the giants. Fearsome lions and dogs aid the Olympians by brutally attacking the necks and heads of the giants...who in turn are aided by large coiling snakes. The giants remain defiant as they fall under a merciless onslaught.

Dillon says the ancient sculptors: "...fill the entire height of the frieze...a mass of human limbs, wings, scaly snakes, and lions. The divine and monstrous figures twist and turn in space...some confront and threaten the viewer...and some even invade real space by spilling out onto the steps of the monumental staircase." [*Encyclo Sculpt*, p 1260]

The 'Athena versus *Alcyoneus*' section of the *Gigantomachy* is considered the most dramatic and skillfully executed.

Lawrence describes it: "On four of the best-preserved slabs, *Athena* pulls a giant's hair...and *Gaia* [earth mother] emerges from the ground to make a grief-stricken appeal for clemency for her sons, the giants." [*Greek & Roman Sculpture*, p 228]

Ignoring the mother's appeal, *Athena* retains her grip on the fallen giant *Alcyoneus* and prepares to slay him. On *Athena's* left, the goddess of victory [*Nike*] arrives on wings to crown *Athena* in her triumph.

[the giant *Alcyoneus* is similar to the doomed priest *Laocoon* #51]

Throughout the frieze, the expressions of the giants show sufferings...while faces of the gods are calm. The giants can only wrestle or throw stones.... while the gods are well-armed.

The Jansons comment: "This unique blend of two traditions – Hellenistic and baroque – brings the development of Greek architectural sculpture to a thundering climax. The muscular bodies rush at each other, and the high relief creates strong accents of light and dark. The beating wings and windblown garments are almost overwhelming in their dynamism." [*Basic History of Western Art,* p. 101-02]

In Greek mythology, the outcome of this Battle symbolized the end of the matriarchal [barbaric] era... and the establishment of a new advanced [civilized] culture. The royal leaders and people of Pergamon associated the outcome of this mythical Battle with their recent victories over the Gauls to the north... interpreting it as a victory of culture over the non-cultured.

Sculptor:

Durant comments: "For a half a century, Pergamon was the finest flower of Hellenic civilization." [p 579]

Bazin adds: "The generosity of the kings of Pergamon attracted artists from all over, and this kingdom in Asia Minor became one of the most brilliant centers of Hellenistic civilization... artistic activity reached a zenith with the construction of the *Great Altar of Zeus.*" [p 155]

Menekrates of Rhodes is said to be the master sculptor. Phyromachos of Athens is mentioned as a principal sculptor. References suggest at least 14 other sculptors helped to complete it.

Visitors to the Pergamon Museum should reserve time to also view the famed *Ishtar Gate* and the *Market Gate of Miletus.*

Travel Note: Yes, Berlin is out-of-the-way. *Solution*: book overnight train-sleeper from Paris to Berlin. Day-visit the *Great Altar... Nefertiti* #4... and *Black Caesar* #54. In evening, take train/sleeper south to Munich... do day-tour. Take train/sleeper to Florence, spend a few days... then, onto Rome. Luggage can be checked at railway stations.

Major References:

Pergamon Altar, 1995, Zabern, p 5, 15

Greek & Roman Sculpture, 1972, Lawrence, p 227-30

Arts of the Ancient Greeks, 1972, Brilliant, p 318-20, 341-42, 347, 351-6

Basic History of Western Art, 1996, Janson & Janson, p 101-02

Art of Crete, Mycenae, and Greece, 1968, Hafner, p 248-252

Hellenistic Sculpture, 1991, Smith, p 155-64, 172-80
Art Through the Ages, 1996, Gardner, p 174-75
Encyclopedia of Sculpture, 2006, Dillon, p 1259-61
The Pergamon Altar, 1995, Max Kunze, all pages
Ancient Greece, 1997, Durando, p 230-5
History of World Sculpture, 1968, Bazin, p 155
Life of Greece, 1939, Durant, p 579

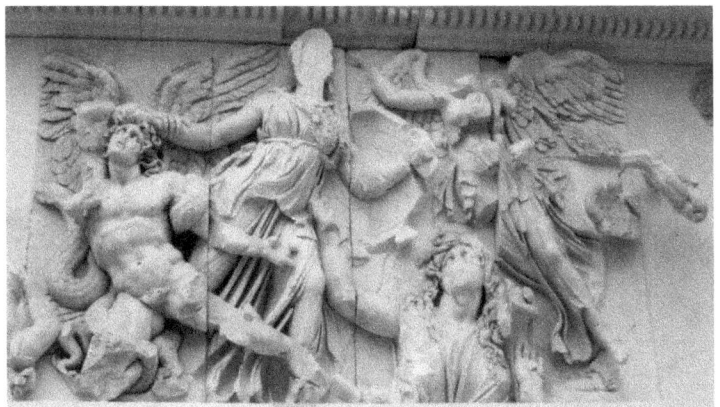

44

THE FARNESE BULL

OR THE PUNISHMENT OF DIRCE

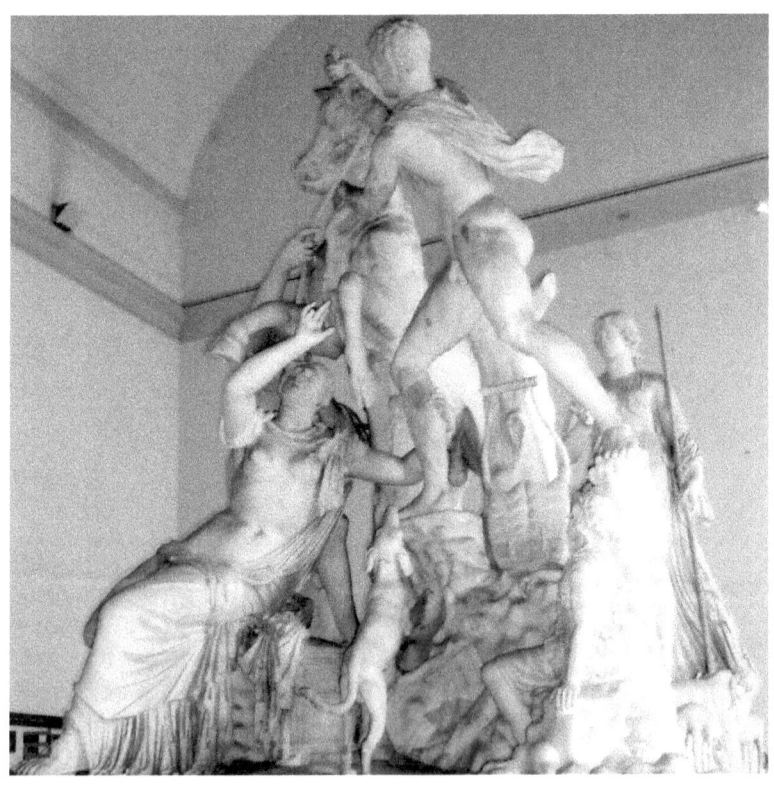

"...a grandiose pyramid of marble figures"
...Smith, *Hellenistic Sculpture*, p 108

Found 1546, Baths of Caracalla, Rome – now, in Naples Mus.
Greco-Roman copy – 150 to 200 AD – Hellenistic Baroque
From: Orig. Greek-Rhodian bronze [lost] – 140 BC
Height: 13.3 feet – marble
Orig. Sculptors: Apollonius & Tauriskos of Tralles

Visitors to the Naples Archaeological Museum approach this dynamic group with growing concern for the woman under the flailing hooves of a raging bull.

Bazin says: "... the group of figures clustering on their rocky base is shot through with <u>the fiery drama of action...in the largest of all known [surviving] ancient statues</u>." Where the hand of the higher man grips the bull's horn, the height is over 13 feet. [*History of World Sculpture,* p 161]

Two men struggle with the bull...while a fully-robed, standing woman calmly watches from behind. In front, a herdsman sits and observes with his dog. The intent of the two struggling men is not to throw the bull off the sitting woman...but to keep the flailing hooves over her.

She raises a hand in a feeble attempt to deflect the hooves. The retribution she receives is dreadful, but infinitely befitting

We need not pity this woman. By Greek myth, her fate is meant to illustrate 'divine punishment' for her arrogance and cruelty. [*Hellenistic Sculpture,* Smith, p 108]

Initially, a visitor must circle the group...to identify and 'fix the positions' of the figures about the maddened bull.

This group was first created in bronze by Hellenistic Greeks on the island of Rhodes in about 140 BC. Some 100 years later, it was 'seized' by the Roman general Asinius Pollio [76 BC to AD 4] who brought it to Rome. Pollio displayed his trophy in Rome's first public library [financed from the spoils of his military victories]. He also donated his vast book collection to the library. Later, the bronze group was lost. [Durant, C & C, p 159]

[histories by Pollio were important sources for Plutarch who wrote one of the most famed works of ancient history; *Plutarch's Lives*]

In approximately 175 AD, when Roman sculptors copied the original bronze in marble, they improved upon it... by adding two important figures: *Antiope*, the standing woman... plus, the sitting herdsman who made possible the retribution. This statuary is also known as *the Punishment of Dirce* [the seated woman under bull]

In 1546, the Roman copy was discovered in the Baths of Caracalla in Rome. Extensive restoration by Renaissance masters was necessary... to replace missing limbs and other pieces... it is said Michelangelo supervised the sculptor Biannichi in this work.

Lawrence reveals that most of the figures were missing "practically half" of their bodies. "As to the aesthetic value [of restoration], it was a more impressive piece of decoration because of the [Roman] elaboration [of the Hellenistic original] ..." [*Greek & Roman Sculpture*, p 298]

Subject:

[the theme resembles the *She-Wolf* #10: wronged mother of twin sons... they right the wrong... one becomes new king]

The rearing bull – its hoofs over the figure of *Dirce* – fights control by the two brothers... *Amphion* and *Zethus*. The higher brother *Amphion* twists the right horn of the bull to bring its head down. His right hip is braced against a tree trunk, where his lyre is displayed.

Zethus helps pull down the opposite horn with a rope.

Dirce – fiendish queen of the Greek city-state Thebes – raises an arm to ward off the thrashing hooves. Her loosely-draped figure is posed on an altar of Dionysus, the Greek god of wine.

The sitting herdsman – for aesthetic purposes – is sculpted half-size, to balance the composition. Behind the bull, the figure of *Antiope* stands and watches... her raised hand may signify abhorrence at what must come.

A popular version of the myth of the Theban queen *Dirce* has her initially meeting the twin brothers *Amphion* and *Zethus* on Mt. Cithaeron...where she is engaged in bacchanalian rites [explains her minimally-draped figure] as a devotee to the deity Dionysus.

The brothers – mesmerized by *Dirce* – agree to help her find her former slave *Antiope*. When *Antiope* is located, *Dirce* encourages the twin brothers to tie *Antiope* to a bull so she will be dragged to her death.

However, at the last moment, the herdsman – who had raised the brothers from childhood – appears and reveals to them that *Antiope* is, in fact, their mother.

With this revelation, the twins decide to deliver to *Dirce* the punishment the evil queen intended for their mother.

Edith Hamilton's *Mythology* reveals: "A queen of Thebes, *Antiope*, bore two sons to the god Zeus, *Zethus* and *Amphion*...*Antiope*, fearing the anger of their mortal 'father' [King Nycteus of Thebes, later usurped by his brother Lycus], left her twins on a lonely mountain...but they were discovered by a herdsman who brought them up. Lycus [new king ruling Thebes] and his wife *Dirce* treated *Antiope* with great cruelty...until she decided to leave Thebes and hide. Finally, she came to a cottage where her sons lived. Somehow they recognized her or she them and, gathering a band of their friends, they went to the palace to avenge her. They killed [king] Lycus and brought a terrible death upon *Dirce*, tying her by the hair to a bull." [p 425]

Bulfinch's Mythology differs slightly: "*Amphion* was the son of Jupiter [Roman for *Zeus*] and *Antiope*, queen of Thebes. With his twin brother *Zethus*, they were exposed at birth [but survived] where they grew up among the shepherds, not knowing their parentage. Mercury gave *Amphion* a lyre and taught him to play upon it, and his brother occupied himself in hunting and tending the flocks. Meanwhile *Antiope*, their mother...found means to inform her children of their rights and summon them to her assistance. With a band of their fellow-herdsmen they attacked and slew King

Lycus…and, tying *Dirce* by the hair of her head to a bull, let the bull drag her till she was dead. *Amphion*, becoming the next king of Thebes, fortified the city with a wall. It is said that when he played on his lyre the stones moved of their own accord and took their places in the wall." [p 199]

In 1546, when the *Farnese Bull* was discovered in pieces during excavations at the ruins of the Baths of Caracalla, it had been sadly mutilated…possibly during a sack of Rome or by a religious sect. The Baths of Caracalla were known as "the Palace of Roman Water"… at 270,000 square feet, the complex was larger than the combined Houses of Parliament and Westminster Hall. Only the Baths of Diocletion [built by the Emperor Maximian in 295 AD] would be larger.

Pope Paul III, a member of the wealthy and influential Farnese family, had ordered excavations at the Baths to decorate his Roman residence with ancient statuary. Over time, many pieces also came into the hands of Cardinal Farnese and were displayed in his palace…to be called *the Farnese Collection*. When the family died out in 1731, the *Collection* was willed to the King of Naples. However, for almost half a century, most of it remained in Rome in the hands of the Vatican. It was not until 1777 – when King Ferdinand of Naples [1759-1825] requested the *Collection* – that it came to Naples, where Ferdinand established the current museum with the *Collection* as its base.

Sculptors:

The original Greek *Punishment of Dirce* was created in Rhodes by the Greek-Rhodian sculptor/brothers Apollonius and Tauriskos of Tralles. Their father Menecrates is "doubtfully identified as one of the sculptors of the *Great Altar/Gigantomachy* #43 of Pergamon." [Lawrence, p 298]

The era of the work of Apollonius and Tauriskos is estimated in the second century BC. The later sculptor(s) of the Roman copy are unknown. They were either Roman or imported Greek artists.

A painting, by Henryk Seimieradzki entitled "A Christian Dirce", illustrates how the myth of Dirce may have been re-enacted for the blood-lust of the crowds in the Roman arena.

Major References:

Caesar and Christ, 1944, Durant, p 159, 634

Mythology, 1942, Hamilton, 1942, p 425

Bulfinch's Mythology, 1968, foreword by Graves, p. 199

Hellenistic Sculpture, 1991, Smith, p 108, fig 142

The Life of Greece, 1939, Durant, p 623

Greek and Roman Sculpture, 1972, Lawrence, p 298, fig 92a

Arts of the Ancient Greeks, 1972, Brilliant, p 343

History of World Sculpture, 1968, Bazin, p 161

45

ALEXANDER MOSAIC
OR BATTLE OF ALEXANDER
& THE PERSIANS

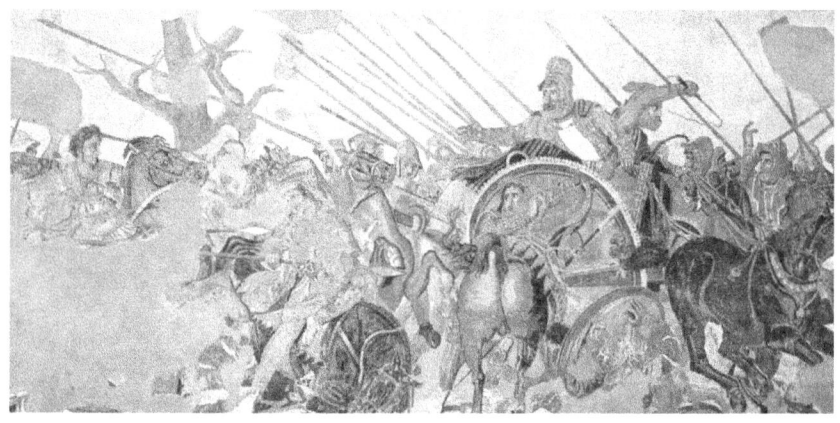

"One of the finest surviving ancient figural works...
extraordinary." ... *30,000 Years of Art*, 2007, p 284

Found 1831, *House of the Faun*, Pompeii – now Naples Mus.
Orig. Greco-Roman mosaic – approx. 100 BC – Hellenistic
<u>From</u>; painting [lost] by Greek Philoxenos or Aristides – 315 BC
Ht. 9', width 17' [3.2m x 5.5m] – 1.5 million marble & glass cubes
Sculptor: unknown Greco-Roman(s)

[see Alexander 'lancing' Oxyathres at chapter end]

T he mammoth 17-foot-wide *Alexander Mosaic* astounds...in both dimension and drama.

Durant's *Life of Greece* states: "There is no greater mosaic than this. The representation of complex emotions in [Persian king] Darius' face is the outstanding accomplishment of the work...but the most attractive head in the composition is that of Bucephalas, Alexander the Great's horse." [p 621]

The relentless Alexander is also persuasively presented. [at far left]. In the heat of battle, his face is mottled by dirt and sweat...his hair disheveled. Under a creased brow, his glaring eye is over-sized...to 'give the eye' to his opponents. [better view chapt end]

His lance appears to impale the brave Persian prince Oxyathres [younger brother of King Darius III].

A sneer curls Alexander's upper lip.

In the royal chariot, the mouth of Darius falls open...at the sight of his younger brother diverting Alexander's lance from the king.

At the "thundering, relentless charge" of Alexander and his Companion Cavalry, the chariot driver of Darius whips his horses to flee in panic. The royal Persian Guard [Immortals] will follow close behind.

Historical records indicate the Battle of Issus was not lost...yet.

By most accounts, Darius' 'surprise' at Alexander's sudden assault caused the king's chariot to prematurely leave the Persian front. It is unknown whether Darius or his chariot driver initiated their withdrawal.

One version has the driver wounded...Darius seizes the reins "and was the first to fly. The fall of the charioteer had been seen by neighboring Persians...the chariot's flight convinced them that it was the king who had fallen and died. The center disintegrated; a signal for general rout." [*Nature of Alexander*, Renault, p 122].

After a second battle at Gaugamela, Darius lost the Persian throne.

The Jansons describe this work as: "...an exceptionally large and technically masterful floor mosaic...surely an excellent copy of an early Hellenistic painting of c. 330-300 BC...The crowding, the air of frantic excitement, the powerfully modeled and foreshortened forms…and the precise shadows make the scene far more complicated and dramatic than any other work of Greek art from the period. … this picture explores a new world: the clash of civilizations and the triumphs and tragedies of men of awesome power…In effect, its realism turns us into eyewitnesses of these events." [*Basic History of Western Art,* p 77-8]

Subject:

This mosaic most likely depicts the 'Battle of Issus' in 333 BC, the first of two battles Alexander the Great fought against the Persian king, Darius III. The decisive 'Battle of Gaugamela' occurred 2 years later. It is possible the sculptor incorporated elements of both battles in this work.

At each battle, Darius positioned his war chariot at 'command center' of his massive armies…which vastly outnumbered Alexander's forces. On each occasion, Alexander sent a wing of his army in 'oblique attack' toward the Persian front…creating a reacting imbalance at the center of the Persian line. Alexander then led a massive cavalry charge into the weakened Persian front…aiming directly at the royal chariot of Darius. [Fox, p 173-77]

Panic is visible in the expression of Darius [especially the eyes] as Alexander drives Bucephalas toward the king. The head of the beloved horse is rendered with tenderness and beauty…in contrast to the otherwise violent scene.

The King's brother, courageous Prince Oxyathres – who *appears* to be pierced by Alexander's lance – did not die of this wound…if he was wounded at all. Oxyathres may have pushed the lance aside. Or, the point of the lance may have passed through his garment…missing his body.

Renault adds, after the battle: "Oxyathres arrived voluntarily to accept Alexander as King…Alexander recruited him at once into the Companions." The Companions were personally-selected Macedonian aristocrats who composed an elite cavalry unit which fought at the side of Alexander. According to the ancient historian

Diodorus, Prince Oxyathres lived many years after this battle; and his daughter Amastris in 324 BC became the bride of Alexander's general Craterus. [p 137]

After Alexander's victories, his strategy of treating the defeated soldiers humanely – seldom killing or enslaving those who surrendered or had fought valiantly – permitted him to assimilate most of the countries he conquered with minimal bloodshed.

This approach also served to ease and encourage the introduction of Greek culture and political ideas throughout the Mediterranean, Near East, and as far as India. His founding of Alexandria in Egypt – as a center of learning in the Mediterranean world – became one of the most influential events in Western culture.

Alexander is often credited for the blossoming of the Hellenistic Age [323 to 23 BC]. The role of his boyhood mentor Aristotle – selected by King Philip II of Macedonia [father of Alexander] – was instrumental.

Aristotle counseled his student: "... the intellectual soul must be trained to rule, like a king, over all lesser and baser appetites ... to covet as riches only honor, nobility, and glory." [Renault, p 48] Alexander is believed to have said: "I am indebted to my father for living, but to my teacher for living well."

'Nobility' above refers to 'principled, magnanimous, fair, etc.'

Alexander, mindful of his eventual place in history, often made benevolent decisions minimizing his immediate benefit... for improved judgment by historians.

Military historian E.W. Marsden states Alexander: "possessed that rare ability to sift conflicting reports, to make correct observations, and – remaining cool and un-flurried – to issue swift and well-considered orders in such circumstances. Alexander had this ability in a pronounced degree." [Renault, 124]

Following his untimely death in 323 BC [recent studies indicate typhoid] the next 300 years were called the Hellenistic Age. The benefits of this enlightened age are still being realized.

Alexander's Appearance

Most of Alexander's surviving images are believed to be idealized in varying degrees. From sculptures executed within a few centuries following his life – mostly copies of originals – it is conjectured Alexander had a protruding brow, pointed nose, and narrow mouth.

Robin Fox, in *Search for Alexander*, reports: "texts imply he was a smallish man … he was brisk, men later believe, in speech and walk … his many wounds are proof of his exceptional strength and toughness … his bold and handsome features, brownish hair, and brown eyes are well caught in the *Alexander Mosaic*, a close Roman copy of a contemporary painting [315 BC] … Alexander cut a fine figure before his new army …" [p 98]

Bucephalas, Horse of Alexander:

Perhaps, the most famous warhorse in history, Bucephalas is said to have saved the life of his master 5 times. Renault relates how Alexander acquired his favorite steed: "It is a well-worn tale: the fiery charger offered at a high price to Philip II … refusing to be mounted … and turned down as useless … the boy Alexander insisting that a great horse was being wasted … the father challenging him to do better than his elders … their bet on it: the horse to be bought for Alexander if he could manage it, and if not, paid for by him … the horse's instant trust when it felt Alexander's hands … [the boy easily mounted] … Philip, buying him as agreed, showed great pride in his son's achievement. No other incident in Alexander's life is related by Plutarch in so much detail." [*Nature of Alexander*, p 39-41]

It is suggested Alexander earlier had observed Bucephalas was afraid of his own shadow. Therefore, the boy, upon receiving the reins, eased the head of the horse away from a view of his shadow. He then mounted Bucephalas without difficulty and galloped away.

Discovery:

The mosaic, found in Pompeii, was excavated in the House of the Faun in 1830 and 1831. It composed the floor of a large room, open on one side. The excavated villa is considered one of the richest from ancient times due to its dimensions [32,000 feet], varied architecture [2 atriums, 2 peristyles, and 4 dining rooms placed according to the seasons], superb wall paintings, plus many other excellent mosaics. It may have been the home of P. Sulla [appointed by his uncle, the dictator Sulla, to organize the Roman colony of Pompeii].

The *Alexander Mosaic* is now framed on a wall like a painting...where the perspective is much improved over 'a floor placement'. Though one-sixth of the marble cubes are missing, the vacant areas are not vital to the composition. The eruption of Mt. Vesuvius in AD 79 and earthquakes may have 'disrupted' the lower corner of the mosaic. [Pompeii-AD 79, p 112]

In 2005, a full-scale replica was completed in Ravenna, Italy...then installed in the position of the original at the House of the Faun in Pompeii. The 2-year project involved 16,000 man-hours at a cost of $215,000.

Sculptor:

The ancient mosaic artist could have been either Roman or Greek, though Greek artists were usually more highly-skilled in mosaics.

The material for the mosaic is mostly tesserae – smooth-surfaced cubes cut from marble. The tesserae are in varying sizes [none larger than 4 millimeters] depending on the detail desired. The surfaces of the cubes are flatter than water-worn pebbles used previously in mosaic floor art...therefore, tesserae withstands wear and tear better. Four basic colors are utilized in varying shades: white, yellow, red, and black.

The editors of *30,000 Years of Art* add: "the entire work was made...using extremely small stone tesserae...nearly limitless detail allowing the viewer to appreciate both the dramatic battle and decorative minutiae on every figure, fine fittings on weapons and armor, and trapping on horses." [p 284]

The model for the mosaic may be a famous painting by a Greek artist in about 315 BC [*described by Pliny*]. Most references suggest the painter was one of Alexander's court artists: Philoxenos of Eretria, or Aristides.

Finley & Pleket state: "The original painting, now lost – commissioned by Cassander, one of Alexander's generals – was taken to Rome as booty after the Roman defeat of Macedon in the Battle of Pydna in 168 BC." [*The Olympic Games* , p 54]

Alexander, ever conscious of his place in history, selected with care those artists he permitted to reproduce his image. He favored the sculptor Lysippos of Sicyon because – according to the Plutarch – his work expressed those aspects of his subject's character that Alexander thought most appropriate to emphasize, such as "his manly and leonine quality."

This mosaic is far more meaningful to those who've reviewed the life of Alexander the Great. Excellent sources are Renault's *The Nature of Alexander*...and Fox's *Search for Alexander*...both illustrated.

Other notable Alexander sculptures:

...Azara Herm #28 – believed copied from Lysippos original
...Alexander Sarcophagus – pose similar to *Alexander Mosaic*
...Pella mosaic – A's foot pinned by lion, Craterus to kill lion
...Stag Hunt mosaic – A. w/raised sword, grips antler of deer

Major References:

Basic History of Western Art, 2006, Janson & Janson, p 77-8

History of Art, 1977, Janson, p 145

30,000 Years of Art, 2007, Phaidon, p 284

Nature of Alexander, 1975, Renault, p 39-41, 48, 122, 124, 137

Search for Alexander, 1980, Fox, p 98, 99, 163, 173-77, 179

Art in the Western World, 1953, Robb & Garrison, p 591-92

Alexander Mosaic: Stories of Victory and Defeat, Ada Cohen (new)

World History, Diodorus, 17.34.1-5

Arts of the Ancient Greeks, 1972, Brilliant, p 276, p 274-5

Pompeii – AD 79, 1979, Brilliant, p 112-13

Birth of Western Civilization, 1964, Grant, p 66 large image

Ancient Rome, 1996, Liberati and Bourbon, p 180-1 large image

Search for Alexander: An Exhibition, 1980-1982

Art Through the Ages, 1980, Gardner, p 182-83

British Museum Book of Greek & Roman Art, 1991, p.130

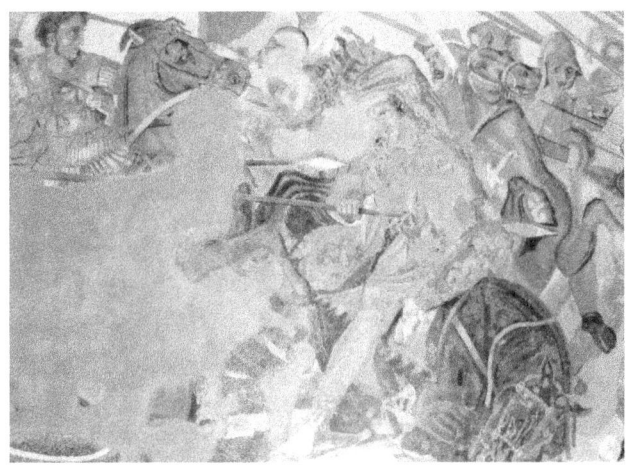

46

MAN OF DELOS

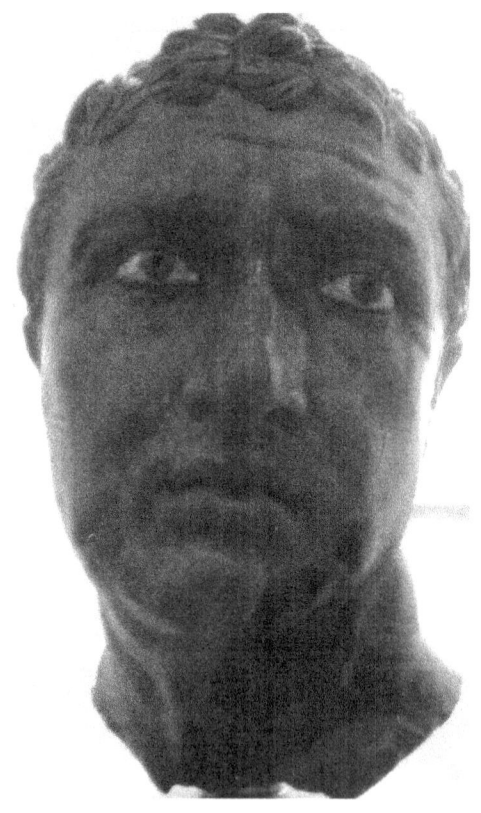

"... the fine Hellenistic portrait from Delos.... extremely
persuasive likeness... impresses us with its subtle
grasp of the sitter's psychology."
...Janson, *History of Art,* p 167

Found 1912, island of Delos – now, Nat. Museum of Athens
Orig. Greek portrait – 100 BC – Late Hellenistic style
Ht. 13 inches – bronze, with dark green patina
Sculptor: Agasias, son of Dositheos of Ephesus
      [or a cousin, also named *Agasias*]

The ancient *Man of Delos* is a rare, surviving Greek portrait with realistic features. His <u>extremely melancholy portrait is one of the most expressive from any era</u>. The grieving eyes – "marvelously well-preserved" – elicit our sense of sympathy. [Meletzis, p 130]

Smith says, with the advent of the Late Hellenistic Age: "The new portrait mode appears... Its external features are easily recognized: middle-aged, short-cropped hair, and a hard, objective style. The portraits have... apparent realism, of a particular mortal individual 'as he really was'... This was something quite new." [*Hellen. Sculpt,* p 256]

In 1912, this head was discovered under the ruins of the Arena of Delos – an open stadium for training or exercise in wrestling and other athletic sports. References suggest the head represents an unidentified Delian leader or wealthy merchant in approximately 100 BC. Prominence of the subject is implied by the high quality of its execution.

Janson observes: "One of the few original [Greek portraits] is the very vivid bronze head from Delos... it was not made as a bust, but, in accordance with Greek custom, as part of a full-length statue. The identity of the sitter is unknown. Whoever he was, we get an intensely private view of him that immediately captures our interest. The fluid modeling of the somewhat flabby features... the uncertain, plaintive mouth... the unhappy eyes under furrowed brows... <u>reveal an individual beset by doubts and anxieties... an extremely human, un-heroic personality</u>... it is significant that the inner complexity of such men could be conveyed by a work of art only when Greek independence, culturally as well as politically, was about to come to an end." [*History of Art,* p 143]

R. Brilliant is more incisive: "By early in the 1st century – as demonstrated in the affecting bronze head of an unknown man found in the palestra on Delos – <u>sensitivity has become 'pathetic</u>

ROBERT LAWRENCE HOLT

anxiety' and spirituality 'emotional disturbance'... the structure of the head seems to dissolve as the bone begins to disappear beneath puffy, not quite sagging flesh ... and the bronze surface becomes a rich field for the rapid play of ever-changing intensities of light." [*Arts of the Ancient Greeks*, p 396]

Ragghianti adds: "The fleshy modeling ... has a capricious 'pictorial' treatment in the hair, the eyebrows ... emphasized by the protruding chin and the wrinkled forehead." [p 158]

A possible explanation for the excellent condition – particularly facial surfaces and eyes – of the *Man of Delos* is the relatively short period of time [a few decades] between its creation and 'burial' in the Arena of Delos. Most references date its creation to about 100 BC ... within a few decades of two foreign invasions of Delos.

In 88 BC, a general serving under Mithridates the Great was ordered to sack Delos because its native population had taken the side of Rome in a local war. Later, in 69 BC, pirates sacked Delos again, and the population never fully recovered. It is conceivable the original owner of this bronze head – in a desperate effort to save it before a sack – had the head torn from its body and secretly buried.

Smith explains how the *Man of Delos* may have been commissioned. "The new realistic Roman portrait style first emerged during the 2nd century BC in Rome. There, Hellenistic sculptors were enlisted to produce portraits that would embody the Roman aristocrat's ideas of his defining qualities: his 'sternness, honesty, gravity, experience, and hardened military courage'. Minor kings in the Greek East, known from coins and in sculptured heads, chose this [Roman] style as opposed to the prevailing, highly idealized royal norms. These kings, it turns out, were all client rulers who owed their thrones to Rome, and for them this portrait manner clearly signified their 'Roman loyalty'. [p 256-57]

Island of Delos

The Aegean Sea, between Greece and Crete, contains hundreds of islands of which Delos is near the center ... explaining why Delos became one of the most important sanctuaries of ancient Greece.

Durant adds: "On Delos, according to Greek storytellers, Apollo himself had been born. So sacred was the island as his sanctuary that both death and birth were forbidden within its borders ... those about to give birth or to die were hurriedly conveyed from its shores ... and all known graves were emptied that the island might be purified. There, after the repulse of the Persian invasions, Athens and her Ionian allies agreed to keep the treasure of the Delian Confederacy. Later, of course, Pericles moved it to Athens for 'safekeeping'... eventually, these funds would finance his grandiose building plans.

Smith adds: "Every 4th year, the [Greek] Ionians met in pious but convivial assemblage to celebrate the festival of the handsome god [Apollo]." [p 131] "...island sanctuaries, like Delos and Samothrace, experienced their greatest prosperity from Hellenistic royal patronage. The sanctuaries were often the context for the most prestigious royal dedications – imposing portrait statues and victory monuments." [p 241]

After 168 BC, some 70 years before the *Man of Delos* is tentatively dated, the Romans had turned the island of Delos into a thriving "free port ... crowded with alien merchants, business offices, palaces and hovels, and the diverse temples of exotic faiths." [Durant, p 570]

Subject:

On Delos, Smith informs us: "The Romans had their own monumental marketplace [the Agora of the Italians]. For them, Delos was particularly important as a clearinghouse for the slave trade from the East to Italy." [p 255]

Therefore, the subject matter of the *Head of Delos* might even be a slave ... perhaps, a father who has witnessed his wife and children auctioned separately to different bidders at the famed slave market.

Conceivably, the head also could represent a Roman citizen during the 88 BC sack of Delos. Now ... he is 'in stark fear for his life'... having received further news of the massacre of 80,000 Romans by Greeks throughout the Aegean islands.

Or, the head might even be a prominent Greek citizen of Delos after the 88 BC massacre ... who now fears for his own life ... as the

Roman fleet and legions will surely seek revenge for the massacre of Roman citizens.

Lawrence suggests a higher station for the *Man of Delos*: "Pergamene heads, gaining their effect by lumpy modeling...illustrated in the remaining bronze head...probably of a ruler." [*Greek & Roman Sculpture,* p 241]

The Jansons' *Basic History of Western Art* [2006] even suggests: "...he may have been a local politician." [p 103]

Sculptor:

Most references attribute this head to Agasias, an active Greek sculptor early in the 1st century BC. Ragghianti, in *Nat. Arch. Museum of Athens*, says the *Man of Delos* head: "has been attributed to Agasias...on the basis of a comparison with the head of the so-called *Borghese Gladiator* #47 in the Louvre, signed by this eclectic sculptor." [p 158] It is also possible that a cousin, also named Agasias, made the Delos head.

Major References:

History of Art, 1977, Janson, p 143, 145, 167, color pl. 14
Basic History of Western Art, 2006, Janson & Janson, p 103
Ancient Greece, 1997, Durando, p 64, 216-24
Hellenistic Sculpture, 1991, Smith, p 241, 256-57
Nat. Arch. Museum of Athens, 1980, Ragghianti, p 158-9, ph 159
Nat. Arch. Museum, 1988, Meletzis & Papadakis, p 11, 130
Greek and Roman Sculpture, 1972, Lawrence, p 241, pl. 71b
Greek Sculpture, 1960, Carpenter, p 241-3, pl XLIV
Arts of the Ancient Greeks, 1972, Brilliant, p 395-56
The Life of Greece, 1939, Durant, p 131, 245, 251, 570

47

Borghese Warrior

or Gladiator

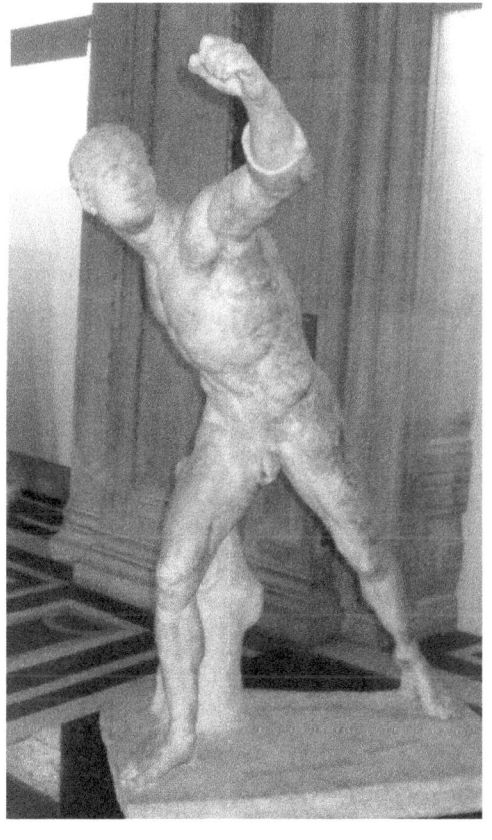

"an original masterpiece ... embodies the artistic endeavors
of the late Hellenistic period, most notably in its mastery
of three-dimensional representation."
... Louvre Museum website, Nov 2010

Found 1611, Nettuno, Italy – now, in the Louvre
Greco-Roman copy or orig. – 100 BC – Late Hellenistic
Or, possibly: Orig. Greek marble – 2nd C. BC
Ht: 1.99 m. – life-size – marble
   Sculptor: Agasias, son of Dositheos of Ephesus

From wherever we stand before the *Borghese Gladiator,* we receive a new and dynamic view. Some 2,100 years ago, this was revolutionary.

The Louvre Museum states this figure is "an original master-piece of the late Hellenistic period, created about 100 BC... one of the very few signed statues to have survived. An inscription on the tree trunk reveals its sculptor: *Agasius of Ephesus*..." [2010]

Pasquier says: "the *Gladiator's* display of musculature makes it of the time... which was the twilight of the Hellenistic period... though a superb twilight." [*Louvre: Greek, Etruscan, & Roman Antiquities,* p 53]

The statue was discovered in 1611 at Nettuno, south of Rome in the Anzio region of Italy... originally, without sword, shield or its right arm. In the 2 centuries following its discovery, it became one of the most copied of ancient statues. The right arm is believed to have been restored in the 17th century.

Two years after its discovery, *the Gladiator* entered the collection of the wealthy Borghese Family. It was displayed in the Villa Borghese of Rome... where Bernini studied it when creating his *David* #70.

Nearly 200 years later, in 1807, Prince Camillo Borghese* sold *the Gladiator* 'under pressure' to his brother-in-law, Napoleon... who transported it to Paris where it entered the Louvre collection. A bronze copy can be seen in Windsor Castle.

*Camillo's other misfortune was to marry his sister Pauline #80.

Subject:

In the arena, *the Gladiator* faces off against a charging horseman. His right hand is believed to have held a sword. The left arm displays the 'remains' of a shield.

Though vastly over-matched by a mounted combatant, *the Gladiator* stands his ground ... aware of the impossible odds ... knowing the end will be violent and bloody.

However, he also knows, while the gods can be capricious – should he display great courage, the gods may condescend to care ... and thereby favor him. Protected by his [unseen] shield, *the Gladiator* prepares to deal a counter-blow in a gesture that forms a powerful diagonal ... slicing through space. His shield and sword are ready!

Bazin states: "The artist who carved this young *Warrior* exploits to the full the possibilities of the 3rd dimension, which had been introduced into Greek sculpture by Lysippos. The <u>body thrusts forward along a forceful diagonal ... and the figure takes complete possession of its surrounding space</u>." [*History of World Sculpture,* p 161]

Rhys Carpenter says the figure was designed to "yield expressive contours from every viewpoint. The refinements of pose ... pass into every plane ... being based on progressive rotation of the horizontal axes of the human body. If we draw an imaginary line through the two ears ... another through both shoulders ... another through both hips ... another through both knees ... another through both ankles ... we shall have the five horizontal axes." [*Esthetics of Greek Sculpture,* p 62]

Carpenter [former director of Amer. Sch. of Classical Studies in Athens]* further explains: "the axes gradually turn like the needle of a compass so that the lowest one points at right angles or even in the opposite direction to the topmost ... from the employment of this [Lyssipic] formula comes the extraordinary completeness of each aspect under which the statue can be viewed ... and <u>the remarkably harmonious manner in which each aspect arises out of the preceding and melts into the succeeding one</u>, as we move around the statue." [p 63]

*later, Professor-in-Charge of Amer. Academy in Rome

Other "excellent illustrations of this use of [Lysippan] formula" are the *Dancing Satyr* from Pompeii, the *Seated Hermes* from

Herculaneum, and the *Listening Dionysus* – all in the Nat. Arch. Museum of Naples. [Carpenter, p 63]

Stripped Muscle Style:

Smith adds: "The tall proportions of the Lysippan canon and a 'stripped' muscle style evolved further…in both athletic and other heroic males. An extreme is reached in works like the *Borghese Warrior.*" [*Hellenistic Sculpture,* p 53, 59]

In fact, the sculptor may have selected the subject of a warrior in mortal combat in order to display the body with every muscle and sinew under maximum strain. His feet are widely separated…his left arm bears a shield [remains] stretched out as far as possible to meet the coming blow…the right arm – holding the hilt of the [unseen] sword – is posed to strike back. This position is referred to as the *'heroic diagonal'.*

The Louvre Museum states: "The head here is much reduced in size…and the supple, slender muscle structure…echoes the artists of the Pergamon baroque." [website, 2010]

Carpenter says: "So vivid is the muscular articulation of the tensely straining figure that *the Warrior* has been stigmatized as representing a flayed body rather than a living form. On the purely technical side, I believe that the flayed effect is due solely to the deeply grooved demarcation of the muscular divisions…the anatomical pattern, while founded on natural truth, has been intensified beyond natural limits in the interest of dynamic expression of strength of body, agility of action, and vehemence of will." [p 220]

Thiersch's *Epoch der Bildenden Kunst* speculates the hero was Achilles opposing the mounted Amazon, Penthesilea. [1816-25]

Sculptor:

The Gladiator by Agaias is sometimes considered an adaptation of an earlier but unknown Hellenistic work, possibly a bronze. If Agaias copied from another figure, he is thought to have varied his own version considerably. The proud Agaias may have intended to produce an image of such perfection that it would bring him wide renown, even immortality. If so, he succeeded.

In the National Museum of Athens, the *Man of Delos* head #46 is suspected to be by the same sculptor, or a cousin.

Major References:

Louvre website, 2010
History of World Sculpture, 1968, Bazin, p 161
Hellenistic Sculpture, 1991, Smith, p 53, 59
Esthetics of Greek Sculpture, 1959, Carpenter, p 62-3
Greek Sculpture, 1960, Carpenter, p 219-21
Louvre: Greek, Etruscan, & Roman Antiquities, 1998, Pasquier, p 53
Greek and Roman Sculpture, 1972, Lawrence, p 239-40, pl 70c
Handbook of Sculpture, 1897, II; Gardner, p 475-77
Epoch der Bildenden Kunst, 1816-25, Thiersch

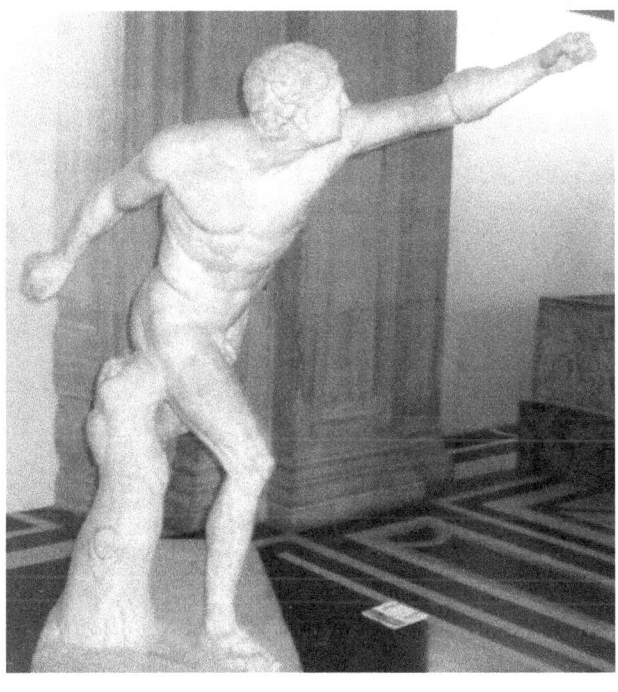

48

Venus de Milo

or aphrodite of melos [greek]

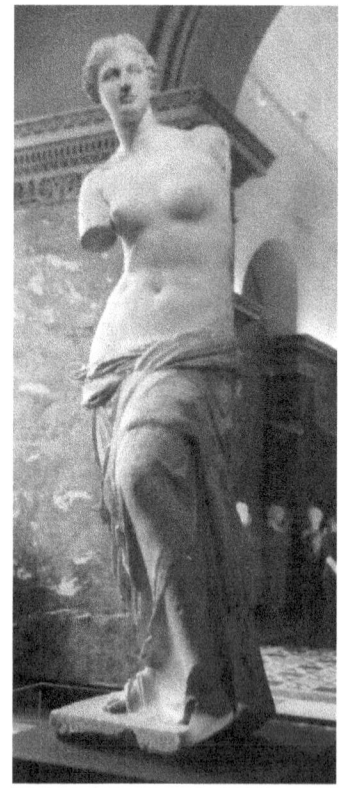

"... a timeless masterpiece"
... 30,000 Years of Art, 2007, p 288

Found 1820 by Greek farmer* on Melos – now, in Louvre
Orig. Greek statue [over life-size] – 80 BC – late Hellenistic
Ht. 6 feet, 8 inches [2.04 m] – Parian marble [cleaned 2010]
Sculptor: Alexandros of Antioch on Meander [now Turkey]
*observed by French Navy Lieutenant Olivier Voutier

[slipping drapery photo at chapter end]

This Grecian goddess, explains Curtis in *Disarmed*: "…has fascinated artists for generations…great masses of tourists arrive at the Louvre each day to see her…because the statue is beautiful in a way even an untrained eye immediately understands." [p 201]

Historian Will Durant describes her as "the most famous statue in the Western World…a poem of that health whose natural flower is beauty…the wasp waist finds no encouragement in this full body and sturdy hips." [*Life of Greece*, p 133, 624]

Equally charmed, Rodin: "praised her splendid belly as wide as the sea." [Louvre website 2004]

As a mother of 5 children, *Venus* had fair reason for a splendid belly. Save for arms, she was intact when discovered in 1820. For a 2,100 year-old statue, it is a miracle she survived in superb condition.

Approach *Venus de Milo* [in her alcove] from the other end of the hall of *Antiquites Grecque* [Greek Antiquities]. Pause often in the long hall…to contemplate her emerging 'perfection of proportion'. Note the long Nordic legs. At 6 feet, 8 inches, she hardly needs a pedestal.

30,000 Years adds: "In this Hellenistic sculpture, the artist gives the figure more dramatic drapery…and soft sensuous flesh, adapting and innovating to create a timeless masterpiece." [p 288]

Clark declares this Venus "is fruitful and robust beyond the other nude *Aphrodites* of antiquity…and remains one of the most splendid physical ideals of humanity." [*The Nude…Ideal Form*, p 89]

Curtis comments: "The flesh appears so real that one expects it to be warm to the touch. Some of that is due to the translucence of the [Parian] marble, but mostly it's the result of the delicate skill

Alexandros had with a chisel." [p 203] Curtis suggests the sculptor intended his statue to be viewed from its right front... yielding a three-quarter view of the face. From this viewpoint, "her expression is neither disdainful nor blank but completely absorbed. She is pondering [the Golden Apple awarded for] her beauty." [p 203-04]

The slightest of smiles teases the viewer.

For the finest overall view of the entire statue, move slightly to your right until the face is full and direct... here, the figure stands gracefully and is even more engaging.

Natural light in the arched alcove is inferior. Therefore, any time of day, circle her pedestal and search through shadows for other attractive views.

On the island of Milo/Melos, the first impression of French Navy Lieutenant Olivier Voutier – 'co-discoverer' with a Greek farmer – is described by Curtis: "Stains, nicks, and scrapes covered the surface of the statue. But despite these imperfections, Voutier sensed from the first glance that he was seeing something extraordinary. This torso was more glorious than anything he could have hoped to find when he set out that morning with the two sailors and a few picks and shovels.

Voutier later wrote a single sentence to describe these first few moments: 'Those who have seen the *Venus de Milo* are able to understand my stupefaction'." [p 5-7]

Subject:

In the Louvre, a nearby glass-case displays fragments of hands, an apple, and an upper arm... discovered with the statue. Part of the upper arm matches her left shoulder... if attached, it would extend to the left... suggesting the left hand had received the apple. [p 191]

These fragments reveal the theme of this particular *Venus* – her acceptance of the 'Golden Apple' from the Trojan prince Paris... known as *the Judgement of Paris*. In Greek myth, Zeus [supreme deity of the Olympian gods] faced a dilemma. "All the gods had been invited to the wedding of Peleus and Thetis... except Eris, the goddess of discord... who avenged the affront by throwing among the guests a golden apple inscribed with the words: 'For the most beautiful.'

Hera, Athena and Aphrodite squabbled over the precious apple until Zeus intervened ..." [*Louvre*, 2007, Scala, p 100[

Zeus feared dire consequences if he did not choose Hera [his wife]. Therefore, he asked the most handsome of mortal men, Paris of Troy, to make the selection. When Paris accepted the task, each of the goddesses offered him inducements.

"*Hera* promised to make him Lord of Europe and Asia ... *Athena*: that he would lead the Trojans to victory against the Greeks ... *Aphrodite*: that the fairest mortal woman in the world should be his." [*Mythology*, Hamilton, p 256-259]

The sliding gown of *Aphrodite* offers Paris even more enticement. Robb and Garrison reveal: "the effect of the figure is rather disquieting ... the draperies could hardly remain in place if the figure were to take a step ...." [*Art in Western World*, p 447] Lenaghan describes *Venus* "who wears a slipping mantle draped over her lower body ... the right hand reached downward across her body and held the drapery ..." [*Encyclo Sculpt*, p 1714]

The hand barely restrains the slipping mantle as Paris gives her the Golden Apple. Later, *Aphrodite* kept her promise by persuading Helen [of Sparta] to run off with Paris to Troy. [see the Lion Gate. #6]

The statue has holes in its earlobes for earrings and more in the right arm for a metal armlet. Curtis explains: "She wore jewels on her head, ears, and arms. Her hair was painted gold, her eyes and lips were red. Probably her flesh was left unpainted, but the exposed marble would have been highly polished to a high shine and might even have been waxed." This caused marble "statues to appear more life-like to the ancient Greeks." [p 191]

Discovery

The statue was unearthed April 8, 1820 on Melos in "a lonely, isolated farmer's pasture" near "remains of a theater ... stone bleachers ... remnants of walls ... and occasional parts of marble columns of an ancient Greek settlement." [Curtis, p. x]

Melos/Milo is a 51-square-mile island among the Cyclades, a group of islands off the southeast coast of Greece...90 miles from Athens and 40 miles from Paros, where its marble was quarried.

As Lieutenant Voutier and 2 sailors were breaking earth in search of antiquities, a nearby Greek peasant farmer named Yorgos [20 paces distant] had already uncovered half the statue before Voutier saw the find. Yorgos was "...trying to remove the stones from an ancient wall to use in a structure he was building on his farm. Voutier saw that the man had stopped digging for the moment and was staring at something in a niche he had uncovered in the wall...his posture was curious enough that Voutier went to look for himself." [p 5]

The 'niche' was arched and built into the stone wall. A nearby inscription indicated the presence of an ancient outdoor gymnasium, where nude statues personifying physical beauty were normal décor. From the lettering of the inscription, the statue could be dated between 150 and 50 BC.

By April 19th, news of the find reached the French counsel in Constantinople [Istanbul] who sent his secretary Count Marcellus to make the purchase. When Marcellus arrived at Melos on May 22nd, he learned the statue was already on an anchored Russian ship, whose captain had been bribed by a representative of the Turks [who controlled Greece at the time] to safeguard the statue [or even take it to Constantinople for the Turkish pasha]. After 24 hours of bluffing and bargaining by Count Marcellus, the local Greeks agreed to sell him the statue for 1,000 francs [750 to Yorgas and 250 to the 3-man island council]. Voutier, in a lifeboat with other French officers and sailors, recovered *the Venus* without a fight from the Russian captain. [p 7, 12-23, 26-30]

When the statue arrived in Paris in February 1821, it was gifted to King Louis XVIII, who donated it to the Louvre. Museum officials were extremely disappointed upon realizing their new acquisition could not be claimed to be from the 'Classic Age' of Greece [450 to 323 BC].

A separated fragment from its inscribed base indicated the *Venus* could not be older than "Antioch on the Meander" [now, in modern Turkey] – an ancient Greek city not established until 270 BC…. well into the Hellenistic Age. The inscribed base also proved the statue was the work of 'Alexandros of Antioch on the Meander'. [p 75, 187]

Louvre 'Disposes' Inscribed Broken Base & Left Foot

England had recently acquired the 'Classic' *Elgin Marbles*, and the French wished to make a similar 'Classic' claim with their *Venus*…though it was clearly from the Hellenistic Age. Their solution was to 'dispose of' the separated [inscribed] portion of the statue's base…including the left foot. Curtis tells us: "…the slab disappeared…Forbin either had it destroyed or hid it so deeply in some recess of the warehouses of the Louvre that it has never been found." [p 76]

Louvre officials would have succeeded in this subterfuge…except for the actions of 2 prominent French citizens: a curious artist in Brussels and a forthright conservator of antiquities at the Louvre.

The self-exiled <u>artist</u> David in Brussels [a few decades earlier, Napoleon's favorite painter]: "wanted to see what it [*Venus*] looked like. He wrote to Paris to ask to have a drawing sent to him. David's request fell to a former sculptor Debay, who had been a student in David's school. Now, Debay was 'curator in charge of antique restorations' at the Louvre. He gave the task to his 16-year-old son, Auguste who – either unconcerned or unaware of the debate over the 'base' and 'its inscription' – <u>drew them both quite clearly</u>…then gave the original to his father…a tracing went to David." [p 77]

The <u>Count of Clarac</u>, a titled Frenchman and <u>conservator</u> of antiquities at the Louvre, vehemently disagreed with the museum's decision to 'dispose' of the inscribed base…and he put his opinions in writing. "Clarac titled his paper: 'On the antique statue of *Venus Victory*, with a drawing by Debay the younger.' And there on the cover of the pamphlet was the Debay drawing. The fragment of left arm was attached at the shoulder and stuck straight out parallel to the ground. And, against the left side of the statue's base, fitting perfectly against the jagged edge, was the broken base with the inscription. The Greek letters were clearly legible." [p 88]

The Louvre ignored the protests of Count Clarac.

It was not until 1893, when the German archeologist Furtwangler published his *Masterpieces of Greek Sculpture* – with a definitive and accurate chapter devoted to the *Venus de Milo* – that world opinion began to sway to the correct conclusion that the Venus was a Hellenic statue.

A half-century later in 1951, Jean Charbonneaux, a conservator at the Louvre, would finally admit the true Hellenistic origins of the *Venus*... but, at the same time, this official acknowledged his countrymen still preferred to believe otherwise. [p 185]

Note to museum: since the Louvre admits 'deliberately losing' the left foot and broken base, why does the museum not re-create and replace them... based on Debay's sketch?

Sculptor:

The sculptor of the Aphrodite of Melos inscribed his name on the original base: "*Agesandros* [Alexandros] *son of Menides, from Antioch on the Meander*". There are no reliable references revealing more statuary by this sculptor.

Curtis does reveal: "the name of the artist [Alexandros from Antioch] is on an inscription from Thespiae, a city near Mount Helicon on the mainland of Greece where an important contest of poetry and theatrical arts was held every 5 years. In an inscription from around 80 BC, Alexandros of Antioch is mentioned twice, as a victor in singing and at composing. As a sculptor... he is indisputably a genius, whose name deserves to be mentioned in the same breath as Phidias, Praxiteles, and the other ancient masters." [p 188-89]

The *Venus* was carved from 2 large blocks of marble plus several smaller pieces for her gown. The unclothed upper half of the figure [includes a few inches of the draped gown] is designed to rest upon the lower half. This resulted in a lack of stability for the finished statue... and may be responsible for its damaged arms... especially in a region prone to earthquakes.

Alexandros was certainly familiar with the style of Lysippos – royal sculptor to Alexander the Great. The head and body also reveal a body style similar to that of Praxiteles' *Aphrodite*...though the *Venus de Milo* exhibits far more complex movement. [see *Aphrodite of Cyrene*, #20]

The *Venus de Milo* was likely commissioned by a wealthy land-owner who frequented or even financed the ancient outdoor gymnasium where it was found...or by civic leaders from the nearby Greek settlement [now in ruins].

Louvre visitors wishing to experience the mystique and allure of this iconic statue are advised to arrive early or late in the day, especially during summer. By mid-mornings, a sea of bodies and heads often surrounds the *Venus*...and other icons of the Louvre. Overly-loud tour guides begin to arrive 'in force' by mid-morning and well into afternoon.

The museum is open 2 evenings a week...early summer evenings [on clear days] may provide superior natural light for the Venus.

Note: look for 'the S-curve figure' inside the Notre Dame Cathedral.

Finding *Venus de Milo* in the Louvre

Venus is moved from time to time...therefore, consult the Main Information Desk beneath the Pyramid entrance for specific directions [get them in writing]. Ask how to approach *Venus de Milo* from the opposite end of the Antiquites Grecques corridor. If offered a confusing 'Plan/Information' handout [its terms often do not agree with Louvre signage], ask a second clerk for written assistance.

Be forewarned: uniformed museum employees are often security; and therefore, they may know little or nothing about the art they protect and its location.

Major References:

Disarmed...Story of the Venus de Milo, 2003, Curtis
Louvre Museum, pamphlet, 2008
The Nude, a Study in Ideal Form, 1956, Clark, p 89
The Life of Greece, 1939, Durant, p 133, 624

Louvre, 2007, Scala, p 100
Art in the Western World, 1953, Robb & Garrison, p 447-48
30,000 Years of Art, 2007, Phaidon, p 288
Ancient Greece, 1997, Durando, p 154
Encyclopedia of Sculpture, 2006, Lenghan, p 1716
Greek and Roman Sculpture, 1972, Lawrence, p 237
Arts of the Ancient Greeks, 1972, Brilliant, p 365-6, 368-9, 372, 388
Classical Myths in Sculpture, 1951, Agard, p 19-20
Greek Sculpture, 1960, Carpenter, p 197
Art Through the Ages, Vol I, 1980, Gardner, p 141, 148
Smithsonian, Oct/2003, Curtis, p 106-07
Mythology, 1942, Hamilton p 256, 259

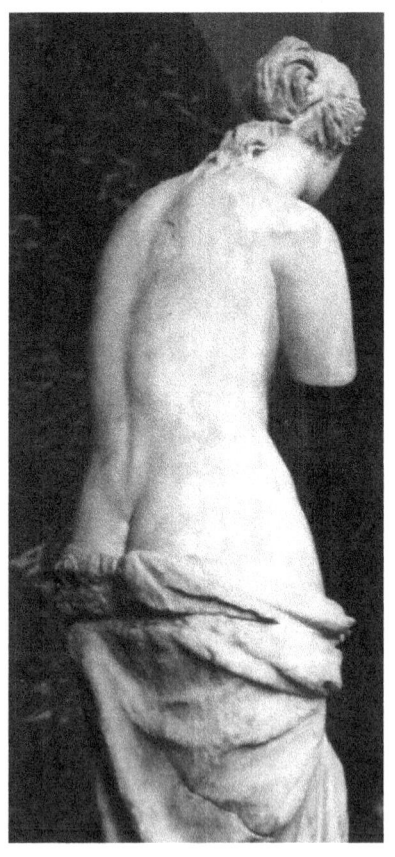

49

THE BELVEDERE TORSO

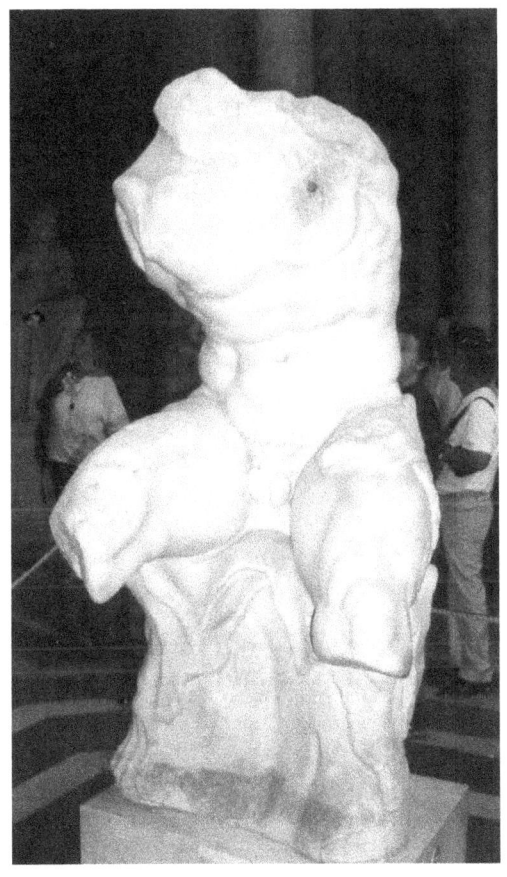

"The *Torso* is grand, noble, from the realm of heroic myth."
...Smith, *Hellenistic Sculpture*, p 54

First documented 1432-35, Rome – in Vatican since 1532
Greek Orig. [or Roman copy] – 60 BC – Late Hellenistic Baroque
Ht: 62.5 in [1.59 m] over-life-size – Parian marble
Sculptor: Apollonios of Athens, or an unknown copyist

Were the *Belvedere Torso* whole, it could hardly be more impressive.

This work may have influenced Rodin … *the Thinker* #87 compares. Even the enamored Michelangelo was inspired … over and over.

Bazin comments: "This mutilated torso – <u>hailed as a miracle</u> – has been variously identified as Hercules, Marsyas, and, most recently, the wounded Philoctetes." [*History of World Sculpture*, p 160]

Nolan describes it as: "<u>a powerful and moving heroic nude</u> with super-human muscular development … seated on a rock covered by a panther skin. No known source from Antiquity directly mentions the *Belvedere Torso* or the artist. Instead, it became a famed icon through its reincarnation during the Renaissance in Rome … first documented about 1432-35 as part of the collection of Cardinal Prospero Colonna. Documents place it in the Vatican by 1532, where it was installed in the sculpture court of the Belvedere … from which the *Torso* takes its name." [*Encyclo Sculpt.*, p 145-6] Many copies and casts were created for art academies throughout Europe.

O'Neill observes: "The powerful body of a man of advanced age is seated on a rock. The upper torso bends forward, to the right, as the body turns left. The right arm was lowered, perhaps leaning on the thigh, while the left arm was raised at the side … correspondingly, the left leg extended forward and the right one somewhat back." [*Vatican Collections*, p 64]

That the marble legs, buttocks, and the arms are missing may be because its sculptor made these parts detachable. Dowel holes and unaltered joining surfaces suggest these body parts were originally detachable. Unfortunately, detachability may have made these parts more attractive to workers in Antiquity who broke down marble for the making of lime. [Nolan, p 145]

The 1968 *Vatican Museums, Rome* says it is: "of uncertain provenance [but certainly Roman]...one of the few marbles to have escaped the dangerous and often fanciful 'completions' by restorers who, from the Renaissance on, falsified masterpieces found in fragmentary condition...until 19th century historicism created greater respect for originals..." [p 22, 25]

Unconfirmed traditions suggest the original Rome location of the *Belvedere Torso* could have been at the Campo di Fiori,.. the Baths of Caracalla...the Baths of Constantine...or on the Quirinal Hill. [Nolan, p 146]

Michelangelo Influenced

In *Rome, Eternally Beautiful,* Fattorusso says: "The accuracy of its anatomy is so perfect, that <u>its discovery caused a revolution in the field of art...Michelangelo studied it to such a degree that he was wont to call himself pupil of the *Torso*</u>." [p 161]

It was held in wide high esteem "largely from Michelangelo's admiration for it and the belief that he had discovered in it a 'certain principle...which principle gave his works a grandeur of gusto equal to the best antiques...'." [Bullfinch, 269]

The *Torso* also may have influenced Michelangelo due to the "emphatic anatomy of the large and compact muscular masses, which are not inert but 'in action'." Michelangelo modeled "exact counterparts" of the back and front of the *Torso* in the modeling of his *Ignudi* on the Sistine Chapel ceiling and St. Bartholomew of the *Last Judgement* respectively.... plus, in his figure *Day* in the Medici Chapel of the Church of San Lorenzo in Florence. [Nolan, p 146]

References suggest Michelangelo, impressed by the fragmentary nature of the *Torso*, therefore left many of his own works unfinished. Other sources say he simply did not have adequate time to finish such works due to being "overwhelmed with commissions". [Bullfinch, 269] [Nolan, p 146]

That the *Torso* remained unrestored is said to be due "to the sentiments of Michelangelo, who was quoted as saying that he was unqualified to restore the ancient fragment by Apollonios." [Nolan, p 146]

After this declaration, no one else dared.

Subject:

There are two schools of thought concerning its subject. The first and oldest suggests this marble represents a divine being...such as Hercules, mortal son of Zeus. *Bullfinch* states: "the heavy muscularity of the torso and the animal skin upon which it is seated suggest that the completed statue represented Hercules." [p 269] The Vatican Museum also offers Hercules as the subject.

Nolan suggests other subjects: "Recent interpretations of the *Torso* based on comparisons with images preserved in vase paintings, gems, and silver include Philoctetes...the satyr Marsyas with his arms bound behind him...Marsyas playing the pipes...and a pensive Ajax..." [p 147]

Smith references a painting in Herculaneum – *Olympos & Marsyas* – in suggesting the subject is *Marsyas*: "If one wants to visualize a sculptured version of such a *Marsyas*, the *Belvedere Torso* might serve well. The famous *Torso* is seated, not on a lion-skin of Hercules, but on a panther-skin, the regular animal-wear of satyrs. It sits on a rocky base which indicates a figure of the outdoors, and it has a hole in the small of the back that can be explained as a dowel hole for the addition of the short stub of a satyr's tail. The panther-like-skin shows the *Torso* must belong to the realm of Dionysus..." [*Hellenistic Sculpture,*, p 133]

Hamilton describes the fate of *Marsyas*: "The flute was invented by Athena, but she threw it away because in order to play it she had to puff out her cheeks and disfigure her face. *Marsyas*, a satyr, found it and played so enchantingly upon it that he dared to challenge Apollo to a contest. The god won, of course, and punished *Marsyas* by flaying him." [author of *Mythology*, p 435]

Note: The Uffizi in Florence displays a bound *Marsyas*.

The *Torso* is stylistically associated with the *Laocoon* #52 and the sculptural frieze from the *Altar of Zeus* #43 from Pergamon, which places the *Torso* stylistically in the Hellenistic Baroque period." [Nolan, p 145-6]

Coveted by Napoleon, the *Belvedere Torso* was taken to Paris in 1797...and not returned until 1816.

Sculptor:

Opinions vary sharply among art authorities concerning the sculptor: between the Greek Apollonius ... or an unknown artist [approx. 100 years earlier] who labored on the *Gigantomachy* [*Great Altar of Pergamon* #43] ... or a Neo-Attic copyist.

Bazin favors Apollonius: "... it seems to be an original creation of the Athenian sculptor Apollonius, son of Nestor, whose signature appears on the rough-hewn base. Apollonius may have been among the most important of the Neo-Attic sculptors working in Rome during the lst C. BC." [p 160]

Lawrence states: "... the extremely powerful physique conforms with the style of the *Gigantomachy*, so that the statue might be a copy from a Pergamese original."

Smith suggests, even though the signature of Apollonius appears on the *Torso*, we cannot be certain the signature is valid. "The *Belvedere Torso*... is the product [surely a copy] of a neo-Attic sculptor. In short, these sculptors could supply any statue or sculptural artifact that a client might want reproduced in marble. It was these same sculptors, the 'copyists', who also made for the Romans their portrait statues, the cult images of their gods, and their historical reliefs..." [p 261]

A completely restored copy is in the Albert and Victoria Museum of London.

Major References:

Vatican Collections, 1982, O'Neill, p 64-5

History of World Sculpture, 1968, Bazin, p 160

Vatican Museums, Rome, 1968, text contributors (4), p 22-5

Rome: Eternally Beautiful, 1937, Fattorusso, p 161

Vatican Museums & City, 1986, Papafava, p 46

Encyclopedia of Sculpture, 2004, Nolan, p 145-6

Greek Art and Roman Sculpture, 1972, Lawrence, p 250-51

Mythology, 1942, Hamilton, p 435

Bullfinch Guide to Art History, 1996, Shearer West (editor), p 269

Hellenistic Sculpture, 1991, Smith, 54, 133, pl 165, 261

50
THE SEATED BOXER

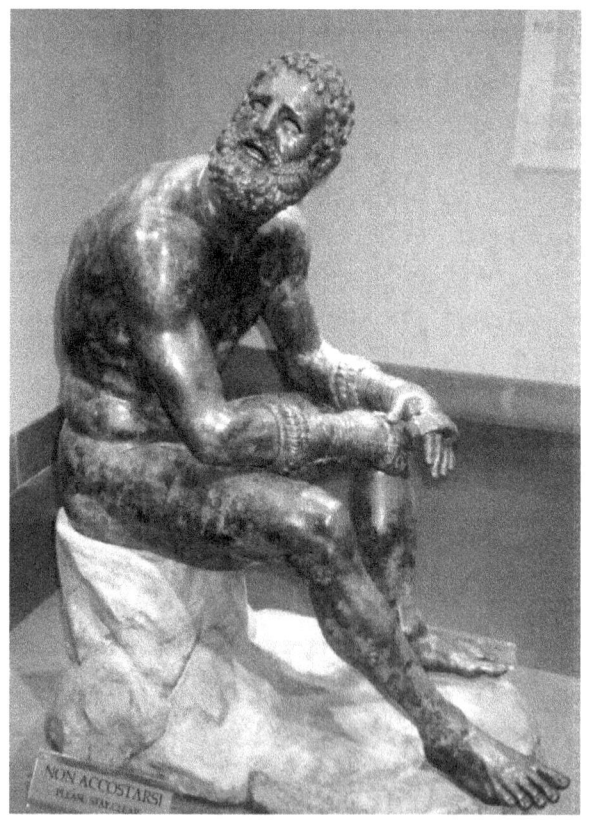

"...a masterpiece that vividly reflects
Hellenistic athletic professionalism."
...Smith, *Hellenistic Sculpture*, p 54

Found 1884, Baths of Diocletion – now, Terme, Rome
Greco-Roman Orig. bronze – 50 BC – Late Hellenistic
Height: 2.3 feet [1.2 m] – life-size
Sculptor: unknown Greco-Roman copyist
　　*buy guide book, as museum offers scant info on displays

This ancient Roman pugilist – with his brutally realistic head – is better described as a brawler. He is more an entertainer than an athlete... performing for the blood-lust of the crowd [not unlike modern kick-boxers]. In his time, at the Colosseum and other ancient arenas, the blood was plentiful and the outcome often lethal.

Durant's *Life of Greece* identifies this boxer as *the Prize Fighter*... surviving in a grand era of excess: "No student with a mind of his own will join in any sweeping judgment about Hellenistic decay... we feel in this period a slackening of creative impulse... but we are compensated by the <u>lavish abundance of an art now completely master of its tools</u>... never in its isolated youth had the Greek passion for beauty, or the Greek power and patience to embody it, spread so triumphantly, or with such rich stimulation and result, into the sleeping cities of the East. There Rome would find it, and pass it on." [p 626 & fig 64]

Reddish stains on the *Seated Boxer* are not from 2,000 years of aging. They depict: "... drops of blood [damascened in red copper] from wounds on the face... scattered over the boxer's body to show signs of combat... the hematoma under the right eye is represented with a darker alloy of bronze... copper inserts indicate metal parts of the gloves." [*Nat. Museums, Rome*, Caderio, p 28]

Pain is clearly visible on the bruised face. In the man's slumping shoulders, we see fatigue... his fight continued without interruption until one boxer surrendered. If the contest has ended... by his despair, he may have lost. Or... if victorious, he senses relief more than satisfaction.

This statue is said to have been discovered on the Quirinal Hill in Rome, in what may have been a private residence. Other references suggest, at one time, it was displayed in the nearby Baths of Diocletion.

Bazin observes: "The figure takes approximately the same position as the *Belvedere Torso* #49 ... brutal realism combines oddly with such classical stylistic elements as the treatment of the beard and hair. The contrast points up this boxer's actual remoteness from the idealized representations of athletes in the Classical period." [*History of World Sculpture,* p 161]

Lawrence adds: "... the bronze *Boxer* 'may' also be by Apollonius because the letter 'A' is clearly legible on both feet ... while the eye can discern his complete signature in some blurred markings on the left gauntlet. This statue must, in any event, date from Apollonius' time ... it may have been freely adapted from an earlier figure. The monstrous slabs of muscle and the battered face parody the style of the *Gigantomachy* on the Pergamon Altar #43." [*Greek & Roman Sculpture,* p 251]

Subject:

Gardner suggests this is: "a heavily battered veteran of the arena resting, perhaps beaten and listening to the berating of his manager. The boxer's smashed face, broken nose, and deep scars tell the gist of the story. The sculptor appeals not to our intellect but to our emotions, as he strives to evoke compassion for the battered hulk of a once-mighty fighter." [*Art Through the Ages,* p 148]

Caderio offers fine detail: "After a devastating contest – as is apparent from numerous wounds on the head – the boxer has sat down to take a rest, still breathless and with his mustache glued to his lips by sweat ... The chest is hairy and muscular, but the layer of fat and the face are those of a mature man. The marks of the last match are mixed up with the scars of a long career ... the right eye is wounded, the ears are so swollen that we have to suppose a considerable loss of hearing, the nose has previously been broken and the upper teeth are missing from the mouth. From a series of cuts evident on the forehead, cheeks, and ears ... the blood shed in the recent fight has run down the right arm and the leg." [p 26-8]

Robb & Garrison suggest the turned head and upraised eyes indicate the presence of an [unseen] fight-manager. "The sense of actuality...is heightened by its momentary pose, the head being turned to one side as if in response to a question while the jolted brain seeks painfully for an answer." [*Art in the Western World,* p 453-54]

Boxing in ancient Rome bore little resemblance to the competitive boxing introduced at the 23rd Olympic Games in 688 BC...or to traditional pugilists of today.

The early Olympian boxers, wearing leather gloves, could neither clinch nor throw hooks or uppercuts. There were no rounds or decisions by judges or technical knockouts due to injury. The contest ended when a boxer conceded defeat by raising an index finger...or, in other boxing competitions, by tapping the shoulder or back of the opponent. Homer gives us the earliest record of boxing in the 23rd book of *The Illiad*:

> "Amid the circle now each champion stands,
> And poises high in the air his iron hands,
> With clashing gauntlets now they fiercely close,
> Their crackling jaws re-echo to the blows,
> And painful sweat from all their members flow,
> At length Epeus dealt a weighty blow
> Full on the cheek of his unwary foe."

Some 700 years later, the ancient Romans introduced their version of boxing...with the cesti [caestus] – gloves of stiff leather reinforced with inserts or studs of bronze, iron or lead. Later, spikes would be introduced. The hardened leather also covered the wrists and forearms as seen in the statue. Virgil, the famed poet of Rome, gives us this account:

> "From somewhere he produced the gloves of Eryx
> And tossed them into the ring, all stiff and heavy,
> Seven layers of hide and insewn lead and iron.
> You can still see the blood and splash of brains
> That stained them long ago."

Caderio adds: "The painstaking representation of the marks left by the fight... is intended to show the boxer's toughness, a quality extolled as a symbol of the capacity to overcome any difficulty in order to attain virtue [and victory]. It is no accident that the boxer is assimilated to Hercules in his posture and features, with the aim of presenting the image of a victorious and morally worthy athlete. The statue, which almost seems to illustrate a literary paradigm, may have been the reconstructed portrait of a famous boxer." [p 28]

E.V. Lucas concludes: "... the old pugilist in bronze so conscious that pugilists cannot be successful forever." [*A Wanderer in Rome,* p 214]

Sculptor:

R. Brilliant identifies the sculptor as Apollonius of Athens, who immigrated to Rome. [p 364]

Other sources believe an obscure Roman or Greek created [or copied] the piece. Though signed 'Apollonius of Nestor', another artist may have signed that name to create the impression it was carved by the famed sculptor.

The *Boxer* could have been commissioned by either a Roman or Greek aristocrat.

Other boxers listed in book are *Agias* #26... and *Milo of Crotona* #75.

Major References:

Life of Greece, 1939, Durant, p 664
History of World Sculpture, 1968, Bazin, p 161
Museo Naztonale. Romano, 2005, Caderio, p 27-9
Art Through the Ages, 1980, Gardner, p 148
Hellenistic Sculpture, 1991, Smith, p 54, 62
Arts of the Ancient Greeks, 1972, Brilliant, 361, 364
A Wanderer in Rome, 1926, E. V. Lucas, p 214
Ancient Rome, 1996, Liberati, p 12-3, 112-3
Art in the Western World, 1953, Robb & Garrison, p 453-54,
Greek and Roman Sculpture, 1972, Lawrence, p 251

51

VENUS GENETRIX

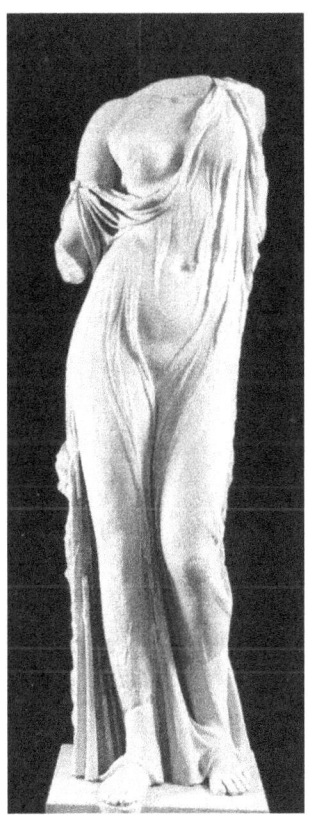

"... considered a splendid masterpiece ...
adorned with [rare] pearls from Britain."
...Clement, *Eternal City, Rome*, p 362

Found in Rome – now, Palatine Museum & Getty Villa*
Greco-Roman copy – 40 BC to 200 AD
From: Orig. marble – 46 BC – Classic & Roman style
Height: 38.5 inches [97.7 m] – marble
Sculptor: Arcesilaus, a Greek in Italy
    *copies: Terme, Louvre, Vatican, Boston, Florence, Athens, etc.

A sublime *Venus Genetrix* stands in a quiet corner of the Getty Villa in Malibu.

An equally serene and graceful *Genetrix* poses among ancient statuary in the Palatine Museum of Rome. Both are among the finest surviving copies of one of the most popular statues of Imperial Rome.

Clement states the figure: "…was considered a splendid masterpiece, and was adorned with…[rare] pearls from Britain. It is a draped figure, but the form is scarcely concealed…" [*The Eternal City: Rome,* p 362-363]

The Getty's *G&R Sculpture*…declares: "Illusionary transparency is evident in this *Venus*. The pattern of carved ridges gives the impression of a diaphanous, transparent fabric and reveals the voluptuous forms of her body." [Grossman, p 29]

Lawrence says this figure was: "The final stage of the development of 'wet' clinging drapery…it appeared on Roman coins with the legend '*Venus Genetrix*' soon after Arcesilaus made a statue so called for the Forum of Julius Caesar…who claimed descent from the goddess through Aeneas [of Troy]. A hand [missing] of the goddess lifts the end of her drapery over her shoulder…in her other hand [also missing] she holds the apple awarded by Paris to the most beautiful of goddesses." [*Greek & Roman Sculpt,* p 161-62]

The hand of this *Venus* receives the same golden apple as *Venus de Milo* #48. Both figures intrigue.

On the eve before Caesar's decisive battle against his rival Pompey at Pharsalus in 48 BC, Caesar made a vow to the goddess *Venus Genetrix*…he would dedicate a temple to her in Rome if he were victorious. Upon his triumphant return to Rome, he fulfilled that vow and also commissioned the Greco-Roman sculptor Arceilaus to create her statue. Caesar spared no expense in constructing Rome's most resplendent temple to display the statue. The temple dominated his new Forum. [today, its sparse ruins are to the right of the ascending Sacred Way as we move past the Arch of Severus]

The Forum of Julius Caesar and its temple – though incomplete – were dedicated on the final day of Caesar's greatest triumphal parade, September 26 in 46 BC. Each year, on this date by long tradition, ancient Romans held an annual festival to honor *Venus* as their ancestral goddess.

Mozzati reveals: "the Forum of Caesar, begun by him in 46 BC, was completed by Augustus... extended and rebuilt by Trajan in 113 AD... and substantially restored by Diocletian after the fire of 283 AD. This was the oldest of the Imperial forums..." and included "the equestrian statue of the dictator in the center, and the temple at the far end..." [*Rome: Sites & Monuments,* p 10-11, 58]

"The Temple of Venus Genetrix stood on a high podium... it had 8 columns on each side... its fourth side was originally built up against the saddle of the Capitoline Hill. The cella [enclosed central chamber] – probably vaulted and decorated with valuable columns of *giallo antico* marble – ended in an apse and housed the statue of *Venus.* The Temple also displayed many pictures and other statues dedicated to Cleopatra and perhaps Caesar himself." [p 58]

Eventually... Caesar's *Venus Genetrix* was lost... due to fire, theft, or otherwise. A statue commissioned by Julius Caesar would have been highly coveted as a trophy by any invader. Countless copies, mostly low quality, were sculpted during the Empire. An 'average' one is seen in the Capitoline Museum of Rome. The Louvre copy is poorly restored.

Further background concerning Julius Caesar appears in 2 chapters: *the She-Wolf* #10 and *the Black Caesar* #54.

Subject:

Venus, by Roman legend, gave birth to Aeneas, the Trojan hero whose ancestors – Romulus and Remus – were the founders of Rome and of Caesar's *Julian* clan.

Caesar wished his version of the Greek goddess to firmly illustrate and reinforce his family's claim of descent from Venus. Consequently, its 'fertility aspect' is clearly distinguished by the figure's reproductive attributes.

Two folds of her translucent gown delineate the gateway of birth … and, above, a breast is bared in the manner of a nursing mother. The Getty Museum is academic: "Venus, the goddess of love, stands clothed in a sheer, clinging garment that leaves one breast bare and emphasizes her body underneath, especially her genitalia." [www.getty.edu, 2009]

When Caesar commissioned the *Venus Genetrix*, he also may have had a practical reason. Durant reveals: in 45 BC, Caesar … "Long disturbed by the fall in the birth rate … had given precedence in land allotments to fathers of 3 children … now he promulgated rewards for large families and forbade childless women under 45 to ride in litters or wear jewelry." [C&C, p 193]

Janson asserts the Forum of Julius Caesar: "… set the pattern for all the later Imperial forums, which were linked to it by a common major axis, forming the most magnificent architectural sight of the Roman world …" [*History of Art*, p 157]

As testimony to <u>the opulence</u> of Caesar's Forum, it was disgracefully pillaged during the Renaissance for its fine marbles. His Forum now consists of little more than 3 restored columns with an entablature … though both the columns and table are richly carved and suggest the splendor of the temple.

[Durant discloses: "In just 4 years, 1546-9, new builders destroyed or dismantled the temples of Castor and Pollux, Julius Caesar, and Augustus. Material for the Sistine Chapel was quarried from the mausoleum of Hadrian. Practically all the marble used in raising St. Peter's was taken from classic buildings; and to the same shrine went the podium, steps, and pediment of the temple of Antoninus and Faustina, the triumphal arches of Fabius Maximus and Augusta, and the temple of Romulus, son of Maxientius." p 495]

Other Ancient Motherhood
& Fertility Figures:

In this compendium, they include: the *Snake Goddess...She-Wolf...Demeter...Altar of Aphrodite...* the *Crouching Aphrodite...* the *Venus de Milo...* the *Tellus* relief on the Ara Pacis...Michaelangelo's *Pieta...* Moore's *Recumbent* figure...and Vigeland's wealth of mothers in Oslo. *Aphrodite* also is one of the *Three Goddesses* #17. Similar themes appear in pre-historic figures such as the limestone *Venus of Willendorf* [21,000 BC] illustrating pregnancy by exceptional swelling of the abdomen and prominence of the birth gateway. [Bazin, p 92]

Sculptor:

Arcesilaus, a Greek sculptor who worked in Rome, is believed to have created Caesar's *Venus Genetrix*. Durant says he was considered one of "the greatest of...artists working in Italy, who drew high fees and lived in peripatetic [itinerant] luxury. The Roman Lucullus gave Arcesilaus a million sesterces to make a statue of the goddess Felicitas..." [C&C, p 342]

Several references refer to Caesar's *Genetrix* as an adaptation of an earlier work by the Classic Greek sculptor Callimachus. It is known he created a similar statue in about 410 BC, which proved highly popular at the time. How much Caesar's *Venus Genetrix* resembled the work of Callimachus is unknown.

The Louvre copy of the *Genetrix* [known as *Venus of Frejus*] is cold in comparison to the *Venus* on the Palatine or in the Getty Villa. Lesser examples are also found in the Boston Museum of Fine Arts...Borghese Gallery...Palazzo Colonna...Detroit Institute of Arts...the Uffizi in Florence...the Glyptothek in Copenhagen...the Naples National Museum...Holkam Hall...Mantua...Montpellier...and other locations.

Major References:

Rome: Sites & Monuments, 2006, Mozzati, p 10-11, 58
Greek and Roman Sculpture, 1972, Lawrence, p 161-62, 166
The Eternal City: Rome, 1896, Clara Erskine Clement, p 362-63

Ancient Rome: Past and Present, 1959, Wiley, p 52-3

Caesar and Christ, 1944, Durant, p 193, 342, 349

Arts of the Ancient Greeks, 1972, Brilliant, p 241-42

Greek and Roman Sculpture in Stone, 2003, Grossman, p 29

History of Art, 1977, Janson, p 157-59

History of World Sculpture, 1968, Bazin, p 92

30,000 Years of Art, 2007, Phaidon, p 5

52

THE LAOCOON

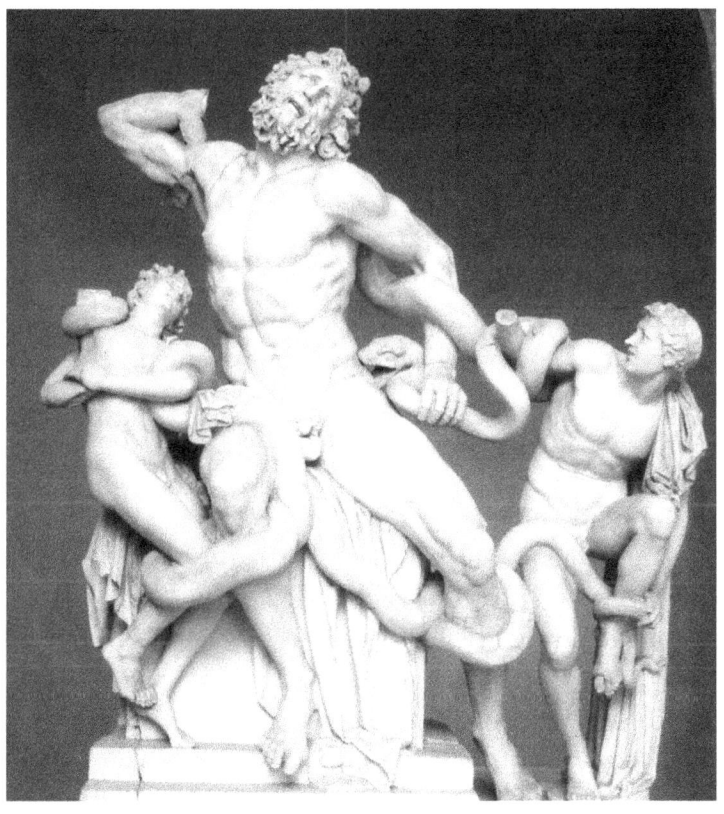

"One of the most famous statues in classic antiquity...
hailed as a masterpiece of the finest period of Greek sculpture."
...Robb & Garrision , *Art in the Western World*, p 452.

Found Jan 14, 1506, Esquiline Hill, Rome – now, Vatican
Greco-Roman Orig. – 30 BC-20 AD – Hellenistic High Baroque
or: adapted from [lost] Orig. Greek bronze – 200 BC
Ht. 8 feet [2.44 meters] – Luna marble [outside Rome]
Sculptors: Agesander, Polydoros, & Athanadoros of Rhodes

Virgil, Roman author/poet, [70-19 BC]:
... the sea-serpents: "seize and bind in mighty folds ... the father
strains his hands to burst the knots ... his flesh steeped in blood
and black venom ... he lifts to heaven hideous cries ... like the
bellowing of a wonnded bull that has fled from the altar ... and
shaken from its neck the ill-aimed axe." [Gardner, p 148]

A gony of the father and sons builds ... as the snakes entrap them
and sink fangs into their flesh.

30,000 Years declares: "The *Laocoon* is one of the most famous,
admired, and debated sculptures in the Western World ... experts
are divided on whether it is a Hellenistic original ... or a later
Roman copy of the lst century AD. The style is typical of Hellenistic
baroque with its complex composition, dramatic poses, and exaggerated expressions." [p 289]

In the Vatican Museum ... approach this group from your left.

Focus on the younger son ... a serpent bites into his ribcage. His
left hand attempts to push it away ... but both arms are trapped in
thick coils ... his legs also are caught. He has no hope of escape. The
same serpent entraps the father's left leg.

A second serpent sinks fangs into the father's left hip. His left hand
tries to push it away ... a coil blocks the arm. The snake winds around
behind his back and entwines his other arm. [see Brilliant, p 361].

Black venom will soon incapacitate the father and younger son.

The first snake wraps its tail around the older son's left ankle.
He reaches down, attempting to push it off.

The second snake half-winds a coil around the backside of the
older son's right arm. If he can yank his right arm away and also

free his ankle, he has a chance…unless the nearest snakehead turns to him.

Bazin says: "…conflicting tensions are set up as the father and younger son sink to the left, dying, against the altar behind them…while the elder son pulls to the right in an attempt to free himself. The faces express the same paroxysm of pain that grips the giants of the Pergamon Frieze #43 where we find quite similar melodramatic chiaroscuro effects produced by the same sunken eyes, mouths half open in an agonizing cry, and tortuous strands of beards and hair." [*History of World Sculpture*, p 159]

Voorhis comments: "The naturalistic anatomy and agonized expressions of the figures were highly praised by and profoundly influential for Michelangelo and his contemporaries…as well as for successive generations of artists…" including Rubens, Titian, and Raphael. [*Encyclo Sculpt*, p 918]

The Durants tell us the interior of the extravagant Golden House built by the Roman emperor Nero "gleamed with marble, bronze, and gold…with thousands of statues, reliefs, paintings, and objects of art bought or looted from the classic world…among them *the Laocoon*." [p 345]

Later, another Roman author Pliny the Elder remarked: "The *Laocoon* – placed in the house of the emperor Titus – should be rated <u>above all works of art</u>, whether in painting or sculpture." [Lawrence, p 249]

Subject:

The legend of this epic struggle has both Greek and Roman versions. The older Greek account describes the *Laocoon* as a priest who offended the god Apollo by breaking an oath of celibacy and fathering children…procreating on holy ground sacred to Poseidon. While the *Laocoon* prepares a sacrifice at an altar along the seashore with his sons [Antipha and Thymbraeus], two serpents sent by Poseidon [or Apollo] emerge from the sea to crush and poison the father and sons. [Voorhis, p 917; Boardman, p 189]

The better known Roman version [from Virgil] begins near the end of the Trojan War … when neither side has won a decisive victory. The Greeks pretend to withdraw. As a parting 'offering of peace', the Greeks construct and leave a giant hollow horse … [within which their finest warriors hide].

The Trojan priest *Laocoon* forewarns Troy not to accept gifts from the Greeks. When he is ignored, *Laocoon* throws his lance at the wooden horse.

Gombrich's *Story of Art* says: "The gods [Poseidon and Athena on the side of the Greeks] – seeing their plans of destroying Troy threatened – send two gigantic snakes from the sea which catch the priest and his two unfortunate sons in their coils and suffocate them." [p 111]

Versions of the fate of father and sons vary. Most often, all 3 are crushed by the snakes … and poisoned as well. Or, the father is first blinded, then strangled with his sons. Or, the blinded father survives his sons to suffer the agony of their loss. Quintus of Smryna, about 300 AD, wrote that Athena blinded the father [uplifted eyes suggest blindness] before sending snakes to kill his sons.

In another ending not wholly tragic: the blinded father, unable to fend off the coiling serpents, dies with his younger son, while the older son pushes the snake off his body and survives to serve as a witness to the tragedy. [Smith, p 109] Brilliant concurs: "The slight distancing of the elder son suggests the possibility of his escape from the serpents' coils, as in the version of this episode by Arctinus of Miletus." [*My Laocoon*, p 10]

Bazin semi-agrees with Brilliant. [p 159]

That the Greeks fought long and hard at Troy may be true.

Durant informs us: "An Egyptian inscription of Ramses III reports that 'the [Greek] isles were restless' toward 1196 BC … and Pliny alludes to a Ramses 'in whose time Troy fell'. The great Alexandrian scholar Eratosthenes – on the basis of traditional genealogies collated late in the 6th century before Christ by the geographer-historian Hecataeus – calculated the date of the siege as 1194 BC." [*Life of Greece*, p 55]

Durant mentions a practical goal of the Greeks. "Euripides attributed the expedition to excess population in Greece, and the consequent urge to expansion...in the struggle of two groups of powers for possession of the Hellespont and the rich lands lying about the Black Sea. Nevertheless, it is possible that some story, such as the abduction of a beautiful woman [Helen of Troy], was used to make the adventure digestible for the common Greek...men must have phrases to give their lives." [p 55]

Discovery:

In Rome, on January 14, 1506, this remarkable sculptural group [in pieces] was unearthed from the ruins of the giant holding tanks at the Baths of Trajan. When word of its discovery reached Pope Julius II, he immediately instructed his architect Giuliano de Sangallo [with whom Michelangelo was visiting at the time] to investigate the extraordinary find. They rushed to the site, where Sangallo promptly exclaimed:

"This is the *Laocoon* mentioned by Pliny!" [Voorhis, p 918]

"Marvelous!" exclaimed Michelangelo.

Julius II purchased the statuary from the finder and his son by offering them a lifetime annuity of 600 ducats [$7,500]. Though the existence of the *Laocoon* had been well-known from Pliny the Elder's description in 70 AD, it had not been seen in more than a 1,000 years.

Michelangelo attempted a poor restoration of the lost right arm. Bernini also worked on it, placing it upright. In 1906, the original right arm [hand still missing] was recovered in an artist's studio...in 1942, it was incorrectly attached...and, finally in 1960, properly reattached. [Voorhis, p 918]

Sculptors:

Agesander, his son Athanadoros, and Polydoros from the island of Rhodes [settled by Greeks 3,500 years ago] are believed to have sculpted this group from 7 or 8 blocks of Luna marble [quarried near Rome]. It might have been carved shortly after the Roman author Virgil popularized the myth of the *Laocoon* in his *Aeneid II*.

The *Laocoon* may have been adapted from an original Greek bronze at Pergamon...however, there is little evidence other than ancient Greek vases, gems, and Pompeii frescos on which the subject appears. [Lawrence, p 249-50]

The identity of the 3 Greeks sculptors comes from two sources. When the monument was in the house of the emperor Titus, Pliny the Elder named them.

[Tiberius, emperor 14 to 37 AD, owned a large seaside villa south of Rome containing the *Sperlonga* pieces...which show close similarities to the *Laocoon*. They are signed by the same 3 artists. [Voorhis, p 917; Lawrence, p 250] The 4 marble groups of the *Sperlonga Sculptures* – hammered into 5,000 fragments by Christian monks about 511 AD – were discovered in 1957. The reassembled fragments are exhibited in the Sperlonga Museum, 60 miles south of Rome.]

These 3 sculptors may have studied the earlier *Altar of Zeus* #43 in ancient Pergamon as Smith tells us. "In composition and heightened theatrical pathos, the *Laocoon* is close to the *Giant* who opposes *Athena* on the east frieze of the *Great Altar of Pergamon*." [Smith, p 109, 161]

Influence of *The Laocoon*:

...Michelangelo: *Bound Slave* in Louvre: knotted muscles similar to *Laocoon*; Sistine Chapel's *Brazen Serpent* & *Punishment of Hamen*
...Rubens: *15 drawings of Laocoon* – musculature and pathos passed into works of Rubens, especially extravagance of figures [see online]
...Titian: *Meeting of Bacchus & Ariadne*, Nat. Gallery, London
...Raphael: *Galatea* – Villa Farnesina, Rome

Major references:

The Story of Art, 1995, Gombrich, p 110-11, 129, 178, 440, 626

Hellenistic Sculpture, 1991, Smith, p 12, 108-9, 111, 161

The Eternal City...Rome, 1896, Clement, p 194

Arts of the Ancient Greeks, 1972, Brilliant, p 339, 357-60, 370, 372

My Laocoon, 2000, Brilliant, p xiv, 2-5, 10, 98

Greek and Roman Sculpture, 1972, Lawrence, p 249-50

Greek Art, 1973, Boardman, p 188-9

Art Through the Ages, 1980, Gardner, p. 144-47

Birth of Western Civilization, 1964, Grant, p 171

The Life of Greece, 1939, Durant, p 55

Encyclopedia of Sculpture, 2004, Voorhis, p 916-18

The Eternal City (2 Vol), 1896, Clara Erskine Clement, p 194

Art in the Western World, 1953, Robb & Garrison, p 452-53

History of World Sculpture, 1968, Bazin, p 159

Caesar & Christ, 1944, Durants, p 345

53

THE SPINARIO OR THORN PULLER

(SPINA IS LATIN FOR THORN)

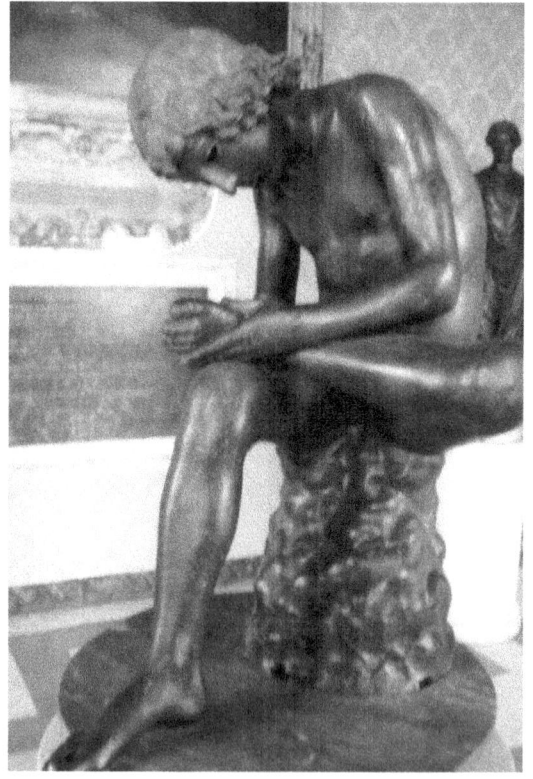

"... one of the most renowned pieces of ancient bronze sculpture"
...Janson, *History of Art*, p 14

1st recorded in 12th Cent. AD – now, Conservatori Mus, Rome*

Body: possibly Orig. [or Roman copy] – 25 BC – late Hellenistic
Head: possibly Greek Orig. – 425 BC – severe Classic style
Height: 28.75 in. [73 cm.] – bronze
Sculptors: unknown, likely from Greek school of Pasiteles
    *copy in British Museum displays grimace.

J anson says: "The *Thorn Puller*, <u>one of the most renowned pieces</u> <u>of ancient bronze sculpture</u>...enjoys considerable fame as a work of art today..." [*History of Art,* p 14] It is uncertain whether it is an original or a Roman copy. The head is likely older than the body...and may be an original Greek creation.

Clement says: "Probably no piece of *genre* [everyday subject] sculpture is more universally admired than *the Spinario*...this boy, picking a thorn from his foot, is natural and graceful, and so simple in style as apparently to belong to the best period of ancient sculpture..." [*Eternal City, Rome,* p 732]

The first record of *the Spinario* indicates the statue was placed outside the Lateran Palace of Rome in the 1160s. [*Bullfinch,* p 815]

Napoleon, in 1797, coveted the statue and ordered it transported to Paris for display in the Louvre. It was returned in 1815.

Lenaghan states: "The excellent condition of the statue and the fact that its existence is recorded in the 12th century – prior to any campaigns of excavation – indicate [possibly] that it has stood above ground from its creation until today...it was one of the few large-scale [life-size] ancient bronzes known to scholars and artists of the Renaissance...who admired the piece for its antiquity and aesthetic charm...during the Renaissance it was extremely influential and is significant to our understanding of Late Hellenistic and ancient Roman sculpture production." [*Encyclo Sculpt.* p 1600-01]

That this ancient bronze survived – with an even older head – the upheavals of some 2,000 years may be due to a subject-matter that could hardly offend anyone. If anything, it draws empathy. The statue's longevity also may be due to its relatively small size, which offered little raw material for other purposes...and it could be hidden [during invasions] more readily than larger sculptures.

Pope Sixtus IV in 1471 gifted it to the Conservatori Museum on the Capitoline Hill. The only other major ancient bronzes in Rome with similar credentials – believed to have been openly displayed since their creation – are the *She-Wolf* #10 and the *Marcus Aurelius Equestrian* #60.

In 1926, travel author E.V. Lucas opined: "The most famous possession [in the Capitoline Museum] is the bronze figure of the boy removing a thorn from his foot..." [p 164]

Subject:

Lenaghan explains: "The statue was popularly believed to represent a shepherd named Martius who diligently delivered a message to the Roman Senate... only *afterward* stopping to remove a thorn from his foot." [p 1601] Bullfinch adds, "... the Roman Senate commissioned it to commemorate a conscientious messenger boy...inspiring its popular Italian name, *Il Fedele*, 'the Faithful One'." [p 815-16]

Hafner describes the *Thorn Puller* as: "an insignificant act used to portray the beauty of the youthful body. He is a well-bred boy, nicely groomed, whose tender foot has been injured...and this trivial incident shows the painful discovery of...raw nature – a nature which he seeks out, all the same. The significance of this piece would be lost if the boy were a mere peasant lad." [*Art of Crete, Mycenae, & Greece*, p 239]

Monti observes: "The sculpture is based on Hellenistic models, perhaps of the 2nd C. BC...in this eclectic remake, each realistic element has been cleverly softened in order to compose a calm and balanced figure...the sculptor – almost certainly of the *Augustan* period – has added a young head in the '*Severe*' style to the youthful body..." [*Capitoline Museums*, p 67-8]

During the Hellenistic Age, Lenaghan says: "highly naturalistic genre scenes, which provided glimpses of country life and that often had – through their outdoor setting, nakedness, or drunkenness – connections to the world of Dionysus, were for the first time made on a life-size scale, with delightfully virtuoso handling." [p 1601]

Smith agrees: "*The Spinario* ... is an attractive life-size figure ... The thorn-in-foot motif was popular for satyr and Pan figures, and connects *Spinario* to the Dionysian world." [*Hellenistic Sculpture,* p 137]

The reason for the 'added' head is unknown – the original head may have been removed as 'booty' by a marauding army ... or by a thief. Or ... a Greco-Roman sculptor [or his patron] may have changed their mind [after completion of the statue] and preferred a head with an entirely different expression. The practice of borrowing Greek heads from an earlier era was not uncommon in Rome during the 1st century BC.

The British Museum displays the *Castellani Spinario* found on the Esquiline Hill of Rome ... the museum claims this copy retains its original head. It offers a 'grimace' instead of the more serious and contemplative expression on the Capitoline figure.

Lawrence reports: "the *Spinario* [in Rome] combines an old type of head with a Lysippic-type body which bore in the original a less pretty head ... such as that seen on a copy in the British Museum. The hair of the *Spinario*, whose head is bent forward so sharply, should of course fall over the face instead of maintaining its original position." [*Greek & Roman Sculpture,* p 244-45]

During the Renaissance, numerous copies were commissioned, often as diplomatic gifts. Surviving statues include 5 marble copies of the body ... and 10 separate heads.

Lenaghan concludes: "... it seems probable that both original models [Capitoline Mus. and British Mus.] date after the late 2nd C. BC ... and were intended to depict no subject more specific than a country boy with a thorn in his foot." [p 1602]

Sculptor:

The Greco-Roman sculptor remains unknown ... but is likely from the school of Pasiteles.

Lawrence informs us: "The prominent Greek sculptors of Rome commanded a high price for work but seldom signed their names ... Most celebrated of these artists was Pasiteles ... To a large extent his rivals and pupils adapted or imitated older sculptures…The athlete signed by Stephanus, pupil of Pasiteles, suggests that to this school should be assigned such statues as the *Resting Hermes,* and the boy removing a thorn from his foot." [p 244]

Major References:

Capitoline Museums, Rome, 1984, Monti, p 67-8

History of Art, 1977, Janson, p 12, 14-5

Encyclopedia of Sculpture, 2004, Lenaghan, p 1600-02

A Wanderer in Rome, 1926, Lucas, p 164

Hellenistic Sculpture, 1991, Smith, p 136-37

Rome, the Eternal City, 1896, Clement, p 732

Bullfinch Guide to Art History, 1996, p 815-16

Greek and Roman Sculptures, 1972, Lawrence, p 244, pl.72c

Art of Crete, Mycenae, and Greece, 1968, Hafner, p 239

Art & Architecture of Rome, 2005, Hintzen-Bohlen, p 53

54

THE BLACK CAESAR

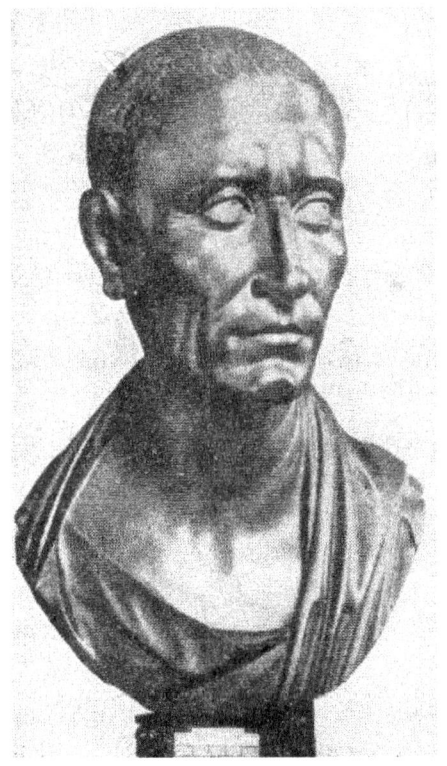

"The greatest of the portrait busts..."

... *Caesar & Christ*, 1944, Durant, p 350

"...suggests the keen and incisive mind of the man...burning
ambition...evident in every line of the ravaged countenance."

Art in Western World, 1953, Robb & Garrison , p 458

Acquired 1790 by Frederick the Great –now, Classical Mus. Berlin
Greco-Egyptian Orig. [or copy of Roman orig.] – 50 AD – realistic
Height: 13 in. [41 cm] – green-black Egyptian basalt
Sculptor: unknown Greek or Roman

> The language in England and the United States might
> not have been English ... if the military genius of Caesar
> had not repelled most of the Germanic invasions into
> Gaul during his lifetime. It might have become German.
> ... *Caesar & Christ*, Durant, p 174-78
> ... *Anchor Atlas-World History*, 1974, p 90-154

The finest surviving sculpture of Julius Caesar is the inscrutable *Black Caesar*. Ironically, today, this bust of the victor over the ancient Germans receives a place of honor in the principal city of Germany.

Durant describes it as: "The greatest of the portrait busts ... the sparse hair and sharp chin, thin and bony face, the heavy lines of weary thought, the resolution yielding to disillusionment, accord well with the traditional attribution." [C&C, p 350]

In approx. 1790, it was purchased in Paris by Frederick the Great, King of Prussia. The bust is now in the Berlin Museum of Classical Antiquities. [Scott, p 125]

30,000 Years states: "...this portrait shows little idealization...facial wrinkles and sunken cheeks are appropriate for an authoritative, patrician Roman...giving the portrait a majestic presence...enhanced by the rich sheen of the polished green-black Egyptian basalt...and the characterful gaze of the inlaid rock crystal eyes. It is probably a copy [Egyptian] of an original for which Caesar would have sat. Its Egyptian origin is based on the stone type...and ancient cities in the [Roman] empire [wished] to curry favor with its emperors." [p 319]

Robb & Garrison say: "the sculptor omitted no detail essential to an exact likeness of the living man...taut muscles of the lean throat, the furrowed brow, the lines around the mouth and chin... are specific and individual traits. At the same time...the bust <u>suggests</u> <u>the keen and incisive mind of the man.</u> The sensuality for which Caesar was famous in a sensual age can be read in the thin lips, no less than the burning ambition whose implacable demands are evident in every line of the ravaged countenance." [*Art in the Western World*, p 458]

30,000 Years estimates the bust was created near the middle of the first century AD, because: "Republican patrician busts usually ended at the neck, but this piece includes some of the chest and toga, not common until the first century AD." [p 319]

In the Berlin museum, *the Black Caesar* commands the center of a large, shadowed reception hall. He is presented alone, unadorned. His immortality rivals that of Alexander...neither man requires a more distinguished setting than himself.

Visitors can approach the *Black Caesar* at close quarters. He appreciated a quick mind. Face to face, we might inquire of him:

'How did you survive on the field of battle? You were outnumbered almost every time.'

His response: '*With patience... and discipline. In intervals of peace, I worked my soldiers so hard they begged for battle instead.*'

Caesar's victories were rewarded by an unprecedented 5 triumphs – grand processions through Rome...along the Sacred Way...and up the Capitoline Hill. We may ask: 'Why did your legions follow you so blindly?'

We see a slight smile. '*My boys believed the blood in my veins came from the gods... therefore, I could not lose.*'

His Julian clan claimed ancestry from Ascanius, son of the Trojan warrior Aeneas...by legend, offspring of *Venus*. [Durant, III, p 167]

'*And my boys loved me,*' he adds.

Though born a patrician, Caesar was fluent in the coarse slang of his legions and could entertain them with their own ribald humor...which they freely returned. As they paraded in his triumphs, Suetonius reports his 'boys' chanted:

'*Home, we bring our bald whoremonger.*
Romans... lock your wives away!

All the bags of gold you lent him
Went his Gallic tarts to pay.' [*Twelve Caesars*, Seutonius, p 34]

Our final query: 'How could you have walked undefended into the Senate that day?'

Silence. His fatal decision remains an enigma.

Subject:

Seutonius, in *The Twelve Caesars*, reveals: "Caesar is said to have been tall, fair, and well-built, with a rather broad face and keen, dark-brown eyes. He was something of a dandy, always keeping his head carefully trimmed and shaved…His baldness was a disfigurement which his enemies harped upon, much to his exasperation…he used to comb the thin strands of his hair forward…and, of all the honors voted him by the Senate and the People, none pleased him so much as the privilege of wearing a gold laurel-wreath on all occasions…" [p 32]

The 'gold wreath' was awarded to Roman soldiers [Caesar at 20] for exceptional bravery in saving the life of another soldier. When a Roman so honored wore his gold wreath and entered a building, all persons within were required to rise, including members of the Roman Senate. The award automatically gave the recipient membership in the Senate. The gold-wreathed Caesar took particular pleasure entering the Curia [Senate building]…compelling even his senatorial enemies to stand in respect.

Caesar was noted for brevity. In 47 BC, when he "defeated Pharnaces [son of Mithridates the Great] at Zela, Caesar sent to a friend in Rome the laconic report: "Veni, vidi, vici" (I came, I saw, I conquered) [Durant, III, p 188]

Suetonius adds: "This refers not to the events of the war…but to the speed with which it had been won." [p 30] The unique, rhythmic phrase entered the lexicon of European languages…taking on broader, popular meanings through the centuries.

Durant describes Julius Caesar as "the most complete man that antiquity produced." [II, p 197] Seutonius concurs: "Caesar equalled, if he did not surpass, the greatest orators and generals the world had ever known." [p 34]

The famed Roman orator Cicero – though hostile to Caesar – humbly wrote: 'Very well, then! Do you know any man who – even if he has concentrated on the art of oratory to the exclusion of all else – can speak better than Caesar? Or…anyone who makes so many witty remarks? Or…whose vocabulary is so varied and yet so exact?'" [p 34]

Clement confirms: "Even his enemy, Cicero, admits that he was a genius, and possessed of superior understanding, taste, precision, reflection, industry, and memory." [*Eternal City, Rome,* II, p 616]

Seutonius also wrote: "Caesar was a most skilled swordsman and horseman, and showed surprising powers of endurance. He always led his army, more often on foot than in the saddle…went bare-headed in sun and rain alike…and could travel for long distances at incredible speed in a gig, taking very little luggage. If he reached an unfordable river, he would either swim or propel himself across on an inflated skin…and often arrived at his destination before the messengers whom he had sent ahead to announce his approach." [p 35]

The Assassinaton:

Durant speculates the body and mind of Caesar at 55 – prematurely aged by the hardships of military campaigns – may have been too weary to take precautions. Or, he may have had an incurable illness. [C&C, p 190]

Seutonius wrote: "Some of his friends suspected that, having no desire to live much longer because of his failing health, he had taken no precautions against the conspiracy, and neglected the warnings of soothsayers and well-wishers. On the day before his murder, he had dined at Marcus Lepidus' house, where a topic discussed happened to be 'the best sort of death', and Caesar cried out: *Let it come swiftly and unexpectedly!*" [p 45]

Clement reviews reactions: "Seneca condemns the murder with abhorrence…the Greeks regarded it as atrocious…Tacitus is non-committal…Plutarch regards Caesar as one sent by Providence to establish a monarchy…Livy agrees with him." [II, p 615]

Durant cautions: "The past would be startled if it could see itself in the pages of the historians."

He adds: "The assassination of Caesar was one of the major tragedies of history...it interrupted a great labor of statesmanship and led to 15 more years of chaos and war...probably both parties were right: the conspirators in thinking that Caesar meditated monarchy, Caesar in thinking that disorder and empire had made monarchy inevitable. Men have divided on the issue ever since the Senate sat for a moment in consternation at the deed...and then fled in tumult and terror from the hall." [p 198]

Suetonius concludes: "Very few, indeed, of the assassins outlived Caesar for more than 3 years. Some died naturally. All were condemned, and all perished in different ways – some in shipwreck, some in battle, some using the very daggers with which they had murdered Caesar to take their own lives." [p 45]

Sculptor and Commission:

The sculptor of the *Black Caesar* was likely Greek...and the bust may have been commissioned in Egypt. Or, the bust could have been secretly spirited out of Egypt in much the same manner as the bust of *Nefertiti* #4.

Or...a block of green-black Egyptian basalt was exported from Egypt to Europe, where a highly-skilled sculptor fashioned it into this bust.

In Paris, the Louvre exhibits a striding *Caesar* by Nicholas Coustou [1658-1733] completed in 1722. In imperial finery, he wears the famed golden wreath. [see last photo at chapter end]

A realistic image of Caesar in his final years is seen in the Capitoline Museum bust [with Medusa cuirass], a portrayal of a rapidly-aging man. [in Naples, the same Medusa cuirass is worn by the charging *Alexander* #45] Medusa was a talisman of good fortune for the wearer and bad luck to an opponent. In ancient myth, if a man made the mistake of looking directly at the snake-haired Medusa, he would turn to stone.

In the Forum of Rome … near the ruins of the Temple of Venus Genetrix, we find a standing bronze of *Caesar* [facing Via Fori Imperiale]. The darkly-mottled bronze is hardly recognizable as a statue of Caesar, except in the morning sun. It is a modern reproduction of the excellent *Caesar* inside the virtually-inaccessible Town Hall of Rome – better known as the Palazzo Senatorio [City Council of Rome] atop the Capitoline Hill.

The Vatican Museum displays a notable bust of Caesar … with whom we may *converse* at eye-level. [below]

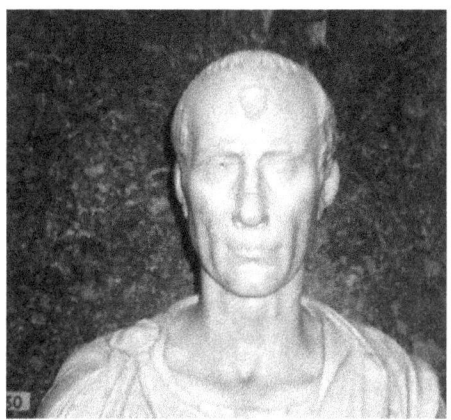

Major References:

Anchor Atlas of World History, Vol 1, 1974, p 90-154

Ancient Rome, 1996, Liberati & Bourbon, p 42

Art in the Western World, 1953, Robb and Garrison, p 458

The Twelve Caesars, Suetonius, 119 AD, (Penguin, 1980, Graves)

Life of Greece, Vol II, 1939, Durant, p 122, 197, 425, 615, 616

Caesar & Christ, Vol III, 1944, Durant, p 167, 188, 190, 198, 224, 350

The Eternal City, Rome; II, 1896, Clement, p 615-16

30,000 Years of Art, 2007, Phaidon Press, p 319

A Traveler in Rome, 1957, H. V. Morton, p 217

Portraitures of Julius Caesar, 1903, Scott, p 125

Alexander and Actium, 1990, Green, p 665

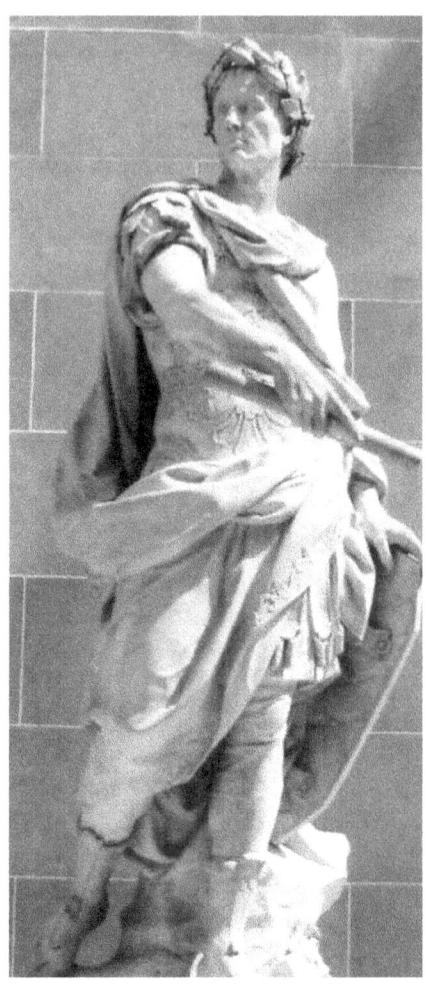

55

ARA PACIS

OR ALTAR OF PEACE, AUGUSTAE

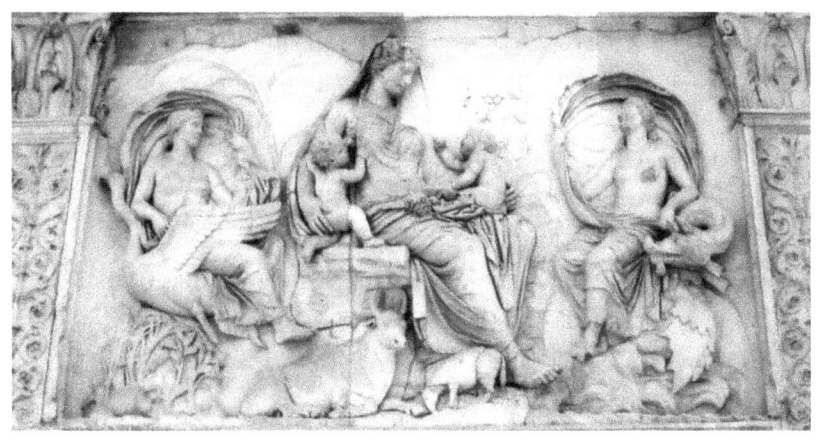

Tellus relief – "... the noblest of all the sculptural remains of Rome."
... Durant, *Caesar & Christ*, 1944, p 348

Dedicated 9 BC, Rome ... re-discovered 1568/ 1859/ 1903
Greco-Roman – marble altar – Classic Greek & Roman
Size: Ht. 11.5 m; rectangular 35.5' x 39' [11.6 m x 10.6 m]
Sculptors: unknown Greco-Romans
        *restored & enclosed in large pavilion near original location,
        between the Tiber and ruins of Augustus Mausoleum

A third of the statuary listed earlier in this book symbolizes victory – either military or athletic.

Here ... *peace* is celebrated.

We may stand near the <u>first Imperial family of Rome</u> ... in parade: Augustus ... wife Livia ... her son Tiberias ... Agrippa ... and Julia, daughter of Augustus.

Hintzen-Bohlen's *Art & Architecture: Rome* explains the *Altar*: "<u>symbolized the age of peace that had dawned</u> – after centuries of conflict – with the policies introduced by the new imperial autocracy." Not only had Augustus ended the civil war between those who supported Caesar and those who did not, he militarily defeated all others who threatened his own leadership ... including Anthony and Cleopatra, at the Battle of Actium. [p 215]

The *Altar of Peace* displays the exceptional artistic skill of the Imperial Romans, who now ruled – by force of arms – the civilized Western world. To a significant degree, it was the Romans who 'introduced' civilization to the Western world ... following the brief 'example' of the Greeks.

Bullfinch agrees the *Ara Pacis* is a: "carving of extremely high quality ... one of the principal works of sculpture in Augustan Rome. The *Altar* has been referred to ... as <u>a masterpiece of political and social propaganda</u>." [p 224]

> [several references erroneously claim the *Ara Pacis* was dedicated by the Senate in 13 BC "to celebrate the safe return of Augustus from Gaul and Spain" or "to commemorate pacification of Gaul and Spain."]

The *Encyclo Sculpt* states: "Although Augustus refused official senatorial triumphs for his achievements in Spain and Gaul, he granted permission for an *Altar* dedicated to the grander concept of Augustan peace and material prosperity." [p 74]

30,000 Years concurs: "The *Altar*, constructed between 13 and 9 BC, was used for ceremonial offerings to the Augustan peace ... after decades of civil war. It also acknowledges Augustus' special position in Rome, even though he insisted on calling himself 'first among equals'." [p 306]

Durant concludes: "... despite a 100 defects and half a dozen idiots on the throne, the strange and subtle 'principate' that he [Augustus] had established would give the Empire the longest period of prosperity ever known to mankind [507 years*] ... the *Pax Augusta*. It would – in the perspective of time – be accounted the supreme achievement in the history of statesmanship." [*Caesar & Christ*, p 232]

*[*Pax Augustus* began in 31 BC with the Battle of Actium, became the *Pax Romana*... and lasted until 476 AD]

Subject:

The *Altar's* famed *Tellus* relief displays the theme of the *Ara Pacis*.

Durant says: "The central figure is unsurpassed ... in its union of mature motherhood and womanly beauty, tenderness, and grace ... there is a soft perfection unmatched by the stately goddesses of the Parthenon ... never again would Roman sculpture show such mastery of drapery, such natural and effective grouping, such modulations of light and shade." [p 348]

Mother Earth "holds 2 children in her arms, corn and flowers grow beside her, and animals lie contentedly at her feet. These were the leading ideas of the Augustan reformation: the family restored to parentage ... the nation to agriculture ... the Empire to peace...." [Durant, p 348]

'Mother Earth' is another aspect of Venus as the divine mother "through whom all men, animals, and plants thrive and prosper." Two younger women hold cloaks to catch favorable winds. "One figure – representing sea breezes – rides a water beast as waves flow out from beneath her; whereas the other – symbolizing freshwater breezes – pours water from a jug while sitting astride a swan." [*Encyclo*, p 74]

Other important reliefs on the *Altar* include:

... the procession of the Imperial family of Augustus [see next section],

... the Trojan Aeneas offering sacrifices to the penates [gods of agriculture],

... Mars [Roman god of war] who – mating with virgin Rhea Silva – fathered twin sons Romulus and Remus, legendary founders of Rome.

Augustan Family Procession:

The reliefs of Imperial Romans are often compared to those on the Parthenon frieze created 400 years earlier. Figures on the Parthenon represent the gods... on the *Ara Pacis* they represent people.

The realistic heads and figures of the Imperial Family includes the emperor Augustus... his stern wife Livia... her son and future emperor Tiberias... the military genius Agrippa who built the Pantheon... and Augustus' daughter Julia [unwilling wife to Tiberias and later famed for her charms, but doomed by her Imperial position]. These individuals are well-known to anyone who has read historical accounts of Imperial Rome. [or viewed reenactments on PBS]

The *Encyclo Sculpt.* says: "On the south frieze... the figure wearing the cap of *pontifex maximus* is Augustus. ... accompanied by official lictors [officials who cleared the path] and flamines [priests devoted to individual gods]." [p 75]

Durant comments, Augustus "had no pretentiousness... he is not set apart from the other citizens..." [p 229] He stands near the front of the procession, slightly taller than the others and has a somewhat younger face." [Liberati, p 132]

Behind Augustus is a consul, who holds Augustus' left elbow. The four Flaminian priests wear skullcaps with a T-shaped décor. The man holding the hand-axe is a lector. Next is Marcus Agrippa. [Liberati, p 133]

Agrippa was the most trusted minister to his father-in-law Augustus. He initially built the famed Pantheon. [rebuilt by Hadrian]. Agrippa is easily identified by a veil draped over his head... indicating he died after *Altar* construction began [but before its dedication]. [p 133]

One of his 5 children [Caius Caesar... by Julia, daughter of Augustus] grips his father's toga and looks back to his mother Julia... she is appealingly presented. Behind her is Tiberius – unwilling new husband to Julia [her third]. <u>Tiberius</u> would become the next emperor. He holds his toga with both hands." [p 133]

30,000 Years comments: "The identity of children is controversial, but they hint at 'family values'... a message that politicians still find irresistible." [p 306]

Sculptor(s):

The designer and sculptors of the *Altar* are unknown. Undoubtedly, Augustus and his principal advisors were involved in the design and progress of the monument.

The original *Ara Pacis*, erected on unstable soil too close to the Tiber River, was periodically flooded, and eventually buried under layers of mud, then forgotten. In 1568, the first slabs of its reliefs were unearthed...in 1859 and 1903, more parts were found. Further excavations took place in the 1930s...before final restoration was completed in 1938.

It is one of a handful of major architectural structures – erected during the 'glory' of ancient Rome – which still appears basically intact. Other major, surviving, ancient structures in Rome include the Pantheon...Hadrian's Mausoleum [also known as Castel Sant'Angelo, much modified]...and the Senate [Curia] building, rebuilt during the Empire in the Forum.

Major References:

Roman Art, 1974, Brilliant, p 241

Caesar and Christ, 1944, Durant, p 229, 348-9

A Traveler in Rome, 1957, Morton, p 256-57

30,000 Years of Art, 2007, p 306

Encyclopedia of Sculpture, 2006, Grash, p 74-5

Bullfinch Guide to Art, 1996, (editor) West, p 224

Art and Architecture – Rome, 2005, Hintzen-Bohlen, 215, 218

Roman Art and Architecture, 1964, Wheeler, p 9-10, 163-67

History of Art, 1977, Janson, p 169-70

Ancient Rome, 1996, Liberati and Bourbon, p 132-33

Gardner's Art Through the Ages, 1980, Gardner, p 195-96

History of World Sculpture, 1968, Bazin, p 166

56

THE PORTLAND VASE

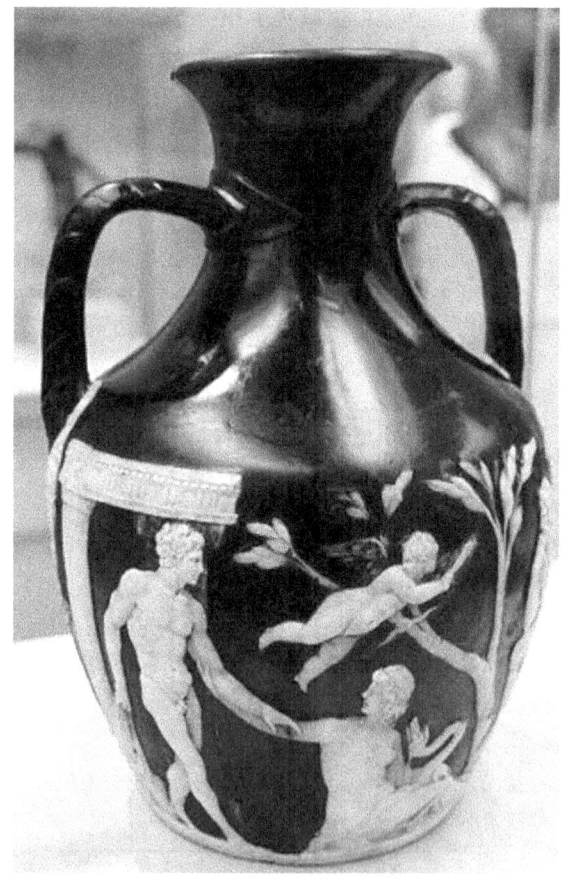

"the most beautiful cameo-glass
vessel surviving from antiquity."
...Walker, *The Portland Vase*, 2004

Found before 1600 outside Rome – now, British Museum
Orig. Greco-Roman vase – AD 10 – Classic & Augustan
Ht. 9.5 inches [24.5 cm] – double-layered cameo-glass
Sculptor: possibly Dioscurides, or an Egyptian artisan

O n the above half-view of the vase: Cupid leads Mark Antony into the garden of Queen Cleopatra...she embraces the arm of Antony. From the other side of the tree, Hercules [far right] watches...he sees the asp...and suspects this will not end well.*

*by Roman legend, Hercules founded the line of Antony

The *Portland Vase* – created 2,000 years ago with extraordinary skill and difficulty – is said by the British Museum to be the "most famous cameo-glass vessel to have survived from antiquity." [website 2004]

Its cobalt-blue glass core is coated with an opaque white layer of glass; on which members of Augustus' Imperial family are carved. Most references suggest the vase was made during the reign of the first Roman emperor, Augustus [31 BC to AD 14].

In 1633, the Italian engraver Bernardino Capitelli referred to the vase as a "precious pearl" and an "engraving of such cunning and industry that, if the heavens could breathe life into figures in pictures, it would be the most elegant to be seen." [*Portland Vase*, Walker, p 31]

Durant reveals: "The *Portland Vase* – very likely a product of Alexandria – shows this art at its best...Alexandria became famous for its goldsmiths and silversmiths...delightful cameos...blue and green faience...skillfully glazed pottery...and its delicately designed and many-colored glass." [*Life of Greece*, p 616]

Prior to 1600, the history of this vase is speculative. It might have been a possession of the Roman Emperor Severus Alexander [AD 222-35]. Reportedly...it was in a tomb containing his sarcophagus...and held the ashes of this emperor. [Walker, p 7]

Whoever commissioned this vase was immensely wealthy to afford its cost. Durant says: "In the reign of Tiberius, the art of glass blowing was brought from Sidon or Alexandria to Rome... and soon polychrome vials, cups, bowls, and other forms of such delicate beauty were produced that they became for a time the favorite prey of collectors and millionaires. In Nero's reign, 6000 sesterces were paid for two small cups of blown glass... Even more prized were the 'Murrhine' vases imported from Asia and Africa. They were made by placing white and purple glass filaments side by side to form a desired pattern ... or pieces of colored glass were embedded in a transparent white body... Augustus, though he melted down Cleopatra's gold plate, kept for himself her goblet of Murrhine glass. Nero paid a million sesterces for one such cup... Petronius, dying, broke another lest it should fall into Nero's hands." [p 347]

Since the time of Augustus – with each barbarian invasion of ancient Rome and later incursions by hostile armies during the medieval era [476 to 1450 AD] – the *Portland Vase* must have been secreted away. Its small size – 9.5 inches high – aided its survival.

The first glass used by man was volcano-made obsidian, highly prized as long as 75,000 years ago or more. In Egypt and Mesopotamia, 3,500 years ago, man began making a glaze of crude glass for fusing onto ceramics. In Egypt, glass beads and small vessels were made. Finally, in the 1st century came a revolutionary event. "The advent of the blowpipe extended the use of glass greatly and made glass production in Roman times into a major industry." Glassware was expensive and benefited mostly the wealthy. [*Collecting Bottles*, Munsey, p 6-7]

Subject:

While ancient vases often illustrated subjects in mythical literature and poetry, the *Portland Vase* exhibits historical persons [with 'related' Greek gods]'

It is fairly obvious that members of the Imperial Family of Augustus are displayed around the side of *the Portland Vase*.

The fore-mentioned *Mark Antony* [above view] drops his robe as he is led by *Cupid* to the wiles of *Cleopatra*. The seated, half-nude Queen of Egypt reaches to draw *Antony* nearer. An asp winds around her other hand... omen of her future.

On the other [unshown] side of the vase, *Octavian* [soon-to-be Emperor Augustus] is seated in a position of authority... he consoles his sister *Octavia* [abandoned wife of Mark Antony]. [Walker, p 62]

Octavia – reclining and holding her downcast head – had married *Mark Antony* for political reasons in 34 BC.

Prior to this marriage, Durant explains: *Antony* had raised an army to overthrow *Octavian*, but: "The armies, showing more sense than their leaders – refused to fight each other – and compelled them to a peaceable agreement. As a pledge of good behavior, *Antony* married *Octavian*'s sister, the gentle and virtuous *Octavia*. Everybody was briefly happy..." [C&C, p 205]

Three years later, *Antony* left *Octavia* for *Cleopatra*. [p 50]

It is believed the *Portland Vase* originally had a lid... now lost. The current base – either original or a replacement – appears to have been broken in antiquity. On the base is the figure of Paris of Troy... the mortal who judged the 3 divine goddesses and selected *Venus* as the most beautiful. [p 10-1]

Circumstantial evidence suggests the vase was found by F. Lazzaro about 1582 in a conical tomb [just outside Rome] holding a marble sarcophagus "believed to contain the ashes of Roman emperor Severus Alexander..." [AD 222 to 235]. Lazzario sold it to his neighbor, Cardinal Francesco del Monte. [Walker, p 17]

Ever since, the *Portland Vase* has experienced an illustrious international reputation.

In 1600, the vase was "first observed" by a Nicholas de Peiresc in the collection of del Monte [appointed by a Medici as Florence's representative to Rome]. Upon the death of del Monte, a relative [Alessandro] sold the vase to another cardinal, Antonio Barberini in about 1626.

By the early 1700s, this vase [then known as the Barbarini Vase'] ... was an essential item on the Grand Tour of European aristocracy. By the 1770s, the fortunes of the Barbarini family declined and – though the "pope forbade the export of Barberini antiquities from Italy" – the vase was sold in Rome to James Byres.

Byres, in turn, sold it to Sir William Hamilton, envoy of King George III to the Bourbon court at Naples in about 1782. By 1783, Hamilton secretly took the vase to London. [p 19] In 1784, Hamilton sold it to the second Duchess of Portland. When she died the following year, her heirs put the vase up for auction…the third Duke of Portland – first son of the Duchess "and largely spurned in her will" – bought the vase. Henceforth, the vase became known as the *Portland Vase.* [p 21]

"In an alarming episode, the base disc was dislodged [damaged] by the Duchess of Gordon…after which it was replaced with a smaller disc 'to which were cemented the sides of the vase'. Increasingly worried for its future safety, the fourth Duke of Portland entrusted the vase to the care of the British Museum, where it was deposited on loan in 1810." [p 25]

In 1848, a thick glass showcase did not prevent a "drunken Irish university dropout" from seizing a nearby stone sculpture and smashing the vase into more than 200 fragments. Six months later, the museum's restorer, John Doubleday, had returned the vase to a satisfactory state for viewing. The drunk dropout was excused "from his fine and sentence of two months' hard labor" by the [current] Duke of Portland, who felt pity for the man's family. [p 25]

In the early 1870s, a competition to produce an exact replica of the vase was begun by Benjamin Richardson – senior member of British glassmakers – who offered 1,000 pounds for such a replica. The competition lasted 3 years and generated considerably more publicity for the vase. [p 27]

The famed manufacturer of ceramics, Josiah Wedgewood, required four years to perfect ceramic-cameo copies [40 to 50] made with black jasperware. Popularity of Wedgwood copies of the vase, in many sizes, has continued. [p 27]

In 1929, when the [current] Duke of Portland solicited offers for the vase, a bid of $152,000 was received…and rejected as too low. [Durant, C&C, p 347]

In <u>1945</u>, the British Museum purchased the vase from the Portland family for 5,000 pounds.

Sculptor:

For several decades, Dioscurides was the gem-cutter for the family of the emperor Augustus. There is "an affinity between the airy, elegant style of *the Portland Vase* and surviving gems signed by Dioscurides." [Walker, p 62]

Though the sculptor/carver of *the Portland Vase* is uncertain, he may have been inspired by the frieze of the Erechtheum on the Acropolis in Athens…. where white Pentelic marble figures were set against a background of blue limestone. Remains of this frieze can be viewed at the Acropolis Museum in Athens.

After cobalt-blue glass was partially blown into the shape of the vase, it was dipped into melted opaque white glass. Reheated, it was blown to full-size…possibly in a mold…or the shoulders and rim might have been shaped. Handles were then attached. When the vase cooled, a gem-cutter carved on the white layer to create figures in cameo fashion.

Another famed Roman cameo – second only to *the Portland Vase* – from the 1st century AD is the *Gemma Augusta*. [displayed at the Kunsthistorisches Museum in Vienna] "Tiberius [astride a chariot] is portrayed in *triumph* in the presence of the [seated] Augustus…Roman soldiers are hoisting the spoils won from defeated enemies in front of a group of prisoners. Tiberius had already shown himself to be a brave commander before Augustus designated him as his successor." [Liberati, p 46]

Major References:

Collecting Bottles, 1970, Munsey, p 6-7
The Portland Vase, 2004, Walker, p 7, 31, 17-9, 21, 25, 27, 31, 48-9, 51, 56, 62
30,000 Years of Art, 2007, p 309
Archaeology of the Roman Empire, 1982, King, p 142
Life of Greece, II, 1939, Durant, p 616
Caesar and Christ, III, 1944, Durant, p 347
The Portland Vase, 1975, D.E.I Haynes
Art in the Western World, 1953, Robb & Garrison, p 887-888
Ancient Rome, Liberati & Bourbon, 1996, p 46

57

AUGUSTUS

PRIMA-PORTA

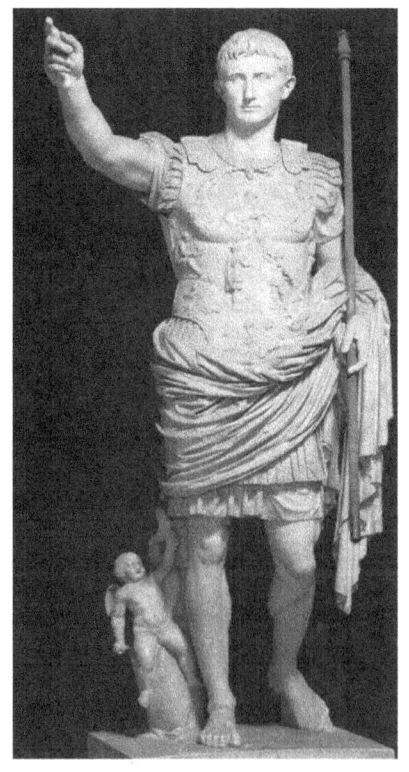

"Roman portraiture ... finds its climax ...
in the splendid statue from the Prima-Porta"
...Janson, *History of Art*, 1977, p 168

Found 1863, Imperial Villa of Livia – now, Vatican, Rome
Greco-Roman copy – 14 BC to AD 20
From: Orig. bronze – 20 BC – Classic & Roman style
Height: 6'8" feet [203 cm] – white marble
Sculptor: unknown Greek in Italy
   * Prima-porta – the Imperial villa of Augustus' wife Livia

Augustus – who reigned as the first Roman emperor, 27 BC to 14 AD – is said to be "the greatest statesman in Roman history." [Durant, III, p 200]

In 44 BC…Octavian [later, renamed Augustus] was 18 when his great-uncle Julius Caesar was assassinated. Slight and sickly, Octavian was barely a man; yet the written will of Caesar named him heir to three-quarters of Caesar's immense wealth. By the same will, Caesar legally adopted Octavian as his son. Durant tells us that, in the previous 3 years, Octavian "had lived a good part of the time in Caesar's palace…and was carefully instructed in the arts of war and government." [p 200]

History would prove Caesar judged his great-nephew well. In the 17-year civil war following Caesar's assassination, Octavian outwitted and eliminated all rivals – initially, the assassins Brutus and Cassius in a battle which would not have been won without the generalship of Mark Antony. "*Octavian was confined to his tent with illness.*" [p 203]

Later, when Antony formed a threatening alliance [and romance] with Cleopatra of Egypt, it became necessary to eliminate even Antony. In the Battle of Actium, 31 BC, Octavian soundly defeated Antony, who escaped with Cleopatra back to Egypt. Octavian did not immediately pursue them.

In the following year, Octavian – now in control of the entire Mediterranean world – entered Alexandria [Egypt] and initiated conflict with forces led by Antony. After a temporary victory over Octavian, Antony received a report of Cleopatra's death. Disillusioned, Antony stabbed himself…then, learned her death had been falsely reported. He asked to die in her arms, to which

Octavian assented. Shortly thereafter, Cleopatra, rather than submit to the terms of Octavian, ended her life with an asp. [p 206-08]

Before Octavian left Alexandria, he visited the tomb of *Alexander the Great*. Octavian was 32 years old, one year younger than Alexander at his death.

Earlier... when Octavian, at 18, began his rise to power, he had been 2 years younger than Alexander when the latter became king of the Macedonians and crossed the Hellespont to challenge the Persians. [see *Alex. Mosaic* #45]

The ancient Roman historian Suetonius describes Augustus at 35 [near when bronze original of his *Prima-Porta* was cast]: "He had sandy hair, a strangely triangular head, merging eyebrows, clear and penetrating eyes; yet his expression was so calm and mild, that a Gaul who came to kill him changed his mind." [p 227]

Robb & Garrison describe the *Prima-Porta* head: "...the skull tapering sharply toward the chin, the high cheek bones, deeply recessed eyes and the arrangement of the hair are all details that can be observed in other portraits of Augustus...and the expression of the face is calm and self-contained." [*Art in the Western World,* p 458-59]

Janson adds: "...small details are suppressed, and the focusing of attention on the eyes gives it something of the 'inspired' look we find in portraits of *Alexander the Great* #28. Nevertheless, the face is a definite likeness..." [*History of Art,* p 168]

In statuary of both Alexander and Augustus, their forelocks [hair at the forehead] were carved with unique and idealized designs... the intent being to distinguish their statues from all others.

Subject:

Durant summarizes Octavian/Augustus as: "...refined, delicate, serious, at once diffident and resolute, yielding and tenacious... an idealist forced to be a realist, a man of thought painfully learning to be a man of action. He was thin and pale and suffered from poor digestion. He ate little, drank less, and outlived strong men around him by abstinence and the regularity of his life." [p 200]

Augustus was known as a strong admirer of Classic Greek art. The pose of the *Augustus Prima-Porta* closely resembles the *Doryphorus/Spear Carrier* #15 of <u>440 BC</u>. Leg positions are the same, both left arms carry a spear/rod, and the heads face to their right front...only the right arm positions differ, the *Doryphorus'* arm is relaxed by its side.

The [lost] original bronze was created at the beginning of Augustus' reign to offer an image of strong leadership – to both warn his enemies of his ability to exact vengeance and, at the same time, to extend a message of peace. The military cuirass [breast-plate] signifies his supreme authority.

30,000 Years of Art reveals: "...when Octavian ended the civil war that marked the end of the Roman Republic...his hands were as bloody as any, so he shrewdly crafted a propagandistic program – both political and artistic – designed to accustom the Roman state and citizens to his authority. Key messages appear in this famous statue...These concern especially the peace-making diplomacy and a return to the putative [reputed] 'good old days' of Roman respectability and virtue." [p 307]

The gentle face of *Augustus* is sensitive, that of a humble man. His hands do not hold weapons. The long, thin staff resting in his left hand was likely a scepter, a symbol of sovereignty. He is not ready for action. The raised right hand normally indicates a general addressing his troops...in this instance, he may be pointing to a better future. These messages were intended to pacify the many dangerous political enemies of Augustus after the civil war...particularly among the Republican aristocracy whose corrupt control of the Senate had been ended.

The Jansons say: "Here we meet a concept...the godlike, even divine ruler. Alexander the Great adopted it, as did his successors...the idea of giving the emperor the divine stature appropriate to his godlike status, authority, and power soon became official policy...the *Prima-Porta* statue clearly shows him enveloped in an air of divinity." [*Basic History of Western Art*, p 121]

R. Brilliant tells us: "The cuirass statue was a Greek invention, quickly adopted by Roman generals to honor themselves after successful campaigns against the Greeks in the late Republic." [*Roman Art,* p 31]

The highly-detailed cuirass worn by *Augustus* is a masterpiece of sculpture in itself. Prominent at its center is the return by a Parthian king of a gold Eagle standard...captured from defeated Roman legions led by Crassus in 53 BC. Tiberius, as a delegate of Augustus, receives the standard from the Parthians in 20 BC. This was celebrated as a significant 'diplomatic victory' by Augustus. A Roman legion's Eagle standard was rarely captured.

Lawrence says: "At the top...the sky-god Caelus spreads the mantle of the heavenly vault above the sun-god [Apollo], who drives his chariot in pursuit of two goddesses...identifiable as Dew and Dawn by the jug and torch they carry." [p 256] Gardner adds: "Together the figures [on the cuirass] symbolize blessings of the new Golden Age expected to come with the Augustan peace." [p 194-95]

At the right foot of the *Augustus* statue, Cupid rides a dolphin...symbolic of the "divine ancestry of the Julian family which claimed descent from Aenaes, the mortal son of Venus and half-brother to Cupid." [Robb & Garr., p 459-60]

Multiple copies of the *Prima-Porta* were distributed throughout the Roman Empire. This was one of many measures taken by Augustus that permitted him to rule from the age of 32 – without serious opposition – until his death at the age of 76.

The statue became an icon of Rome and the Empire.

Durant concludes: "Augustus was at once dull and fascinating; no one was more prosaic, yet half the world adored him; a physical weakling not particularly brave, but able to overcome all enemies, regulate kingdoms, and fashion a government that would give the vast realm an unexampled prosperity for 200 years." [p 227]

Sculptor:

This marble statue [and the orig. bronze] undoubtedly were created by the most skilled sculptors available in the Mediterranean world...yet they remain unidentified. The marble copy was likely commissioned by his wife, Livia, after the death of Augustus in AD

14. That it survived in excellent condition – with only minor restorations of the limbs – may indicate it was intentionally and carefully buried at one time... to avoid destruction or pillage. Lawrence says: "The Cupid... as well as the right arm and left leg, may be ancient restorations." [p 257]

In the Vatican, it stands near a bust known as the *Young Augustus*... and another complete statue of the aging emperor veiled as a priest.

The root of the word emperor is *imperator,* meaning 'victor in battle'.

Major References:

The Twelve Caesars, 1957, Suetonius/Graves, p 88-9

Roman Art, 1974, R. Brilliant, 1974, p 111-12

Art in the Western World, 1977, Robb & Garrison, p 458-459

History of Art, 1977, Janson, p 168

Janson & Janson, 2006, Basic History of Western Art, p 121

Caesar & Christ, III, 1944, Durant, p 227-9

Art Through the Ages, 1980, Gardner, p 194-5

Greek and Roman Sculpture, 1972, Lawrence, p 252-58

Ancient Rome, 1996, Liberati & Bourbon, p 43-5

Vatican Museums-Rome, 1968, Newsweek, p 34-5

30,000 Years of Art, 2007, Phaidon Press, p 307

The Eternal City, Rome, 1896, Clement, p 140-2

A Traveler in Rome, 1957, Morton, p 217-18

58
Arch of Titus

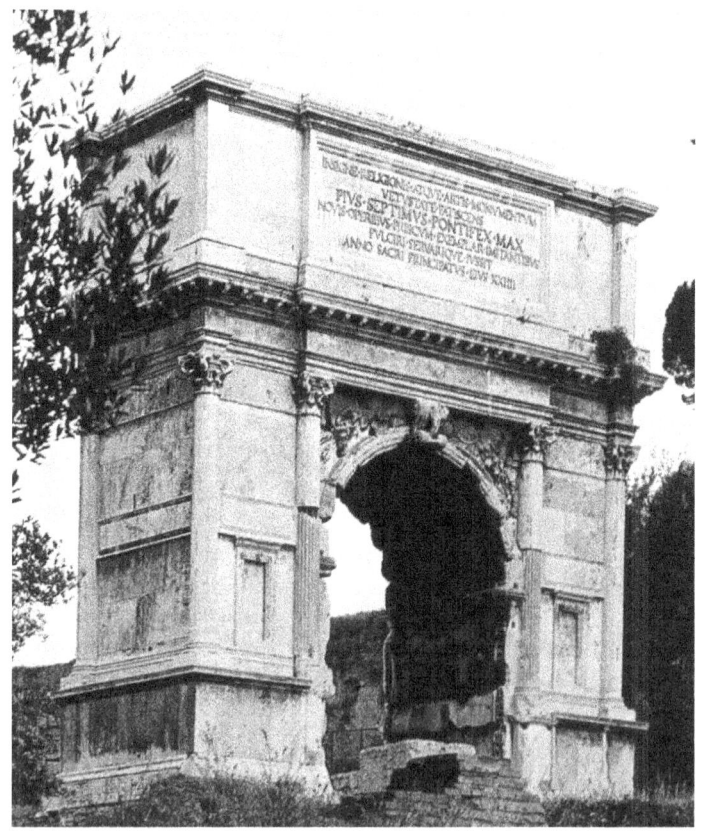

Of all the Roman arches, Durant states:
"The finest survivor is *the Arch of Titus...*"
... Caesar & Christ, p 348

Erected 81 AD on the Sacred Way – south entry to Forum
Greco-Roman reliefs – marble-facing – Roman style
Arch Ht. 47 ft. [15 m] – Relief Panels Ht. 7 ft. 10 inches
Sculptors: unknown Greek and Romans
    *purchase guidebook at gift store [at east entry of Forum]
    **also buy hand-book comparing original & current views

Manzione's *Rome & the Vatican* declares: "...as if to mark the center of Rome and of the whole world stands the *Arch of Titus*." [p 12] It is the earliest of surviving triumphal arches.

Its elevated location – during the Roman Empire – was perhaps the most prominent in Rome...aside from the Capitoline Hill where the Sacred Way ends. [*Encyclo,* p 1686]

First-time visitors to the Forum are advised to approach from the direction of the Colosseum...via the Sacred Way...the oldest street of Rome. The gradual walkway leads up to the *Arch of Titus*...where the 'high ground' offers a sudden view of the Roman Forum.

The ancient privilege of passing under the *Arch of Titus* was "restricted to Roman generals or emperors awarded a 'triumph' for an exceptional military victory over a foreign enemy, resulting in expansion of territory." [Carpenter, p. 308]

In 71 AD, General Titus [a future emperor] rode his 4-horse parade chariot along this route during his triumphal procession...awarded for the capture of Jerusalem during the Jewish wars of 66-70 AD.

Brilliant describes the 'celebration of the ceremonial triumph' as "a dazzling parade...with trains of spoils and captives offering tangible proof of victory...the whole symbolized by the appearance of the *triumphator* in his gleaming chariot dressed in the robes of Jupiter. Often, the soldiers of the victorious general carried large paintings, describing his and their exploits in battle...while temporary arches and trophies of captured weapons were erected along the parade route to add greater splendor to the occasion." [*Roman Art,* p 85]

Carpenter adds: "a long procession of horse-drawn floats, laden with booty and followed by captive princes and generals walking in chains, was assembled in the Field of Mars, [now, at bend of Tiber opposite St. Peter's]. Thence the senators and magistrates escorted the triumphal procession along an established route through the city streets...swung past the Colosseum and followed the paved Sacred Way under the triumphal *Arch of Titus*...and up the winding ascent to the Temple of Jupiter atop the Capitoline Hill. Sacrifices and offerings were made at the temple...then the prisoners were led away, traditionally to their death. A sumptuous feast followed, to which soldiery and populace were invited." [p 308]

As Titus rode in his triumph, by tradition, "so did a slave who whispered in his ear, 'Sic transit Gloria mundi', warning him of the brevity of fame despite the immediate glory of victory and stunning spectacle of the *pompa triumphalis*." [Brilliant, p 85]

Or, the slave might repeat words to the effect: "You are only a man."

The free-standing, Roman triumphal arch developed from the arched town gates built by the earlier Etruscans and similar gateways in Asia Minor. Brilliant concludes: "Above all, the arches stood as monumental instruments of propaganda in the permanent service of the triumphant Imperator and of the Roman state, both at Rome and in the wide Empire." [p 119]

"Although it is believed that nearly every Roman city throughout the far reaches of the Roman Empire had at least one triumphal arch, the surviving 'remains' today number only slightly more than 120." [*Encyclo Sculpt.*, p 1685]

Subject:

At the time Titus captured Jerusalem in 70 AD, he was the older son of Emperor Vespasian, who began construction of the Colosseum in 72 AD.

When Titus became the next emperor in 79 AD, he ruled only two years before succumbing to a fever at the age of 42...while still the "darling of mankind" due to his many accomplishments and the benevolence of his rule. He "made his government a model of wisdom and honor"... opened the Colosseum [though uncompleted] begun by his father...and built another municipal bath. No one suffered capital punishment...he swore that he would rather be killed than kill. When two patricians were detected in a conspiracy to depose him, he contented himself with sending them a warning...then he dispatched a courier to relieve the anxiety of a conspirator's mother by telling her that her son was safe." [Durant, 288-89]

Grant tells us: "Titus' generosity gained for him the reputation of being the most popular of Roman emperors." [p 255] Durant adds: "he showed not merely the concern of an emperor, but a father's surpassing love. All of Rome mourned him...except the younger brother [Domitian] who succeeded to his throne." [p 289]

Of all Roman arches, Durant adds: "The finest survivor is *the Arch of Titus*.... the artists here experimented bravely: they chiseled the background to give the illusion of depth...the action is shown not in separate episodes but in continuity...as seen later on the column of Trajan...so the sense of motion and life is better conveyed. The figures were not idealized and softened...they were taken from the flesh and the dirt, and carved in the earthy tradition of Italian realism and vitality." [p 348-49]

In *Rome: Eternally Beautiful*, Fattorusso states, "This splendid arch...is one of the gems of the first century." [p 30]

Narrative Panels on Inner Walls:

On the inner walls "...one panel [*Spoils from the Temple of Jerusalem*] shows part of the procession celebrating the conquest of Jerusalem in AD 70. The movement of the crowd of figures in depth is conveyed with striking success...the procession passes...hurrying us along with it. It then turns away and disappears through a triumphal arch, placed obliquely...so that only the nearer half is actually visible – a radical but effective compositional device...and transports us back to Titus' real triumph of AD 71..." [*Basic History of Western Art*, p 125-26]

The Jewish historian and general Josephus – who viewed this triumph – tells us: "Most of the spoils that were carried were heaped up discriminately, but more prominent than all the rest were those captured in the Temple of Jerusalem – a golden table weighing several 100-weight...and a lampstand [candelabrum] similarly made of gold...After these, came the Jewish Law...Next came a large group carrying images of *Victory*, all fashioned of ivory and gold. Behind them drove Vespasian [father and still emperor]...with Titus behind him. Domitian [the brother] rode alongside, magnificently adorned, with his horse..." [Gardner, p 197]

The second panel [*Triumph of Titus*] shows Titus, now emperor, riding his imperial chariot in triumphal procession. A *Winged Victory* behind Titus holds a laurel-wreath crown to his head.

A third panel depicts 'the burning city of Jerusalem'. Its citizens appear "wild with fear, its wealth looted by legionnaires. Another [panel] has 'Titus riding into Rome in his chariot' amid soldiers, animals, magistrates, priests, prisoners..." [Durant, p 348-49]

At the top of the vault of the *Arch of Titus*, a small relief shows: "the Emperor borne up to heaven on the back of an eagle...this indicates that the *Arch of Titus* is a posthumous dedication, made by Domitian his brother and successor...." [Brilliant, p 124]

Irregular holes along the upper edge of this relief were made during the Middle Ages by the Frangipani family, who inserted support beams for a second story in the vault when they incorporated the arch into their family fortress. In 1822, Giuseppe Valadier re-erected the arch from the ruins of the Frangipani fortress. [*Encyclo.*, p 1686]

Originally, as with most Roman arches, the *Arch of Titus* was surmounted by a bronze quadriga – four horses pulling a 2-wheeled chariot. Brilliant tells us this group would have been: "brightly visible from a distance...carrying the triumphator(s) in the company of Victoria [*Victory* or *Nike*], and flanked by subsidiary figures representing the conquered enemy." [p 123]

Sculptors:

The designer and sculptors of the *Arch of Titus* are unknown. They could have been Greek, Roman, or both. Carpenter describes the

Arch as "constructed of Greek Parian marble ... inadequately patched and rebuilt with Italian travertine early in the 19th century." [p 289]

In Paris, the impressive *Carrousel Arch* – celebrating victories of Napoleon in 1805 – was modeled by the French in 1806-08 after Rome's nearby *Arch of Constantine*. After Napoleon 'confiscated' the *Four Horses of St. Mark* #29, he placed them atop the arch ... until the French returned them to Venice in 1815. Copies of the horses were made, to which the French later added a chariot carrying a statue of Peace.

Major References:

Rome & the Vatican, 1983, Manzione, p 12-3
Rome: Eternally Beautiful, 1937, G.Fattorusso, p 30
Roman Art, 1974. Brilliant, p 119, 122-24
Caesar & Christ, 1944, Durant, p 288-89, 348-49
The Colosseum, 1971, Quennell, p 22-3, 26-7
Basic History of Western Art, 2006, Janson & Janson, p 125-26
Art Through the Ages, 1980, Gardner, p 196-97
Encyclopedia of Sculpture, 2004, Tchkine, p 1684-6
The Birth of Western Civilization, 1964, Grant, p 255
All Paris, 1975, Giovanna Magi, p 28
Everyday Life in Ancient Times, 1958, Carpenter, p 289, 308-09

59

Trajan's Column

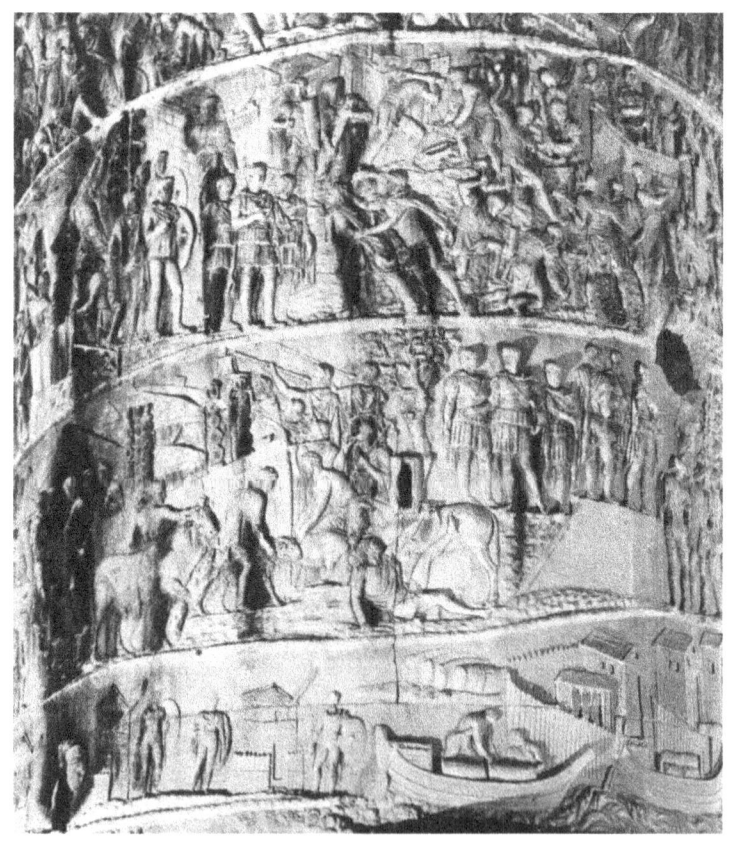

"... the most masterly narrative relief in sculptural history."
... Durant, *Caesar & Christ*, p 412]

Erected 106 to 114 AD – in Forum of Trajan, Rome
Greco-Roman – white Parian marble – Classic Greek & Roman
Ht. 130 feet [39.7 m], Width [bottom] 12 feet [4.7 m]
Ht. shaft: 98 feet [29.8 m] – 155 scenes with 2600 + figures
Spiraling Relief: 625 ft. [200 m]; Ht. 36" bottom to 50" at top
Sculptor: possible architect, Apollodorus of Damascus

[above section of 625-foot spiraling band depicts battle
of Romans & Dacians, their surrender, & a Roman fort]

At first sight, *Trajan's Column* – a victory and funerary monument – is a considerable surprise. Among the ruins of Rome's ancient forums, this column is not a ruin. It is basically intact... because, for 7 centuries, it served as a 'bell-tower' of a Christian church [the San Nicola de Columna].

Hintzen-Bohlen's *Art & Architecture* describes this monument as "...an impressive sculptural masterpiece and a valuable historical source..." [p 141]

The figures on it are usually two-thirds life-size.

Initially, a bronze statue of the emperor Trajan – holding a globe of the world – stood on its summit. Within its square base was a mausoleum containing a golden urn [lost] with his ashes.

When the San Nicola church was 'removed' in the 9th century, *Trajan's Column* became the first archeological monument to be officially designated for protection by the papal rulers of Rome. Some 600 years later [1588], they replaced its statue of Trajan [now lost] with a bronze statue of St. Peter.

The *Column* was completed in 114 AD within the Forum of Trajan – northwest of the center of the adjacent Roman Forum. The *Column* displays scenes from two wars – 102 AD and 105 AD – when Trajan fought the Dacians... usually depicted with dignity and as formidable opponents. The Dacians occupied lands – now Hungary and Romania – north of the Danube River.

30,000 Years reveals: "The Roman Empire reached it geographical zenith when Trajan conquered Dacia. The emperor maintained the popularity engendered by this victory by commissioning vast public works, a law court, library, and this carved column. War spoils decorate the base of the column, reminding Romans that Dacian war booty paid for Trajan's projects." [p 332]

The figures on the *Column* grow larger with the ascending band. Height of the band begins at 36 inches and expands to 50 inches by the top. The marble reliefs record 155 episodes – displaying more than 2,600 carved figures.

Within the column, an interior spiral staircase of 185 marble steps was carved... a unique achievement by ancient Roman engineers. [not open to public]

To best view most of the reliefs requires binoculars... and circling the *Column* 22 times. [providing Trajan's Forum is open to the public]

In 114 AD when the *Column* was completed, it was surrounded by a small courtyard between two-story buildings with rooftop gardens... from which the ancient Romans had far better views than now.

Today, the west side of *Trajan's Column* can be viewed from a public park [elevated in relation to column's base] some 35 yards distant. Viewing [w/binoculars] in mid-afternoon is advised... as the sun then will be behind the viewer's back.

Subject:

Trajan is often described as one of 'the good emperors'. He ruled from 98 to 117 AD. During his reign, the Roman Empire experienced its greatest size and glory. He was the first and last Roman emperor to conquer lands as far west as the Indian Ocean.

Durant tells us he: "never ceased to be a general. His carriage was military, his presence commanding... tall and robust, he was wont to march on foot with his troops and ford with full armament the 100 rivers they had to cross... his mind was clear and direct... he took no advantage of his office... his simplicity, geniality, and moderation readily won a people so lately acquainted with tyranny... he was an able and tireless administrator, a sound financier, a just judge..." [p 408-09]

Durant explains why Trajan fought his Dacian campaigns. "Nurtured on war, the Emperor was a frank imperialist... hardly a year after his arrival in Rome, he set out for the conquest of Dacia. The lands of the Dacians plunged like a fist into the heart of German tribal lands, and would therefore be of great military value in the struggle Trajan foresaw between the Germans and Italy." [p 410]

Figures on the *Column* are carved in low relief to reduce heavy shadows. In ancient times, the figures were painted with color, improving visibility. The scenes are not idealized, but done in the Roman style... vivid, active individuals engaging in the turmoil of war:

> ... "Roman cohorts issuing from their stations in full armor
> ... crossing the Danube River on a pontoon bridge
> ... pitching a Roman fortification in enemy land
> ... the confused conflict of spears, arrows, sickles, stones
> ... captured Dacians in humane prison camps
> ... a Dacian village set to the torch
> ... Dacian women begging Trajan for mercy
> ... Dacian women torturing Roman prisoners
> ... Trajan giving rewards to his soldiers
> ... Dacian princes [defeated] drinking from cup of poison
> ... head of Dacian leader brought as a trophy to Trajan
> ... file of captive men, women, & children led into slavery."
> [Durant, p 412]

Durant declares: "The finest figure in the scroll is that of a Dacian king."

The Baths of Diocletian Museum in Rome displays a magnificent, colossal statue of another Dacian... if a king, he appears anything but barbarian. The museum guidebook describes it as: "an attractive but highly restored colossal statue of a Dacian in ethnic costume – the earliest pants with cuffs, a heavy cloak with a painted head." [La Regina, p 120, 122]

In the Vatican Museum, within its Hall of Marbles [Section 32], another impressive, colossal Dacian [from hips up] is titled: "The

Barbarian Leader in Massimo" [chieftain]. The upper portion is sculpted in pavonazetto [peacock-colored Phrygian] marble from the era of Trajan. It is magnificent.

Sculptor:

The designer/sculptor of Trajan's Column may have been Apollodorus of Damascus. [Gardner, p 198] He is said to have been Trajan's favorite architect and military engineer, who also designed the Forum of Trajan [370 by 354 feet].

The exceedingly-difficult round 'format' of the *Column* helped ensure its permanence. Traditional temples and similar monuments – constructed with rectangular blocks of stone – were more likely to be pillaged for building materials by later generations.

Marble of the column was quarried from the island of Paros – the same source as *Venus de Milo* – and arrived in Rome in the form of 18 cubes, each weighing about 50 tons. Each cube was recut into 32 blocks. The pedestal required 8 blocks. Three sides of the pedestal were sculpted … the fourth side was opened for a spiral staircase. The shaft of the column is 98 feet high, and at the bottom, 12 feet in diameter, tapering toward the top. Reliefs were carved on blocks before they were raised to their positions. [Durant, p 411]

Digital versions of *Trajan's Column* may be available at larger libraries.

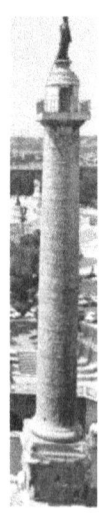

Major References:

Art & Architecture: Rome, 2005, Hintzen-Bohlen, p 140-41, 213

Caesar & Christ, 1944, Durant, p 408-13, 442-43

30,000 Years of Art, 2007, Phaidon, p 332

History of World Sculpture, 1968, Bazin, p 33-34, 178-79

Art Through the Ages, 1980, Gardner, p 198-99

The Story of Art, 16th edition, 1995, Gombrich, p. 122

Greek and Roman Sculpture, Lawrence, 1972, p 272-278

History of Art, 1977, Janson, p 171-73

Roman Art, 1974, Brilliant, p 123-28

Museo Nazionale Romano, 2005, La Regina, p 120, 122

60

MARCUS AURELIUS –

EQUESTRIAN

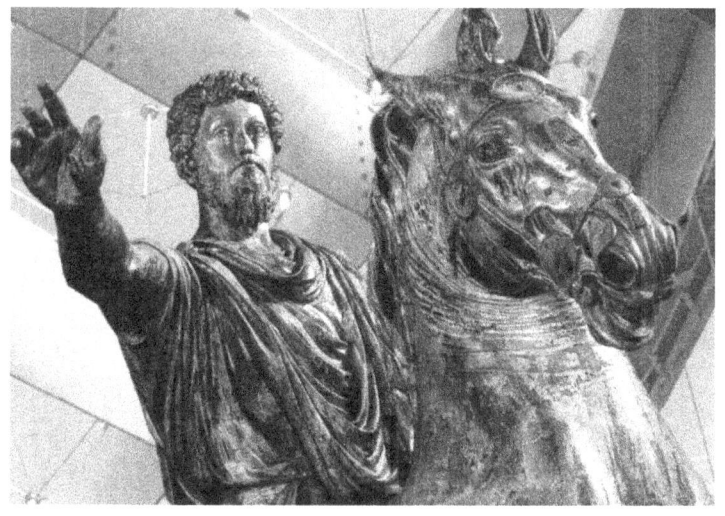

"exudes majesty and power... one of the most continuously
celebrated and influential statues in Western art."
...Lenaghan, *Encyclopedia of Sculpture, p 523*

Equestrian bronze, orig. gilded in gold – Capitoline Mus., Rome
Original Roman sculpture – 161-192 AD – Classic style
Height: 13.5 feet [4.24 m] – almost double life-size
Sculptor: unknown
    *original [above] inside museum, replica outside since 1997

T his is believed to be the only ancient equestrian statue of a Roman emperor to survive.

Lenaghan says the statue: "<u>exudes majesty and power</u>... it has never been buried or lost... <u>one of the most continuously celebrated and influential statues in Western art</u>." [*Encyclo Sculpt,* p 523]

Man and horse are almost double life-size. In 1538, they were installed in the Piazza Campidoglio, atop the Capitoline Hill. They were cast sometime between 161 AD [when Marcus Aurelius became emperor] and 192 AD [last year in reign of his son, Commodus].

In 1981, due to environmental damage, the 'original' statue was removed from its outside pedestal. After restoration, it was installed <u>inside</u> the Capitoline Museum at almost eye-level.

In 1997, a replica was placed on the original 12-foot high pedestal <u>outside</u>. The revered 'philosopher-emperor' of Imperial Rome remains the Piazza's centerpiece; however, it is said to be "controversial and far less refined... much to the dismay of Romans who loved the original." [Hintzen-Bohlen, p 57] [WSJ, 6/12/11, Freudenheim, p. C13]

Still, the replica outside is worthy of attention... as its greater height [compared to the *original* now indoors] provides a viewing experience nearer to what the ancient Romans saw.

Bazin suggests the original "likely adorned the upper part of a triumphal arch." [*History of World Sculpture,* p 180]

The replica [outside] appears: "massive... overwhelming and even intimidating... the horse and rider declare power and demand our attention... the horse itself has an immense torso with bulging musculature and swelling veins, which we [can] see from under-neath." [WSJ, Freudenheim]

Before entering the Capitoline Museum, note the heads of M. Aurelius and his horse in the Piazza. Inside the museum, their 'original' faces are more finitely sculpted.

Inside the museum, Freudenheim favorably observes: "The close-up, even intimate view... affords the visitor the opportunity to marvel at the surface complexity of the ancient bronze. The work was severely pitted and corroded after 19 centuries outside, but has been sensitively restored...now we see remnants of the original overall [gold] gilding, which plays beautifully against the green bronze patina. The remaining gilt on the faces of both emperor and horse is especially alluring." [p C13]

The original statue may have remained intact due to its 'adoption' and deliberate mis-identification by early Christians as a statue of Constantine...who was the first Roman emperor [306-337 AD] to protect, support, and eventually prefer Christianity.

In the years 761-762 AD – when Holy Roman Emperor Charlemagne first visited Rome – historic accounts note this equestrian statue stood near a Christian basilica built by Constantine. Lanaghan adds the placement of the statue "was a symbol of the Church's authority..." [p 524]

Before it was moved to the Capitoline Hill in 1538, Michelangelo redesigned the Piazza for its prominent display. Durant reveals: "Michelangelo used one of the columns of the temple of Castor and Pollux [from the Forum] to create a pedestal for the equestrian statue..." [Vol. III, p. 495]

By 1600, the identity of the equestrian had been re-established as Marcus Aurelius.

Subject:

Russell's *Art in the World* muses: "The imposing equestrian bronze figure...celebrated the Emperor M. Aurelius, highly-regarded for his leadership and philosophical convictions. Having carefully studied the Greek philosopher Stoic, he based his writings on a similar kinship with nature and universal brotherhood...Aurelius seems perfectly balanced on his splendid mount in an attitude of deep thought, projecting the same patient Stoic philosophy for which his *Meditations* was widely read." [p 270]

The figure of M. Aurelius appears to pause in parade: "The emperor commands 'order' with an outstretched right arm while holding the horse's reins [missing] in his left hand." Originally, a [defeated] kneeling barbarian appeared near the horse's raised right leg. M. Aurelius is neither armed nor dressed in armor...his clothing is described as "a tunic and *paludamentum* [general's cloak]" worn while traveling on a military campaign. His horse is "decorated with parade paraphernalia". [Lenaghan, p 524]

Gardner observes: "His gesture here, magisterial, benignly authoritative – much like a later papal blessing – conveys at once the awesome and universal significance of the Roman imperium... the almost godlike presiding of the emperor over the whole world... we see... a man calmly aloof, meditative, a little resigned. The magnificent, high-stepping charger, a war horse mettlesome and impatient with the tameness of the parade, breathes hotly through dilated nostrils. The superb bronze was the inspiration and sometimes 'despair' of [aspiring] sculptors of the Renaissance." [*Art Through the Ages*, p 202]

Durant describes the early life and education of M. Aurelius: "... born in Rome in 121 AD... 3 months after birth, his father died, and he was taken into the house of his rich grandfather, then a consul." [C&C, p 425]

"Emperor Hadrian, a frequent visitor to the house, took a fancy to the boy and saw in him the stuff of kings. Seldom has any lad had so propitious a youth... good grandparents, parents, a good sister, good teachers, good kinsmen [gave him] modesty, patience, manliness, abstemiousness [moderate in eating & drinking], piety, benevolence and 'a simplicity of life far removed from the habits of the rich' – though wealth surrounded him on every side. Never was a boy so persistently educated." [C&C, p 425]

Durant relates how Hadrian, at the end of his life [138 AD]: "called to his bedside... a man with an unblemished reputation for integrity and wisdom – Titus Aurelius Antonius – and adopted him as his son and successor [Emperor Antonius]. Looking far ahead, Hadrian advised Antonius to adopt in turn, and educate for government two youths then growing up at the court: Marcus Annius Verus [later Emperor Marcus Aurelius] then 17, and Lucius Aelius Verus..."

Emperor Antonius – after reigning 23 years – followed the advice of Hadrian and chose 'Marcus Annius Versus' as the next emperor: Marcus Aurelius, in 161. [p 421-22, 424]

As emperor, M. Aurelius "allowed himself no luxury, treated all men with simple fellowship…paid the Senate every courtesy…the people loved him…The spirit of the Emperor had helped to form the art and morals of his time. The games were less cruel, the laws more considerate of the weak; marriage was apparently more lasting and content." [Durant, p 427, 443]

The 19-year reign of M. Aurelius has been described "as the calm before the storm." In the next century, Rome was "in almost perpetual crisis. Barbarians endangered its frontiers while internal conflicts undermined the authority of the imperial office. To hold the throne became a matter of naked force, succession by murder a common habit…" [Janson, p 174]

Sculptor:

While the sculptor is unknown, he almost certainly was Greek and assisted by Roman artists. The statue could have been commissioned by either M. Aurelius or his son Commodus.

Because this imperial equestrian statue survived, it became 'the prototype' for later equestrian statues. "It heavily influenced Renaissance equestrian designs – for instance, Donatello's *Gattamelata* monument in Padua, Verrochio's monument in Venice, and Leonardo's sketches for a monument." [Lanaghan, p 524]

Since the equestrian statue was cast in bronze and originally gilded in gold, it is surprising it survived the sacks of Rome during the long decline of the Roman Empire…the Visigoths under Alaric sacked Rome in AD 410…the Vandals under Genseric in 455 carried off treasures including the gold-plated roof tiles from the Temple of Jupiter on the Capitoline Hill. [Liberati, p 57] [Durant, III, p 670]

Contrary to Lenaghan's earlier statement that this work was 'never buried'… the *Author* believes it is possible this equestrian statue was temporarily 'buried' for safe-keeping when foreign armies threatened Rome. Standing plans could have been executed to sequester the statue – plus the *She-Wolf* #10, the *Hellenistic Ruler* #42, *the Laocoon* #52, and other important works – in pre-prepared, hidden locations.

Those involved in such measures – to insure secrecy – would have fled Rome [even Italy] until it was safe to return.

Major References:

History of World Sculpture, 1968, Bazin, p 180

Art in the World, 1975, Russell, p 270

Art Through the Ages, I, 1980, Gardner, p 201-02

Ancient Rome, 2007, Hill, p 207

Art and Architecture of Rome, 2001, Hintzen-Bohlen, p 56-7, 158

Encyclopedia of Sculpture, 2007, p 523-25

Caesar and Christ, Vol III, 1944, Durant, p 425, 670

Ancient Rome, 1996, Liberati, p 49, 57

History of Art, 1977, Janson, p 174-75

The Renaissance, Vol V, 1953 , Durant, p 495

Wall Street Journal, 6/12/11, Freudenheim, p. C13

61

MARCUS AURELIUS COLUMN

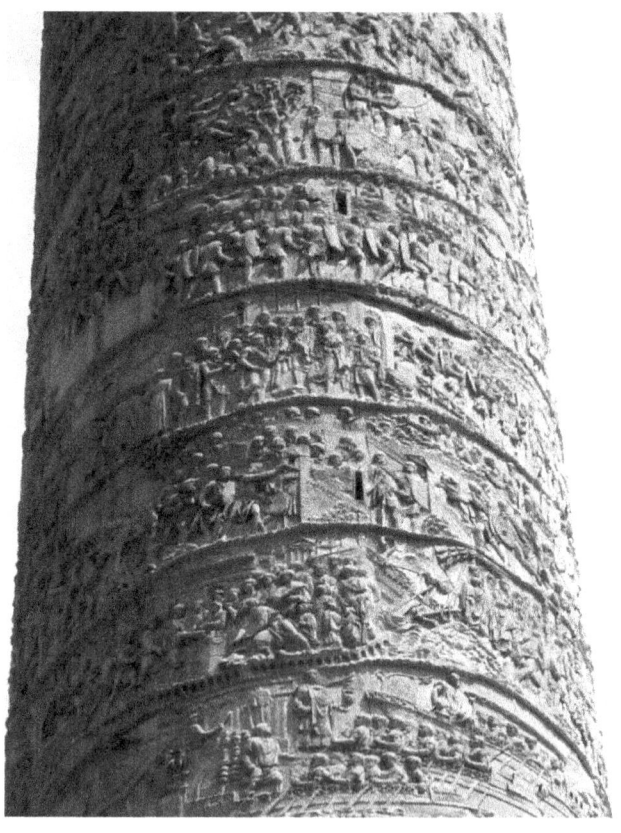

"the wars of M. Aurelius are rendered in simplified pictures in
stronger relief... sacrificing Classical proportions for the sake
of clarity and immediacy.... Rome, 2003, Kindersley, p 113

Erected AD 180-193, Rome – in the Piazza Colonna*, Rome
Roman sculpture – white marble – realistic Roman style
Ht. 136 feet [42 m]; shaft 98 ft. [30 m]; 21 spiral bands
Sculptor: unknown
    *on the Corso, 7 blocks north of *Trajan's Column*
    **binoculars recommended

The *Marcus Aurelius Column* [193 AD] – completed 80 years after *Trajan's Column* – displays far more realism. In an open plaza, it is also more viewer-friendly.

Lenaghan states: "The greater attention given to the human figures and their expressions may be explained by a deliberate attempt to create greater legibility and to correct the mistakes made by the sculptors of the *Column of Trajan*. Fewer figures with more pronounced expressions are easier for a spectator looking up at a tall relief column to understand." Reliefs on the *M. Aurelius Column* also display "deeper carving ... more animated action ... more violent war scenes." [*Encyclo Sculpt.* p 351-52]

Bazin adds: "this monument is decorated in a very different spirit. The high relief, worked with a drill, expresses in dramatic chiaroscuro [light and shadow] the sufferings caused by a ferocious war." [*History of World Sculpture,* p 179]

Initially, the open space surrounding the *Column* was bordered by a temple dedicated to Marcus Aurelius and the ancient Via Flaminia ... [now the Via del Corso] which still bisects Rome north to south.

Hooker declares: "The helical reliefs of the *M. Aurelius Column* ... follow the model of *Trajan's Column,* but ... the *M. Aurelius* reliefs are more schematic [graphic] ... the emperor's presence dominates the composition more insistently ... and an unprecedented expression of savagery and anxiety manifests itself in violent scenes of battle ..." [*History of Western Art,* p 42-3]

In 1589, papal 'restoration' resulted in a statue of St. Paul being placed atop the column. This 'restoration' included the destruction [scraping off] of reliefs on sides of the column's base. The reliefs had displayed: "Victories with garlands and a scene of M. Aurelius with defeated barbarians." [Lenaghan, p 350]

[St. Peter bronze installed atop *Trajan's Column* 1 year earlier]

The carved staircase of the *Column* is not available to the public.

Subject:

M. Aurelius became emperor in 161 AD … and reigned for 19 years.

The spiral reliefs of his *Column* illustrate the 2 wars he fought between the years 172 AD and 175 AD. The first involved the Quadi and Marcommani [Germanic] tribes [172-73] … the second, the Sarmatians [174-75]

Bazin states the *Column* was: "… designed to celebrate the victories of a philosopher-emperor who hated war and yet had to wage it throughout his reign … the reliefs on the column … bear the marks of a spiritual unease that had begun to affect both private citizens and public men in the later 2nd century … the faces of both barbarians and Romans reflect the virulence of battle … the relentless mechanical force of the legions turning to ferocity … the primitive violence of the barbarians turning into fury. With their flaming beards and hair, their coarse, ravaged features, and their burning eyes, the Sarmatians and Germanics have an aura both 'demonic and pitiful'." [p 33]

While victories of Roman legions often led to the building of roads which fostered the growth of trade and prosperity within the Empire, the *Column* also illustrates the negative consequences of these victories.

Bazin explains: "The demon raging them [barbarians] on is against their invaders … all the evils that conquest brings upon them – torture, burned villages, razed towns, mass deportations – are fully pictured here." [p 33-34]

"The *Pax Romana* advanced with cataclysm and misery. The victorious army took booty, not only gold and precious materials, but even more … human cattle. One result of the Roman victories was an enormous increase in slavery. Many of those slaves had to fight again … against each other in the arena. Some deep sense of remorse regarding so many outraged human lives must have tormented [some of] the Romans, for they depicted insistently the tortures inflicted on their enemies." [p 33-34]

Sculptural art from the era of Marcus Aurelius would later adorn the *Arch of Constantine.*

Durant reveals: "Of 11 panels surviving from triumphal arches erected to commemorate the campaigns of Marcus Aurelius – 8 adorn the *Arch of Constantine*…and 3 are in the Museo de' Conservatori. [on Capitoline Hill] They show the naturalistic style in perfection; no one is idealized, every participant is individualized … Marcus Aurelius receiving without pride the submission of a fallen enemy is an appealing human figure … and the defeated are shown not as barbarians but as men worthy of their long struggle for freedom." [p 443]

Sculptor:

The designer and sculptors of the *M. Aurelius Column* remain unknown. It is possible they were Roman. By this time, the skill of the Roman sculptor had improved to the degree that it equaled the skill of the Greeks.

Lenaghan says: "At the end of the second century AD, artists in the Imperial service could work to the highest foreign standards. Elegant portraits of the family of Marcus Aurelius as well as the fine relief panels of the period attest to this notion." [p 351]

Note: To study casts up close of the *M. Aurelius* reliefs, visit the Museo della Civilta Romana at EUR [in southern Rome].

Major References:

History of Western Art, 1994, Hooker, p 42-3

ROME, 2003, Kindersley, p 113

Art & Architecture: Rome, 2005, Hintzen-Bohlen, p 56-7, 213

Caesar & Christ, 1944, Durant, p 408-13, 442-43

History of World Sculpture, 1968, Bazin, p 33-34, 178-79

Art Through the Ages, 1980, Gardner, p 199-202

Encyclopedia of Sculpture, 2006, Lehagnan, p 350-53
Roman Art, 1974, Brilliant, p 123-28
History of Art, 1977, Janson, p 174-75
Ancient Rome, 1996, Liberati, p 4-5, 50, 57

62

CONSTANTINE ...

COLOSSAL HEAD

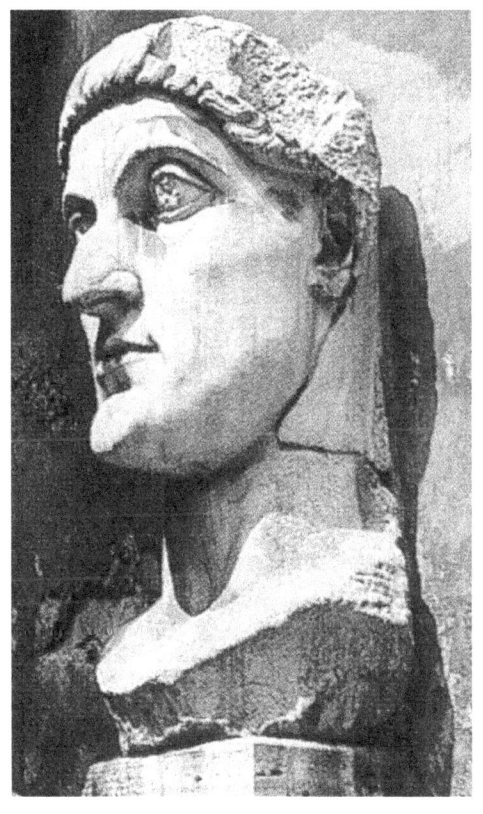

"....one of the most awesome portraits in Western art"
...Thomas Hoving, *Greatest Works of Art...* , p 201

Found, Forum, Basilica of Constantine* – now, Capitoline Mus.
Original Roman sculpture – 324 AD – Classic / Roman style
Height of head: 8 ft. 6 in. [2.6 m] – marble
Sculptor: unknown Roman
    *initially *Basilica of Maxientius*…before Battle of Mulvian
    Bridge

Constantine the Great [272-337 AD] is said to be one of the finest Roman emperors. At first view of his 8.5-foot-tall colossal head, the over-sized melancholy eyes draw our attention.

Hoving comments: "Those huge eyes stare into one's soul with chilling power…there is a sacrifice of finesse for brute force…in imperial portraits, abstract power was preferred over realism or idealism…for the emperor had become an idea of godhead, not a man." [*Greatest Works*…, p 201]

The Jansons say: "We enter a different universe with the *Head of Constantine the Great*…the first 'Christian' emperor and reorganizer of the Roman state. Its face is not a true portrait. Everything is so out-of-proportion to ourselves that we feel crushed by its size. An image more of imperial majesty than a living, breathing man…it was clearly intended to give the viewer the impression of being in the presence of a superhuman power." [*Basic History of Western Art*, p 124]

Hartt adds the eyes: "… stare above and beyond us as if…his godlike gaze were fixed on eternity. Enormous enlargement of the eyes – as an indication of sanctity or of inspiration – became a convention in Early Christian and Byzantine art. No accusation of technical decline can be leveled at this magnificent head. The features and neck muscles are superbly modeled, showing a full understanding of Hellenistic tradition …" [*Art: History*…, p 274]

Subject:

Durant describes the man: "He was a masterly general, a remarkable administrator, a superlative statesman. He inherited and completed the restorative work of Diocletion…through them, the Empire lived 1,150 more years. [*Caesar & Christ*, p 653-6]

Byzantium was an ancient Greek city on the Bosphorus. A few miles south was Nicomedia, which had become the imperial headquarters of Diocletion after he abandoned Rome. When Constantine rebuilt Byzantium…it was re-named Constantinople. [present-day Istanbul]

Durant declares: "Wiser than Diocletion, Constantine gave new life to an aging Empire by associating it with a young religion…a vigorous organization with a fresh morality. By his aid, Christianity became a state as well as a church, and the mold – for 14 centuries – of European life and thought. Perhaps, if we except Augustus, the grateful Church was right in naming him the greatest of the emperors." [C&C, p 664]

The above explains why he earned the rare sobriquet: …'the Great'.

Constantine's father Constantius – a 'co-Caesar' appointed during the reign of Emperor Diocletion – had an "illegitimate son by his legal concubine, Helena, a barmaid from Bithynia." Young Constantine, though poorly schooled, soon became a valiant soldier.

Durant adds: "The Gallic army – deeply loyal to the humane Constantius – came to love his handsome, brave, and energetic son…and when the father died at York, the troops acclaimed Constantine not merely as 'Caesar' but as *Augustus* – their emperor. Constantine fought successfully against the invading Franks, and fed the beasts of the Gallic amphitheaters with barbarian kings." He was 34 years old. [C&C, p 653]

After Emperor Diocletian's abdication in 305 AD, Constantine proved to be the most capable general during the inevitable battles between the 4 sub-rulers [and others] who would be emperor.

The Jansons describe the deciding battle in 312 AD. "Constantine's 'conversion' begins on the eve of the battle against his rival Maxientius at the Mulvian Bridge over the Tiber River in Rome. According to the emperor's recounting of the event, there appeared in the sky the sign of the cross with the inscription, *'In this sign, conquer.'* The next night, Christ came to Constantine in a dream with a sign – the 'Chi Rho' monogram – and commanded him to copy it. He had the insignia inscribed on his helmet and on military standards for his soldiers. After his victory, Constantine accepted the faith...although he was not baptized until on his deathbed." [p 142-43]

Durant offers this account by the ancient historian Eusebius: 'Constantine saw a flaming cross in the sky...with Greek words [in this sign, conquer]. Early the next morning, Constantine dreamed a voice commanded him to have his soldiers mark upon their shields the letter X with a line drawn through it and curled around the top – the symbol of Christ.' Constantine cast in his lot with the Christians...who were numerous in his army...and made the engagement [victory] a turning point in religion." [p 654]

The colossal head of Constantine [and fragments] were found in the Roman Forum within the Basilica of Constantine.

After the Battle of the Mulvian Bridge, Constantine 'inherited' this basilica...almost finished by Maxientius. Constantine left a colossal statue of Maxientius in place...but had it remodeled to represent himself. He also gave the basilica his name. [Jansons, p 118]

Lawrence adds: "Fragments indicate the exposed arms and lower legs were marble...attached to a torso core likely composed of brick and wood covered with gilded bronze or even sheets of gold. [*Greek & Roman Sculpture,* p 309]

In 313 AD, Constantine [with co-emperor Licinius] issued the 'Edict of Milan' that confirmed the same religious tolerance proclaimed earlier [in 261] by the Roman Emperor Galerius...recognizing Christianity as a permitted religion. In 323 AD, Constantine fought Licinius and won his final battle of succession to become the sole Emperor. [C& C, Durant, p 655]

When Constantine built his new capital in Constantinople [330 AD], he "used pagan as well as Christian rites in dedicating" the city. He also "restored pagan temples, and...used pagan magic formulas to protect crops and heal disease." [p 656]

Durant suggests: "While still proclaiming liberty of worship for all, he now invited his subjects to join him in embracing the new faith. Was his conversion sincere – was it an act of religious belief, or a consummate stroke of political wisdom? Probably, the latter." [p 655]

Hoving says Constantine the Great was "able to sit for hours at a time to greet the hundreds of supplicants that were presented to him on 'public days' without moving a muscle or twitching an eye. Possibly, the *Colossal Head's* unknown sculptor captured him in this mode ... for there is an impassivity in the great face ..." [*Greatest Works...*, p 201]

Sculptor:

The unknown Roman sculptor(s) of the *Head* – when creating the image of Constantine the Great – undoubtedly had in mind similar colossal works by the famed Greek Pheidias [490-432 BC].

Pheidias had designed and directed the creation of the 38-feet tall, standing *Athena Parthenos* on the Acropolis in 438 BC. Later, he created the seated *Zeus* [60-feet-tall] at Olympia ... which became one of the *Seven Wonders of the Ancient World*. Neither survived ... having been too richly adorned in valuable metals, ivory, and precious jewels. [Durant, Vol. II, p 324-26]

Major References:

Arts of the Ancient Greeks, 1972, Brilliant, p 273

History of Art, 1977, Janson, p 176

Basic History of Western Art, 2006, Janson & Janson, p 124

Greatest Works of Art of Western Civilization, 1997, Hoving, p 201

A Wanderer in Rome, 1926, E V Lucas, p 190

Art: A History... 1989, Hartt, p 273-74

Greek and Roman Sculpture, 1972, Lawrence, p 309-10

Art Through the Ages, I, 1954, Gardner, p 206

Caesar and Christ, III, 1944, Durant, p 653-56, 664

Life of Greece, II, 1939, Durant, p 325-26

Roman Art and Architecture, 1964, Wheeler, p 114-15

Ancient Rome, 2000, Liberati, p 55

63

THE NORTH ROSE

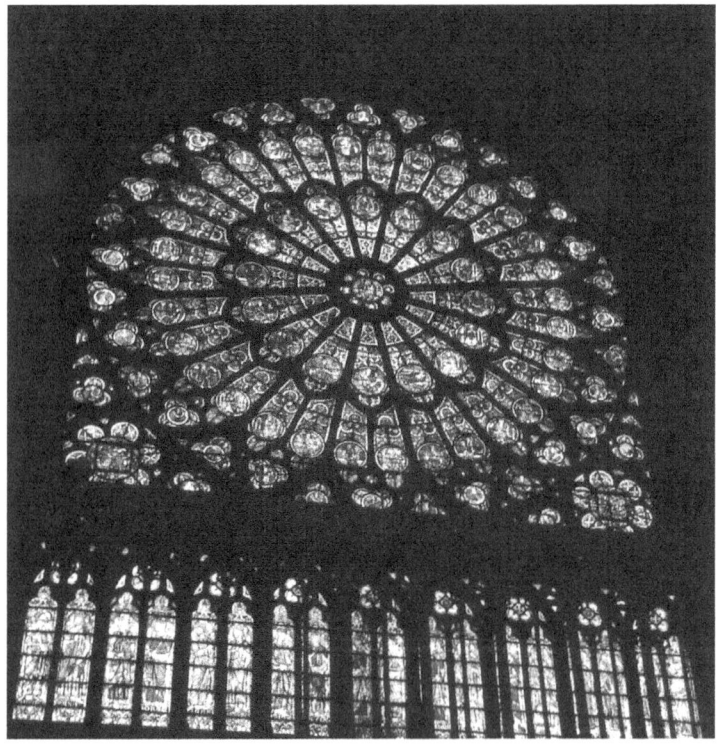

"The rose windows of *Our Lady of Paris* are masterpieces
of bar tracery and coloring..." ... Durant, IV, p 877

North Rose window of Notre-Dame Cathedral – Paris
Stained Glass & Tracery [85% original] – 1250-1265 AD

Diameter: 42 feet [12.9 m] – carved glass and stone
Style: rayonnant [wheel-radiating tracery]
Architect [master mason]: Jean de Chelles.

66 T he great rose windows of Paris and Chartres take the breath away ... with their spectacular webs of glass, lead, and stone ... a perfection which, as Rodin says, 'speaks to our hearts because it is the general principle of things'." [*Rose Windows*, Cowan, p 8]

To optimally view *the North Rose* in the Notre-Dame, arrive within an hour of noon ... when the colored glass is bathed in the most brilliant light.

Initially ... sit in a back row of the cathedral ... an excellent refuge for weary legs ... permit your vision to adjust in the dim light. The immense space slowly reveals itself. Towering columns and arches climb 11 stories before disappearing in shadows. The far end of the cathedral is 420 feet [128 m.] distant.

[after the streets of Paris, the relative silence can be refreshing]

Varicolored rays of light stream down from the tall windows. A rare linear-rainbow may appear. Search out soft rays of white sunlight streaming through the highest glass ... some call it *god-light*. With the eyes adjusted, stroll down the center aisle toward the altar. [if this aisle is closed, use far-left aisle]

Glance neither right nor left.

A great spherical apse gradually opens before you.

Nearing the altar, still resist glancing left or right.

If altar area is crowded with milling people, join them.

Within 10 yards of the altar ... abruptly turn left, and

Raise your eyes to the violet-blues of *the North Rose*

An explosion of color fills the senses ...

At mid-day, its radiance can be almost blinding.

Shift attention to the dark walls on either side of the great window ... close eyes to clear their retinas ... then, return to *the North Rose*.

Winston accurately declares: "the glorious rose window built by Jean de Chelles in about 1250 – [blue, red, green, brown, and yellow, but predominantly blue] – is breathtaking." [*Notre-Dame de Paris, p* 74]

Turn about to view *the South Rose*. Many believe its dominant reds to be equally spectacular.

After 750 years, *the North Rose* is said to retain 85% of its original glass. The *South Rose* has far less original glass, due to restorations required by its southern exposure.

Cowen adds: "The sheer size and strength of form of the greatest [rose windows] cannot fail to hold the attention and provoke a moment's reflection in wonder. To the people who first saw them, the impact must have been astounding. Even in sophisticated people of the 20th century – with a lifetime's experience of electric light – rose windows still promote a sense of awe..." [p 98]

When leaving the cathedral, check when *Vespers* [evening song] begins in the late afternoon.

If you return for Vespers [music and/or singing], walk down the aisles to sit as close as possible to the performers. This again may provide spectacular views of the giant roses. For the *Author*, Vespers *with the rose windows* is a highlight of any Paris visit.

As daylight fades, the Notre-Dame offers a final visual treat...sunset through the smaller west rose window. Rodin maintains the "magnificence [of] these rose windows...was inspired by the setting sun or by the dawn..." [*Notre-Dame de Paris*, p 142]

Visitors of all spiritual persuasions [including without] are welcome in the Notre-Dame. Two centuries ago, the Revolution nationalized this sanctuary...it is now owned by the people of France. Thoughtful visitors respect its serenity...speak in low voices...and minimize the flash of cameras.

Anytime of day or evening, visitors may stroll the perimeter passageways [outer aisles] of the cathedral. During a Sunday service, when seated, it is polite to remain seated until the service ends.

The Cathedral of Chartres [hour train-ride from Paris] possesses another famed stained-glass window... *the Rose of France.*

During the Middle Ages, Chartres became a major pilgrimage cathedral of Europe. It is famed for the excellence of its free tours morning/exterior & afternoon/interior. [guides accept gratuities – *not required* – from appreciative visitors]

Subject:

Hendrik Willem Van Loon, in *The Arts*, says it well: "A stained glass window is a symphony in color just as an orchestra is a symphony in sound." [p 216]

The goal of the original architects of the giant 'roses' was to open up the new Gothic cathedrals to more light ... to stun the faithful by its beauty ... so they might become 'more receptive to the gospel'.

Some 200 years before the Renaissance – about 1170 – these 'giant flowers' began to bloom in Gothic cathedrals. They were a refinement of smaller Roman innovations [as early as the 1st century].

Gardner states: "Perfection of the technology must have been gradual, with the greatest advances during the 10th and 11th centuries. The first accurately-dated rose windows – in the Choir of St. Denis [Paris] in 1144 – show a high degree of skill ..." [*Art Thru the Ages*, p 337]

Durant comments: "... radiating tracery generated the term 'rayonnant' for the style that began at Notre-Dame in 1230." [p 875]

Cowen states: "Built on the geometry of the number 16, *the North Rose* is the ultimate in sheer delicacy, the ratio of stone to glass having been reduced to an absolute minimum." [p 135]

Between 1250 and 1265, the *North Rose* of the Notre-Dame was carved with such elaborate expertise that later artists – restoring lost or damaged stained glass – have been unable to match its quality.

The window depicts Old Testament prophets, judges, kings, and high priests ... down to the time of *Christ*. Each figure appears in a circular medallion among the 3 rings which enclose the central figure of *Mary* with the infant *Jesus*. The Inner Ring of medallions (*prophets, plus a pharaoh*) number 16. The Middle Ring (*judges and kings)* doubles to 32. The Outer Ring, also 32, offers more kings, plus high priests.

Binoculars are necessary to distinguish figures in the medallions. Solomon, Abraham, Moses, and David can be located as follows. In the Inner Ring … the top medallion is *Hosea*. Directly above *Hosea* are *Ozias* and *Deborah* in the Middle Ring. To the right (ours) of *Deborah* is *Solomon*.

In the Inner Ring, the bottom medallion is *Zephaniah*. Directly below *Zephaniah* are *Ahiud* and *Abraham* (our right) in the Middle Ring. To the right of *Abraham* is *Moses*. To the right of *Moses* is *David*.

Readers wishing to identify other figures can refer to page 135 of the book: *Rose Windows* by Cowen, 1979. Or, go online.

Sculptor:

The North Rose is believed to have been designed and built primarily under the direction of the French architect Jean de Chelles … also known as the *Master of the Notre-Dame*. Little is known of him, as the first name is common … and Chelles denotes the place where he was born. After completing the design and installation of *the North Rose*, he died before finishing the South Rose.

Several other equally-talented but unknown architects worked on the cathedral. The workers who fashioned, cut, and leaded the stained glass were skilled tradesmen and remain unnamed … as are the stone masons who carved the tracery.

Color was fused into glass as it was made. The chemical secrets – proportions, temperatures, quality of sand, etc. – were guarded closely by the master glass-makers and passed down through their families.

In the Notre-Dame, 18-foot-wide rose windows were installed before 1250 … but taken down when the original buttresses had to be replaced. New rose windows [current] – more than twice the size – were installed between 1250 and 1270.

Ancient Romans had built a temple where the cathedral now stands. Evidence of earlier primitive altars also has been found … suggesting the space has been hallowed through several millenniums.

Some visitors claim to sense 'a collective energy' or electricity in the vicinity of the altar...a residuum resulting from millions of past visitors. [breathe deeply a few moments...then look up into the shadows overhead some 20 to 30 seconds]. Hearts of mammals create electricity through the combining of certain elements...it is not a miracle.

When it rains in Paris, water pours from the dragon-spouts of the cathedral. Kotaro Takamura [studied with Rodin] wrote a poem: *Cathedral in the Thrashing Rain.* Below is the first stanza. When it rains in Paris, stand outside the Notre-Dame by a dragon-spout and boldly read aloud:

"This morning
A terrible storm, increasing since daybreak
Now rages in the four corners of Paris.
I cannot distinguish east from west,
Nor even which way the storm is moving,
as it runs amok here in the Ile de France...
But here I am again...
Oh Notre-Dame of Paris!
Soaked with rain...just to gaze at you, to touch you,
To steal a kiss from you...your flesh of stone..."
    *there are 5 more stanzas.

Major References:

Art Through the Ages, 1980, Gardner, p 317, 332, 336-37
Wonders of the World, 2002, Burton & Cavendish, p 28-9
The Age of Faith, 1950, Durant, p 875, 880-1
Notre-Dame de Paris, 1971, Winston, p 36, 74, 142, 165
    (*North Rose* is on above dust-jacket)
Rose Windows, 1979, Cowen, 15, 81, 83, 96-9, 102
A History of Art, 1977, Janson, p 288, 297, 306
Notre-Dame de Paris, 1952, Temko
The Arts, 1939, Hendrik Willem Van Loon, p 216
Wonders of the World, 2002, Burton & Cavendish, p 28-9

64

THE GATES OF PARADISE

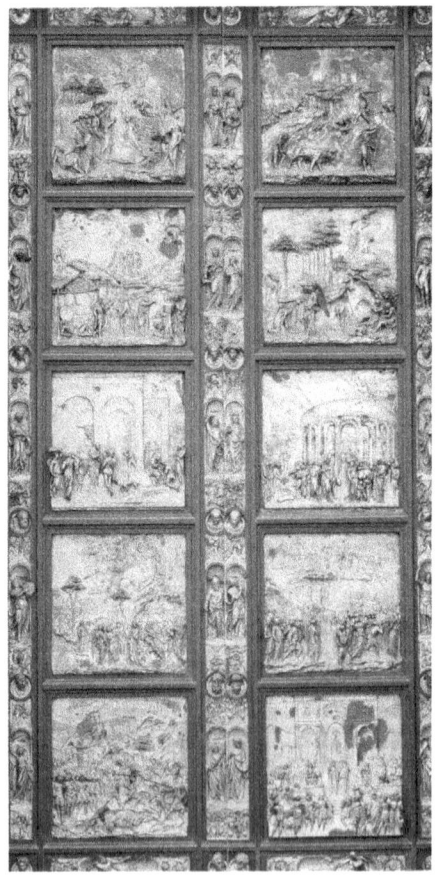

"these gilded bronze doors are the finest ever made"
Hoving, *Greatest Works ...*, p 44

Bronze Doors, 1452, Florence – now, <u>Museo d' Opera d' Dumo</u>
        [restored original door re-installed 2012 at Museo d' Opera d' Dumo]
Orig. Italian sculpture – 1425 to 1437 – Classic style
Ht. 15 feet [or 4.57 m] – gold-gilded bronze
Sculptor: Lorenzo Ghiberti [1378-1455]

During the Italian Renaissance, these doors were remark-able...as the skill of sculptors had been in long decline fol-lowing the fall of Rome. During that interval, most of the subjects of Western sculpture had been religious, repetitive, and/or largely uninspired.

Ghiberti received a commission to create the bronze doors for the Florence Baptistry in 1425...most of his work was completed by 1437...and the finished doors were installed in 1452.

In 1990, they were removed for conservation. In 2012, the original bronze doors were re-installed inside the <u>Museo dell' Opera d' Dumo</u>.

The replacement copies currently on the Baptistry are described as "extremely precise" however we are warned they "suffer from the limitations of modern gilding technology...which is safer than the mercury-based method Ghiberti used...but much thicker and less luminous, masking much of the finer detail." [*Wall Street Journal*, 9/13/2012, Rocca, p D6]

Therefore, visitors to Florence are advised to <u>view the original Gates </u>in their new, nearby location...the <u>Museo d' Opera d' Dumo</u>.

In describing the original *Gates of Paradise*, Hoving states: "Lorenzo Ghiberti was one of the giants of the Renaissance who truly combined nature and the antique to create something new, lively, graceful, and everlastingly beautiful." [*Greatest Works of Art*, p 46]

Janson says: "The present title of the doors derives from the fact that they [originally] opened on the *paradiso* – the Italian term for the area between a baptistry and the entrance to its cathedral. Michelangelo – playing on this word – is reported to have said that the doors were truly worthy to be the 'Gates of Paradise', and the nickname stuck." [*History of Art,* p 196]

Hoving adds: "Michelangelo ... was so enthralled with them I'm convinced he loosely-patterned the Sistine Ceiling after their Old Testament subject matter and borrowed freely from their classical majesty." Hoving also suggests Rodin used the *Doors* as inspiration for his *Gates of Hell* in Paris. [p 44]

Janson singles out the 'Jacob and Esau' panel to illustrate the beauty of all the panels. "The setting for Ghiberti's narrative is a spacious hall ... a fine example of Early Renaissance architectural design reflecting the mature art of Brunelleschi ... ." [p 387]

Hartt adds: "The last traces of Gothicism in line and pose have been transmuted into Hellenic grace and ease. Despite their diminutive scale, such figures as the angry Esau standing before his perplexed father or the three beautiful female figures at the left can be set against the masterpieces of Greek sculpture." [Vol. II of *Art...,* p 531]

The original location of the doors, the octagonal Baptistry of St. John the Baptist – one of the oldest Tuscan Romanesque buildings – was the cathedral of Florence until 1128. Surprisingly, the Baptistry contains the tomb of the licentious and deposed Anti-Pope John XXIII. This may be due to his sizeable 'donation' prior to his death. John had transferred the Vatican's banking affairs to Florence – into the hands of Giovanni de Medici. Vastly enriched, the Medici family "helped bankroll the artists, the architects, and the glory of Florence ... ." [Hall, 56]

Subject:

Each panel depicts an event from the first 5 books of the Old Testament. Their illusion of depth is highly convincing ..."enhanced by the use of gold over the entire relief, giving the feeling that the space is pervaded by a kind of golden atmosphere." [Hartt, History ..., p 196-99]

The Biblical themes of each panel were ordered by Leonardo Bruni, then Chancellor of the Republic of Florence. Beginning from the top panels, they are:

1. Creation of Adam and Eve ... the Original Sin
2. Adam and Eve, with Cain and Abel
3. Story of Noah: leaves ark after Flood
4. Story of Abraham; Angels appear to Abraham
5. <u>Story of Jacob and Esau: Esau sells birthright</u>
6. Story of Joseph: bros. put him in well & sell to merchants
7. Story of Moses: receives Tablets of the Law
8. Story of Joshua: The crossing of the Jordan
9. Story of Saul and David: David kills Goliath
10. King Solomon solemnly receives the Queen of Sheba

Sculptor:

Lorenzo Ghiberti received training as a goldsmith, painter, architect, and sculptor. He won a competition in 1400 for an initial pair of bronze doors on the Baptistry – with 28 panels depicting events from the *New Testament*. Ghiberti completed them by 1424 ... with the help of Donatello and other artists. These doors are now on the north side of the Baptistry. Ghiberti then received a commission for two more doors.

When Ghiberti completed his masterpiece – *the Gates of Paradise* – in 1452, he was 74 ... and had spent most of his adult life working on 4 bronze doors. Three years later, he died. Due to private commissions, Ghiberti also completed other works.

Hoving says: "Ghiberti was aided to a significant extent by the young Leon Battista Alberti, a humanist scholar ... they experimented with fresh ways of forming pictorial space and invented figures that moved naturally ... in which there's a matchless combination of the grace." [p 46]

Ghiberti also excelled with his 2 *Madonna and Child* [painted terra cotta] sculptures now displayed in the NY Met. Museum of Art. The 'tenderness' of Mary's face is rarely equaled.

Major References:

History of Renaissance Art, 1974, Hartt, p 196-99
Art: History of Painting, Sculpture, Architecture, Vol II, Hartt, p 531
Greatest Works of Art in Western World, 1997, Hoving, p 44-46

Art Through the Ages, 1991, Gardner, p 589-91
History of Art, 1977, Janson, p 385-86
A Wanderer in Florence, 1912, E.V. Lucas, p 43-7
National Geographic Traveler, 1992 , Hall, p 51-68
How To Visit the Beauties of Florence, 1971, Bonechi, p 8-14
History of World Sculpture, 1968, Bazin, p 330-31
Wall Street Journal, 9/13/2012, Rocca, p D6

65
MARY MAGDALENE

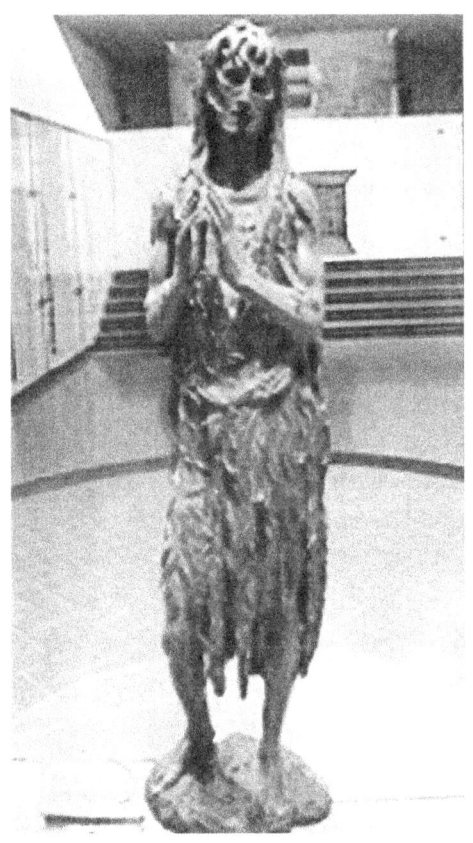

"Of all the magnificent works by the 15th century sculptor
Donatello, none surpasses the poignant *Mary Magdalene*..."
... *Greatest Works of Art*, 1997, Hoving, p 84

Mary Magdalene – now, Mus. d' Opera d' Dumo, Florence
Italian – 1454-55 – French Baroque style
Ht. 6 feet 2 inches [1.88 m] – poly-chromed wood, gilded
Sculptor: Donatello [1386-1466

F rom a distance, *the Magdalene* appears to be a woman deep in prayer.

The wooden surface modeled by Donatello – considered the finest sculptor of the 15th century – is so realistic she seems almost alive. [*Bullfinch History of Art*, p 392] Though she is much aged, her poly-chrome finish creates the impression she is quivering with passion.

Hoving, in *Greatest Works of Art*, says: "Of all the magnificent works by the 15th century sculptor Donatello, none surpasses the poignant *Mary Magdalene*..." [p 84]

J. White, in *History of Western Art*, is equally effusive: "...it is only in the Renaissance, and in the light of the new knowledge, that such an image could have been brought into being. In her youth, *Mary Magdalene* herself was famous for her beauty. Now, all her flesh is eaten up in fasting and remorse and by her love of God and of the Christ who died to wash her free of sin. Her flame-like hands burn with the intensity of her longing and her love. Her matted hair flickers with flames, consuming the emaciated remnants of corporeal being and transmuting body into soul." [*History of Western Art*, p 141]

In 1966, after floodwaters in Florence damaged the wooden statue, restoration revealed the original multi-colored finish had been coated with a "thick layer of brown paint." With this paint removed, it was possible to "see the tan of the *Magdalene's* face, arms, and legs setting off the intense blue of her eyes and, even more, the flickering highlights of gold in her hair..." [Russell, p 144]

Gardner notes her 'sway': "The repentant saint in old age, after years of wasting mortification, stands... hands clasped in prayer. The beautiful woman has withered, but her soul has been saved... This figure... is nude, 'clothed' only in her extraordinary long hair… and her body sways gently in a contrapposto stance…" [*Art Through the Ages,* p 690]

Donatello did not carve *Magdalene* until near the end of his own life. Gardner adds: "His last period is marked by an intensely personal kind of expression, in which his earlier realism returns… but with purposeful exaggeration and distortion. He turns away from Classical beauty and grandeur toward a kind of expressionism <u>that seems deliberately calculated to jar the sensibilities</u>…" [p 689]

Hoving describes Donatello as: "Powerful, sensitive, subtle, amusing, quirky, and lyrical… there's just no one like him. He was a man of simple tastes who seems to have insisted upon utter artistic freedom and received it… in a day when there were strict guild regulations and when artists were considered craftspeople." [p 84]

Durant, reviewing the work of Donatello, says: "Only one sculptor would reach greater heights, and then by 'inheriting' what Donatello had learned, achieved, and taught. Bertoldo was Donatello's pupil… and the teacher of Michelangelo." [p 95]

Subject:

Mary Magdalene is a Biblical figure described in *Webster's Encyclopedic Dictionary* as "traditionally identified with the repentant woman who Jesus forgave. Luke 7:37-50." [p 880]

The *Gideon Bible, St. Luke* [7:37] explains how Jesus met Mary Magdalene at the house of Simon the Pharisee:

"And, behold, a woman in the city, who was a sinner – when she knew that *Jesus* sat at meat in the Pharisee's house – brought an alabaster box of ointment. 38.And stood at his feet weeping, and began to wash his feet with tears, and did wipe *them* with the hairs of her head, and kissed his feet, and anointed *them* with the ointment. 39.Now when the Pharisee Simon who had bidden him saw *it*, he spake, 'This man, if he were a prophet, would have known who and what manner of woman *this* is that toucheth him: for she is a sinner…'

44.And *Jesus* turned to the woman, and said unto Simon, 'Seest thou this woman? I entered into thine house, thou gavest me no water for my feet: but she hath washed my feet with tears, and wiped *them* with the hairs of her head. 45.Thou gavest me no kiss: but this woman since the time I came in hath not ceased to kiss my feet. 46.My feet with oil thou didst not anoint: but this woman hath anointed my feet with ointment. 47.Wherefore, I say unto thee, Her sins, which are many, are forgiven; for she loved much: but to whom little is forgiven, the same loveth little.' 48.And he said unto her, 'Thy sins are forgiven.'

49.And they that sat at meat with him began to say within themselves, 'Who is this that forgiveth sins also?' 50.And he said to the woman, 'Thy faith hath saved thee; go in peace'."

Durant provides a description of Mary Magdalene's presence during the crucifixion and resurrection of Jesus. At the crucifixion: "Of all the apostles, only John was present; with him were three Marys – Christ's mother, her sister Mary, and Mary Magdalene ... Two days later, Mary Magdalene – whose love of Jesus partook of that nervous intensity which characterized all her feelings – visited the tomb with 'Mary the mother of James, and Salome.' They found it empty. Frightened and yet overjoyed, they ran to tell the news to the disciples. On the way they met one whom they thought to be Jesus; they bowed down before him and clasped his feet ... Forty days after his 'appearance' to Mary Magdalene, says the beginning of the Book of Acts, Christ ascended physically into heaven." [p 572-3]

On September 18, 2012, Professor Karen King – Harvard's Hollis Professor of Divinity – at the International Congress of Coptic Studies [in Rome] "sparked intense debate with her discovery of a 1,600-year-old papyrus fragment referring to Jesus' wife." [*Smithsonian*, Nov, 2014, Sabar, p 74-5]

Prof. King "had come upon an ancient scrap of papyrus on which a scribe had written the words, 'Jesus said to them, 'My wife … She will be able to be my disciple … I dwell with her.' The words on the fragment, scattered across 14 incomplete lines, leave a good deal to interpretation. But in King's analysis, the 'wife' Jesus refers to is probably Mary Magdalene … and Jesus appears to be defending her against someone, perhaps one of the male disciples." [*Smithsonian*, p 76]

"Professor King believes the fragment's origin is a 4th-century Coptic book from a previous Greek text. King states: 'If the 2nd century date of composition is correct,' it provides 'direct evidence that claims about Jesus' marital status first arose over a century after the death of Jesus in the context of intra-Christian controversies over sexuality, marriage, and discipleship'." [p 76]

Further scholarship may or may not confirm King's conclusions … which will remain controversial in either case.

Sculptor:

Donatello was initially apprenticed to Ghiberti – famed for "linear elegance" and the bronze *Gates of Paradise* #64 doors in Florence.

Bullfinch states: "Donatello's influence was enormous, affecting painters and sculptors alike, throughout Italy. Castagno and Botticelli saw the linear possibilities of Donatello's wiry and expressive contours … although his last dramatically emotional works seem to have been beyond the comprehension of most of his contemporaries, they were profoundly admired by a later generation of artists and especially by Michelangelo." [*History of Art,* p 392-93]

His principal patron was Cosimo De Medici, who first commissioned from Donatello his famed *David* in the Bargello in 1430. "Patron and artist grew old together"… and after numerous other commissions from his benefactor, Donatello – at the age of 80 – was buried beside Cosimo in the crypt of San Lorenzo in 1466.

Among other masterpieces by Donatello, the most notable are the marble 6'10" *St. George* and his equestrian bronze *Gattamelata.*

Another outstanding *St. Magdalene* – by Gregor Erhart, [1540?], polychrome limewood – is in the Louvre. She is a far younger

Mary Magdalene than envisioned by Donatello. The saintly face is idealized.

Major References:

The Renaissance, Vol V, 1953, Durant, p 92-5

History of Western Art, 1994, Hooker (Prof. John White), p 141

Greatest Works of Art of Western Civilization, 1997, Hoving, p 84-85

Art Through the Ages, 10th Ed., Gardner, 1996, p 689-09

Italian Renaissance Art, 1974, Hartt, p 250

Art, A History of Painting, Sculpture … 1985, Hartt, p 529

Art in the World, 1993, Russell, p 144

Bullfinch's History of Art, 1996, West, p 392-93

Art Through the Ages, Vol II, Gardner, p 488-89

66
THE PIETA

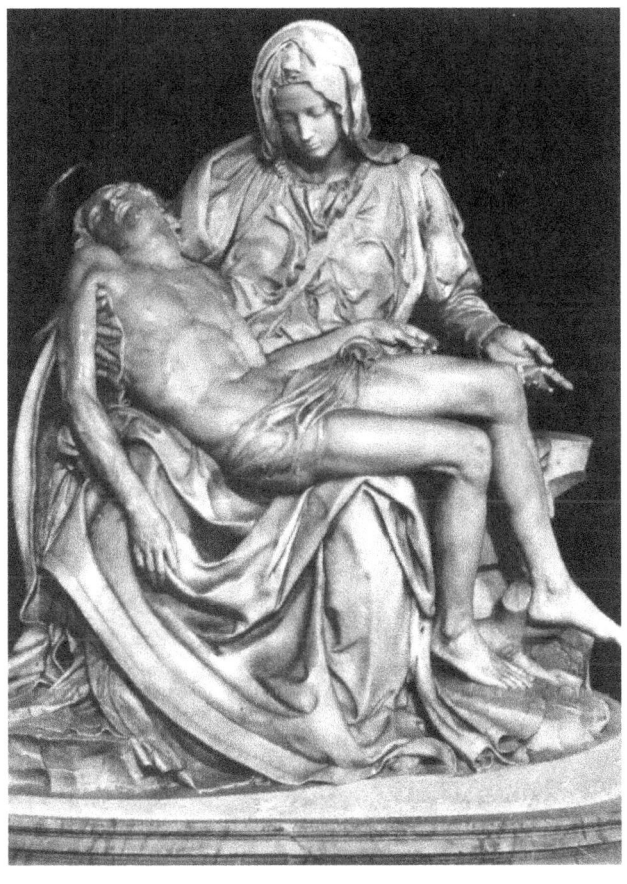

"His earliest masterpiece ... excited the intense admiration
of Michelangelo's contemporaries." ... Hartt, *History---*, p 610

Mary cradling body of *Jesus* – now, in St. Peter's, Rome
Italian sculpture – 1498 to 1499 – Hellenistic style
Ht. 68.5 inches – Carrara marble
Sculptor: Michelangelo Buonarroti [1475-1564]

In 1497, at the age of 23, Michelangelo received a commission to carve *the Pieta.* Most references pay this work high compliment.

In 1964, *the Pieta* became a popular attraction at the New York World's Fair where it astounded American viewers [including the *Author*] by <u>its grace and tenderness.</u>

Hartt says: "His earliest masterpiece ... excited the intense admiration of Michelangelo's contemporaries. The exquisite Virgin, whose left hand is extended less in grief than in exposition, looks as young as her son ... The extreme delicacy in the handling of the marble and the contrast between the long lines of Christ's figure and the crumpled drapery folds produce <u>passages of beauty Michelangelo was never to surpass</u>, despite the grandeur of his mature and late work." [*History of Painting-Sculpt.-Arch.,* p 610-11]

Bazin mentions Da Vinci's impact on the younger artist: "Leonardo's influence appears in the gentleness of the face and in the firmly built pyramidal composition turning around a core, while the perfectly polished marble-figures, especially the Madonna, belong still in the refined tradition of the Florentine Early Renaissance sculpture." [*History of World Sculpture,* p 346]

Wide acclaim for *the Pieta* [and later his *David*] assured Michelangelo commissions and money for the rest of his life. Nevertheless, neither sculpture escaped adverse comment.

Durant observes: "There are some blemishes in this glorious group of the Virgin Mother holding her dead son in her lap: the drapery seems excessive, the Virgin's head is too small for her body, her left hand is extended in an inappropriate gesture; her face is that of a young woman clearly younger than her son." [p 467]

Clement defends the artist: "This marvelous group of the Virgin Mary holding her dead son upon her knee was at first much criticized for the youthful face of the Blessed Mother, which the sculptor defended by saying that her purity of thought kept her ever young. When a courtier asked where a mother could be found who looked younger than her son, Michelangelo replied, 'In Paradise'." [*Rome, the Eternal City*, p 747-48]

Holmes adds: "Michelangelo had achieved a very early command of realism and was always therefore drawn to go beyond realism to a refinement of the body's movements in an unreal weightless space." [*The Renaissance*, p 173]

Close observers of *the Pieta* may sense Jesus appears much younger than a 33-year-old man. Michelangelo's wealthy patrons – anxious to obtain his services – ignored his detractors. They also tolerated his demand for artistic freedom...and forgave the artist for his deliberate deviations from reality. Engrossing biographies of Michelangelo describe a difficult artist whose haughty personality generated much controversy throughout his lifetime.

An irregular childhood may have influenced both his life and work. Within a month of his birth – due to a sickly mother – Michelangelo was 'turned over' to a wet nurse in a village in the hills of Florence...where he was raised in a stone-cutter's family. When the boy reached the age of 6, his natural mother expired.

Putnam states: "No words record his feelings about her [his mother], yet pathos and a sense of irretrievable loss would mark his greatest works, and the women he portrayed would often seem cold and distant, as if viewed through gauze." [*The Renaissance: Maker of Modern Man*, p 148]

Subject:

The subject of Jesus is universally recognized and requires no further description.

The Italian word 'pieta' means pity, compassion, sorrow. In the form of a proper-noun, it refers to any work displaying the Virgin Mary holding her dead son in her arms.

The loving expression on the face of Michelangelo's *Mary* can be described as both sad and serene. The calm face of *Jesus* appears to be that of a person either dreaming or sleeping.

The *Pieta* was commissioned by Cardinal Lagraulus, French ambassador to the Vatican. In the contract, Michelangelo, then 23, boasted it would be "the most beautiful work in marble which exists today in Rome." It was intended for display in St. Peter's Basilica, within the Chapel of the Kings of France. Since its completion in 1498, it has been displayed at several locations within St. Peter's.

Damage and repairs to the sculpture include: 1736, repair of fractured fingers... 1972, damage from 15 blows of a hammer held by a deranged man, repaired 1973... also 1973, repair of holes on head supporting metal halos [removed].

Sculptor:

As a child, Michelangelo became adept at the play of "chipping at stone" with the sons of stone-cutters. Later, Michelangelo would recall: "With my nurse's milk, I sucked in the hammer and chisels I use for my statues." [Putnam, p 148]

When his failing mother died in 1481, Michelangelo "had been lonely and unwanted except by his grandmother... and the stone-cutter's family." [Stone, 19]

When Michelangelo rejoined his real family, his passion to carve stone and draw continued... though he was beaten by a father who believed this activity interfered with the boy's school studies. The 'non-working' father had counted on his second son to help support the family by entering the wool trade. [Stone, 13-19]

In April of 1488, at the age of 13, Michelangelo was indentured – over the initial protests of his father – to the studio of Ghirlandaio, a successful Florentine artist. The father changed his mind upon learning he would receive money *from* Ghirlandaio – the reverse of the normal indenture contract. Ghirlandaio, much impressed by sketches from the precocious boy, immediately had him assist in the carving of marble reliefs already under commission at his studio.

As the teen sculptor received wider recognition in Florence, he accepted an invitation to an art school whose patron was Lorenzo de' Medici. Medici treated Michelangelo as one of his family and introduced him to the finest artists in Italy.

Most of the famed works of Michelangelo have gone unsigned, except for the *Pieta*. Giorgio Vasari, an art historian and contemporary of the artist, relates: "... one day Michelangelo was in St. Peter's when a group of visitors from Lombardy greatly admired his *Pieta,* and he heard one of them say that the artist was: *our Hunchback of Milan.* Michelangelo returned at night with a lantern and carved in Latin on the band across the Virgin's robe: "MICHAEL-ANGELUS-BONAROTUS-FLORENTINUS-FACIEBA[T]" Translation: 'Michelangelo Buonarroti, The Florentine Made It.'

Major References:

Greatest Works of Art of Western Civilization, 1997, Hoving, p 53
History of World Sculpture, 1968, Bazin, p 346
History of Painting-Sculpture-Architecture, 1985, Hartt, p 610-11
Renaissance, 1996, Holmes, p 173
The Renaissance: Maker of Modern Man, 1970, Putnam, p 148-50
History of Italian Renaissance Art, 1974, Hartt, p 415-17
Michelangelo, 2009, Paris, p 137-39, 143
Michelangelo: Pieta, 1975, Hupka (photos and essay)
Rome, the Eternal City, Vol II, 1896, Clement, p 747-48
The Agony and the Ecstasy, 1961, Stone, 13-19
The Renaissance, 1953, Durant, p 467, 495
A Wanderer in Rome, 1926, E.V. Lucas, p 56-7

67

DAVID

[BY MICHELANGELO]

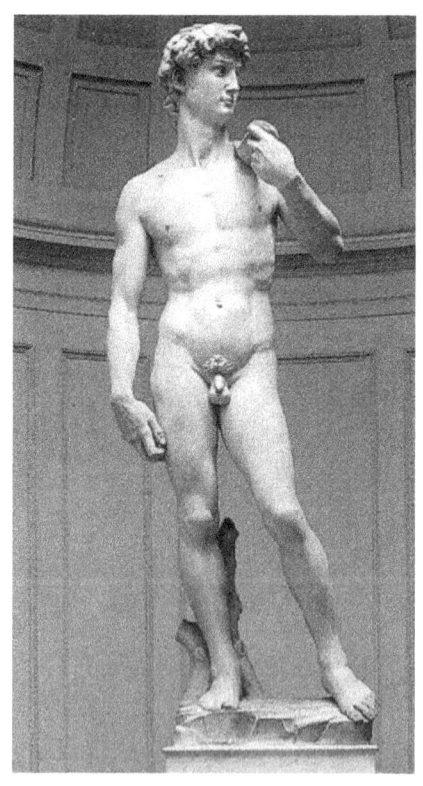

"Every aspect of Michelangelo's sculpture *David* is stupendous.
There is not a single imperfection in the entire majestic work."
... *Greatest Works of Art,* Hoving, 1997, p 52

Colossal *David* – now, in the Accademia, Florence
Italian sculpture – 1501-04 – Classic style
Ht. 13 ft., 5 inches – Carrara marble
Sculptor: Michelangelo Buonarroti [1475-1564]

The *David* by Michelangelo is one of the most recognized statues in the world. High praise comes from numerous art authorities.

Turner states: "The significance of *David* is powerful and unequivocal. He was the symbol of constant vigilance and strength to the citizens of a free republic surrounded by hostile city states … many under autocratic rule. With the strap of the sling pulled across his back and the stone in his raised hand, *David* looks intently to his left into a space that we must understand as containing the approaching giant. His right side is flexed and closed, his left relaxed and ready for the engagement. By changing the moment from that chosen by his predecessors, Michelangelo drove home <u>the symbol of eternal vigilance</u>." [*History of Western Art,* p 181]

The civic goal of this colossal figure for the citizens of Florence was similar to the intent of the *She-Wolf* #10 for the ancient Romans. Both symbolize 'a guardian of the city'.

The Jansons say: "By omitting the head of *Goliath*, Michelangelo transforms his *David* from a victorious hero into the champion of a just cause. To Michelangelo … the figure has a civic rather than a moral significance." [*Basic History of Western Art,* p 287]

Hoving reverently states: "Every aspect of Michelangelo's sculpture *David* is stupendous – the concept, the execution … the god-like anatomy of David's body, the turn of his head, the anxiety in his eyes and across his brow, his casual stance disguising his fear, the crispness of his eyes, the head's impressive mass of curls. There is not a single imperfection in <u>the entire majestic work</u>." [*Greatest Works of Art* … , p 52]

Durant agrees: "The total effect of the work silences criticism: the splendid frame, not yet swollen with the muscles of Michelangelo's later heroes … the finished texture of the flesh … the strong yet refined features … the nostrils tense with excitement … the frown of anger ... and the look of resolution subtly tinged with diffidence as the youth faces the fearsome Goliath ..." [*The Renaissance*, p 468-69]

E.V. Lucas prefers another *David* by the artist: "Personally, I put Michelangelo's small *David* [in the Bargello] first... it is the one in which, apart from its beauty, you can best believe. His colossal *David* seems to me one of the most glorious things in the world; but it is not David; not the simple, ruddy shepherd lad of the Bible." [*Wanderer in Florence*, p 187]

Hartt counters: "Any attempt to translate a painting or sculpture by Michelangelo into terms of literal reality arrives at absurdity, because throughout his life this artist was interested in the inner meaning of his works, not the literal illustration of anecdotes." [*History of Italian Renaissance Art*, p 417]

Subject:

David is an historical figure, recognized as the second king of Israel... thought to have reigned from about 1015 BC until his death in about 970 BC.

That the young David struck down the giant Goliath with a sling and stone may sound improbable ... yet legends often offer some element of truth.

Durant states there is no surviving contemporary mention of Saul or David outside of the Bible. He further cautions that biblical accounts of Saul and David may be "merely a masterpiece of literary creation." With these reservations, Durant says: "... this first king [Saul], after a bloody interlude, was succeeded by David, heroic slayer of Goliath, tender lover of Jonathan and many maidens, half-naked dancer of wild dances, seductive player of the harp, sweet singer of marvelous songs, and able king of the Jews for almost forty years." [p 304-05]

To the citizens of Florence, as previously explained, this *David* was a patriotic symbol of their republic... during its extended struggle for economic prosperity and independence from neighboring Italian city-states and also foreign armies. The steady glare of *David* signifies the watchful eye of Florence against all adversaries – whether ancient or contemporary.

Sculptor: [for formative years of artist, see final pages of previous chapter]

Michelangelo, at the age of 26, accepted a 2-year contract to carve *David* from an irregular-shaped block of Carrara marble [known as the *Giant*] which had been worked by another sculptor before being abandoned as unusable. Michelangelo required an additional 6 months to complete the statue...which was then exhibited outside until 1873, when weathering encouraged an indoor location in the current Accademia.

On May 3, 2014, *The Los Angeles Times* reported: "...*David* is at risk of collapse due to weakening of the artwork's legs and ankles... micro-fractures in the ankle and leg areas... researchers found that the carved tree stump at the base of the statue is also at risk because it may also contain micro-fractures in the marble Michelangelo used. Much of the sculpture's 5.5 tons rests on the left leg and the tree stump." [Mikhail Wood]

The NY Met. Museum of Art displays Donatello's impressive *David*, who stands with his left foot on the head of Goliath. This self-satisfied *David* – with raised brows – appears to be staring down the Philistines.

Major References:

History of Western Art, 1994, Turner, p 181

Janson & Janson, 2006, Basic History of Western Art, p 287

Our Oriental Heritage, 1935, Durant, 304-5

The Renaissance, 1953, Durant, p 468-9

Michelangelo, 1980, Murray, p 13-22, 33-5

Life of Michelangelo, 1550, GiorgioVasari

Art Through the Ages, 1991, Gardner, p 651

The Agony and the Ecstasy, 1958, Stone, 19-22

History of Italian Renaissance Art, 1974, Hartt, p 417

Greatest Works of Art..., 1997, Hoving, p 52

30,000 Years of Art, 2007, Phaidon Press, p 719

History of Art, 1977, Janson, p 424-25

Art in the Western World, 1935, Robb and Garrison, p 532

Los Angeles Times, May 3, 2014, Mikhail Wood

A Wanderer in Florence, 1912, E. V. Lucas, p 187

How To Look At Sculpture, 1984, Finn, p 73

History of World Sculpture, 1968, Bazin, p 346

68

MOSES

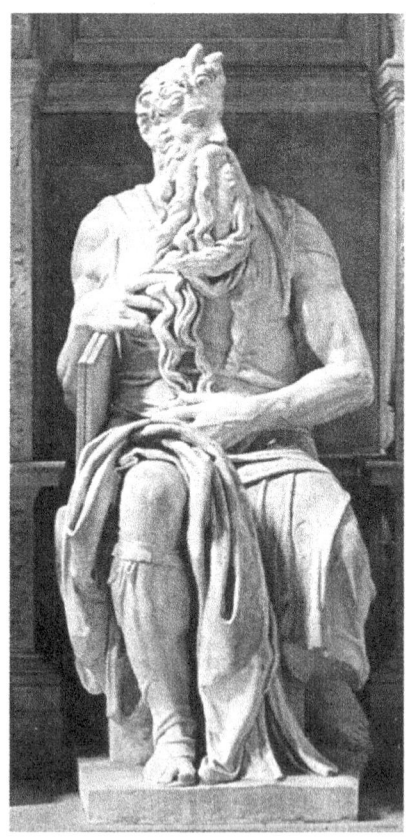

"...the turned head... concentrates the expression of fury...
The muscles bulge, the veins swell... The holy rage of Moses
mounts to the bursting point..." ... *Art Thru Ages*, '91, Gardner, p 652

Over life-size Moses – San Pietro in Vincoli Church, Rome*
Italian sculpture – 1513-1515 – Classic style
Height. 7.7 feet [2.35 m.] – Carrara marble
Sculptor: Michelangelo Buonarroti [1475-1564]
    *church may close for 3-hour siesta [12:30 to 3:30 pm],
    contact Rome's Visitor Info Booths for latest hours

Michelangleo lived to the age of 89, a long life in any century. His first toys were a hammer and a chisel.

Janson states: "The majestic *Moses,* meant to be seen from below, has the awesome force which the artist's contemporaries called *terribilita* – a concept akin to the sublime. His pose, both watchful and meditative, suggests a man capable of wise leadership as well as towering wrath." [*History of Art,* p 425]

Ancient tradition and texts disclose Moses led his people – an unruly mixture of Hebrew clans – out of Egypt some 3,300 years ago. For his people to survive, it became necessary to establish just and lasting laws. With the *Ten Commandments,* Moses is said to have accomplished this.

Originally, the statue was to have adorned a corner of the second story of the façade of a large, ornate, free-standing mausoleum – designed to be walked through – for the warrior pope Julius II [1443-1513] within St. Peter's.

However...Julius II died before completion of his tomb...too soon to ensure the intended location of his ostentatious memorial. [at the time, St. Peter's also was unfinished]

Gardner *says:* "The leader of Israel is shown seated – the tables of the Law under one arm, his other hand gripping the coils of his beard...after the 'ecstasy' of receiving the Law on Mount Sinai. In the valley below, the people of Israel give themselves up once more to idolatry. Michelangelo uses the turned head, which concentrates the expression of fury that now begins to stir in the mighty frame and eyes. The muscles bulge, the veins swell, the great legs begin to move. The holy rage of Moses mounts to the bursting point..." [*Art Through the Ages,* p 652]

Hartt declares: "*Moses'* head, with its two-tailed beard, is one of the artist's most formidable creations; the locks of the beard, lightly drawn aside by several fingers of the right hand, are a veritable Niagara of shapes." [*Art, A History...*, p 612]

Giorgio Vasari – friend of Michelangelo, fellow sculptor, and famed biographer of Renaissance artists in *Lives of the Painters, Sculptors, & Architects* wrote: "...in an attitude of great dignity, he rests his right arm and hand on the Tables while the fingers interlock with thick strands of his great beard... this beard, long and waving, is carved in the marble in such care, that the hairs are wrought with the greatest delicacy, soft, feathery, and detailed... to say nothing of the beauty of the face, which has all the air of a true Saint, the most dread Prince."

The San Pietro in Vincoli Church displaying *the Moses* is believed to have been built in 432 AD, on ground where St. Peter – four centuries earlier, in the time of Nero – received his death sentence. This small church [in *English* known as St. Peter in Chains] is a few blocks north of the Colosseum. According to religious tradition, its main altar holds the venerated chains of St. Peter... two sets: one bound Peter in Jerusalem... the other in Rome's Mamertine Prison. When the two chains were placed beside each other, they are said to have miraculously fused together.

Clement adds: "As much as Michelangelo was permitted to do was completed in 1545, and the monument now stands in the unattractive, lonely, and neglected church of S. Pietro in Vincoli. But although the church does not seem appropriate to *the Moses*, the prophet fills the place..." [*The Eternal City: Rome,* Vol. II, p 749]

A common reaction of many modern visitors, upon entering the church is to wonder: 'Why did the Vatican place *the Moses* of Michelangelo in such a small, out-of-way location?'

Four-hundred years ago, it is possible the Vatican suspected *the Moses* might draw unduly numbers of non-Christians – Moses having been an Israelite – into St. Peter's basilica. Or... succeeding popes may have been concerned that Julius II's enormous tomb would compete with that of St. Peter in the basilica. Or... Julius

II had been cardinal of San Pietro in Vinoli for 34 years before becoming a pope, and the façade of his tomb would fit neatly into the diminutive church. [Hartt, Ital. Ren., p 458]

Lucas [in 1926] says of the small Vincoli church: "Well may the Hebrews continue to go there, as they do every Sabbath, both men and women, like flocks of starlings, to visit and adore that statue...for they are adoring a thing not human but divine." [*A Wanderer in Rome,* p 101]

Recently, while the *Author* visited this small church, a 25+ tour group from Israel arrived...as their numbers crowded into the nave, their animated discourse revealed widely-divergent opinions concerning the appearance and meaning of *the Moses.*

Similarly loud public discourse [by visitors of all nations] periodically disturbs the Sistine Chapel...which, surprisingly, utilized an even louder bull-horn to quiet the unruly.

Subject:

Non-clerical historians generally suggest Moses led his people out of Egypt somewhere between 1447 BC and 1220 BC. Reasons for this exodus vary: a plague among Hebrews in Egypt...their labor strike against the Pharaoh...or a need to flee from persecution on the accession of Thutmose III...among many other possibilities.

According to tradition, Moses and his nomadic followers – for some 40 years – wandered in the desert during which he led them to Mt. Sinai...where *the 10 Commandments* 'appeared'.

The Dutch theologian Erasmus [1466-1536] is said to have "smiled at the traditions that Minos and Numa persuaded their peoples to obey uncongenial legislation by fathering it upon the gods...and probably suspected Moses of similar statesmanship." [*In Praise of Folly,* p. 48]

Durant describes Moses as "a patient statesman..." who "ruled...by inventing interviews with God..." [Durant, Vol. I, p 301-02]

References suggest Michelangelo's *Moses* is furious because – after he has 'received' two tables of law [including *the 10 Commandants*] and come down from the heights of Mt. Sinai – he discovers a disobedient segment of his people dancing and worshipping around a golden calf. Immensely angered, Moses smashes his stone tables to the ground. [Exodus 32:15 and 32:19, Catholic Bible]

Religious references then suggest Moses made a second trip up Mt. Sinai to obtain a replacement set of stone tables...and, at that time, he acquired his horns/radiant beams 'from Heaven'. As a visitor to San Pietro in Vincoli Church comes nearer *the Moses*, the horns/beams become more evident.

Sculptor:

In 1505, Pope Julius II commissioned the 30-year-old Michelangelo to create a massive tomb which was to include 40 sculptures...to be installed eventually in [yet unfinished] St. Peter's. After the artist completed *the Moses* and a few other statues [some by assistants], Michelangelo received more pressing commissions, including the Sistine Chapel [also from Julius II].

Michelangelo worked sporadically on the Tomb of Julius II over a period of 4 decades...sculpting most of *the Moses* from 1513 to 1516. His bulging, tightly-clenched muscles are not dissimilar to the musculature displayed on *the Laocoon* #52 which Michelangelo described as "marvelous" when he first saw it in 1506.

Major References:

Italian Renaissance Art, 1974, Hartt, p 294, 457-58, 463, 499, 578

Art: A History of Painting, Sculpture, & Arch..., 1985, Hartt, p 612

History of Art, 1977, Janson, p 425, 429

Art Through the Ages, II, 1991, Gardner, p 652

Catholic Bible, Exodus 32:15 and 32:19

Lives of Artists, G. Vasari (contemp. of M, architect of Uffizi)

The Eternal City: Rome, Vol. II , 1896, Clement, p 749

Guide to Vatican, 1986, p 94

A Wanderer in Rome, 1926, E.V. Lucas, p 97, 100-01

Our Oriental Heritage, 1935, Durant, Vol. I, p 301-02

In Praise of Folly, Erasmus, p. 48

69

ABDUCTION OF THE SABINE

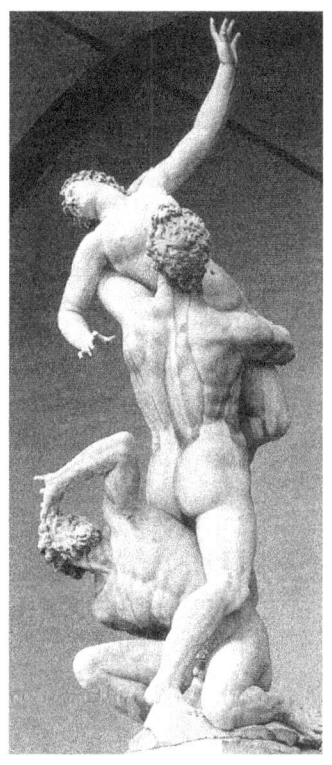

"...wonderfully exemplifies the Mannerist
principles of figure composition."
... Gardner, *Art through the Ages*, p 672

[see other side of statue at chapter end]

Over life-size group – now, Piazza della Signoria, Florence
Orig. Italian sculpture – approx. 1581 – Mannerist style
Ht. 13 ft. 6 in – from single block of marble
Sculptor: Giambologna [or Giovanni da Bologna]
  Flemish-born as *Jean de Boulogne* [1529-1608]

T he period from 1520 to 1600 – between Michelangelo and
  Bernini – is known as the Era of Mannerism... when a new and
invigorating form of artistic expression flourished. It compares with
the Hellenistic era, when artists radically broke from the Classic
Greek traditions.

Giambologna is described by Gardner as: "the most important
sculptor in Italy after Michelangelo... and his [Mannerist] work
provides the stylistic link between the sculpture of that great master and that of the Baroque sculptor Lorenzo Bernini." [*Art Thru
Ages*, p 672]

Hartt concurs: "his vitality appears as a refreshing antidote... to
the stiffened intellectual climate... in freedom of invention and
quality of execution, he surpassed any of his native Italian contemporaries, save only Michelangelo himself. His chief interest lay
in the energy of the spiral movement and the splendid vitality of
the male and female figures... he succeeded so well in their rendi-
tion that Baroque sculptors, particularly Bernini, never forgot this
group." [*History of Italian Renaissance Art*, p 591]

In Florence's popular Piazza della Signoria, this over life-sized
statuary is swiftly recognized even from across the broad square. It
accompanies several large statues meant to impress visitors to the
city... but none approach the stunning vitality of *Abduction of the
Sabine* by Giambologna. The tame *David* [copy] pales in comparison.

Gardner adds the *Sabine*: "wonderfully exemplifies the Mannerist
principles... in which the compositions, as well as the fanciful gestures and attitudes, are deliberately intricate. Where the art of the
High Renaissance strives for balance, Mannerism seeks 'instability'.
The calm equilibrium of the former is replaced by a restlessness
that leads to distortions, exaggerations, and bizarre posturing on

one hand ... and <u>sinuously graceful, often athletic attitudes on the other.</u>" [p 668, 672]

When Giambologna attended the Academy of Design – established by Vasari in 1562 [with support of Cosimo I de Medici] – he chose the challenge of creating 3 contrasting figures within a single, spiraling, massive exertion.

Borghini wrote in *Il Riposo*: "Giambologna wanted to display here the art of making nude figures – demonstrating the weakness of old age ... the strength of youth ... and female delicacy – solely to show the excellence of his art, not to tell any story." [Vossilla, *Encyclo Sculpt*, p 665]

The Jansons say: "the sculptural composition was to be seen from all sides. This had previously been attempted only in bronze and on a much smaller scale." [*History of Western Art*, p 316]

Today, as we circle *the Sabine*, each viewpoint alters radically from the previous one. Though the figures twist in complete opposition to each other, they remain within their closed space. Due to these multiple aspects, several references [*including this one*] provide more than one photo of the sculpture. [Janson, p 455] [Hartt, p 590]

Subject:

The title attached to this sculpture – *Abduction of the Sabine* – was not selected [or intended] by the sculptor.

Hartt says Giambologna considered several other titles, including: "Paris and Helen ... Pluto and Proserpina ... or Phineus and Andromeda ..." [p 591]

Janson concurs ... he: "designed the group – with no specific subject in mind – to silence those critics who doubted his ability as a monumental sculptor in marble." [p 454]

Vossilla adds: the statue "received a title only after its completion ..." [p 665]

Raffaello <u>Borghini</u>, a Florentine writer and member of the Academy of Design suggested the title ... which was 'approved' by the Medici family member who acquired the work – <u>Francesco</u> de

Medici, the Grand Duke of Tuscany – "the greatest art patron of the day." [*Encyclo,* p 666] [Jansons, p 316]

The Grand Duke made the decision to install the group in Florence on the Piazza della Signoria... since the piazza of the city-state was recognized as a "theater of Renaissance sculpture." [p 666]

To accommodate the 'naming' of his work by <u>Borghini</u> and <u>Francesco</u>, Giambologna "created a relief [for the base] showing a relevant episode from Rome's history – the capture of the Sabine women by the Romans – a story known to even the least erudite of Florence's citizens." [p 666]

The Jansons summarize this 'legend': "... the city's founders, an adventurous band of men from across the sea, tried in vain to find wives among their neighbors, the Sabines. Finally, they resorted to a trick. Having invited the entire Sabine tribe into Rome for a festival, they attacked them, took the women away by force, and thus ensured the future of their stock." [p 316]

Livy [59 BC-AD 17] – in *History of Rome, Vol. I* – provides the following account. How much is legend is unknown.

"Romulus prepared to celebrate solemn games in honor of Neptune... he then ordered the celebration to be proclaimed among the neighboring nations. Great numbers of people assembled... induced, in some measure, by a desire of seeing the new city... the whole multitude of the Sabines came with their wives and children. When the show began and every person's thoughts and eyes were attentively engaged on it... then according to the pre-concerted plan, on a signal being given... the Roman youth ran different ways to carry off the young [Sabine] women. Some they bore away as they happened to meet them, without making a choice... but others, of extraordinary beauty – being designed for the principal senators – were conveyed to their houses.... The terror occasioned by this outrage put an end to the sports... and the parents of the young women retired, full of grief. Romulus went about in person and told them [the abducted women], that this proceeding had been occasioned by the haughtiness of their parents, who refused to allow their neighbors to marry among them... He begged of them to soften their resentment, and to bestow their affections on those men on whom chance had bestowed their persons. To these persuasions was added: the soothing behavior of their husbands. [when one city-state fielded an army in protest, Romulus easily defeated it, killed their king, and seized his spoils] He "marched up in procession to the capitol, carrying on a frame...the spoils...and marked out with his eye the bounds of a temple for Jupiter [repository of spoils] in acknowledgement of the victory..." [p 15-18]

Just as Michelangelo and other 16th century artists were influenced by *the Laocoon* #52, so was Giambologna. The facial expression of his 'older man' and his hand gesture borrow aspects from *the Laocoon*. The woman's figure also has aspects of the older youth on the left side of *the Laocoon* group. [Robb & Garrison, 534]]

Sculptor:

Giambologna also was known as *Giovanni da Bologna*...or by his original Flemish name: *Jean de Boulogne.*

At 26, Jean de Boulogne left Flanders [now Belgium] to study in Rome, moving to Florence 2 years later. He stayed so long – more than a half-century – that his name became Italianized to Giovanni Bologna...hence, Giambologna. His bold works, both colossal and smaller scale, encouraged the Mannerist style throughout Europe.

Unlike sculptors before him, Giambologna exhibited "a daring willingness to cut right through the block" of his colossal statuary in the creation of his "multiple viewpoints, complex twisting poses." [Bulfinch, 284] Examples are his *Samson Killing the Philistine* [Albert & Victoria Museum, London] and the *Florence Triumphant over Pisa* [Bargello, Florence].

He left many other masterpieces in Florence...including the first equestrian statue cast in that city...for Grand Duke Cosimo I "which influenced many later examples throughout Europe." [p 284]

A few references, including Gombrich, select Giambologna's *Mercury* as the sculptor's most popular work...in the National Gallery of Art in Washington, DC...the NY Met. Museum of Art...and the Bargello Museum in Florence, Italy.

Major References:

Encyclopedia of Sculpture, 2006, Vossilla, p 664-66

30,000 Years of Art, 2007, Phaidon, p 753

Art in the Western World, 1935, Robb & Garrison, p 533-34

Basic History of Western Art, Jansons, 2006, p 315-16

History of Art, 1977, Janson, p 439-40, 449, 454-55

Italian Renaissance Art, 1974, Hartt, p 590-91s

The Story of Art, 1995, Gombrich, 366-68

Bulfinch Guide to Art, 1996, West, p 284-85

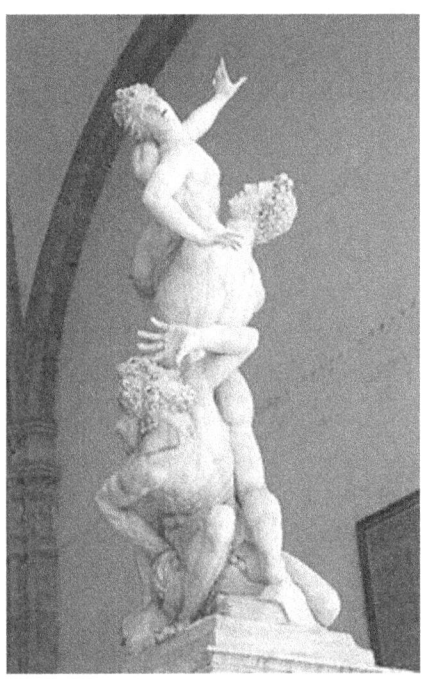

70

DAVID

BY BERNINI

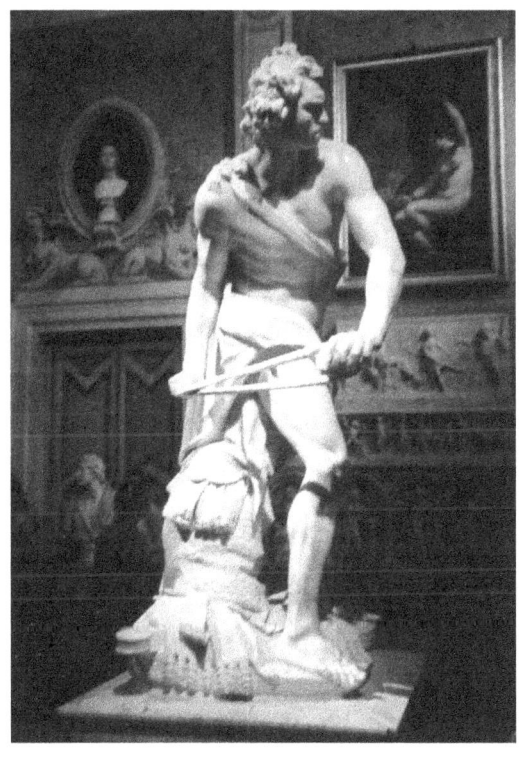

"Bernini presents us with 'the moment of action'...
not just the contemplation of it as in Michelangelo's work"
... *History of Western Art*, Jansons, 2006, p 369

Sculpted at age 25 – now, in Borghese Gallery, Rome
Italian sculpture – 1623 – Roman High Baroque style
Ht. 67 in. [1.7 m.] – white marble
Sculptor: Giovanni Lorenzo Bernini [1598-1680]

T his *David* was completed 129 years after Michelangelo's version. In the Borghese Gallery of Rome, the youth with a sling
is more than determined. The presence of his adversary Goliath is
easily imagined.

Gardner declares: "Bernini's version of *David* <u>aims at catching
the split-second action of the figure</u>...and differs markedly from
the restful and tense figures of *David* portrayed by Donatello,
Verrocchio, and Michelangelo." [*Art Thru the Ages,* p 758]

"Bernini's *David* – his muscular legs widely and firmly planted –
is beginning the violent, pivoting motion that will launch the
stone from his sling. The implied continuum [sequence of poses]
imparts a dynamic quality to the statue that suggests a bursting
forth of energy one sees confined in Michelangelo's figures. For the
first time since the Hellenistic era, a sculptured figure moves out
into and partakes of the physical space that surrounds it and the
observer." [p 758]

In the Borghese Galley, it is a rare privilege to stand near [almost
beside] the *David*. His figure is slightly elevated, and we are able to
closely examine the straining muscles of his legs, shoulders, and
arms the precise moment before he slings his stone at the forehead
of Goliath. This *David* is totally believable.

The Jansons concur: Bernini's "...figure shares with Hellenistic
works that unison of body and spirit, of motion and emotion, which
Michelangelo so consciously avoids. The Baroque often suggests a
heightened vitality and energy." [*History of Western Art,* p 369]

Hartt states: "A brilliant youthful work...done for Cardinal
Scipione Borghese when Bernini was 25...has captured...the [war-
rior] prophet – now a full-grown youth of about 17 or 18 – twisting
vigorously, about to launch the stone. The left hand's tightening
about the sling and stone produces sharp tensions in the muscles

and veins of the arm ... and the expression – unprecedented even in Hellenistic sculpture – shows the boy biting his lips with the strain." [*Art: History of Paint., Sculpt.*, p 699]

The impassioned face of *David* is said to be a mirrored reflection of the face of Bernini. The 'threatening attitude' of the [Louvre's] ancient *Borghese Warrior* #47 may have inspired the fierce expression. At the time Bernini created his *David*, the *Warrior* was in the same Borghese collection. [Martin, p 258]

The Borghese Gallery – built specifically to house the rich collection of sculpture gathered by Cardinal Borghese, the immensely wealthy, powerful manager of the papal government for his uncle Pope Paul V – displays 3 additional high-drama masterpieces by Bernini: *Aeneas, Anchises, & Ascanius Fleeing Troy* ... the *Rape of Proserpina* ... and *Apollo & Daphne* #71.

Durant adds that Cardinal Borghese "earned a moderate immortality in marble from his protégé Bernini." [Durant, p 238]

All Rome would become a gallery for Bernini. Durant describes him as "the greatest sculptor" of his age. [p 225] Bernini also designed and/or created numerous majestic works, including *the Fountain of 4 Rivers* #73... the great piazza and colossal colonnade before St. Peter's ... its interior 94-foot twisting baldacchino, and more. Several weeks in Rome can be devoted exclusively to 'exploring' his works.

The *Oxford Companion to Western Art* states: "It is only since the revival of interest in the art of the Baroque in the secular second half of the 20th century that Bernini has taken his rightful place among the greatest artists in the Western canon." He is generally considered to be "the outstanding figure of the Italian Baroque and the greatest formative influence within it." [p 66-7]

Subject:

David is a historical figure, the second king of Israel, thought to have reigned from about 1015 BC until his death in 970 BC. He succeeded Saul.

[Moses lived about 1330 BC ... give or take 100 years]

Durant states there is no surviving contemporary mention of Saul or David outside the Bible. He further warns that biblical accounts of Saul and David may be "merely a masterpiece of literary creation." With these reservations, Durant writes: "... this first king [Saul], after a bloody interlude, was succeeded by David, heroic slayer of Goliath, tender lover of Jonathan and many maidens, half-naked dancer of wild dances, seductive player of the harp, sweet singer of marvelous songs, and able king of the Jews for almost forty years." [*Our Oriental Heritage*, p 305]

That the young David struck down the giant Goliath with a sling and stone may sound improbable ... nevertheless, there is often an element of truth in legends. The Bible relates, for 40 days the great Philistine Goliath had put forward his challenge to the Israelites. Only young David had the courage to step forward. When King Saul lent him his armor, the boy dropped it and faced the giant with only a sling.

On the pedestal of Bernini's statue, Saul's 'armor' lies on the ground by David's feet. There also is his harp, which he will play after victory. [eagle decorating end of harp is emblem of Borghese family] According to the biblical account, David struck Goliath on the forehead with his stone ... then seized the sword of the giant and killed him. [*Bible*, Samuel I, chapter 17]

Sculptor:

Gianlorenzo Bernini began to sculpt at an early age in the studio of his father Pietro Bernini ... a Mannerist sculptor in Florence. Moving his family to Rome in 1604-05, the father is best known for creating the 'sunken ship' fountain at the base of the Spanish Steps ... among the most popular drinking fountains in Rome. Pietro was well-connected "with the powerful Borghese and Barberini families of Rome, who fostered and employed Gianlorenzo's talent. The father may have helped his son in carving the *Aeneas, Anchises, and Ascanius Leaving Troy* ... in the Borghese Gallery. [*Encyclo Sculpt.*, Avery, p 154]

The younger Bernini's earliest surviving work, said to have been carved when he was 16, is the group: *Goat Amalthea Nursing the Infant*

Zeus and a Young Satyr [also in Borghese Gallery], which long passed for a Hellenistic original...a tribute to his precocious virtuosity." [*Oxford*, p 66]

The monumental *Ecstasy of St. Theresa* #72 is the centerpiece of the most notable small church in Rome – the S. Maria della Vittoria.

His famed self-portrait as a dark, self-assured, handsome youth can be seen in the Uffizi Gallery of Florence.

"Bernini also was a witty conversationalist, a writer of comedies, a caricaturist, and a painter." [*Oxford*, p 67]

Major References:

Oxford Companion to Western Art, 2001, p 66-7
Encyclopedia of Sculpture, 2004, Avery, p 154
Baroque, 1977, Martin, p 74-5, 78
Reality Through the Arts, 2004, Sporre, p 308
History of Western Art, 2006, Jansons, p 369
History of Art, 1977, Janson, p 487
Art: History of Painting, Sculpture..., 1985, Vol II, Hartt, p 698-99
Our Oriental Heritage, 1954, Durant, p 305
Age of Reason, 1961, Durant, p 225, 238, 270-3
Art & Architecture, 2001, Hintzen-Bohlen, p 248-53, 479-82, 599
Art Through the Ages II, 1991, Gardner, p 755-58
Key to Baroque Art, Triando, p 39

71
Apollo and Daphne

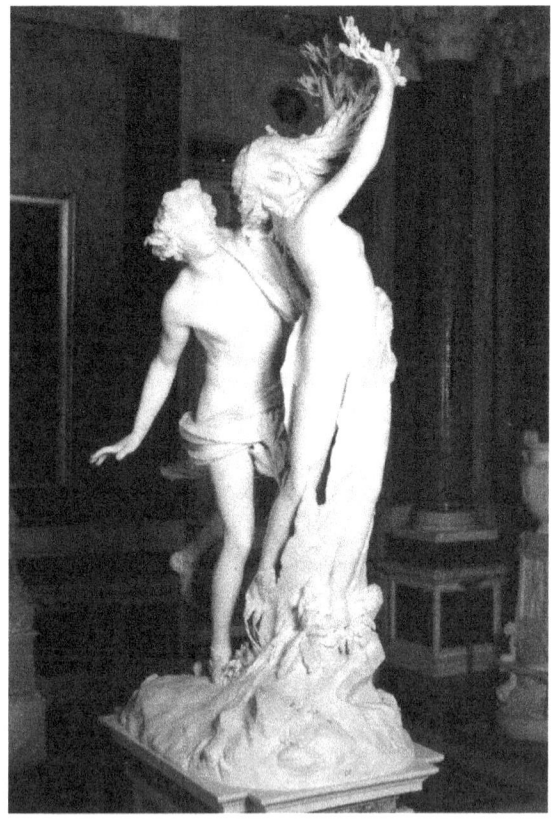

"With supreme virtuosity, the sculptor gave this
marble the translucency of wax"...
...Bazin, *History of World Sculpture*, p 389

Apollo pursues *Daphne* – in Borghese Gallery, Rome
Italian sculpture – 1625 – Roman High Baroque
Ht. [2.43 m] – Carrara marble
Sculptor: Giovanni Lorenzo Bernini [1598-1680]

   *Bernini interrupted work on this group to complete his *David*

These marvelously presented figures – the romantically-inclined god *Apollo* pursuing the chaste, young huntress *Daphne* – have been described as '*Virtue* flees *Temptation*'.

In 1625, Lorenzo Bernini's new creation: "...a tour-de-force... was instantly the talk of Rome." [Knight, p E-5]

With this sculptural group, Bernini invites us to hallucinate. *Oxford Companion to Western Art* says the artist involves: "... the spectator not just in an act of aesthetic contemplation, but in a moment of theater." [p 66]

The face of *Apollo* displays desire... the clouding face of *Daphne* shows terror. [Hartt, p 699]

We see the moment when panicking *Daphne* – chased by *Apollo* – calls to her river-god father Peneus to transmute her body into a laurel tree. Instantly and miraculously, toes of her left foot take root... bark sprouts around *Daphne's* left leg and wraps about her waist... her fingers and hair transform into leaves and branches.

Bazin observes: "...one forgets that the figures were carved from a block of marble, for they seem to take flight into space. With supreme virtuosity the sculptor gave this marble the translucency of wax. His satiny smooth polished surfaces succeed in conjuring up the fresh complexion of the girl and the blondness of her hair." [*History World Sculpture*, p 388-89]

The viewer must resist an urge to touch the "smooth surfaces" of this racing couple.* It is difficult to comprehend how any sculptor could have carved stone so intricately... notice the extremely narrow roots stemming from Daphne's toes and even finer twigs and leaves sprouting from her hands and fingers. *do not touch... body oils stain marble

Hartt adds: "Evanescent [fleeting] effects of melting texture, translucency, and sparkle dissolve the group into the surrounding space ... it is as if Bernini had been able to carve light and air as well as marble. The fidelity with which the softness of female flesh, the lithe body of *Apollo* ... and the textures of the hair, bark, and leaves are rendered is no more dazzling than Bernini's craftsmanship in carving the scores of minute and slender projections from fragile marble." [p 699]

Hartt concludes: "He has reached in his mid-20s the height of his ability at pictorial sculpture ... the negation of everything Michelangelo stood for ... and the fulfillment of promises made by the daring Ghiberti in the *Gates of Paradise* #64 ..." [p 699]

The *Oxford* reference describes the Borghese Gallery in the early 17th century: "The Villa Borghese was an elite, private space which acted as a showcase for the young Bernini and his discerning patron ... it was filled with contemporary High Renaissance and ancient works which allowed informed [and usually male] visitors to judge how recent developments either built on or surpassed the art of the past." [p 210]

Subject:

The Roman poet Ovid [43 BC–AD 17] in *Metamorphoses* relates the myth of *Apollo & Daphne*.

Apollo [*son of Zeus*] was the Sun God to the ancient Greeks ... [in addition to being their god of Light, Truth, Prophecy, Music, Archery, and Health].

Daphne was a young virgin huntress and the daughter of the River god Alpheus [Peneus]. She is in permanent mourning for her prince Leucippus ... killed by her companions for disguising himself as a woman in order to hunt with Daphne.

Cupid – offended earlier by an insult from Apollo – strikes him with a gold, sharp-pointed arrow ... causing him to be seized with love for Daphne. Then, Cupid strikes Daphne with a blunt arrow, tipped with lead ... causing her to be abhorred at the thought of love.

When Apollo comes upon Daphne hunting in the forest, he is enchanted by her beauty and pursues her.

Edith Hamilton's *Mythology* provides a version of what follows: "But, she is an excellent runner and he is hard-pressed to overtake her. *'Do not fear,'* he calls to Daphne. *'Stop and find out who I am… no rude rustic or shepherd. I am the Lord of Delphi, and I love you.'* But Daphne flies on, even more frightened than before. If Apollo is indeed following her, the case is hopeless… but she is determined to struggle to the very end. She feels his breath upon her neck, but there in front of her the trees open and she sees her father's river. She screams to him, *'Help me! Father, help me!'*

"At the words, a dragging numbness comes upon her… her feet seem rooted in the earth she has been so swiftly speeding over. Bark is enclosing her; leaves are sprouting forth. She is changing to a tree, a laurel. Apollo watches the transformation with dismay and grief.

" *'O fairest of maidens, you are lost to me,'* he mourns. *'But at least you shall be my tree. With your leaves, my victors shall wreathe their brows. You shall have your part in all my triumphs. Apollo and his laurel shall be joined together wherever songs are sung and stories told'.* " [p 155-56]

For 1,000 years, the victors at Olympia in Greece were crowned with laurel-leaf wreaths. Ancient Rome also selected leaves of the laurel tree as models for golden wreaths they awarded Roman soldiers for exceptional bravery in battle. Julius Caesar [#54] wore his 'golden wreath' often and with great pride. [see photo, #54 end]

Hintzen-Bohlen summarizes the historical significance of Bernini's group: "… an achievement unprecedented in large sculptures; the depiction of something described in literary terms as *a continuous process.*" No other sculptor had demonstrated an ability to give the impression of different colors by diversifying "surface structures by polishing, boring, and roughening them… the smoothly polished areas of the naked bodies contrast with the god's smooth but unpolished fabric cloak and the rough bark of the tree… Apollo's tousled mane of curls is in contrast to the fine strands of the nymph's hair." [p 249]

Hooker relates: "Bernini describes how, when he was carving the *Apollo and Daphne* for Cardinal Scipione Borghese, the patron and several other clerics came to see it. One of the visitors suggested that he would have scruples about having such a beautiful young woman in his home. The cardinal replied that he could solve the problem with some verses, and composed an epigram in Latin to the effect that anyone who pursues the delights of love will end up [like *Apollo*] with only withered leaves in his hands. Bernini added the lines to the grotesque cartouche on the pedestal, but it was not part of his original conception nor was it a common moral for the story." [*History of Western Art,* p 238-39]

Sculptor: [see previous
chapter describing Bernini's David]

Avery in *Encyclo Sculpt* reveals of Bernini: "His only statue that survived the almost universal disfavor into which his oeuvre [works] fell for two and a half centuries was the group *Apollo and Daphne*..." [p 155]

Major References:

Oxford History of Western Art, 2000, Kemp, p 210-12

Encyclopedia of Sculpture, 2004, Avery, p 154-55

Art: A History of Painting, Sculpture,.Vol II, 1985, Hartt, p 699

History of World Sculpture, 1968, Bazin, p 388, 389

Precious Stone, 8-5-08 Los Angeles Times, Knight, p E-5

Baroque, 1975, Martin, p 199-200

Age of Reason, 1961, Durants, p 270-3

Bullfinch Guide to Art History, 1996, West (editor), p 273

Art & Arch: Rome, 2001, Hintzen-Bohlen, p 248-53, 479-82, 599

Mythology, 1942, Hamilton, p 29, 155-6

Titans and Olympians, 2003, Allan & Maitland, p 131

Bullfinch's Mythology, 1968, R. Graves (editor), p7, 22-4

History of Western Art, 1994, Hooker, p 238-39

72

ECSTASY OF ST. THERESA

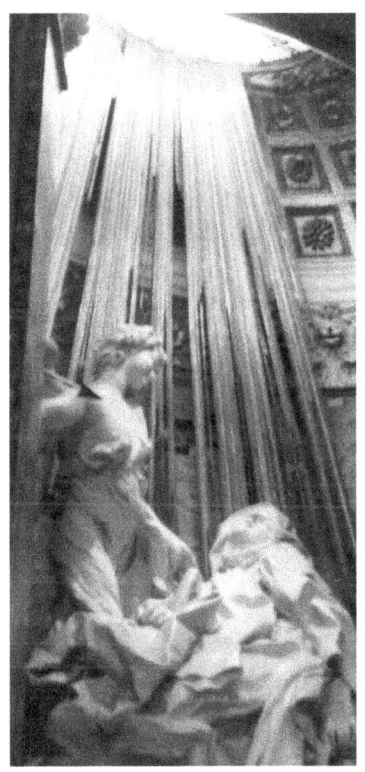

"...merges sculpture, painting, and architecture in emotional
and entertaining ways...unsurpassed in all of art."
...Hoving, *Greatest Works of Art*, p 178

[see face of *Theresa* at chapter end]

Saint's 'Vision' – in Santa Maria d' Victoria Church, Rome
Italian statuary – 1645-52 – Roman High Baroque
Ht. 11 feet 6 in. [350 cm] – marble
Sculptor: Giovanni Lorenzo Bernini [1598-1680]
　　*church closes for 4-hour siesta [11 am-3 pm, Mon.-Sat.]
　　& 5 hours [10 am-3 pm, Sunday] check at tourist kiosks

As art and learning revived during the Renaissance – encompassing the 14th, 15th, and 16th centuries – artists in the Western world still found commissions primarily from the Christian Church. This work by Bernini was perhaps the sculptural highpoint of that age.

Hoving's *Greatest Works of Art* declares it "...<u>merges sculpture, painting, and architecture in entertaining and emotional ways and is unsurpassed in all of art</u>." [p 178]

Gilbert & McCarter state: "With a taste for drama and over-statement, a flair for the grand gesture, Bernini found great success in an era that appreciated such expression...all these talents were brought to bear in his masterpiece, the Cornaro Chapel." [*Living With Art*, p 401]

In 16th century Spain, a Carmelite nun named Theresa "claimed to be subject for many years to religious trances...visions of Heaven and Hell...and visits by angels and others. The Catholic Church declared the visions miraculous...and proclaimed Theresa a saint.

Federigo Cornaro, a Venetian cardinal, selected this 'event' as the theme of a 'mortuary chapel' to eventually house his body and also to commemorate his family.

In the Cornaro Chapel within this small church, *Theresa* and the angelic *Cupid* appear to float on a cloud...bathed in golden rays from the 'sun' [a heavenly blessing?]. The bright illumination is from a high window above. Kitson explains: "Nature is brought into the work of art by the use of light from a concealed source...filtered through yellow glass, to reinforce the symbolic light represented by metal rays." [*Age of Baroque,* p 16-7]

Initially...*St. Theresa* and *Cupid* are best viewed from a dis-tance...at least 15 yards...where the entire ensemble of the chapel is visible. Colored-marble columns enclose the figures and support an ornate, tri-pointed canopy in white marble ... which serves to isolate [highlight] the figures from a dome.

Also, notice 'spectators' sitting on balconies to either side of the saint and *Cupid*. The balconies are marble, as are the spectators ... modeled from members of the Cornaro family ... to provide the illusion of an audience for the miraculous event. Some pray and ... for realism, others talk or even read.

Gombrich explains, during the blossoming of Roman High Baroque: "Architects, painters and sculptors were called upon to transform churches into grand showpieces ... whose splendor and vision nearly swept you off your feet. This supreme art of theatrical decoration had mainly been developed by one artist, Gian Lorenzo Bernini. He has deliberately cast off all restraint ... If we compare the face of his swooning saint [photo at chapter end] with any work done in previous centuries, we find that he achieved an intensity of facial expression which until then was never attempted in art. Even Bernini's handling of draperies was [for the Renaissance] completely new. Instead of letting them fall in dignified folds in the approved classical manner, he made them writhe and whirl." [recalling *Winged Victory of Samothrace* #38] "In all these effects, he was soon imitated all over Europe." [*Story of Art*, p 437-40]

*Bernini never saw *the Winged Victory*, unearthed 1863

Subject:

St. Theresa is described as "a Spanish mystic, founder of a strict order of nuns, and an important figure in the Counter-Reformation." [Gilbert, p 401] Her visions and trances were accompanied by a mysterious pain in her side ... she presumed the cause was a "fire-tipped dart of Divine love ... which an angel had thrust into her bosom and which she described as making her swoon in delightful anguish." [Gardner, 758]

[Theresa did not identify her angel as *Cupid*. The 'Greek' title followed Bernini's creation.]

From the *Journals of St. Theresa of Avila*, Gilbert quotes her: "Beside me, on the left hand, appeared an angel…short, and very beautiful; and his face was so aflame…In his hands I saw a great golden spear, and at the iron tip there appeared to be a point of fire. This he plunged into my heart several times…and left me utterly consumed by the sweet love of God. The pain was so severe that it made me utter several moans. The sweetness caused by this intense pain is so extreme that one cannot possibly wish it to cease." [p 401-02]

The Jansons offer a slightly different interpretation: "The pain was so great that I screamed aloud; but at the same time I felt such infinite sweetness that I wished the pain to last forever. It was the sweetest caressing of the soul by God." [p 370]

Hoving is flamboyant: "Saint Theresa's eyes are closed, and a look of orgasmic pleasure shines upon her face. But this is a pleasure that is far from one of the flesh. It is the ultimate ecstatic transport to a spiritual paradise – the departure of the spirit from the soul to unite with the divine spirit…. among the most beautiful portrayals of a woman in all of art." [p 178]

Gilbert concludes: "Bernini shows the saint in a swoon, ready for another thrust of the angel's spear. She falls backwards, yet is lifted up on a cloud, the extreme turbulence of her garments revealing her emotional frenzy. We can almost hear the moans Theresa spoke of in describing her passionate experience." [p 402]

Art in the Counter-Reformation:

The Jansons reveal the significance of this work to the Catholic Church: "The Counter-Reformation was a movement that began in the mid-sixteenth century and was created specifically to counter the attacks of the Protestant Reformation. In 1622…Ignatius Loyola, Filippo Neri, Francis Xavier, and the mystic Theresa of Avila achieved sainthood. With these saints – contemporary figures – new imagery, ideas, and a revitalization of the Catholic Church were possible. Art, with these exemplary figures as its subject, abounded and was used to spread the teachings of the saints and the church." [p 358]

Sculptor: [see previous chapter
#70 describing Bernini]

To create such masterpieces, Bernini – like other renowned art-ists – employed a large team of assistants for rough shaping of the marble blocks, transferring figures from clay models to stone, and the casting of bronze. Bernini directed the entire production, making the finishing touches himself.

Hoving states: "A child prodigy, Bernini was working in full flower at the age of 14, even before he was admitted into the sculptor's guild. His first major work, a *Pan* leaping into a tree, is in the NY Metropolitan Museum of Art." [p 178]

Note: In Rome, the Santa Maria d' Victoria Church is at the quiet intersection of Via XX Septembre and Via Barberini. [some 750 meters northwest of Termini (train) Station] Carry a good street map ... and double-check open hours beforehand.

Major References:

Living with Art, 2nd Ed., 1987, Gilbert and McCarter, p 400-02

The Story of Art, 1989, Gombrich, p 438-40

Basic History of Western Art, 2006, Jansons, p 370-71

Greatest Works of Art of Western Civilization, 1997, Hoving, p 178

30,000 Years of Art, 2007, Phaidon, p 783

Baroque, 1975, Martin, p 105-07

Art in the Western World, 1935, Robb & Garrison, p 538-40

Art Through the Ages II, 1991, Gardner, p 755-761

The Age of Baroque, 1966, Kitson, p 16-7

History of Western Art, 1994, Hooker, p 228-29

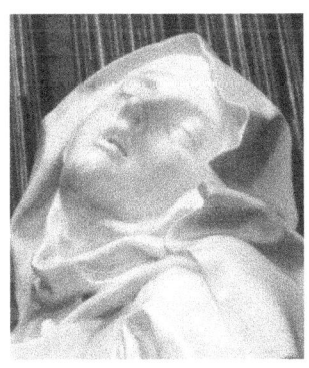

73

FOUNTAIN OF FOUR RIVERS

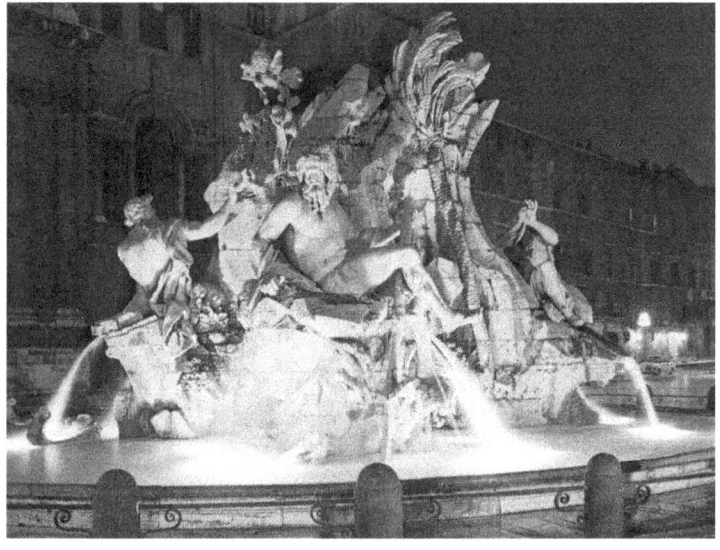

"... one of the great achievements of Baroque sculpture."
...*Rome & Vatican City*, 2001, Hintzen-Bohlen, p 178

Monumental statuary [1648-1651] – Piazza Navona, Rome
Double life-size marble figures – High Baroque style
Architect/Designer: Gian Lorenzo Bernini
[he clay-modeled *River Gods*; assistants carved them]

[in Rome, begin after-dinner stroll here...or at Trevi
Fountain]

A very in *Encyclo Sculpt* declares: "Most famous and a symbol of Rome is the *Fountain of Four Rivers* that animates the Piazza Navona... commissioned by Pope Innocent X [1644-55] to enhance the outlook from and approach to the Pamphili Palace. It is a bizarre amalgam of ideas that succeeds in enthralling even today." [p 154-55]

*some claim *Trevi Fountain* #76 to be 'most famous'

Hintzen-Bohlen states: "Bernini's magnificent *Fountain of 4 Rivers*... is masterly in its presentation... and is regarded as <u>one of the great achievements of Baroque sculpture</u>." [p 178]

The *Fountain* was commissioned in 1648 by the Pope as part of his Baroque transformation of the Piazza. His family's Pamphili Palace [since 1960, the Brazilian Embassy] borders the Piazza's southwest side and was constructed 10 years after the *Fountain.*

Hughes says: "No great Roman family was more bound up with an architectural feature of Rome than the Pamphili clan with the Piazza Navona. It was 'their' square – actually, an elongated horse-shoe which almost exactly follows the track of the ancient Stadium of Domitian." [*Rome... a History,* p 291]

Wurman's *Rome* reveals Bernini received the fountain commission "by bribing the Pope's 'lady-friend' Donna Olympia... Bernini gave this unscrupulous papal sister-in-law a solid silver model of his design for the fountain... insisting that it must be left out [in the Vatican] so that Innocent X would see it... which he did. The Pope then incurred the wrath of the Roman population by taxing bread [during a famine] to raise a vast sum in gold coins to finance the fountain. Both Innocent X and Donna Olympia were publicly reviled." [p 109]

Morton adds: "Innocent X was 72 at the time of his election, a gentle and compassionate man... but completely dominated by his widowed [and avaricious] sister-in-law. [When] the Vatican grew shrill with feminine disputes from which the poor Pope tried to hide himself... the Pamphili Palace became the place where most [of his] decisions were made." [*Traveler in Rome,* p 240]

Piazza Navona:

The dimensions of the Piazza are vast... 787 by 213 feet [240 x 65 m.].

Remains of the ancient Stadium – some 20 feet beneath the 'built-up' Piazza – can be viewed through a barrier at the northwest end of the Piazza. The Emperor Domitian built the stadium in AD 86 "for games and sporting competitions... The structures bordering the Piazza stand on the ancient rows of stone-bleacher seats which could hold 30,000 spectators." [Hintzen-Bohlen, p 174]

Hughes reveals, in the time of Bernini: "... the Piazza had evolved into one of the greatest festive precincts in Rome, frequented alike by the grandees taking their evening *passeggiata*... and every kind of jongleur, contortionist, hawker, and gawker... whose descendants still throng the square as the day's light is fading." [p 291]

Today... entertainers continue well into the night... grateful for gratuities from their audiences. Artists offer paintings/prints of favorite Rome views, often well-executed. On stays in Rome, the *Author* and family are irresistibly drawn to the Piazza for after-dinner/gelato strolls... which often include the *Trevi Fountain* as well.

Subject:

The *Fountain* displays double life-size figures that symbolize the 4 greatest rivers recognized by Europeans in the 1600s: the Nile... the Rio de la Plata [in silver-rich Uruguay] ... the Ganges of India... and the Danube. "These [gigantic river gods] were carved by 4 assistant sculptors... from Bernini's drawings and clay models." [Avery, p 155]

The northeast river-god personifies the Nile... with a cloth partially draped over his head as the source of the Nile was still a mystery. Errant tourist-guides suggest the head was covered by Bernini so it could not see the 'façade' of the St. Agnese Church [built by his competitor Borromini]. The *Fountain* was completed 6 years *before* the 'façade'.

The northwest river-god of the Rio de La Plata reclines on a pile of coins representing the promise of New World riches. [*plata* meaning silver] The figure, with a raised hand, appears to tumble backwards, as if in fear of something unseen...perhaps, someone who would steal his riches. Again, guides mislead by suggesting the hand is raised to 'keep Borromini's church from falling on the *Fountain.*'

The <u>southeast</u> river-god for the Ganges River in India holds a long oar...to indicate the navigability of the Ganges. He is heavily-bearded with his body at rest.

The <u>southwest</u> river-god for the Danube – representing Europe – sits upright and touches the ornate papal 'coat of arms' of Pope Innocent X. The tall hooded-hat above the coat of arms resembles ceremonial headgear worn by popes on formal occasions.

Bernini 'enlivened' his *Fountain* by adding a mix of flora and fauna related to the foreign lands where the Church sought new converts and wealth. A lion is seen creeping down to drink the rushing water...a horse emerges from a cavern in the rock. Circle the *Fountain* for more surprises.

Symmes adds: "Seated at the base of an obelisk [a stylized sun-ray], the river gods twist, gesticulate, or look away as if to shield themselves from blinding light...water copiously streams from the rocky base beneath...this grand monument celebrates the pope's extension of the Aqua Vergine* to this plaza." [*Encyclo Sculpt,* p 583]

*an aqueduct for delivery of water

The Roman obelisk that surmounts the *Fountain* originally was erected by Emperor Domitian [AD 61-96] for the Temple of Isis in Rome. "Roman emperors commissioned obelisks as often as they stole them...the hieroglyphics on this one record Domitian's devotion to the goddess." [*Rome & Vatican City,* p 178] The bronze dove atop the obelisk is a symbol of the Pamphili family.

Martin states: "For all its complexity and multiplicity of parts, the work possesses a powerful unity, which can be felt building up from the rough and 'haphazard' forms at the bottom ... to its climax in the soaring obelisk." [*Baroque,* p 22-3]

Sculptor:
[also see 2 previous chapters]

Hughes explains that Bernini, like most famed sculptors, employed "a cast of skilled assistants ... on a project like this, Bernini was more 'the master' of the works than the carver ... although he reputedly did the horse, the palm tree, the lion, some of the rock, and possibly the bizarre hybrid creature next to the figure of the river Plata."

Bernini intended this 'hybrid' to portray an armadillo. At the time, no one in Rome had ever seen this exotic creature, not even Bernini ... which explains its questionable resemblance. [p 293-94]

Avery tells us: "Bernini felt that he was at the apex of the tradition that had come down to him from antiquity ... which he could meaningfully re-interpret – often to rather different ends – in the light of the styles of his prestigious predecessors, Michelangelo and Giambologna #69 ..." [p 155]

A special treat for travelers who love to walk Rome – in late afternoon – are Bernini's 'angels' on the Ponte San Angelo *bridge*... [10 short blocks west of Piazza Navona]. These magnificent, over-sized angels [1668-69] were designed by Bernini [he carved 3] and are best viewed when illuminated in the setting sun.

References:

Encyclopedia of Sculpture, 2004, Symmes, p 583
Encyclopedia of Sculpture, 2004, Avery, 154-55
Rome & Vatican City, 2001, Hintzen-Bohlen, p 174-78
Rome, a History, 2011, Hughes, p 291-95
Rome, Facaros & Pauls, 1993, p 160
Baroque, Martin, 1977, p 22-3
Art: Painting, Sculpture ..., 1985, Hartt, p 700-01
Age of Baroque, 1966, Myers, p 36
Rome, 1993, Furman, p 107-09
Morton's A Traveler in Rome, 1957, Morton, p 238-241

74

FOUNTAINS OF VERSAILLES

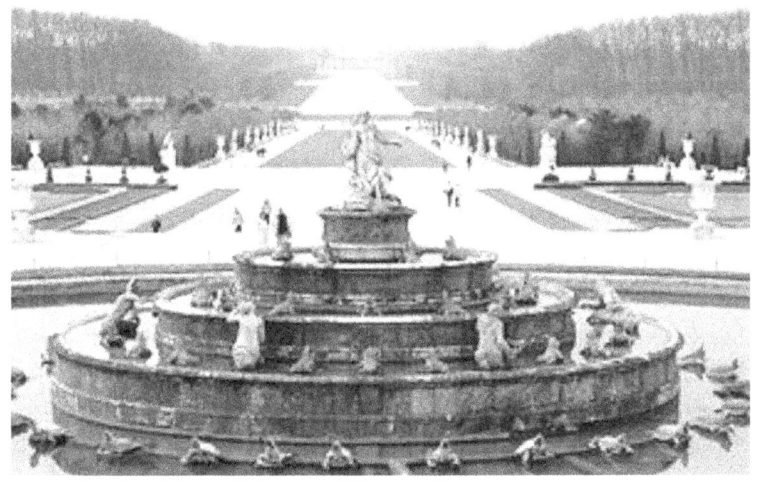

"the park of Versailles must rank among
the world's greatest works of art"
...Gardner, *Art Through the Ages*, p 808

Designed, Andre Le Notre [1613-1700] – Versailles, France
French – 1663-1750 – French Baroque or Style of Louis XIV
Varying Sizes – in lead, bronze, and/or marble
Sculptors: leading French sculptors of late 17th century
    *bring hat, sunglasses, blanket-roll & purchase 'Gardens'
    guide

T he Durants describe the park of *Versailles* as "a <u>garden of the gods</u>...after 350 years, it remains <u>one of the meccas of mankind</u>." [p 92]

In 1661, 10 years after Bernini completed the *Fountain of the 4 Rivers*, Louis XIV ordered his architect Andre Le Notre to design the 'fountain park' of Versailles.

Five years later, Louis XIV established the French Academy of Rome [for French artists who won the *Prix-de-Rome*] ...under the direction of Bernini, Jean-Baptiste Colbert, and Charles <u>Le Brun</u>. The latter two became assistants to Le Notre in creating the *Gardens of Versailles*.

Smith in *France, A History of Art*, says: "The king wanted a place to play. As a child, he had often stayed at his father's hunting lodge near the village of Versailles. So this dedicated outdoorsman, who hated Paris, made a decision. He resolved to build a spacious palace near Versailles... thus giving him the opportunity to lead, at least part of the time, the outdoor life." [p 131]

Janson states: "Apart from its magnificent interior [especially, the Hall of Mirrors], the most impressive aspect of Versailles is the park extending west of the Garden Front for several miles...these formal gardens form a series of 'outdoor rooms' for the splendid fetes and spectacles that Louis XIV so enjoyed." [*History of Art*, p 526]

While one tour of the Palace may suffice for most... visitors to Versailles often return again and again to be enchanted by the gardens and fountains. [the experienced know to schedule visits around grand performances of the *Fountain of Neptune*]

The Gardens:

A treatise in Hoog's *Garden of Versailles* says: "Louis XIV loved the gardens of Versailles as much and maybe even more than he did the Chateau. Practically up until the day he died, he presided over the work they involved, walked in them often, set his most sumptuous festivities in them, and accompanied his most important guests there as well as foreign ambassadors. Toward the end of his reign, the king wrote an itinerary – *The Manner of Presenting the Gardens of Versailles* [1689] – which can still be followed today." [p 4]

In 1663, Le Notre's work started [continuing 40 years]...undertaken simultaneously with the building of the great Palace.

The king insisted on reviewing all plans, studying every detail. Tens of thousands of men were employed, including military units. What had been woodland and marsh would become the most famous garden in the world. Most of the initial fountains remain intact.

The Durants reveal: "In 1662, Le Notre presented to Louis XIV a general plan for *the grounds*...It was to be not so much a masterpiece of architecture as an invitation to live outdoors...amid a nature tamed and improved by art...to breathe the fragrances of flowers and trees...to feast the eyes and fancied touch on classically sculptured forms...to hunt prey and playful friends in the woods...to dance and picnic on the grass...to boat on the canal and the lake...to hear Lully and Moliere under the open sky." [p 91-2]

Visitors wishing to see in one day the Palace and the important fountains in the *Gardens* should arrive early and in good physical condition. [bring small blanket or towel to recline on grass]

Since summer lines to enter the Palace may involve one to two hours standing under the sun...many visitors visit the *Gardens* first. [its line is seldom more than a few minutes] By mid-afternoon, the line for the Palace is usually much shorter.

Visiting Major Fountains: [*Garden Guide* necessary]

At the ticket office, check the hours of 'water shows' at the vast *Fountain of Neptune*...plan to arrive at least 20 minutes before a show begins [prime seating is on grass]. It is a brief walk from the north wing of the Palace.

A century was required to complete this fountain in 1741. Its elaborate show has been staged since the time of Louis XV. As a grand finale for a visit to Versailles, it includes 28 water jets and sprays coordinated to create 99 different water-effects. The fast, high-flying water is marvelous.

Having planned *Neptune's* show...begin a tour of the fountains of Versailles on the broad terrace [Garden Front] on the west side of the Palace.

The memorable view to the west – across the length of the _Grand Canal_ – appears unending.

Within the _Gardens_ [and unseen] are 14 distinct _Groves_. Janson describes their past…and present. "One withdrew there to partake of a light supper, listen to music or to dance, and the King could thus indulge his taste for spectacle and for play. Adorned with fountains, vases, and statues, they bring an element of surprise and fantasy to the interior of the great Garden." [p 526]

Initially…walk west from the Palace…along the Royal Avenue…toward the Grand Canal…down the majestic staircase to the grand fountain.

Fountain of Latona   [see first photo]

Hibbert informs us: "The _Fountain of Latona_ occupies the place of honor in the gardens of Versailles…" [_Versailles_ [1972] p 35]

Bizarre figures [giant frogs and humans becoming more frogs] – all howl at the statuesque Latona…who stands at fountain center protecting her 2 children [Apollo and Diana].

Their story: Zeus fathered with lovely Latona her two children. Hera [jealous wife of Zeus] had Latona banished when pregnant…forced to wander, Latona gave birth and comes upon a pure spring where she wishes to bathe her children and drink…but peasants [encouraged by Hera] insult her and try to drive her away…enraged, Latona calls out to Zeus…who turns the threatening peasants into frogs. [Hoog, p 14]

On the grounds nearby, copies of important sculptures appear on their pedestals.

When Louis XIV established the French Academy in Rome, one of its goals was to identify the finest statues in Italy, make copies, and return them to decorate his gardens. Copies from other foreign countries also were 'ordered', and "seldom have copies so rivaled their originals" according to Durant. [p 88]

Resume walking down the _Royal Avenue_ – in the direction of the Grand Canal. Before reaching the large _Apollo Fountain_ at the end of the Royal Avenue, detour left into _the Colonnade_…a tranquil setting to rest in shade. Louis XIV held many festivities in this grove. Return to the Royal Avenue and continue west to:

The *Apollo Fountain*

Apollo was the son of Latona. As the Sun-God, he faces east ... toward the Palace and the rising sun. In a spectacular gushing of water, *Apollo* and his golden 4-horse chariot emerge from the depths to greet the new day [and race across the sky].

Apollo is 'associated' with Louis XIV ... who was often referred to as the 'Sun-King'.

For refreshments, backtrack along the Royal Avenue a short distance ... and ask directions to nearby food-stands and restaurants 'hidden' within the groves to the south [your right].

Use *Guide* map to visit the nearby *Fountain of Bacchus*. Directly north along the same corridor is the *Fountain of Saturn* [winter] created by the famed Francis Girardon. Return to the grand *Fountain of Apollo* to resume a tour of the northern groves.

Visit the *Fountain of Flora* [spring] ... and the *Fountain of Ceres* [summer].

Locate on *Guide* map the:

Apollo Served by Nymphs of Thetis

This large group [aka *Fountain of the Nymphs* or *the Bathing Apollo*] by Francis Girardon is considered "the sculptural masterpiece of Versailles. It depicts the morning ablutions of the deity as he prepares for his daily course, after having rested at the nymph Thetis' abode." [Versailles, Meyer/Saule, 2000, p 86]

Its original site was suggested by Madame de Montespan – favorite mistress [for 19 years] of Louis XIV. It includes two other groups: *Horses of the Sun* ... and *Groomed by Tritons*.

With adequate time, many visitors continue west to view the intimate mini-mansions which once provided 'play and privacy' to Marie Antoinette ... and later 'privacy' to Napoleon Bonaparte.

[to visit the 'mansions' on a later visit to Versailles, know that it is possible to park a car in residential areas outside *the Gardens* [north-side] and walk in. Consult city map]

The Palace:

The Durants offer this assessment of the *Palace*: "Architecturally ... too complex and haphazard to approach perfection. The chapel is brilliant ... parts of the *Palace* are beautiful ... sometimes the proliferating pile leaves an impression of cold monotony – one room after another ... [many] appear too small for comfort ... only the *Hall of Mirrors* is spacious ..." [p 92-3] The *Author* shares this viewpoint.

However, the *Hall of Mirrors* itself is worth the price of admission ... particularly, when not crowded. This may depend on the number and size of tour groups.

[Mad King Ludwig II's perfect replica of the Hall of Mirrors – in his palace on Lake Chiemsee in Bavaria, an hour train-ride east of Munich – is a pleasant, un-crowded alternative]

Robb & Garrison describe the Versailles Palace's long-term political consequences: "... its swallowing up the taxes of decades for initial construction, and the exhaustive drain upon the state that its subsequent maintenance involved ... in some measure, hastened the revolt which took place toward the close of the 18th century [the French Revolution]." [p 254]

Caution: before hiring a horse-drawn carriage in the Park, inquire if the ride includes cobble-stone surfaces ... they can be bone-rattling. Do not enter carriage unless driver, *in clear English,* confirms there will be no cobble-stones.

Architects:

Andre Le Notre, master landscape architect of the *Gardens*, was aided by his able assistants Jean-Baptiste Colbert and Charles Le Brun.

The French were adept in designing what many describe as the finest public park in the world. However, LeNotre found it necessary to hire experienced <u>Italian</u> hydraulic engineers to create the 'water effects' of the aquatic architecture.

Major References:

The Garden of Versailles, 2003, Hoog, all

Versailles, 1972, Hibbert, p 35

Versailles, 2000, Meyer/Saule, p 86

Wonders of the World, 2002, Burton & Cavendish, p 50-51

Versailles, Strolling the Royal Estate, 1986, Van Der Kemp, p 76-97

France, A History of Art, 1984, Smith, p 131-34

Encyclopedia of Sculpture, 2007, p 682-3

Age of Louis XIV, 1963, Durants, p 88, 92-3

Art Through the Ages, 1991, Gardner, p 806-09

History of Art, 1977, Janson, p 521-27

Art in the Western World, 1935, Robb & Garrison, p 249-254

75
MILO OF CROTON

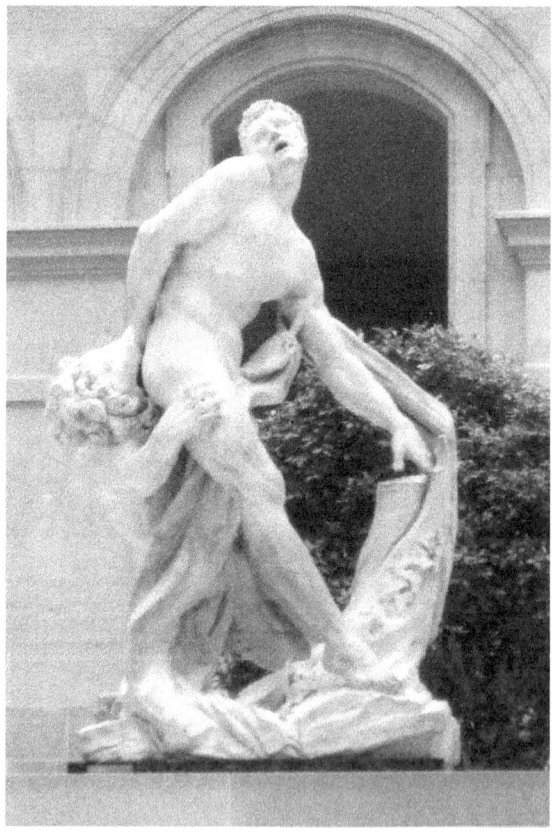

"... the fullest expression of the Baroque in France ...
monumental, multi-faceted, and technically brilliant..."
... Campe, *Encyclo of Sculpture*, p 1373-74

Erected 1683, Versailles – to Paris, 1779 – now, Louvre*
Orig. French sculpture – 1670-82 – French Baroque style
Ht. 8 feet 10.5 inches [275.5 cm] – Carrara marble
Sculptor: Pierre Puget [1620-1694]
  *small bronze copy in Baltimore Museum of Arts

T his historical event – recreated by French sculptor Pierre Puget – occurred some 2,500 years ago near Crotona, a Greek colony on the boot of Italy.

A ravenous lion clamps its jaws around the flesh of the man's buttock.

Excruciating pain distorts the face of *Milo* as he attempts to push away the beast. Its claws rip into his thigh and back. If he could face the lion, he might prevail. But he cannot turn.

The displeased gods of Mt. Olympus do not favor him.

Hoving declares Pierre Puget to be: "<u>one of the most accomplished sculptors in history</u>... at his best when depicting scenes of violence and passion... and no work is a more fitting example than his monumental *Milo of Croton*... almost nine feet tall in beautifully finished white marble. The story on which it is based is Greek, and it's about hubris – arrogance caused by excessive pride. His sculptures have <u>a ferocious energy and eclat combined with a mountainous solidity</u> that is unique in art." [*Greatest Works of Art,* p 236]

The Jansons comment: "... the agony of the hero attacked by the lion – while one hand is trapped in a tree stump – has such force that its impact is almost physical. The internal tension fills the statue with an intense life that also recalls Hellenistic sculpture. That, one suspects, is what made it acceptable to Louis XIV." [*History of Western Art,* p 40]

Originally... *Milo of Croton* "was placed in the Gardens of Versailles... on an exceptionally high pedestal, in a prime position. He immediately drew all eyes... the sculpture was heralded as <u>the fullest expression of the Baroque in France... monumental, multifaceted, and technically brilliant</u> – a theatrical expression of suffering and destiny." [*Encyclo Sculpt,* p 1373-4]

Today, *Milo* is displayed within a tall, glass-enclosed atrium of the Louvre. The sunny location highlights his dilemma.

Subject:

Milo of Croton – famed for his super-human strength and skill as an Olympic wrestler – was one of the most revered Greeks of his time.

Campe in *Encyclo Sculpt* says: "In the late 6th century BC, the Greeks revered him during his lifetime for his wisdom ... but especially for his immense strength ... as a military hero and as an athlete ... [as one of] the most renowned wrestlers in Antiquity, he remained unbeaten over more than a quarter of a century in 32 events at the Olympic Games." [p 1373]

[200 years later, *Agias* #26 was undefeated in the Olympic pankration for a period of 30 years]

Durant reveals the younger Milo: "... had developed his strength ... by carrying a calf every day of its life until it was a full-grown bull ... he would hold a pomegranate so fast in his fist that no one could get it from him, and yet the fruit was uninjured ... he would stand on an oiled quoit and resist all efforts to dislodge him." [*Greece*, p 214]

"Milo's adulation reached a peak after he led the Crotonate army to victory over the Sybarites in southern Italy about 510 BC." [*Encyclo.* p 1374]

Pausanias, the ancient Greek traveler/author, in 175 AD, wrote: "Milo chanced on a withered tree, into which some wedges had been driven to separate the wood ... he took it into his head to tear the wood apart with his hands. But the wedges slipped out ... he was imprisoned by the tree and became prey to the <u>wolves</u>." [Durant, p 215]

Storytellers/artists, for greater drama, altered the 'wolves' to more regal lion.

In his tragic end, *Encyclo Sculpt* suggests this representation of *Milo* may be of a man "unable to accept the ravages of age"... or, he displays an "inability to adjust to his altered condition ... as a warning to aging rulers." [p 1373]

Sculptor:

Pierre Puget – born in Marseilles in 1620 – sculpted primarily in this city...far from Paris and Versailles where the finest sculptors were most likely to receive commissions from wealthy patrons.

Durant describes Puget as: "...the most powerful sculptor of his land and time. Dreaming of Italian masters, he had walked from Marseilles to Genoa to Florence to Rome. He worked eagerly...in decorating the Barbarini Palace...he absorbed every echo and vestige from Buonarroti [Michelangelo]...and envied Bernini's varied fame." [*Louis XIV*, p 101]

In Rome, Puget may have studied *the Laocoon* #51...a reference compares *Milo*'s "anguish and despair of the lonely dying hero" with the father's expression in the Hellenistic *Laocoon* group: "his head jerked back in agony and toes clenched with pain, fully realizing his plight." [*Encyclo*, p 1374]

In Rome, Puget may have observed the painting by Pordenone, *Milo Attacked by Lions* [1520-35]. Like Pordenone, Puget "replaced the wolves – which most Classical writers described as devouring Milo – with nobler lions." [p 1374]

Early in his career, Puget declined to be politically-correct...and consequently, until late in life, he did not enjoy patronage among the privileged of French society.

Durant reveals: "defying the soft idealism of official sculpture, Puget made his chisel the voice of the anger and misery of France...he modeled his marble on the toiling porters of the dock figures and gave almost a revolutionary cry to their straining muscles and pain-distorted faces – the oppressed proletariat upholding the world. This would hardly do at Versailles." [*Age of Louis XIV*, p 100-01]

Martin's *Baroque* reports: "Puget, whose style was considered too Italian and too un-classical by Colbert, was over 50 years of age before he succeeded in placing any of his works at Versailles." [p 319] Hartt describes Puget as: "The maverick among French Baroque sculptors...whose independence of official taste cost him popularity at court. [p 721]

Finally, after the death of Louis XIV's leading statesman and conservative finance minister [Jean-Baptiste Colbert], Puget was asked: "...for statuary, preferably in a harmless mythological vein." Puget sent 3 pieces [now in Louvre]: "the violent *Milo*...the *Meeting of Alexander and Diogenes* relief...plus a laborious and overdone *Perseus and Andromedia*..." [*Louis XIV*, p 101]

Encyclo Sculpt adds: "...court painter Charles Le Brun wrote to congratulate Puget for the beauty of his work...Queen Marie-Therese was moved by the suffering expressed by the figure. Viewers widely remarked on the successful representation of the pathos of the human condition through energy, rage, and despair...and the king, after some hesitation, gave it his approval." [p 1373]

In 1799, after the *Milo* had weathered 116 years in the Gardens of Versailles, it was transferred to Paris...to be displayed inside the Louvre where, for the next two centuries, the *Milo* became the primary model for the academic instruction of French sculptors.

Note: In the Louvre, visit Puget's huge relief, *Meeting of Alexander and Diogenes*. Alexander meets the Cynic philosopher who reclines on the ground. After shifting his horse to create shade for the philosopher, the Greek leader said:

"I am Alexander the Great king." To which the philosopher replied, "I am Diogenes the dog." Alexander respectfully responded: "Ask of me any favor you choose." Diogenes said, "Stand out of the sun." Unfazed, the young king shifted his horse and replied, "If I were not Alexander, I would be Diogenes."

Durant adds: "but we do not hear that the philosopher returned the compliment. The two men died, we are asked to believe, on the same day, in 323 BC...Alexander at Babylon in his thirty-third year, Diogenes at Corinth in his 90s." [*Greece*, p 507]

Major References:

Encyclopedia of Sculpture, 2006, Campe, p 1373-74

Basic History of Western Art, 2006, Janson & Janson, p 406-07

Bullfinch Guide to Art, 1996, West, p 732

Art: A History of Painting, Sculpture..., 1985, Hartt, p 721

Greatest Works of Art of Western Civilization, 1997, Hoving, p 236

Art Through the Ages, 1991, Gardner, p 811-12

History of Art, 1977, Janson, p 528

Life of Greece, Vol 2, 1939, Durant, p 215, 507

Age of Louis XIV, Vol 8. 1963, Durants, p 100-01

Baroque, 1977, Martin, p 77, 319

76

THE TREVI FOUNTAIN

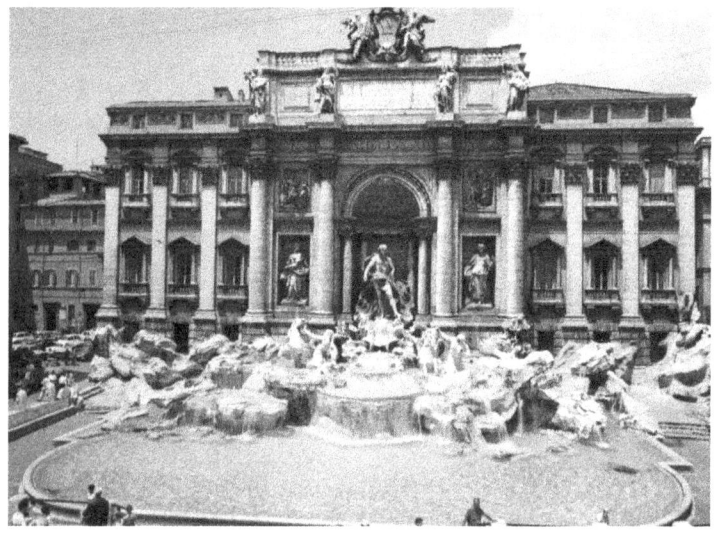

"...the most celebrated of all fountains...
renowned for the purity of its water."
...*Encyclo of Sculpture*, Symmes, p 583

Monumental fountain and facade, 1762 – Rome
Italian marble – created 1732-1762 – High Baroque style
Ht. 85 feet [25.9 m], Width 65 feet [19.8 m]
Architect: Niccolo Salvi – Sculptors: Bracci & della Valle

Rome's Afternoon / Evening Stroll (either direction):
Trevi + Pantheon + Gioletti's Gelato + Piazza Navona

In a world capital known as 'the city of fountains', the *Trevi* is known as the 'Queen of Fountains'.

Lucas' *Wanderer in Rome* describes the atmosphere and music of the *Trevi*: "three primary streams broken by rocks into a score of minor torrents... which in their total exuberance make one of the coolest and most delicious melodies of Rome." [p 31]

Its bountiful water splashing over marble refreshes the senses... and offers constant theater to Romans and others drawn by its healing waters. The *Trevi* also is unique among fountains in that it provides 'intimate amphitheater seating'... a lesson for architects of waterworks.

Symmes in *Encyclo Sculpt* states: "Rome's Trevi is the most celebrated of all fountains ... the location dates to 19 BC, when Agrippa [son-in-law to Augustus] first completed the Aqua Virgo. The original *Trevi* fountain – located at an intersection of 3 streets [*fountain title*] – marked the aqueduct's terminus." [p 583] Water travelled from a spring 12 miles east in the Alban Hills, mostly by underground conduit.

McGregor remarks: "Inspired by Bernini's *Fountain of Four Rivers* #73 in Piazza Navona, the *Trevi* translates his work in the round as... an architectural backdrop. Seats along this fountain's curve are ideal to view the spectacle..." [p 240] Hughes' *Rome* suggests: "Bernini had a hand in the original design..." [*Rome*, p 295]

In *Rambles in Rome* [1892], Forbes describes a tradition: "If you wish to return, come here on the last day of your visit, take a drink with your left hand, then turn and throw into the water, over your left shoulder, a half-penny."

Hughes, in 2011, adds: "... legend of the fountain holds that if a lover drinks a cup of its water in the presence of his beloved, he will never be able to get her out of his heart." [p 295]

To safely drink the water, use the Roman 'water jets' at the far right of the walkway along the rim of the basin. Note how locals use their index finger. This water is said to be the purest and sweetest in the Eternal City. [the *Author* has quenched his thirst here for 60+ years]

Subject:

Behind the rocky landscape and waterfalls is a High Baroque façade that resembles the front of a small palace. In fact... the 85-foot facade is attached to the south wall of the Palazzo Poli. [note windows on upper floors]

A bold triumphal arch dominates the fountain's facade.

Under the arch, Neptune – father of the sea gods – stands in a shell-shaped chariot. To his right, an allegory statue for *Abundance* pours water from her urn. The figure on the left is *Healing* [healthy water]. She holds a cup from which a snake drinks. The theme of this group is 'Taming of the Waters'.

Neptune's chariot is drawn by 2 winged sea-horses, partially submerged. They are led by Tritons – Greek sea gods with tails of a fish and bodies of a man. The Triton on our *left* struggles to control his thrashing horse... while the other sea god, leading a calmed horse, announces his arrival with blasts from a conch shell. The thrashing and calmed horses display the contrasting nature of the ocean.

Above each 'allegory' statue is a high relief related to the water's source. The relief [on our right] displays the source, a spring – to which a virgin girl has led Roman soldiers. The left relief has Agrippa approving the design of his aqueduct. The top of the facade is inscribed with the name of Pope Clement XII, who commissioned the fountain's primary architect and builder Niccolo Salvi.

At the end of each week, the basin is drained and cleaned, including the statuary. Tossed coins are gathered and distributed to charity.

To hear the 'music' of the *Trevi* unmarred by a multitude of voices, visit in the morning before 9 am.

In late evening – when the fountains are flood-lighted – the water [when gushing] can momentarily take one's breath away.

If the central staircase and nearby seating are over-crowded, circle to the far left [west] side of the amphitheater where a second staircase leads down to seating and access to the basin rim. This 'west' approach may provide quicker access [along basin rim] to the 'east' side where drinking water is available.

Lovers of romantic movies filmed in Rome – *Three Coins in a Fountain, Roman Holiday, La Dolce Vita,* etc. – will find scenes featuring the *Trevi*. After Anita Ekberg's memorable dip in *La Dolce Vita,* it is said visitors to the fountain doubled... then tripled.

To gain 'polite' passage through a crowd at this iconic fountain [and elsewhere in Rome], quietly murmur the word 'scusi'... and, only when necessary, add the 'gentlest tap' on the shoulder. Romans are among the most courteous and tolerant hosts on the Continent... and, invariably, they graciously yield to the equally courteous. [never push or bump... this is not Paris]

Designer/Sculptor:

The current fountain, in 1762, replaced a smaller one of 1453.

The chronology and men who created current *Trevi* are:

... 1730-32, Pope Clement XII held competition to finish *Trevi*
... architect Salvi's proposal is approved, with elegant façade
... Salvi's chief sculptor is Giovanni Maini... both die in 1751
... new architect is Giuseppe Panini, new sculptor Pietro Bracci
... Bracci sculpts central group with Maini's models
... Filippo della Valle creates figures *Abundance* & *Healing*
... 1762, architect Panini & sculptor Bracci complete work
[Encyclo Sculpt, p 563]

To the far right [east] and facing the fountain, a gigantic stone-wave is seen crashing high above the boundary wall. A dubious story [Rome is old enough to have many] has Salvi designing this wave in retaliation to a barber who loudly and continually protested the noisy construction of the fountain near his place of business... frequently shouting to Salvi how much he detested its presence. The tall wave was positioned directly in front of the barber's shop... so his customers might hear the fountain, but not see it.

To our left of the fountain is a small 'square', where a fruit-stand offers fresh snacks [including sweetest peaches in Rome]. Forty steps directly west of the fountain is an excellent pizzeria. Across the street is a deli offering a fine blend of 'walnuts & cheese'... to complement your freshly-baked whole-wheat bread from *Il Fornaio Bakery* on Via dei Baullari. [off northwest corner of Campo de Fiori]

References:

Rome, Hughes, 2011, p 295

Rome Eternally Beautiful, 1937, Fattorusso, p 293

Encyclopedia of Sculpture, 2006, p 583

Rome, From Ground Up, 2005, McGregor, 240-42, 244, 250, 284, 301-02

Art and Architecture: Rome, 2005, Hintzen-Bohlen, 285, 290

Rousseau and Revolution, X, 1967, Durants, p 247

H.V. Morton, A Traveler in Rome, p. 22-25

A Wanderer in Rome, 1926, E.V. Lucas, p 30-2

Rome in History, 1977, Fox, p 293

77
NYMPH & SATYR

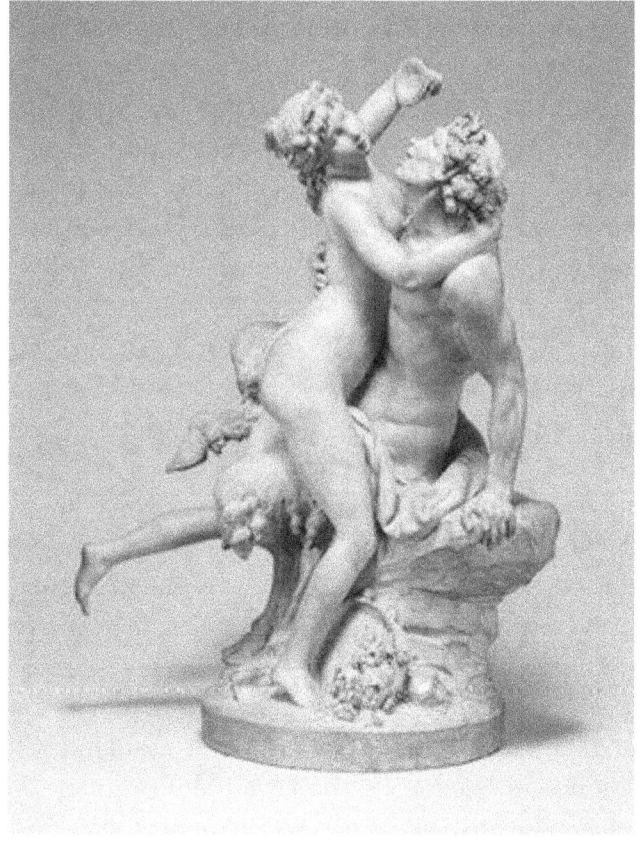

"All the ecstasy of the flesh sings in the *Nymph & Satyr*..."
...Durant, *Rousseau & Revolution*, 1967, p 911

Created in Paris – now, Met. Mus. of Art, NY
Orig. French sculpture – 1775 – French Rococo
Ht. 23 in. – terra cotta [baked earthenware]
Sculptor: Clodion [or Claude Michel] 1738-1814

F estivity … merriment … romance …
One-sixth of the 100 statues herein – directly or indirectly – address the pleasures.

Robb & Garrison describe Clodian: "The greater part of his work consists of small statuettes such as the *Nymph & Satyr*, designed primarily for interior ornament and as appropriate to the boudoir … as the heroic 17th century figures were to the formal gardens in which they were placed." [p 545]

In 1715, the crown of France passed to a new king, Louis XV … . whose name is associated with a style created by French designers called 'rococo'. With the arrival of the Rococo Era, the subject matter of artists abruptly altered from Classic gods/heroes and religious subjects.

Artists and their clients now embraced lavish ornamentation to an extreme … yet, delicate in appearance … with light-hearted themes.

In describing Clodion's statuary, Janson says: "Their coquettish eroticism is another form of the 'miniature Baroque,' a playful echo of the ecstasies of Bernini and Puget …" [*History of Art*, p 539-40]

Janson explains why Rococo sculpture is often compact: "After the death of Louis XIV … the nobility, hitherto attached to the court of Versailles, were now freer of royal surveillance. Many of them chose not to return to their ancestral chateaux in the provinces, but to live instead in Paris, where they built elegant town houses, known as *hotels*. Because available sites in the French capital were usually cramped and irregular – they offered scant opportunity for [large] impressive exteriors – the layout and décor of the rooms became the architects' main concern." [p 538]

Gardner adds: "the Rococo proved so appealing to the nobility that it spread rapidly throughout Europe … replacing the earlier, heavier Baroque style." [*Art Thru the Ages*, p 819]

Wealthy private patrons of sculpture also included members of the new business class. They purchased the intimate Rococo statuary for both their salons [to entertain friends] and their boudoirs [a lady's bedroom or private sitting room].

Clodian's Rococo statuary was relatively small and intimate...meant for a tabletop and viewable at close range...even touched. Consequently, his lively and rapturous nymphs, satyrs, and shepherds were much in demand.

As Durant says, "Clodion carved a way to prosperity with terracotta groups slightly erotic. All the ecstasy of the flesh sings in the *Nymph & Satyr*..." [p 911]

Yet...Clodian is ever graceful. For the first time, it is acceptable for a major sculptor to present a thoroughly enticing embrace that is both dynamic and amorous.

In the next century [1869], the vigor and "coquettish gaiety" of this couple would be celebrated again by Dionysus and his nymphs in *the Dance* by Carpeaux. [Janson, p 603]

Subject:

Gardner suggests: "The *Nymph & Satyr* has an open and vivid composition suggestive of its dynamic Baroque roots" plus "the erotic playfulness of Boucher and Fragonard to energize the eager nymph and the laughing satyr into whose mouth she pours a cup of wine." [p 892]

Instead of Bernini's *Apollo* chasing unwilling *Daphne* #71...now, in this Rococo group, the female is the 'assertive' party...and she is welcomed.

With uninhibited enthusiasm, she thrusts herself at the seated *Satyr*...splashing wine over his face and into his willing mouth. In turn, the *Satyr* wraps his arm around the *Nymph* and pulls her to him.

She grips the back of the *Satyr's* neck with purpose...and presses into him. Her momentum may very well bowl him over...as they meld into one.

"The feminine look of the Rococo style suggests that the age was dominated by the taste and social initiative of women – Madame de Pompadour in France ... Maria Theresa in Austria ... Elizabeth in England ... and Catherine in Russia – who held some of the highest positions in Europe ... and female influence was felt in any number of smaller courts." [p 821]

Smith describes Madame Pompadour ... also known as the Marquise de Pompadour: "Jeanne Antoinette Poisson – born into a wealthy banking family – had intelligence, charm, and beauty. Her friends included Voltaire and Montesquieu. She became the mistress and confidant of Louis XV who made her Marquise de Pompadour. Almost from the time of her romantic meeting with Louis XV at a masked ball at Versailles – *she costumed as Diana and he as a yew tree* – Pompadour became the king's mistress and often his advisor. For her, he had the formal apartments built by Louis XIV redecorated in the new, exaggerated and spritely Rococo style." [*France, History in Art,* p 147-48]

The Durants' *Age of Voltaire* reveals: "The ascendancy of a woman over a sensual and sensitive king [Louis XV] gave new prestige to delicacy and sentiment ... the sublime gave place to the delight-ful ... the dignified to the graceful ... the grandeur of size to the charm of elegance ... subjects shunned tragedy to stress the bright potentialities of life. Rococo was the last stage of Baroque, of the rebellion of imagination against reality, of freedom from order and rules. Despite its coquettish prettiness, Rococo produced thousands of objects unsurpassed in finish and elegance." [p 303, 306]

Hartt reveals Clodian's particular technique: "His groups of accurately modeled figures in erotic abandon are made all the fresher and more alluring by his knowing use of pinkish terra-cotta [a hard brown-red earthware ... carved, then baked] as if it were actual pulsating flesh, rendering each incipient embrace 'forever warm and still to be enjoyed'." [*Art: History of Painting, Sculpture ...,* Vol II, p 766-67]

Sculptor:

Clodian, as son-in-law to French sculptor Augustin Pajou – and with early training from his uncle Adam and another sculptor,

Pigalle – advanced rapidly as an artist. In 1759, at 21, he won the Prix de Rome which enabled him to attend the French Academy in Rome from 1762 to 1771. During those studies and active sculpting in Italy, his abilities and style attracted a widening circle of French patrons. Upon his return to France, Clodian already was a popular artist, and his success as a sculptor was ensured.

He preferred creating small-scale statuary for private collectors, though he also sculpted a large-scale *Montesquieu* for the king, Louis XVI. When the French revolution altered demand for art, Clodion adapted his work to the more acceptable and serious Neo-Classical style.

In 1806, Napoleon engaged him to provide reliefs for two monuments in Paris – the Vendome Column [1806-10] and the Carrousel Arch [1806-9] near the Louvre.

In the 19th and early 20th centuries, the continued popularity of Clodian's statuary encouraged many fake copies of his work. Accurately attributed examples of his work can be seen in the Louvre, the Victoria & Albert Museum in London, and the Met. Mus. of Art in New York. [Brigstocke, p 134]

Major References:

Age of Voltaire, 1965, Durants, p 303, 306

Rousseau and Revolution, 1967, Durants, p 106, 911

History of Art, 1977, Janson, p 539-40, 603

Art: History of Painting, Sculpture ... Vol II, 1985, Hartt, p 766-77

Bullfinch Guide to Art History, 1996, West, 346

Art in the Western World, 1935, Robb and Garrison, p 545, 945

Gardner's Art Through the Ages, 1996, Tansey & Kleiner, p 892

Art History, 2005, Stokstad, p 908-09

Oxford Companion of Western Art, 2001, Brigstocke, p 134

78
DIANA THE HUNTRESS

[<u>NOT</u> THE LOUVRE'S VERSAILLES DIANA]

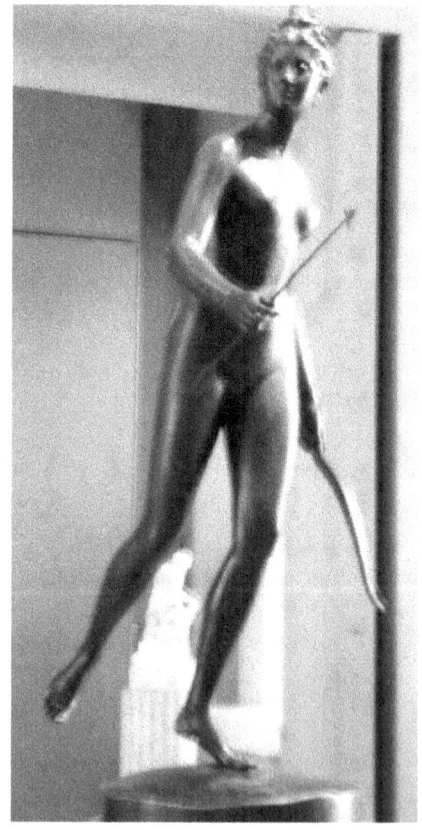

"...acclaimed for its beauty worthy of classical statuary."
...Louvre, website, 2010

[ancient Greeks called their goddess of the hunt *Artemis*…
the Romans called their goddess of the hunt *Diana*]
Bronze, 1790, from plaster model – now, Louvre*
From: Houdon's marble Original 1776 – Neo-Classic style
Height: 6 ft. 11 in. – bronze
Sculptor: Jean-Antoine Houden [1744-1828]
      *see Huntington Mus., LA, for earlier bronze [more chaste]

In the Louvre, this graceful huntress reigns like the ancient goddess. As the afternoon sun envelopes her, she acquires a lovely golden halo. [above]

O'Rourke says: "Since Antiquity, *Diana* was depicted either as running and clothed…or nude and reclining: Houdon's treatment combines these two characteristics in a work whose realism shocked some of his contemporaries." [*Encyclo Sculpt,* p 765]

The Durants describe Houdon as: "the supreme sculptor of the age"…before and after the French Revolution. "In Paris he carved or cast a succession of *Dianas;* one in bronze [modest, Huntington Collection] is a marvel of classic features and French grace." [*Rousseau & Revolution,* p 911]

"More famous is the [later] bronze *Diana* in the Louvre [Hall of Late French Sculpture]. It was refused a place in the Salon of 1785, perhaps because [said a critic] 'she was too beautiful and too nude to be exposed to the public'… more probably because the statue violated the traditional [semi-clothed] conception of *Diana* as chaste." [p 911}

Subject:

The *Louvre* website says: "The slender Diana…leaning slightly forward on one foot, gives the statue an ethereal and dynamic allure…Diana was habitually portrayed in a short tunic belted at the waist, in the manner of the often-copied *Artemis the Huntress* [also in Louvre]. Her nudity here – considered improper for hunting – scandalized Houdon's contemporaries." [2010]

Gardner declares: "The fleet goddess of the hunt is caught in one swift movement, elegantly poised. The suavely modeled volumes, the supple contours, and the compact silhouette contribute to her <u>cool simplicity and dignity</u>. All traces of Rococo complexity, asymmetry, and restlessness have vanished." [*Art Thru Ages*, 1970, p 791]

Today...in the center of the great hall in the Louvre,
... the running *Diana* comes alive
... her long legs flow effortlessly
... bow in hand, she chases prey
... she balances on a single foot
... shimmering light on her body heightens its energy
... her head twists right (though she runs slightly left)
... she has noticed sudden movement
... now, she knows her 'first' arrow hit its mark
... and a wounded prey can be dangerous
Cautiously, Diana alters her direction further away from her prey.

This is one of many interpretations Houdon's creation invites us to consider.

Edith Hamilton, in *Mythology*, describes the goddess *Diana/ Artemis* as: "lover of woods and the wild chase over the mountains... Apollo's twin sister... a good hunter, but careful to preserve the young... fierce and revengeful... and [to her] all wild animals were sacred, especially the deer." [p 31-2]

Bullfinch adds the tall "goddess of the woods" was a "virgin... an athletically-built woman... attended by nymphs" at her cave in the woods. In one episode of her being... when the prince Actaeon unintentionally happens upon Diana at bath with her nymphs, she: "dashed water into the face of the intruder, adding these words: 'Now go and tell, if you can, that you have seen Diana un-apparelled.' Immediately, a pair of branching stag's horns grew out of his head"... and the balance of his body also became that of a stag. Soon, Actaeon's own hunting dogs found him, chased him down and finished him." [p 36]

As sweet and lovely as Diana/Artemis appears in both sculpture and paintings, this goddess was also vengeful. In another episode, she and her brother Apollo were the Olympian deities who, in myth, destroyed the children of *Niobe* #16.

Sculptor:

Jean-Antoine Houdon was born in the city of Versailles, where he had ample time to study statues in the gardens of the Palace. At 20, he won the Prix de Rome and sailed to Italy in 1764. During 4 years at the French Academy in Rome, Houdon decided to sculpt in the Classic style … and eventually became known as the greatest Neo-Classical sculptor of his time. [*Encyclo.* p 791]

His gift to the world of art was to add realism – a precise record of individual appearance – to the Classic style.

In *History of Painting, Sculpture…*, Hartt says: "Houdon was devoted to perfection of naturalness … he studied anatomy with exhaustive care, and did not disdain the use of plaster casts from life and meticulous measurements. None the less, his scientific precision in no way deadens his work. He declared that his purpose was to 'present with all the realism of form and to render almost immortal the image of the men who have contributed the most to the glory or happiness of their country'… shown in a characteristic pose and in a moment of thought, feeling, or speech." [p 795]

Gardner [1991] adds: "In all his portraits, Houdon's strong, perceptive realism penetrates at once to personality, catching its most subtle shade." [p 837]

During his long productive life, many of the most celebrated men of his time had "telling and powerful" busts sculpted by Houdon. They include Voltaire, Rousseau, Franklin, Jefferson, Lafayette, Washington [in Louvre], Napoleon, Moliere, Fulton, John Paul Jones, Diderot, Louis XVI, Marshal Ney, etc. [p 836]

His life-like busts of famed Americans would become models for the Jefferson nickel … the Washington quarter … and the Franklin half-dollar. [Durant, p 912]

In Paris, following the success of his bust of Benjamin Franklin [1778], the State of Virginia [assisted by Thomas Jefferson, ambassador to France] invited Houdon in 1785 to execute, from life, a

<u>complete</u> statue of George Washington [1791]…now displayed in Richmond. A busy Washington begrudged the time…but Houdon remained at Mount Vernon for two weeks and created the most reliable surviving image of his subject…in common colonial attire. He would have preferred to portray the *first president* in Classical robes.

Later, the American sculptor Greenough would use the head of Houdon's *Washington* [at Richmond] as a realistic model for the head of his 'Classical' *Washington* #83 now in the Smithsonian's Museum of American History.

Due to the wide popularity of Houdon's works, they were frequently reproduced by others without his knowledge. This may explain the large number of cities and museums displaying 'his works'.

To view another *Diana* standing high on her left foot and releasing an arrow, see the 18-foot bronze by Augustus-Saint Gaudens, 1893 [Philadelphia's Museum of Art]…or the 9-foot bronze in the New York Met. Mus. of Art [cast in 1928 from 1893 bronze].

Major References:

Bullfinch Guide to Art History, 1996, West, p 515-16

Art Through the Ages, 1970, Gardner, p 791

Art Through the Ages, 1991, Gardner, p 836-7

Art in the Western World, 1935, Robb & Harrison, p 545-47

The History of World Sculpture, 1968, Bazin, p 417-18

History of Painting, Sculpture…, 1985, Hartt, p 795

Rousseau and Revolution, Vol X, 1967, Durants, p 911-12

Encyclopedia of Sculpture, 2004, O'Rourke, p 765-67

Wall Street Journal, July 24, 2008, p D5

Mythology, 1942, Hamilton, p 31-2

Bulfinch's Mythology, 1968, Graves, p 36

79

CUPID AWAKENING PSYCHE

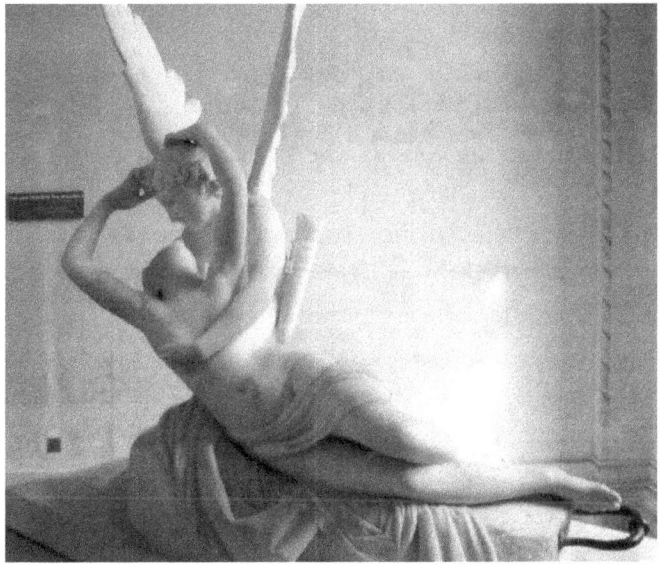

"This gentle eroticism … further distinguished Canova from other sculptors." … *Encyclo Sculpture*, Fogelman, p 150

Earliest masterpiece by Canova – now, in the Louvre
Italian Orig. – first version 1789-1793* – Neo-Classic style
Height/Width: 6'1" by 6'8" [1.55 m by 1.73 m] – marble
Antonio Canova [1757-1822]

    *not to be confused with 1796 'standing' version, also in Louvre

'Sublime' describes Canova's first masterpiece, *Cupid Awakening Psyche*. The back is as exquisite as the front. His 'theme of romantic love' remained unequalled for 100 years ... until arrival of Rodin's *the Kiss* #86 in 1886-87.

In the Louvre, visitors of all ages pause to contemplate the tender 'awakening' of *Cupid* and *Psyche*. Many undoubtedly imagine themselves in such an embrace. The young – having the least savoir-faire – linger the longest.

Antonio Canova, with this masterpiece, became widely recognized as one of the finest sculptors of his time. [1783 to 1822] He brilliantly proved the prime of the Classical past could be recaptured.

Fogelman in *Encyclo Sculpt* states: "Among his most famous mythological groups, Canova's *Cupid Awakening Psyche* depicted semi-recumbent, embracing lovers ... their almost-touching lips framed by the circle of *Psyche's* arms. This gentle eroticism, heightened by the glossy finish of the surface, further distinguished Canova from other sculptors." [p 250]

Castellani captures the essence of this mythical couple. "It needed the delicacy of an artist like Canova to create an image so remote from earthly reality. In fact, the story of *Cupid & Psyche* represents ... the encounter of the human soul and heavenly love in an embrace ... that for a moment makes them dream of being able to fuse into a single entity. But desire remains unfulfilled ... the arms of the two lovers do not clasp ... fingers brush each other's hair and skin without taking hold ... and their kiss remains in suspense. The languid abandon of the woman's body in the arms of her lover is a vivid image of an impulse that is checked ... their embracing arms frame the splendid heads as they approach one another ... ." [*The Louvre*, p 266-67]

The beguiling robe 'lightly' draped over the figure of *Psyche* is on the fringe of movement ... similar to garments of the *Winged Victory* #38 and *Venus de Milo* #48 ... an alluring detail Canova did not borrow from either. [*Victory* found 1863, *Venus* in 1820]

Agard's *Classical Myths in Sculpture* concludes: "There is a very sweet and genuine quality in the soft flesh and gentle faces, and the composition reinforces the effect by the smoothly encircling rhythm of the arms... here there are no counter thrusts as in baroque sculpture, no violent contrasts..." [p 110-11]

Due to popularity of *Cupid Awakening Psyche*, the Louvre exhibits this statuary in a spacious corner.

Subject:

The legend of *Cupid* & *Psyche* has widely varying interpretations.

Hamilton's *Mythology* says: "a king had 3 daughters, all lovely maidens, but the youngest, *Psyche*, excelled her sisters so greatly that beside them she seemed a very goddess consorting with mere mortals." [p 121]

Castellani tells us: "The very young *Psyche* was so beautiful that she aroused the envy of Venus, who sent *Cupid* [her winged son, invisible to mortals] to make *Psyche* fall in love with the most despicable of men. But *Cupid*, as soon as he saw *Psyche,* was so struck by her extraordinary beauty that he fell in love with her himself. *Cupid* secretly began to visit *Psyche* [she could only hear his voice] as it was forbidden for a mortal to love a god and they could not meet in the light of day." [*The Louvre,* p 266]

Hamilton [from Apuleius, Roman author of 2nd C. AD] reports that, one night, *Psyche* lighted a candle to reveal the face of *Cupid*...but a drop of hot oil from the candle fell on his skin and burnt him... *Cupid*, hurt and disappointed, fled back to his mother...Venus, furious upon discovering their visits, used guile and magical powers to cause the overly-curious *Psyche* to fall into an indefinite heavy sleep. [p 129-33]

Bullfinch's Mythology relates: "*Cupid*...no longer able to bear the absence of his beloved *Psyche*...flew to the spot where she lay...and gathering up the sleep from her body...waked *Psyche* with a light touch of one of his arrows. Then, *Cupid* presented himself before Zeus/Jupiter with his supplication. Zeus lent a favoring ear, and pleaded the cause of the lovers so earnestly with Venus that he won her consent. On this, Zeus sent Mercury to bring *Psyche* up to the heavenly assembly...and when she arrived, Zeus handed her a cup of ambrosia and said, 'Drink this, *Psyche*, and be immortal...' thus, *Psyche* became at last united with *Cupid*, and in due time they had a daughter born to them whose name was *Pleasure*." [p 92]

In mythology, *Cupid* was symbolic *of love*, and *Psyche* was symbolic of *the soul.*

Hamilton, concludes her version of their love story. "So all came to a most happy end. 'Love' and the 'Soul' had sought and – after sore trials – found each other... and that union could never be broken." [p 134]

Bullfinch adds: "The fable of *Cupid* & *Psyche* is usually considered allegorical. The Greek name for 'butterfly' is *Psyche*... though, the same word means the 'soul'. There is no illustration of the immortality of the soul so striking and beautiful as the butterfly... bursting on brilliant wings from a dull caterpillar existence... to flutter in the blaze of day and feed on the most fragrant and delicate productions of spring. *Psyche*, then, is the human soul, which is purified by sufferings and misfortunes... and is thus prepared for the enjoyment of true and pure happiness." [p 92]

This bears some resemblance to the 'promise' of several religions.

Sculptor:

Canova's father and grandfather were stonemasons. As a boy, Canova's enthusiasm and skill in carving encouraged a wealthy patron to provide funds in 1775 for his study in Venice... resulting in his first successful work, *Orpheus and Eurydice.*

After Canova settled in Rome in 1779-81, he embraced the Neo-Classic style. His *Theseus and the Minotaur* [1783] brought him international fame. By 1800, he had executed two more Neo-Classic works, *Perseus* and *the Pugilist*, which the Vatican accepted and displayed with their finest Classic works from antiquity.

With the success of these works, Canova became one of the most sought-after European sculptors of the period. He devoted his energy to the creation of public monuments for leaders of Europe... "and erotic mythological subjects, such *as Cupid Awakening Psyche* for the pleasure of private collectors." [Stokstad, *Art History* p 913]

Describing Canova's work, Agard observes: "The best of it ... does achieve a satisfying simplicity, purity of line, and serene tranquility in picturing the mythological episodes ... his work mirrors his gracious personality, having tender sentiment beyond that of any other sculpture of the period. The scenes he represented from classical mythology were chiefly romantic ones ... he preferred quiet attitudes." [p 110]

His other widely-recognized statuary include the *Pauline Borghese* #80 and the *Three Graces* #81. He also created an over-sized *Napoleon*, the *Venus Italica*, and the *tomb of Pope Clement XIV*.

Fogelman concludes: "Canova set a precedent that the best Neo-Classical sculpture was associated with a high level of executive precision and elegance and subtlety of surface finishing." [p 1170]

[see two following chapters for more biography]

Major References:

Classical Myths in Sculpture, 1951, Agard, p 109, 110

30,000 Years of Art, 2007, Phaidon, p 858

Encyclopedia of Sculpture, 2004, Fogelman, p 250, 1170

Art History, 2005, Stokstad, p 913

The Louvre, 2007, Castellani, p 266-67

Hamilton, 1942, Mythology, p 121-34

Bullfinch's Mythology, 1968, Robert Graves foreword, p 84-94

80

THE PAULINE BORGHESE

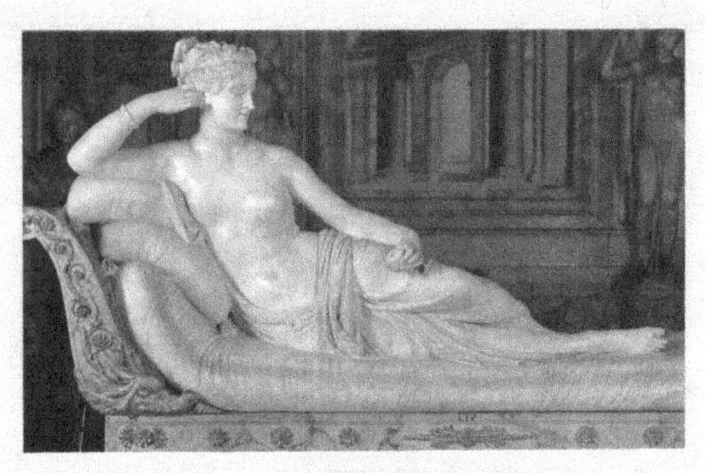

"There is simply not another portrait – either in paint or
in stone – that is as gripping, provocative, and at the
same time, endearing." ... Hoving, *Greatest Works*, p 78

Created in 1808 – now, in the Villa Borghese, Rome
Orig. Italian marble – Pauline, sister of Napoleon
Size: 63 by 78 inches [1.6 x 2 m] – Neo-Classic style
Sculptor: Antonio Canova [1757-1822]

Antonio Canova's provocative *Pauline* reclines in a 'semi-Classic' pose ... not unlike the haughty *Aphrodite* of the Parthenon's *Three Goddesses* #17.

Canova was familiar with this *Aphrodite*, as: "He studied enthusiastically the Parthenon sculptures brought to London by Lord Elgin." [Hartt, p 779] Upon receiving an invitation to restore them, Canova wisely declined.

The Durants explain the revival of interest in Classic sculpture. "Italy's sculptors were inspired – by the excavations at Herculaneum – to discard the eccentricities of baroque and the exuberance of rococo ... to seek the grace and calm and simple lines of classic statuary. One of these sculptors [Canova] left us work that still stops the eye, tempts the touch, and lives in the memory." [p 554]

Canova further alludes to the classical *Aphrodite* by having *Pauline* delicately but visibly holding the 'apple awarded to the most beautiful goddess' by the mortal Paris.

The Durants add: "Canova finished the work in two years, and then exposed it to the judgment of the public and his peers. They marveled at its proud beauty and loving finish ... here was no mere imitation of some ancient masterpiece, but a living woman of her time ... Canova made her a gift to the generations." [p 555]

Morton reports his first impression upon viewing *Pauline* at the Villa Borghese: "One might have been in the presence of Pauline herself ... and the pose was one she adopted to the end of her life. [another 17 years] Even in an age when nudity was fashionable, the statue was thought to be rather daring, except by Pauline. A woman friend once asked how she could have posed almost naked. 'Oh, there was a stove in the studio,' was her reply." [*Traveller in Rome*, 1955 , p 227]

Bazin suggests the "modeling throbs with life. The formal purity of the art of Canova ... is demonstrated in this work." [*History of World Sculpture*, p 419]

Canova may have been inspired by a reproduction of Jacques-Louis David's famed portrait, *Madame Recamier* [1800] ... who also reclines alluringly on a couch.

The *Encyclo Sculpt* states the *Pauline* "with its nude torso and luminous, velvety surface, was one of the most risqué productions in the history of official portraiture." [p 250]

Gardner adds: "With remarkable discretion, Canova created a daring image of seductive charm, generalized enough to personify the goddess of love, yet still suggestive of the living person. Despite a lingering Rococo charm, this work shows the artist to have been firmly Neo-Classical in his approach." [*Art Through the Ages*, II, p 868]

The Durants best describe *Pauline*: "beautiful and scandalously gay, who...still holds court, in Canova's softly contoured marble in the Galleria Borghese...as one of the lasting delights of Rome." [p 92]

Subject:

As the sister of Napoleon Bonaparte, Pauline [1780-1825] lived like royalty during the time her brother dominated most of Europe.

The Durants report: "She was fated to spread happiness and trouble, for she was rated the most beautiful woman of her time. The men who saw her never forgot her...and the women who saw her never forgave her. She was not well adapted for monogamy...but she was apparently a loving wife [married at 17 in 1798] to her first husband, General Le Clerc...sharing his danger and yellow fever in St.-Domingue. When he died [1802], she returned to Paris...opened a salon, charmed husbands by her beauty and some by her generosity. Napoleon hurried to marry her to the rich and handsome Prince Camillo Borghese [1803]." [p 771]

At 23, Pauline was wife again...to: "the dull but worthy Prince Borghese, who, though he covered her with the family diamonds, got little from her but contempt and tantrums..." plus the embarrassment of a "long procession of lovers." [Morton, p 226]

The Durants declare that Canova "persuaded Pauline Borghese...to pose for the sensuous figure." [p 555]

Morton counters: "Pauline sat for it at her own suggestion, soon after her marriage to Borghese, when she was still thrilled to find herself a wealthy princess. Canova...at first...tried to persuade her to be shown as Diana. This did not please her at all. She insisted on revealing herself as Venus." [p 227]

According to the Durants, Canova "used only her face as a model...for the drapery and the limbs he drew upon his imagination, his dreams, and his memories." [p 555]

Morton claims the memoirs of Madame Junot [close friend to Pauline] reveal Canova had no need to alter her flawless features other than to correct her rimless ears. [p 230]

Hoving analyzes the work: "Madame Pauline is portrayed as sexy, arrogant, willful, intelligent, beautiful, profound, fashionable, and dangerous. Semi-nude, Pauline seems at first glance to be a reclining Venus after a classical model...rendered impeccably in glistening ivory marble. She is imperious as a deity from ancient mythology – the type is called 'Venus Victrix' – but she's also as wanton as a street cat." [p 78-9]

The Durants describe the person. Pauline "was also a model of kindness...gave abundantly, won many lasting friendships, even among her discarded lovers, and was more loyal to Napoleon than any other Bonaparte, except his mother...When he left for his last gamble, Pauline gave him her finest necklace...She followed him to Elba, played hostess for him, and enlivened his life..." [p 772]

In 1825, when Pauline was stricken with cancer at the age of 45, Prince Borghese returned. "Her husband forgave her sins, rejoined her in her last year, and closed her eyes when she died...'After all,' he said, 'she was the kindest creature in the world'." [Durant, p 220, 772]

Sculptor: [see previous chapter for more biography]

When Canova became Napoleon's favorite sculptor in 1802, he left a successful career in Italy and moved to Paris where he executed numerous portraits – all Classical – of the emperor [*Napoleon as Mars*] and his family. After Napoleon fell, Canova was asked by the Pope to coordinate the recovery of many Italian works of art which the French had seized. And he did.

Other well-known statuary by Canova include *Cupid Awakening Psyche* #79, the *Three Graces* #81 ... and the *Venus Italica.*

In 1802, Napoleon seized the *Medici Venus* at the Uffizi Gallery in Florence and took it to Paris. When the Florentines asked Canova to make a replacement, he assented ... then proceeded to sculpt 4 versions of his own ... called *the Venus Italica.* None reached the Uffizi. They stand in the Pitti Palace of Florence ... the Hearst Castle in California ... the Residence Museum in Munich ... and the Leeds City Gallery in England.

Napoleon as Mars, in white marble, is a colossal nude [11 feet high] with Napoleon posed as the Greek god of war. Canova "was inspired by portraits of ancient rulers whose nudity indicates their status as divinities." [Janson, p 592] When it arrived in Paris [1811], Napoleon immediately rejected it ... "allegedly, because the little *Winged Victory* placed in his right hand seemed to be flying away from him." [Durant, p 555]

In 1816, the British government purchased the statue from the Bourbon dynasty and presented it to the victor of Waterloo – the Duke of Wellington. It now dominates the grand staircase in the Wellington Museum. [by Hyde Park in London]

Durant concludes: "Canova was a good man, known for modesty, piety, and charity, and capable of appreciating his competitors. He worked hard ... on October 13, 1822, he died ... mourned by all literate Italy." [p 556] He had designed his own tomb, a small replica of the Pantheon of Rome.

Major References:

Greatest Works of Art of Western Civilization, 1997, Hoving, 78-9

History of World Sculpture, 1968, Bazin, p 419

Art: History of Painting, Sculpture, II, 1985, Hartt, p 796-97

Art in the Western World, 1953, Robb & Garrison, p 548-9

Encyclopedia of Sculpture, 2006, p 249-51

Bullfinch Guide to Art, 1996, West, 318

Age of Napoleon, XI, 1975, Durants, p 92, 220, 554-56, 771-2

Art Through the Ages, 1991, Gardner, p 867-68

A Wanderer in Rome, 1926, E.V. Lucas, p 223

History of Art, 1977, Janson, p 591-92

Art History, 2005, Stokstad, p 913

Traveler in Rome, 1957, Morton, p 226-31

81

THE THREE GRACES

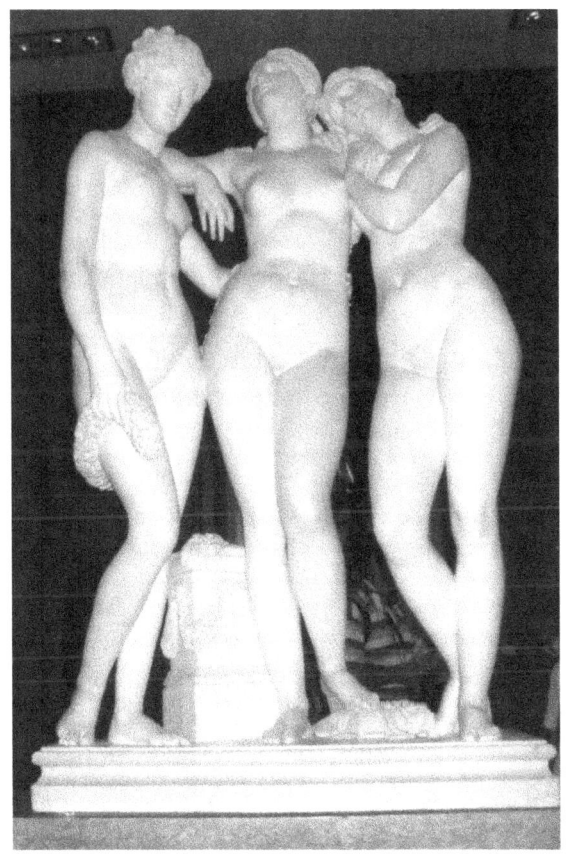

"epitomizes the beauties of Neo-Classical sculpture ..."
... *30,000 Years of Art*, 2007, p 858

1819, Victoria & Albert Mus. or Nat. Gallery Scotland* [+Hearst]
Italian orig. – 1st version, 1817[Hermitage]; 2nd version, 1819
Height: 5 feet 8 in. [1.73 m] – marble – Neo-Classic style
Sculptor: Antonio Canova [1757-1822]

    *rotates every 3 years
    **also Hearst Castle, Calif.

The Durants declare Antonio Canova: "…left us work that still stops the eye, tempts the touch and lives in the memory." [*Age of Napoleon*, p 554]

These three friends fully succeed.

Canova presents his *Three Graces* as one cohesive group, closely-joined by embracing arms. Previous artists commonly placed the center figure facing the other two, her back to viewers. Other artists gave identifying attributes to each sister, but Canova declines to distinguish them in this manner.

Fogelman says: "*The Three Graces* became famous even before they left Canova's studio. Most critics applauded Canova for capturing the essence of Grace as a concept… and for creating an unrivaled vehicle for the appreciation of Divine Beauty." The trio appear to be absorbed "in their own intimate exchange…" rendering "them oblivious to the viewer's presence…" [*Encyclo Sculpt*, p 252-53]

30,000 Years states: "The work epitomizes the beauties of Neo-Classical sculpture…with its erotic, curvaceous nudes and highly polished finish…an adventurous work…it was universally admired…" [p 858]

Josephine de Beauharnais, divorced wife of Napoleon, had commissioned the first version from Canova in 1812. When Napoleon was forced to abdicate, and the fortunes of his family became uncertain, John Russell [Duke of Bedford] offered to purchase the 'first' version. Canova declined to sell it to the British duke…who then commissioned a 'second' version in 1816. [Fogelman, p 253]

Josephine died in 1814 before her 'first' version was completed [1817]…and her son Eugene purchased it. Later, this group was acquired by the Hermitage Museum in St. Petersburg where it remains.

John Russell's 'second' version [completed in 1819] was "installed in the Temple of the Graces … built to house the group … for his Woburn estate." [Fogelman, p 253]

In 1994, it was acquired by the British nation in a highly-publicized campaign … to prevent the Getty Museum in Los Angeles from purchasing it. After the British government declined to grant an export license, "the sales price [7.6 million pounds] to the Getty was matched by a British company, the Victoria & Albert Museum, and the National Gallery of Scotland … with help from the National Heritage Memorial Fund … and, surprisingly, John Paul Getty II." [BBC website, 5/25/10]

Every 3 years, the 'second' version rotates between the Victoria & Albert Museum in London … and the Nat. Gallery of Scotland in Edinburg.

A fine copy of Canova's 'second' version – by French sculptor Emile Boyer [1877-1948] – stands on a tall pedestal in the gardens of the Hearst Castle in California. From all viewpoints, in bright sunlight, the embracing women are stunning.

Subject:

References offer several variations of the mythical origins of *the Three Graces*. It is generally accepted they were sisters who became handmaidens to *Venus*, the goddess of love.

The Durants describe one variation involving Zeus/Jupiter: "Gradually … he becomes the calm and mighty ruler of gods and men, bestriding Olympus in bearded dignity. His one failing is the youthful readiness with which he falls in love. His first mate is Dione … later, his first wife is Metis [she births Athena from his head]… lonely, he takes Thetis for his mate and by her begats the 12 Hours … then takes Eurynome and begats the *Three Graces* …" [*Life of Greece* p 181-82] His amours continue.

The *Encyclo Sculpt.* views *the Graces* from three contexts: divine origin … through ancient authors … and by Renaissance theorists.

First: "The *Graces* were of <u>divine origin</u>, the Latin *Gratiae* [or Greek *Charites*] – Aglaia [the Radiant], Thalia [the Flowering], and Euphrosyne [Joy]." [p 252]

Second: "To ancient authors, *the Graces* represented '<u>benevolence'…the three aspects of generosity</u> – giving, receiving, and returning gifts." [p 252] Their 'benevolence' explains why many artists, over the millenniums, presented two sisters frontally with one facing backwards…to signify reciprocity.

Third: "Renaissance theorists saw them as <u>Beauty, Desire, and Fulfillment – the three stages of love</u>…or Chastity, Beauty, and Love." [p 252] In this context, all 3 sisters normally face frontally.

Fogelman says: "Throughout his career, Canova sought the perfect balance between naturalism and idealization, on the basis of the principles of ancient art. *The Three Graces* represent the most sophisticated and most famous embodiment of this aesthetic exploration." [p 252]

Sculptor:

[also see 2 previous chapters]

The popularity of Canova's Neo-Classic style strongly influenced other artists of his time…until "the Romantic movement subordinated line and form to color and feeling…" [p 556]

30,000 Years concludes: "During his lifetime, Canova achieved wide reputation as the greatest of the living sculptors. He received orders of knighthood from the Pope, the king of England, and commissions from Catherine the Great of Russia." [p 858]

In 1818, Canova began carving a marble statue of George Washington, commissioned by the state of North Carolina for its Capitol building in Raleigh. Canova's *Washington* was seated like a Caesar in Rome and dressed in the uniform of a Roman general. Delivered in 1821, this statue was destroyed by fire in 1830 and never replaced. [*200 Years of American Sculpture*, p 34]

Major References:

Greatest Works of Western Art, 1997, Hoving p 198-89

Encyclopedia of Sculpture, 2004, Fogelman, p 249-53

Life of Greece, II, 1939, Durant, p 181-2

Age of Napoleon, XI, 1975, Durants, p 301, 550, 554-56, 771-72

30,000 Years of Art, 2007, Phaidon, p 858

Hearst Castle, Curator of Art

BBC, Britain, website, Nov 13, 2002

200 Years of American Sculpture, p 34

Hearst Castle, Coffman, 1985, p 90

82

Departure of the Volunteers

or, the Marseillaise

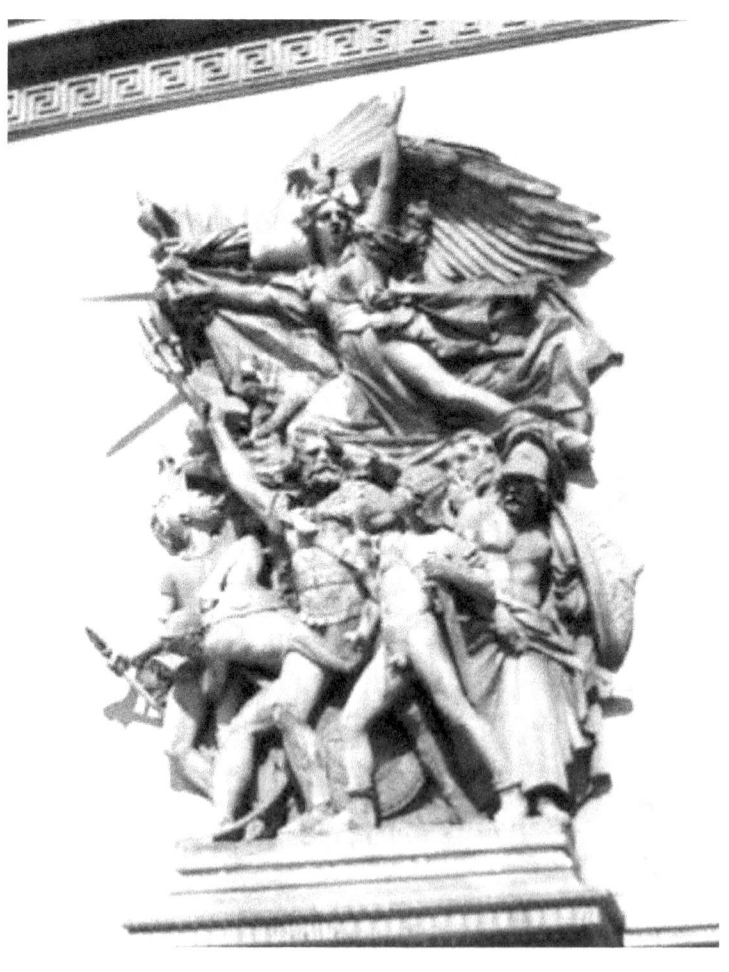

"In this epic work – rooted in public sentiment and
patriotism – the shouting figure of *the Marseillaise* is
incomparable for its passion and movement."
... Bazin, *History of World Sculpture*, 1968, p 421

Monumental high-relief*, Arch of Triumph – Paris
French orig., 1833-36 – Romantic/ Realism/ Baroque
Height: 42' ft., Width 26 ft. – marble
Sculptor: Francois Rude [1784-1855]

*more than half of figure/volume projects from vertical
surface

Napoleon assumed leadership of France in 1799 and
crowned himself in 1804. In 1806, he began construction of
the Arch ... to commemorate military victories of the revolutionary armies and his empire. Over next 30 years, kings
Louis 18th and Louis Philippe continued and finished it.
[Smith, p 157, 190]

The Jansons state: "Francois Rude's nationalistic fervor explodes
out at us in his <u>masterpiece</u>. Rude's scene ... evokes an eternal,
all-powerful nationalistic spirit that emanates from the people and
arises as need requires." [*Basic History of Western Art*, p 473-74]

Today, *the Departure of the Volunteers* – facing east down the
Champs-Elysees toward the Place de la Concorde – is famed as <u>the
finest work on the Arch of Triumph</u>.

Durants' *Age of Napoleon* says: "This is one of the high moments of
19th century sculpture. Frankly imitating the Arch of Constantine
in Rome, it surpassed it – and any Roman arch – in beauty, partly
because of its marble bas-reliefs ..." [p 280]

Bazin declares: "Rude was one of the masters of Romantic
sculpture ... his stone relief representing *the Departure of the Volunteers
of 1792* ... is rooted in public sentiment and patriotism, <u>the shouting
figure is incomparable for its passion and movement</u> ... Rude used
his wife as a model, crying out to her *'Louder! Louder!'*" [*History of
World Sculpture*, p 421]

Rude had received a commission to create 1 of 4 colossal reliefs for the Arch – each 42 feet high and 26 feet wide. His relief was to be symbolic of the conscription of 200,000 men by the Legislative Assembly... to defend the borders of France from foreign opponents of the Revolution of 1792. Expected 'opponents' were the emperors and aristocracies of Prussia and Austria... who feared similar citizen-uprisings in their own lands.

Hartt adds, among Romantic sculpture in the 1800s, "the grandest is *the Marseillaise*. Under the thundering folds of Liberty's flying garments, the massed figures – with their rich light-and-dark contrasts – are deployed to great effect against the cliff-like surface of the Napoleonic Arc de Triomphe..." [*History of Painting, Sculpture*, p 812]

Claudon reveals: "Francois Rude... caused a sensation with his figures for *the Marseillaise*... which were both dynamic and contained..." [*Encyclo Romanticism*, p 121]

Rude required 3 years [1833 to 1836] to sculpt the giant relief. His work initially offended a conservative element in France.

The *Encyclo Sculpt* describes Rude's relief as: "controversial in its time... his preference for deep carving violated the Arch's flat façade and effectively upstaged the architecture... the group was the most emphatic example of the new tendency... to exploit dramatic and pictorial effects and anatomic realism. Contemporaries perceived these qualities as dangerous, because they were signs of Romantic artists' rejection of sculpture's traditional public functions..." [p 1477-78]

Ultimately, the success and fame of Rude's high-relief was due to the 'supposed fault' found by these mid-19th century critics... who frowned upon its "instantaneous moment charged with historic significance". [p 1478]

The *Encyclo Sculpt* concludes: "the *Departure of the Volunteers of 1792* served as the basis for all subsequent sculpted images of the Republic and has enjoyed an unprecedented influence on French patriotic art generally." [p 1479]

Subject:

Bouvet disagrees with early critics of Rude's relief: "If Rude represented a real episode in the history of France, he nonetheless treated his subject in an allegorical manner: he employed neither costumes of the epoch, nor contemporary Revolutionary arms. Instead, the upper relief strives to achieve a universal dimension and to symbolize the struggle of a people – whoever they be – in defense of their territory." [*Arc de Triomphe de l'Etoile,* p 30]

Rude's masterpiece highlights 6 colossal figures, each clearly distinct from the others by ultra-high relief. A 7th figure is mostly obscured.

The <u>winged woman – brandishing her sword</u> – dominates the scene as she shouts the battle cry – giving warning of enemy invasion, and urging the militia to follow. She is variously described as: the Roman war goddess Bellona, the Goddess of Liberty, the Genius of Liberty, genie wearing a Phrygin cap, or Nike the Goddess of Victory [see #38 discovered 30 years after Rude created this one].

Robb & Garrison observe that she: "<u>imparts her great forward-rushing movement to the entire group</u>...a furiously animated personification of the violently clashing emotions attendant upon physical combat." [*Art of the Western World,* p 553]

The male figures, attired in Roman armor, represent all ages, from the unclothed youthful man to the old bearded man [w/o helmet] behind him who appears – with raised finger – to urge caution.

The <u>youthful man, gripping the hilt of a sword</u>, wears sandals and a small helmet. His left upper-arm is held firmly by the left hand of the largest man – a cuirass identifies him as a leader – possibly father or an elder to the youth. The basically-nude 'vulnerable' youth may be symbolic of the greater sacrifice made by the young in war.

The <u>breast-plated, heavily-bearded leader</u> also waves his helmet to order departure... indifferent to the caution of the bearded older man.

To the far right, <u>a darkly-shadowed, helmeted man carries a shield</u> ... his left arm and lower body draped by a cloak. Though his body fails to move forward with the others, the turn of his head suggests he may soon follow after all.

To the left, <u>an archer</u> stoops to bend and string his bow ... displaying the musculature of his back. Another <u>man, holding a spear and wearing a plumed helmet, sounds his trumpet</u>. Behind him, a mostly-unseen figure struggles to rein in a frenzied war horse.

Gardner tells us: "The Classical accessories do not disguise the essentially Baroque qualities of the group – the densely-packed masses, jagged contours, violence of motion. If we think here of the Classical at all, it would be of the 'post-classical baroque' of Hellenistic works like the great frieze #43 of Pergamon." [p 870]

Robb & Garrison state: "The popular name – *La Marseillaise* – bestowed upon the group is sufficient proof of its effective interpretation of French patriotism, for its forms arouse the same sentiment as the stirring lines and music of the song whose title it shares. Its Romanticism lies in the fact that it is so directly addressed to the emotions rather than ... to reason and intellect." [p 552-53]

The massive conscription – symbolized in the *Departure of the Volunteers* – secured the first victory of the Revolution against a foreign power: the Battle of Valmy, against Prussia in September 1792 ... and another victory, in November of the same year, over Austria at Jemmapes.

Sculptor:

Bazin says: "The only sculptor in the 2nd quarter of the century who had any real sense of sculptural volumes was Francois Rude ... a fervent supporter of the Revolution and Napoleon ... Rude had the epic sense; he knew how to fix a commemorative statue firmly in the changing light of the open air, or to evoke some great historical event, such as *the Departure of the Volunteers*." [p 84]

His early training was in the Neo-Classical style at an art school in Dijon, France. Moving in 1807 to Paris, he won the Prix de Rome in 1812, but did not go to Italy due to a lack of public funding. In

1814, when Napoleon abdicated, Rude moved to Brussels for his safety and remained there until 1827.

The State of France purchased Rude's first major success, *Neapolitan Fisher Boy* [1831-33] ... which led to his receiving the commission for the colossal relief on the Arch of Triumph. Though Rude created successful statuary which combined Classical and Baroque styles, he was recognized as the principal French sculptor of the Romantic Period.

As a loyal follower of Napoleon, Rude sculpted his *Napoleon Reawakening to Immortality* [1845] in bronze as a private commission [free of charge] for another Bonapartist, Captain Claude Noisot. A plaster cast is in the Musee d' Orsay. [Bulfinch, 773]

Major References:

France, A History of Art, 1984, Smith, p 157, 190
Basic History of Western Art, 2006, p 473-74
The Age of Napoleon, 1975, Durants, p 206, 280
History of World Sculpture, 1968, Bazin, p 84, 421
History of Painting, Sculpture..., II, 1985, Hartt, p 812
Arc de Triomphe de l'Etoile, 2000, Bouvet, p 29-31
Art through the Ages, II, 1991, Gardner, p 870
Encyclopedia of Romanticism, 1980, Claudon, p 121
Encyclopedia of Sculpture, 2006, Tripodes, p 1476
Bulfinch, 1996, West, p 773
Art of the Western World, 1935, Robb & Garrison, p 552-53

83

WASHINGTON ... SEATED

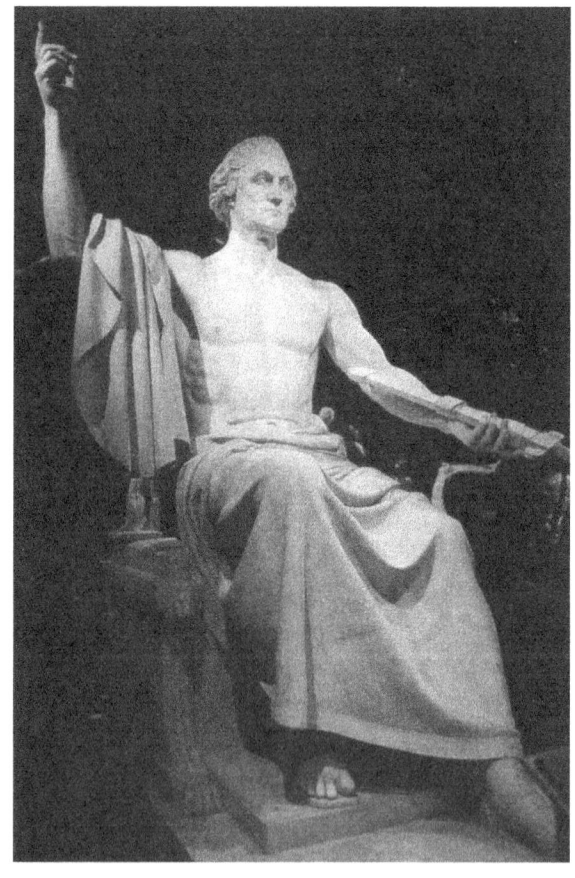

"... a splendid sculpture and superbly finished piece"
... Craven, *American Art*, p 250

1832-41 – Mus. of American History, Washington, DC
Orig. American sculpture – Neo-Classical style
Ht. 11' 4" – marble
Sculptor: Horatio Greenough [1805-1852]

Craven's *American Art* states: "Congress, in 1832, turned to a native son for the execution of an extremely important commission. The result is <u>noble and impressive ... a splendid sculpture and superbly finished piece.</u>" [p 250]

Washington's face is grave, his jaw solid, his gaze firm and steady. The wide shoulders and torso are well-defined ... an accurate portrayal of the physically-endowed man.

Self-assurance is evident in the general who relentlessly led the Revolutionary Army to victory over the British ... and served as the first president of the United States. [1789-1797]

More than any other American, his military leadership and extraordinary patience made possible the permanent establishment of a self-governing republic ... which continues to serve as a model for democracies throughout the world.

Brigstocke's *Oxford Companion* describes the statue as a "<u>landmark in the evolution of American public sculpture</u>" and says the head of the first President is a "realistic portrait ... derived from Houdon's famous bust of Washington." (as stipulated by Congress) [p 322]

Hamilton, in *Encyclo Sculpt*, informs us: "Greenough based his statue at least in part on a 19th century reconstruction of Pheidias' colossal 5th C. BC statue of Zeus." [p 715] At the site of the ancient Olympics, Pheidias had created the original Greek masterpiece in the 'calm grandeur' of the Classic style ... "which came to be ranked among the *7 Wonders of the Ancient World* ..." [p 1270]

Hamilton adds: "Greenough's *Washington* is seated with a sheathed sword in his left hand, with his right hand raised in a gesture of address. That the figure was presented as nude from the waist up ... proved to be its most crucial attribute. Greenough was interested in <u>invoking virtue and nobility</u> ... rather than portraying any single aspect of Washington's life as a statesman or military leader." [p 715]

His 'raised arm' also appears on the *Augustus Prima-Porta* #57 in the Vatican...a pose first popularized by victorious Greek and Roman generals.

Gardner says the sheathed sword is: "offered hilt forward...to symbolize 'Washington the peacemaker', rather than 'Washington the revolutionary war general'." [*Art Through the Ages,* p 868] It may also connote his return to civilian life after the war, when he declined to assume dictatorial powers.

Prior to the 1841 official unveiling of the *Seated Washington,* American sculptor Hiram Powers – the leading portraitist of his time – presented in 1835 his bust of President Andrew Jackson...also draped with a toga in the Classic manner. [NY Met. Mus. of Art]

Nevertheless...when the *Seated Washington* first arrived from Florence, it generated immediate controversy. *Chronicles of America* provides this 1840 newspaper quote: "Washington Statue, In Toga, Stirs Furor – Many American citizens are outraged to learn that a barely-clad statue of George Washington has been completed by Horatio Greenough, the expatriate sculptor who lives in Italy. He has depicted Washington in the manner of a classical figure, draped in Roman toga and wearing sandals...Americans would prefer to see the first President attired in full Revolutionary uniform." [p 313, 316]

Craven adds: "After Greenough's *Jovian Washington* was unveiled in 1841, it drew more censure than praise. Nevertheless, the precedent had been established...and in the second quarter of the 19th century, those Americans who aspired to be sculptors almost unanimously looked to Neo-Classicism as the determinant style in their work. [p 35]

[80 years later, Henry Bacon, architect of *Lincoln Memorial* #93, also was criticized for modeling the *Memorial* in classic style]

Modern scholars – describing Greenough's *Washington* – declare: "...it does have an imperious majesty appropriate to the national memory of its subject." [*Art Through the Ages,* p 868]

In 1841, when the monumental statue was installed in the rotunda of the Capitol, its heavy marble began to crack the floor. At 11-feet in height, it also 'diminished' life-size statuary of congressional leaders in the rotunda...which may have contributed to the initial negative reception.

Hamilton reveals: "Greenough himself was disappointed with the sculpture's placement in the rotunda. Poor lighting and an inappropriate pedestal prompted him to insist in 1843 that the statue be moved to another location on the Capitol grounds. It remained outside until 1908 when it was moved to the Smithsonian Institution." [p 716] In 1964, it was transferred to its current location in the Museum of American History on the National Mall.

Author conjecture: if *Washington* had been displayed in a freestanding temple – similar in stature to the *Lincoln Memorial* – it would draw a comparable number of visitors.

Subject:

During his lifetime, Washington acquired diverse titles, including: *Sword of the Revolution...Atlas of America...* and the *Sage of Mount Vernon.*
1732...born Wakefield, Virginia; wealthy parents from England
1749...after excellent education, appointed land surveyor
1751...joined military [as major] to protect Virginia frontier
1754...led Virginia regiment in French and Indian War
1755...served as aide-de-camp to British General Braddock
1755...appointed Commander in Chief of Virginia military
1758...elected to Virginia House of Burgesses
1774...appointed delegate to first Continental Congress
1775...appointed commander of Continental Army
1781...received surrender of Cornwallis at Yorktown
1783...retired to Mount Vernon
1787...delegate to Constitutional Convention, chosen its president
1789...elected first President at 57, re-elected...declined 3rd term

An example of Washington's 'creative' leadership occurred in 1781...when he devised an artifice that convinced Lord

Cornwallis – after French and American artillery had bombarded the British army in Yorktown – to prematurely surrender.

His 'artifice', drawn up with Alexander Hamilton, was recorded by Elias Boudinot [a president of Continental Congress during Revolution] in the *Journal of the American Revolution* or *Historical Recollections of American Events* [published in a limited edition of 350. New York City Public Library holds # 47]

"Genl Washington…fell upon the following expedient. He sent out Col [Alexander] Hamilton with some other Officers with a Flag of Truce…they carried with them something to eat and drink. They were met half way by a number of British Officers. In conversation, they mentioned to the British Officers their concern for them as Gentn & Soldiers…<u>That</u> the American Army had determined to Storm their lines…<u>That</u> the American Soldiery and Country People were so exasperated at the British [atrocities] to the Southward [in Carolinas] <u>that</u> they did not think they could be restrained by authority and Discipline. <u>That</u> they knew Genl Washington's humane Temper, and his wish to avoid unnecessary shedding of blood. <u>That</u>, in the case of Capitulation, the same terms the British gave our Troops at CharlesTown – with the addition of the Officers wearing side-arms and being immediately sent on their Parole to New York – might be obtained. <u>That</u> they did not wish their names to be mentioned. Within a few Hours after their return, a [British] proposal for surrendering on Terms was sent out…and the Capitulation took place." [p 37-8]

This 'artifice' is also mentioned in Schachner's *Alexander Hamilton* [1946]:

"…Hamilton and other officers sauntered over to the British lines under a flag of truce. During casual conversation – the amicable sortie was supposedly a private venture – they mentioned that an assault in force was in the making; that everyone was so exasperated at the Conduct of the British to the Southward [south of Virginia] that they could not answer for the Consequences, as they did not think they could be restrained by authority and Discipline. However, they added deftly, they knew Washington's 'humane

Temper,' and if the British would surrender now, before the attack commenced, he would certainly grant them favorable terms and hold them harmless. [p 142] The stratagem worked. A few hours later, Cornwallis proposed an armistice. On the 18th, commissioners met. On the 19th, Cornwallis surrendered." [p 143]

Prior to the British surrender, Schachner also reveals Washington's dilemma:

"Difficulties arose in a new and unexpected quarter. [French] Comte de Grasse had suddenly decided to withdraw his troops within 48 hours. Washington remonstrated that he had too few men on his own to assault a fortified position [Yorktown] and he would be compelled to raise the siege on the very brink of victory. De Grasse refused to change his mind." [p 142-43]

Sculptor:

Horatio Greenough [1805-1852] was one of the first American sculptors to receive a national commission and gain international fame.

His interest in the arts inspired him – at age of 12 – to model in chalk a statue of William Penn. In 1821, he enrolled at Harvard, obtaining a Classical education … and created minor sculptures.

Brown's *Amer. Art to 1900* describes Greenough: "…a proper Bostonian … friend of Emerson … and a brilliant conversationalist, he moved with grace in the highest social and intellectual circles at home and abroad. He was as sophisticated an intellectual as American culture produced at that time." [p 373]

When he travelled to Rome in 1825 to heighten his sculptural skills, it is said the *Laocoon* #52 and the *Apollo Belvedere* in the Vatican were among his favorite statuary. He studied with Thorvaldsen … who followed Canova as the most prominent sculptor in Europe.

After producing several busts and statues, Greenough returned to the United States in 1827 where he sculpted busts of prominent citizens … including Pres. John Quincy Adams and Chief Justice John Marshall. Both Daniel Webster and James Fenimore Cooper urged Congress to select Greenough as the sculptor of *George Washington*.

In 1828, Greenough settled in Italy and established a studio in Florence. He remained in this Renaissance city the remainder of his professional life...producing other full-size statues including *Marquis de Lafayette* [1831-32], *James Fenimore Cooper* [1831], *The Rescue* [1837-50], and a *Castor & Pollux* [1847].

He also acquired fame as an author...the phrase "form follows function" can be traced to Greenough. The *Oxford Companion to Western Art* adds: his theory of function/form "inspired architects including Louis Sullivan and Frank Lloyd Wright." [p 322]

Greenough died relatively young at 47, in 1852, of a sudden high fever.

Other important Washington statues:
Houdon's *Washington* in Richmond, VA .
Houdon's *Washington* in Capitol Rotunda, life-size bronze.
Houdon's *Washington,* Trafalgar Square, London, gift, 1921, VA.
Canova's *Washington in No. Carolina* "contributed to establishment of sculpture as a fully developed art form in America." [Craven, p 34] Lost in 1830 fire.

Major References:
Encyclopedia of Sculpture, 2006, Hamilton, p 715

American Art, 1994, Craven, p 249-51

Art and History of Washington DC, 1997, Smith, p 19-20

Age of Napoleon, 1975, Durant, p 912

Classical Myths in Sculpture, 1951, Agard, p 142-43

Wall Street Journal, July 3-4, 2010, Margaret Lough, p W12

Art Through the Ages, 1991, Gardner, p 868

Oxford Companion to Western Art, 2001, Brigstocke, 322

200 Years of American Sculpture, 1976, Craven, p 34-5, 91

New Encyclopedia Britannica, Vol 5, p 473

Bulfinch Guide to Art History, 1996, West, p 485

Rousseau and Revolution, X, 1967, Durant, p 912

American Art to 1900, 1977, Brown, p 373-74

Chronicles of America, 1989, JL Intr. Publ. p 313, 316

Treasures of the Smithsonian, 1983, Parks, p 120-21

Lightning Rods & Sideshows, 5-21-09, Weber, Book Review p 22

Alexander Hamilton, 1946, Schachner, p 142-3

Leckie, 1993. G. Washington's War, p 631-2, 638, 641, 643-4, 656, 658

Rakove, 2010, Revolutionaries, p 270

84

THE DANCE!

OR LA DANSE!

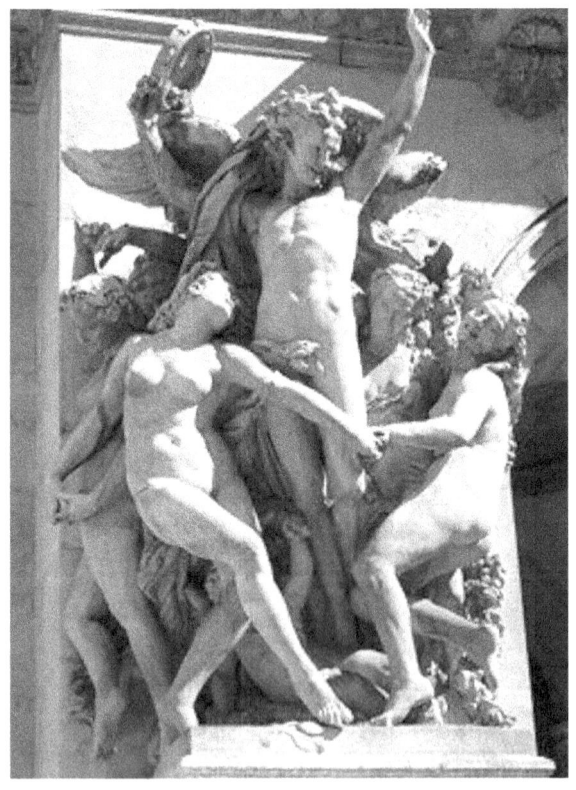

"A masterpiece of animation, rhythm and grace..."
...Bazin. *History of World Sculpture*, p 422

On façade of Paris Opera – orig. now Musee de' Orsay
French orig. – 1869 – [copy made for Opera, 1964]
Ht. 15 ft. [420 cm] – Marble – Romantic style
Sculptor: Jean-Baptiste Carpeaux [1827-75]
Architect: Charles Garnier [selected Carpeaux]

A visit to *the Dance!* on the façade of the Paris Opera House is best planned near noon...when sunlight overhead creates highlights...and deep shadows richly define the figures.

Dionysus and his circling bacchantes are *alive!* This spirited group is a delight and inspiration for all who love to dance...and frolic under the sun. Carpeaux's winsome nymphs swing and twirl in carefree abandon.

To spur their frenzy, the Greek god of wine and revelry beats a tambourine. In his name, the ancient Greeks celebrated 3-day harvest festivals of unrestrained feasting, drinking, and dancing...a ritual of mankind since time immemorial.

Celebration was well-deserved...after men and women had toiled in the fields and hills through spring and summer to cultivate grains and other foods.

Their fondest reward in the fall came from the conversion of grapes to wine...and their favorite god, of course, was Dionysus...central figure of Carpeaux's creation.

[in 1964, due to outdoor pollution, the original *Dance!* on the Paris Opera was moved inside to the Louvre...then, in 1986, transferred to the Musee de Orsay. The copy now on the Paris Opera was carved by Paul Belmondo]

In 1863, Charles Garnier, as architect of the new Paris Opera, had commissioned his friend Jean-Baptiste Carpeaux to carve an allegorical scene representing the theme of dance...to decorate one of four piers on the façade of the Opera.

Bazin says: "The result was *La Danse!* which provoked a typical Parisian scandal. <u>A masterpiece of animation, rhythm and grace,</u>

this ring of 6 nymphs around a leaping sylph [*an imaginary being supposed to inhabit the air*] reflects the round of feverish pleasure to which the Second Empire abandoned itself." [*History of World Sculpture,* p 422]

Janson observes: "*The Dance!* perfectly matches the Paris Opera Neo-Baroque architecture. Its plaster model [also, in Musee de Orsay] is both livelier and more precise than the final stone group. Its coquettish gaiety derives from small Rococo groups such as Clodian's *Nymph & Satyr* #77 ..." [*History of Art,* p 603]

Hooker states: "*The Dance!*...infused fresh life into traditional artistic formulae ... it aroused great controversy when it was unveiled in 1869, because of the lifelikeness and dynamic energy of its naked figures, in marked contrast to the static Neo-Classical groups by other artists elsewhere on the façade ..." [*History of Western Art,* p 319]

Editors of *Musee de' Orsay* [1987] reveal Paris' reaction in 1869 to Carpeaux's group: "When the work was unveiled, there was a popular outcry. The prudes joined forces with the opponents of the regime [Napoleon III]* and demanded action." [p 48-51]

"The architect Garnier himself – apparently lost in admiration for the life-like modeling – famously and cleverly said, 'Well, if the monument suffers a little from the exuberance of my sculptor, that will be a small price to pay ... but, the price would be huge if I stuck rigidly to my ideas and deprived France of a work that will certainly be a masterpiece'." [p 48-51]

Bulfinch describes the conclusion: "Following its unveiling ... the work was greeted with extreme hostility ... the exuberance of the nude figures and the fleshy realism of their bodies was shocking to a public accustomed to the bland generalized surfaces of establishment sculpture --- the other three groups of the façade all work safely within the prevailing Neo-Classical taste. It was intended that the offending sculpture should be removed ... but the Franco-Prussian War intervened ... the Third Republic was established ... the original scandal was largely forgotten ... and <u>La Danse! came to be hailed as Carpeaux's masterpiece</u>. It typifies his other works with the lively chiaroscuro of its modeling and confirms him as Rodin's principal precursor." [*History of Art,* p 323]

Six years earlier, Emperor Napoleon III had settled the future of another 'scandalous' masterpiece – Cabanel's colossal painting *The Birth of Venus* exhibited at the 'Salon of 1863' [now, in Musee de Orsay & NY Met]. Described "as audaciously erotic a nude as has ever been put on public exhibition, critics admitted this *Venus* was 'wanton' but were able to discover refinements in Cabanel's painting to counteract its lasciviousness." [*Mainstreams of Modern Art*, Canaday, p 170-01] When the Emperor then purchased the painting, Parisians rushed to view it... as did art connoisseurs throughout Europe. Prints, lithographs, and replicas proliferated... even in America, where the 4'x 6' *Venus in the Clouds* below, 1896 [signed by 'Mabel Hollister' aka New York socialite Mrs Arthur Amory Houghton] undulated over the 60-foot bar of the famed Silver Dollar Saloon... within the luxurious Windsor Hotel of Denver.

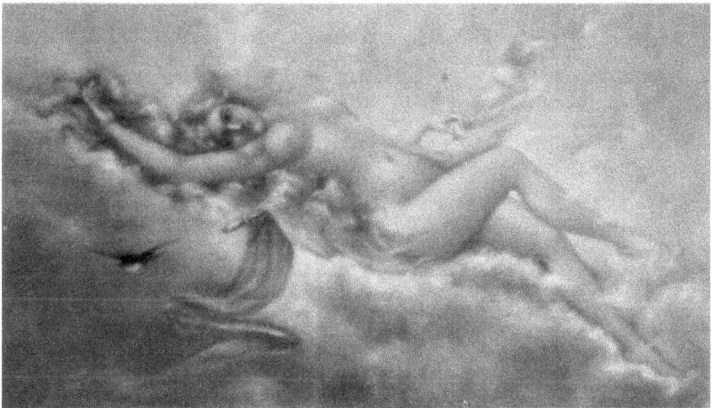

Subject:

Edith Hamilton's *Mythology* describes the Greek god of wine: "The worship of Dionysus was centered in these two ideas so far apart – of freedom and ecstatic joy... he was man's benefactor and he was man's destroyer. The 'God of Wine' could give either to his worshipers. The reason Dionysus was so different at one time from another was because of the double nature of wine. On his beneficent side, he was not only the god that makes men merry, his cup also was life-giving, healing every ill. Under his influence, courage was quickened and fear banished... he uplifted his worshipers, he made them feel that they could do what they had thought they could not. All this happy freedom and confidence passed away, of course, as they either grew sober *or got drunk*, but while it lasted it was like being possessed by a power greater than themselves." [p 72-3]

Another Dionysus festival – in the spring – was quite sober. "What was done at his Great [Spring] Festival was open to all the world and is a living influence today. No other festival in Greece could compare with it. It took place when the vine begins to put forth its branches... and it lasted for five days. Days of perfect peace and enjoyment. It was a theater; and the ceremony was the performance of a play. The greatest poetry in Greece, and among the greatest in the world, was written for Dionysus. The performances were sacred; the spectators, too, along with the writers and the performers, were engaged in an act of worship." [p 73-4]

Nearly all the mythical gods of the ancient Greeks possessed characteristics which were contradictory... not unlike mortals.

Sculptor:

Carpeaux was the son of a mason and trained with François Rude [*La Marseillaise* #82]. After Carpeaux entered the School of Fine Arts in Paris in 1844, he received the Prix de Rome in 1854. During 7 years in Rome, he was inspired to combine the Baroque style with the spontaneity and movement of the Romantic style.

He sculpted a plaster version of his smiling *Neapolitan Fisherboy* when in Italy... and, several years later, submitted it to the Salon of 1863. It was well received and purchased by Eugenie, Napoleon III's empress. It is now in the Louvre. [copy now in Nat. Gallery of Art, Washington, DC]

Soon thereafter, Carpeaux began to receive many commissions, including his *Flora relief* on the south façade of the Pavillon de Flore [1863-66]. Other renowned sculptures include the *Four Continents* and the despairing bronze *Ugolino* – both in the Musee de' Orsay.

Carpeaux also was a painter...a representative collection of his paintings may be seen at the Petit Palais, Paris.

Major References:

Musee d' Orsay, 1987, Editors, p 48-51

Mainstreams of Modern Art, 1959, Canaday, p 170-01

History of World Sculpture, 1968, Bazin, p 422

History of Western Art, 1994, Hooker, p 319

Website, Musee de' Orsay, Paris, 2009

Art in the Western World, 1953, Robb and Garrison, p 553-54

Mythology, 1942, Hamilton, p 64-76

History of Art, 1977, Janson, p 603, 605, 616

Bulfinch Guide to Art History, 1996, West, p 323

Art: History of Painting, Sculpture...II, 1985, Hartt, p 812

Musee de' Orsay, 2001, Gartner, p 40-45

85

THE STATUE OF LIBERTY

*OR LIBERTY ENLIGHTENING

THE WORLD

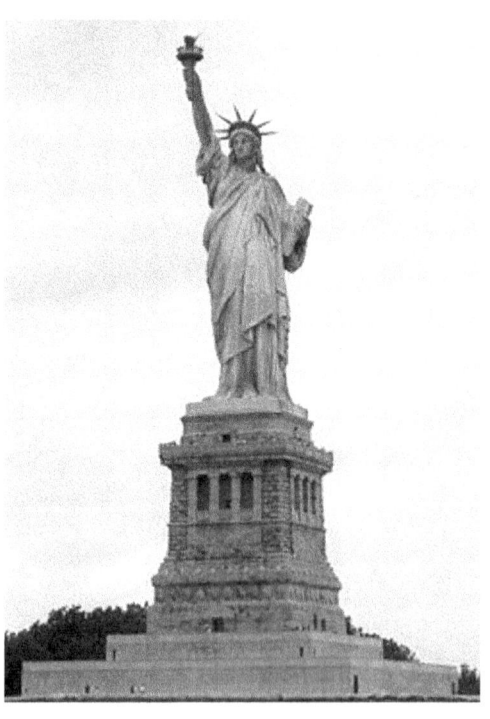

"best-known statue in North America … perhaps, the world."
… *Wonders of the World*, 2002, Burton & Cavendish, p 220-21

Gift of France, 1884 – erected 1886, New York City Harbor
Copper plates on iron frame – Neo-Classical
Statue Ht. 151 ft. [46 m]; Pedestal Ht. 154 ft. [46.8 m]
Conceived 1865: Edouard de Laboulaye [scholar & statesman]
Co-creator/Sculptor: Auguste Bartholdi [1834-1904]
Architect: Viollet-le-Duc [restorer of Notre-Dame, 1845-65]
Engineer: Gustave Eiffel [designed/built Eiffel Tower, 1889]

F or an American returning from a lengthy trip to Europe, the sight of the *Statue of Liberty* can be a heart-warming experience.*
No other statue offers so grand a *Welcome*.

*particularly, when returning by ocean-liner

Ambrosini in *Encyclo Sculpt* states: "Its flexibility as an image…its testimony to 19th-century progressive ideals…and the technical genius of its construction set it apart from all other sculptures." [p 133]

Most important…it is <u>the world's most recognizable symbol of freedom</u>.

Under unique circumstances, a liberty-minded group of French intellectuals would gift this colossal statue to the United States on July 4th 1884 in Paris. Two years later, it was erected in the harbor of New York City.

[one century earlier, in 1781, a French fleet had blockaded the British in Yorktown, and their artillery joined Washington in bombarding Yorktown…leading to the surrender of Lord Cornwallis and ending the American Revolutionary War. Freedom followed for the grateful citizens of the united 13 states of America. See *Washington*, #83]

In <u>1852</u>, Auguste Bartholdi – 'eventual' sculptor of *the Statue of Liberty* – received a commission to create a bronze of General Jean Rapp, marshal to Napoleon. "This statue – unveiled in 1856 when Bartholdi was 22 – immediately made his reputation." [*Stat. Lib.*, p 15, 18]

"In <u>1865</u>, Professor Edouard de Laboulaye – French legal scholar, statesman, and admirer of the U.S. Constitution – conceived the notion of giving a monument to the U.S for its 1876 Centennial." Laboulaye and his liberty-minded friends in Paris believed this gift "would <u>reflect back</u> to the people of France the benefits of America's freedoms." Therefore, they formed the Franco-American Union to create the statue and attempt to gain American support for their political struggle "against Napoleon III's repressive Second Empire." [*Encyclo Sculpt*, p 132]

In <u>1866</u>, Auguste Bartholdi created a bust of Professor Laboulaye...who invited the young sculptor to join his circle of political friends.

In <u>1869</u>, Bartholdi traveled to Egypt "to propose an idea worthy of the pharaohs: a gigantic sculpture of a fellah [torch-bearing female figure] to serve as a lighthouse at the entrance of the new Suez Canal." The ruler of Egypt was not interested. [*Encyclo*, p 130]

In <u>1870</u>, Bartholdi "recycled his concept of 'a huge, torch-bearing female figure" for a *Liberty* sculpture ..." [p 130]

Subsequent Events Leading to *Statue of Liberty*:

1870 ... outbreak of Franco-Prussian War

1871 ... France loses, Napoleon III abdicates

1871 ... Bartholdi U.S. trip promotes *Liberty* statue, meets Grant

1871 ... Americans offer no financing [Handlin, p 23]

1875 ... Bartholdi makes 4-foot *Liberty* model

1875 ... Laboulaye plans financing, with Franco-American Union

1876 ... Bartholdi's 'colossal arm with torch' at U.S. Expo. & NYC

1881 ... Franco-American Union raises $400,000 to construct statue

1881 ... Americans begin work on a pedestal

1883 ... Emma Lazuras pens *"The New Colossus"* for pedestal fund

1884 ... in Paris, the colossal statue is erected [temporarily]

1885 ... Joseph Pulitzer, publisher, raises final $100,000 for pedestal

1886... Oct 28, Pres. Grover Cleveland* presides over dedication.

*as NY governor, he had vetoed bill providing $50,000 for pedestal

French and American members of the Franco-American Union – rarely lauded for their contributions – deserve primary credit for construction of the *Statue of Liberty.* Newspaper publisher Joseph Pulitzer also deserves strong credit. Had Pulitzer not stepped forward, the French statue might have been installed in Boston, Philadelphia, or Washington, DC... or even remained in Paris.

The model for the face on the *Statue of Liberty* is believed to be the mother of the sculptor, which Bartholdi neither confirmed nor denied. Other sources suggest it was the face of a U.S. Liberty silver dollar during Bartholdi's visit to the United States.

Subject:

The *'official'* French title assigned by Laboulaye and Bartholdi was: *Liberty Enlightening the World.*

However, their primary intention was to 'enlighten' the people of France ... to encourage their countrymen to establish a democracy similar to that enjoyed by the American people. Eventually... the *Statue of Liberty* would fulfill this goal.

Its powerful message has again and again 'enlightened' peoples across the face of the Earth to establish democracies.

The renowned 14-line poem, *The New Colossus,* written in 1883 by 32-year-old American poet Emma Lazarus [1840-1887] is often condensed to its most powerful lines:

'Give me your tired, your poor,
Your huddled masses yearning to breathe free,
The wretched refuse of your teeming shore.
Send these, the homeless, tempest-tost to me,
I lift my lamp beside the golden door!"

Sculptor ... Architect ... Engineer:

Auguste Bartholdi created his statue in a Neo-Classical style. Its outer surface consists of sheets of hammered copper "and then the lead templates [molds] ... 300 segments that were later riveted together to create the sculpture's final surface." [Ambrosini, p 132]

The architect E.E. Viollet-le-Duc – who had restored the Notre-Dame [1845-1865] – assisted Bartholdi in designing the framework.

The engineer Gustave Eiffel – famed for his steel bridges, and later his great 'Tower' [1889] – finalized the framework design and manufactured the iron-pylons to which the sculpture was attached.

Later, Bartholdi would sculpt a statue of *Lafayette* for New York City.

Both France [on the Seine] and Japan [on island in Tokyo Bay] have erected scaled-down versions of *the Statue of Liberty*.

Conditions for visiting *the Statue of Liberty* change often. For current information concerning visiting hours and reservations, see: www.nps.gove/stli

Major References:

Statue of Liberty, 1977, Handlin, p 15-18-9, 22-3, 25, 29 51

Wonders of the World, 2002, Burton & Cavendish, p 168-69

Encyclopedia of Sculpture, 2006, p 129-33

Living with Art, 1987, Gilbert & McCarter, p 289

The New Colossus, 1983, Moreno

Chronicles of America, 1993, Daniel, p 466-7, 473, 892

New York Times, June 28-29, 2008, Scherer, p W12

The Statue of Liberty Revisited, 1994, Dillon, Smithsonian Press

Webster's Encyclopedic Unabridged Dictionary, 1989, p 826

86
THE KISS

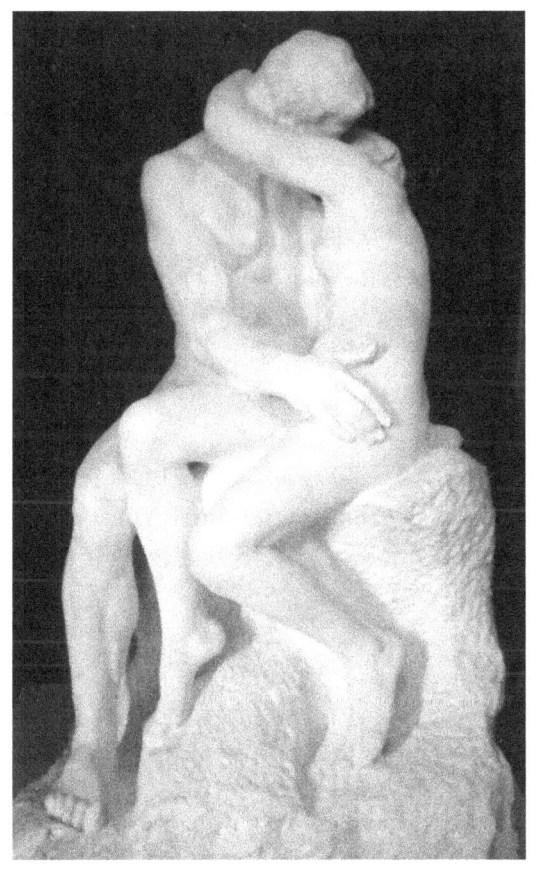

"...sometimes considered his masterpiece"
....Kingston, *Arts and Artists*, p 133

French, over life-size statue – 1886-87* – Rodin Museum, Paris
Ht: 5 ft. 10 in. [1.8 m.] – marble – Impressionistic / Romantic
Sculptor: Auguste Rodin [1840-1917[
   *date from *Rodin: Sculpture*, 2001, p 38

T *he Kiss* inspires its viewers no less than *the Thinker*.
   Visitors in the Rodin Museum often stand for some time
before *the Kiss,* then circle it... pausing often. We may imagine ourselves
in the warmth of such an embrace. When Rodin began to exhibit this
marble, it was the viewing public who gave the statuary its title.

Among 'romantic couples' masterfully carved in stone, Canova's
Cupid & Psyche #79 one century earlier compares.

When Rodin first presented this work in 1887, "its immediate success was due to its "harmonious and sensual vision of love... and the
soft voluptuousness of the embracing couple... Visitors were astonished
by the disconcerted originality of these couplings... that no [contem-
porary] sculptor had previously dared treat." [Herpin, p 13, 44, 38]

Robb & Garrison state: "Rodin's sculptures appear amazingly
real by virtue of the play of light and shade created by the expressive modeling of the surfaces... which also bestows psychological
validity upon the ideas they embody. All of this is apparent in *the
Kiss*..." [*Art of West. World*, 554-56]

Janson observes: "*The Kiss* was planned from the start to include
the mass of roughhewn marble to which the lovers are attached,
and which thus becomes symbolic of their earthbound passion.
The contrast of textures emphasizes the veiled, sensuous softness
of the bodies." [*History of Art*, p 617]

Contrary to the cold reception given to many of Rodin's major
sculptures, both the academic Salon of Paris and the public swiftly
accepted this work. "Indeed, he was highly praised for it... two replicas of it being created after 1890." [*Rodin*, p 44]

Chronology of *the Kiss*:

1880 *Gates of Hell* commissioned [from which came *the Kiss*]
1886-87 *the Kiss* is altered & enlarged from *Gates of Hell*

1888 State commissions marble *Kiss* for 1889 Univ. Exhibition
1889 Rodin exhibits *the Kiss* at Galerie Georges Petit
1889 Rodin exhibits *the Kiss* at joint exhibition with Monet
1900 the *Kiss* is exhibited in Rodin/s pavilion near Expo.

Subject:

Eisenwerth reveals *the Kiss*: "dates back to the period around 1880, when the sculptor was doing studies…for the *Gates of Hell*. The *Kiss* was originally conceived as an illustration of the story of Paolo…and Francesca…in Dante's *Divine Comedy*." [*Rodin & Camille Claudel*, p 50]

When Rodin expanded this work to slightly over life-size, he also chose to introduce a light theme…it may remain unnoticed to a hurried viewer. It is described as 'reverse reciprocity.'

Gardner explains: "Rodin's mastery of dramatic gesture…finds expression in *the Kiss*…a subtle, if explicit, essay in a contrast of ardent approach and clumsily shy response. The artist may have carried in his mind a memory of Michelangelo's *Temptation of Adam and Eve*, one of the masterpieces of the Sistine Ceiling." [*Art Thru Ages*, p 879-80]

For Auguste Rodin, the mysteries of human sensuality were a constant theme. "The exotic nature of Rodin's work has often been noted…and it is true to say that couples like those depicted in *The Kiss* and *Eternal Spring* are perfect representations of his gently erotic sensuality." [Herpin, p 15]

Here, Rodin presents the 'deliberate' female…versus a 'reluctant' male.

The woman alluringly leans into her lover.

Yet, the male, with a stiffened back, maintains distance. His right hand, without passion, rests on her hip. His other hand rests on stone.

The woman, with clearly apparent enthusiasm, lifts the heels of her feet off the stone.

Both feet of the reserved man remain planted on stone.

She gives notice of desire by placing her soft under-thigh over his knee, trapping his leg.

Eisenworth adds: "She eagerly throws her arm around her lover's neck, drawing him toward her and exacting a kiss from him. One of her legs rests on his thigh...a common symbol of sexual union in Mannerist art." [p 50]

Rodin's male may be "clumsily shy"... or he may hesitate for good reason. Her affection might be suspect...if due to generous wine. Or, he may believe she only teases...and a serious response on his part might end in frustration and embarrassment...even rejection.

Herpin observes: "...for Rodin, women were distant...even cruel, in awakening desires that they refuse to satisfy." [p 44]

Notwithstanding the male's hesitance, Rodin's couple remains among the most admired embraces in the Western world. Kingston's *Arts and Artists* says it is the "most sensuous of the many passionate couples that make up a great proportion of Rodin's output." [p 133] Gilbert & McCarter describe the lovers as: "modeled to a smooth perfection and grace." [*Living with Art*, p 434]

Robb & Garrison observe: "...contrasts in the group are eloquent of the passion animating the figures. But where the effect would be sensual and suggestive in the hands of an artist who aimed at nothing more than representation of the entwined forms, Rodin deliberately made it abstract by veiling the heads in shadow and thereby achieved a more powerful expression." [p 554-56]

Among Rodin's other embraces, the enticing dance of the passionate couple in *Eternal Spring* suggests a less mysterious conclusion.

Since its creation, *the Kiss* is one of several works by Rodin which "has been reproduced in large quantities" by reducing scale. [*Rodin*, p 34, 100]

Sculptor:

Gardner says: "Rodin, who declared that his encounter with the art of Michelangelo had been decisive in the formation of his style, was struck by that master's many uncompleted sculptures and admired the half-finished figures left in the rough block, as here." [p 880]

The Rodin Museum exhibiting *the Kiss* originally was a private mansion built in 1730 by a wealthy wigmaker, Abraham Peyrenc.

Later, it was occupied by a succession of owners until it became a convent school in 1820...and then, a secondary school.

Major exhibits of Rodin's sculptures are found in Philadelphia and Stanford University. In London, the Victoria & Albert Museum has a rich trove of his works.

Major References:

Rodin: Sculpture & Drawings, 2001, Normand-Romain, p 38, 1-82

Art in the Western World, 1953, Robb & Garrison, p 554-56

Rodin & Camille Claudel, 1994, Eisenwerth, p 50

Art Through the Ages, 1980, Gardner, p 879-880

Encyclopedia of Sculpture, 2004, p 1444-46

Living With Art, 1987, Gilbert & McCarter, p 434

Arts and Artists, 1989, Kingston, p 132-33

History of Art, 1977, Janson, p 614-17

Rodin, 2002, Herpin, p 14-5, 34, 44, 100

87

THE THINKER

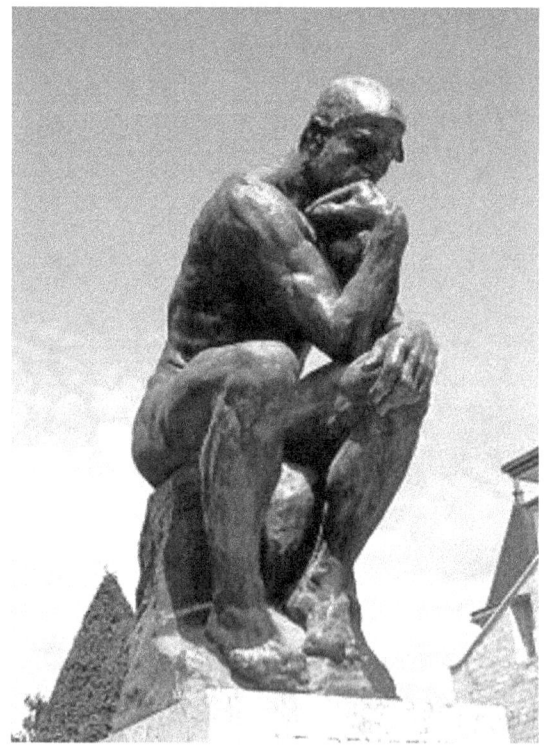

"Its attitude and powerful modeling give it ... an anguished
concentration in the face of mankind's tragic destiny."
... Bazin, 1968. *History of World Sculpture*, p 423

Monumental Bronze, 1888 – at Rodin Museum, Paris
From: small plaster figure on *Gates of Hell*, 1881
French – Ht. 6.5 ft – Impressionistic/Romantic style
Sculptor: Auguste Rodin [1840-1917]
    *numerous locations, including the Oval Office.

T his universally-recognized work of art speaks to everyone.
    In 1880, Rodin began work on his initial small-scale figure – atop his monumental *Gates of Hell*. It was 8 years before he produced the full-scale figure.

Thomas Hoving [former director of NY Met Museum of Art] describes *the Thinker* as "<u>one of the most unforgettable images...</u> <u>What more vivid single act of sculpture in the 19th or 20th centuries is there</u>?" [*Greatest Works of Art...* p 265]

The Jansons identify Auguste Rodin as: "...perhaps, the first Western sculptor of genius since Bernini." [*Basic History of Western Art*, 2006, p 504]

Rodin's style was new and distinct – a combination of Modernism with Impressionism and Romanticism. Yet, Rodin also was influenced by the masterpieces of antiquity...such as *the Belvedere Torso*. [Hoving, p 265] In 1904, he wrote: "On Sundays, when I go up to the *Winged Victory o] Samothrace* #38, I feel an eternal youth, an inspiration of happiness." [*Rodin*, p 16]

Levkoff in *Encyclo Sculpt* observes: "This seated *Thinker* became one of the most frequently reproduced [and parodied] sculptures in Western art...Deceptively, the body is unnaturally twisted so that the right elbow is supported on the left knee, resulting in a contortion that endows the form with remarkable physical intensity." [p 1445]

Gombrich reveals the initial works of Rodin: "...were the object of violent quarrels among the critics. To the average public...artistic perfection still meant that everything should be neat and polished. Rodin despised the outward appearance of 'finish'..." [*Story of Art*, p 528]

Robb & Garrison explain: "Rodin's sculptures appear astonishingly real by virtue of the play of light and shade created by expressive modeling of surfaces. [p 554-55] Sporre adds: "Rodin's textures, more than anything else, reflect Impressionism – his surfaces appear to shimmer as light plays on their irregular features..." [*Reality Thru the Arts*, p 342]

The artist went to great lengths to accomplish these effects.

Russell reveals: "Rodin was said to have worked by the light of a flickering candle, as an apprentice slowly illumined his models from head to foot in order to simulate the effect of broken light desired by the Impressionists." [*Art in the World*, p 58-9]

Rodin told his contemporaries: "Sculpture is thus the art of hollows and mounds, not smoothness, or even polished planes." [*Gardner*, 911]

As Rodin's most popular work, *the Thinker* established his name. He chose it for company at his grave.

Subject:

Considering his ultimate fame, it is surprising Rodin struggled so long for recognition. His early critics were cruel...failing to see merit in his new 'abnormal' style.

Finally, the Salon of 1877-78 accepted for exhibit his *Age of Bronze*...a standing male nude. This provided him invaluable status as an officially-recognized French sculptor. Rodin also received widespread publicity due to 'false' accusations he had cast the impressive figure from a living model. Nevertheless, this initial success led to a commission from the State of France...meaning he would be furnished a shared studio, technicians, and a constant supply of models.

Bazin says: in 1880 "...Rodin received a [State] commission for a monumental door intended for a future museum. He worked at this grandiose, many-figured *Gates of Hell* – inspired by Dante's poem – for the rest of his life. Some figures conceived for the door he [later] isolated and enlarged... the bronze *Thinker* is one of these. Its attitude and the powerful modeling give it...an anguished concentration in the face of mankind's tragic destiny." [*History World Sculpt*, p 423]

In <u>1885</u>, Rodin announced "his *Gates of Hell* would be ready for casting in six months." However, the construction of its museum was cancelled.

In <u>1888</u>, Rodin first exhibited his full-size *Thinker* in Copenhagen... but under the temporary name, *the Poet*. Rodin did not assign a permanent title to this sculpture... nor did he choose to explain it in detail. Perhaps, because *the Thinker* is "infinite", Rodin anticipated mankind eventually would find the place of this statue.

During the next decade, Rodin and many of his fellow artists – particularly Impressionist painters – formed new 'art societies' and organized their own annual 'salons' or 'exhibitions' to display works rejected for violating 'the norms.'

In <u>1899</u>, Rodin worked on a full-sized plaster cast of the *Gates of Hell* for a personal exhibition he arranged at the Pavilion de l'Alma – on the fringe of the Universal Exposition of 1900 – during which he exhibited 168 of his other sculptures, paintings, and drawings.

"The Exposition confirmed Rodin's fame as the greatest living sculptor. He became a celebrity and was much in demand – royalty, politicians, society" came to visit his studios, and "orders flowed from museums and many patrons, especially English and Americans..." [Rodin, 143]

In <u>1903</u>, Rodin exhibited his large-format plaster cast of *the Thinker* in London, and later at the Salon in Paris. In <u>1906</u>, *the Thinker* in bronze was installed in front of the Pantheon in Paris. [later, this statue would be moved to mark Rodin's grave]

The world-wide popularity of this iconic work soon became synonymous with the name of Rodin.

Its source – the *Gates of Hell* – would not be cast in bronze in Rodin's lifetime.

Sculptor:

In his 20s, Rodin thrice failed the entrance exams to the prestigious School of Fine Arts in Paris... and would spend 15 frustrating years as a novice sculptor. His inability to attend this School severely limited his access to the studios of the most prestigious sculptors…whose endorsements, in turn, normally were necessary for new artists to enter works in the yearly Salon. In addition, when Rodin did receive an early commission, it was often cancelled after his design was submitted…or when he refused requests to change it.

After Rodin spent a winter in Italy – studying the master sculptors of the past, especially Michelangelo and Donatello – he combined what he'd learned with the lessons of Puget and Houdon.

In Paris again, Rodin discarded the chisel…following the method of the earliest sculptors who used no more than fingers and palms to model clay.

Gardner informs us: "… Rodin worked his surfaces with fingers sensitive to the subtlest variations of plane, catching the fugitive play of living motion as it changed fluidly under light…His goal, as he put it, was 'to render inner feelings through muscular movement'." [p 911-13]

The result was a more powerful display of emotion and character in the sculpted figure than the world had previously known.

In 1916, the year before Rodin died, he gave the French State his sculptures and drawings, plus his other collections. The Rodin Museum opened in 1919 and is now one of the 4 most-visited art museums in France. With the exception of a Van Gogh self-portrait and a few other works, the Museum shows the art of only one person.

[in a formal garden, Philadelphia's Rodin Museum showcases the largest collection of Rodin's sculptures outside of France]

Thinker Best Viewed:

In bustling, noisy Paris, an afternoon in the tranquil park of the Rodin Museum is a pleasant retreat. Refreshments are available. Before entering the Museum, stroll about its courtyard and garden to view 4 of the 5 principal sculptures created by Rodin: *the Thinker… Burghers of Calais* #88 … *Gates of Hell…* and *Balzac.* Inside the Museum is *the Kiss* #86.

At *the Gates of Hell,* contemplate why Rodin said this is "where I lived for a whole year in Dante's Inferno." He meant it to overwhelm and it does. In the Musee de Orsay, a white plaster version of this group offers better definition than the dark bronze in the Museum garden. At both locations…visitors cannot view distinctly the small figures at the top of *the Gates*…particularly, *the Thinker.* [3-step viewing platforms along-side are needed]

In front of the museum is the full-scale *Thinker.* Sit with him. Sense why Rodin declared he "thinks with every muscle of his arms, back, and legs, with his clenched fist and gripping toes."

In 1937, the famed, blind Helen Keller – given permission to 'view' the statue with her hands – said: "In every limb, I felt the throes of emerging mind."

Major References:

Rodin: Sculpture and Drawings, 2001, Nat. Gallery Australia, p 1-80

Greatest Works of Art of Western Civilization., 1997, Hoving, p 264-65

Encyclopedia of Sculpture, 2004, p 1444-46

The Story of Art, 1995, Gombrich, p 527-530

History of World Sculpture, 1968, Bazin, p 423

Art in the World, 1993, Russell, p 58-59

30,000 Years of Art, 2007, Phaidon, p 903

Art Through the Ages, 1991, Gardner, p 911-13

Arts and Artists, 1989, Kingston, p 132-33

History of Art, 1977, Janson, p 614-17

Basic History of Western Art, 2006, Jansons, p 504-05

How To Look At Sculpture, 1989, Finn, p 81-2, 142

Reality Through the Arts, 2004, Sporre, p 342

88

THE BURGHERS OF CALAIS

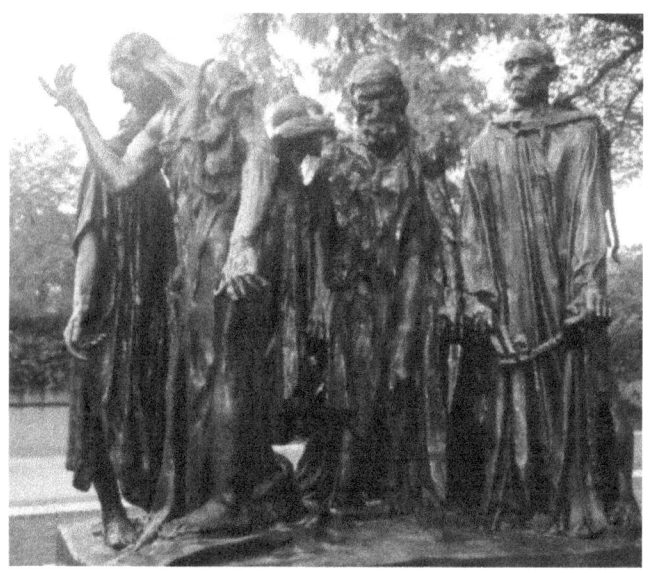

"... a testament to Rodin's greatness as a bronze sculptor."
... Hartt, *Art: History of Painting, Sculpture*, II, 1985, p 856

French, final version 1889 – Rodin Museum, Paris*
Monumental bronze – Impressionistic/Romantic style
Height: 6 ft. 10 in. [2.1 m] – 6 figures
Sculptor: Auguste Rodin [1840-1917]
* plus: Calais, Musee de Orsay, London, Washington, Copenhagen, etc.

[on our right...Jean d'Aire, hands down, stares straight ahead, perhaps thinking of his two beautiful daughters]

The plight of the *Burghers of Calais* is a well-documented event in the history of France and England. It occurred some 670 years ago at Calais [port on northern coast of France].

August 3, 1347...following 11 months of bloody conflict, the English king *Edward III* drove off the army of French king *Philip IV*...who left the citizens of Calais to suffer whatever fate might befall them.

What happened next was recorded by French historian Jean Froissart in *Chronicles of the 100 Years War*. He was only 10 years old in 1347...coincidentally, much later he would serve as 'secretary' to *Queen Philippa of England*, an important participant at this event.

Rodin, in 1884, received a commission from the city of Calais to create a monument to Eustache de St. Pierre – once the bravest [and richest] man in Calais – and 5 other volunteers...men of prominence and wealth who offered their lives to save other citizens of Calais from the wrath of the English king during the 100 Years War. The French seaport of Calais, directly across the English Channel from Dover, had long been a haven for pirates preying on English ships.

The *Burghers of Calais* display a wide range of emotions as they stand in the market square of their city and prepare to leave loved ones. Rodin treats all 6 equally...by their common nooses, sackcloths, and bare feet. They stand in a rough circle, with no distinguishable leader. All heads are presented on the same level...a few appear more pitiable than others...a few are noble. Each figure is alone in his anguish...and waits without glancing or gesturing to another.

Hartt observes: "The roughness of the drapery surfaces is masterfully exploited, in heavy folds and masses, against which the twisted gestures, taut limbs, and tragic faces communicate heroism, self-sacrifice, and the fear and inevitability of death ..." [*Art: History Paint, Sculpt,* p 856]

When Rodin made public an early model in July 1885, civic leaders of Calais were dismayed by the destitute figures ... they "did not appreciate finding in the gestures and attitudes of *the Burghers* an expression of suffering that made them appear like criminals on the way to punishment rather than as heroic martyrs." [*Rodin,* p 55, 57]

The final version of *the Burghers* was completed in 1889. [Rodin Museum website, 2016]

30,000 Years reveals: "The artist made a robust defense of his work, commenting, "I only ask to be allowed to make a master-piece ... for me the question of art takes precedence over anything else." [p 903] Kingston adds: "Rodin imagined the emotional state of the doomed men, their uncertainty and despair, and charged the group of 6 figures with supreme dignity and pathos. One of his undoubted masterpieces ...." [*Art and Artists,* p 132]

Gardner states: "The officials in Calais found the realism of Rodin's vision so offensive, however, that they banished the monument to an out-of-the-way site and modified the impact of the work by placing it high on an isolating pedestal." [*Art Thru Ages,* 1991, p 912-13]

The high pedestal disappointed Rodin. He preferred a level pedestal so the burghers would appear: "very low to enable the spectators to penetrate the heart of the subject, like entombments in churches, where the group is almost ground level ... and plunges viewers deeper into the tragedy and sacrifice of the drama." [Rodin to Dewavrin, Dec 8, 1893]

Years later, the city of Calais would lower their monument to the level preferred by Rodin.

Again, as in his previous sculptures, Rodin catches "the fugitive play of living motion as it changed fluidly under light ... to render inner feelings ... the play of light and shade ... bestows psychological validity upon the ideas they embody." [Gardner, p 911-13]

Subject:

In the crestfallen men, we see mostly resignation, despair, and even anger. One figure [Jean d'Aire] appears erect and determined, calmly accepting his fate. Though the Governor of Calais, [Jean de Fiennes], was not one of the citizens who offered up their lives that day...Rodin chose to include the Governor in the monument. His hands are spread wide, as if asking "What have we done?"

How to Identify the 5 Volunteers and Feinnes:

...Eustache de Saint Pierre – center, head lowered, hands down
...Pierre de Weissant – right arm up, head down and turned right
...Jacques de Weissant – right arm raised, behind Eustache
...Jean d'Aire – stares straight ahead, somber yet determined
...Andrieu d'Aires – holds lowered head with both hands
...Governor Jean de Fiennes [not a volunteer] – hands spread

Rodin is said to have been inspired by Froissart's *"Chronicles of the One Hundred Years War"* [1369, earliest edition] from which the following is abridged:

The siege of Calais continued for almost a year...until, in 1347, the French king Philip withdrew his army and ceded the city to the English.

"After the departure of Philip, the people of Calais were so weakened by hunger that they took counsel together and decided it would be better to throw themselves on the mercy of the king of England. So their Governor, Jean de Fiennes, went onto the battlements and signaled to those outside that he wished to talk. When King Edward heard of this, he sent out Sir Walter Manny and Sir Ralph Basset.

Jean de Fiennes, said to them: 'My dear lords, you are gallant knights, and you know that the king of France whom we serve has ordered us to hold the town and castle for as long as our honor and his interest might require it. But now his help has failed us and you are pressing us so hard that we have nothing left to eat. We must all die of hunger if the noble king whom you serve does not take pity on us. We beg you, in the kindness of your heart, go to the king of England and entreat him to spare us.'

'Indeed, yes,' said Sir Walter Manny. 'I will do that willingly.'

King Edward was eager to have news. Walter Manny began, 'Sire, it appears that the captain of Calais and his companions in arms as well as the citizens would be quite ready to surrender, on the condition that they are allowed to leave unharmed.'

'Walter,' replied the king, 'there is not the slightest hope of my changing my mind.' [the king's intention was to let the citizens starve to death]

Walter Manny went closer to the king. 'My lord, you may be setting a bad example for us. Suppose one day you sent us to defend one of your fortresses. We should go cheerfully. If you have these people put to death, then their countrymen would do the same to us if they had a chance.'

'Walter, go back to Calais and tell its commander that this is the limit of my clemency: Six of the principal citizens are to come out, with their heads and their feet bare, halters around their necks, and the keys of the city and castle in their hands. With these 6, I shall do as I please … and the rest I will spare.'

Walter Manny went back to Calais to Jean de Fiennes and told him what the king had said. Fiennes had the bells rung to summon the people together and quietly repeated all that had been said. The people began to cry out and weep.

At last the richest citizen of the town, Eustache de Saint-Pierre, said, 'Sirs, it would be a cruel and miserable thing to allow such a population as this to die. I wish to be the first to come forward. I am willing to deliver myself into the king of England's hands.'

Men and women flung themselves at his feet, weeping bitterly. Then another respected and wealthy citizen, who had two beautiful daughters, stood up and said he would go with his friend. His name was Jean d'Aire. A third, called Jacques de Wissant, who owned a rich family estate, offered to accompany them. Then his brother, Pierre de Wissant, and a fifth and sixth, said they would go, too.

These six burghers stripped to their shirts and breeches there and then in the marketplace, placed halters round their necks and took the keys in their hands, each holding a bunch. Jean de Fiennes mounted a pony – for he could only walk with great difficulty – and led them to the gates. The men, women, and children of Calais followed them weeping and wringing their hands. Outside the gates with the 6 burghers, Fiennes said to Walter Manny:

'Sir Manny, as military commander of Calais and with the consent of the poor people of this town, I deliver up to you these burghers. I swear that they have been and are to this day the most honorable and prominent citizens of Calais, and that they carry with them all the keys of the town and citadel.'

Manny led the 6 burghers to the king, who hearing that the men of Calais were coming, went out to an open space, followed by his nobles and by great numbers of others. Even the queen of England – Philippa of Hainault, far advanced in pregnancy – went out with her lord the king. Manny went up to the king and said, 'Sire, here is the deputation from Calais at your orders.'

King Edward looked at them fiercely, for he hated the people of Calais because of the losses they had inflicted on his forces at sea in the past. The 6 burghers knelt down before him and clasped their hands in supplication. One said, 'Most noble lord and king, we surrender to you the keys of the town and the castle, to do with as you will. We put ourselves as you see us entirely in your hands, in order to save the remaining inhabitants of Calais, who have already undergone great privations.'

It was indeed a moving sight to see men so humiliated and in such mortal danger. The king continued to glare at them savagely, his heart so bursting with anger that he could not speak. When at last he did, it was to order their heads to be struck off immediately.

All the nobles and knights who were there murmured in protest, but the king would not listen. Then Walter Manny spoke loudly for them, 'Noble sire, you have a reputation for royal clemency. Do not perform an act which might tarnish it and allow you to be spoken of dishonorably.'

At this the king ground his teeth. 'That is enough! Sir Walter, my mind is made up. Let the executioner be sent for. The people of Calais have killed so many of my men that it is right that these should die in their turn.'

Then the noble queen of England, pregnant as she was, humbly threw herself on her knees before the king and said, 'Ah, my dear lord, since I crossed the sea at great danger to myself, you know that I have never asked a single favor from you. But now I ask you in all humility, in the name of the Son of the Blessed Mary, and by the love you bear me, to have mercy on these 6 men.'

The king remained silent for a time, looking at his gentle wife as she knelt in tears before him. His heart was softened, for he would not willingly have distressed her in the state she was in. At last, he said, 'My lady, I could wish you were anywhere else but here. Your appeal has so touched me that I cannot refuse it. So, although I do this against my will, here, take them. They are yours to do what you like with.'

The queen thanked him, then rose to her feet and told the burghers to rise also. She had the halters taken from their necks and led them into her apartment. They were given new clothes and an ample dinner. Then each was presented with 6 nobles and they were escorted safely through the English army and went to live in various towns in Picardy. Later, the heroic Eustache de Saint-Pierre was confirmed of his possessions and given a post of special responsibility in Calais." [Froissart Chronicles, transl. Brereton, 1968, p 103-09]

For almost 200 years, Calais became an English colony.

Sculptor:

Using live models, Rodin modeled in clay each of the 6 men – first their nude bodies...then cloaked in "flimsy garments with ropes around their necks." [30,000 Years, p 903]

Before entering the Rodin Museum in Paris, stroll about its courtyard to view *the Burghers* and 3 other principal sculptures by

Rodin. At *the Burghers*, walk around them until each man is identified by his futile gestures and posture.

The blind Helen Keller, in 1937 – given permission to 'view' them solely with her hands – said they were "sadder to touch than a grave."

Currently, there are 9 other bronze casts of *the Burghers*... in London – Victoria Tower Gardens, Copenhagen, Philadelphia, Washington – Hirshhorn Gardens, Stanford Univ., Jerusalem, Canberra, etc. In Paris' Musee 'de Orsay, their full-size plaster casts are on display. Scores of museums throughout the world own copies from figures of this monument.

Avid admirers of Rodin may wish to visit his other museum outside of Paris in Meudon – the Villa des Brillants. Before it became a museum, it was both his home and a studio, although he made daily trips to his main studio in Paris. The Meudon studio was popular in its time... even Edward VII, King of England, visited in 1908. It holds the principal plaster cast figures and studies for the monuments sculpted by Rodin.

Note: check Rodin Museum website [www.musee-rodin.fr] for 'newsletter' announcing cultural events such as lectures, concerts, special exhibitions, etc. Be certain to view one of its finest paintings – *Venus Showing Cupid the Ardor of his Arrows* by Francois Lemoyne.

[Acting Out the Calais Event: at outdoor *Burghers* (Hirshorn) in Washington, the *Author* and family enjoyed reading aloud the above portion of the *'Chronicles'*. Assume roles of Governor de Fiennes, Sir Walter Meany, King Edward III, and Queen Phillipa]

Major References:

Froissart Chronicles, transl. Brereton, 1968, p 103-09
Rodin: Sculpture & Drawings, 2001, Nat. Gallery Australia, p 1-82
Greatest Works of Art of West-Civ., 1997, Hoving, p 264-65
The Story of Art, 1995, Gombrich, p 527-530

Encyclopedia of Sculpture, 2004, p 1444-46
Art in the Western World, 1935, Robb and Garrison, p 554-56
30,000 Years of Art, 2007, Phaidon, p 903
Art Through the Ages, 1980, Gardner, p 879-80
Art Through the Ages, 1991, Gardner, p 911-13
Living with Art, 1987, Gilbert & McCarter, p 284, 294-5, 434
Arts and Artists, 1989, Kingston, p 132-33
History of Art, 1977, Janson, p 614-17

89

END OF THE TRAIL

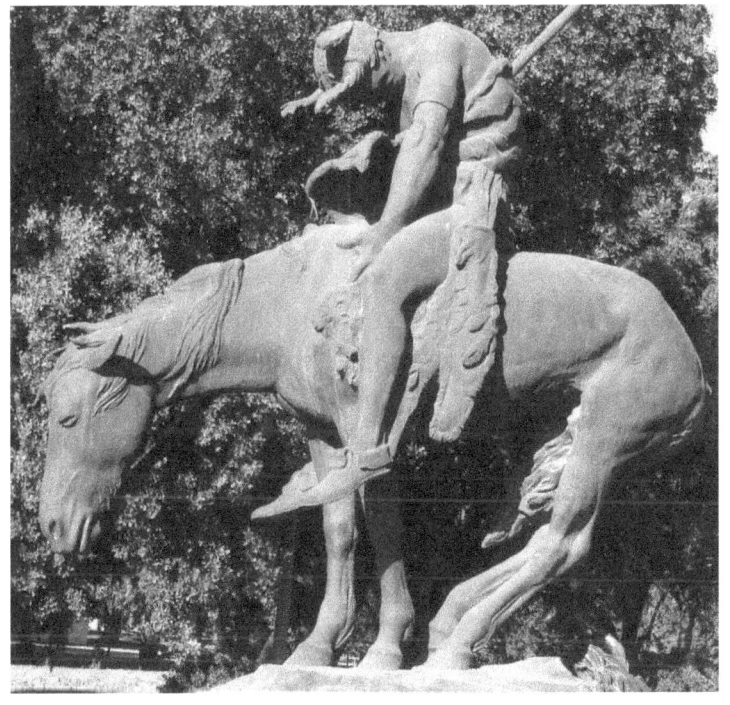

"... best-known sculpture in America."
... *NY Times*, 1953, James Fraser obit.

[frontal view at chapter end]

Plaster/stucco, 1915 – now, Nat. Cowboy Mus., Okla. City
Bronze, 1971 – also double-life-size – in Visalia, CA
From: Original 18" bronze – 1894
Ht: 18 ft. x 14 ft. x 5 ft. – Classic/Baroque/Romantic
Sculptor: James Earle Fraser [1876-1953]
    *also Brookgreen Gardens, So. Carolina, & Waupun, Wis.

M an and horse halt… heads down… eyes shut.
    The right hand of the man spreads over the shoulder of his horse… feeling a faint heartbeat. The lance is loosely held to the man's ribs by the crook of his arm. <u>The brutal wind behind horse and man will not relent</u>.

The hard wind is a metaphor for the relentless western march of the white settler.

Reynolds' *Masters of American Sculpture* says: "Fraser infused the theme of the Indian's despair with dramatic power… a lone Indian – scantily clad in an animal skin, his spear pointing down – is slumped over and can barely sit his horse. The emaciated animal – unsteadily perched on a rocky peak – peers down as if looking into a bottomless crevasse. Its tail and mane and the fur of the Indian's wrap are blown by a wind from behind… making the stance of the horse even more precarious… and the hopeless fate of the Native American crystal clear." [p 201-2]

In 1894, when James Earle Fraser completed his 18-inch *End of the Trail*, he was only 17… <u>one of the youngest sculptors</u> to create what became a world-famous statue.

Twenty years later… Fraser sculpted a monumental 18-foot, plaster/stucco version for the 1915 San Francisco Panama-Pacific Exposition. Collins & Bergren describe its reception:

"<u>One of the most dramatic displays</u> was a giant statue of a weary Native American seated on his downcast steed. The plaque beneath the statue read: 'The drooping, storm-beaten figure of the Indian on the spent pony symbolizes the end of the race which was once a mighty people'." [*Ishi, the Last of His People*, p 76-7]

The 'storm-beaten figure'... greeted 19 million visitors...won the Exposition's 'Gold Medal'... and gave Fraser immediate international recognition. [*LA Times*, 1-4-15]

[in San Francisco, Fraser followed the example of Frederic Remington who had displayed his colossal *Coming Through the Rye* at the 1904 St. Louis Exposition and again at the 1905 Lewis & Clark Exposition in Portland, Oregon]

Fraser's *End of the Trail* became an icon of the American Wild West – one of the most recognizable images in the United States – and still is.

Morrison, in *Buffalo Nickel*, reveals the Fraser "sculpture was based <u>on a sad phrase</u> he remembered about the Sioux [Lakota] being moved west, away from their homelands: *'The Native Americans will be pushed into the Pacific Ocean'.*" [p 16]

Editors of *Artists' America* explain: "After the Native American had been completely subdued and pushed aside, guilt and nostalgia led to his re-creation in a new image, as represented by James Earle Fraser's sentimental and sad sculpture, *the End of the Trail*. It is Fraser's most celebrated work...with the exception of his design for the famous Buffalo nickel with a Native American's profile on the reverse side." [p 276]

The 18-foot plaster/stucco *End of the Trail* is now superbly displayed within the Nat. Cowboy & Western Heritage Museum [formerly Cowboy Hall of Fame] in Oklahoma City.

When visitors enter its soaring, glass-paneled display hall at mid-day, they are near-blinded by unrestrained sunlight reflecting off the albino-white monolith. The harsh light serves to magnify the tragic man and horse.

Though most viewers may have seen countless images of *End of the Trail* beforehand, prior familiarity does not prepare one for the emotional force of the double life-size figures. It touches the soul of anyone familiar with the history of the American West.

Chapin quotes Civil War General George Crook, who later served in the West: "when asked what he found hardest in the Native

American Wars, he said, 'The hardest thing is to fight against those whom you know are right'." [*Great Masterpieces of Frederic Remington* p 7]

Subject:

History textbooks in America have often given short shrift [usually by errors of omission] to the treatment of Native Americans. Ignorance and shame suppressed facts.

Before the 19th century, Native Americans existed on the Great Plains in essential balance with their environment. Change began with the arrival of European fur-trappers, who cleared the rivers of beaver. Later, white hunters reduced the buffalo herds for hides...limiting the Native Americans' food supply. Finally, whites fired their buffalo guns for 'sport of the kill'. During the mid-1800s, discovery of silver and gold in the Rockies, Black Hills, and Sierras inspired a flood of opportunists from the east.

Virtually all U.S. Government treaties with Native Americans – drawn up to 'guarantee they had sufficient land to subsist' – were broken in Washington, DC.

When the Lakotas [with the Cheyenne] in 1876 took arms against the invasion of their lands, they easily defeated an attack by a unit of U.S. Cavalry led by George Custer. But, it proved to be a short-lived victory.

Frederic Remington, after sculpting a riding warrior he called *The Cheyenne*, in 1899 commented: "They were fighting for their land – they fought to the death – they gave no quarter, and they never asked for it. There was a nobility of purpose about their resistance which commends itself now that it is passed."

Fraser's *End of the Trail* was and is a painful memorial to Native Americans. It is a reminder of their ultimate military defeats...attrition through meager or spoiled rations...virulent diseases deliberately spread by white men...the introduction of toxic alcohol...and, finally, enforced existence all too often on desolate, infertile reservations.

Sculptor:

Born in 1876, Fraser's boyhood began on the prairie of the American frontier. His family lived in a train-yard, out of a railroad boxcar, until a ranch house was built by his father, an engineer working for the Chicago-Milwaukee Railroad. Frazier grew up in the Dakota Territory – ancestral land of the Lakota Nation [misnamed 'Sioux' by a French missionary].

In his youth, he played with children of the Lakota. Frontiersmen and other friendly Native Americans frequently visited their home. Fraser had no illusions concerning their circumstances. On the Great Plains, he watched the near-extinction of the buffalo and how it crippled the culture and livelihood of the Native Americans.

At the age of 8, his family moved to Mitchell, South Dakota. Fraser made friends with the 'town whittler' who showed him how to carve white chalk-stone [from a nearby quarry] into animals and people. When his family moved to Minneapolis, he won a city-wide competition for drawing and composition. They moved to Chicago, where Fraser attended a polytechnic school offering courses in architectural drawing.

At the age of 13, he applied for study at the famed Art Institute of Chicago. Its director – brother to sculptor Daniel Chester French [see *Lincoln Memorial,* #93] – encouraged the young boy; and, one year later, Fraser would attend night school at the Institute. The next year, he worked in the sculptor studio of Richard Book.

At 17, he was inspired to sculpt his 18-inch bronze *End of the Trail* by other statuary of Native Americans he'd seen while arranging displays at the 1893 World Fair. In 1897, he travelled to Paris … and the following year exhibited his *End of the Trail* at a competition and won a $1,000 prize [a fair sum at that time] sponsored by the American Art Association for American artists.

One of the judges was the American sculptor, Augustus Saint-Gaudens, who asked Fraser to become his assistant. Fraser spent 4 years in Saint-Gaudens' studio, first in Paris, [then in Vermont].

During his final year of study in Paris [at the School of Fine Arts], Fraser visited Italy and viewed the works of Michelangelo. After

Fraser and Saint-Gaudens returned to the United States, President Theodore Roosevelt in 1905 requested that Saint-Gaudens do his portrait…but the aging artist strongly recommended Fraser. The *Fraser Bust of Roosevelt*, as it is known, was a favorite of Roosevelt and is now displayed in the main corridor of the Capitol's Senate Wing.

In 1911, Fraser competed to design the new nickel. As models, he employed 3 Native American chiefs he knew: Chief Iron Trail, Chief John Big Tree, and Chief Two Moons. [Masters, p 189]…the buffalo on the opposite side was modeled from a zoo animal named Black Diamond. Two years later, Fraser's *Buffalo Nickel* became known as "the first uniquely American coin." More than 1.2 billion were minted.

In 1914-1915, he created the fore-mentioned 18-foot stucco/plaster *End of the Trail* for the San Francisco Panama-Pacific Exposition. After the Exposition, he intended to cast the monumental sculpture in bronze, to be placed on Presidio Point overlooking San Francisco Bay. However, scarcity of metal during World War I made that impossible. Instead, the plaster statue was consigned to storage. In 1919, the citizens of Tulare County, California 'rescued' the statue and placed it within Mooney Grove Park in Visalia, California.

In 1968, the Cowboy Hall of Fame in Oklahoma City acquired [by trade] the colossal plaster/stucco version of *End of the Trail* from Tulare County. After its full restoration, the museum cast a double life-size <u>bronze</u> copy for Tulare County…. dedicated in 1971 at Mooney Grove Park in Visalia.

In 1929, a life-size bronze – commissioned by Charles Shaler – was cast and dedicated in Waupun, Wisconsin. Reportedly, "The Native American who modeled for the sculpture, Chief John Big Tree, was the honored guest at Waupun's 125th Jubilee celebration on July 1st thru 4th, 1964." A third large bronze *End of the Trail* stands in Brookgreen Gardens, Murrells Inlet, So. Carolina.

There are many more notable Frazier statues: Thomas Jefferson, Lewis & Clark, Alexander Hamilton, Benjamin Franklin, Abraham Lincoln, Thomas Edison, Daniel Boone, Gen. George Patton, etc.

Fraser also sculpted an impressive, 60-foot plaster statue of *George Washington* for the New York World's Fair of 1939-1940. It was known briefly as the largest portrait statue in modern times. After the fair, its steel armature was contributed to the coming war effort. [see photos online]

Major References:

Ishi, The Last of His People, 2000, Collins & Bergren, p 76-77

www.natiinalcowboymuseum.org

Masters of American Sculpture, 1993, Reynolds, p 36, 91, 189, 201-02

Artists' America, 1973, American Heritage, p 276

Dickinson Research Center, [nationalcowboymuseum.org/research]

"Project Proposal for Exec. Committee", Nat. Cowboy Hall of Fame, Mar 1969

"Nickel Series", [usmint.gov/mintprograms/nickel/index]

200 Years of American Sculpture, 1976, Whitney Mus., p 272-73

The Buffalo Nickel, 2002, Morrison

Frederic Remington Art Museum Collection, 2001, Abrams, p 132

Great Masterpieces of Frederic Remington, Chapin, p 7

[colossal bronze in Visalia, California]

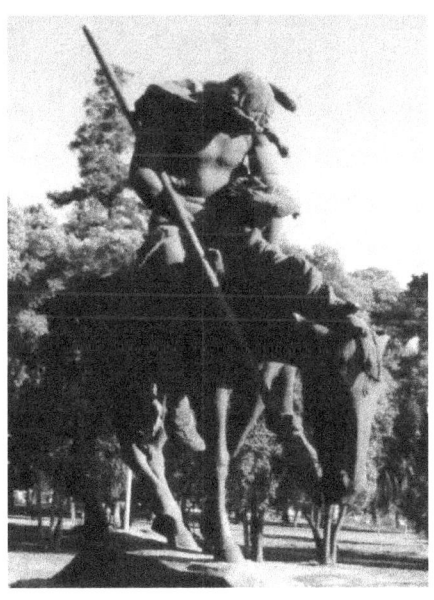

90

THE BRONCO BUSTER

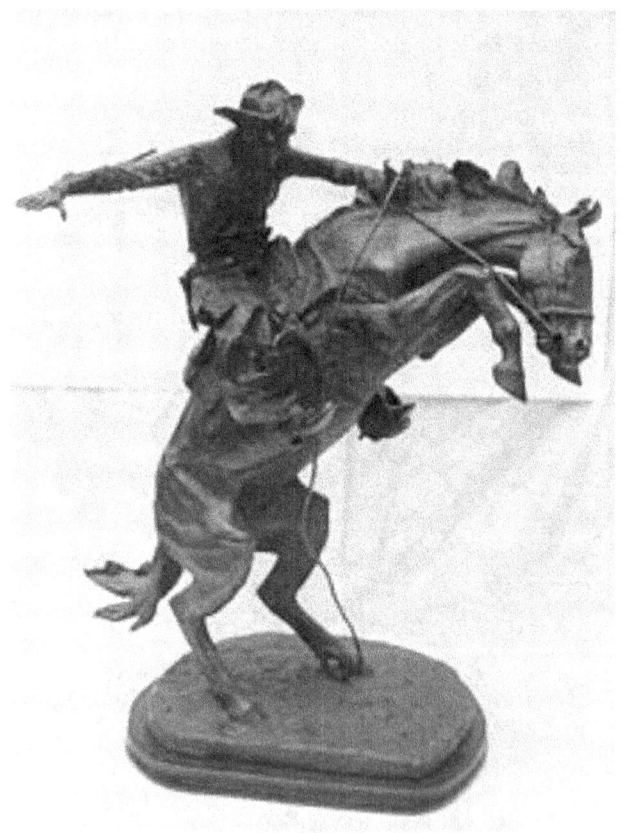

"the most popular American bronze statuette
of the 19th and 20th centuries"
... *Remington Art Mus. Collections*, Dippie, p 116

Statuette 1895 ... now, Oval Office, NY Met. Mus. of Art*
Statuette Ht. 29 in. [31 cm] – bronze – 23 in x 20 [59 cm x 50]
Life-size bronze, 1908 [Philadelphia] – Classic/Romantic style
Sculptor: Frederic Remington [1861-1909]
    *and LA Autry Center, Denver Art Mus., etc.

T *he Bronco Buster* often appears in media photos with the
President in the Oval Office. Acquired as a gift during the
Carter administration, the 'spirited' horse and rider are a constant
reminder to the occupant of the Oval Office ... expect a mercurial,
rough-and-tumble, unsettling experience at best.

Reynolds' *Masters of American Sculpture* describes Remington
as "first and foremost a narrator of the vanishing West as he saw
and imagined it in the 1880s and 1890s – the cowboys and Native
Americans, ranchers and mountain men, soldiers and outlaws,
horses and cattle." [p 218]

A bow-legged cowpuncher – if he possessed adequate courage
and acquired the necessary survival skills – often worked alone, in a
hostile, unforgiving environment. Common dangers in the late 1800s
included wild beasts, extremes of temperature, cattle rustlers, and
Native Americans fighting to preserve their land and livelihood. How
cowboys [and Native Americans] of the American West met these
challenges led to a new genre of both art and literature for tens of
millions of 'romantic-minded' individuals – in both America and
Europe – many of whom dreamed of escaping to such an 'exciting
and colorful' existence.

In 1895, Remington's 19-inch statuette was his first attempt at
bronze ... it became an "instant classic."

The subject-matter and grace displayed in *the Bronco Buster*
accounted for its popularity at the 1901 Pan American Exposition
in Buffalo, New York ... where it sold more than 200 copies ... a considerable number at that time. More than a century later, demand
for the statuette remains strong.

Subject:

The skill of an early cowboy, of necessity, included the ability to catch a wild horse and bust [tame] it... then train the horse to herd cattle.

In 1889, Frederic Remington observed: "only those who have ridden a bronco the first time it was saddled – or have lived through a train accident – can form any conception of the solemnity of such experiences. Few eastern people appreciate the sky-rocket bounds, and grunts, and stiff-legged striking..." [F.Rem. Art Mus, 2001, Dippie, 112]

Busting a wild horse begins by getting aboard long enough to tightly wrap the knees and legs around its torso. Assistance of a few experienced cowboys holding the animal in place within a narrow stall can be beneficial.

Once aboard, the wary cowboy grips both reins with a fistful of mane. His other hand may or may not hold a quirt. It might take a deathgrip on the saddle horn.

Freed from the stall, the horse instantly tries to buck away the unwelcome weight. That failing, it may switch into a twirling corkscrew.

At a rodeo, it is near impossible to follow the rapidity of opposing movements between the lurching horse and reacting rider... or predict what will occur next. The battle may last little more than a few seconds... depending on the cowboy's skill and the horse's savvy.

The rider may begin losing a stirrup... start sliding off the saddle at an awkward angle, or any one of scores of scenarios ending in a climactic and inglorious descent into dirt.

As the man, in a whirl of flailing limbs, separates from the horse, he prays not for a good landing but to be far enough from the still kicking, angry horse to not take a hoof in the head.

The next step is to get back in the saddle... and get the job done.

Before Remington, such fury between man and horse had not been sculpted with exceptional skill.

Even when tamed, a horse can be dangerous.

[... the *Author's* father related this experience from his youth. As he haltered a new horse, its jaws 'chomped down' on his shoulder. After wrenching his shoulder free, he took up a thick wooden yoke and dropped the horse in one blow – a crude but necessary remedy to 'get the attention' of a vicious equine. Recovering its senses after a few minutes, the horse came to its feet. The shoulder remained sore more than a year. The horse never bit again.]

Theodore Roosevelt, when a rancher, eloquently remarked that cowboys were: "wild spirits from *every* land ... yet the latter soon become indistinguishable from their American companions ... the passing of a few years leaves printed on their faces certain lines which tell of dangers quietly fronted and hardships uncomplainingly endured." Roosevelt also observed [in 1885] they would "shortly pass away from the plains as completely as the red and white hunters have vanished from before our herds." [*American Heritage*, p 276]

One year later, on Sept 4, 1886, Geronimo – among the greatest of America's warriors – voluntarily ended hostilities with the U.S. Government. For 15 years, he and his Chiricahua Apaches – had fought and outwitted the U.S. Cavalry. [during Remington's travels in the West, he at one time accompanied a U.S. Cavalry unit in a lengthy, fruitless search for Geronimo]

Later, at the St. Louis World's Fair, Geronimo would be a popular celebrity. His autograph was highly prized. [*Chron*, p 472, 565]

His name – exclaimed with great vigor – became a part of American culture ... and still is. During World War II, '*Geronimo!*' was a battle-cry shouted by paratroopers as they jumped from their aircraft. To this day, it is exclaimed by youths and adults in the exhilaration of acts of courage or unique physical skill. In the 1940s and 1950s, children yelled his name when jumping off high walls or fences. [the *Author's* father gave his sons paratrooper boots ... to protect the ankles]

In 1898, during the 'mustering-out' ceremony of the Rough Riders led by Theodore Roosevelt up San Juan Hill [Spanish-American War], one of the troopers – in the name of the entire regiment – gave Roosevelt an object wrapped in a horse blanket. He later recalled: "they presented me with Remington's fine bronze, '*The Bronco Buster*.' There could have been no more appropriate gift from such a regiment, and I was...deeply touched..." [Dippie, p 250] Remington, as a war correspondent and illustrator, had witnessed the decisive San Juan Hill charge.

Roosevelt, after receiving his *Bronco Buster*, accurately predicted "the cowboy would live for all time in the bronze figures of Remington." [*Am. Herit*, p 276]

When Roosevelt was elected President, he invited Geronimo and other prominent Native American chiefs to attend his inauguration. On horseback and in full regalia, the chieftains were given the honor of leading his Inaugural Parade. The passage of the proud, colorful chieftains down Pennsylvania Avenue received the most acclaim of any group. [this is on film]

Sculptor:

30,000 Years describes Remington as "the artist who created the visual legend of the West...he inspired the imagery of Hollywood movies as well as modern painters of the wilderness." [p 910]

Remington had completed 22 bronze sculptures and more than 3,000 drawings and paintings. His works often tell a subtle story, referred to as 'characterizations'. When visiting any museum with sculptures or paintings by Remington, it is an enjoyable challenge to search out the 'unique story' within each work.

He was born in 1861 and spent a great deal of his formative years hunting and fishing in the Adirondack Mountains of up-state New York...and is said to have "sketched constantly, including on lamp shades."

In 1878, Remington enrolled in the Yale School of Fine Art for 3 semesters, during which he also played varsity football and boxed as a heavyweight. When his father died in 1880, he left Yale at 19 and [with $10,000 inheritance] headed "west to make his fortune...he spent 5 years [at intervals] travelling from cattle roundups in northern Montana to gold miner camps in the Southwest and Old Mexico." [Reynolds, 218]

In 1886, Remington experienced his first creative success when *Outing Magazine* editor Poultney Bigelow – who had published Remington's cartoons at Yale – bought an entire portfolio of Western paintings from the 25-year-old artist.

Soon, *Harper's Weekly* and *Collier's* also were interested in publishing Remington's art.

Bigelow described Remington's characters as "parched in alkali dust, blinking out from barely-opened eyes under the furious rays of an Arizona sun." He may have borrowed these words directly from Remington, who authored several books based on his experiences in the West. They include: *Pony Tracks,* 1895 ... *Crooked Trails,* 1898 ... *John Ermine of Yellowstone,* 1902 ... and *Way of the Indian,* 1905.

By 1889, Remington showed his works at major exhibitions. In France ... one of his paintings won a Silver Medal at the 1889 Paris Exposition.

Originals and copies of Remington's sculptures are exhibited in museums throughout the United States. His first life-size statue – from the 1895 cast of *the Bronco Buster* – was erected in Philadelphia in 1908 on Kelly Drive. [Reynolds, p 219]

In 1909, his life was cut short at 49 ... following an emergency appendectomy.

One of Remington's dreams was to see his dramatic *Coming Through the Rye* #91 in life-size. Smaller versions are on display at the 'tourist visitor' entrance to the White House, the NY Met. Mus. of Art, and the Art Institute of Chicago. Not until 1981 was it cast in life-size ... and prominently displayed in the entry plaza of the National Cowboy and Western Heritage Museum [Oklahoma City].

The Frederic Remington Art Museum is in Ogdenburg, New York. Its website is fredericremington.org.

Major References:

Frederick Remington, 1973, Hassrick, p 182-83

Fred. Remington Art Mus. Collect., 2001, Dippie, p 112, 136, 138, 250
Great Masterpieces of Frederic Remington, Louis Chapin
Encyclopedia of Sculpture, 2004, p 1408-10
GERONIMO, His Own Story [as told to S.M. Barrett], 1984, all pages
GERONIMO, 2012, Robert Utley, all pages
A Western Legacy: The Nat. Cowboy & Western Heritage Museum
Bulfinch Guide to Art History, 1996, West, p 748-49
30,000 Years of Art, 2007, p 910
Masters of American Sculpture, 1993, Reynolds, p 218-20
The Artists' America, 1973, American Heritage, p 274-76

91
COMING THROUGH THE RYE!

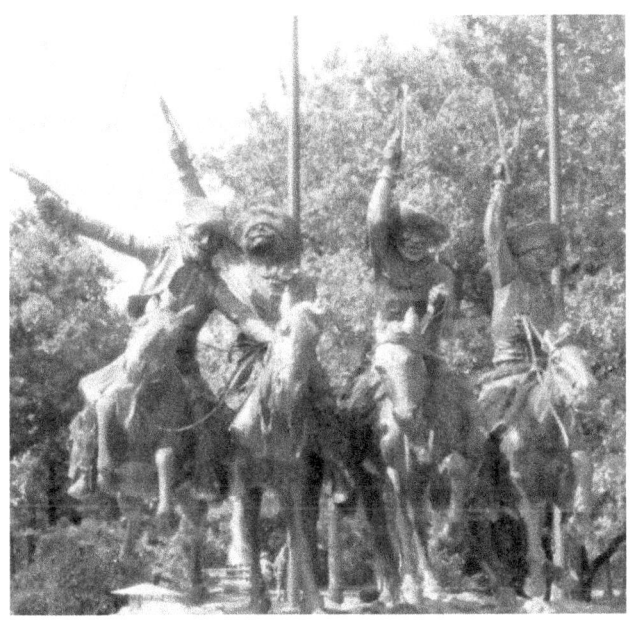

"With its jubilant air, it became Remington's most popular
multi-figured statue..." ... *F. Remington*, Hassrick, p 183

Bronze, 1902 – NY Met. Mus., White House, Art Inst. Chicago
Ht. 27 to 31 in. -– Classic/Romantic
Colossal Bronze, 1981, Nat. Cowboy & Heritage Mus, Okla. City
Life-Size, Ht. 15 ft.
Sculptor: Frederic Remington [1861-1909]

3 *0,000 Years of Art* states: "Frederic Remington established a reputation <u>as the artist of the American West</u>." He "…produced more
than 3,000 drawings and paintings and 22 bronze sculptures. As
the artist who created the visual legend of the West, he inspired
the imagery of Hollywood movies as well as modern painters of the
wilderness." [p 910]

The 'supreme unrestrained spirit' of his life-size *Coming Through
the Rye* is paralleled by only 7 other sculptures* in this compendium. In the presence of these dynamic artworks, we sense their
<u>passion</u>…and – according to our nature – would but join them!
*listed at chapter end

Craven says: "Remington himself loved the carefree life of
the cowboy…and one can sense this in his *Coming Through the
Rye*…Here a group of rowdy cowboys come shooting and yelping
as they ride into town after a long period of lonely days and nights
on the plains. They are indeed lively portrait studies of the <u>jubi-
lant hell-bent cowpokes and their galloping ponies</u>." [*200 Years of
American Sculpture*, p 68]

Hassrick states: "…it became Remington's most popular multi-
figured statue…" [*Frederic Remington*, p 183]

A contemporary of Remington, author Brian Dippie, suggests
the riders already have found their first saloon: "Here are 4 cowboys, wild, harum-scarum devils, shooting up a town from the mere
joy of a healthy existence…plus the exhilaration produced by frontier rum. They are dashing down the street, ponies at top speed,
<u>spurning the ground beneath their feet…and that is the marvelous
part of it</u>…!" [*Fred. Remington Art Collection*, p 136]

['rye' may refer to the tall rye (cereal) grass on the plains…or
the whisky distilled therefrom, also known as 'frontier rum']

The far left horse is entirely off its feet [anchored to next horse].
Its reeling rider throws out an arm to steady himself by the other
horse.

In 1902, this sculptural group – originally cast as a 31-inch
bronze – was reproduced by Remington in a colossal plaster version, entitled *Cowboys Off the Trail*…for exhibition at the 1904 St.

Louis Exposition. It drew large crowds and wide acclaim. In 1905, Remington displayed a similar model at the Lewis and Clark Exposition in Portland, Oregon … re-naming it: *"Shooting Up the Town!"*

Hassrick explains: "But wherever the place or whatever its title, the sculpture struck a festive note, recalling 'the days when the Saturday night frolic of the cowboys who came to town was the chief social institution of the week in border towns'." [p 183]

Remington's dream was to see this work reproduced in a colossal bronze. Due to the high cost, this did not happen in his lifetime. The eventual casting of the colossal bronze – now prominently displayed in front of the National Cowboy … Museum in Oklahoma City – was completed in 1981 by Cesare Contini with Franco Vianello.

Levathes declares: "Remington's work is as immensely popular now as it was in his lifetime. Pieces like *Coming Through the Rye* … have become symbols etched in the public consciousness of the unrestrained spirit of the West." [*Nat. Geographic,* Aug. 1988, p 226]

[the 'Cowboy Hall of Fame' in Oklahoma City was renamed 'Nat. Cowboy & Western Heritage Museum'. It houses the largest and finest collection of Western art and lore in the world … well worth a visit to Oklahoma City]

Subject:

Hassrick comments: "Cowboys 'hoorahing' the town were as much a part of the cattle-frontier legend as the lariat, the long horn, and the red bandana. In sight of an outpost of civilization, the boss had no way of restraining his men … who for weeks had drank nothing but dust washed down a couple of times a day with the rust-colored water they called coffee." [p 182]

Gibson adds: "… the great mass of 4 galloping, hootin' and hollerin' cowboys on horseback is supported by almost nothing—only 6 of the 16 hooves anchor the sculpture to its base." For stability, all 4 men are joined at their knees. [*Wall Street Jour,* 1-14 2014]

Craven says: "Remington knew his subject so intimately that he could give all the color of the wiry, raw-boned cowboy and his costume, the horse and its trappings, and the wild, noisy commotion of the breaking of a wild bronco. There is a roughness to his style, an unsophisticated directness in the making of his image … that seems totally appropriate to this subject. Remington insisted upon authenticity of every detail…" [p 67-8]

A related Remington work [an oil] titled "Painting the Town Red" (or "Dissolute Cowpunchers") depicts celebrating cowboys riding their horses into the saloon. This work was originally an illustration in *Century Magazine.* [Oct 1888]

Another notable Remington [oil] presents 4 horses charging directly at the viewer, titled: "Dismounted: The Fourth Trooper Leading the Horses" [*30,000 Years…*, p 910]

In museums with multiple works by Remington, viewers often 'make a contest' of seeking out the subtle 'theme' within each painting or sculpture.

In 1989, an original 27-inch bronze-casting of *Coming Through the Rye* sold for more than $4,000,000. Copies of these 'tabletop' bronzes continue in strong demand.

The public-visitor entrance* to the White House offers the same statue as a greeting. [pre-arranged pass required…contact local Congressman's office]

Sculptor:
[also see *Bronco Buster* #90]

In 1878, Remington enrolled in the Yale School of Fine Art for 3 semesters, during which he also played varsity football and boxed as a heavyweight. When his father died in 1880, he dropped out at 19 and headed west. *American Heritage* tells us: "He tried ranching and saloon-keeping in the West; he also worked as a cowboy, and did some prospecting…" [p 274]

Reynolds adds: "Remington followed the cattle trails, got to know the Native Americans, and rode with the United States Cavalry." [p 218] He is described as "first and foremost a narrator of the vanishing West as he saw and imagined it in the 1880s and 1890s – the cowboys and Native Americans, ranchers and mountain men, soldiers and outlaws, horse and cattle." [*Masters of American Sculpture*, p 218]

In 1886, Remington experienced his first creative success when editor Poultney Bigelow with "Outing Magazine" – [he had published Remington's cartoons at Yale] – bought an entire portfolio of Western paintings from the 25-year-old artist. Bigelow described Remington's characters as "parched in alkali dust, blinking out from barely-opened eyes under the furious rays of an Arizona sun." Soon other magazines, such as *Harper's Weekly* and *Colliers,* showed interest in Remington's art.

By 1889, the growing popularity of Remington's works in major exhibitions led him to Paris where his paintings won a Silver Medal at the 1889 Paris Exposition.

His first life-size statue – from a 1895 cast of *the Bronco Buster* #90 – was erected in Philadelphia in 1908 on Kelly Drive. [Reynolds, p 219]

In 1909, his life was cut short at the age of 49 ... in the aftermath of an emergency appendectomy.

Later ... the Frederic Remington Art Museum – in Ogdenburg, New York – was established by his wife. Its website: fredericremington.org.

Seven Other 'Supreme Unrestrained Spirits':

250 BC	Jockey of Artemsion #34
220 BC	Winged Victory of Samothrace #38
120 BC	Alexander Mosaic #45
1775	Nymph & Satyr #77
1836	Departure of Volunteers #82
1865	Le Dance! #84
1954	U.S. Marine Memorial #98

Major References:

200 Years of American Sculpture, 1976, Whitney Museum (Craven), p 68-69

Frederick Remington, 1973, Hassrick, p 182-83

Frederick Remington Art Museum Collection, 2001, Dippie, p 136, 138

Great Masterpieces of Frederic Remington, Louis Chapin
Encyclopedia of Sculpture, 2004, p 1408-10
A Western Legacy: Nat. Cowboy & West. Heritage Mus.(website)
Bulfinch Guide to Art History, 1996, West, p 748-49
30,000 Years of Art, 2007, p 910
Masters of American Sculpture, 1993, Reynolds, p 218-20
The Artists' America, 1973, American Heritage, p 274-76

92

THE LITTLE MERMAID

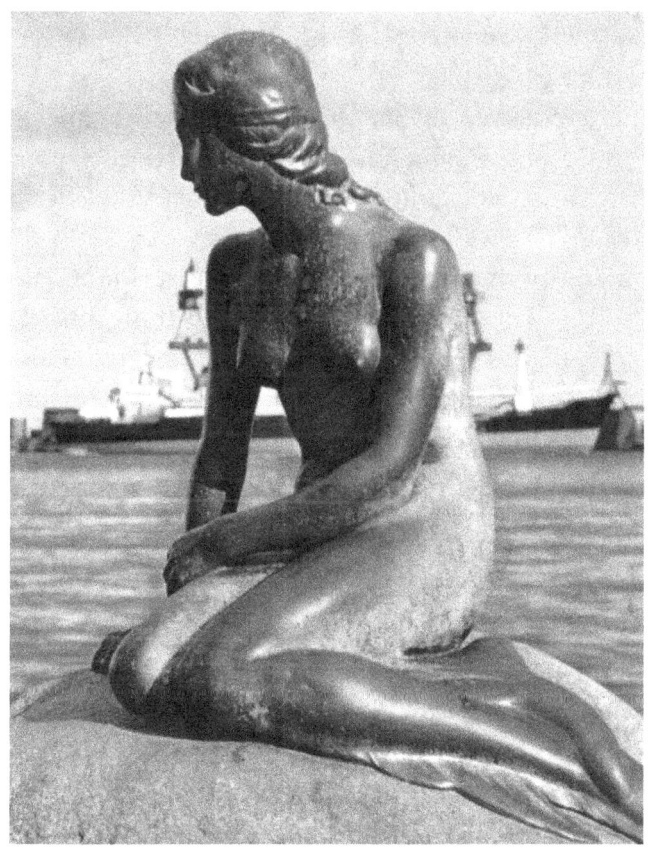

"world famous statue, stunning salute to the classic story"
...Playhouse Theatre, 1984

Danish sea nymph, 1913 – Langelinie Pier, Copenhagen
Ht. 4 ft. [1.2 meter] – bronze – Realistic
Sculptor: Edvard Erikson [1876-1959]
    *due to vandalism, a copy is displayed

This winsome sea maiden – one of the most widely-recognized and popular statues in the world – reclines on a rock in the harbor of Copenhagen. She captures the hearts of those who view her...and share her dreams.

The Mermaid was created by the Danish sculptor Edvard Erikson...borrowed from the classic fairy-tale by Hans Christian Andersen [1837]. In the story, she aspires for the affection of a human prince.

As she languishes on her pedestal along the Langeline Pier, her gaze is far across the water. Though demure and reserved, the young nymph is determined...as she ponders the sacrifices she must make to 'live' with a human.

Along the promenade of the pier, the reclining *Mermaid* is separated from her 21st-century admirers by only a brief span of water – intended to discourage human interaction. This accords with the fairy-tale...inasmuch as 'human contact' for this courageous maiden will result in either triumph...or her undoing.

Though diminutive and derived from a fairy tale, the *Mermaid* statue is often in international news...most frequently when mischievous admirers and others [mostly Danish] decide to alter her. The *Mermaid* alongside the pier is not the original. An exact replica became necessary after: "the original had been attacked repeatedly – parts removed such as arms, even the head [several times]...she may be painted in pink or other decor...even draped in a burka, etc. The original is stored in a secret location." [*WSJ*, July 27, 2009]

On occasion, the entire statue has disappeared...she is now securely bolted to a large boulder.

On May 26, 2010: "Denmark shipped its most famous sculpture, *the Little Mermaid* – not a replica, but the real thing – outside the country for the first time." The occasion was the World Exposition of 2010 in Shanghai, China. As the centerpiece of the Danish Pavilion, she became one of the most popular attractions at the Expo. [*LA Times,* 6- 27-10]

Subject:

Edvard Erikson unveiled his statue in 1913...76 years after Hans Christian Andersen's book was published. The bittersweet tale – the young *Mermaid's* rescue of the handsome prince, followed by her extreme sacrifices to win his heart – became one of the most widely-published children's stories ever written.

Over the past 175 years, Andersen's original tale has been retold in countless versions...often 'gentled' to the detriment of its theme.

In the 20th century, Walt Disney offered an immensely-popular movie with a cheery, fluffy ending...which 'loses' the original ending, plus the theme.

[the Faerie Tale Theatre version – featuring the voices of Helen Mirren, Treat Williams, and Brian Dennehy – is closer to Andersen's original story and provides a more truthful and still satisfying ending]

Edvard Erikson's sculpture portrays the *Mermaid's* yearning and loneliness...following her initial encounter with the Prince. At the age of 15, she is hopelessly in love. Her expression is both warm and slightly sad.

She senses comfort with the memory of having held the unconscious Prince in her arms...after rescuing him at sea. Now, she wishes to again hold him in her arms.

When our sea nymph shares these yearnings with her sisters, one knows the location of the Prince's palace and guides her to it. From a distance, the maiden secretly views the Prince...and yearns to become human and join his world.

After consulting the wicked Sorceress, the *Mermaid* becomes despondent. She learned transforming to a human is possible...however, to do so, she must 'trade' her beautiful voice to the Sorceress and thereby become mute...plus, the transformation cannot be reversed … and, if the Prince fails to return her love with marriage, the consequences can be dire.

Torn between love and fear, she contemplates her choices in anguish. [Disney minimizes this]

With the passage of time … she is a year older at 16 … not quite an adult. Sitting on the rock, *the Mermaid* makes a momentous decision … she will break all ties with her past … and become human.

She goes to the Sorceress where her webbed tail is transformed to legs of a human. She relinquishes her 'lovely' voice to the Sorceress. Now mute, she also must endure a new and constant pain in her feet … of which she had been warned.

Silently, she pursues her quest for the Prince's love.

[the Disney version has the Prince marrying the sea nymph … she recovers her voice … and loses the pain in her feet – all contrary to Andersen's original story]

The Faerie Tale Theatre conclusion is more traditional. When the Prince plans to marry a human wife, the former mermaid acquires a ghost-like presence … she remains 'about and near' the Prince and continues a platonic, one-way relationship. She takes comfort in this … in her mind, she has partially succeeded. When the Prince marries another, she accepts her fate with little remorse.

In the traditional Andersen ending [from the beautifully-illustrated Unicorn Publishing House book edition, 1990] she then acquires an angelic existence as one of:

"… the daughters of the air, although they do not possess an immortal soul, [they] can, by their good deeds, procure one. 'We carry the perfume of flowers to spread health and restoration. After 300 years, thus shall we float into the kingdom of heaven … and we may even get there sooner. Unseen, we can enter the houses of children, and for every day we find a good child, who is the joy of her/his parents and deserves their love, our time of probation is shortened... for we can count one less year of our 300 years'." [p 15]

The indomitable courage of Andersen's *Little Mermaid's* inspires readers and audiences of all ages... to seek their fondest dreams... to not be deterred by fear of failure... to make the most of whatever results... and to realize, that when we try our best, we can be satisfied in knowing that. There can be no regrets.

For young and old who know this fairy-tale, the example of *the Little Mermaid* may explain why the sculpture became one of the most beloved in the world.

Sculptor:

Edvard Eriksen, born in 1876, was trained as a sculptor before the age of 20. At 26, his first statue *the Sufferer* was accepted for exhibition. The Danish State Museum of Art purchased his *Hope* sculpture in 1904, a turning point of his career. In 1908, he was commissioned to create 3 marble statues: *Grief... Memory...* and *Love...* for the sarcophagus of a Danish king and queen in Roskilde Cathedral. Later, Eriksen spent several years in Florence [and nearby Carrara] developing his skill in carving marble.

Erikson received the commission for the mermaid statue from Carl Jacobsen [son of the founder of Denmark's Carlsberg Brewery] who had attended a ballet in 1909 featuring 'the Little Mermaid' based on Andersen's story. Jacobsen, smitten by the performing prima-ballerina, asked Eriksen to sculpt a 'little mermaid' using the prima-ballerina as the model. When she declined to pose unclothed, only her head was modeled. Eriksen's wife, Eline, modeled the balance.

Both *the Little Mermaid* and Rodin's *Thinker* sit... deep in thought. This may not be a coincidence.

When Erikson was 12 years old [1888], Rodin selected Copenhagen as the first city to exhibit his *Thinker*. Eriksen, born in Copenhagen, developed his skills as a sculptor in the city. If he viewed and admired *the Thinker* in Copenhagen, it is possible

Rodin's most popular statue inspired him to create his own 'contemplating figure' in 1912-1913.

The original mold for *the Mermaid* still exists, allowing damaged or 'missing' parts to be recast and seamlessly welded back onto the statue.

The famed Danish-American entertainer Victor Borge chose a copy of *the Little Mermaid* to accompany his grave in Greenwich, Connecticut.

The 'yearning for love' theme is seen in many well-known works...including: *Ares/Mars* #27......Clodian's *Nymph & Satyr* #77...Canova's *Cupid & Psyche* #79...Rodin's *the Kiss* #86...and often in *Vigeland Park* #97.

Major References:

Hans Christian Andersen, 1990, Unicorn Publishing House, p 15

The Little Mermaid, 2005, Larkin

History of World Sculpture, 1968, p 423

Encyclopedia of Sculpture, 2004, Levkoff, p 1445

National Geographic, April, 2005

The Little Mermaid, 1984, Faerie Tale Theatre (Shelley Duval)

The Little Mermaid, 1989, Walt Disney

Partnership of Sculptor Edvard Eriksen Heirs

www.mermaidsculpture.dk/thesculptor.php

Los Angeles Times, May 27, 2010

Wall Street Journal, July 27, 2009, p A12

93

ABRAHAM LINCOLN MEMORIAL

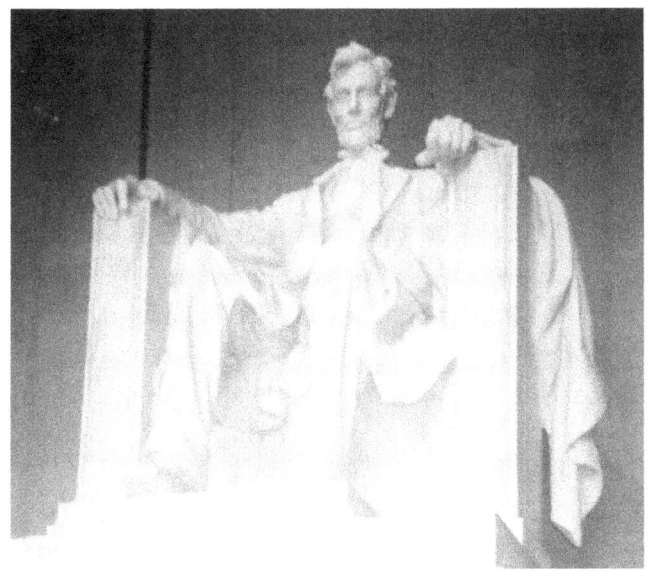

"...dignified, restrained, and moving tribute to the man &
to the virtues of tolerance, honesty, and constancy."
... *Wonders of the World*, 2002, p 171

Colossal Statue, 1922 – Lincoln Memorial, Wash., DC
White Georgia marble – Realistic style
Ht. 19-feet [5.8 m] not including 10-foot base
Sculptor: Daniel Chester French [1850-1931]
Architect: Henry Bacon [co-designer with French]

[arrive early... or late... to avoid crowds]

Visitors to the Lincoln Memorial usually converse in hushed tones; consequently, its interior is usually quieter than the Sistine Chapel.

T he rising sun reveals a meditative expression on Lincoln's face. In the early hours, some believe he broods.

By standing well back from his massive chair of state, our eyes can meet his. The seated figure is 19 feet high, atop a 10-foot base.

His exceptionally strong hands... triple life-size... symbolize the power of the American union. The left hand makes a closed fist. The other, relaxed, grips the pillar of his chair.

His face is not idealized. "... Daniel Chester French worked hard to make his huge *Lincoln* a man and not a god. This is one rumpled icon. The imperfections are hard to miss. His hair is uncombed. His tie is askew. His hands betray a fidgety disposition, and his eyes aren't quite symmetrical." [*Wall Street Jour.*, 5-24-08]

Visitors often enter the adjoining South Chamber to review his *Gettysburg Address* carved over an immense stone wall. At the southwest corner of this chamber, if we face the 16th president and study his right profile, we see a *slight smile*. In the North Chamber, from its northwest corner... we see a *sadness* in his left profile.

Lough states: "Despite criticisms that a [classic] temple was an inappropriate image in American politics, architect Henry Bacon insisted on modeling the building after the Parthenon... a nod to the Greek roots of American democracy." [*Wall Street Jour.*, 7-3-4, 2010]

The perimeter of the Memorial is 614 feet... the Parthenon is 658. The long side of the Memorial has 12 Doric columns, the Parthenon has 17. Their short sides both have 8 columns.

Subject:

Lincoln was born February 12, 1809 in a log cabin on Nolan Creek in the wilderness of Kentucky. His senseless assassination occurred

5 days after the Civil War ended. His final breaths were on April 15, 1865. He was 56.

"Now he belongs to the ages," voiced Edwin Stanton, Lincoln's Secretary of War and close friend. [*Lincoln*, McGovern, p 145]

The following Lincoln anecdote – there are several versions – explains the origin of *Honest Abe*: "He worked as a clerk in Denton Offut's store. One day, a woman bought several yards of calico. After she left, Abe discovered he had charged her 6 cents too much. That evening he walked 6 miles to give her the money. He was always doing things like that, and people began to call him 'Honest Abe'." [Cavanah, p 78]

A Civil War anecdote describes a visit by Lincoln to a hospital for wounded soldiers, both Union and Confederate. 'A young officer from the South – badly-injured and blinded in battle and not realizing who had greeted him – asked the President if he could help prepare a will. Lincoln, having been an attorney before entering politics, allowed that he'd had some experience and sat down. He wrote out the will.... never revealing his identity.'

During the war, Lincoln – confronted by seemingly insurmountable challenges – displayed consummate skill in transforming words into action. McGovern explains a key to his success:

"He was determined to leave the world a better place for his existence. And he was convinced that the best way to deal with political adversaries was to apply a friendly touch...for, he believed, a man's judgment and opinions could best be reached through his heart." [*A. Lincoln*, McGovern. p 7, 153; & *Lincoln in American Memory*, Peterson. p 31]

The 'friendly touch' often included a well-delivered joke...or humorous story, of which Lincoln had unlimited supply.

Mere words by others cannot describe Abraham Lincoln.

His actions and his words speak for themselves.

Chronology of Statue & Memorial:

1911   Congress passes bill creating a planning commission
1912   site selected at west end of Potomac Park [then swampy]

1913   Congress & Pres. Taft approve Commission conclusions
1915   ground broken on Lincoln's birthday, February 12th
1922   completed…dedicated Memorial Day, 1922

Senator Shelby Cullon – who had personally known Lincoln – proposed numerous bills in Congress to establish the commission and build the monument. Finally, in 1911, a bill passed allotting $2,000,000 for the *Memorial*. [total cost would be $3 million] Senator Cullon would die 2 weeks before its 1922 dedication…fully aware of his success.

The Commission selected as architect the young and highly-successful Henry Bacon of New York City. He submitted his plans in the fall of 1912…and recommended the self-taught and well-known 65-year-old artist Daniel Chester French to create a design for the statue. French and Bacon initially agreed on a 7-foot-tall, bronze statue. French devoted the next 6 years to creating a clay model…aided by a copy of the life mask of Lincoln's head, plus plaster casts of his over-sized hands.

In the spring of 1918, French submitted a model for an 8-foot sitting Lincoln. When it arrived, both French and Bacon agreed it was not adequate… [an 8-foot tall Lincoln would be dwarfed by the 44-foot temple columns.] French ordered 18-foot and 20-foot photographs of the statue, then mounted them on a chamber wall. The 2 men agreed the statue should be 19-feet high, with a 10-foot pedestal. And, the statue would be marble, not bronze.

French delivered a 7-foot clay model to the stone-cutting Piccirilli family of New York City… [their studios occupied almost an entire city block]. French frequently visited…climbing the scaffolding to chisel on the statue himself. Piccirilli [and 6 sons] required 3 years to cut and carve the statue by sections…from blocks of white Georgia marble. The 28 sections, weighing 175 tons, fit so well that seams are almost unseen. At the time, the finished work was the largest marble statue in the world.

When installed in the Memorial in 1922, French felt the statue was too flat, lifeless, and cold…not compassionate and thoughtful as he'd intended. On new scaffolding, he worked further with his chisel and tinted the marble ... to fine-tune and properly shade the brooding face.

French remained unsatisfied ... now, with the lighting. An outside glare needed to be neutralized. After 7 years of experimentation, he installed powerful, overhead floodlights at the back of the ceiling slats. The effect was immediate. With new and richer light, the cold marble changed ... yielding the thoughtful expression and compassion French sought.

Many historic gatherings have occurred before the eyes of Lincoln ... including in August of 1963 when the Reverend Martin Luther King delivered his famed *"I Have a Dream"* proclamation before 250,000 Americans supporting passage of a civil rights bill. The legislation would pass.

Marble sources – *statue*: white marble from Georgia ... *36 outside columns and walls*: fine white marble from Colorado ... *interior walls and inner columns*: Indiana limestone ... *floor*: Tennessee pink marble ... *ceiling panels*: Alabama marble ... *pedestal*: Tennessee marble.

For families and individuals interested in an educational *Abraham Lincoln* field-trip including Washington, Nashville, and Springfield, Ill. – see *lookingforlincoln.com* and *alplm.org*

[in Nashville, see full-scale replica of original Parthenon ... includes re-creation of 42-foot tall *Athena Parthenos*. Built for 1897 Tennessee Centennial Exposition]

Sculptor & Co-Designer:

Daniel Chester French was born in New Hampshire in 1850. Following a year at MIT, he went to New York City and spent a month in the studio of John Quincy Adams Ward ... after which French began working on commissions.

In 1874, his friend and neighbor Ralph Waldo Emerson helped him obtain a commission to create the *Minuteman* statue in Concord ... he thereby gained instant fame at the age of 24.

In 1876, French travelled to Florence, Italy and spent a year in the studio of Thomas Ball. After 2 more years in Paris studying with Fine Arts Academy sculptor Mercie, he returned to the United States. In 1879, French made a bust of Emerson.

In 1893, French created his sculpture *Republic* [symbolizing America] for the Chicago Exposition. He had quickly become one of the nation's leading sculptors.

The Lincoln Memorial is open every day except December 25th.

Other Notable Daniel Chester French statues:

... *Standing Lincoln*, Lincoln, Nebraska

... *Memory* (*Seated Female Nude*), 1896 and 1919, Metropolitan Museum, NY

... *Winged Victory* (15' & gilded, atop World War I Memorial). Washington, DC

... *History* (10.5' tall, plaster painted in ivory, Rotunda, Library of Congress, DC

... *DuPont Circle Fountain*, Washington, DC

Major References:

Wall Street Journal, May 24-25, 2008, Ferguson, p W12

Wonders of the World, 2002, Burton & Cavendish, p 174

Masters of American Sculpture, 1993, Reynolds, p 94-7

Artists' America, 1973, Davidson, p 230, 234

The Story of the Lincoln Memorial, 1966, Miller

The Lincoln Memorial, 1996, Kent

Abe Lincoln Gets His Chance, 1959, Cavanah, p 78

Los Angeles Times, Feb 13, 2009, "Invoking the Lincoln Mystique", Nicholas

Wall Street Journal, July 3-4, 2010, Margaret Lough, p W12

Lincoln in American Memory, Peterson, p 31

Abraham Lincoln, 2009, McGovern, p 7

94

CHRIST THE REDEEMER

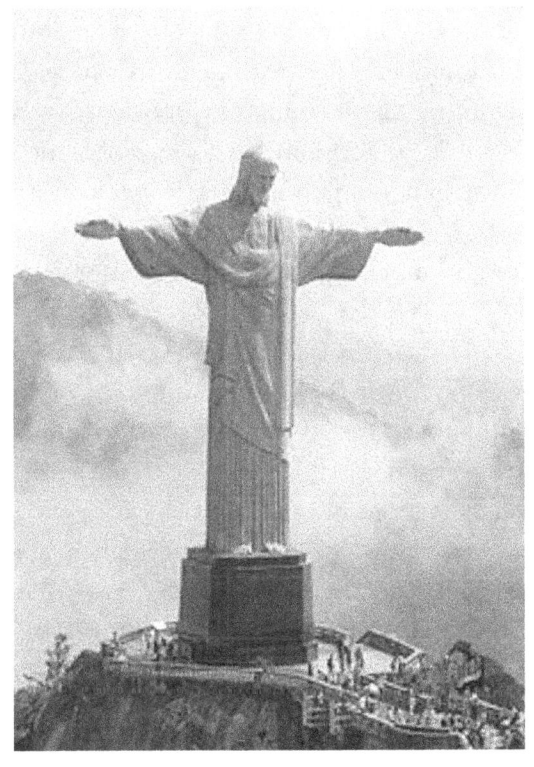

"one of the world's greatest landmarks"
... *Rio de Janeiro*, Wynne-Jones, 2005, p 26

Erected 1931 – on Mt. Corcovado, in Rio de Janeiro, Brazil
Soapstone mosaic over reinforced concrete – Art Deco style
Ht. 98 feet [30 m], pedestal 26 ft. [8 m]; Weight: 635 tons
Designer: Brazilian engineer Heitor da Silva Costa
Sculptor: Paul Landowski (Polish-French) [1875-1961]

As an icon of both Brazil and Rio de Janeiro, *the Redeemer* receives instant recognition throughout the world.

It enjoys an unparalleled setting on the pinnacle of 2,425-foot Mt. Corcovado ... near the famed beaches of the city. Ten stories tall, its extended arms provide a warm welcome to all people. The arms slightly exceed the 98-foot height of the towering figure.

Burton & Cavendish state: "with arms spread wide on a mountain peak to embrace the teeming city, the statue was intended to express both divine compassion and a sense of achievement at the centenary of Brazilian independence." [*Wonders of the World,* p 220]

[references give more credence to the 'centenary']

A visitor's first view of the figure may be from 3 to 4 miles ... where its pose suggests an Olympic diving champion ... or even an Andes condor preparing for flight. Above a thick layer of morning mist, it appears to float in midair. In the evening, floodlights illuminating the spectacular statue again isolate it in the sky.

Visitors to Mt. Corcovado [*humpback* in English] should set aside the better part of a morning or afternoon. Plan a leisurely lunch, snack or picnic on the mountaintop ... few natural dining locations in the Western World compare.

Select only clear or semi-clear days to visit the mountain statue.

To circumvent crowds, arrive before mid-morning or in the late afternoon ... Monday through Friday. [weekends are more crowded]

An inexpensive taxi in Rio is a common means of ascending the mountain. However, for first-time visitors, the Red Cog-Wheel Tram is suggested. Seats are assigned. [on occasion, tickets must be purchased with cash]

The slow-moving tram [20-minute-ride] meanders along a narrow-gauge railway … climbing through an exotic tangle of vines, trees, flowers, and bushes that offer the occasional comfort of shade as the colors of Rio unfold.

Throughout the city and along its coast, lovely dark-green camel-back mountains [of surprising symmetry] spring up. They appear as pleasant islands among the discordant structures of man. Their steepness has usually discouraged development.

The tram halts 130 feet below the statue, from where gradual walkways or escalators/elevators deliver visitors near the base of *the Redeemer*. Walkways are suggested … let the views build … unrushed. Sunglasses and hats/visors are essential.

Visit the statue first … the 'views to infinity' will stay.

The Redeemer's sudden height and immensity overwhelms. Camera buffs contend with sharply-ascending viewpoints by lying down on their backs.

When staring at the statue begins to strain the neck, transfer attention to other wonders of Rio de Janeiro.

The brilliant blue Atlantic stretches forever. Light blue lagoons weave among the deep-greens humpbacks and man's creations. Views in every direction are enthralling.

Botting asserts: "…from here you look down on the most dazzling urban panorama … poised between air and water. Rio seems a dream city – the most beautiful in the world." [*Rio de Janeiro*, 1978, p 22] The *Author* concurs.

The Redeemer faces the deep-green pinnacle of Mt. Sugarloaf on the edge of the gleaming Atlantic … 3 miles distant … though it seems nearer. Sugarloaf also has a tram. Take it, following an evening dinner, for the night-view back at Mt. Corcovado. [night helicopter tours are available at Sugarloaf]

The right arm of *the Redeemer* points over a wide lagoon to the white sands of Ipanema Beach … immortalized by poet Vinicius de Morales and songwriter Tom Jobim. Day after day, they were enamored by the same vision: "A beautiful schoolgirl walking past their favorite haunt [café] on her way to the beach." The result was *'The*

Girl from Ipanema'. The cafe is easy to find … as it assumed the title of the song.

To the far left is the 2.5-mile-long stretch of white sand known as Rio's favorite playground, Copacabana Beach … stretching from Ipanema to Sugarloaf. On the Copacabana, bikinis compete for attention [and often lose] with the feet of fuss-volleyball enthusiasts … who use only a bare foot to both serve and volley over a high net.

The Redeemer's other arm extends northward, pointing over the broad city to a coastal horizon that wraps around blue water and mountains like no other place in the world. A distant second is lovely, charming San Francisco.

Subject:

In the mid-1850s, Pedro Maria Boss first suggested such a statue. In 1921, a group of citizens began raising donations to build it. From several proposals, a statue of Christ with welcoming arms was selected. The Brazilian architect and engineer Heitor da Silva Costa created a general design. In 1924 and 1925, he began discussions with the French-Polish sculptor Paul Landowski [of Paris] … who submitted specific designs.

The monument's surface would be reinforced concrete with an outer layer of soapstone tiles … made in France. In 1927, Landowski commenced work … which continued until 1931 at a cost of $250,000. Dedicated on October 12, 1931, *the Redeemer* was recognized as the largest Art Deco sculpture in the world at the time. In 2006, its 75th anniversary, a small chapel was placed below the statue for weddings and baptisms.

Sunlight gives the statue's surface a greyish off-white. In the shadow of clouds, it can become close to black. At night, floodlights transform it to stark-white … a beacon visible to ships 100 miles off the coast.

Due to strong winds, heavy tropical rains, lightning strikes, and sun exposure, the soapstone mosaic covering the statue receives periodic restoration.

Sculptor:

In 1875, Paul Landowski was born of Polish parents in Paris. Initially interested in philosophy and drama, he switched to drawing and entered the Academy Julian in 1893. By 1895, his skill led to acceptance in the Ecole des Beaux Arts [School of Fine Arts].

With his *Fighting David* in 1900, he earned the Prix de Rome for sculpture and 4 years attendance at the Villa Medici in Rome. During this time, he travelled to Tunisia and completed 3 bronzes: *the Orange Thief... Bedouin with a Jug...* and *the Blind Water Carriers.*

Upon his return to Paris, Landowski sculpted the *Sons of Cain* for which he received critical acclaim at the yearly Salon and wider recognition at 31. When the state of France purchased this work, it was installed in the Jardins [*Garden*] des Tuileries. This success was followed by the *Monument to Unknown Artists...* installed at the Pantheon in Paris... and the *Reformation Wall* [co-created with Henri Bouchard] now in Geneva, Switzerland.

In 1912, he completed matching statues – *Agriculture* and *Industry* – for the façade of the Piratini Palace in Porto Alegre, Brazil. This success helped earn him the eventual commission for *the Redeemer.*

At the end of World War I, Landowski sculpted a series of monuments to the fallen... including *The Phantoms* [8 giant granite figures] on the battlefield of Butte de Chalmont. He also created monuments to heroic accomplishments of modern man, including the *Monument to Wilbur Wright and the Forerunners of Aviation* erected at Le Mans in 1920.

In 1933, Landowski was named director of the Académie de France in Rome... and, later in 1937, served as the director of the Ecole des Beaux-Arts.

Major References:

Rio de Janeiro, 2005, Wynne-Jones, p 26-29

Wonders of the World, 2002, Burton & Cavendish, p 220-21
Rio de Janeiro, 1996, Kent, p 4-7, 16, 57
Rio Days, 2006, Lieberman, San Diego Union, p D1
Brazil's Towering Icon, 2007, U.S. News & World Report, p 59
Latin America's Bright Future, 2009, Kraul, Los Angeles Times, p B2
Rio de Janeiro, 1978, Botting, p 22

95

RECUMBENT (RECLINING) FIGURE

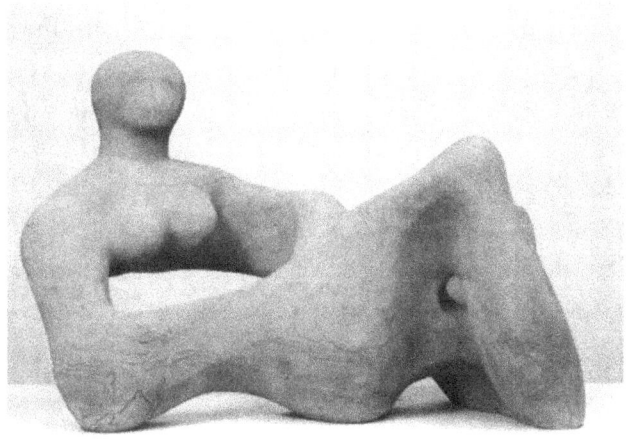

H. Moore's "…work found virtually universal favor. It was
loved by people the world over – and not least by those
who had never looked at the work of another sculptor."
…John Russell, art critic, *New York Times*, Sept 1, 1986

Recumbent Figure [1938] – now, Tate Museum, London*
Length: 52 in [133 cm] – green Hornton stone – Modernism
Sculptor: Henry Moore [1898-1986]

*Moore's works are found in major cities, museums, and
parks

At the *Recumbent Figure* in the Tate, we quickly recognize her
head, bust, and arms…then the broad hip and thigh…plus a
thin knee and widening calf.

Is this a mother watching over her children? A woman preparing to give birth? A reclining woman at rest, inviting us to join her? It could be any of the three...and many more.

Henry Moore's work is deliberately mysterious...offering a multitude of meanings. He invites us to discover whatever we wish. This is his gift to us.

When the *reader*–with family or friends – visits the Tate Museum in London, bring them to Moore's *Recumbent Figure*. Ask each person to silently study the reclining *Figure* for 10 to 15 seconds...then briefly describe what they see. All interpretations can be respected. Expect surprises...humor...honesty...feelings, etc.

Moore's surprises appear in public parks throughout the world. His reclining figures often prove as irresistible to adults as they are to children. They invite us: *Come play with me...climb on me...enjoy me...rest on me.*

Interaction with Moore's abstract works is expected in public parks.

Gaitlein in *Living with Art* says: "Moore's particular fascination lay in abstracting the body to explore its visual harmonies with landscape...especially with the sea-smoothed rock formations of his native English coast." [p 270]

Lynton suggests: "The timeless theme of women – lover, earth-goddess, and giver of life – dominates [almost] all Moore's work..." [*History of Art*, Myers, p 872]

The Tate Museum describes their *Figure* by Moore as "one of the earliest works in which Moore shows the female figure undulating like the landscape. It was commissioned by the architect Serge Chermayeff to stand on the terrace of his home on the Downs. Visually, the figure would have acted as a bridge between the rolling hills and the ultra-modern house." [Tate brochure, 2007]

Moore adds: "My figure looked out across a great sweep of the Downs, and her gaze gathered in the horizon. The sculpture had no specific relationship to the architecture. It had its own identity...I think it became a humanizing element; it became a mediator between modern house and ageless land." [*European Sculpture...*, Valantiner, p 27-8]

Later, in 1955, Moore declared: "I would rather have a piece of my sculpture put in a landscape, almost any landscape, than in the most beautiful building I know."

Kosinski declares: "Moore's <u>staggering success and popularity define his reputation and simultaneously render the man and his work untouchable... beyond critical discourse</u>." [*Henry Moore: Sculpting...*, p 21]

However, some early critics were not complimentary. They called his colossal reclining figure in Paris – created for UNESCO's headquarters in 1956-58 – an "eroded dowager" and an "antiquated modernity." A half-century later, the 2004 *Encyclopedia of Sculpture* selected this work as one of 150 sculptures considered <u>most notable</u> in the Western World. [p 1121-23]

The term "antiquated modernity" references that Moore's work has been compared to Cycladic art – from 2750 to 2250 BC – discovered on a ring of islands near Delos in the south Aegean Sea.

Burn says: "... these are the figures whose great, elemental simplicity was so admired by... Henry Moore. The finest Cycladic figurines are very striking in their restraint and quiet power. Since the majority are female – some are pregnant and the genital area is often strongly marked – it is reasonable to suppose that they are associated with fertility, but exactly how they were used will probably always remain a mystery." [*Brit. Mus. Book of Greek & Roman Ar,t* p 8-9, 12]

Finn describes visits with Moore: "His personal treasures in his home included a collection of Cycladic sculpture, a number of excellent African and Oceanic sculptures, several Rodin sculptures, a great stone carving from a medieval church, an ancient sculpture of a lynx, and a miscellany of stones... <u>these were among the sources of his inspiration, and out of them he created what became the archetypal sculptural forms of his time</u>." [*How To Look at Sculpture,* p 113-15]

Finn advises: "Moore's sculptures are mysterious. Each is an encyclopedia of aesthetic experiences. One can look at it endlessly and always find something new to appreciate. He sometimes gave different explanations for the same sculpture, almost as if they were ideas that occurred to him after he produced his work…indeed Moore's work makes us wonder if the greatness of any sculpture may be measured by the number of spellbinding discoveries one can make in it." [p 115, 119]

Valantiner comments: "More than any other contemporary sculptor, he <u>expresses our deep longing for a closer connection with the elemental forces of nature</u> as found in primeval deserts, mountains, and forests, away from cities…Moore's sculptures conjure up the spirit of the wild, uninhabited nature in a manner never to be found in other sculptors of recent times." [*European Sculpture…*, p 27]

Moore never discouraged a wide variety of viewpoints for his works.

Subject:

Moore preferred subtle communication with his viewer. His sculptures strive to stimulate the mind. Titles are not important.

For lack of a better term, '*Moore's Madonnas'* is a term used to describe many of his most famed figurative works.

The *Encyclo Sculpt.* says: "A decision to avoid ideological references led to Moore's choice of the reclining figure motif…which, as he said in 1962, 'seeks to tell no story at all, I wanted to avoid any kind of allegorical interpretation that is now trite'." [p 1122]

Moore was strongly influenced by the countless thousands of people he had seen during World War II in 'reclined positions' within the crowded underground passages of London subways…seeking shelter during the terror of repeated aerial bombings. [Kosinski. p 22]

Finn cogently adds: "There is something glorious in the way his forms writhe around each other…as they sweep up and around…the ever graceful lines that one's eye can discover as one explores the bulges and cavities…the way the light falls on the forms, creating delicate shadings in some areas and monumental abstractions in others...the surprise of different shapes and forms appearing out of nowhere as one looks at the sculpture in different angles." [p 118-19]

Canady is conclusive: "Inside a house or in a museum, Moore's sculpture may be reduced to an effective demonstration of a theory or to a piece of brilliant but eccentric design. Out of doors, where they properly belong, they share the serene and powerful unity of trees and rocks and air, which live, and change..." [*Mainstreams of Modern Art,* p 500]

Sculptor:

Moore was born in 1898, child of a miner in the mining town of Castleford in the Yorkshire moors of northern England. In 1916, he became a teacher before going to war in France in 1917...where he 'endured' mustard gas. Returning to England, he attended Leeds School of Art.

At the age of 23, he entered the Royal College of Art. In the same year, Moore visited Paris and was impressed by the work of Cezanne. Rejecting 'classical' art, he researched ancient and primitive art at the British Museum before carving his first *Mother and Child.*

In 1924, he became an instructor at Royal College. Two years later, he received his first important commission from the London Underground Railway.

In 1925, he travelled to Italy and found he preferred Indian-Egyptian-Mexican sculpture to that of the Renaissance [excepting late Michelangelo]. He returned to Royal College in 1928 for his first solo show.

In 1929, he completed a *Reclining Figure* inspired by a photograph of a Toltec carving. In 1931, he made his first foreign sale and also became head of the Sculpture Department at Chelsea College of Art.

In 1938, Moore exhibited at an Amsterdam museum with Klee, Mondrian, and Brancusi. He sold his first *Reclining Figure* [in elm-wood] to the Buffalo Museum in 1939.

Major References:

Gaitlein, Living with Art, 2002, p 270

European Sculpture After 1945, Valantiner, p 27-8

British Museum Book of Greek & Roman Art, 1991, L. Burn, p 8-10

Mainstreams of Modern Art, 1962, Canady, p 499-500

Henry Moore: Sculpting the 20th Century, 2001, Kosinski, 62-9

The Story of Art (16th Edition) 1995, Gombrich, p 584-85

Art Through the Ages, 1991, scholars, p 991-92

Art in the Western World, 1953, Robb & Garrison, p 568-69

Bulfinch Guide to Art History, 1996, West, p 641-2

How To Look at Sculpture, 1989, David Finn, 113-19

Art of Crete, Mycenae, and Greece, 1968, Hafner, p 15

Museum w/o Walls: Henry Moore: in NYC, 1985

History of Art {Myers], 1985

96
Mount Rushmore

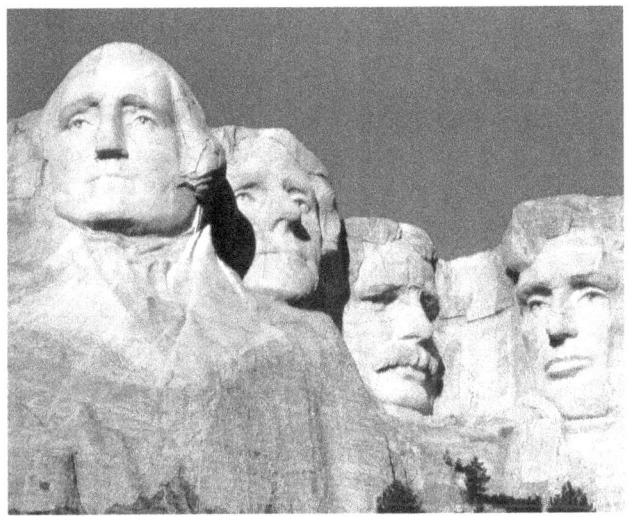

"a remarkable shrine to democracy in the Black Hills"
... *Wonders of the World*, 2002, Burton & Cavendish, p 176

Colossal Presidential busts, 1927-41 – Black Hills. South Dakota
Bust Ht. 60' [to scale of 465-foot-tall person] – Realistic style
Sculptor: Gutzon Borglum [1867-1941]

arrive at <u>8 am opening</u> ... by 9, *Jefferson* and
Roosevelt may be hidden in indistinct shadows

F rom the heights of a 1,300-foot granite cliff in the Black Hills, the towering busts of 4 American presidents watch over the land. They were never solemn sentries. Today, their faces are life-like and full of scrutiny … as if measuring the durability of their legacies.

We may envision … Washington weighs the decline of courtesy and compromise … Jefferson deplores a narrowing of democratic ideals … . outdoorsman T.R. Roosevelt scolds us for the warming climate … and Lincoln broods over spiritual intolerance.

Their vigilant eyes are as wide as 11 feet. Of the 800-million pounds of rock removed from the mountain, 90 percent was 'carved away' by dynamite … the rest was sculpted with jackhammers, chisels, and brawn.

Smith's *Carving of Mt Rushmore* says: "Created as a monument not only to those 4 men but also to the aspirations and ideals of the nation they did so much to mold, the faces together constitute the world's most gigantic piece of sculpture … at this time. Men of the same proportions would stand shoulder-even with a 40-story building and could wade the Mississippi River without dampening their knees." [p 13]

In August of 1936, President Franklin Delano Roosevelt – arriving at Mt Rushmore to unveil *Jefferson* – observed: "I had seen the photographs and the drawings of this great work. And yet, until 10 minutes ago, I had no conception of its magnitude, its permanent beauty, and its importance." [Smith, p 1]

In 1925 when Gutzon Borglum accepted his commission, he was a strong 58-year-old. He dedicated the rest of his life [16 years] to the project. Cohen adds: "The increased progress of the final years was often overshadowed by financial crises and bitter controversy … An artistic genius with an unyielding personality, Borglum himself agitated the situation by clashing with others …" [p vi]

His nature is described by Smith: "… no matter how much those who became associated with him might be impressed by his artistic talents, they soon became even more impressed by his capacity for affection, wrath, generosity, stinginess, nobility, pettiness, charm, and sheer obnoxiousness. Of modesty and humility, it was true, Borglum had but a meager supply. Of pure, mulish stubbornness, on the other hand, he had an abundance. But most of all, <u>Borglum thought big and dreamed big, and talked big, and he was not afraid to tackle any undertaking</u>. This, combined with his talents, made him ideally suited to the times and to the carving of mountains." [p 17-18]

Construction continued intermittently for 14 years…only 6 years of which were fully-productive. Some years, as few as 1 to 4 men toiled on the mountain. At times, Borglum expended his own funds. In 1937, he worked with no pay until the following year. Nearing the end of his life, Borglum set out for another fund-raising tour…and did not make it back to the mountain he loved. He died in Chicago in 1941…at 74.

The total expenditure for the presidential memorial "amounted to over $989,000…the federal government contributed $836,000…private sources, the remainder." [Cohen, 62] "South Dakota spent $2 million, mostly on roads." [Chron. p 694]

According to the wishes of Borglum, his name does not appear any place on Mt Rushmore. At the site of his first studio – some 500 feet from the mountain – his bust is mounted on a waist-high platform.

Crazy Horse & Mt. Rushmore:

The Crazy Horse Memorial – 17 miles from the 4 presidents – was begun by sculptor Korczak Ziokowski. He "took on the project at the invitation of Lakota* Chief Henry Standing Bear who, referring to nearby Mt Rushmore, wrote a letter to him saying, 'We would like the white man to know the red men have great heroes also'." [Walker, *Associated Press*, May 25, 2014]   *[the *Lakota* were mis-named *Sioux* by French missionaries]

In 1876, Crazy Horse was 34 when he helped lead some 1,500 Lakota and Cheyenne Native American warriors in the Battle of Little Big Horn…vanquishing the rash, overly-ambitious Lt. Colonel George Custer and 260 other members of the Seventh Cavalry. Custer, knowing he was vastly outnumbered, attacked." [*Custer*, 2012, L McMurtry, p 100, 130]

[Custer – undone by hubris – is often harshly disparaged for this defeat. It overshadowed his extremely-courageous and 'overly-ambitious' yet remarkable cavalry charges which were instrumental in winning the day at Gettysburg]

This monument to Crazy Horse, when complete, will depict the Lakota warrior/leader astride his stallion ... left arm pointing east and declaring "my lands are where my dead lie buried." [Wagner]

The face of *Crazy Horse* – finished in 1998 – is 87.5 feet high, nearly a third larger than each of the 4 presidents at Mt Rushmore.

The free and spacious museum at the Crazy Horse Memorial includes one of the most complete collections of Native American artifacts in America.

The Black Hills – straddling the borders of Wyoming and So. Dakota – were sacred to the Lakota. Rich in animal life [including buffalo], the Hills sheltered the Lakota from bitter winters and spring winds. By the *Treaty of 1868*, the U.S. government confirmed Lakota ownership of the Hills "as long as the rivers run, and grass grows, and trees bear leaves." [*Wonders of World*, p 177]

Eight years later, in 1874, an 'invasive' military expedition into the Hills by Custer led to the discovery of gold.

Viola, in *Smithsonian Chron. No. Amer. Indian*, explains: "The construction of the Northern Pacific Railroad through Dakota and Montana territories – the heart of Sioux/Lakota country – triggered the next confrontation. The military decided that a new fort was necessary to guard the railroad and the ideal site for the structure lay somewhere inside the Black Hills.... a sacred precinct in the southwestern portion of the great Lakota reservation. Colonel George Custer led an expedition into the Black Hills to establish a precise site for the fort and, in the process, discovered gold. Prospectors soon overran the country, and the army faced a losing battle trying to keep them off Lakota land. When a move to purchase the Black Hills failed in 1875, commissioners recommended government action against the Lakota ..." [p 169]

McMurtry adds: "Throughout 1875, travel by whites in the Black Hills was an extremely chancy thing. The government took a hands-off policy: anyone who wanted to head into those hills was taking a big chance, but the [gold] discoveries at first were rich enough to keep the miners coming. The extra-legal process by which we took back the Black Hills was clearly a disgrace." [p 95]

It was one year later, on June 25, 1876, when the Lakota and Cheyenne took revenge on Custer in a one-sided, brief skirmish at Little Bighorn Creek. Custer's loss, however, had the effect of bringing overwhelming military resources against the Plains Native Americans... resulting in the eventual elimination of their independence.

Subjects:

Washington's head is the only one carved entirely in the round. Due to configuration of the original granite wall, it would have been prohibitively expensive in the 1930s to carve the other 3 heads fully in the round.

When the face of Thomas Jefferson was completed in 1936, Cohen says: "Borglum reveals the refined, inventive spirit of the Virginia statesman, whose forwarding of the principle of self-government insured that the nation would be governed by the people." [p 70]

Abraham Lincoln's face was considered finished in 1937. Though missing a neck, collar, and lapels, its profile is remarkable and perhaps the most famed. Cohen adds: "Borglum captures the depth of the sad face of Abraham Lincoln, a president who braved the arduous task of preserving the Union through its bloodiest war." [p 71]

The head of Theodore Roosevelt, 26th President, was completed in 1938. His selection involved 5 factors: "Roosevelt's vigor and ability to think big typified the character and thought of Americanism" [Cohen, 71] ... T.R. was a "frank admirer of the American West who stamped an ever-lasting influence on the spirit of the nation"... his "2 years as a cowboy in the Lakota Territory" [Daniel. 694] ... Borglum, his friend, strongly spoke out for him.... and President Coolidge's endorsement. [the deciding factor]

Sculptor:

Gutzon Borglum was born 1867 in Idaho. His Danish emigrant parents moved to Nebraska where his father was a doctor. He showed artistic talent in both grade school and high school. When he moved to Los Angeles and became an artist, Mrs. John C. Fremont [wife of explorer-general] urged him to travel to Paris for training. Upon doing so, Borglum enrolled at the Julien Academy before being accepted at the Ecole des Beaux-Arts [School of Fine Arts]. In France, he met and admired Rodin, who encouraged him to become a sculptor instead of a painter.

Borglum returned to California in 1891, before moving to England. In 1902 he opened a studio in New York City...and, in 1904, won a medal for his *Mares of Diomedes* at the St. Louis World's Fair. He soon received commissions from throughout the country...including several bronzes [one is the head of *Lincoln* now in the Capitol rotunda]. He also became well known for bronzes of Native Americans and Civil War heroes. As one of the finest sculptors in the United States, Borglum even "had a hand in upgrading the torch on the *Statue of Liberty*." [Cohen, 6]

In 1916, Borglum accepted a commission for a 'Confederacy' memorial on Stone Mountain in Georgia. He worked on this project – developing many of the skills he would later utilize at *Rushmore* – until 1925..."when differences between Borglum and the Stone Mt. Monument Association boiled over..." [Cohen, 12]

After taking the *Rushmore* commission, Borglum purchased a ranch in the Black Hills.

Viewing the Memorial:

Arrive at parking lot at 8 AM opening. Within the hour, significant portions of *Jefferson* and *Roosevelt* will pass into dark shadows and no longer offer dramatic views...or yield inclusive photos.

Entry to the Memorial is free...after an $11 parking lot fee. [as of 2013]

From the entrance, briskly walk a long promenade [12 to 15 minutes] ... as the 4 presidents become ever larger.

Following an 8 AM arrival, it soon becomes apparent how swiftly the shadows fill recesses on the south-facing Memorial. At the Visitor Center, [skip its excellent exhibits, for now]. Pass through onto its broad outdoor viewing balcony. Do not tarry too long here for a group photo ... if you wish to obtain superior views close-up.

On your left, a gentle half-mile Presidential Trail leads to the base of the *Memorial,* where the presidents are framed by attractive foliage.

Up close, their life-like heads are overwhelming in size and dignity. If a visit is within the first hour of the *Memorial's* opening [before crowds pack the trail], the visit will be far more personal and rewarding.

With the gigantic heads so near, a reasonably-good photo including the face of a companion may require the camera-person to kneel or even lie down on the trail.

A fruitful hour or more then can be spent in the Visitor Center. This includes an excellent orientation film. Give yourself time to read each surprisingly well-prepared exhibit.

During spring-break and summer months, prudent travelers book rooms well-in-advance at closeby Keystone ... only a few minutes from the *Memorial's* fee parking lot. Rapid City is 25 miles distant.

Several references suggest a sundown visit, also ... to watch a 45-minute program that concludes with illumination of the 4 presidents. Check online for schedules ... which change with the seasons. Phone number: (605) 574-2515.

Major References:

The Carving of Mount Rushmore, 1985, Smith, p 1, 13-21

Masters of American Sculpture, '93, Reynolds, p 85-9, 90, 148, 180, 202

Mount Rushmore, 1952, Fite

Borglum's Mountain, 1983, Cohen, p 1-83

Chronicle of America, 1989, Daniel, p 634, 694, cover
Northern Plains Map, 1986, National Geographic Society (Dec. 1986)
"Crazy Horse Sculpture", 2010, Wagner, SD Union (2/28/2010)
"70 Years Ago...", Smithsonian, Oct '11, McLean, p 21
Smithsonian Chron. of No. American Indian, 1990, Viola, p 169
Associated Press, May 25, 2014, Carson Walker
Custer, 2012, L McMurtry, p 95, 100, 130

97

VIGELAND SCULPTURE PARK

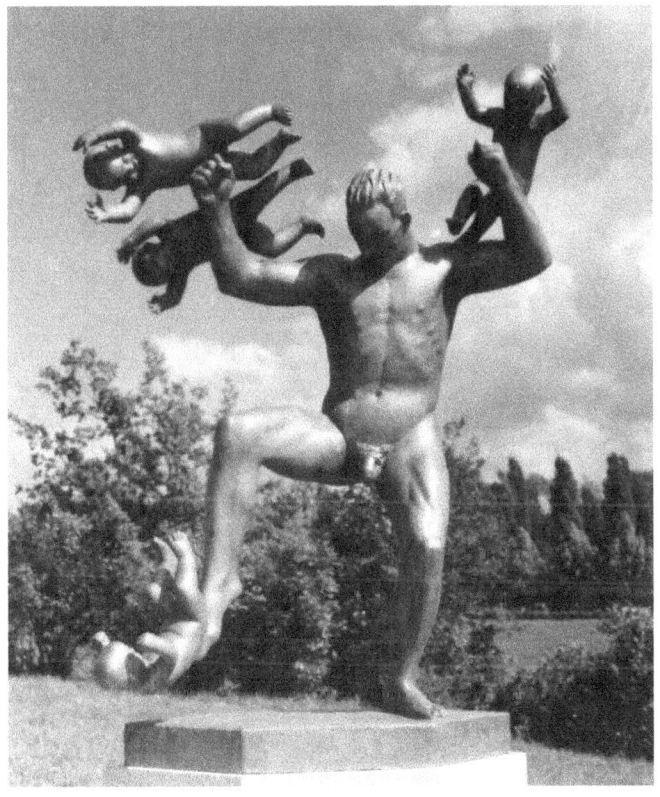

"... the scope of his production ... its power of expression
and forcefulness have never been surpassed in modern times."
...Dreyers, *Norway Today*, 1970, p 50-1

Vigeland Sculpture Park, 1905-1942 – Oslo, Norway
650+ figures – granite and bronze – Realistic / Contemporary
Sculptor: Gustav Vigeland [1869-1943]
    *purchase park's guidebook
    [*Monolith* photo at chapter end]

A proud father – blessed with quadruplets – juggles all four! This group is a superb example of Gustav Vigeland's work.

In Oslo's vast Vigeland Sculpture Park, many more works can be described as "mind-blowing." [*SD Union*, 10-9-05]

Spring, summer, and fall... natives of Norway and others flock to the 80-acre park. They stroll, picnic, and play in the inspiring presence of 650+ bronze and granite figures – men, women, and children of all ages.

On a scale unrivaled in the Western world, the figures chronicle the 12 'stages' of life: *Amour*... Birth... Nurturing... Childhood ... Adolescence... Coming of Age... *Amour Again*... Motherhood & Fatherhood... Middle age... Grand-Parenting... Old age... and *Peace*.

So often... we think: *Wish that were me!*

Vigeland's sculptures bring to mind the pleasures and trials of life. They are honest in expressing the inevitable... such as natural aging. Yet, they also remind us aging can be amazingly enriching and fabulous with <u>the arrival of children and then grandchildren</u>.

The energy of Vigeland's statues encourages us to be free... to be in the moment.

Others invite quiet pursuits... cloud-gazing, intimate conversation, cuddling, smelling the roses [in the garden], napping, sunbathing, reading, etc.

Some figures encourage contemplation of choices... desires... expectations... the range of aspirations that make living exciting.

At the end of a visit to Vigeland Park, we too may have *seized the day!*

The old 'status quo' may no longer be acceptable.

Gustav Vigeland:

Vigeland's career began in 1889 during an era of growing naturalism. His distinctive style was 'earthy and direct'. Tone Wikborg, a curator of the Vigeland Museum, explains: "In order to make the figures timeless and universal, they are rendered in the nude..." [*Vigeland Park*, p 35]

In 1900, at the age of 30, Vigeland took the initial step eventually leading to the *sculpture park*. He conceived the concept of a massive *Fountain*. [originally, intending it for an Oslo city square]

In 1901, he designed the Nobel Peace Prize...and was knighted by King Olaf "in recognition of his contribution to the cultural heritage of Norway and his growing stature as one of the leading artists in Northern Europe." [*Ency World Bio*,Vol 25]

Two years later, he began modeling *20 Tree Groups* to encircle his massive *Fountain*. [*Encyclo. Sculpt*, p 1725] In 1905, a committee formed to finance the *Fountain*.

Ten years later, Vigeland began sketches for a 57-foot-tall *Monolith*... [now, an icon of Norway]. And, he made the critical decision to open his studio to the public.

As a setting for his planned *Fountain*...an 80-acre Sculpture Park was conceived. It would include the *20 Tree Groups*...the *Monolith*...and more.

Finally, in 1921, Vigeland signed a contract with Oslo, making the capital of Norway the owner of all works of art in his possession, plus future works. In return, Oslo agreed to finance the Sculpture Park...construct a home and studio for Vigeland [in park]...to provide lifetime funding...and to build a museum for his works. [p 1725]

[5 years earlier, Rodin made a similar agreement with Paris]

Today, the Vigeland Museum contains approximately 1,600 works [including plaster or clay models of all park statuary], 12,000 drawings, and 420 woodcuts.

Sculpture Groups in the Park [in order of appearance]:

1. the Bridge
2. Children's Playground

3. the Fountain
4. 20 Tree Groups
5. the Labyrinth [maze]
6. 36 Granite Groups
7. the Monolith
8. Wheel of Life
9. the Clan

The Park's 930-yard promenade [850-m] commences across a broad lawn.

At the 100-meter Bridge, visitors are greeted by 58 life-size bronzes: the ties between woman and man…and between children and adults. "Figures in repose alternate with dynamic figures…" [Wikborg, p 7]

Below the *Bridge*, a <u>Children's Playground</u> displays 8 bronze youths… [most can be touched or climbed upon, by children]. A pond, in season, is refuge to ducks and geese.

Visitors then enter a wide and fragrant <u>rose garden</u>.

This leads to the giant, double-tiered <u>Fountain</u>. Six bronze giants hold a wide saucer-vessel aloft from which a curtain of water skims over their heads. They are said to "toil with the burden of life…" [p 15]

Around the Fountain's pool are <u>20 Tree Groups</u> "representing Man's romantic relationship to nature." [p 15] Each bronze tree holds one or more inter-active figures in the evolving stages of life.

The *Fountain* is also the center of <u>the Labyrinth</u> – a 1,800-square-foot maze. Its black-and-white mosaic paving-stones are a unique playground…a source of joy for all ages…especially youths in need of diversion…who can race from opposite ends of the maze. [a speedy winner requires about 30 minutes]

From every direction, broad lawns and giant trees beckon visitors who wish to picnic…play games…rest in shade…or otherwise frolic under the sun.

Past *the Fountain*, 3 ascending terraces lead to the highest point in the park…<u>the Monolith</u>. This massive 57-foot column [from a single block of granite] displays 121 figures. Three stone-carvers – guided by Vigeland's plaster models – worked from 1929 to 1942 to complete it.

The Monolith is circled by a 360-degree staircase. Spaced evenly around the staircase are 36 Granite Groups ... [view them after climbing to base of *Monolith*].

From the base of the Monolith, a mass of men, women and children strive to ascend the column. Some pause to rest ... embrace ... or even sleep. At the crest of the column, a lively cluster of young children enjoy the grand view.

Gustav Vigeland said: "... the Column belongs to the world of fantasy. The granite groups are easy to understand ... *the Monolith* may be interpreted in many ways." [p 33]

Dreyer, in *Norway Today*, concludes: "... the *Monolith* exercises an abiding and almost magical effect. Visitors from all over the world depart, shaken or moved, but never indifferent ..." [p 50]

Arranged around the circular staircase are 36 Granite Groups. They – depict the drama of life. At the top, an endearing *Swarm of Babies* faces the Fountain ... 6 steps lower, at mid-level, the *Man & Woman with Baby* is precious.

To view the next 12 chronological sculptures, walk clockwise. At the lowest level, note the exquisite *Embracing Couple* ['the kneeling man behind the woman' competes with Canova's *Cupid & Psyche* #79 ... and Rodin's *Kiss* #89]

The famed Wheel of Life is at the far end of the park promenade. Four adults and 3 children [arranged in a vertical circle] symbolize our eternity and "... emphasize the interdependence of all human beings." [p 33]

In the 21st century, the *Wheel of Life* has become a symbol of the growing movement to confront and halt Climate-Change.

Another masterpiece is *the Clan* ... located north of the *Fountain*. This 21-figure group was created in 1934-1936. Limited funding kept its plaster model in storage until 1985 ... when IBM funded a bronze version ... installed in 1988. [p 33]

"The [Clan} figures are disposed in minor groups, all repeating the motif of protection: a mother shields her children, older children care for smaller ones, the eldest ones huddle together." A muscular male stands at each end of the group...to guard against menacing threats. "Vigeland's intention was to portray one of Man's deepest instincts, the protection of kin." [p 33]

The creation of *the Clan* preceded the horrors of World War II by 3 years...when Norway mounted an active resistance [underground] to the invading Nazi military.

The Clan now gathers against the ravages of Global-Warming. In that context, it is <u>one of the most significant sculptures</u> in this compendium.

Sculptor:

Gustav Vigeland created most of the Park's granite figures in clay...then master stonecutters fashioned them in stone.

In 1869, he was born in Mandel, Norway. His father, a master carpenter, apprenticed his son at 14 to a master woodcarver in Oslo [1884]. In evenings, Gustav drew at the Royal School of Design and decided his primary artistic interest lay in sculpting. When his father died suddenly in 1886, Gustav left Oslo to help his family.

During the winter of 1889, Gustav [hungry and without shelter] knocked on the door of sculptor Brynjulf Bergslien [in Oslo] to show his sketches. Bergslien – impressed by Gustav's work – agreed to become his first teacher, found him shelter, and allowed him to work in his studio." [*Ency. of Sculpt.*, p 1724]

In 1894, Vigeland gave his first solo exhibition of 51 sculptures. In Paris, Florence, and Rome [1896], he studied "art of the Renaissance, ancient Egypt, and Classical Greece..." before returning to Norway to create gargoyles for the National [Coronation] Cathedral in Trondheim. A second solo exhibition in 1899 was "unequivocally well-received by Norwegian critics." Vigeland returned to Paris in 1900-1901 "...making sketches for large, public monuments, a form that became his specialty." [*Encyclo. Bio.*, Vol. 25]

The *Encyclo of Sculpture* reveals: "Vigeland also produced a small equestrian statue, *Theodore Roosevelt Riding At a Trot*, cast for North Dakota." [p 1725]

To enjoy all the monuments at Vigeland Park ... arrive at opening.
[10 am in summer, noon from Sept thru April]

Major References:

Gustav Vigeland, the Sculptor and his Works, 1965, Stang, p 15, 48, 118-35, 144-51

Gustav Vigeland: Sculpture Park and Museum, 1991, Wikborg

Norway Today, 1970, Dreyers, p 48-50

Embrace of Life: The Sculpture of Gustav Vigeland, 1968, Hale

Encyclopedia of World Biography Supplement, Vol. 25, 2005, Thomson Gale

Encyclopedia of Sculpture, 2004, p 1725

Vigeland Park, 1991, Wikborg, p 5, 7, 15-17, 25, 33-35

Oslo, 1993, Brun, p 48-55

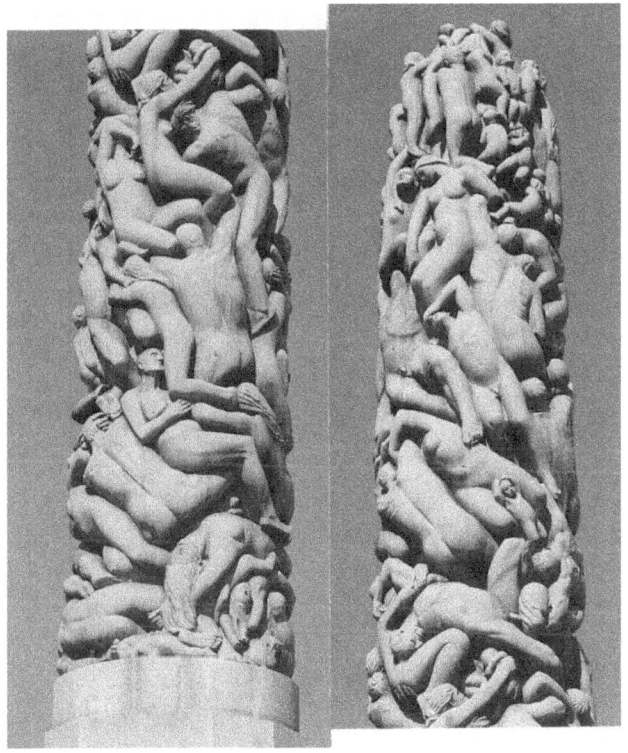

98
MARINE MEMORIAL
OR IWO JIMA MEMORIAL

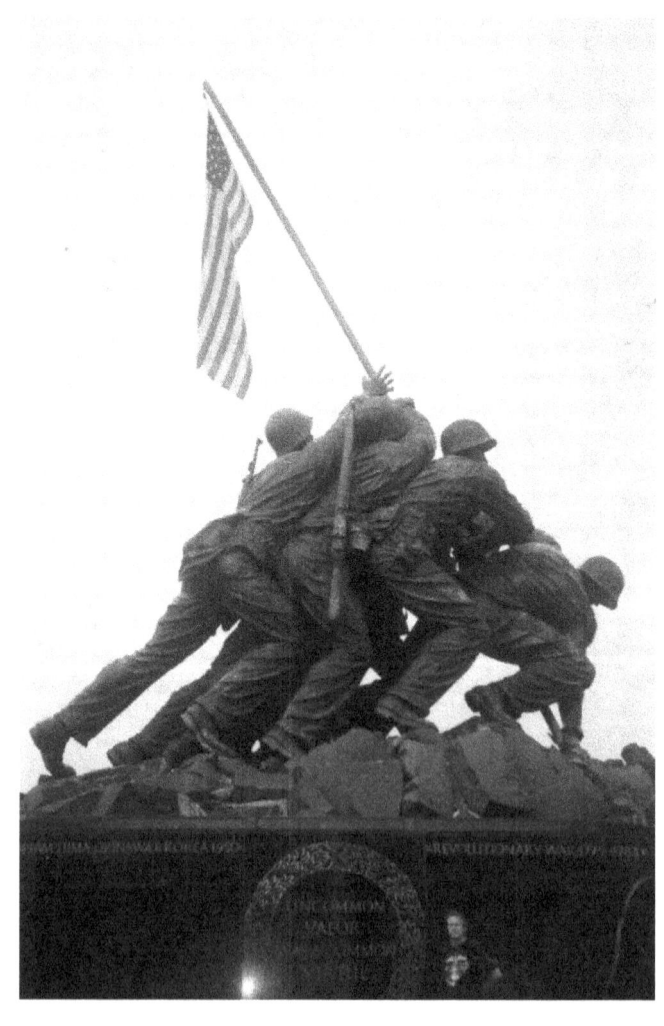

"the single most powerful image of democratic solidarity in
our culture ... 'it has set the standard for collective action ...
individuals working together ... rising as one'."
... Hariman & Lucaites, *LA Times*, 8-22-06

Colossal bronze, 1954 – Wash, DC & Camp Pendleton, Calif.
From: photo, top Mt. Suribachi – Joe Rosenthal – 2/23/1945
Ht. 78-ft. Wt. 100 tons – 6 times life-size – Realistic
Sculptor: Dr. Felix de Weldon [U.S. Navy artist]
    [14 more sculptures addressing 'democracy' list at chapter
end]

T he *Marine Corps War Memorial* symbolizes <u>courage</u> and <u>collec-</u>
<u>tive action</u> ... a necessary path for a people seeking freedom or
to protect it.

The 'model' for this sculpture was a rushed photograph at the
raising of the second American flag over Mt. Suribachi ... the 556-
foot volcanic cone dominating Iwo Jima. The date: February 23,
1945.

The 5-mile-long island of Iwo Jima – fortified and manned by
22,000 Japanese soldiers during World War II – was strategically
important for American bombing missions over Japan, 660 miles
distant. Enemy soldiers hid in 16 miles of reinforced tunnels and
1,500 man-made caverns ... supporting 750 blockhouses and pill-
boxes ... constructed of "rounded concrete, reinforced with steel
rods to make them impervious even to artillery rounds." [*Flags of
Our Fathers,* Bradley, p 8, 141]

Bradley describes the initial Japanese gunfire, deliberately
delayed one hour until Marines had landed and filled a narrow
beachhead: "... smoke and earsplitting noise suddenly filled the
universe. The almost unnoticed blockhouses on the flat ground
facing the ocean began raking the exposed troops with machine-
gun bullets. But the real firestorm erupted from the mountain,
from Suribachi: mortars, heavy artillery shells, and machine-gun
rounds ripped into the stunned Americans. Suribachi turned into a

monstrous Christmas tree with blinking lights. The lights were gun barrels discharging ammunition ...” [p 155-56]

Combat correspondent Joe Rosenthal, who took the Pulitzer Prize-winning photo on Mt. Suribachi, later declared: “No man who survived that beach can tell you how he did it. It was like walking through rain and not getting wet.” [*LA Times*, 8-22-06]

Twenty-seven Congressional Medals of Honor – 14 posthumous – were awarded on Iwo Jima ... the highest total “in any battle in the history of the United States.” A third of all Marines killed during World War II died on the island. [*LA Times*, Luther, 8-22-06] [Bradley, p 10]

“Although the flag-raising inspired the forces trying to take the tiny island [2 x 5 mi.], it could not minimize the heavy casualties suffered by the Americans. Before the battle ended on March 25, 1945 – more than a month <u>after</u> the capture of Mt. Suribachi – 5,931 Marines lost their lives and 17,372 more Marines were wounded ...” [*Arlington Nat. Cemetery*, Peters, 2000]

In Washington: “At the White House, President Roosevelt shuddered when told of Iwo’s first day. ‘It was the first time in the war, through good news and bad, that anyone had seen the President gasp in horror’.” [Bradley, p 166-67]

Subjects: [Suribachi – Flag-Raisings – the Photo – Battle]

Mt. Suribachi was 300 yards south of the Marine beachhead. A narrow neck of land – 700 yards wide – connected Suribachi to the island. On the first day, the 28th Marine Regiment was assigned to isolate Suribachi from the island ... and this was done. The 250-man Marine company which led the “700-yard near-suicidal dash across [the neck of] the island ... was down to 37.” [p 166]

On the second day, the 28th assaulted Suribachi. Its well-armed defenders included 1,300 soldiers and 640 Navy troops. The bloody assault to take the 200 to 300 yards of terrain to the base of Suribachi lasted 3 days.

First Flag-Raising: On Feb. 23, 1945, 4 days after landing on Iwo Jima, the Marines 'secured' Mt. Suribachi and planted 2 successive American flags on its summit, the tallest point on the island.

Initially, a 4-man patrol had reconnoitered a route to the summit, encountering no opposition...then, a 40-man patrol climbed to the top with a flag. A fragmented pipe was found, the Marines threaded a rope through holes, and "thrust the pole [and flag] upward in the gusty wind..." [p 205]

Staff Sergeant Louis Lowery – a photographer for *Leatherneck Magazine* who had accompanied the 40-man patrol – documented the proceedings with a steady succession of camera shots." [*Flags...*, 2000, Bantam, p 311]

From the ground below and surrounding ships, Marine and Navy personnel had been watching the patrol. "When the small swatch of color fluttered, Iwo Jima was transformed, for a few moments, into Times Square on New Year's Eve. Infantrymen cheered, whistled, and waved their helmets. Ships offshore opened up their deep, honking whistles." [p 205]

"Just moments after the Stars and Stripes went up, Hot Rock's summit got hot again." [p 205] Three disturbed Japanese soldiers popped out of a nearby tunnel and were immediately gunned down. Others threw hand grenades at the Marines. "The firefight lasted several minutes, and no American casualties were taken. And then the invisible enemy was silent again." The Marines atop Suribachi "spent the ensuing hour securing the mountain. 'We used the flamethrowers or demolition charges...we burned them out. We didn't know what side the Japanese would be coming up from, so we had to work fast'." [p 206]

Of the 6 Marines who raised the first flag, all returned to combat on the island...3 would not survive. The names of the first flag-raisers are: Corporal Charles W. Lindberg *(awarded Silver Star)*...Sergeant Hank Hansen, Jr. *(did not survive)*...Sergeant Boots Thomas *(did not survive)*...Private 1st Class James Michaels...First Lt. George Schrier *(did not survive)*...and Private 1st Class Louis Charlo.

Second Flag Raising: The second flag-raising over Mt. Suribachi occurred 4 hours after the first. During the jubilant celebration of the first flag-raising, a landing craft carrying Secretary of the Navy James Forrestal came ashore. Forrestal "decided he wanted the Suribachi flag as a souvenir...news of this did not sit well with Colonel Chandler Johnson of the 28th Regiment...'The hell with that' the colonel spat when the message reached him. The flag belonged to his unit as far as he was concerned." [p 207] Johnson ordered another flag be found – larger – and sent a 6-man detail from Company E to raise it and return the first flag.

[Johnson placed the first flag in his battalion safe. He would survive 8 more days]

The 6 Marines raising the second flag are: Sergeant Michael Strank *(did not survive)*...Corporal Harlon Block *(did not survive)*...Private First Class Rene Gagnon...Private First Class Ira Hayes...Private First Class Harold Schultz*...and Private First Class Franklin Sousley *(did not survive).*

*recently identified – *Los Angeles Times*, June 24, 2016

<u>*The Photograph*</u>: Joe Rosenthal, Associated Press photographer, having spotted the first flag atop the mountain, started up Suribachi. As he climbed, he learned of a second flag going up the slope ahead of him. Reaching the summit just in time, Rosenthal scrambled to the best position for a photo...then saw the first flag coming down and the other starting up. Without looking through his view-finder, he pointed his camera toward the flag-raisers and snapped the shutter. [*LA Times*, 8-22-06]

Later, Rosenthal said: "No photographer could have asked for a better break. The sun was just right. The wind was just right to flow the flag. The pipe – it must have weighed 100 pounds – was so heavy the guy holding it was struggling...." [*LA Times*, 1987]

"Their collective image…became the most recognized and the most reproduced in the history of photography." [Bradley, p 3] Within days, the second flag-raising photograph was on front-pages of newspapers throughout the United States…in countless magazines and movie reels. Within months, its image "had been engraved on 150-million 3-cent stamps and emblazoned on 3.5 million posters and thousands of outdoor panels and car panels…" Almost overnight, Rosenthal's photo of the second flag-raising "became an indelible image of courage and fortitude" in the minds of all Americans. [*LA Times*, 8-22-06]

Congressman Joseph Hendricks [Fl.] introduced a bill in the House of Representatives to authorize the erection of a monument based on the photograph by Rosenthal. [Bradley, p 233]

The Battle: After the Marines landed on February 19, 1945…the combat continued for 36 days. *Time Magazine* declared: "No battle of World War II, not even Normandy, was watched with more intensity by the American people." [Mar 5, 1945]

The Navy's brief bombardment of Iwo Jima prior to the Marine landing remains controversial. Some historians describe it as overly brief. General 'Howling Mad' Smith, a Marine veteran of amphibious warfare, requested Navy ships provide 10 days bombardment before the assault. The Navy "stunned" Smith by offering only 3 days. Smith strongly protested. Bradley reports: "Smith knew 3 day's shelling would spell death for many of his Marines. But the Navy would have their headlines…the Navy was eager to grab headlines and show that they too – not only the Army Air Force – could 'shell' mainland Japan. And so, ships [of Task Force 58] were diverted to the high-profile but strategically dubious mission of bombing the enemy's homeland." [p 144] & [Moskin, p 359-60]

The Navy commitment to bombard Iwo Jima on February 16, 17, and 18 was reduced to little more than one day – due to 'less than optimal weather' in the stated opinion of the Navy. Consequently "only February 17 saw a complete day of bombardment." [Bradley, p 144-45]

The *New York Times* reported: "...3,650 Marines were dead, wounded, or missing after only 2 days of fighting...more than the total casualties of Tarawa...about as many as all the Marine casualties of Guadalcanal in 5 months of jungle combat." [p 219]

On March 16, Marine General Holland Smith stood at the ceremony dedicating the 5th Marine Division cemetery on Iwo Jima. His "eyes filled with tears as he said to his aide: 'This is the worst yet'." [Bradley, p 242]

Outside the cemetery, a Marine had chiseled in stone:

"When you go home...Tell them for us and say

For your tomorrow...We gave our today."

This 'recalls' the Greek epitaph to the 300 Spartans at Thermoplyae in 480 BC:

"Go tell to Sparta, thou who passest by...

That here, obedient to her laws, we lie."

[*How Civilization Began*, 1932, Kelty, p 138]

Hearing of the dedication ceremony on Iwo Jima, President Roosevelt stated: "The Japanese know what it means that '*The United States Marines have landed*.' And I think I may add – having Iwo Jima in mind – '*The situation is well in hand*'." [p 242]

The *Author*, a Marine Corps officer in the 1960s, can attest: later generations of Marines oft repeat the under-scored words above.

"The [costly] American victory unquestionably hastened the end of the war. In the ensuing months, about 2,400 distressed B-29 bombers, carrying 27,000 crewmen, would make emergency, life-saving landings on the island." [Bradley, p 377]

Photographer:

Joseph Rosenthal was born in Washington, DC in 1911. In high school, photography was his hobby. After graduation, he moved to San Francisco and worked for a photo service acquired by the Associated Press. He also was a reporter and photographer for the *San Francisco News* and the *New York Times-Wide World Photos*. After Pearl Harbor, he attempted to enlist, but his eyes were too impaired.

He joined the Maritime Service until 1944, when the Associated Press gave him an opportunity to shoot photos with the Wartime Still Pictures Pool. Before the invasion of Iwo Jima, Rosenthal had covered the invasion of Guam. [*San Diego Union*, 8-22-06]

In 1981, Rosenthal recalled: "I preferred going with the Marines because of the types of pictures that were available. Assault landings appealed to me. All you had to do was screw up your courage and go with them." When interviewed about his iconic photo, he "repeatedly said that he was not the story, that the Marines were the story. 'What difference does it make who took the picture? I took it, but the Marines took Iwo Jima'." [*LA Times*, 8-22-06]

[Rosenthal never claimed to have taken the first photograph of an American flag being raised over Iwo Jima. On the other hand, Marine Sergeant Lowery – who took photographs at the initial flag-raising – suffered many unwarranted indignities when he correctly claimed to have taken the first photo of the American flag being raised.]

Sculptor:

Dr. Felix W. de Weldon – originally a European with a doctorate in art from the University of Vienna – came to Canada to sculpt a portrait bust of its prime minister ... and decided to settle in the United States. During World War II, Weldon enlisted in the U.S. Navy. In 1945, he became an American citizen.

Bradley describes Weldon's initial interest in Rosenthal's photo: "News pros were not the only ones bedazzled by the photo. Navy Captain T.B. Clark was on duty at Patuxent Air Station in Maryland when it came humming off the wire. He studied it for a minute, then thrust it under the gaze of Navy Petty Officer Felix de Weldon ... who could not take his eyes off the photo. In its classic triangular lines, he recognized similarities with ancient statues he had studied. He reflexively reached for some sculptor's clay and tools. With the photograph before him he labored through the night. By dawn, he had replicated the 6 men pushing a pole, raising a flag." [Bradley, p 220]

In 1951, Congress commissioned Weldon to design and create the *Memorial*. His final version required 36 plaster models. With the assistance of several hundred assistant sculptors, Weldon completed the monument in 3 years.

Five faces of the 6 'second flag-raising group' appear accurately on the *Memorial*. The sixth face is currently [2017] incorrect. The correct face would be that of <u>Private First Class Harold Schultz</u> *[who died naturally in 1995]*. Schultz was not identified during the ongoing heat of battle. This oversight did not become known until 2014. Schultz "had never spoken publicly about appearing on the photo." [*LA Times*, 6-24-16, p A7] [*SD Union*, June 24, 2016, p a10]

> After the flag-raising, "Schultz sustained wounds to his arm and stomach, and he was sent home. Several months later, Schultz...was discharged from the Marines. Many Marines who had fought on Iwo Jima suffered from post-traumatic stress disorder, but little was known about the condition at the time. To cope, many Marines simply never talked about their military experience. One of the other men pictured in the flag-raising, Ira Hayes, had asked men in his unit not to identify him as being in the photograph, but they could not keep it a secret." [*SD Union*, June 24, 2016, p a10]
>
> Charles Neimeyer, Chief Historian of the Marines [who served on the USMC panel investigating the photograph] adds: "I think Hayes and Schultz believed that if they were identified as flag-raisers, not a day would go by without them being reminded of combat and being on Iwo Jima." [*SD Union*, June 24, 2016, p a10]

Inscribed around the granite base of the monument is mention of every major Marine Corps engagement since 1775. The base bears a World War II quote from Admiral Chester Nimitz: *"Uncommon Valor was a Common Virtue."*

The *Memorial* is best viewed during a 'Sunset Parade' – a Marine ceremonial marching performance which includes the Marine

Silent Drill Platoon. [contact: (202) 433-4173 for schedule] Early evening views, including the flood-lighted Washington Monument and the Capitol Building, are impressive.

Other sculptures within this book voicing man's quest for freedom are: the Tyrannicides ... She-Wolf ... Pericles ... Demosthenes ... L Junius Brutus ... Winged Victory of Samothrace ... Moses ... Depart ure of Volunteers ... George Washington ... Statue of Liberty ... End of the Trail ... Lincoln Memorial ... Mount Rushmore ... the Vietnam Veterans Memorial.

Major References:

Journal of Military History, Oct 2004, Robert Burrell, p 1143-1186

Amer Jour. Speech, 2002, Hariman & Lucaites [LA Times, 8-22-06]

Impact, Sept-Oct 1945, Assistant Chief of Air Staff, p 69-71

Victory in the Pacific, 1945, Morison

Arlington Nat. Cemetery: Shrine to Amer. Heroes. 2000, Peters

Flags of Our Fathers, 2006 (Bantam), Bradley, *(multiple pages)*

The U.S. Marine Corps Story, 1992, Moskin, p 359-360

Washington Post, July 30, 2008, Hubbard,

The 1st Battalion, 28th Marines on Iwo Jima, 2004, Allen

Associated Press, August 22, 2006, Justin Norton

Associated Press, July 1, 2007, Chris Williams

How Civilization Began, 1932, Kelty, p 138

Los Angeles Times, August 22, 2006, Luther

Los Angeles Times, October 20, 2006, Turan

San Diego Union-Tribune, August 22, 2006, Norton

Flags of Our Fathers (movie), October 2006, Clint Eastwood

Los Angeles Times, June 24, 2016, p A7, Evans

99
ALBERT EINSTEIN MEMORIAL

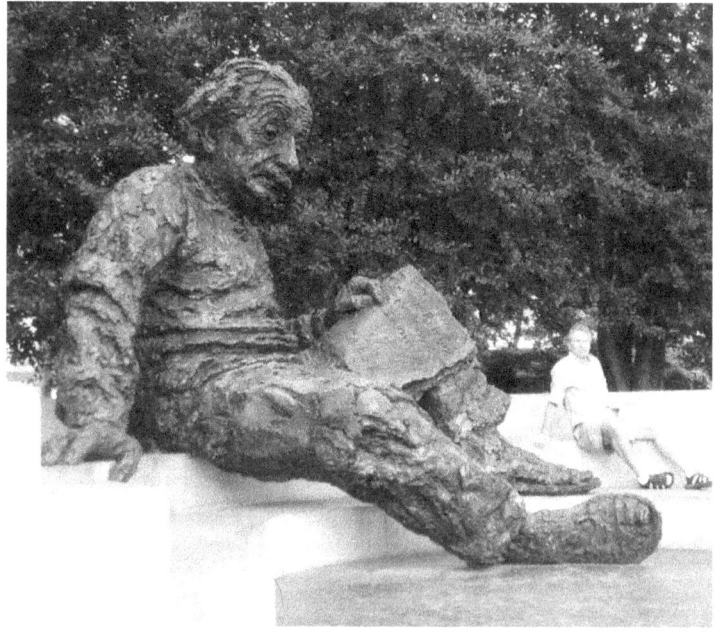

Einstein received the Nobel Prize "mainly for his work on the
photoelectric effect ... that led to the tapping of solar power."
....*Einstein, 100 Years of Relativity,* 2005, Robinson, p 35

Colossal bronze, 1979 – Nat. Acad. of Sciences, Wash., DC*
Ht. 12 ft., Length 22 ft., Wt. 4 tons – triple life-size – Modern
Albert Einstein [1879 to 1955]

Sculptor: Robert Berks, [1922 –]
  *copies in NYC and Jerusalem

Children – their future *pursuit of happiness* problematic – delight in climbing on the grandfatherly *Albert Einstein* in Washington, DC. His colossal bronze – 12 ft. high by 22 ft. – can easily accommodate a dozen children.

The future well-being of children and grandchildren
depends upon the timely success in harnessing
the sun's rays to reverse Global-Warming.

95 years ago, Einstein revealed how this could be done

Before 1922, Einstein had been nominated 10 times for the Nobel Prize in Physics.

In 1922 ... he finally received it "mainly for his work on the photoelectric effect that led to the tapping of solar power." [*Einstein, Robinson*, p 235]

On his *Memorial*, in Washington, a prominent inscription states Einstein: "described light as a stream of energy particles called 'quanta'. He explained the already observed photo-electric effect – that beams of light cause metals to release electrons that can be converted into electric current." In other words ... solar power.

Can Solar Power Reverse Global-Warming/Climate-Change?
  Yes ... it can.
  Will solar power reverse Global-Warming/Climate-Change?
  Currently ... *NO.*
  An Associated Press-Stanford University poll in 2009 reports: "Three of every 4 Americans view Climate-Change as a serious problem that will harm future generations if not addressed." [*San Diego Union*, 12-20-09]

  However... 8 years later, in 2017, a Coalition of corporate CEOs and politicians control the U.S. Congress ... by majorities in each house. The Coalition <u>denies</u> Climate-Change is 'serious'. Therefore, the Coalition <u>continues to block legislation</u> that might reverse Climate-Change.

This is foolhardy.

The price of avarice* may be too high ... when it threatens the lives of children and grandchildren. *<u>definition of avarice</u>: *greed for money*

Nevertheless… in 2017 ... we are in *stalemate.*

The Coalition remains unconcerned that Climate-Change is a time-bomb. Everyday we are in *stalemate* is one day closer to the *cut-off date* – when Global-Warming becomes *irreversible.*

When and if that occurs, the future for children and grand-children will darken. The young will pay the ultimate price for the avarice* of the Coalition.

Why?

There is no acceptable answer.

No excuse.

See 'EXXON 1982 Cover-Up' at chapter-end.

Also see the *Addendum* if solutions are sought.

Abraham Lincoln counseled:

"The dogmas of the past are inadequate
  to the stormy present.
The occasion is piled high with difficulty.
As our case is anew,
  so we must think anew... and act anew..."
        `[*Annual Message to Congress,* Dec 1, 1862]

Subject:

Albert Einstein was chosen *Person of the Century* in 1999.

In 1905, he presented 5 papers "scientists ranked among the greatest bursts of creative genius in history." They explained: Quanta... Molecular Dimensions... Brownian Movement... Special Relativity... and Energy = mass X speed of light squared.

In 1915, when Einstein was 36, his "general theory of relativity" broke tradition and "would revolutionize people's ideas about the physical world and guarantee that the rest of his life would be lived in the glare of a celebrity that made heads of state and Hollywood stars go tongue-tied in his presence." [*LA Times*, 1/29/2007]

In 1917, he theorized "stimulated emission of radiation" was "at the heart of the laser."

In 1919, the 40-year-old Einstein was recognized as the world's greatest physicist...when British astronomers observed a solar eclipse [May 29] which confirmed the bending of starlight by the sun...as predicted by Einstein's general theory of relativity...thereby validating the theory. Following this, Einstein's heavily-furled face with its leonine mane "and a look of wide-eyed innocence became better known than any other human being." [Neffe, all pages]

Einstein preferred to work in solitude at a desk near a window offering a peaceful, private view of a garden with bushes and trees.

Therefore, in 1992, his colossal bronze statue in Washington, DC was screened by the thick foliage of holly bushes and elm trees. Now [2017], he has lost that solitude...as most of the foliage has been stripped away...to make him visible from all directions.

Einstein greets us with a weary face. His reclining figure spreads over a broad, 3-tiered stone bench. He might doze off at any moment. [before the surrounding foliage was stripped away, scientists from nearby buildings often lunched and napped alongside Einstein]

His statue has an unusually rugged surface...fitting to its subject. In real life, Einstein's face was described as craggy. In public, he chose to wear slightly-disheveled suits and favored a wildly-flaring hairstyle. [flared in advance for photographers]

At his Memorial, *Einstein* contemplates the 28-foot-wide circle of emerald-pearl granite before him. Embedded in the granite are 2,700 stainless-steel studs – size denotes magnitude – representing the location of the sun, moon, planets, and other celestial bodies on the 100th anniversary of his birthdate [April 22, 1879]. The *Memorial* was dedicated on this anniversary.

In his left hand, he holds a folder displaying the equations for his 3 primary discoveries: <u>the photoelectric effect [solar power]</u>...the <u>theory of general relativity...and the equivalence of energy and matter</u>.

Visitors' words spoken from the epicenter of the emerald-pearl granite surface may amplify and generate an echo from the giant bronze figure...explaining why some persons appear in conversation with *Einstein*. At the epicenter, Einstein's thoughtful gaze meets our own...and might ask of us:

Do you contemplate the future of your own celestial body?

Important Events of Einstein's Life:

1921...visits U.S. after receiving 'personal' attacks in Germany

1930-33...makes 3 research visits to Calif. Inst. of Technology

1933...announces he will not return to Germany

1933....spends next 22 years at Princeton Inst. for Advanced Study

1939...sent letters to Roosevelt, warning Germany making A-bomb

1946...championed need for arms control & world government

1950...opposed building of hydrogen bomb

1953-4...openly and strongly opposed McCarthyism

1955...signed Russell/Einstein Manifesto against nuclear weapons

1955...passed, April 18, at Princeton   [Robinson, p 240-41]

Sculptor:

Robert Berks is Boston-born [1922]...his parents were artists. From 13 to 19, he studied at the School of the Boston Mus. of Fine Arts. As World War II approached, he designed keels of wooden mine sweepers and, during the war, crafted military devices at Harvard. After the war, he resumed painting and sculpture, moving to New York in 1948. He has sculpted more than 300 portrait bronzes and a dozen monuments.

His *Einstein* in Washington is based on a bust of the scientist sculpted from life in 1953. Another bronze *Einstein* is currently exhibited at the American Natural History Museum in New York City.

Berks also created the colossal portrait head [similar in style & 8-feet tall] of JFK inside Washington's Kennedy Center. This work alone justifies a visit to the Center.

Berks "primary career choice has been to create for future generations a visual record of people who have shaped our time." [as did Houdon 2 centuries ago] They include Abraham Lincoln, Enrico Fermi, FDR, Harry Truman, Lyndon Johnson, Martin Luther King, Pablo Casals, Alistar Cooke, Robert F. Kennedy, Golda Meir, Pope Paul, and more.

A work-in-progress is his *Great Buffalo Herd Monument* – 1,000 life-sized bronze buffalo, grazing and facing into prevailing winds in Wyoming's Wind River Basin. When completed, the monument will be one of the largest in the world. [*Nat. Geographic*, Oct. 1994]

His website states: "To Berks, his tribute to the near extinction of the buffalo carries a strong cautionary message to future generations. Berks intends that the monument will awaken the understanding that, like the buffalo, all resources are finite; that they require respect and thoughtful management." [2013]

The *Einstein Memorial* is 175 yards north of the *Lincoln Memorial*... at the northeast corner of Constitution and 22nd Street. Bring lunch.

References:

American Declaration of Independence, 1776
The Lessons of History, 1968, Will & Ariel Durant
Winston Churchill, 1983, William Manchester, p 873
Los Angeles Times, p A22, April 5, 2015
Einstein, 2005, Jurgen Neffe, all pages
Elnstein, A 100 Years of Relativity, 2005, Robinson, all pages
Art & History of Washington, DC, Smith, 1997, p 86-7
Robert Berks website: www.robertberksstudios.com
National Academy of Sciences website
"Sincerely, a Human Einstein", Jan. 27, 2007/LA Times, Johnson
National Geographic, October 1994, p 76-77)
Los Angeles Times, Jan. 29, 2015, Charles Townes, p 1, 14

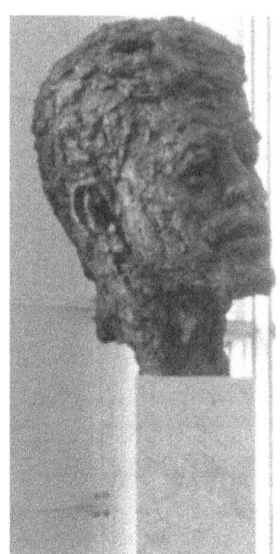

EXXON COVER-UP of CLIMATE-CHANGE:
Los Angeles Times, 2-15-2016

On Feb 15, 2016, economist Neva Rockefeller Goodwin described "catastrophic events" related to climate-change.

> [Neva is great grand-daughter to John D. Rockefeller Sr who founded the Standard Oil Company...from which EXXON was a spin-off. Her inherited shares have been sold, the proceeds will help fight global warming.]

"Giving Up on Exxon-Mobil. In shareholder resolutions and meetings with company representatives, I and other members of my family have argued that it is shortsighted for EXXON to insist on remaining 'an oil and gas company' – rather than evolving into an energy company prepared to transition to a post-carbon economy. I thought the company was being foolish. But we now know it was worse...it was being deceitful, in a way that is almost unimaginably heartless to future generations."

"Way back in <u>1982</u>, EXXON-MOBIL's environmental affairs office printed a primer on climate-change marked: '<u>*Not* to be distributed externally*'.* It laid out for company leaders the reality that <u>major reductions in fossil fuel combustion would be required to avert potentially catastrophic events.</u> These findings were given to the company's management, but not released to shareholders or securities regulators."

"Since then catastrophic events have become virtually certain. We already feel the oncoming wave in storms, flooding, droughts, hunger, human immiseration and migration. How different things might be if EXXON and others had begun to pivot away from fossil fuels 34 years ago."

"The attorney-generals in New York, California [and Massachusetts] have launched investigations into whether EXXON defrauded its shareholders by hiding what it knew about Climate-Change."

Los Angeles Times, 8-4-2016

On August 4, 2016, the Editorials section of the newspaper reported: "...<u>at least 17 state attorneys general</u> are investigating whether EXXON Mobil lied to investors by publicly denying a link between fossil fuels and global-warming even though their own research dating back to the 1970s established the connection."

<u>Google Los Angeles Times 'headlines' below</u> for articles describing how Exxon secretly used their research – that 'confirmed Global-Warming' – for their economic benefit...at the same time, hiding this information from the public and governmental regulatory authorities...for *34 years!*

What Exxon Knew about Warming in the Arctic... 10-11-2015

Exxon Planned for Warming 10-11-2015

Exxon's Damaging Denial 10-15-2015

Exxon Inquiry Sought 10-16-2015

Exxon's Shifting Stance … on Climate-Change 10-25-2015

New York Investigating Oil Giant 11-6-2015

Big Oil Braces for Warming …

While Fought Regulations 12-31-2015

Giving Up on Exxon 2-5-2016

Exxon Climate-Change Probes Expand 3-30-2016

Oil Giant Fights Inquiry 4-15-2016

⚜ ⚜ ⚜

[see *ADDENDUM* for new solutions]

100
THE WALL
VIETNAM VETERAN'S MEMORIAL

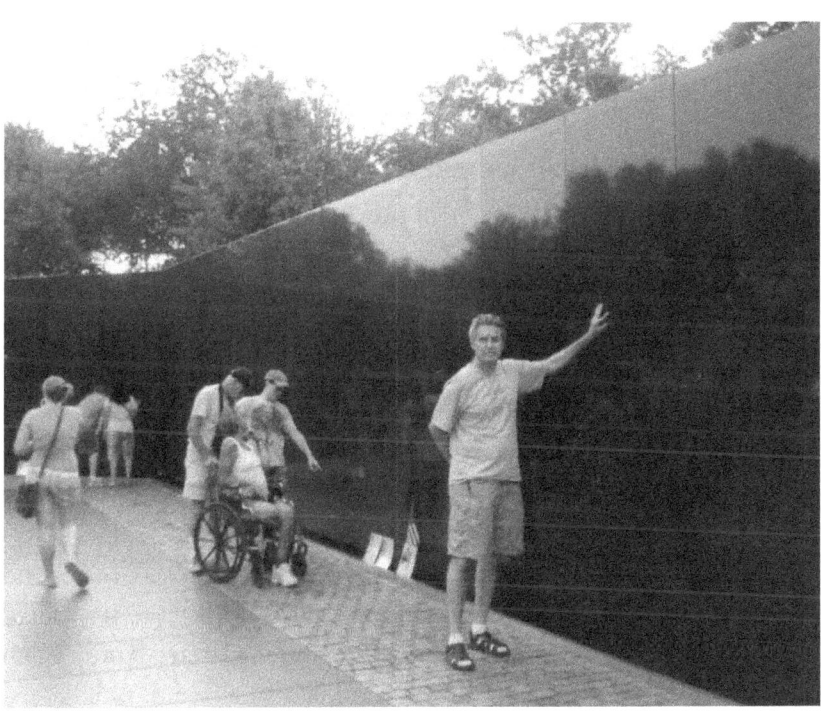

Author joins with Captain John Joseph Livingston

"One of the most dramatic pieces of political art created
in the 20th century..." Gardner, '91, *Art Through Ages*, p 1092

Dedicated Nov 13, 1982 – west end, Nat. Mall, Washington
Two black granite walls form a wide V – Realistic style
Ht. 10.1 ft. [from base]; Length each wall: 246.75 ft. [75 m.]
Sculptor: Maya Lin [1959–]

The Wall honors the memory of 58,300 American servicemen and women lost during the Vietnam conflict. Each is individually commemorated by their name, deeply-inscribed in highly-polished black granite.

Completed in 1982, *the Wall* swiftly became one of the most visited monuments in the world. With more than 5.6 million visitors in 2015, only the *Lincoln Memorial* draws more in Washington.

The war memorial's *Directory* includes:

John Joseph Livingston   William Leroy Johnson
Captain U. S. Army   Captain U.S. Army
Born 25 Nov 1939   Born 21 Jan 1937
Killed 11 Nov 1966   Killed 10 Oct 1965
Cody, Wyoming   Cleveland, Tennessee

Joey Livingston, 14 days short of 27…deserved more. Until I scanned his brief bio in the 'Directory' at *the Wall*, I hadn't known he hailed from Cody. I did know he was finest-kind company…with a perpetual smile…we played basketball together. At Frankfurt Amer. High School, Joey's athletic acumen helped our team win the 1956-57 Basketball League Championship.

Leroy Johnson reached 28…and deserved more. His proud accent confirmed a Tennessee birth. A natural-born leader, Leroy was captain of our 1954-55 basketball team at Salzburg Amer. High School. In the '55 Tournament, we won every game but one.

In the photograph, my hand marks Joey's name. Beside his name and up close, a reflection of my face appears on the polished granite. As I searched for my friends on the *Memorial*, I constantly saw myself reflected on the granite…and, when I found them, we became one.

This bonding is the wonderful mystique <u>and blessing</u> of *the Wall*.

For families and friends of those who have been lost, plus surviving veterans, a visit to *the Wall* is profound. The 2004 *Encyclopedia of Sculpture* adds: "The reflective black granite implicates the spectator in the act of remembering: one cannot see the dead [and missing] without seeing oneself." [p 1049]

Gardner's *Art Through the Ages* says: "the extraordinary simplicity of Lin's monument touches the hearts of those who visit it in ways that... have helped to heal the divisions caused in the United States by the prolonged 'police action' in Southeast Asia... all who come are filled with the enormity of the loss... the columns of names unroll as one walks along the adjacent path. Unlike other [memorial] monuments, the names carved here do not vanish into the comfort of a list ordered by rank or alphabetical placement. Each life lost in Vietnam has equal importance, equal value." [p 1092-93]

Gardner's *Art...* adds: "Rare is the visitor to this monument who is not drawn into silent meditation on the immeasurable cost of human life lost in the Vietnam conflict. Yet, the power of *the Wall* to heal has been so great that replicas of the panels have been made and sent on tour throughout the country... at each stop this traveling monument attracts crowds who come to make connections with the silent rows of names." [p 1093]

Tony Cordero of Los Angeles was 4 years old when his father – Air Force Major William Cordero – was lost when his plane was shot down in the mountains of Laos. The son's words – 42 years later – describe *the Wall*:

"It reinforces to me, whenever I see his name there, that he
is special and unique to me and my family. But it also
reminds me every time I visit that he is one of many."
[*Los Angeles Times*, 11-12-07]

Some visitors – as part of their healing process – leave a wide array of personal items... flowers, letters, photos, wedding rings, medals, clothing, insignia, a motorcycle, and other mementos along the base of *the Wall*. National Park Service rangers collect these items daily...each is catalogued and stored...including a *Congressional Medal of Honor* [Army Chaplain Charlie Liteky 1931-2017].

Following the Vietnam War, Jan Scruggs – a former U.S. Army corporal wounded in the conflict – had the idea to create the *Memorial*. For many years, he had "studied the effects of post-traumatic stress disorder and guilt complexes surrounding survivors of traumatic events. He believed that the nation had been scarred emotionally and politically...and that it needed healing." [*LA Times*, 11-12-07]

With similar-minded veterans, he founded the Vietnam Veterans Memorial Fund...its goal being "to create an area of contemplation, where individual sacrifice – not political division – would be the focus." [*Nat. Park Serv.* brochure, 2007]

They decided upon 4 criteria, that it: "1. be reflective and contemplative in character...2. harmonize with its surroundings...3. contain the names of all those who died or remain missing...and 4. makes no political statement about the war." [*NPS*, 2007]

As the person most responsible for the creation of *the Wall*, Scruggs recently commented, "It's changed – in a societal sense – the way that people have to mourn...as we search for a sense of community, a sense of shared values." [*LA Times*, 11- 12-07]

The National Park Service states: "Maya Ying Lin conceived her design as creating a park within a park – a quiet protected place unto itself, yet harmonious with the site. To achieve this effect, she chose polished black granite for the walls. Their mirror-like surfaces reflect the surrounding trees, lawns, monuments, and the people looking for names.

The names are inscribed in <u>chronological order of the date of casualty [or missing]</u>, showing the war as a series of individual human sacrifices and giving each name a special place in history. Lin said, "The names would become the monument." [*NPS*, 2007]

In 2009, Joanne Hanley, superintendent of the *Flight 93 Memorial*, observed: "It used to be, you visited memorials, you paid your respects, and you left." [that changed with the *Vietnam Veterans Memorial*...a spare, dramatic roster of names that was designed and built in less than 3 years ... and opened in Washington within a decade of the war's end.] "Now, visitors expect to be transformed ... to have a life-changing experience." [*USA Today*, 9-11-2009]

The Wall is at the northwest end of the National Mall. From the *Lincoln Memorial*, walk northeast for 2 to 3 minutes. If needed, ask directions of anyone in the vicinity.

Searching for Names:

The Wall is entered at ground-level from either end. Its west-end points to the *Lincoln Memorial*, the east-end points to the *Washington Monument*. The design of the *Memorial* – "2 low, polished black granite walls that seem to grow from the earth and converge in a shallow V at the center of the monument" – is minimal yet bold.

As visitors move along its walkway, they gradually descend to a depth of 10 feet at its midpoint [vertex] ... where the walls meet at an angle [125 degrees]. The top of the 2 sections of wall remains 8 inches above ground. [*Encyclo Sculpture*, p 961]

Volunteers wearing yellow jackets or hats assist visitors ... including how to find a name ... create a 'rubbing' of a loved one's name ... to take a photo, etc.

To locate a name on *the Wall*, visitors check a '*Directory*' [located at either end of the monument]. With each name, a 'section code' is provided for its chronological location. If a 'volunteer' is nearby, their help can speed your search.

The National Park Service provides these vital instructions: "The names begin at the vertex [middle] of the walls ... below the date of the first casualty ... and continue to the end of the east wall. They resume at the tip of the west wall ... ending at the 'vertex' above the date of the last death. With the meeting of the beginning and ending, a major epoch in American history is denoted." [NPS brochure]

The names of the nearly 1,000 '*missing*' casualties are designated by a 'cross' [on the west wall, *before* their names .... on the east wall, *following* their names]. If a missing casualty becomes 'accounted for', their cross is superimposed by a diamond.

In 1984, to satisfy veterans who voiced preference for a more traditional figurative memorial, a bronze group – *Three Soldiers* – by Frederick Hart was dedicated in a nearby grove of trees. They stand looking toward *the Wall.* In 1993, a *Vietnam Women's Memorial* by Glenna Goodacre was dedicated to the 8 servicewomen killed in Vietnam. In 2004, a memorial plaque was dedicated to honor veterans who died after the war, as a result of injuries incurred in Vietnam.

Commission:

After the 'Jan Scruggs' Vietnam Veterans Memorial Fund motivated national leaders to create the monument, they determined it would be constructed in the Constitution Gardens section of the National Mall. It was to blend with the landscape, in addition to being more horizontal than vertical. [*Encyclo Sculpt*, p 961]

A nationwide competition for its design was announced July 1, 1980, with a prize of $50,000. By March 31, 1981, 1,420 designs were submitted and displayed in an airport hangar to be judged. Entries were identified by number only, for anonymity of the entrants. A selection committee initially narrowed the entries to 232...then to 39. On May 6, 1981, an 8-member jury unanimously selected the design of Maya Lin.

Sculptor/Designer:

In 1980 and 1981, Maya Lin [born in Athens, Ohio] was a 21-year-old Yale University senior attending a course in funerary architecture. Each student in the course was required to submit an entry. Her formal training in the fields of sculpting and architecture afforded Lin an advantage over other entrants. Currently, as an architect, Lin holds both a BA and MA.

When Lin won the design competition, her critics were numerous and outspoken. They claimed: the horizontal design was neither heroic nor in white marble...it was a gloomy depression in the earth...the design did not exalt the sacrifice of lives...it did not explicitly honor the veterans who had returned. They even criticized Maya Lin's gender. [*Encyclo Sculpt.*, p 1369]

Lin envisioned 'regeneration' in her design...and she responded:

"Take a knife and cut open the earth and with time the grass will heal it. A walk along *the Wall* takes the visitor into the dark earth, past the etched names of every single American killed in the war, and out again into the light and air."

The *Encyclo Sculpture* adds: "This same focus on the individual within the larger issue is seen throughout Lin's other monuments...and along with the sculptor's success in engaging the viewer in the *Memorial's* space, it serves as Lin's lasting contribution to the field." [p 962]

It would not be until after *the Wall* was dedicated that the public could realize its true impact. Only then was Maya Lin's design acknowledged as an astounding success.

It is said of the early critics: "They went expecting to hate it...and they wept."

Major References:

Thousands Pay Tribute at 'the Wall', LA Times, 11- 12- 07, Yager
Art and History of Washington, D.C., 1997, Smith, p. 3, 70-1
Encyclopedia of Sculpture, 2004, p. 961-2, 1049, 1369
Vietnam Veterans Memorial Brochure, 2008, National Park Service
For Flight 93 Memorial...Moore, USA Today, 11 Nov 2009

Addendum

We cannot know at what point Climate-Change becomes irreversible. It will be silent. Then...higher temperatures will create increasingly-violent storms leading to permanent harm.

In 2017, the United States is burdened by an <u>ineffective</u> Congress, a <u>co-opted</u> Supreme Court And a new President <u>uninterested</u> in Climate Change. Our legislative, judicial, and executive branches have proven incapable of jointly addressing and controlling Climate-Change.

If this Inaction continues, cataclysmic Climate-Change can and will result in <u>Severe Social Disruption</u>...beyond control of local and State law enforcement agencies.

In recent decades, Social Disruptions – due to other causes – have occurred on most continents of the world...resulting in 'failure' of elected officials...national chaos...and 'broken' countries.

Under these circumstances, military leaders often have – willingly or unwillingly – assumed a quasi-leadership role.

> [the Roman Republic – enduring for 500 years – often resorted to this 'temporary' solution in the face of severe foreign threats]

On Feb. 16, 2016, the editorial board of the *San Diego Union-Tribune* recommended:

"Use the Pentagon to Fight Global Warming"

"In a 2015 report to Congress, the Pentagon depicted global Climate-Change as a huge national security issue. The report warned that global warming was expected to increase environmental degradation, poverty and political instability.

It cited problems scientists linked to Climate-Change – severe weather events in North America, the sea level rising in the Pacific and flooding in South Asia. Most ominously, it raised the possibility of an international-showdown over Russia's attempts to lay claims to oil and mineral wealth in vast swaths of the Artic that are becoming accessible because of higher temperatures.

"This is not an ivory tower bloviating. This is generals and admirals looking at the evidence coming from around the world, hypothesizing about what's coming next and growing deeply worried about the scary effects of a hotter, less predictable climate.

"Perhaps the next time the president makes a speech about global warming, he shouldn't be flanked by EPA officials but by the Joint Chiefs of Staff."

www.ingramcontent.com/pod-product-compliance
Lightning Source LLC
Chambersburg PA
CBHW071245220526
45468CB00001B/4